Writing That Makes Sense

Writing That Makes Sense

Critical Thinking in College Composition

DAVID S. HOGSETTE

RESOURCE *Publications* · Eugene, Oregon

WRITING THAT MAKES SENSE
Critical Thinking in College Composition

Resource Publications
A division of Wipf and Stock Publishers
199 W. 8th Ave., Suite 3
Eugene, OR 97401

www.wipfandstock.com

ISBN 13: 978-1-55635-861-6

Manufactured in the U.S.A.

Brief Contents

Detailed Contents

Introduction

What Am I Trying to Say, Anyway, and Why Does It Even Matter?

THINKING BEING OR REACTIVE MECHANISM

YOUR ABILITY TO WRITE is contingent upon your being able to think. However, have you ever thought about what it really means to be a thinking creature? What is this thing called mind, and what exactly is thinking? Clearly, we cannot empirically measure the mind: we don't know what it looks like, what color it is, how much it weighs, how large it is, or how small it is. The mind is immaterial, yet it exists all the same. There are some people who believe the mind isn't real, or that it is merely a chemical reaction of the brain. Ironically, a person must have a mind to even utter the statement that there is no true mind. You can point to the *brain* as material matter, but the *mind* is not merely brain. Indeed, the existence and function of the mind has something to do with the brain, but it is a problematic reduction in logic (a fallacy or error) to suggest that mind is nothing but brain.

Let's assume for a moment that only matter and energy exist, that there is no such thing as the immaterial, the metaphysical, or the spiritual. What would it mean if this were true? Well, for starters, we would have a hard time explaining our discussion right now—how could you be conceptualizing a strictly materialistic world within the immaterial mind if in fact the immaterial didn't really exist? Thoughts and concepts are immaterial, so you wouldn't even be able to think conceptually about these questions if there were no such thing as the immaterial. Science would have a hard time doing its work, too, since scientific practice depends so much upon numbers, which are immaterial concepts describing quantity. Also, scientific precepts, principles, theories, and presuppositions are immaterial and could not exist in a strictly materialistic universe. Isn't it interesting that it requires the immaterial mind to even posit the possibility that there is no immaterial reality?

A strictly materialistic reality in which there is absolutely no immateriality is a pretty disturbing possibility. Some people who are attracted to this materialistic worldview for one reason or another must still deal with the undeniable reality of mind and mindfulness. They implicitly understand the deeper spiritual consequences of acknowledging a mind that is separate from the body, and for various reasons they do not want this to be true. (For example, if the immaterial mind exists, then possibly an immaterial God exists who created that mind, and if God exists and created our minds, then possibly we are accountable to Him for our actions. Some people do not want to be held accountable.) Realizing that it is quite difficult to ignore or argue away the existence of the mind (because, again, to do so requires the use of the mind, the very thing being denied or argued away), some try to suggest that the mind is mere illusion presented to us by the brain. Others claim that the mind is the "shadow" of the physical processes of the brain, or that it is an "epiphenomenon" of the brain (a by-product or a phenomenon that is itself not tangibly real but merely a consequence of something else, in this case, the brain).

These ideas are fascinating possibilities. But, let's explore the logical ramifications of such views. If the mind is mere illusion, then so too are emotions, thoughts, ideas, feelings, loves, fears, cares, concerns, desires, joy, sadness, right, wrong, good, bad, victory, defeat, and so on. The various things that give life meaning are immaterial values, "things" associated with the mind that are, in the materialistic worldview, mere illusion and ultimately meaningless. But are these values truly illusory and without any real meaning? Moreover, without true mind, there is no free will. Think about it: free will requires choice and the ability to make choices, and the ability to choose requires a thinking mind capable of rational decision making. If there is no true mind, then there is no real faculty of reason; if there is no true reason, then there is no ability to make actual rational choices; if there is no ability to make real choices, then there is no free will.

In short, in the absence of mind, there is no true freedom and we are merely reactive mechanisms. But don't our everyday experiences and basic common sense tell us that we have freedom of mind and are thus more than mere reactive mechanisms or biological robots? Another consideration on this point: if we are merely reactive mechanisms, then we are not moral agents who choose to do good or to do evil. Rather, we are merely reacting to our environment according to a program written in our DNA. (This begs the larger questions of how that DNA got there and who or what wrote the program of the DNA. Can such a complex biochemical program spontaneously exist on its own from purely mindless or unintelligent material processes?) If we are merely reactive mechanisms and not moral agents, then we cannot be, nor should we ever be, held accountable for our actions. This is a frightening possibility, to say the least.

Just the fact that you are reading these words and thinking about these ideas strongly suggests that you are more than a mere biochemical mechanism. You are in no way materialistically compelled to read these words. You could decide on your own to close the book. I'm hoping that you won't, but you are clearly free to do so from a rationalistic perspective. Of course, there would be ramifications from that choice, like not learning some important concepts or receiving a low grade on an assignment in your writing class that expected you to have read the content in this book. My point is that it would require a rational mind that is real and not illusory to enable you to think through these choices and ramifications and to make a decision (hopefully, the right one).

In other words, you are more than a mere mechanism. You are a thinking being. As a thinking being you have a mind, and there is soulishness to your material existence. This soulishness is related to your having a mind that then allows for reason, imagination, thinking, feeling, creativity, and willfulness. These metaphysical qualities are what make you uniquely you. You are a being, not a mere thing, and as a being you are more than just material substance. In addition to a body, you have a mind, and thus you are not merely a reactive mechanism but, rather, a thinking being. Since you are a thinking being, you are thus able to write, because writing is the material manifestation on paper or on a computer screen of the thoughts you produce freely in your mind. Writing is the material expression of your immaterial thoughts.

THINKING TO WRITE AND WRITING TO THINK

If we were nothing more than material bodies and if our minds were really nothing but mechanical brain, then it really wouldn't matter one whit what you, I, or anyone had to say. Speaking or writing would be a mere reaction to external stimuli beyond our control. If we are nothing more than complex machines, then nothing we have to say to ourselves or anyone else is of any real importance. Yet, we seem to know implicitly that we as individuals and as communities of individuals do in fact matter and that what we say very often is important. Since we are indeed much more than mere matter in motion, since we have minds that are aware of ourselves and our relationship to the world around us, and since we have the quality of soulishness that is characterized by volition (will) and that characterizes our identity, then we do in fact have value beyond our material composition and what we have to say matters very much. What we say, how we say it, why we say it, and to whom we say it make all the difference in the world, and it is precisely this act of thinking, speaking, and writing that helps us discover the meaning of our lives, understand this world in which we live, and communicate our discoveries and ideas to other thinking beings.

Good writing, therefore, depends upon good thinking. In order for us to develop and communicate our thoughts through writing, we have to be able to think. Thinking not only establishes our being and our identity, but thinking also is the foundation for our writing. Consider this question for a minute or two (or, at least, for a few seconds): Can someone with an empty mind write? Arguably, we really cannot achieve a truly empty mind, because even the concept of nothingness in our minds is itself a cognitive something that occupies our thoughts. In some philosophical worldviews, the empty mind is that which is ultimately sought. Yet even in these systems of thought, the reality of true and utter cognitive emptiness or no mindedness is recognized as not truly obtainable, for one cannot ever totally empty the mind of all things unless the mind is utterly an-nihilated, at which point the thinking self no longer exists and there is no longer any individual mind. In the absence of mind, there can be no thinking self and thus no writing. So, we are back to the beginning—there must be a thinking mind for there to be any writing. Our thinking is what informs our writing and calls it into being.

Yet, this process of translating thinking into writing is not exclu-sively a linear progression. In other words, it is not a one-way street from thinking to writing. Rather, there exists a recursive process from thinking to writing and from writing to thinking. In addition to thinking in order to write, we also write in order to think. Writing informs and develops our thinking. Indeed, if we were mere unthinking, mindless, mechanical clockworks (or wind-up toys), then our writing would be mere reactionary reflex, determined by some programmed response or procedure that would be completely independent of any kind of self-conscious mindfulness. In such a scenario, writing would have no connection whatsoever to thinking, for there would be no true thinking at all, and writing would merely be a robotic operation. However, because we are thinking beings, our writing grows out of our thinking, and our writing can then allow us to reflect back upon our thinking and then encourage more thinking. Therein we find the recursive nature of thinking leading to writing which leads to more thinking. Therefore, good writing and good thinking are mutually dependent and complementary cognitive operations.

WRITING AS DISCOVERY

Writing and thinking are recursively interactive, but to what end? Are we simply trapped in an endless loop of thinking, writing, thinking, writing, thinking, writing, ad infinitum? It is common these days to value a process over the product resulting from the process, and there are some constructive points to be made here, as we'll see in chapter 1. Process is undeniably important. However, there is a problem with overemphasizing process to the utter diminishment or even exclusion of product. It's similar to the aphorism that says life is all about the journey, as if it doesn't matter at all where we end up. If we apply this adage to a real situation, say traveling on a road that leads to an abyss as opposed to traveling on a road that leads to a comfortable lodge, then we see that traveling is not just about the journey alone. It does matter very much what road we are on and the ultimate destination of that road. Not thinking about the end of a process is, ultimately, irrational. So, what is the end or goal or purpose of writing and thinking? The discovery of knowledge and truth.

Wait a minute. What's this about knowledge and truth? Hasn't all the collective wisdom of the great thinkers of Western civilization since the eighteenth-century Enlightenment taught us that truth is relative and that we really cannot know anything for sure? Indeed, many people today do believe that truth is relative and that knowledge is at best uncertain. If these people are right, then why am I saying that the purpose of writing and thinking is the discovery of knowledge and truth? We will discuss this a bit more in chapters 4 and 5, but suffice it to say at this point that the ideas claiming there is no absolute truth and that knowledge is unknowable are actually self-defeating statements. Those who hold these beliefs presuppose that it is absolutely true that there is no absolute truth, and they seem to know with great certainty that we cannot know anything with any certainty. See the problem? Uttering the claims actually falsifies them and demonstrates they are not true. Yet, many go on irrationally believing quite adamantly that these ideas are fundamentally true.

I encourage you to think a bit more deeply about such contemporary "truths" (the false notions that there is no truth and that nothing can be known with any certainty). Many people today believe that knowledge is a mere personal or social or historical construction. They believe that knowledge is not true in any real sense, but that knowledge is arbitrarily created by groups of people within certain historical time periods and cultural contexts and that these people groups assert the knowledge as true. According to this view (often called constructivism), knowledge is a mere social construction that is true or false depending upon what the constructors of the knowledge happen to believe. Constructivism teaches that truth is based merely upon what you believe to be true, that truth has no objective meaning, value, or legitimacy beyond what an individual or culture happens to believe. The value of any knowledge, constructivism suggests, is determined by the community constructing the knowledge. Moreover, adherents of this view of knowledge are less concerned about knowledge being true and are more interested in it being efficacious. If it works to the satisfaction of the group or the community considering the idea, then the knowledge is considered valid or viable but not necessarily true.

The obvious problem with this constructivist notion of knowledge is that first it assumes its own view to be true in an absolute sense, even as it denies the reality of absolute truth. In other words, it assumes its own view to be an accurate description of reality, even though it denies the existence of any absolute by which to determine if a view is accurate to reality or not. As such, it contradicts its own view of reality and the nature of truth. Second, constructivism assumes that all knowledge is mere social construction and that the validity and significance of knowledge is socially, culturally, and historically contingent. But if this is true for all knowledge, then it is equally true for constructivism as a knowledge system. Therefore, there is no reason for you or me to accept this theory of knowledge over any other theory of knowledge, since all knowledge is supposedly communally constructed and only relatively truthful. If you wanted to, you could simply dismiss this view as a constructed bit of knowledge, because it was created by other people and is not relevant to your lived experience or your own individually or socially constructed understanding of reality. In other words, there is no rational basis to accept constructivism as being any truer than any other concept about the nature of reality, knowledge, and truth. (Yet, proponents of constructivism want other people to accept it as true.)

So what's the larger point to this logical analysis of the self-defeating nature of constructivism? Mainly, I want us to realize that thinking and writing are ultimately about the discovery of knowledge and truth, not the construction of it. Sure, some people or groups of people may "construct" or create a new bit of knowledge, but we must ask if this is really a construction of their own making or a discovery of what has always been in existence, which we simply did not realize up until the point of discovery. For example, when Sir Isaac Newton theorized about gravity, he didn't construct this knowledge; rather, he formalized an understanding of reality (the existence of gravity) that had existed from the creation of the universe. He did not create or construct the laws and principles of gravity; rather, he discovered them. His process of thinking, writing, testing, and questioning led him to more thinking and writing and questioning, that led him to formulate his various postulates concerning the laws of gravity. He did not "construct" this truth such that it was a relative truth contingent upon the society and historical period in which he worked. Rather, he discovered a truth that has always been true as part and parcel of the created universe, and his process of thinking and writing made it collectively known to others during his life and for centuries ever since. In a very similar way, our own processes of thinking and writing lead us to discover knowledge and truths that may be new to us, but are not constructed by us. Writing and thinking are dynamic acts of discovery, and they are processes as wondrous and mysterious as the mind itself. When you think and write, what do you expect to happen? I encourage you to expect wonder, mystery, and discovery.

WRITING AS EXPRESSION

Writing is an act of discovery, and very often this can be self-discovery. But, the discovery is not limited to what we learn about ourselves; we also learn about the external world and our relationship to it. Clearly, we are not alone in this world. Therefore, what we discover and learn through our writing and thinking may actually help others to learn various truths and to delight in the knowledge discovered through their own writing and thinking. Writing, then, should be viewed as more than mere self-discovery and self-communication, although writing does involve communication with the self. We carry out conversations, debates, discussions, rants, diatribes, and orations in our own minds all the time. Come on, admit it. You've done this, too. It's perfectly normal. Some writers call this the writer's mind or writer-based prose. It is writing that is written with the author in mind as the audience. It is the writer writing to him- or herself. This is the start of good writing and discovery.

However, at some point good writers move beyond this self-communication and desire to share what is going on in their heads with others. This is the nature of true communication—it is the formation of community through the expression of thoughts and ideas common to the group. Community is the desire to find unity within the diversity of the many. In a community, people join in an intimate state of unity or togetherness, sharing common goals, interests, concerns, hopes, dreams, and desires. We achieve this mutual sensitivity through the expression of ourselves to others through language. Community is achieved through communication. Therefore, writing must at some point move beyond the subjective or the self and reach out to and invite in other people. Writing is an expression of self to another so as to enter into a state of cognitive and emotional community. Writing as expression seeks not only to know the self, but it also desires to express the self to the other and to attempt an understanding of the other in relation to the self. Indeed, the self and the other may never meet. We are not required nor compelled to embrace all things or to accept all ideas; however, thinking and writing enable us to express the self so as to approach the other in a community of thought and emotion.

Through the interchange of expressive selves, mutual understanding can be reached, and in some cases we can even achieve true intimacy in a community of shared ideas. This is a rare blessing and is to be cherished when it is accomplished in spirit and in truth. At other times, such expression reveals too great a gulf, such that the self and the other shall never meet. This reality is not necessarily to be mourned, for indeed some things are not to be joined in intimate community. Thinking and writing allow us to know the self, meet the other, express the self to the other, and then discern the degree to which community ought to be formed. As you explore writing and thinking, try to move beyond the purely academic notion that writing is merely another tool by which you accomplish your academic goals. Writing is indeed crucial for academic success. However, you should also consider the degree to which writing is an expression of the self and how your writing can be offered up as a gift to another with the potential hope of community governed by the spirit of truth

WRITING AND THE CONSEQUENCES OF IDEAS

You may be thinking to yourself, oh come now. What's all this nonsense about community and the spirit of truth? It's just writing, right? It's just ideas and thoughts; what's the big deal? Aren't we making way too much out of writing with all this philosophical mumbo jumbo about the community of self and other? This reaction is understandable. Sometimes professors have a tendency to get carried away. But, is it really so unreasonable to view writing and thinking as having profound effects upon both individuals and communities? We might approach this question by rephrasing it: what do we risk by not realizing that writing has a powerful influence upon people and society? In other words, do ideas and the expression of thought have consequences? This is a vitally important question to ask, one I fear that is not asked frequently enough these days. There is a sense among many people, both in academia and the general public, that ideas are somehow value neutral, and that thoughts, concepts, and theories are in themselves amoral or without moral determination and ethical effect. Is this a reasonable view?

Let's consider first the relationship between ideas and actions. Do we ever really act without thinking? OK, sure, we are sometimes scolded by our family and friends when we do something hurtful or stupid. They (rightly) chastise us for not thinking before we acted badly or said something really destructive. But, are they really saying that our minds were blank or empty and that we weren't thinking anything before we said something shameful or behaved immorally? No. What they are saying is that we didn't *think about* our statements and how they would affect other people, or that we didn't *think through* the ramifications of our actions upon others around us. Implicit in the chastisement is the truth that our thoughts, ideas, and behaviors have consequences, and we can really hurt people when we don't consider carefully what we are saying and why we are doing what we are doing. As we discussed earlier, we are thinking beings with real minds, and therefore our actions are related to and grow out of our thinking processes and cognitive choices. Actions presuppose ideas. Thoughts give rise to behavior. Whether we want to admit it or not, ideas have consequences. Therefore, it matters what we think. It matters very much what we write. As we learn to think logically and to write critically, let's carefully consider the ways in which ideas have consequences. Let's remember that the thinker and the writer have ethical responsibilities.

A powerful example from history may serve us well here. A painful but undeniable truth is that the twentieth century was the bloodiest century in recorded human history. Hitler's Nazi government is but one of many murderous regimes we could examine, and the Nazi vision that informed its various policies of genocide and conquest was not comprised of mere value-neutral ideas. Viktor Frankl, a Holocaust survivor who went on to become a renowned philosopher and psychologist, once noted:

> If we present man with a concept of man which is not true, we may well corrupt him. When we present him as an automation of reflexes, as a mind machine, as a bundle of instincts, as a pawn of drive and reactions, as mere product of heredity and environment, we feed the nihilism to which modern man is, in any case, prone. I became acquainted with the last stage of corruption in my second concentration camp, Auschwitz. The gas chambers of Auschwitz were the ultimate consequence of the theory that man is nothing but the product of heredity and environment—or, as the Nazis liked to say, "of blood and soil." I am absolutely convinced that the gas chambers of Auschwitz, Treblinka, and Maidanek were ultimately prepared not in some ministry or other in Berlin, but rather at the desks and in lecture halls of nihilistic scientists and philosophers.[1]

Think about that for a moment. Frankl clearly says that theories (ideas) have consequences. He explains, quite convincingly, that what some philosophers and scientists believed and taught had a very real affect upon millions of people's lives in history. These philosophers and scientists wrote books and taught ideas that basically denied the reality of the metaphysical or the spiritual and presupposed that the human being is nothing but bits of material randomly and violently thrown into an arbitrary universe that is devoid of meaning and purpose. Some may think these are value-neutral philosophical musings or harmless scientific theories, but Frankl forces us to consider the historically real consequences of these

---

1. Frankl, *The Doctor and the Soul*, xxi.

ideas upon individuals, families, communities, cultures, nations, and civilizations. These ideas were not value neutral; rather, they were built upon a controversial assumption about the nature of reality and the human being, and they served as the presuppositional framework upon which the cruel and immoral policies of the Nazis were built.

A plaque in Auschwitz displays these words from Hitler: "I freed Germany from the stupid and degrading fallacies of conscience and morality.... We will train young people before whom the world will tremble. I want young people capable of violence—imperious, relentless and cruel."[2] Materialistic, existential, and nihilistic principles served his purposes neatly, efficiently, perfectly, and effectively. It is more than naïve to think ideas are without consequences; it is irresponsible and can result in horrifically catastrophic ramifications. If you think Hitler's regime is but an extreme and isolated example, consider Joseph Stalin's Soviet Union and Pol Pot's Khmer Rouge of Cambodia. Both regimes justified horrific acts of cataclysmic violence with very similar philosophical and ideological views grounded in materialism, existentialism, and nihilism.[3] Ideas have consequences, and because writing is the expression of ideas, writing itself also has consequences. Moreover, because there are ramifications to our thinking and writing, we must carefully consider the moral and ethical dimensions to our writing.

CONCLUSION: CONSIDERING THE ETHICS OF WRITING AND THINKING

As we learn more about critical thinking and the writing it produces, let us never forget the fundamental truth that ideas have consequences. It matters very much what we think, because our thinking directly informs our decisions and determines our actions. Remember, we are more than mere matter and energy in motion. We are more than the product of blood and soil. We are more than reactive robots or mechanistic clockworks. We are thinking agents with independent reasoning minds that afford us free will, or the volitional ability to think and act.

2. Zacharias, *The Real Face of Atheism*, 62.

3. For a more developed discussion of the horrific application of materialistic and nihilistic ideologies in the twentieth century, see Zacharias, *The Real Face of Atheism*, 51–69.

However, with free will comes responsibility, because there are always consequences to choices. Therefore, we must remember that we are also moral agents who are responsible for what we think, write, say, and do. When we think up ideas, formulate them in writing, and then communicate them to others, we are acting upon and influencing other thinking agents. Yes, these agents are responsible for themselves, but we are also responsible for what we express to others and how we influence them. If we convince someone else that an evil act or concept is actually good, then we are ethically responsible for the corruption of another moral being and for the misrepresentation of evil as good. Conversely, if we convince another moral being that an apparent evil is in fact an actual evil and we encourage that person toward the good through our thinking and writing, then we have served a powerfully moral end through the means of our thinking and writing. In short, it is vitally important that we discover and know to the best of our ability exactly what it is we are trying to say, and it is equally important that we firmly understand and believe that it really does matter what we think and what we write. May we be blessed through our exploration of critical thinking and writing, and may our lives as explored in thought, expressed in writing, and revealed in action make a positive difference in this truly wondrous world in which we live.

PART ONE

Composition and Critical Thinking

1

Writing as Process: Overcoming the Blank Page

QUESTIONS TO CONSIDER BEFORE READING

1. What are your attitudes toward writing?

2. Do you consider yourself a good writer? Why or why not?

3. What do you think are the characteristics of a good writer?

4. How do you approach a writing assignment or task?

INTRODUCTION

FEW THINGS ARE AS discouraging to a writer as staring at a blank page. At some point in our lives, we have all faced this formidable foe by tapping out the rhythm of a favorite tune with a gnawed pencil over and over, hoping beyond hope that such repetitive behavior will somehow magically cause words and sentences to appear out of thin air. Even worse is trying to stare down the incessantly blinking cursor at the top of a completely empty computer screen. Blink . . . blink . . . blink. In such moments this steady blinking represents the only action which, really, is an indication of our inaction, and it mocks our frustrating inability to produce writing. Why is it sometimes so hard to get started on a writing project? We seem to be able to start other projects. When is the last time someone experienced gardener's block? Do we ever need to prime ourselves to mow the lawn? Sure, we may not *want* to mow the lawn, but do we just stare at the mower wondering how to get started? And how about cooking a nice meal for a friend or the family? Maybe we struggle

15

deciding what to prepare, but once we decide, do we experience cooker's block? Probably not.

But when we sit down to write an essay, a report, a research paper, a memo, or an important e-mail message, suddenly all kinds of blocks pop up. There we are, staring at the empty page, wondering how to begin, what to write, where to go next with the ideas running through our minds. Or, if no ideas present themselves, we worry about getting some ideas into our head so that we can transfer them to the page or computer screen. Also, most of us lead busy lives. We have things to do, places to go, and people to see. Notice how all of these activities seem to flood our consciousness whenever we have a significant piece of writing to produce. Isn't it interesting how the phone rings more frequently, or the instant message (IM) chat windows suddenly light up with activity, or the e-mail inbox gets more flooded whenever we need to write a report or an important letter? When we have a writing assignment to complete, suddenly we are crazily busy with so many other things that we cannot find the time to write, and when we do finally carve out a bit of time for writing, suddenly we do not have anything to say (even though we had been saying things all day with very little trouble).

Writing isn't always easy, and our daily lives sometimes make it difficult to complete our writing tasks. There are two key initial steps to consider when facing a writing project. First, commit to spending a significant amount of time working on your writing in a comfortable, personalized writing space. Successful writers note that it is extremely important to have a familiar space in which to write, and it is equally important to be disciplined in scheduling blocks of time for writing. Grabbing a few minutes here and there usually is not sufficient. Try to leave a good hour or so for each writing session. Second, you should view writing as a process. Too often we shut our creative minds down by fretting about the final product. Such fear of the uncreated or the unknown stifles the imagination and reduces morale, making it difficult to start the process. However, if we view writing as a manageable process and focus on the various stages in appropriate ways, then we can more effectively work our way through the writing process and complete our task in a timely manner. This chapter provides an overview of the basic stages of the writing process: invention, planning, drafting, revision, editing, and production. By analyzing these phases and adapting your writing practices to these principles, you will become a more productive, confident, and capable writer. You may not become a Hemingway, a Toni Morrison, or a Shakespeare (if you do, please let me know!), but you will have a better understanding of how to engage any writing task and complete it successfully.

UNDERSTANDING THE WRITING TASK AND THE RHETORICAL SITUATION

We encounter different kinds of writing every day, and believe it or not, we are generating quite a bit of that writing ourselves. Everyone, to some extent, is a writer. We may not view ourselves as such, but it is important that we recognize the degree to which writing is an integral part of our lives. Try to recall all the writing you did yesterday or the day before. Maybe you wrote a to-do list or a shopping list, maybe you wrote a note to your sibling or roommate about cleaning up after themselves, maybe you wrote an e-mail message to a friend making plans for lunch, maybe you wrote a mushy love letter to that special someone, maybe you wrote out a nice birthday card, maybe you chatted on IM with a bunch of friends about a movie you just watched, maybe you posted an insightful entry on a blog site, maybe you wrote a bunch of notes in your history class, maybe you wrote an essay exam in your literature class, maybe you started writing an early draft of your sociology research paper, and so on. We write more than we think. Let's face it—we are writers. It is actually rather difficult for must of us to get through the day without ever writing something. Let's start thinking of ourselves as writers.

Okay, so we are writers. But are we good writers? Do we know the criteria for being a good writer? There are some key behaviors, strategies, and practices that mark a good writer, and we will be learning about them throughout this book. For starters, a good writer generally begins by carefully considering the expectations of the writing task or assignment. This is often referred to as *identifying the rhetorical situation*. In other words, the good writer tries to determine as early as possible the main requirements of the writing task. To complete the writing project successfully, the writer needs to understand the purpose for writing, the message being communicated, and the intended audience for the message. These three components make up the rhetorical situation of a writing task, the context (situation) in which language is used in particular ways to achieve some end or goal (rhetoric).

The purpose is the reason behind the writing, that which motivates or drives the composition effort. For example, sometimes we write to inform our readers about some news item or current event. Other times we write to instruct or to explain how something works or how to perform some task. We see this type of writing in the technical professions in the form of sets of instructions or manuals. Also, we may write in order to present an argument in favor of a point of view or to persuade an opposing audience to embrace our view on an issue. There are many different purposes for writing. Once we understand our purpose, we need to consider the message of our writing. What are we trying to communicate? What do we want to give to our readers? What do we want them to take away from our writing? Lastly, we need to consider our readers, our audience. Who is reading our work? Why are they reading it? How do we expect them to react? How do we want them to respond? Taking some time to think about these elements of the rhetorical situation will help us better understand the writing task, and it will aid us in making crucial drafting and revision choices later in the writing process.

Writing Tips:

1. At the beginning of all writing tasks, get into the habit of contemplating your purpose, message, and audience (determining the rhetorical situation).

2. Consider writing down your thoughts about the rhetorical situation of your writing task or assignment. Incorporate this process into the invention phase of writing (see below).

3. On shorter writing tasks (like e-mail messages or IM chat sessions), at least consider your purpose, message, and audience in your mind before and as you write.

WRITING AS PROCESS, NOT JUST PRODUCT

Before actually beginning to write, the good writer first thinks about the writing task—what is the purpose, what is the message, who is the audience? We must mentally prepare ourselves for writing by considering the rhetorical situation of the writing task. However, even if we understand the rhetorical situation, we sometimes have a difficult time getting started.

We worry about the finished product to the point of crippling our ability to begin writing. To avoid experiencing writer's block or unreasonable anxiety about writing, we should learn to focus on the process of writing and not obsess about the final product.

But let's not be naïve: we are judged by our writing. Readers do not generally care how long we spent writing a report; they just want the report to be informative, clear, organized, and interesting. How can we make our reports and other writing interesting, engaging, and clear? The best way to accomplish good, effective writing is to adopt a process approach to writing. Like all complex procedures or activities, writing can be better understood if we break it down into its various stages. If we engage each stage on its own, while keeping in mind how the individual stages contribute to the larger project, we will be more successful in completing the task. Do you think Einstein developed his theory of relativity in one step? Even God saw fit to engage a sequential process when creating the universe, and He took rest when He was finished. So, it seems reasonable that we also can take a process approach to our writing (and also rest to enjoy and reflect upon what we have written and, hopefully, declare it "good").

Generally speaking, the writing process is comprised of six main steps. Please note that this is a descriptive model and not a prescriptive mandate on how to engage writing as process. In other words, this is an outline revealing the general pattern used by most successful writers; however, these stages contain a significant degree of flexibility. Each writer engages this process in one form or another. That there is a process to writing is absolute, but how a writer engages this process is very individualistic. Once we learn about the various stages in the writing process, it is then up to us as writers to apply these patterns to our own writing practices. We have to determine what areas in our own writing process need to be improved and what areas are already strong. Good writers continuously reflect upon their own writing habits and try to make adjustments so as to improve their writing with each major writing task. Good writers also understand that this process is flexible and can be abbreviated or expanded depending upon the writing task. For example, writing a letter is very different than writing a formal research project, but both tasks follow a process. The exact nature of the processes will differ, but there is a process for both tasks. To be effective writers, we need to recognize how to adapt the general writing process to any writing assignment. Let's examine the basic steps in the writing process.

Six General Steps to the Writing Process

Step 1: Invention

This stage is sometimes called *prewriting*, but this term suggests the writer is not yet writing, which may not necessarily be the case. *Invention* is a more comprehensive term, because in this phase of writing you are creating ideas, developing content, discovering material, and compiling information. You are *inventing*. Some writers like to do some invention work right from the start, and then reflect upon the rhetorical situation. Most writers find this rather difficult, because how can you know what to invent if you do not yet have some understanding of the task and the situation for writing? So, invention may actually begin when you are examining the rhetorical situation and reviewing the requirements of the writing task. What is the purpose, what is the message, and who is the audience? Note that you should continually ask these questions throughout the writing process to help keep you focused on achieving your rhetorical goals.

You can invent early in the writing process as you are getting your thoughts together, and you can invent later in the drafting and revision stage when you need to develop specific sections of your paper, report, or essay. Basically, whenever you need to generate material or information for your document, you can engage in some invention. Below are some of the key invention strategies that writers use to come up with ideas and content for their documents. Experiment with these different techniques and discover which ones work best for you. If at some point one technique is not producing good material, then shift to another one and keep trying to develop information. Consider using a few different strategies on any given writing assignment.

BRAINSTORMING. This strategy involves writing a list of thoughts and ideas that come to mind. Brainstorming can help you generate material on a paper topic, or it can even help you discover a topic. Just get out a sheet of paper or open a blank word processing document and create a bullet list of words and phrases that pop into your head. Eventually, your mind will focus upon some issues and themes you find important, and you will discover a topic. Or, you can perform a focused brainstorming session in which you brainstorm about a topic you already have in mind. Just write the topic heading at the top of the page (or screen) and then create a bullet list of ideas, concepts, words, and phrases related to the general topic. This type of invention is associational (leading freely from one thought to another) and unstructured (no sentences or paragraphs). Do not worry about spelling or grammar, and do not censor yourself at this point. You are exploring what you already know and trying to discover what or how much you do not know. You are trying to get what is in your mind and memory onto the page. You will sort through the material and make sense of it later. When brainstorming, you are concerned only with transferring information from your head to the page. The following is an example of a focused brainstorming session:

Topic: Media Bias

- bias
- slant
- neutrality
- objectivity
- personal feelings
- personal views
- reporter involvement in story
- political perspective
- worldview of reporter
- seeing the world through lenses
- bias is relative
- bias is in eye of beholder
- bias is real
- bias is observable
- bias has been documented
- bias affects readers
- need for multiple news outlets
- denial of bias by mainstream press

- vilification of those in the press revealing bias
- news as propaganda
- polemics
- opinion versus reporting
- opinion in reporting
- reporting as opinion

Such a list can go on and on. Keep brainstorming until you get tired, rest a bit, and then brainstorm some more. The objective is to discover as many ideas as possible. Then, you can go back to the list, identify some key issues and points, and group the content into related sections or categories of thought. (Note: grouping content is the beginning of planning, which is the second major phase in the writing process.)

Writing Tips:

1. Use the bullet list feature in your word processor and brainstorm on the computer.

2. When brainstorming, resist the temptation to correct mistakes (spelling and grammar), as this may interfere with the generation of ideas and material. If you are brainstorming on a computer with a word processor that identifies errors with colored squiggly lines, try to ignore them and keep on brainstorming. Avoid the temptation to hit the Backspace key to make corrections. Just keep typing and pressing Enter to build your brainstorming list.

FREEWRITING. Freewriting is very similar to brainstorming in that it is free associational and spontaneous. However, instead of creating a list of ideas as in brainstorming, freewriting involves writing out your thoughts in complete sentences. Some people process thoughts in list form and find brainstorming very productive, but others think in sentence form and thus find freewriting more conducive to generating information. You need to decide what works best for you.

When you are freewriting, avoid self-censorship—it does not matter (yet) if the information is good or interesting, right or wrong, meaningful or nonsensical. Just write. Do not worry about spelling, grammar, syntax, or clarity. Just write. Get your ideas out of your head and onto the page. Freewriting can also be used when you have no idea what topic to write about. Just sit down and start writing whatever comes to mind, and hopefully you may stumble upon a topic that interests you. Or, if you already have an idea for a topic, write it at the top of the page and then start writing whatever comes to mind about that topic. Here is an example of using freewriting to discover a topic:

> It is really getting late, and I'm not sure what I want to write about. I tried to watch some television, but nothing was really interesting on. Oh, I saw a movie trailer for The Lion, the Witch and the Wardrobe that will be coming out in December. That looks really good. I loved that book as a child, and I have such fond memories of it. I sure hope they don't mess it up. I think the same production company that worked on Lord of the Rings will be doing some design work for LWW. If that's the case, then it should be pretty good. I think they did a really good job with the special effects in LOTR, and I'm sure they've learned so much from making those films that they can do even more with LWW. I'm really interested in computer graphics. Hey, maybe I can do a paper on advances in computer graphics and how they are used in feature films, particularly fantasy films in which the director needs to create a convincing fantasy realm, like Middle Earth or Narnia.

In just a short period of time, this writer went from no topic at all to a possible topic on advances in the use of computer graphics in film. The writer still has a long way to go with this topic, but at least there are some ideas and a clear direction for further invention, development, and planning.

Writing Tips:

1. Try to freewrite on the computer using a word processor.

2. Ignore the spelling and grammar indicators in your word processor as you are freewriting—concentrate on your ideas.

3. Consider turning your monitor off as you are freewriting so that you do not get hung up on spelling, grammar, and syntax. Or, if it is inconvenient to turn off your monitor (as is the case for laptops and tablet computers), then consider changing the font color to white (on white background) so that you cannot see your typing. When you are finished freewriting, choose "Select all" from the Edit menu and change the font back to default (or black).

BRANCHING OR CLUSTERING. This is another free associational invention strategy, but it is more graphically and spatially oriented. Writers who are more visual learners often use this invention strategy very effectively. When branching or clustering, start in the middle of the page and write a word or phrase that comes to mind, usually in relation to some issue or topic you are already considering. Draw a circle around that word. Then when an associated word or thought comes to mind, write that word down, draw a circle around it, and connect the two bubbles with a line. Keep doing this until you have a branching mess of clusters on the page. This strategy is challenging for some people and is thus not appropriate for everyone. But it does have one compelling advantage. When you step back and examine the resulting web of ideas, you can often see organizational patterns emerging. You can then create an outline from the (apparent) mess on the page. Below is an example of a cluster session focused on the topic of providing evidence for theism:

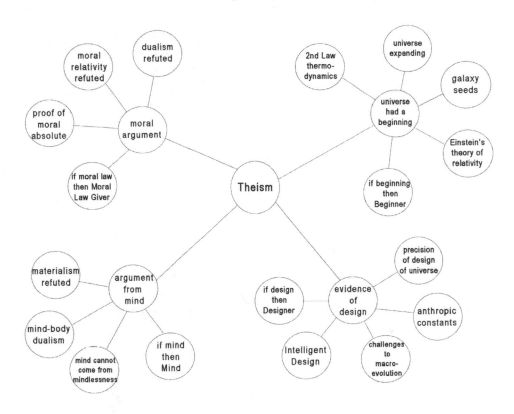

Figure 1: Example of Clustering or Branching

Indeed, theism (the belief in the existence of a personal God) is a complex topic involving principles of logic and philosophy as well as empirical scientific evidence. One significant challenge is how to organize these concepts and data. This example cluster visually organizes some key points, and we can see a logical organization developing from the clustering process: four lines of argumentation, two philosophical and two scientific, each with its own logical reasoning and supporting evidence. The clustering invention strategy not only helps us generate information, but it can also help us develop effective organizational plans or outlines for writing an early draft.

Writing Tip:

After you create a cluster or web, consider conducting a focused brain-storming or freewriting session, using the cluster as a rough outline for your thoughts.

QUESTIONING OR THE JOURNALISTIC MODEL. In this invention technique, you basically come up with a series of probing questions that get you to think more deeply about an issue or topic. You generate information by attempting to answer the questions as thoroughly and completely as you can. Think of yourself as a reporter or investigator and ask questions dealing with who, what, when, where, why, and how. The trick is to come up with interesting, meaningful questions that are open-ended, allow for good contemplation, and help you generate detailed content. The better the questions, the more interesting the information you will generate. For example, if you are working on a topic dealing with crime on campus, you might pose such questions as the following:

- Who has experienced crime?
- Who has been perpetrating the crimes?
- Who has been involved in trying to solve these crimes?
- What crimes are being committed?
- What are students doing to protect themselves?
- What are the authorities doing to improve safety?
- What prevention classes or self-defense courses are being offered?
- When are the crimes occurring?
- When will campus police or security implement new safety policies?
- Were there more or fewer crimes than previous years?
- Where are the crimes taking place?
- Where are the safe zones on campus?
- Why is crime on the rise (or decreasing)?

- Why are certain people or groups targeted?
- Why are certain dorms or buildings or parking lots targeted?
- How can an individual make a difference?
- How can the crime be reduced?
- How can community safety be improved?

Once you formulate your list of questions, you then must answer them to the best of your ability, thus generating specific information and details that can be used to develop your essay. This questioning method can reveal rather quickly how much or how little you actually know about a particular topic. You can then decide how much additional research you may have to perform in order to complete the essay on that given topic.

INTERVIEWING. If you are not an expert on a given topic, you will be able to generate only so much information by yourself. In addition to tapping your own mind, experience, and memory with your journalistic questions, you may also want to consider interviewing other knowledgeable people about your topic. You can use the journalistic model to develop your questions, and then seek out an expert to answer the questions through an interview. Please note that your roommate and your Uncle Bob are probably not the best individuals to interview for your academic paper, unless of course they happen to be leading experts on your topic. You can interview someone in person, taking careful notes and recording the interview (on tape or video), as long as you ask permission first. Or, you can request an e-mail interview, in which you simply e-mail the questions and the interviewee replies to your questions via e-mail. Some individuals may even agree to an IM chat interview or an interview over the phone. Always inform your interviewee when you are recording the session or if you are planning to save or print any electronic exchanges (like e-mail, IM chats, blogs, newsgroup sessions, or listserv interactions). Interviews are common practice in journalistic writing, but they are also used extensively in professional and academic writing.

FORMAL RESEARCH. Another key method for gathering information for an academic paper is formal research. Depending upon the curriculum design of your college composition course, your instructor may or may not require research when writing your papers. Be sure to clarify with your instructor any questions you have about the requirements of the writing assignment before you begin writing, and definitely before you submit the finished draft. There are many strategies for conducting research, and chapter 13 of this book provides more detailed information about the research writing process. At this point, it is important to keep in mind that your college library, local library, and various online database systems offer excellent resources for finding information about a variety of topics. Whenever you are conducting formal research, be sure to follow appropriate academic standards concerning incorporating material into your own writing and citing your sources so as to avoid plagiarism. Again, chapter 13 provides more specific information on strategies for effective research writing.

Step 2: Planning

You have thought about the rhetorical situation (your purpose, message, and audience), you have some idea what your topic is, and you have generated a lot of good material by using a variety of invention strategies. Now, you need to decide what to do with this material. You need to spend some time planning.

There are two key aspects of planning in the writing process: planning your time and planning the document. First, you should plan your time—set deadlines and meet them. Deadlines are set externally and internally. External deadlines are those set by agents outside of yourself, like the instructor or the course syllabus. The course may be designed with a series of predetermined deadlines for various phases of the assignment. Make sure you know about these deadlines and plan your time accordingly. In other situations, you are only given the final assignment deadline. In such cases you must be disciplined enough to establish your own deadlines, which are known as internal deadlines. Carefully look over your schedule—other classes, major assignments, work, and socializing—and make reasonable decisions about what can and cannot be accomplished in the amount of time you have. Create your own deadlines and stick to them. Also, if the assignment is a group project or a collaborative paper, consider that there will be others involved in the process. When working collaboratively, create a group timeline indicating when different parts of the assignment will be due, and then make sure everyone is accountable to the group so that the project is completed on time. Sometimes designating a group manager helps keep the group focused and provides some degree of accountability. In either case (an individual or collaborative assignment), practice good time management skills.

In addition to planning your time, you also need to plan your document. You should have already thought about your purpose, message, and audience (rhetorical situation), but now is the time to identify these elements more specifically. It is nearly impossible to create a plan for writing your essay if you have no idea what your purpose is for writing, what basic message you want to convey, and what audience you are trying to reach. Indeed, it is important to note that writing is discovery, and you may discover more about these things as you write. However, you should try as hard as possible to develop some clear sense of the rhetorical situation by the time you reach this phase of writing. Decide what your purpose is (to inform, to instruct, to persuade, to evaluate, to entertain), what your message is (your main point or thesis), and who your audience is (college students, professionals, politicians, friends, family members, some combination of such audiences), and then develop a plan to write an essay that meets the expectations of this rhetorical situation.

An effective way to develop a writing plan is to create an outline. At this phase of writing, I do not recommend an overly rigid outline. However, if you are more comfortable as a writer with a highly detailed outline, then by all means create one. But, try not to limit yourself too much this early in the writing process. I recommend creating an electronic outline that is structured enough to provide guidance as you are writing, but one that is also flexible enough to be altered if you discover a new structural pattern as you are writing. In my own experience, I have found electronic outlines to provide a productive combination of structure and flexibility. In a word processor I create an outline that is divided into main Roman numeral sections. Within these sections, I create a bullet-point list of the main issues or topics to be covered in that section. When I am ready to start writing, I split the word processing screen on my computer into two spaces—the top is my writing space and the bottom is my electronic outline. I keep the outline open as I am writing, so that I can glance down from my writing space to check my outline and to keep myself focused and on target. Sometimes as I am writing, I discover a better organization for a section. Because my outline is a word processing document that is open as I write, I can quickly make changes to my outline and then continue writing. I have found this to be a very effective writing strategy. Your task as writer is to experiment with different strategies and to find some that work well for you. It is necessary to have some kind of plan, road map, or outline to help guide your writing and to keep you focused. It is up to you as a writer to discover the best planning or organizational mechanism that will help you be an effective and efficient writer. Below is an example of using a split screen or multiple windows in a word processor for drafting an essay. Notice that the electronic outline is open in a window beneath the draft.

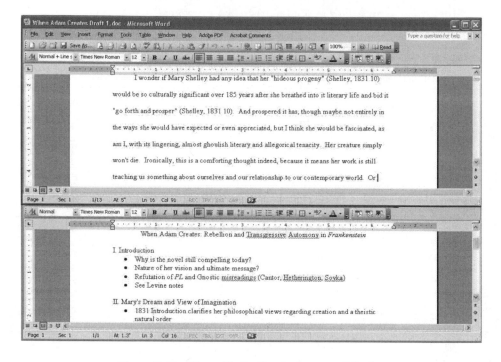

Figure 2: Drafting with Outline in Separate Window

Writing Tip:

When creating your outline, consider using the outline feature in your word processor.

Step 3: Drafting

If you have spent some time generating a significant amount of material, planning your time, and planning your document, then you should have little trouble actually writing an initial draft. A lot of writing has already been accomplished. Now you just need to shape the material and make it look like an essay. We call this the drafting phase of writing. Follow your document plan or outline and write a complete early draft of the essay. Try to write it straight through if you can, and be sure to have a beginning, a middle, and an end to your draft. Do not get bogged down in grammar, spelling, and sentence structure at this point. You can worry about these mechanics issues later in the editing phase. At this point, you simply want to produce a solid draft that has an introduction, several supporting paragraphs, and a concluding paragraph. Try not to obsess about each word or sentence, because after you revise a few times, that word or sentence may not even appear in your final version. Therefore, any time you spend agonizing over that word or sentence will be wasted. Your main task during the drafting phase is to follow your plan or outline and to write a complete rough draft.

Once you have finished the draft, set it aside for a day or two. This will give your mind time to rest, and it will put some cognitive distance between you and the draft. When you later sit down to revise it, you will have a fresher, more objective perspective on your work. If you are composing on a computer, which I advise you to do, consider saving each draft as a new file by simply renaming the file using the "Save as" command in your word processor. By saving each draft separately as a new document, you will have an electronic trail of the different versions of your paper. You never know what can happen in the writing process. Sometimes, you may take your paper in a direction that just does not work in the end, and you may decide to go back to an earlier version and develop it in a different direction. You will not be able to do so if you have saved over the earlier versions. But, if you have been creating new files for each new draft, you can easily go back to an earlier draft and pick up where it left off.

Step 4: Revising

After you have rested a bit and have not looked at the draft for a while, go back to it with a fresh, objective perspective and start revising. Revision means "to see again" or to look at the draft as if you have never seen it before. This is really hard to do. You are the writer, you basically know what you are trying to say (most of the time), and your mind does a really good job of making your unclear writing sound really good in your head. Have you ever noticed that? You can read something you just wrote and think it sounds wonderful. Let it sit for a while, and the wonder starts to diminish. That is because you are looking at the draft more objectively. The goal here is to move the draft from writer-based prose to reader-based prose. Writer-based prose is writing that makes sense to the writer, because the writer is the main audience and already knows what is trying to be said. Unless you are writing a personal diary for your eyes only, you will want to transform your writing into prose that makes sense to other readers. We call this reader-based prose. The revision process is instrumental in transforming a draft from one that makes sense only to the writer to one that makes sense to other readers.

Read the draft as if you have never seen it before, keeping your purpose, message, and audience in mind. Make sure you are accomplishing your goals. Review the large or "global" issues of writing. At this point, you should not worry about grammar, sentence mechanics, or style. You will deal with these important issues later in the editing phase. During the revision process, consider such writing issues as the following:

1. Is your thesis clear and focused?

2. Are you reaching your audience?

3. Are you providing your readers with relevant, interesting, and engaging information?

4. Do you have a compelling introduction, effective supporting paragraphs, and a satisfying conclusion?

5. Are your paragraphs focused, coherent, unified, and well developed?

6. Is the essay focused, and are you leading your readers to a clear and compelling conclusion?

7. Are your paragraphs logically arranged?

Keep these questions in mind as you review your draft, and make appropriate changes to the draft where necessary.

We are not always the best reviewers of our own work, and it is helpful to have other peers read our drafts to provide constructive feedback. We call this revision strategy peer revision. Your instructor may divide your class into peer revision groups. Working collaboratively in such peer groups obviously helps writers improve their papers, assuming everyone in the group takes the peer review sessions seriously and provides constructive feedback. Such peer group work also should help you become a better reviewer of your own writing. It is easier to review someone else's work than to critique your own. However, as you practice reviewing and commenting on other people's writing, you develop the necessary skills to become an effective reviewer of your own writing.

We are not born knowing how to review our own work or another person's draft. We have to develop the necessary skills for effective revision. It may be helpful to consider some key revision questions to ask as you read a draft. Below is a list of revision questions you may want to follow as you comment on another student's draft or as you read through and revise your own draft. Answering such questions as these will help you provide more specific feedback to other students, in addition to helping you revise your own papers.

Invention:

- Is the topic interesting and engaging?
- Has the writer spent enough time generating material for this essay?
- What would make the essay more interesting?

Purpose:

- What is the purpose of the essay?
- What do you think the writer is trying to accomplish in the essay?
- Is the essay focused around a main theme or thesis?
- How could the writer focus the essay more carefully?

Content/Development:

- Does the writer provide enough description and detail?

- What ideas and areas in the essay should the writer describe more carefully?

- What needs more careful defining?

- Is the essay carefully organized? How might the writer better organize his/her material?

Audience:

- Does the writer consider the needs and interests of the reader?

- Is the essay effectively introduced and concluded?

- How might the writer better open and close the essay to make it more appealing to readers?

Language Use:

- Is the writing clear and understandable?

- Are the sentences carefully written and grammatically correct?

Remember, the objective is to provide specific feedback to help the writer focus, structure, and develop the draft so that he or she can accomplish the purpose, communicate the intended message, and reach the target audience. Also, by providing such feedback on other people's papers, we learn how to become better reviewers and revisers of our own writing.

Try to repeat the drafting and revising process as many times as your schedule permits. The problem is that few people really like to revise their writing. Most of us have such limited schedules that we are fortunate if we complete only one good drafting-revision cycle. Since we are so busy, we often view revision as taking up valuable time. Moreover, most of us unfortunately view revision as punishment, because we have been taught, explicitly or not, that revision is a sign of failure. We all remember getting a paper back from a teacher that is all marked up (usually in red) with "See me" or "Write over" or "Revise" scrawled in big letters across the top of the page. Writing a paper over again in such cases is clearly a form of punishment for not doing it right the first time. In our minds, revision necessarily becomes identified with failure. In other areas of life, we are often admonished to "do it right the first time." If we mess up and have to do it over again, we feel we are wasting time.

However, when it comes to writing and other forms of creative expression, we have to unlearn this problematic view of revision. It is simply unrealistic to expect to get it exactly right the first time around. The truth is that good writers revise, poor writers do not. Revision is not punishment nor is it a sign of failure. Rather, revision is an opportunity for success. It is a chance to make sure you are saying what you really want to say, a chance to make sure you are accomplishing your writing purposes and goals, and a chance to make sure you are reaching your intended audience. Revision is a chance for excellence. If you happen to have a negative view of revision, try to remember that revision is not an indication of bad writing; rather, it is an opportunity to express your thoughts and feelings in good writing. Revision is not a sign of failure but an opportunity for excellence. Revision is the trademark of a good writer.

Writing Tips:

1. When revising your work, try to use peer commenting groups.

2. Use specific criteria questions like the ones listed above to guide your own revision practices and to provide suggestions on how to comment on other people's writing.

3. Consider using your university writing center or learning center to get another fresh perspective on your draft.

4. Read your draft out loud to yourself and listen for problematic areas that can be revised.

5. Have someone else read your draft out loud to you and listen for sections that can be revised.

Step 5: Editing

Some people confuse revision with editing, or they lump the two together under the same heading, considering them to be equivalent or part of the same basic writing operation. In actuality, revision and editing are completely different, because they focus on two separate areas of concern. Revision means to look again, to examine the draft as if for the first time, focusing on the larger, global issues. Editing, on the other hand, means to make presentable, to polish, or to clean up. Once you have your paper focused, organized, and developed the way you want it through drafting and revision, then you can go back and sweat the small stuff. If revision deals with the global or larger issues, then editing deals with the local or the sentence-level stuff, like spelling, diction (word choice), grammar, sentence clarity, punctuation, and the mechanics of writing. Most word processors have editing tools like spelling and grammar checkers, but you must not rely too heavily on them. A machine cannot think, so your computer is unable to understand your intentions and message, and it cannot know if you are using a word properly or not.

For example, you may have written the word "hat" but really meant to write "that." Both words are spelled correctly, and the computer will not tell you that there is an error. Also, the grammar checker does not always understand complex sentences and will mark a sentence as ungrammatical when it really may not be. So, you will still need to review your writing carefully on your own. You might also want to have someone else (who happens to be a good editor) review your paper to identify and correct some errors you might have missed. Another helpful hint is to read the essay backwards, word by word or sentence by sentence. This process isolates each word or sentence from the flow of the essay, thus making it easier to notice errors. In addition to sentence-level things like spelling and grammar, editing also involves checking the format of the document. Clarify with your teacher what essay format you are supposed to use, and then check the format of your document during the editing phase. Consider such things as line spacing, indenting for paragraphs, margin sizes, font style, and font size. Remember that the main objective of editing is to polish the draft and to make it presentable.

Writing Tips:

1. Be careful if you use the spelling and grammar checker in your word processor. Do not rely too heavily upon these automated tools. Review the draft carefully yourself.

2. Read your writing out loud and listen for awkward phrasing and grammatical errors.

3. Consider reading your text backwards to isolate each word and sentence.

4. Ask other good writers to edit your work. Be willing to serve as editor for someone else.

Step 6: Production

Once you have written, revised, and edited your document, then you are ready to produce it. For academic writing and producing essays for a college course, production may be as simple as loading paper in your printer and clicking the print button in your word processor. For professional situations, production might be more complicated, involving illustrators, the art department, and the print department. In recent years, more colleges and businesses are relying on electronic modes of production and dissemination (delivering the document to the readers). For example, documents can be sent via e-mail, posted on discussion boards or blogs, published on Web sites, posted in online databases, or published on college or business intranets. If your class is using an online course delivery system like Blackboard or WebCT, your instructor may ask you to post your final draft to a discussion board or an assignment submission area. Whatever method of producing and submitting your document happens to need, make sure you plan ahead to accommodate extra time for your particular production requirements.

Writing Tips:

1. Produce a clean and sharp final product—with today's printing technology there is no excuse for creating a sloppy final document.

2. Save a backup copy just in case an error occurs when printing your document or submitting it online.

Now that we have discussed the details of these various steps in the writing process, take some time to think about your own writing habits and processes. Do you notice how you already engage (or do not engage) these various stages? Can you see how you might adapt your practices toward a more productive strategy? Can you see how these stages factor in both simple and complex writing tasks? For example, when you reply to an e-mail message, you are engaging each of these stages, though you may not fully realize it because some of the steps are abbreviated or performed in your head. *Invention*: reading the message and thinking of a reply; *planning*: outlining your response in your head or filing the messages into folders to be answered later; *drafting*: writing out your reply; *revising*: reading through the message once or twice and making some changes; *editing*: clicking the spell check button and rereading for grammar; *production*: clicking send. We started the chapter noting that we are all writers and that we write all the time. Whenever we write, we are engaging the process of writing in one form or another. To become better writers, we should try to review all of our writing tasks in terms of these six stages and learn how to improve our writing by engaging the various steps appropriately as we complete different writing projects.

STUDENT EXAMPLE

Below is an example from a first-year college composition student at the New York Institute of Technology. This student wrote an essay about the media coverage of two hurricanes that hit the Gulf Coast of the United States in 2005. A note about this student example: the different stages of the writing process reproduced here are accurate to the student's original work, including misspellings and grammatical errors in the early phases of writing. Remember that grammatical errors are permissible early in the process and should be addressed mainly in the later editing stage.

Invention

Topic: Hurricane Katrina and Hurricane Rita

- difference between storms
- how were each of the storms handled?
- role of Bush and administration
- how Bush/administration are viewd after each sctorm
- suggestions as to why Rita was tended to faster
- compare/contrast "Newsview: in Two Storms, Two Worlds Seen: and "This Time Around, Govn't Present and Accounted For"
- compare/contrast "Administration Prepares for Rita" and "After Katrina's Lesson, Bush is Heading to Texas"

Secondary Invention

- Hurricane Rita happened just three weeks after Hurricane Katrina.

- In NY Times article, author Richard W. Stevenson states that President Bush is "under intense pressure to show he has learned practical/political lessons."—Who is putting the pressure on Bush?

- Stevenson also mentions photograph of Bush playing a guitair in San Diego on the morning New Orleans was flooded.—puts Bush in a bad light

- "Until now, Bush has stayed away from disaster zones until the worst is past . . . but after criticism for a less hands on approach immediately after Hurricane Katrina—implies Bush doesn't really care; he is only doing it to save his reputation

- CNN presents more well-rounded and mostly factual info as opposed to NY Times article

- CNN focuses on What Bush/administration are doing now, not what they failed to do earlier.

- "This Time Around . . ." brings up how criticism of the handling of hurricane Katrina, but doesn't use it to imply Bush doesn't care.

- NEWSVIEW presents idea that response to Katrina was so slow because that area is thickly populated with poor blacks whereas Rita took place in Texas, the president's home state.

- NEWSVIEW writer doesn't provide sufficient evidence to support claims.

Draft

Lyra Juinio

Dr. Hogsette

WRIT 101-WH8

   Media bias has existed for as long as the media has been around. However, the use of bias in the media has become more and more prominent in today's society. From newspapers to magazines to live news broadcasts, media bias is being used to sway the audience's view on what seems like every topic being reported. With the recent hurricanes in Louisiana and Texas, media bias has become the most powerful weapon Democrats have against Bush and his administration. Everyone from the Associated Press to *The New York Times* is cashing in on the mistakes made by Bush and his administration during Hurricane Katrina as well as their much improved response to Hurricane Rita.

   Hurricane Katrina left Louisiana in ruins. The 135 mile-per-hour winds and the torrential downpour left many of the residents of New Orleans stranded on their rooftops desperately waiting for help to arrive. The 10,000 people that filled the Superdome were told to eat before arriving and were left in the stadium without food and water. The residents of nursing homes and hospitals were left behind, and many died as a result. As the storm progressed, so did the violence and lootings. So, what took so long for help to arrive?

According to the Associated Press article, "Newsview: in Two Storms, Two Worlds Seen", the author, Tom Raum, suggests that the reason Bush didn't arrive with help until much later is because of the race, political stance, and economic status of the people that populate New Orleans. In other words, Bush didn't help the suffering people any sooner than he did because the majority of the victims of Hurricane Katrina were poor, black, and democratic. Like many other news articles written on the subject, Raum fails to mention how the severity of the storm left anyone trying to get into that region incapable of doing so. Raum also fails to mention the failures of the local government and their equally poor response to the disaster. To back up his claim that Bush didn't provide help sooner because the victims were poor black democrats, Raum presents the results of an Ap-Ipsos poll taken earlier in the month. The results show that 75 percent of the blacks surveyed felt that Bush's response time would have been quicker, had the victims not been poor and predominantly black; only 25 percent of whites felt the same. However, Bush was unpopular with blacks prior to this storm for various other reasons. Even if he had come sooner, it still would not have done much to help his image among blacks. The way Raum presents his information and the lack of sufficient evidence to back up his suggestions shows this article to be a perfect example of media bias.

When the news spread that yet another hurricane was to hit the gulf region, Texas in particular, Bush and his administration made sure that they would be ready. From the *LA Times* article "This Time Around, Government Present and Accounted For", the author states: "This time, the federal government dispatched troops sooner, sent supplies earlier and coordinated more smoothly with local authorities. The consensus is that the response helped minimize the loss of life from a storm that was damaging, though less

Juinio 4

powerful than Katrina." Regardless of the 23
seniors killed in a bus fire and the horrible
traffic jam, the government's response to
Hurricane Rita was well planned out and definitely more successful than the government's
response to Hurricane Katrina. The government was well prepared for this storm and
handled it well, so why is it still causing
controversy?

Well, one reason is the significant difference in the way Hurricane Katrina and
Hurricane Rita were handled. From the CNN
article, "Administration prepares for Rita",
a spokeswoman for Senate Democratic leader
Harry Reid of Nevada says: "It's nice to have
the Bush administration recognize the importance of a federal response to Rita, but
why weren?t they proactively mobilizing and
organizing like this for Katrina?" Tom Raum,
the author of "Newsview: in Two Storms, Two
Worlds Seen", suggests that Texas got much
better treatment by Bush and his administration because Texas is President Bush's home
state, has a Republican governor, and is the
home of big oil. What Raum doesn't mention is
that Bush learned his lesson from Hurricane

Katrina. With all the criticism Bush received as a result to his handling of the first hurricane, why wouldn't he improve his preparation strategies to make things run more smoothly for Hurricane Rita? In this article, Raum implies that Bush only cares about his own Republican home state and not about the Democratic African-Americans in Louisiana.

Similarly, Richard W. Stevenson, author of *The New York Times* article "After Katrina's Lesson, Bush is Heading to Texas", states: "Mr. Bush, who was photographed strumming a guitar in San Diego on the morning that New Orleans was being flooded 23 days ago, appeared intent on ensuring there would be no off-message pictures this time and no question of where his attention was focused." The statement implies that Bush would be better prepared for Hurricane Rita so not to cause anymore damage to his political image.

Today, media bias has become more noticeable; it seems as though it is everywhere. The presentation of unbiased material in the media has become a rarity in today's society. Even during tragedies like Hurricane Katrina and Hurricane Rita, the media uses bias to

Juinio   6

sway its audience to believe what they believe. The fact of the matter is, newspapers,
radio stations, and television networks are
all privately owned organizations, thus reporters can report whatever they see fit.
Therefore, it is up to us as readers, listeners, and viewers to take into consideration
multiple reports on the same topic in order
to get a more well-rounded view of the story.
It is imperative that we as the audience keep
an open mind and remember that these reports
are not always purely factual.

Revised Draft

Lyra Juinio
Dr. Hogsette
WRIT 101-WH8
October 6, 2005

Hurricane Katrina and Hurricane Rita:
Why All the Controversy?

Media bias has existed for as long as the
media has been around. However, the use of
bias in the media has become more and more

prominent in today's society. From newspapers to magazines to live news broadcasts,
media bias is being used to sway the audience's view on what seems like every topic
being reported. With the recent hurricanes
in Louisiana and Texas, media bias has become the most powerful weapon Democrats use
against President Bush and his administration. Everyone from the Associated Press to
The New York Times is cashing in on the mistakes made by President Bush and his administration during Hurricane Katrina, and they
are even trying to use the administration's
much improved response to Hurricane Rita
against Bush.

    Hurricane Katrina left Louisiana in ru-
ins. The 135 mile-per-hour winds and the torrential downpour left many of the residents
of New Orleans stranded on their rooftops
desperately waiting for help to arrive. The
10,000 people who filled the Superdome were
told to eat before arriving and were left
in the stadium without food and water. The
residents of nursing homes and hospitals were
left behind, and many died as a result. As
the storm progressed, so did the violence and

lootings. So, what took so long for help to arrive?

According to the Associated Press article, "Newsview: in Two Storms, Two Worlds Seen", the author, Tom Raum, suggests that the reason President Bush didn't arrive with help until much later is because of the race, political stance, and economic status of the people who populate New Orleans. In other words, President Bush didn't help the suffering people any sooner than he did because the majority of the victims of Hurricane Katrina were poor, black, and Democrats. Like many other news articles written on the subject, Raum fails to mention how the severity of the storm made it difficult for anyone to get into that region. Raum also fails to mention the failures of the local government (which is made up mostly of Democrats) and its equally poor response to the disaster. To back up his claim that Bush didn't provide help sooner because the victims were poor black Democrats, Raum presents the results of an AP/Ipsos poll taken earlier in the month. The results show that 75 percent of the blacks surveyed felt that President Bush's response time would have been quicker had the victims not been poor and predominantly black; only 25 percent of whites felt the same. However, President Bush was unpopular with blacks prior to this storm for various other reasons. Even if he had come sooner, it still would not have done much to help his image among blacks. The way Raum presents his information and the lack of sufficient evidence to back up his charges of neglect shows this article to be a perfect example of media bias.

When the news spread that yet another hurricane was going to hit the gulf region, Texas in particular, President Bush and his administration made sure that they were ready. In the *LA Times* article "This Time Around, Government Present and Accounted For," the author states: "This time, the federal government dispatched troops sooner, sent supplies earlier and coordinated more smoothly with local authorities. The consensus is that the response helped minimize the loss of life from a storm that was damaging, though less powerful than Katrina." Regardless of the 23 seniors killed in a bus

Juinio   5

fire and the monstrous traffic jam, the government's response to Hurricane Rita was well planned out and definitely more successful than the government's response to Hurricane Katrina. The government was well prepared for this storm and handled it well. So why is it still causing controversy?

Well, one reason is the significant difference in the way Hurricane Katrina and Hurricane Rita were handled. From the CNN article, "Administration prepares for Rita", a spokeswoman for Senate Democratic leader Harry Reid of Nevada says: "It's nice to have the Bush administration recognize the importance of a federal response to Rita, but why weren't they proactively mobilizing and organizing like this for Katrina?" Tom Raum, the author of "Newsview: in Two Storms, Two Worlds Seen," suggests that Texas got much better treatment by President Bush and his administration because Texas is President Bush's home state, has a Republican governor, and is the home of big oil. What Raum doesn't mention is that President Bush learned his lesson from Hurricane Katrina. With all the criticism President Bush received as a result

to his handling of the first hurricane, why
wouldn't he improve his preparation strategies to make things run more smoothly for
Hurricane Rita? In this article, Raum implies
that Bush only cares about his own Republican
home state and not about the Democratic
African-Americans in Louisiana.

Similarly, Richard W. Stevenson, author of
The New York Times article "After Katrina's
Lesson, Bush is Heading to Texas," states,
"Mr. Bush, who was photographed strumming a
guitar in San Diego on the morning that New
Orleans was being flooded 23 days ago, appeared intent on ensuring there would be no
off-message pictures this time and no question of where his attention was focused." The
statement implies that President Bush would
be better prepared for Hurricane Rita so not
to cause anymore damage to his political image. The idea that President Bush is solely
concerned with his political image and not
the American public is used over and over
again in articles such as this. Just because
President Bush wants to be more well prepared
the second time around, doesn't mean he is

Juinio   7

doing it just to salvage his image among the
public.

Today, media bias has become more noticeable; it seems as though it is everywhere.
The presentation of unbiased material in the
media has become a rarity in today's society.
Even during tragedies like Hurricane Katrina
and Hurricane Rita, the media uses bias to
sway its audience to believe what they want
the audience to believe. The fact of the
matter is newspapers, radio stations, and
television networks are all privately owned
organizations; thus reporters can report
whatever they see fit. Therefore, it is up to
us as readers, listeners, and viewers to take
into consideration multiple views on the same
topic in order to get a more well-rounded
view of the story. It is imperative that we
as the audience keep an open mind and remember that these reports are not always purely
factual.

CONCLUSION

When you think about it, we really take writing for granted. We often do
not think of ourselves as writers, but if we stop for a moment and retrace
our steps each day, we find that for the most part, we do quite a bit of

writing. Of course, some write more than others, but each of us does a fair amount of writing every day. If we understand the different types of writing (personal, interpretive, analytical, professional, academic) and if we approach writing from a process perspective, then we will be better equipped to handle the various challenges of writing.

As you approach the assignments in your composition class and in your other college courses, try to put the writing into its proper context (analyze the rhetorical situation) and approach the writing task as a process. We can easily overwhelm ourselves if we obsess from the very beginning about the final product that must be completed. What generally happens is that we stare at a blank page or computer screen, and our heart pounds louder and louder, almost in rhythm with the idle, blinking cursor. However, if we break the writing task down into its various stages and then tackle each stage separately, concentrating mainly on what needs to be done for that particular stage only, then we can control the chaos of writing and proceed through the phases in a relatively calm fashion. As we successfully complete more and more writing tasks using some form of the writing process, we become more comfortable with writing, and hopefully, we will also become more capable and confident writers.

DISCUSSION QUESTIONS

1. Where do you usually begin when you have a writing assignment looming ahead? Are you going to start somewhere else after reading this chapter? Why or why not?

2. How do you normally approach a writing task? Will you modify your writing habits after reading this chapter? Why or why not?

3. Which of the steps in the writing process is a challenge for you and why?

4. What is your understanding of revision? Has your view of revision changed at all after reading this chapter? Explain.

5. Why is viewing writing as process important to building successful writing habits?

GROUP ACTIVITIES

1. Discuss the kinds of writing you generally perform. How can you adapt the writing process to these specific writing tasks to improve your writing?

2. As a group, pick a single topic. Each member in the group should pick a different invention strategy and then develop some initial ideas using that strategy. Spend 10–15 minutes generating material. When you are done, compare your invention results and discuss your experiences with using these invention strategies.

3. As you begin working on an essay assignment for your writing course, get into peer review groups and discuss everyone's drafts using the sample revision questions listed in this chapter (or those provided by your instructor). If your instructor is using an online writing environment like Blackboard or WebCT, consider posting your drafts in a group forum and then post replies to each other's drafts. Also, consider using the chat feature or virtual classroom to discuss the drafts online outside of class.

4. When you have revised your drafts several times and are ready for the editing phase, get into peer editing groups and conduct round-robin editing sessions. Exchange drafts, start reading the draft, and underline or circle grammatical and spelling errors in the text (but do not make corrections). After 2–3 minutes stop where you are, mark where you stopped editing, and exchange drafts. Start the same process where the previous reader left off. Continue rotating drafts until all the drafts have been read and marked. When you are finished, get your own draft back and then look at the editing marks. Your group members should have underlined or circled any errors they noticed. Try to figure out what the errors are and fix them. Consult your grammar handbook and discuss with your group members. Be sure to clarify with your instructor any questions you may have about the grammar and sentence structure errors.

WRITING ACTIVITIES

1. Practice different invention strategies discussed in this chapter. Spend some time over the course of a week or two investigating the different ways of generating ideas. Which ones seem to work best for you and why? Can you see yourself using some of the strategies in different writing tasks? Why or why not?

2. After you generate some material and information by using various invention strategies, develop a plan or an outline for a possible essay. Consider using this outline for your next essay assignment, if it meets your instructor's requirements.

3. Write an early draft of an essay based upon the material you generated and the outline you created. Reflect upon the usefulness of your outline. Was it helpful to have generated information before you began writing? Now that you have written a draft, consider how you might use invention strategies to develop your draft even further.

2

Understanding Rhetoric:
Achieving Your Goals in Writing

Questions to Consider Before Reading

1. What comes to mind when you think of the word *rhetoric*?

2. How are purpose, message, audience, and the use of language related?

3. How can we use language to reveal our minds and intentions to other people?

4. How can we use "rhetorical strategies" to develop our ideas?

Introduction

In the previous chapter, we spent a long time reviewing the process of writing. Remember that there is no single way to write a document, and different people complete writing tasks in different ways. Some people spend a lot of time drafting and revising their writing. Other people focus on planning and outlining their projects. Some writers like to remain in the invention phase for as long as possible, generating vast amounts of information before structuring the content into an essay. And still others complete a highly structured outline and then methodically write a detailed draft, revising as they proceed through the document. The universal reality here is that each type of writer engages some kind of process, even though the specific expressions of the process differ. This variability in process is fine, as long as the processes are ultimately productive or profitable to accomplishing certain writing goals. In other words, we should keep in mind that not all writing processes are equally valuable. Some writers, especially beginning student writers, sometimes allow too much procrastination, resulting in an abbreviated process and a diminished final product. Such writing processes that damage the final product fail to encourage excellence in writing and should be avoided whenever possible. The point here is that we should develop constructive writing habits that result in a productive understanding of writing as process and that encourage success so that we can become confident, capable writers.

Even though different writers use different manifestations of the writing process, one aspect of writing is universal: all writers have a purpose. Note that even the writer who claims to have no apparent purpose actually has a purpose. In this case, the purpose for writing is to have no purpose for writing. But, this is a self-defeating position or a statement that contradicts itself, ultimately proving the exact opposite of its claim (see chapter 4 on critical thinking). All writing has purpose, or to phrase it differently, all writers write with some purpose in mind.

At some point in the writing process, it is the writer's responsibility to determine the purpose for writing. As writers, we must ask ourselves such questions as the following: What is writing? What is the purpose of writing? Why am I writing in this situation? Why is writing important? What do I want to learn? What do I want my readers to learn? The answers to such questions form the fundamentals of what is generally known as rhetoric.

WHAT IS RHETORIC?

How often does this term "rhetoric" come up in general conversation? Most of us do not go around talking about rhetoric. Think for a moment. When was the last time you used this word? Okay, maybe in your writing class you hear about rhetoric (like now as you read this chapter). Or, if you are taking a classics course you probably have heard of rhetoric and the ancient Greek rhetoricians. Possibly in a literature class, a teacher may have made reference to the rhetoric of literature (that is, the way in which a story's narrative structure or a poet's use of imagery encourages readers to think or feel a certain way). Maybe your political science professor has mentioned something about the rhetoric of political punditry. Or, possibly, in a journalism class you have discussed the rhetorical nature of bias in the media. If nothing else, most of us are familiar with rhetorical questions that are not supposed to be answered. (Have you ever wondered why, exactly, we are not supposed to answer a rhetorical question?)

Now that we think about it, maybe we are more familiar with rhetoric than we at first realized; or, in the very least, we have discussed the concept of rhetoric without knowing it. Rhetoric is one of those things that is pervasive and universal to human experience, but that sometimes remains rather invisible or unacknowledged. As the above set of examples suggest, we engage rhetoric all the time. In fact, every time we open our mouths to articulate something—regardless of what this something is—we are engaging rhetoric.

Entire books are written on the subject of rhetoric. Arguably, from the very beginning of human expression in which one person attempted to communicate an interior idea, concept, or emotion to another person, there was rhetoric. However, the study of rhetoric in Western civilization was formalized in ancient Greece during the fifth century b.c., and rhetoric has been a fundamental part of any study of language, communication, literature, and artistic expression ever since. Put simply, rhetoric is communication and its goals. Rhetoric is the use of language or some form of communication to achieve some end or goal or purpose. You may have been wondering about the rhetorical question ever since I mentioned it in the previous paragraph, so let's return to it now as a way to illustrate the basic concept of rhetoric. We usually understand that the rhetorical question is a question that is not meant to be answered. However, not answering the question is not what makes it rhetorical. You do not answer the question precisely *because* it is rhetorical. The rhetorical question is not asked in order to receive an answer; rather, it is posed in order to make a point or a statement. It is the *use of language* (in this case, a question) to *achieve a particular end* (to make a statement). The rhetorical question is not answered because it really is not a question as such; rather, it is a statement masquerading as a question. Why do you suppose some people get annoyed when someone actually answers a rhetorical question? (By the way, that was a rhetorical question.)

Writing, then, is essentially rhetorical because it is a specific use of language in order to achieve some goal or purpose. In chapter 1 we talked about the importance of the writer understanding his or her purpose, message, and audience (determining the rhetorical situation). Now, this principle should make a little more sense, because it is the fundamental idea behind rhetoric. If rhetoric is the use of language to achieve some goal, then to be effective rhetoricians or users of language, we must understand our purpose for writing, the message being communicated, and the audience to whom we are communicating. Only then can we craft our language effectively to reach this audience with our message and thus to achieve our purpose. There are many purposes for writing. We write in order to communicate, to share information, to instruct or to teach, to change people's minds about an issue, to argue a point, to illustrate an idea, to tell a story or share a narrative, to discover new things, and so on. Rhetoric, then, is an integral part of writing.

Determining the Rhetorical Situation

If rhetoric is basically the use of language to achieve some goal, and if writing is a form of communication in which we are using language to present a message to an audience in order to accomplish some purpose, then writing is inherently rhetorical. Thus at some point in the writing process, we should determine our purpose, message, and audience. In chapter 1 we learned that this process is called identifying the rhetorical situation, and we concluded that we should figure out our purpose, message, and audience as early in the writing process as possible.

Ideally, we should consider our rhetorical situation during the invention phase of writing, the very first stage in which we contemplate our topic and start generating information and content for our document. The writing process progresses more smoothly and productively if the writer can identify early on why he or she is writing, what message is to be communicated, and what audience needs to be reached. Knowing this writing context (rhetorical situation) helps the writer make key decisions about focus, content, structure, tone, voice, and language. Considering these points in the invention phase will help you plan the document more carefully, because you will have a better idea as to what kind of material or information to use, what form the document should take, and what tone or voice you should use. However, do not panic or become anxious if you have not completely figured out the rhetorical situation during the invention phase. Sometimes, writers do not figure this out until the planning phase or even the drafting phase. At other times, the writer's understanding of the rhetorical situation shifts a bit, or comes into clearer focus, as the writing process progresses. Regardless of when the writer determines the rhetorical situation, it should be determined with a fair degree of certainty at some point in the writing process (preferably before the very end) so that the document can be properly focused, clearly structured, well developed, and convincingly presented.

Let's look at an example. As a college professor, I regularly deliver scholarly papers (lectures) at academic conferences. Basically, I have to write a ten-page essay and then read from that essay to an audience of interested scholars (at least I hope they are interested). For a national conference on Gothic literature and film, I created a lecture analyzing messianic heroes in the Gothic science fiction films *Blade Runner* and *The Matrix*. In preparing for the lecture, I had to consider the rhetorical situation:

> *Message*: The characters Roy in *Blade Runner* and Neo in *The Matrix* are messianic heroes who physically and emotionally redeem the other human characters in the respective films.

> *Purpose*: To prove that these and other cyberpunk, Gothic science fiction films and novels pose fascinating questions about the relationship between humanity and spirituality, thus disproving the commonly held view that cyberpunk literature is inherently antihuman or somehow "post-human." A secondary purpose was to reveal how these films are more than just entertainment and that they actually present viewers with spiritual truths that apply to our own lived experiences.

> *Audience*: Other scholars and fans of cyberpunk science fiction and Gothic literature.

After determining these three elements of my rhetorical situation, I was able to make clear decisions about content, form, and tone. Because this was an academic paper, I needed the tone to be scholarly so that my interpretive arguments would be carefully considered by the academic audience.

However, I also wanted to lend an air of practical relevance to the talk. I believe these films raise important issues that affect audiences in real ways, so I did not want this to be a purely theoretical discussion. Therefore, I tried to have some conversational elements in the talk and impromptu statements. That is, the whole lecture was not read from a script, as are many academic talks. The content included video clips from the films to illustrate my points and to focus my discussions, and I also integrated other critical materials, like film analyses, reviews, and cultural studies material. Because of the academic setting, the form was a lecture; however, because of the film subject, I also chose to incorporate video clips, thus creating a multimedia presentation. The extemporaneous elements of the talk (ideas spoken from my heart and mind without a specific script) made the material more personal and helped me appear more approachable. As a result, the question-and-answer period (common after an academic talk) was lively and honest, as opposed to being too academic and sterile, thus achieving part of my rhetorical goal. Taking time early in the writing process to determine exactly what I wanted to say, why I wanted to say it, and to whom I wanted to say it helped me shape my presentation into the final product that accomplished my various goals.

All modes of writing will be enhanced if we consider the rhetorical situation. In the professional setting (like an office), good writers go through the same basic steps of determining the rhetorical situation when they have to write a memo, a report, or an e-mail response. When writing a memo to other employees, the office manager must consider the message, purpose, and audience to make sure he or she includes the proper information, presents the information in the appropriate voice, and uses the correct document format. If the manager neglects the rhetorical situation of writing to his or her employees, the writing may not achieve its intended purpose. Students must make the same considerations when writing academic essays. Writing a paper for a professor of contemporary history is a very different context than writing a poetry analysis essay for a renaissance poetry professor. Learn how to identify your purpose, message, and audience so that you can better accomplish your various writing goals.

Writing Tip:

Considering the rhetorical situation is fundamental to successful writing. Take some time to think about your own writing habits. To what extent do you consider message, purpose, and audience before you write? How do these things influence the choices you make about form, content, organization, and tone?

USING RHETORICAL STRATEGIES

If rhetoric is the use of language to achieve some end, then the next logical question to ask is: Are there specific strategies for achieving specific ends? In fact there are, and as you might expect we call them rhetorical strategies. Rhetorical strategies can be used in different situations in order to accomplish different communication goals. For example, if you want to explain a concept to someone who has never heard of it before, then you may want to *define* some of the terms and explain what the concept means. If you are trying to re-create a certain event in the minds of your readers, then use *description*. If you want to explain how something operates or why a process is not working properly, then *process description* and *process analysis* would be useful strategies to use. If you are trying to convince someone that one solution to a problem is better than another proposed solution, then you could *compare* and *contrast* the two recommendations and explain why one is preferable to the other. For just about any communication purpose you can think of, there are rhetorical strategies to help you accomplish your goals. Let's explore some of the major rhetorical strategies of writing and discuss some examples of how these strategies can be used in different situations.

Definition

Definition involves explaining what something means, and it is a useful rhetorical strategy for informative writing. There are two main types of definitions: denotative and connotative. The denotative definition is basically the dictionary meaning of a word or the main meaning that is commonly accepted by society or a specific community. The connotative meaning is an implied meaning or a different meaning that is associated with a particular word or phrase. For example, the denotative meaning of the word *literature* is any printed material, but its main connotative meaning is a highly respected piece of fiction or poetry or drama that has been deemed excellent by learned readers and critics over a long period of time. Similarly, the denotative meaning of the word *culture* is a group of people and its various customs and beliefs. However, a connotative meaning of *culture* refers to someone's elevated social status or familiarity with what is sometimes identified as "high culture." We say someone is "cultured" if he or she has a good education and is knowledgeable about art, literature, history, fine cuisine, and the theater.

As writers, it is important to understand the various denotative and connotative meanings of the words we use. We should choose our words carefully so that we can communicate our intended message to the appropriate audience in meaningful ways. You will see the definition rhetorical strategy used throughout various types of informative writing, including nonfiction essays, text books, technical writing, specialized training manuals, insurance documents, legal documents, tax code materials, and scientific analysis. Review the following example from a scientific discussion of irreducible complexity by William A. Dembski in his book *Intelligent Design: The Bridge Between Science and Theology*:

> In *Darwin's Black Box* Behe presents a powerful argument for actual design in the cell. Central to his argument is his notion of *irreducible complexity*. A system is irreducibly complex if it consists of several interrelated parts so that removing even one part completely destroys the system's function. As an example of irreducible complexity Behe offers the mousetrap. A mousetrap consists of a platform, a hammer, a spring, a catch and a holding bar. Remove any one of these five components and it is impossible to construct a functional mousetrap.
>
> Irreducible complexity needs to be contrasted with *cumulative complexity*. A system is cumulatively complex if the components of the system can be arranged sequentially so that the successive removal of components never leads to complete loss of function. An example of a cumulative complex system is a city. It is possible successively to remove people and services from a city until one is down to a tiny village—all without losing the sense of community, which in this case constitutes function.[1]

In this passage, Dembski defines two different modes of complexity as they relate to different designed systems. Notice that the rhetorical strategy of analogy (comparing one thing to another object, in this case a mousetrap and a city) is used to help define the concept, and the rhetorical strategy of description is used to enhance the definition (details of the mousetrap and the city are described). Dembski also further defines irreducible complexity by contrasting it to cumulative complexity. Often, a few rhetorical strategies (in this case, definition, analogy, description, and contrast) are used simultaneously to achieve a particular writing goal (here, to define and explain irreducible complexity).

1. Dembski, *Intelligent Design,* 147; italics in original.

Description

When you want to explain what something is, or when you are trying to inform an audience about an event or some experience, you can use description. Description attempts to create a vivid image or picture of something in the reader's mind, and effective description relies upon specific details that appeal to the major senses: vision, hearing, taste, smell, and touch. Description uses physical details and empirical observation to explain the characteristics of the object being described or the event being explained so that the reader can visualize it as clearly as possible. Good description makes writing interesting and lively, and it can capture the readers' attentions and imaginations, encouraging them to continue reading the essay.

The following passage is an example of how description can introduce a topic and effectively invite readers into an essay. This introduction is from an essay entitled "Meditation in a Toolshed" by C. S. Lewis:

> I was standing today in the dark toolshed. The sun was shining outside and through the crack at the top of the door came a sunbeam. From where I stood that beam of light, with the specks of dust floating in it, was the most striking thing in the place. Everything else was almost pitch-black. I was seeing the beam, not seeing things by it.
>
> Then I moved, so that the beam fell on my eyes. Instantly the whole previous picture vanished. I saw no toolshed, and (above all) no beam. Instead I saw, framed in the irregular cranny at the top of the door, green leaves moving on the branches of a tree outside and beyond that, 90 odd million miles away, the sun. Looking along the beam, and looking at the beam are very different experiences.[2]

Notice how in this description Lewis also sets up a contrast between *looking at* and *looking along*. These are two different ways of seeing something that lead to different types of knowledge about that object, and this contrast becomes the central focus for Lewis's short essay. In addition to enlivening narrative essays, description can also enhance such writing tasks as process analysis (you have to describe the process in order to understand and analyze it), how-to manuals (describing procedures and materials used in the procedure), and cookbooks (describing ingredients, cooking tips, and the finished dish).

---

2. Lewis, *God in the Dock*, 212.

Narration

Narration means telling a story or an anecdote, and this rhetorical strategy can be used to illustrate a point, provide examples, or make an emotional appeal. Narration can also be an effective way to introduce or conclude an essay. Here is an example of using narration to introduce the main subject of an essay:

> I remember, during my first year at Dartmouth, going to meetings sponsored by the International Students Association. I enjoyed these meetings because they presented a fine opportunity to eat good ethnic food. It was in these venues that I first encountered the most intriguing creature, the multiculturalist. The multiculturalist that I remember most vividly was a white guy who wore a pony-tail and a Neru jacket. He was visibly excited to meet a fellow from India.
>
> "So you're from India," he said. "What a great country."
>
> "Have you ever been there?" I asked.
>
> "No," he confessed. "But I've always wanted to go."
>
> "Why?" I asked, genuinely curious.
>
> "I don't know," he said. "It's just—so liberating!"
>
> Because I had a happy childhood in India, I have many nice things to say about my native country, but if I had to choose one word to describe life there, I probably wouldn't' choose "liberating." I decided to prod my enthusiastic acquaintance a little.
>
> "What is it that you find so liberating about India?" I asked. "Could it be the caste system? Dowry? Arranged marriage?"
>
> My purpose was to challenge him, to generate a discussion. But at this point he lost interest. My question ran into a wall of indifference.
>
> "Got to get another drink," he said, racing toward the bar.[3]

Using a light-hearted personal narrative allows this writer, Dinesh D'Souza, to introduce a rather sensitive topic—the problems with popular, uncritical multiculturalism, which sometimes romanticizes difference and all things "other" or "foreign" without attempting to understand the full picture of these other cultures. Notice how D'Souza provides description and dialog to bring this brief story to life. Narration is most often used in personal writing (also called first-person narrative writing), but you will also encounter narrative in newspaper articles, editorial columns,

---

3. D'Souza, *Letters*, 45–46.

legal testimony, and even scientific or sociological reports (for example, anecdotal evidence is often presented in narrative form).

Quotation/Summary/Paraphrase

When you write an academic paper, you often need to support your ideas by discussing experts or other authorities in the field. Incorporating such outside sources provides information, develops your writing, and also lends authority and credibility to your writing, thus allowing you to achieve your writing goals more effectively. You can directly quote the information, summarize large sections of information by restating the main points in a few sentences, or paraphrase short passages of the content by rephrasing them in your own words. We will discuss these in more detail in chapter 13, "Introduction to Information Literacy and Research Writing." For now, it is important to know that incorporating expert information serves your rhetorical goals by providing information, establishing your credibility, and elevating your authority, thus strengthening your writing. You should also remember that whenever you use material from other sources (research material) and present it in your paper as a quotation, summary, or paraphrase, you need to cite the material appropriately or provide attribution to avoid plagiarism (see chapter 13).

Process Description/Analysis

Process description is an explanation of how something works. Technical and professional writing use process description to create such documents as operation manuals, maintenance manuals, and sets of instructions. The main purpose of this rhetorical strategy is to teach the reader how to accomplish some task or to provide instruction in some process—your basic how-to document. Some examples are recipes, furniture assembly instructions (can those Ikea instructions be any more vague?), and DVD player manuals. Process description can also be used for analysis. In order to understand how a system or process works, you sometimes have to analyze it or break it down into its component parts or procedural steps. Then you can describe each part or procedural step and discuss how the various parts work together to make the whole system function properly.

Cause and Effect

This strategy attempts to explain why certain things happen or why an event occurred. Cause-and-effect analysis (also termed causal analysis) describes and explains the "why" behind the "what," or the cause of a particular effect. Analyzing cause and effect is a very common strategy used in scientific discourse and persuasive writing. Causal analysis is also an effective form of logic thinking, and it can be used to develop a section of your paper; for example, in a paper on cell phones and cancer, you may summarize, describe, and explain some medical relationships between high levels of cell phone use and high rates of cancer in cell phone users.

The following is a short paragraph that summarizes previously elaborated discussions into a series of cause-and-effect statements:

> Secularization left society without shame and with no point of reference for decency, and pluralization left society without reason and with no point of reference for rationality. Privatization—born from the union of the other two—has left people without meaning and with no point of reference for life's coherence. The greatest victim of evil so engendered is the self. We no longer know who we are as people.[4]

The writer, Ravi Zacharias, makes a series of this-leads-to-that (cause-effect) statements in order to create a succinct conclusion that reviews the main ideas of the chapter from which this excerpt is taken and drives his main argument home.

Causal analysis is most often used in making logical appeals in an argument, but it can also be used to justify evaluations (this computer program best suits our company's needs because it provides the most comprehensive solution to our data computing problems) or to substantiate recommendations (this proposal is the best course of action because it produces the best possible solution to our problem, given our unique requirements).

Comparison and Contrast

Comparison involves pointing out and describing the similarities between two or more objects, ideas, or concepts. When comparing things, we are interested in the interrelationships and intersections among the

4. Zacharias, *Deliver*, 108.

various items being compared. Usually, we come to a better understanding of something by comparing it to something else that is already known or understood. We call this strategy of explanation *analogy.* Contrast, on the other hand, involves pointing out the differences between two or more things. When contrasting items, we are interested in describing how they differ and then explaining the significance of these differences. Comparison and contrast rhetorical strategies attempt to understand something by placing it in relation to something else and then discussing the similarities and differences. In the following example, William Wordsworth, a famous English Romantic poet of the late eighteenth and early nineteenth centuries, defines the poet by contrasting him or her to other types of writers:

> The poet writes under one restriction only, namely, that of the necessity of giving immediate pleasure to a human being possessed of that information which may be expected from him, not as a lawyer, a physician, a mariner, an astronomer or a natural philosopher, but as a man. Except this one restriction, there is no object standing between the poet and the image of things; between this, and the biographer and historian there are a thousand.[5]

We use comparison-contrast all the time, often without realizing it. How do you explain something totally new to someone who has not seen it before? You compare it to something he or she already knows. If you want to place something in a positive light, you will contrast it with something that is not generally liked, and if you want to place something in a negative light, then you compare it to something that is generally disliked.

Analysis

Analysis means to break something down into its various parts or components so that we can better understand how the whole thing operates. Science depends upon analysis. Most of us are aware of photosynthesis, the process by which plants convert sunlight into other forms of biologically useable energy. Well, how do you think scientists were able to figure out this marvel of creation? (Note, this process is so complex that scientists are still studying it and trying to figure out this intricately designed biological system.) Scientists had to observe various phenomena and then analyze them. That is, they had to discover the various phases and

5. Wordsworth, Preface, 148.

steps in this complex process and figure out how each step works and how these steps relate to each other in an irreducibly complex system that ultimately is able to convert sunlight energy into a biologically useful source of energy.

Scientists are not the only people who analyze things. Sociologists analyze human social systems to figure out how they operate properly so that they can identify when social systems are dysfunctional and then propose ways to resolve the problems. Literary scholars analyze literature, breaking the text down into various thematic, linguistic, and structural segments or elements so as to better understand how the text was put together and how it communicates various meanings to different audiences. Also, we can use analysis to examine our essays, to see if they are properly structured and logically organized. Such analysis becomes a crucial part of the revision process. Analysis is an important method for discovering truth and for learning about ourselves and the world we inhabit.

Evaluation

Evaluation is another common rhetorical strategy that we use every day of our lives. Think for a moment about what you are wearing right now as you read this chapter. Why are you wearing that outfit? Why did you choose that shirt over the other shirts in your closet or drawer? What did you have to eat for breakfast, or lunch, or dinner today? Why did you eat that particular meal? Why did you choose that particular drink to go along with your meal? Are you going to see a movie later today or sometime this week? What are you going to see? Why are you choosing that film over any other film that is currently out right now? Do you see what relates each of these questions? Choice. We make decisions about hundreds (if not thousands) of things every day, and we do not always realize it. However, when we make a decision, there is a reasoning process behind that decision, whether we want to admit it or not. Generally, there is a standard or a set of expectations against which we measure our choices and then make decisions.

This is the basic process of evaluation. Evaluation is a form of judgment. Gasp! We make judgments? Yes, indeed we do. The word *judge* is a tricky one these days, for no one wants to be labeled "judgmental." But, making judgments does not make one judgmental. To be judgmental means to look down upon someone or to make yourself feel better or superior to someone else. It is perfectly fine to make moral judgments and to discern between a morally right behavior and a morally wrong behavior. It is necessary for us to do so; otherwise, how could there ever be true justice? However, we are not to condemn, or to ridicule, or to demean someone else for their moral decisions. We can judge the action, but we must love the actor. This is indeed difficult, but it is central to true virtue. But also remember that judgments do not always involve people and/or behaviors. You also make judgments about food, clothes, entertainment, and classes you take in college. To judge simply means to evaluate, to measure the worth or value of something based upon a known set of criteria.

The key here is to know the criteria. It is nearly impossible to make sound evaluations or judgments in the absence of a set of criteria or expectations. Evaluations devoid of criteria are mere whim or random action, not true evaluation. So, whenever you make various evaluations, judgments, and choices, be clear on your set of criteria or expectations to support, explain, or justify your decision or evaluation. Also, make sure your criteria and expectations are appropriate. For example, it is not reasonable to criticize a banana because it does not taste like an apple—a banana *is not supposed* to taste like an apple, so we must not evaluate a banana according to criteria used for apples. Similarly it is not reasonable to judge harshly a student drama production because it does not meet the criteria of a Broadway production—the expectations and criteria are not appropriate. Fair and legitimate evaluations start with fair expectations and appropriate criteria.

USING RHETORICAL STRATEGIES TO DEVELOP IDEAS

When you are drafting and revising your essays, one thing you will want to consider is whether or not you are providing your audience with enough information to achieve your writing goals. Good writing is information rich, well developed, and intellectually engaging. You do not want your readers to be left asking, "So what? What's the point? Give me some more information." It is your job as writer to develop your essays well enough to satisfy the interests and needs of your readers. Rhetorical strategies are excellent tools for developing your writing. For example, if you have to define something, then you will need to use words to provide more information in your definition. *Defining* concepts, ideas, words, and theories further develops your writing. Similarly, providing *descriptive details* of an event or an object gives your readers more information and helps them better understand the event or object by appealing to their senses and creating a vivid image of it in their imaginations. Descriptive details produce lively and informative writing.

You can also develop a section of your essay by providing an example from your own lived experience in the form of a brief *narrative*. Then, you can supplement your own experience by *summarizing* or *paraphrasing* information from another source or by *quoting* an expert. These strategies provide specific details and thus develop your writing. Moreover, providing an *analogy*, *comparing* something to a known item, or *contrasting* two items helps your reader better understand the concepts, provides information, and produces developed writing. Additionally, discussing *effects* and their *causes* (causal analysis) requires a great deal of information and explanation. Providing causal analysis thus develops your writing and helps your readers better understand the point you are trying to prove or illustrate. Similarly, when you *analyze* something, you have to systematically break that thing down into its parts and explain each part. A thorough analysis of something necessarily produces detailed, developed writing. Lastly, whenever you *evaluate* something, you have to describe the thing itself, explain your criteria of evaluation, and then discuss your evaluation. Such a detailed evaluation cannot be accomplished with brief, vague writing; rather, it requires developed writing. The point here is that if you use rhetorical strategies effectively, your writing will be informative, specific, detailed, and developed. If you are reviewing a draft and you notice some weak, empty paragraphs, or if your professor asks you to develop your thoughts more fully, consider how you can use rhetorical strategies to develop your paragraphs and to expand upon your thoughts and observations.

Writing Tip:

As you are reading essays, chapters, and books for your other classes, or as you are reading other books and essays on topics you enjoy, try to identify how the writers are using various rhetorical strategies to develop their writing, to explore their thoughts, and to expand their observations. Consider jotting down some examples in a reading journal that can serve as models for your own writing.

USING RHETORICAL STRATEGIES TO STRUCTURE ESSAYS

Rhetorical strategies are specific uses of language that help you achieve certain writing goals. Generally speaking, you will use a variety of rhetorical strategies in order to accomplish your purpose for writing a particular essay. However, there are times when one rhetorical strategy will dominate an essay, or you may use many instances of a rhetorical strategy within a certain essay, or the whole essay may be a single, developed rhetorical strategy. For example, if you were writing an essay about what America means to you, you might use a few different rhetorical strategies: maybe you would introduce your essay with a brief *narrative*, then you might *summarize* information about the U.S. Constitution, then you may *contrast* certain experiences in America with those in other countries, then you might relate a personal example about your family who immigrated to America using *narrative*, and so on. In this case, you are developing an essay using various rhetorical strategies, as do most academic and professional writers. Rarely do professional writers write an essay entirely in a single rhetorical mode; rather, they first consider their rhetorical situation (the purpose, message, and audience) and then decide what rhetorical strategies they will use to accomplish their goals.

There are some instances, however, when a writer is asked to write an entire essay in a single rhetorical mode. Sometimes an editor for a magazine will ask a staff writer to write a film review (*evaluation*), or a teacher may ask a student to write a personal narrative about a recent exciting event that happened in the student's life (*narration*), or a history professor may ask students in an exam to *compare and contrast* the ways in which the United States and the Soviet Union expressed their respective superpower status on the world stage during the twentieth century. In such cases, the writer will use a single rhetorical strategy predominantly throughout the paper, and that rhetorical mode becomes the organizing pattern for the whole essay. The following are some tips and suggestions to keep in mind if you are asked to write an essay using a single rhetorical strategy.

Personal Narrative Essay

Narrative essays are very difficult to write, because you are trying to make an expository point (revealing truth, explaining meaning, or sharing information) by using a creative writing style. Generally, try to organize the personal narrative essay chronologically, telling the event from beginning to end. However, you can add interest by beginning somewhere in the middle or near the end, and then through flashback tell the story, shifting back and forth from present to past. This is very challenging and requires great skill in storytelling. You will want to use lots of description in a personal narrative—bring the events and scenes to life with an abundance of descriptive detail. In a personal narrative you must show without telling. That is, reveal the message or the truth through the sharing of details and events (showing) as opposed to directly stating the moral of the story (telling). Pick an interesting event that will have wide appeal, and make sure you are expressing a truly meaningful message. Finally, consider using dialog to enliven the writing and to provide a keener sense of reality and immediacy.

Definition/Description Essay

The objective of a definition/description essay is to explain what something is and/or what it means. In some ways, this is the heart of expository writing, informing your readers what something truly means. The most relevant example is the basic textbook. The goal of any textbook is to "expose" or to reveal what something is, what it means, what its significance is, and what it is all about. In other words, the book is expository because it is exposing or revealing information, meaning, and truth. When you are writing a definition/description essay, you are basically trying to inform your reader about your topic, to explain what something is and what it means. For example, you could write a definition essay on anime (Japanese animation), or mythopoeic literature, or Reformed theology, or intelligent design theory, or Christian apologetics, or irreducible complexity, or philosophical nihilism, or naturalism, or materialism, or mind-body dualism, or moral relativism, or ethical absolutism. Whatever the topic for a definition essay may be, you will want to spend some time analyzing that topic. Examine the topic and break it down into its various subsections or subtopics and then start describing and explaining these various component parts. Note how in this case a rhetorical strategy (analysis) serves as an invention strategy for generating material. The organization of the essay will depend upon the thing being described or the concept being defined. Consider all the main points or aspects of the topic that you want to explain, and then decide upon a reasonable organization of this information. An object can be described spatially. An event can be described chronologically. An idea or concept can be defined logically and described topically. The arrangement of the paragraphs in the definition/description essay will depend upon what organizational model you choose.

Process Analysis or How-To Essay

You will probably encounter this type of paper in a professional or technical writing class in which you may be asked to write a handbook or a set of instructions. However, you may be asked to write a how-to paper in college composition, or your physics professor may ask you to write a process analysis as part of a lab report, or your art history instructor may ask you to write a report on the creative process of some key artist. Remember your main purpose or goal: for the how-to paper you need to instruct your audience how to perform a task, and for a process analysis paper you need to explain how a mechanistic process operates. Analyze the process by breaking it down into its various steps or subprocesses. For a how-to paper, explain chronologically the necessary steps required to perform the procedure successfully. For a process analysis paper, describe in vivid detail the various stages of the larger process and explain how these processes work together toward the proper function of the whole system. Audience awareness is crucial for a successful how-to paper or process analysis. Figure out what your readers need to know in order to complete the operation or to understand the process, and then provide that information in a clear and logical fashion. Discovering what your audience already knows about the process or understanding their comfort level with the procedures and equipment being described is also quite helpful when inventing, planning, and drafting a how-to paper or process analysis essay.

Comparison/Contrast Essay

The comparison/contrast paper is probably the most common academic assignment, especially on essay exams. Professors never seem to tire of asking their students to compare and contrast various things, mainly because this assignment is a proven way to come to a more complete understanding of the items being compared. There are two main ways to organize a comparison/contrast paper. The first method involves summarizing or describing the items first and then discussing the similarities and differences second. For example, if you are trying to discuss three poems by Samuel Taylor Coleridge (an English poet who wrote at the end of the nineteenth century and into the early nineteenth century), you might first briefly explicate each poem in one section of your paper and then discuss elements that are similar and different in the second section of the paper. One problem with this strategy is that it often results in some repetition when you begin discussing the similarities and differences, because you often will refer back to things you have already described earlier in the paper.

The second method for organizing a comparison/contrast paper is to pick out key points or issues for analysis and then explain how various examples from the items being compared address these main points. This is called point-by-point comparison. Let's return to the example of the three poems. Instead of summarizing the poems first and then pointing out similarities and differences, you can simply organize the paper in terms of the main poetic points or issues you want to discuss (for example, the structure of the poems, the word choice or diction, and a few key thematic issues). In this organizational strategy, you briefly describe a main point and then discuss how each poem treats that one point similarly or differently. Then move to the next main point, describe it, and discuss how each poem deals with that point, and so on down the line, point-by-point, until you have covered all the main points.

Whichever strategy you use, remember that the main goal of the essay is not to compare or contrast for the sake of merely comparing and contrasting different things. Rather, you must have a clear, specific point you are trying to prove by comparing and contrasting the various items.

Writing Tips:

1. When you are given a writing assignment, spend time during the invention phase contemplating the rhetorical situation (purpose, message, and audience) and then carefully consider what rhetorical strategies to use in order to accomplish your goals. Do not be afraid to experiment with different strategies during the drafting and revision phases, be open to different possibilities, and be willing to reject some strategies that are not helping you accomplish your goals.

2. If you are asked to write an essay in one rhetorical mode (a personal narrative, or a comparison/contrast essay, for example), make sure you understand the assignment and the rhetorical mode. Also, be sure to have a clear focus and thesis for the paper, and do not merely use a rhetorical mode for the sake of using a rhetorical mode. The dominant rhetorical mode for the essay should help you organize or structure the paper, express your message, and accomplish your main purpose for writing.

CONCLUSION

Good writing strives to communicate a specific message to an intended audience as effectively as possible. Good writing requires an understanding of rhetoric—the use of language to achieve certain goals. The more we learn about rhetorical strategies and apply them to our own writing, the better writers we will become. Just knowing about each of these types of rhetorical strategies is not enough; we must also use them to enhance our writing and communication. Remember that these strategies can be used as organizational structures for your papers (definition paper, process analysis essay, or comparison/contrast paper, for example). Or, they can be used to organize and develop specific sections or paragraphs of your paper. Also, remember that we are more familiar with these rhetorical strategies than we might at first realize, because they show up all over the place. We use them constantly, almost unconsciously. For example, while listening to a lecture we usually do not think to ourselves, "Ah, that's a contrast." Nor do we blurt out during a friendly conversation, "Look, you just used narration!" No, we just use these rhetorical strategies in various ways, often without thinking about them or realizing we are using them. But, once we are aware of them, we will be able to make more conscious choices and informed decisions about how to use them effectively to accomplish our writing purposes, whatever they may be.

DISCUSSION QUESTIONS

1. Explain in your own words what rhetoric means.

2. What is a rhetorical strategy? Pick one strategy, describe it, and then illustrate it with an example from your own writing.

3. Explain in your own words how rhetorical strategies can be used to develop your writing.

GROUP ACTIVITIES

1. Decide as a group on some topic for a brief essay. Discuss your various views on this topic, and then determine a focus or a working thesis that could be developed into a full essay. Then, decide on some key rhetorical strategies that you could use to develop the different sections of the essay.

2. In a group, pick one of the readings assigned by your instructor, and individually list all of the rhetorical strategies you see the writer using. Then, share with each other the different strategies you identified and discuss how the writer uses these strategies to accomplish his or her goals. Discuss the extent to which the writer successfully used these strategies to achieve the purpose of the essay.

WRITING ACTIVITIES

1. Pick some topic or issue that you find interesting and then brainstorm or freewrite about that topic, using some rhetorical strategies as ways to generate ideas. For example, brainstorm a comparison/contrast of two related items in a double-column bullet list. Or, try to define something by freewriting about it.

2. If you have a draft of an essay that you are currently working on, consider how you might revise the introduction by using narration. Write a draft of a new introduction in which you still introduce your topic, but use a narrative or brief story of an event to bring your readers into the subject.

3. As you revise a draft of an essay you are currently working on, review each of your paragraphs. Identify some weaker paragraphs

that need more information, and then consider how you might use some of the rhetorical strategies discussed in this chapter to develop those paragraphs.

3

Organizing and Developing Your Thoughts with Paragraphs

QUESTIONS TO CONSIDER BEFORE READING

1. What is the function of a paragraph?

2. How is a paragraph similar to an essay?

3. What are the qualities of a good paragraph?

4. What are some organizational patterns for paragraphs?

INTRODUCTION

WHAT IF YOU STARTED to read the first chapter of a book, only to discover it was one long block of text—a twenty-page-long paragraph? You probably would close the book and refuse to read it. Have you ever received an e-mail message from a friend comprised of a single long paragraph that scrolled on and on, randomly talking about anything and everything? We love our friends dearly, to be sure, but receiving such messages can be a bit annoying sometimes and really hard to read. If you were to log onto your favorite blog site and saw a posting that was a single paragraph of a few hundred lines, what is the likelihood that you would actually read that posting? Few of us would bother reading it, and we would scroll to the next message, hoping it would be a bit more manageable.

Long, unwieldy paragraphs are quite uninviting, but what about short, skimpy ones? Would you want to read a magazine article comprised of a bunch of two- or three-sentence paragraphs randomly arranged on the page? Probably not, since we expect magazines and journals to provide detailed information in a coherent manner. What about an editorial that is simply a list of positions or brief arguments with no supporting data or explanations; would you seriously consider that writer's point of view? The discerning reader would question the credibility of a writer who did not bother to explain the logic of an argument or to justify a position with evidence and supporting details.

The common problem in each of these examples is a deficiency in proper paragraphing. We may not always give much thought to the paragraphs that we write ourselves, but when we read other people's writing, we expect the information to be presented in digestible chunks, in clearly focused and informative paragraphs. If the paragraphs are not properly organized, then readers will be lost, or they will have to work extra hard to make sense of the larger message. If the paragraphs are not well developed with details, information, and explanations, then readers will not learn much and will be quite dissatisfied. Readers expect essays to be well written, well structured, and well developed. Effective paragraphs help meet these expectations. To become effective writers, we need to develop our understanding of paragraphs and learn how to use them effectively in our writing.

THE FUNCTION OF PARAGRAPHS

The writer of any document should have a purpose and a message to communicate to a particular audience (this is the rhetorical situation we discussed in chapter 2). Good paragraphs help writers achieve their rhetorical goals. Let's start with an example:

> It happened again the other day as we were in one of the teeming cities of our land. My wife and I were walking hurriedly to keep an appointment. We were elbowing our way through the mass of people, bobbing and weaving, a step here and a turn there, making the best speed we could. When waves of humanity descend from every direction, it is inevitable for one to feel like a minute drop in a mighty torrent—unobserved, unimportant, almost non-existent. It is the way with crowds. Such settings at once multiply and diminish the individual.[1]

Remember that all good writing seeks to accomplish a specific purpose and to communicate a clear message to a particular audience. The purpose

---

1. Zacharias, *Recapture the Wonder*, 1.

of the above sample paragraph is to appeal to the reader's common experience of walking through crowds. Then, the writer moves from the common to the extraordinary to reveal a deeper truth lurking just beneath the surface of everyday experience. The message in this short paragraph concerns the wondrous irony of crowds: within a staggering mass of people, the individual is actually diminished. The audience for this paragraph is anyone who has noticed that even though one is surrounded by so many people, one can feel utterly alone. That is quite a bit of meaning packed into a few sentences. But what makes the paragraph work? Why does it effectively communicate this message and thus achieve its purpose? This paragraph is meaningful because it is concise and effectively structured.

Paragraphs enable the reader to group information into digestible bits. Readers do not like to gulp down immense batches of information all at once. By logically arranging information within themselves, paragraphs allow for the logical progression of an argument or the clear presentation of information. Paragraphs also provide stopping points in a discussion in which certain thoughts or ideas can be explored in greater detail—that is, an essay's focus is developed by examining related subtopics in paragraphs. You could present a list of subtopics in an essay, but that would not be very engaging or fulfilling for the reader. The subtopics must be developed into related discussions, and good paragraphing accomplishes this goal. Each paragraph is like a distinct buffet station at a dinner party, serving up separate food items that work together toward completing the entire essay meal. The trick is to make our essays a delightful and edifying banquet.

QUALITIES OF A GOOD PARAGRAPH

How do we make a successful banquet? We start by creating great dishes. In the case of writing effective essays, we must start with writing good paragraphs. This begs the larger question: what is a good paragraph? That is a great question; let's begin answering it by looking at an example.

> The great German social scientist Max Weber, for example, was the first to provide a penetrating analysis of modern bureaucracy. But his vision is best captured in the novels of Franz Kafka, especially *The Castle* and *The Trial*. The world of *The Castle* is the domain of bureaucratic power and authority. Telephone exchanges produce more muddles than connections. Bureaucracy drowns human be-

ings in a deluge of files and forms. A stifling hierarchy makes it impossible to get through to a person above anyone. Countless petty officials work endless overtime and get nowhere. Innumerable interviews take place, but none of them comes to any purpose. In *The Castle* human beings are reduced to files and in *The Trial* to cases. As Kafka once said of such a world, "the conveyor belt of life carries you on, no one knows where. One is more of an object, a thing, than a living creature."[2]

Strong paragraphs are marked by unity or focus, cohesiveness or internal organization, and development or explanation of evidence and information. A paragraph should say one thing, it should communicate a dominant idea, and it should make a singular point. In the above example, the main point of the paragraph is that bureaucracies are faceless entities that tend to oppress and dehumanize the individual. This focus is clearly achieved by the first two sentences: the first establishes the general focus of analyzing modern bureaucracy, and the second sentence narrows the discussion by specifically focusing on the example of Kafka's fiction. Moreover, paragraphs should be cohesive, which simply means that everything in the paragraph coheres or sticks together and clearly relates to the main focus expressed in the topic sentence. In this example paragraph, the problem of modern bureaucracy is the focus, and the specific examples from Kafka's literature all explain this main focus.

Writing Tips:

As you read books, magazines articles, and essays, take note of how the writer creates paragraphs. How are they focused? Does the information cohere or stick together in ways relevant to the focus of the paragraph? To what extent are the paragraphs developed? Is there enough information provided to accomplish the goals of the paragraph? Studying how other writers use paragraphs will help you develop your own paragraph writing skills.

To be sure, there are different types of paragraphs that can range from short transitional paragraphs to long informational discussions. However, all good paragraphs are similar in that they share the following

2. Guinness, *The Call*, 94.

qualities: unity, cohesiveness, and development. Let's examine these qualities in some more detail and discuss some examples.

ESTABLISHING UNITY WITH TOPIC SENTENCES

The first important quality of a good paragraph is unity or focus. A focused paragraph basically says one main thing or explains one main idea and develops it with information and thoughtful discussion. Unity (the one main idea of the paragraph) is usually achieved by writing a clear topic sentence. A good topic sentence suggests or establishes the focus of the paragraph without drawing attention to the fact that it is identifying the focus. For example, avoid topic sentences that say, "The topic of this next paragraph is ..." or "In this next paragraph we will discuss ..." Instead, simply state the focus. Read the following example and identify the topic sentence:

> First, although we must acknowledge our limitations, biases, and perspectives, we are not doomed by our environment to mere "perspective." Some measure of objectivity is possible. Before examining this issue, however, we should recognize the humbling truth about ourselves: We are limited and never as objective as we'd like to be. Our cultural environment, family background, place in history, and a host of other factors can and often do distort our perceptions. We are not 100 percent bias-free, purely objective individuals. That's the downside. On a more positive note, we can still achieve objectivity despite an array of influences that shape us. To deny the possibility of any truth statements or any objectivity is to declare the following a true and objective fact: It is objectively true that we cannot know something as objectively true! Again, truth is inescapable.[3]

If you identified the first sentence as the topic sentence, you are correct. It clearly and simply establishes the main focus of the paragraph without specifically drawing attention to itself. The writer simply states what the focus is—that although we have limitations, we are not so limited that we cannot come to some knowledge of truth. With this focus in mind, the writer provides information that further discusses and explains that topic. But, this paragraph would be confusing and nearly meaningless without the topic sentence unifying it.

---

3. Copan, *"That's Just Your Interpretation,"* 42.

Topic sentences provide readers with a clear sense of the purpose and focus of a paragraph. Let's examine where we can place topic sentences in our paragraphs.

Topic Sentences at the Beginning of Paragraphs

Generally, topic sentences come at the very beginning of the paragraph. Most readers are familiar with this basic logical pattern: state the main idea and then explain the idea with details and information. Professional writers use this method, especially in memos, reports, and e-mail correspondence. You will also see topic sentences at the beginnings of paragraphs in academic writing, where it is important to establish the main point first and then to prove it with information and analysis. In the following example, the writers are making a sophisticated academic point, so they begin with a clear topic sentence and then explain and prove this point with subsequent sentences:

> We cannot see the eternal realm that we enter through language, but to deny that it exists is tantamount to denying the simplest exercise of choice. For instance, it is to deny all reality to the road not taken (or the cup not dropped). Or it is to assert that any reality attributed to such hypothetical possibilities must be a strictly physical reality, which would be absurd. The cup is still here before me and was not dropped and consequently remains as yet unbroken. If any choice is to be regarded as real, we must accept the fact that the rejected alternative is as real as the one selected, though neither was physically determined before the choice was made. Otherwise there could be no real choice between dropping the cup or not. We could still prove that the choice exists by dropping and breaking the cup even now, but we choose not to because the proof is not needed.[4]

Topic Sentences at the End of Paragraphs

However, there are times when it is appropriate for the topic sentence to come toward the end of the paragraph. We usually see this when a generalization is made after presenting information or when the writer wants to lead the reader along, almost in suspense, and then give the main point or meaning of the discussion at the end of the paragraph. In the following

---

4. Oller and Omdhal, "Origin of the Human Language Capacity," 267.

example, C. S. Lewis opens his essay on miracles with a series of narratives and observations that lead to his main point, which is articulated at the end of the paragraph:

> I have known only one person in my life who claimed to have seen a ghost. It was a woman; and the interesting thing is that she disbelieved in the immortality of the soul before seeing the ghost and still disbelieves after having seen it. She thinks it was a hallucination. In other words, seeing is not believing. This is the first thing to get clear in talking about miracles. Whatever experiences we may have, we shall not regard them as miraculous if we already hold a philosophy which excludes the supernatural. Any event which is claimed as a miracle is, in the last resort, an experience received from the senses; and the senses are not infallible. We can always say we have been the victims of an illusion; if we disbelieve in the supernatural this is what we always shall say. Hence, whether miracles have really ceased or not, they would certainly appear to cease in Western Europe as materialism became the popular creed. For let us make no mistake. If the end of the world appeared in all the literal trappings of the Apocalypse, if the modern materialist saw with his own eyes the heavens rolled up and the great white throne appearing, if he had the sensation of being himself hurled into the Lake of Fire, he would continue forever, in that lake itself, to regard his experience as an illusion and to find the explanation of it in psycho-analysis, or cerebral pathology. Experience by itself proves nothing. If a man doubts whether he is dreaming or waking, no experiment can solve his doubt, since every experiment may itself be part of the dream. Experience proves this, or that, or nothing, according to the preconceptions we bring to it.[5]

Topic Sentences at the Beginning and the End of Paragraphs

There are times when a writer decides that placing a topic sentence either at the beginning or the end of a paragraph just is not sufficient. Instead, the writer will suggest the focus at the beginning of the paragraph, discuss information in support of the focus, and then clarify the main topic with a more specific topic sentence at the end. Writers usually put a topic sentence at the beginning and the end of a paragraph to make sure that readers understand a complex point. In the following example, the theologian R. C. Sproul clarifies an important point about the purposes of philosophy

5. Lewis, *God in the Dock*, 25–26.

by writing a general topic sentence at the beginning and then providing a more specific one at the end:

> Philosophy was born in the ancient quest for ultimate reality, the reality that transcends the proximate and commonplace and that defines and explains the data of everyday experience. Three burdens dominated the thinking of the original philosophers: first, a quest for "monarchy"; second, a quest for unity in the midst of diversity; and third, a quest for cosmos over chaos. Though these quests may be distinguished at one level, at a different level all three involve the search for a metaphysical answer to the physical world.[6]

This is a short paragraph, but it packs quite a punch. Sproul raises some big issues that he goes on to discuss in more detail later in the chapter from which this paragraph is taken. However, in this short paragraph Sproul uses topic sentences at the beginning and the end to explain that a fundamental purpose of philosophy in the ancient world was to find answers in the metaphysical realm (the transcendent ultimate reality) to questions that humans ask about their everyday lives ("the proximate and commonplace" world of physical existence).

Writing Tips:

1. As you read books and articles, pay careful attention to where writers place topic sentences and try to determine why they make the choices they do. Try to model your own writing after the good examples you discover in your reading.

2. When revising your next essay draft, review your paragraphs and the way you are using topic sentences. Revise your paragraphs to make sure you are using topic sentences effectively to establish the proper focus necessary for achieving the rhetorical goals of each paragraph.

6. Sproul, *The Consequences of Ideas*, 13.

Structuring Coherent Paragraphs

Not only must good paragraphs be unified with a main focus or topic, but good paragraphs should also be coherent. To cohere means to stick together, so information in a coherent paragraph sticks together or relates together around the main focus. Remember that when we write, we are trying to communicate a message to a reader in order to accomplish a particular rhetorical goal. Paragraphs help us organize the content of our essays and to present the information in logical ways so that we can accomplish our rhetorical goals. If our paragraphs are incoherent, if they are made up of chaotic arrangements of random information, then our readers will be confused, and we will not effectively communicate our message. To write a good paragraph, first consider how to focus it with a good topic sentence, and then decide how to organize the information so that the paragraph will be clearly structured and coherent. Consider the following strategies for writing coherent paragraphs.

Organize by Spatial Order

When you are describing a physical space or providing descriptive details of a physical object, you can organize the paragraph spatially. In spatial organization the writer describes how something exists in space, providing details while moving into (a room, for example) or around (a building) or through (a forest) the object being described. For example, technical writers may use spatial order to explain how a mechanism works; architects use spatial order to describe a building design; or food critics reviewing a new restaurant use spatial order to describe and evaluate the dining area. You can also use spatial order when writing narrative essays, as in the following example I wrote about a couple preparing for a dinner party (note how the perspective moves from room to room in this narrative paragraph):

> Dan and Rosemary had been planning for this dinner party for a few weeks, but no matter how hard they tried, there never seemed to be enough time to complete all the preparations. Rosemary finished dressing and putting on her makeup and came downstairs only to find that Dan was not as far along in the preparations as she had hoped. In the kitchen, she got him started on making the punch, while she finished putting the appetizers in the oven and turning on the festive twinkling lights above the baker's rack next

to the kitchen table. Glancing into the dining room, she noticed that the candles were not yet lit, so she quickly lit them all and smiled at the soft ambiance they created. What about the living room—was it ready? She scurried into that room to find it dark and uninviting. After she lit the candles, turned on the Christmas tree lights, and started the magical Celtic Christmas CD, her favorite room came mystically to life and filled her heart with wonder. That's much better, she thought. As she moved back into the kitchen, Dan had finished the punch and was taking the appetizers out of the oven. And just in time, because at that moment the doorbell rang announcing that the first guests had arrived. Dan and Rosemary opened the door and welcomed their guests into their charming home, delighting them with the wondrous sights, joyful sounds, and delicious scents of Christmas.

Organize by Chronological Order

In addition to organizing paragraphs by spatial arrangement, writers can also use time or chronology as a dominant cohesive pattern. When using chronology to structure a paragraph, you are arranging information in the order in which its elements occurred in time. Chronological arrangement is often used in technical and scientific writing in which processes, methods, and tasks must be described. In such writing, the information is best organized according to the chronological or sequential steps of the process. Examine the following sample set of instructions I wrote and notice how the procedural steps are arranged sequentially or in chronological order:

> Graphics and illustrations can enhance a document by helping you communicate information and messages in powerfully effective ways. As the old adage says, a picture is worth a thousand words. It is quite easy to insert images into a word-processing document. Before you begin, make sure you have a graphic file saved on your computer. Many word processing programs have their own clip art files, and you can also download free images from the Internet. Open your word processing document and place the cursor where you want the image to appear. Next, click on the "Insert" menu on the word-processing toolbar at the top of the screen. Select the "Picture" option from the dropdown menu, and then select the "From File" option. An "Insert Picture" dialog box will open on your screen. Click on the various folders and locate the graphic file you wish to insert. Double click on the graphic file name, or single

click the file name and then click the "Insert" button. The graphic will be placed into your document. You can move the image by clicking on the image, holding the mouse button down, and then dragging the image to a new location in your document. You can also resize the image by clicking once on the image, grabbing a corner of the image frame, and then dragging the corner to make the image smaller or larger.

Chronological organization can also be used to organize a narrative in which an action or event is described in the order it occurred. Journalists often use chronology when reporting a story, and historians organize their writing by chronology when discussing historical events. Chronological organization is fairly simple but not simplistic. In the hands of a good writer, narration can be used effectively to make persuasive arguments that appeal to both the heart and the mind. The following passage beautifully illustrates how the simple strategy of chronological narration can be used to make a profound point:

> Let me narrate for you an experience my wife and I had several years ago when I was speaking in the Middle East. At that time the political situation in that subcontinent had reached an ignition point. In fact, foreign delegations were in the vicinity trying to stem the tide of hate and hoping to bring some semblance of peace to that troubled spot of the world. Our journey took us by taxi from Jordan to Israel by way of the West Bank, crossing over at the Allenby Bridge.
>
> When we arrived at the bridge, we got out of the taxi on the Jordanian side and walked with the help of the Jordanian porter to the midpoint of the bridge, which was as far as he was allowed to go. At that juncture an Israeli porter picked up our baggage and escorted us to the Israeli side of the bridge. The lines were very clearly drawn. Once on Israeli soil, we were taken into a highly secured immigration building for routine but rigorous questioning, which was to precede our procurement of a visitor's visa. My wife, our small daughter Sarah, and I stood in one of the lines, having been warned to expect an emotionally taxing, drawn-out morning, possibly taking up the entire day.
>
> I really did not know how best to prepare my daughter for the experience as she was barely two years old. We were surrounded on every side by machine-gun-clutching soldiers whose glares led us to believe that we were all guilty of something. There were sandbags piled against every wall, and a real sense of unease pervaded the room.

Finally it was our turn to be interrogated. Unknown to me, as she surveyed the room filled with armed guards, Sarah had locked eyes with a young Israeli soldier who was staring back at her in eye-to-eye "combat." Suddenly and strangely there was a moment of silence in the room, broken by the squeaky little voice of my daughter asking the soldier, "Excuse me, do you have any bubblegum?"

Words alone cannot fully express to you what that little voice and plea did for everyone in the room, where hitherto the weapons of warfare and the world of "adult ideas" had held everyone at bay. All who understood English could not repress a smile, and all who did not understand English knew a soldier's heart had been irresistibly touched. All eyes were now on him.

He paused for a moment, then carefully handed his machine gun to a colleague. He came over to where we were standing, looked endearingly at Sarah, and picked her up in his arms. He took her into a back room and returned a few minutes later with her in one arm, and in the other hand, he carried three glasses of lemonade on a tray—one for my wife, one for Sarah, and one for me. We were in and out of the immigration office in twenty-five minutes. In fact, the young soldier brought his jeep to the door and drove us to the taxi stand, sending us on our way to Jericho. If you will pardon the pun, another wall had fallen! I have often remarked that Sarah earned her year's keep with one little question voiced at the right time.

The incredible power of a child! For one fleeting moment in that room, she brought the war to a standstill. Indeed, such is the strength of innocence, is it not? One soldier at least saw something in her—maybe the face of his own little girl back home—and the sentiments he felt transcended his immediate world of guns, hatred, and distrust. The wonder-filled face of a two-year-old girl made it possible for him to rise above the all-pervading air of suspicion, and for the sake of life's infancy and essential beauty, to momentarily trade away all other fears. The very strength of that child's influence was only buttressed by the fact that she was not even aware of the power she wielded or of what she had accomplished.[7]

7. Zacharias, *Can Man Live without God?*, 75–77.

Organize by Logical Order

Despite all the current talk about chaos, disorder, and meaninglessness in art, literature, film, music, science, and even architecture, isn't it interesting that we still want the analysis of the chaos and disorder to make sense? Isn't it curious that our discussion of apparent meaninglessness is supposed to be meaningful? In other words, we will indeed encounter instances of chaos and disorder and apparent meaninglessness, but our academic discussion of these attributes must itself be coherent. Our analysis must make sense, and our interpretation must be meaningful. (For the daring among you: the next time you are asked to write an essay about chaos in postmodern film, ask your professor if your essay should be chaotic; or, if you are assigned to give an oral presentation on the meaningless-ness of absurdist drama, ask the professor if your presentation should be absurdly meaningless.) Our readers actually expect our writing to make sense, to be meaningful, and to be logically structured. Our writing must make sense, and organizing paragraphs logically is one way to express our thoughts in meaningfully clear ways.

When organizing a paragraph according to logical order, present key points in the paragraph such that they progress toward a significant con-clusion. In the following example, C. S. Lewis presents a logical progres-sion of arguments, leading readers toward a deeper understanding of why ethical dualism (the belief that good and evil are both eternal absolutes) is problematic and does not make logical sense:

> The moral difficulty is that Dualism gives evil a positive, substan-tive, self-consistent nature, like that of good. If this were true, if Ahriman [a mythical evil spirit] existed in his own right no less than Ormuzd [a mythical good spirit], what could we mean by calling Ormuzd good except that we happen to prefer *him*. In what sense can the one party be said to be right and the other wrong? If evil has the same kind of reality as good, the same autonomy and completeness, our allegiance to good becomes the arbitrarily cho-sen loyalty of a partisan. A sound theory of value demands some-thing different. It demands that good should be original and evil a mere perversion; that good should be the tree and evil the ivy; that good should be able to see all around evil (as when sane men understand lunacy) while evil cannot retaliate in kind; that good

should be able to exist on its own while evil requires the good on which it is parasitic in order to continue its parasitic existence.[8]

Another way to organize a paragraph logically is to move from the general to the specific. First present the larger picture, broader concepts, and general ideas and theories, and then move toward specific examples that illustrate the general point or that provide a more focused analysis of the general observation. In the following example, the writer progresses from general observations to specific applications and examples to provide one explanation for why some people are ungrateful:

> In his *Notes from Underground* in 1864, Dostoevsky wrote of humanity, "If he is not stupid, he is monstrously ungrateful! Phenomenally ungrateful. In fact, I believe that the best definition of man is the ungrateful biped." Albert Camus wrote similarly, "Man's first faculty is forgetting." More recently novelist Milan Kundera attacked the Marxist censorship of history as "organized forgetting." Ingratitude and forgetfulness are ultimately moral rather than mental; they are the direct expression of sin. No culture has nourished such tendencies as consistently as ours. We pride ourselves on being autonomous, self-created, and freestanding. A modern world with no need of God produces modern people with no sense of gratitude.[9]

Conversely, writers can also logically arrange paragraphs by moving from the specific to the general. Instead of offering general observations and then explaining them with specific details, writers can organize a paragraph by first listing various specific details and then drawing a general conclusion or making a broader point. In the next example, notice how the writer provides a specific principle, illustrates it with specific examples, and then uses these examples to make his final, general point:

> The laws of physics, I understand, decree that when one billiards ball (A) sets another billiards ball (B) in motion, the momentum lost by A exactly equals the momentum gained by B. This is a *Law*. That is, this is the pattern to which the movement of the two billiards balls must conform. Provided, of course, that something sets ball A in motion. And here comes the snag. The *law* won't set it in motion. It is usually a man with a cue who does that. But a man with a cue would send us back to free-will, so let us assume that it

8. Lewis, *God in the Dock*, 22–23.
9. Guinness, *The Call*, 195–96.

was lying on a table in a [cruise] liner and that what set it in motion was a lurch of the ship. In that case it was not the law which produced the movement; it was a wave. And that wave, though it certainly moved *according* to the laws of physics, was not moved by them. It was shoved by other waves, and by winds, and so forth. And however far you traced the story back you would never find the *laws* of Nature causing anything.[10]

Using Internal Transitions for Coherence

Have you ever read a paragraph and noticed that it was rather choppy or bumpy like a road with too many potholes? What causes the choppy bumpiness? Let's first consider the pothole—it is a portion of road that is missing. If you fill in the potholes, the road becomes smooth again (assuming you fill the holes properly). The same may be true for choppy, bumpy paragraphs. Sometimes, sentences are just placed together without any words or phrases that provide a smooth movement from one sentence to the next. Such words or phrases are called transitions, and they connect sentences together in meaningful ways that reveal a relationship between the sentences and help create a smooth coherence to the whole paragraph. Words like *first, second,* and *third* suggest chronology; *for example* and *for instance* signal evidence and information to illustrate a point; *however, but,* and *on the other hand* indicate contrasting points; and *similarly, likewise,* and *moreover* suggest comparisons or additional information. The following paragraph I wrote about the film *The Matrix* has had many of its transitional words and phrases removed. Read it out loud:

> In *The Matrix* we are presented with a messianic figure and a full-fledged revolutionary band of cyberpunk warriors. Neo is "the one" and the Wachowski brothers go out of their way to mix pop-philosophy, cyberpunk culture, postmodern theories of simulation, Greek mythology, and Judeo-Christian theology to create a virtual reality narrative. Underlying the amazing special effects and VR narrative mind games is a classic story about the powers of faith and love. Neo is the hero and the one who is destined to save humans from their post-industrial horror. He does not and cannot act alone. His success is based upon the faith and hard work of others, the love and sacrifice of others, determination and faith in himself, and, his own sacrificial love. There are some cool

10. Lewis, *God in the Dock*, 77.

training sessions with Morpheus and his team, a curious meeting with a renegade Oracle, and some daring rescues of Morpheus and Trinity. These and other acts reaffirm Morpheus's child-like faith in the virtual messiah he announced, like a post-industrial John the Baptist. Neo develops a new faith in himself, understands sacrificial faith, and takes a few steps closer to his final transfiguration. It is Trinity's deep physical and spiritual love for Neo that transforms him from a doubting Thomas (his construct's name is Thomas Anderson) to a self-aware savior.

The paragraph generally makes sense, but you have to work extra hard to figure out how the various sentences relate to each other. The paragraph is focused and the information is all relevant to the topic, but the sentences are a bit choppy. The flow of the logic would make more sense and the paragraph would be more coherent if there were some transitional words and phrases linking the sentences together. Here is the same paragraph revised to include transitions (in bold):

In *The Matrix* we are presented with a **messianic** figure and a full-fledged revolutionary band of cyberpunk warriors. Neo is "the one" and the Wachowski brothers go out of their way to mix pop-philosophy, **cyberpunk** culture, postmodern theories of simulation, Greek mythology, and Judeo-Christian theology to create a virtual reality **messianic** narrative. Underlying the amazing special effects and VR narrative mind games is a classic story about the **redemptive** powers of faith and love. **Clearly**, Neo is the **redemptive** hero and the **messianic** one who is destined to save humans from their post-industrial horror, **but** he does not and cannot act alone. **That is**, his success is based upon the faith and hard work of others, the love and sacrifice of others, determination and faith in himself, and, **ultimately**, his own sacrificial love. **For example**, there are some cool training sessions with Morpheus and his team of **cyberpunk** warriors, a curious meeting with a renegade and **self-sacrificing** Oracle, and some daring and **self-sacrificing** rescues of Morpheus and Trinity. These and other **such sacrificial** acts reaffirm Morpheus's child-like faith in the virtual messiah he announced, like a post-industrial John the Baptist. **In the process**, Neo develops a new faith in himself, understands sacrificial faith, and takes a few steps closer to his final transfiguration. **In the end**, it is Trinity's deep physical and spiritual love for Neo that transforms him from a doubting Thomas (his construct's name is Thomas Anderson) to a self-aware savior.

There are different strategies for providing transitions between sentences and thus creating greater coherence within a paragraph. In this example, the most frequently used strategy is repetition of key words. Notice how adjectives like *messianic, redemptive, sacrificial,* and *self-sacrificing* are strategically placed and repeated in order to provide more descriptive information and to indicate comparative relationships between these sentences. Other transitions such as *that is, clearly,* and *ultimately* add emphasis; *but* provides contrast; and *in the end* signals a concluding statement.

When you are crafting your paragraphs, be sure to understand clearly the purpose and focus of the paragraph. Then, carefully choose your transitional words and phrases. The transitions themselves do not create the cohesion; they merely signal connections. Rather, you as thinking writer create the connections and then indicate them to your readers by using transitional words and phrases. Also, be sure not to overdo it. Too many transitional elements can turn a choppy paragraph with too few transitions into a clunky paragraph with too many transitions that may obscure the elegance and meaning of your paragraph. The following is a list of transitional words and phrases commonly used in academic and professional writing:

To Indicate Addition:

and, again, and then, besides, equally important, finally, further, furthermore, in addition, moreover, too, what's more

To Indicate Comparison:

again, also, by comparison, compared to, in the same way, likewise, once more, similarly

To Indicate Contrast or Exception:

although, but, conversely, despite, even though, however, in contrast, in spite of, instead, nevertheless, on the contrary, on the other hand, once in a while, regardless, sometimes, still, though, yet

To Indicate Proof:

clearly, evidently, for, for the same reason, furthermore, indeed, in fact, moreover, obviously, since, that is

To Indicate Time:

after a few days, after a few hours, after a while, afterwards, as long as, as soon as, at last, at that time, before, concurrently, earlier, finally, henceforth, immediately, in the meantime, in the past, lately, later, meanwhile, now, presently, previously, simultaneously, since, so far, soon, then, thereafter, until, when

To Indicate Sequence:

A ... B ... C, again, also, and, and then, besides, finally, first ... second ... third, following, following this, last, next, still, subsequently, too

To Indicate Emphasis:

absolutely, always, certainly, definitely, emphatically, eternally, extremely, in any case, in fact, forever, naturally, obviously, positively, surprisingly, undeniably, unquestionably, without a doubt

To Provide an Example:

after all, even, for example, for instance, in this case, in this situation, indeed, of course, on this occasion, specifically, such as, the following example, to demonstrate, to illustrate

To Indicate Cause and Effect:

accordingly, as a result, because, consequently, for this purpose, hence, so, then, therefore, thus, to this end

To Indicate Place or Location or Proximity:

above, adjacent to, below, beyond, closer to, elsewhere, far, farther on, here, near, nearby, on the right, on the left, opposite to, there, to the left, to the right

To Indicate Concession:

admittedly, although it is true that, apparently, granted that, I admit that, it may appear that, naturally, of course, supposedly

To Indicate Summary, Repetition, or Conclusion:

accordingly, as a result, as has been noted, as has been shown, as has been stated, as I have said, as I have shown, as we have seen, as mentioned earlier, hence, in any event, in brief, in conclusion, in other words, in short, on the whole, summing up, therefore, to conclude, to summarize

Writing Tips:

1. Unity and coherence go hand in hand. When revising your paragraphs, make sure they are clearly focused and that all the information and sentences are relevant to the topic of the paragraph.

2. Use transitional phrases strategically. Remember that the writer creates the connections and uses the appropriate transitional words and phrases. Avoid using transitions just for the sake of using transitions. You want your writing to be as natural as possible, and overusing transitions or using them inappropriately can make your writing seem forced, artificial, and sophomoric.

How to Develop Paragraphs

Readers generally read for enjoyment and edification. For many, the enjoyment of reading is directly related to learning—the more insights and information gained, the greater the experience of enjoyment. As writers, we should think about satisfying our readers by providing them with as much specific and relevant information as possible. We can do so by developing our paragraphs. Good paragraphs provide specific details and quality information to satisfy the reader's desire to learn. Let's look at an example paragraph from an early draft of a paper I wrote on Mary Shelley's novel *Frankenstein*:

> Mary Shelley's famous novel *Frankenstein* ponders the question of creation and origins from scientific and theistic perspectives. We now hold knowledge that may allow us to do exactly what Mary only dreamed of through the scientist character Victor. This novel is a speculative narrative that is relevant to our contemporary society.

This paragraph has potential; however, in its current state it is not terribly satisfying, mainly because it doesn't tell us very much. We want more information, more details, and more discussion. Let's look at my revision of this paragraph:

> Mary Shelley's famous novel *Frankenstein* ponders the question of creation and origins from scientific and theistic perspectives, but it does not embrace secular humanism or celebrate a subversion of theistic creation in favor of scientific materialism. On the contrary, this novel grips our imaginations still today because the ultimate transgressive horrors of which it speaks pertain particularly to our scientifically advanced culture. We now hold knowledge that may allow us to do exactly what Mary only dreamed of through the scientist character Victor. In other words, *Frankenstein* may no longer be a vicarious thrill, but a terrifying mirror reflecting a horrific reality we are unprepared to accept. This novel is a speculative narrative that asks, what would happen if man attempted to create in the absence of woman and with indifference to God? What if Adam were to reject his own Creator and create life after his own fleshly or material image? Mary's answer to these questions is not a triumphant humanist manifesto, nor is it an ironic subversion of a supposedly outmoded theistic perspective. Rather, it is a philosophical nightmare revealing the horrific consequences of scientific naturalism taken to its logical conclusion. *Frankenstein* explores the ideological vacuum engendered by materialism and examines the futility of replacing theism with secular humanism.

See the difference? Now we have some ideas to sink our teeth into. Now readers have something to consider, to think about, and to engage in their own minds and imaginations. What are some key differences between the two paragraphs? Sure, the second one is much longer and more developed, but how? First, the basic ideas and concepts are listed, outlined, and described. Second, the main idea is contrasted to an opposing idea (notice the transitional "but" and "on the contrary" statements that provide content through contrast). Third, some key questions are asked and then briefly answered. When drafting and revising essays, it is important to examine each of the paragraphs to make sure they are focused, coherent, and developed. Let's examine some common strategies for developing paragraphs.

Develop with Narration

Narration is basically a story or a description of some event. We have already encountered narration in the earlier section on organizing paragraphs using chronology. Narration is an effective strategy for developing your writing by providing narrative details of an event or by discussing a personal experience that relates to the issue or topic being discussed. Important features of a narration are chronological structure, a general plot line (beginning, conflict or action, climax to the story, and resolution or ending), vivid descriptions (appealing to the senses), and specific details. As you provide details and descriptions, your narrative writing will become more developed. The following paragraph is developed with a narrative example:

> It began with one pig at a British slaughterhouse. Somewhere along the production line it was observed that the animal had blisters in his mouth and was salivating. The worst suspicions were confirmed, and within days borders had been sealed and a course of action determined. Soon all of England and the world watched as hundreds, and then thousands, of pigs, cows, and sheep and their newborn lambs were taken outdoors, shot, thrown into burning pyres, and bulldozed into muddy graves. Reports described terrified cattle being chased by sharpshooters, clambering over one another to escape. Some were still stirring and blinking a day after being shot. The plague meanwhile had slipped into mainland Europe, where the same ritual followed until, when it was all over, more than ten million animals had been disposed of. Completing the story with the requisite happy ending was a calf heard calling from underneath the body of her mother in a mound of carcasses to be set aflame. Christened "Phoenix," after the bird of myth that rose from the ashes, the calf was spared.[11]

Avoid telling stories just for the sake of telling stories; rather, try to use narratives to introduce or illustrate a main point. In the above example, the writer narrates a poignant event to introduce a book-length study of rational, ethical, and religious reasons why we should be merciful toward animals, even though we have dominion over them.

Narratives can also be placed within larger discussions to provide a personal anecdote for the purposes of illustration or emotional appeal. The following sample narrative paragraph by Matthew Scully comes after he first discusses why it is important for humans to provide mercy to animals, particularly since animals cannot ask for mercy nor can they rebuke us for unnecessarily hurting them. This anecdote illustrates that

11. Scully, *Dominion*, ix.

mercy toward animals can come in acts of kindness that on the surface seem violent:

> I felt a similar sense of wonder—to share a less heartwarming story—when I was twelve or so and killed a bird. I was strolling along one day with our family dog when suddenly I heard a peeping noise. Looking over a bridge railing, I saw in the stream below a little robin splashing and flailing about. Just a fledgling, he was badly injured, bleeding from a severed wing and, as I assumed, not long for this world. Perhaps a cat had done it. The memory of what I did then still comes back to me sometimes. I lifted him from the stream and set him on an embankment, I tried to stroke him, I talked to him a bit, telling him how sorry I was for what I had to do, and then to end his misery I crushed him with a large rock.[12]

Scully uses narrative quite effectively to shock readers on an emotional level in order to prepare them for the intellectual challenges of his later discussions regarding the moral responsibilities humans have toward animals. In short, narration develops paragraphs by using anecdotes, personal experience, conflict, details, and description.

Develop with Comparison and Contrast

In addition to narration, we can also develop our paragraphs by using the rhetorical strategy of comparison and contrast. Comparison reveals the similarities between various concepts, ideas, topics, or objects; contrast explains the differences between things. Comparison and contrast are often used as methods for better understanding something by placing it in relationship to something else. By writing comparison or contrast, we necessarily must use more language to describe and explain the relationship (be it a similarity or a difference), resulting in more developed writing. There are two basic methods for structuring a comparison or contrast: block method and alternating method. In the block method, you describe all the aspects of one item in a single block of sentences, and then describe the other item in a separate block of sentences. Usually, a transitional phrase is used between the blocks of sentences to reveal the comparison ("similarly," "in the same way," or "likewise") or the contrast ("on the other hand," "on the contrary," or "by contrast"). Notice how a

---

12. Scully, *Dominion*, 4.

block structure is used in the following contrast paragraph, and look for the transitional phrases signaling the contrast:

> This [materialistic] philosophy controls academic work not only in science but in all fields, including law, literature and psychology. It is promulgated throughout the educational system and the mainstream media, and government backs it. Superficially it seems as immovable as that great log that bars your progress on that mountain road. But on closer examination, the log is marked by cracks. The most important crack in the modernist log is the difference between two distinct definitions of science. On the one hand, modernists say that science is impartial fact-finding, the objective and unprejudiced weighing of evidence. Science in that sense relies on careful observations, calculations, and above all, repeatable experiments. That kind of objective science is what makes technology possible, and where it can be employed it is indeed the most reliable way of determining the facts. On the other hand, the modernists also identify science with naturalistic philosophy. In that case science is committed to finding and endorsing naturalistic explanations for every phenomenon—*regardless of the facts*. That kind of science is not free of prejudice. On the contrary, it is *defined* by prejudice. The prejudice is that all phenomenon can ultimately be explained in terms of purely natural causes, which is to say unintelligent causes.[13]

You can organize a comparison/contrast paragraph by using the block method (as in the above example) or by using the alternating method, also known as the point-by-point method. This simply means that you describe an aspect from the first item followed by a description of an aspect from the second item, explaining the similarity or difference depending upon if you are comparing or contrasting. Alternate back and forth between the two items, discussing them point by point until you have addressed all of the important elements. Notice in the following example how my focus shifts back and forth between the two poems being compared:

> Samuel Taylor Coleridge and Percy Shelley both wrote beautiful poems about the ironic failures of creativity. In "Kubla Khan" Coleridge describes the fantastical realm of Xanadu, built by the powerful ruler Kubla Khan. Shelley in his poem "Ozymandias" describes the ruined remains of a statue built thousands of years ago in honor of the Egyptian king Ozymandias. In Coleridge's

---

13. Johnson, *The Wedge of Truth*, 14.

poem, the speaker has a vision of the wondrous Xanadu, the magical caves of ice, and the majestic pleasure dome, but he loses this vision and is desperate to reclaim it. In Shelley's poem, the ruthless king arrogantly claimed that he was the king of kings and that his impressive city and statue proves his eternal dominion over all things. Ironically, all that is now left of his great empire and art are crumbling ruins mocking his arrogance. Both of these poems explore the sad truth that, despite humanity's best efforts, art is just as physical and temporary as this life on earth. However, the one hope rising from the lost vision and the crumbled statue is the possibility that the imagination itself is eternal. Although the art may someday cease to exist, the imagination lives on forever in the eternal soul of each individual person.

Develop with Illustrations and Examples

The most direct way to develop a paragraph is to provide illustrations and examples. It is not enough to express an observation or opinion divorced from evidence, proof, or explanation; readers want details to illustrate the observations, and they want discussion to explain the details. If you are making general observations, then follow them up with evidence, illustrations, and details. Give examples and your paragraph will be more developed and more interesting to read. Notice how G. K. Chesterton in the following example provides an intense series of illustrations and examples to support his general observation:

> And the fact that [the revolutionist] doubts everything really gets in his way when he wants to denounce anything. For all denunciation implies a moral doctrine of some kind; and the modern revolutionist doubts not only the institution he denounces, but the doctrine by which he denounces it. Thus he writes one book complaining that imperial oppression insults the purity of women, and then he writes another book (about the sex problem) in which he insults it himself. He curses the Sultan because Christian girls lose their virginity, and then curses Mrs. Grundy because they keep it. As a politician he will cry out that war is a waste of life, and then, as a philosopher, that all life is a waste of time. A Russian pessimist will denounce a policeman for killing a peasant, and then prove by the highest philosophical principles that the peasant ought to have killed himself. A man denounces marriage as a lie, and then denounces aristocratic profligates for treating it as a lie. He calls a flag a bauble, and then blames the oppressors of Poland or Ireland

because they take away that bauble. The man of this school goes
first to a political meeting, where he complains that savages are
treated as if they were beasts; then he takes his hat and umbrella
and goes on to a scientific meeting, where he proves that they
practically are beasts. In short, the modern revolutionist, being an
infinite skeptic, is always engaged in undermining his own mines.
In his book on politics he attacks men for trampling on morality;
in his book on ethics he attacks morality for trampling on men.
Therefore the modern man in revolt has become practically useless for all purposes of revolt. By rebelling against everything he
has lost his right to rebel against anything.[14]

Develop with Definitions

A definition is an explanation of what a word, idea, or concept means.
Most of the time, we can assume our readers understand the majority
of the words we are using. However, if you are exploring a new topic or
discovery, or if you are discussing a specialized academic, scientific, or
technical topic, your target audience may not be familiar with certain key
terms. In such situations, you should define these terms. Therefore, you
may find yourself on occasion developing paragraphs by explaining the
definitions of words and relating the terms to your focus or main point.
For example, a discussion in philosophy usually starts with a clarification
of categories or definitions, and then elaborate arguments are fashioned
based upon these definitions. (The next time you attend a philosophy lecture or read a philosophical essay, note how many times words are defined
and terms are clarified before an argument is made and defended.) Here
is an example of carefully defining the meaning of a word:

> What is meant here by *monarch* may be understood by a brief
> analysis of the word's original meaning. The term *monarchy* is
> made up of a prefix and a root. The prefix *mono* means "one, sin-
> gular." The root, which is more significant, is *archē*, which means
> "chief, beginning, or root." It is often used as a prefix in English,
> as in *archbishops, archenemies, archetypes, archheretics,* and *arch-
> angels.* Here, *arch* means "chief, ruler." An archangel is a chief or
> ruling angel, as an archbishop is a chief or ruling bishop. The later
> connotation of *monarch* as a political figure rests on the idea of
> one chief ruler.[15]

14. Chesterton, *Orthodoxy*, 46–47.
15. Sproul, *The Consequences of Ideas*, 13–14.

In addition to explaining the technical meaning of a single word, writers sometimes must also define concepts that are usually expressed in phrases, as in the following example:

> Perhaps you have heard of "chaos physics." This name suggests a kind of commitment to chaos, but the opposite is the case. Chaos physics probes elements of *apparent* chaos in order to discover patterns of order that lurk beneath the surface. These physicists study such things as the dynamics of fluid motion, the topography of seacoasts, the structure of snowflakes, and the patterns of wind currents that influence weather. In some respects modern chaos theory recapitulates in a more technical and sophisticated manner the pursuit of cosmos by ancient philosophers.[16]

Develop with Division

Sometimes, the best way to explain something is to divide it into its component parts. Writers in the technical professions and scientific fields often use division to define technical terms or to explain how complex functions operate. In the following example, the writer uses division as a way to explain how traditional definitions of science try to exclude intelligent design from the field of scientific inquiry:

> The charge is frequently made that design is not science. To make this charge stick, however, one needs to demonstrate that genuine science exhibits some feature that design lacks. Many such features have been proposed to date. Yet none has succeeded in showing that design stands outside science. Either the proposed feature is too lenient (thus including design after all) or too stringent (excluding not just design but other forms of inquiry that we do want to count as science), or it constitutes an arbitrary imposition on science, deliberately defining science so that it excludes design.[17]

Develop with Classification

Related to division is the process of classification. Where division breaks a concept or process into component parts, classification organizes several related items into groups determined by shared characteristics. Each group is a different class (thus the term classification). Writers of phi-

16. Ibid, 15.
17. Dembski, *Intelligent Design*, 252–53.

losophy and law use classification to explain concepts, ideas, or principles. Scientific writers use classification to discuss complex processes. Literary scholars use classification to group different types of literature into such genres as poetry, fiction, nonfiction, and drama. In the following example, notice how the writer combines classification with comparison/contrast to discuss two philosophical schools of thought:

> The Western philosophical tradition has thus bequeathed to us two competing metaphysical models: one in which everything is to be explained ultimately in terms of blind and purposeless forces (the materialistic model); and one in which purposefulness is a fundamental and irreducible reality (the teleological model). The most important question, from an epistemological point of view, is this: where should we locate the presumption of truth, and where the burden of proof? There are compelling grounds for placing the burden of proof on the materialistic model. Even stalwart Darwinists like Richard Dawkins admit that the defining task of biology is to explain the existence of things that appear to be designed. Cicero, in *On the Nature of the Gods*, Book II, reports Aristotle's cave analogy: if a group of people had spent all of their lives underground and then emerged on the surface, they would be bound to think of the biologically rich world they discovered there to be the product of intelligence. Only familiarity dulls our sense of wonder at the craftsmanship of nature.[18]

Develop with Cause and Effect

Common, everyday experience shows us that effects have causes. Such philosophers as David Hume and Immanuel Kant have demonstrated that in some cases it may be difficult (if not impossible) to determine absolutely the specific cause for a given effect. But these philosophers did not suggest or even attempt to prove that there are absolutely no causes for known effects. A cause for an effect may be unknown or even unknowable, but this does not mean the cause is nonexistent. When arguing a point, developing an idea, or explaining a concept, you may need to discuss and explain a cause for a certain effect. Science is predicated upon discovering causes; its whole reason for being is to search out and identify causes for phenomena we witness all around us. (If we were ever to decide that there are no causes for effects or that it is totally impossible

18. Koons, "The Check Is in the Mail," 7.

to discover causes, then science would be out of business.) Discussing cause and effect can be a productive way to develop a paragraph. Basically, describe the effect or phenomena and then explain what the cause is (or may be). Or, you can describe a cause (an action or an idea or a policy or a theory) and then explain the ramifications or effects of that cause, as the following example illustrates:

> As a result, according to critics, the main effect of the inquiry approach to values teaching is to "liberate" students from the moral standards they bring into the classroom from home and church. Moreover, the method offers students no alternative standard, leaving them with nothing higher than their own subjective likes and dislikes—or worse, the pressures of the peer group. One education professor, Thomas Lickona, relates the story of a teacher who used the values clarification strategy with a class of low-achieving eighth-graders. Having worked through the requisite steps, the students concluded that their four most popular activities were "sex, drugs, drinking, and skipping school." The teacher was hamstrung: Her students had clarified their values, and the method gave her no leverage for persuading them that these values were unhealthy, destructive, or morally wrong. Thus the main legacy of pragmatism in moral education is that teachers no longer impart to students the great moral ideals that have inspired virtually all civilizations, but instead train them to probe their own subjective feelings and values.[19]

Develop with Questions and Answers

Readers want information. They have questions and they expect writers to provide some answers, or at least to provide enough information to lead them deeper into their quest for answers. An effective way to organize and develop paragraphs is to pose the questions that are on the readers' minds and then discuss the answers. However, avoid relying too heavily on questions and answers in your paragraphs, because your essay will start to read like an online frequently asked questions (FAQ) page. If you have ever tried to read an FAQ, you know how tedious that can be. Q and A is great, but do not overdo it. In the following example, the writers argue that scientific evidence clearly demonstrates that the universe had a beginning (it is not an eternal steady state, nor is it in an eternal state

19. Pearcey, "Darwin Meets the Berenstein Bears," 67–68.

of expansion and contraction). One strand of evidence they discuss is the unidirectional expansion of the universe. Notice how they begin the paragraph with the obvious question on readers' minds and then develop the paragraph by answering that question:

> How does the expanding universe prove a beginning? Think about it this way: if we could watch a video recording of the history of the universe in reverse, we would see all matter in the universe collapse back to a point, not the size of a basketball, not the size of a golf ball, not even the size of a pinhead, but mathematically and logically to a point that is actually nothing (i.e., no space, no time, and no matter). In other words, once there was nothing, and then, BANG, there was something—the entire universe exploded into being! This, of course, is what is commonly called "the Big Bang."[20]

Develop by Combining Strategies

Writers can organize and develop their paragraphs by using one of these common paragraphing strategies; or, they can combine different development strategies. For example, a definition can be comprised of classifications. Or, illustrations and examples can be used when trying to discuss causes and their effects. Or, when posing a question, comparison and contrast can be used to answer the question. Do not feel confined by these strategies, as if they are static models. They only appear static or rigid because they have to be classified, organized, explained, and then illustrated so that we can understand them individually. Now that you know about these strategies of organization and development, think of them as different writing tools that can be used individually and in combination to achieve specific writing goals. As writer, you need to assess your audience, consider your message, and contemplate your purpose (the rhetorical situation of writing). Then you will be able to make clearer writing choices when deciding how to organize and develop your paragraphs.

20. Geisler and Turek, *I Don't Have Enough Faith to Be an Atheist*, 79.

Writing Tips:

1. As you read different types of writing (journal articles, newspaper articles, magazines, academic essays, textbooks, letters, memos, e-mails, blogs), notice how the paragraphs are structured and developed. Try to establish a general sense of appropriate paragraph development for different modes of writing.

2. When revising your essays, examine each paragraph carefully, keeping these development strategies clearly in mind. Scan your draft and look for short paragraphs that can use more development, and consider various strategies for developing them. Also, look for paragraphs that are too long. One possible problem could be that the paragraph is not properly focused and should be divided into separately focused, yet developed, paragraphs.

TRANSITIONS BETWEEN PARAGRAPHS

We have already considered transitions *within* paragraphs, but we also need to discuss transitions *between* paragraphs. Just as sentences need to flow smoothly from one to the next, so too must paragraphs. A paragraph lacking transitional elements can be very choppy. Similarly, an essay without smooth transitions between paragraphs may read like a laundry list of observations and ideas. It is the responsibility of the writer to arrange the paragraphs in a logical order and to direct the readers smoothly between the paragraphs.

Sometimes, all it takes to provide a smooth transition between paragraphs is simply to use a transitional word or phrase at the beginning of the new paragraph (review the list above in the subsection titled *Using Internal Transitions for Coherence*). Transitions like *however, in addition, on the other hand*, and *consequently* help direct the reader from the last thought in the previous paragraph to the new thought of the next paragraph. Or, you can repeat a word or idea from the last sentence of the previous paragraph in the first sentence of the new paragraph. Whatever strategy you use, keep in mind that your goal is to remind the readers where they have been and then direct them to where they are going. Transitions between paragraphs are like road signs, directing readers through the essay. Just as when we travel we are comforted by clear signs and directions guiding us to our destination, readers are equally comforted and reassured when they encounter helpful transitions directing them through an essay. However, be careful not to be too forceful or overbearing with the transitions, as this will annoy your readers. Also, try to vary your transitions. Using the same transitional technique over and over creates a distracting repetitiveness in your writing.

Writing Tips:

1. Writing effective transitions between paragraphs is an important skill to develop. Learn from the writers you are asked to read in your various classes. You will do a lot of reading in college. Try to learn both the *content* of the writing and the *method* by which the content is expressed. Look for transitional techniques used by the writers you are assigned in your various classes and try to model your own writing after the good examples you encounter.

2. Experiment with different transitional techniques during the drafting phase of writing. Take chances and see what works and what does not.

CHECKLIST FOR HEALTHY PARAGRAPHS

As you draft and revise your essays, review your paragraphs for focus, cohesiveness, and development, and make sure you are providing constructive transitions between your paragraphs. Here is a revision checklist for healthy paragraphs:

✓ Transition element smoothly directing readers into the new paragraph

✓ Topic sentence (placed at the beginning, at the end, or both, depending upon the purpose of the paragraph)

✓ Clear discussion of the topic or issue of the paragraph

✓ Sufficient information, data, evidence, and examples to accomplish the goal of the paragraph

✓ Logical organization of the information

✓ Cohesiveness (all the information in the paragraph is relevant to the topic discussed in the paragraph)

✓ Smooth transitions between the sentences where appropriate

CONCLUSION

Reading an essay, an article, or a chapter in a book is a big commitment. Readers do not want to waste their time trudging through poor writing, and if they sense that a document is poorly written, then chances are they will not bother to read it. By the same token, writing an essay, an article, or a chapter in a book is a big commitment. Few people want to spend a lot of time writing something if no one is going to read it. Basically, we are dealing with a set of reciprocal expectations. Writers expect to be read and readers expect to gain something from reading. If you have an important message to convey and a valuable purpose to accomplish, then you must be sure to understand the needs and expectations of your readers. Accomplishing this difficult task begins with understanding the importance of using paragraphs to organize your thoughts and to present your information in meaningful, digestible chunks. Which is more enjoyable: picking through food arranged haphazardly on a table, or sitting down to a carefully planned banquet with crafted courses designed to complement each other and to delight the palate? More than likely, the chaotic mess on the table will not be eaten (unless, of course, you are really, really hungry). However, the sophisticated banquet will be enjoyed and remembered for a long time to come. When crafting your essays, avoid the messy table and try your best to create a pleasing banquet, one that will delight and edify your readers.

DISCUSSION QUESTIONS

1. Discuss the main function of a paragraph. Why should we bother ourselves with proper paragraphing in our essays?

2. Reflect upon your own writing practices. What will you try to do differently when writing paragraphs that you were not doing before?

3. What is a topic sentence and why should paragraphs have one? Where can topic sentences come in a paragraph? Explain the reasoning behind different placements of topic sentences.

4. Describe one paragraph development technique in your own words and explain why you think it is particularly useful for your writing.

GROUP ACTIVITIES

1. As a group, pick a topic and each person write a paragraph about that topic. Exchange paragraphs and then review the topic sentences. Rewrite the person's paragraph and experiment with making the topic sentence more concrete. Also, try placing the topic sentence in different places (beginning, end, or both). Discuss how the paragraph changes depending upon where the topic sentence is situated.

2. If you are working on a draft of an essay, exchange drafts in your group. Review the draft and pick out a paragraph for revision. Explain how you think the paragraph could be improved, and then write one or two revisions of that paragraph, using different paragraph strategies discussed in this chapter.

3. In your group, exchange drafts of an essay you are working on. Examine the draft carefully and underline the topic sentence(s) in each paragraph. Comment on the quality and placement of the topic sentences and suggest revisions.

4. In your group, pick one draft to be read out loud to the other group members. Listen to the draft and see if you can tell just from hearing when a new paragraph has started. Are there transitions between paragraphs? Are they smooth? Are they jarring or clunky? Suggest revisions to help create smooth transitions between paragraphs. Also, indicate if a paragraph is too long, too short, or unfocused and suggest how it might be revised.

WRITING ACTIVITIES

1. Pick an article from the collection in the back of the book. Browse through the article, paying attention to how the writer constructs paragraphs. Write a brief evaluation (one or two paragraphs) in

which you discuss the strengths and weaknesses of the paragraphs in the article. Comment on such things as the use and placement of topic sentences, organization of content in the paragraphs, internal transitions, development, and transitions between paragraphs.

2. Randomly choose a paragraph from an article collected in the back of the book or from a chapter of this textbook. Carefully read the paragraph and point out any transitional elements within the paragraph. Refresh your memory by reviewing the section above on transitions within paragraphs.

3. Review one of your essay drafts you are currently working on and pick out a clearly underdeveloped paragraph. Analyze the paragraph and first decide if it is properly focused with a clear topic sentence and make any necessary revisions. Then, decide how you could develop the paragraph more fully by using various development strategies described in this chapter. Experiment with a few and revise the paragraph to make it more developed.

4. If your class has a blog or a discussion board (for example in Blackboard or WebCT), browse through some of the postings and review how the student writers use paragraphs. Consider the difference good paragraphing makes when writing online. How will you use paragraphs in the future to write more organized blog postings or discussion board entries?

4

Fundamentals of Critical Thinking

Questions to Consider before Reading

1. What is critical thinking?

2. What does it mean to be critical? Do you have to be negative to be critical? Does positive commentary have a role to play in critical thinking?

3. What is logical thinking? What constitutes a good logical argument?

4. What is the relationship between logical thinking and critical thinking?

5. What is the relationship between critical thinking and academic writing?

Introduction

Too often these days, good thinking and good writing do not necessarily coincide. Of course, one has to think in order to write, because writing is an expression of deliberate thought. After all, how many times have you sat down at the computer and mindlessly typed out a paper? Or, have you ever grabbed a pen for no apparent reason and started scribbling out words and sentences mechanically without ever thinking about what you are writing? I would hazard to guess that few people have done so.

To be fair, there are reports of people experiencing the mystical phenomenon known as automatic writing, where supposedly an individual is guided by spirits to take dictation from the nether world. I do not wish to disparage a person's experience. Certainly, there have been many scientific and psychological explanations for automatic writing, ever since it became popular in the West, particularly during the rise of spiritualism and various psychic societies of the nineteenth and early twentieth centuries. Moreover, various cultures' religious experiences and practices involve this kind of mesmeric expression in which the individual's cognitive self is somehow disconnected from his or her physical experience of writing. But aside from such mystical occurrences that a few people may or may not have experienced, I think it is safe to say that generally speaking, good writing is mindful writing. We must be in control of our minds and be thinking clearly if we want to express ourselves effectively in writing.

Writing in the professional and academic arenas is a natural extension of rational thought. Through our writing we relate proclamations of fact, statements of belief, and expressions of truth. There should be a sound correlation, if not a direct correspondence, between what we say and what is known to be true. Our writing should be logical, it should be supported by factual information and evidence, and it should relate reasonably well to lived experience. In short, our professional and academic writing should be rational, and developing rational writing involves developing our critical thinking skills.

Remember, in the introduction to this book we noted that we think to write and we write to think. We are more than mere wind-up toys, clockworks, or mechanical expressions of DNA. We are not robotic entities operating from a predetermined organic program, for if this were the case, then anything we thought (if it could even be labeled as thought) would not be our own but would be a mere mechanical expression of a program we did not write and over which we have no control or influence. We would have no free thought and no free will, and any verbal or written expression would be at most a mere reaction to environment and not the product of free thought or free agency. (If you think about it, such an extreme materialist view is more akin to the spiritualist idea of automatic writing than the scientific materialist would ever dream—both views reduce the individual to a mere robotic object of another force or causal agent; for the spiritualist it is some spirit and for the materialist it is DNA.)

Of course, this materialistic representation of the human person is rather counterintuitive (that is, it is not consistent with our experience), and it is not sufficiently supported by empirical evidence (such reductions of immaterial mind to mere material brain cannot claim adequate scientific evidence). Moreover, if it were indeed the case that we do not have minds and we are merely overdetermined organic machines, then colleges and universities would have a hard time justifying why they grade student performance in writing classes, because ultimately student ability to write well or not would be beyond individual control, completely determined by material programming. It would be unfair to reward or penalize students for their writing skill or lack thereof, because, in the end, such skill levels would be beyond individual control. The main point, here, is simply this: since we are free agents with the ability to think, and since we express our thinking through writing, then it makes logical sense to conclude that there is a direct relationship between good thinking and good writing. In order to develop our writing skills, we should also work on developing our critical thinking skills.

WHAT IS CRITICAL THINKING?

What comes to mind when you hear the words *critical thinking*? Let's just focus on the word *critical*—what does this mean to you? Maybe you think about negative feedback, or possibly film critics who are always bashing the movies you love. Maybe you think of political pessimists who always seem have something bad to say about the state of the world by concentrating on a few negative facts and ignoring information to the contrary. Or, maybe self-proclaimed realists come to mind, those folks who are really just negative skeptics and rarely have anything good to say about anything. I am confident that for most people, this is the dominant impression of the word *critical*—something negative, harsh, or bad. However, there are other notions that some people may think about when they hear this word *critical*. What about such concepts as *vital*, or *important*, or *essential*? A critical argument is one that is central to someone's position. Or, a critical piece of legislature is one that is vitally important to the nation. Another example is critical care in a hospital; this is medical treatment that is essential to the survival of a severely injured person. So, the word *critical* has a variety of meanings and connotations associated with it, making the concept of critical thinking a bit tricky to define.

However, just because it is hard to pin down the meaning of *critical* does not mean that we cannot know or understand the concept of critical thinking. A constructive way to come to a better understanding of *criti-

cal thinking is to consider the relationship of these two words. The term *critical* here refers to analysis. When we analyze something, we break it down into its various components, evaluate the strengths and weaknesses of those components, and consider how they work together to complete the whole. Being critical, in this case, means being analytical. As such, the final assessment of the analysis or the criticism can be negative, positive, or some combination of the two. The term *thinking* refers to the logical or rational methodology by which we conduct our analysis. Critical thinking, then, is simply the cognitive method by which we analyze and evaluate concepts, ideas, arguments, points of view, and problem-solving strategies. Okay, the word *simply* is misleading here, because the process of critical thinking is rarely simple or easy. But, the concept itself is rather straightforward. Critical thinking is a strategy of analyzing and evaluating topics, issues, and situations so that we can develop sound points of view on a subject, arrive at the best possible solution to a problem, or develop a reasonable course of action when faced with a decision.

Good critical thinking is predicated upon developing proficiency in analysis, evaluation, and logic. As we develop these skills and strengthen our critical thinking, we will be able to develop and strengthen our writing in at least two ways. First, critical thinking sharpens our ability to think clearly and rationally about complex issues, allowing us to express more reasonable points of view that are supported by good logic, sound evidence, and relevant experience. Second, critical thinking presents us with strategies for evaluating our own writing. Most of our critical thinking is directed at analyzing the thoughts, views, and positions of others and to evaluate information we plan to use in our writing. However, we should also learn to direct good critical thinking at our own writing to make sure the views we express and the positions we hold are as solid, valid, and reasonable as possible. Critical thinking helps us accomplish these goals and thus allows us to develop and strengthen our writing.

FIRST PRINCIPLES

Good critical thinking is grounded in logical thinking. Logic is the method of reasoning by which we consider information, arrange arguments, ground positions in assumptions and principles (presuppositions), use evidence, and draw conclusions. Logic distinguishes the content of a thought or conclusion from the method by which the thought or conclusion is derived. To be good critical thinkers, we need to be good logicians or practitioners of logic.

In some circles it has become fashionable to deny the importance of logic or to suggest that logic, traditionally understood, is simply a Western perspective that denies the legitimacy of other systems of thought, like Eastern perspectives. Since this is not a book on the history of philosophical discourses, I do not have the room to analyze all of these important issues. For our purposes, which is learning how to think clearly so that we can be effective writers, it is sufficient to first realize that it is a fallacy (an error in argumentation) to reduce the subject of logical discourse to geographical or cultural categories like "West" and "East." There were Western thinkers who disagreed with traditionally Western logical systems yet who knew nothing of Eastern philosophy. Similarly, there were Western thinkers who developed modes of thinking on their own that resembled traditionally Eastern systems of thought. On the other hand, there were Eastern thinkers who critiqued and disagreed with traditional Eastern logic, arguing from within those systems without resorting to traditionally Western thinking, even though their critiques and objections were in agreement with Western thought.

Basically, logical thinking is rational regardless of where you were born. People in China, for example, look both ways before crossing the street just as people do in the United States of America, because in both countries it is equally true that when entering the street, either the person or the oncoming car will pass, not both of them. (As you will soon learn, this is an example of the principle of noncontradiction.)

Principles of logic are fundamental to good thinking. We simply cannot think soundly or rationally without resorting to logic. Even the attempt to deny the legitimacy of logic requires the use of logic. If anyone tells you logic is not necessary for good thinking, simply ask how that conclusion was reached. Invariably, logic was used to reach that (illogical) conclusion. Note what this statement reveals: the use of logic does not mean you will necessarily arrive at the right answer or the truth. Logic is merely a system of thought by which we derive statements and arrive at conclusions. The truthfulness or falsity of the statement or claim must then be ascertained (more on that later). Sound thinking is based upon appropriate uses of foundational principles or laws of logic. These principles of logic are undeniable and self-evident. You cannot "get behind them" because there is nothing more behind them. They are the most basic or fundamental aspects of concepts and ideas. They are the underlying cognitive structures that must exist prior to rational thinking. They allow for thinking to exist. They are just given. They are, quite simply, undeniable and self-evidently true. That is, they cannot be denied without first using the principle in its own denial. Therefore, they are irreducibly, self-evidently, and undeniably true. Indeed, some may quibble with them or try to deny them, but they must in some way resort to using them in the act of quibbling and denying; therefore, they are inescapable.

For the past two thousand years or so, ever since Aristotle formalized the study of logic in the fourth century B.C. for the Western intellectual tradition, several laws or principles of logic have been discovered and articulated. For our purposes, let's look at five very important principles of logic that when properly understood, help us analyze logically and think critically.

Principle of Noncontradiction

The principle or law of noncontradiction states that something cannot be both true and false at the same time in the same way. Another way of expressing this principle is to say that something cannot both be A and non-A at the same time in the same way. For example, I, David S. Hogsette, cannot be both the writer and not the writer of this book. I either wrote it or I did not. And, since there are no coauthors for this book, we cannot hedge by saying I am a writer of this book but not the only writer of the book. Here is another example: You are walking with your parents in a park, and a person comes up to your parents and asks if the woman holding your father's hand (your mother) is his wife. If your mother says yes and your father says no, you have a real problem! Both of them cannot be right. They may have misunderstood or misheard the question, but both of their answers cannot be correct in relation to the actual question being asked.

In our thinking and writing, we must be careful not to contradict the facts (as best we can know them), or to contradict our own statements or principles. Sound logic tells us that something is either A or non-A (or some reasonable degree in between), but not both at the same time in the same way. Good critical thinking follows this fundamental principle of logic. Indeed, some have tried to deny this basic law of logic, but to do so requires the use of the law being denied, which simply verifies that the law is actually true. (To say the law of noncontradiction is not true presumes that the opposite claim, that it is true, is itself not true, which is a use of the law of noncontradiction, thereby requiring and proving it to be true. In other words, to say something is false requires the opposite to be true, which means that the claim and its opposite are not both true. This is an example of using the law of noncontradiction. Therefore, to say the law of noncontradiction is not true requires you to use it. Denying this law affirms it. Think about it for a moment or two and it will make sense. Trust me.)

Principle of the Excluded Middle

This principle is related to the first principle of noncontradiction, and it basically states that either a statement or its opposite is true and there is no middle or third option between these two opposites. Another way of formulating this principle is to say if a statement is not true then its opposite (or its denial) is true; or, conversely, if a statement is true then its opposite (or denial) is not true. It is clear that this principle logically stems from the law of noncontradiction, but it is not as widely believed or held to be true like the law of noncontradiction. At first glance, it seems reasonable that this law should be undeniable. If the statement "David S. Hogsette wrote this book" is true, then its opposite ("David S. Hogsette did not write this book") is not true. However, some people point out fuzzy situations in which this principle does not apply and thus should not be considered a first principle of logic. For example, what about the case in which a dog is standing on the threshold of a door between two rooms. Is the statement "The dog is in the room" true or false? Those who deny the principle of excluded middle claim that the statement is neither true nor false, but is something in the middle, thus disproving the principle of excluded middle.

Two responses can be made to rescue this principle from this objection. First, the dog is not technically in the room. Maybe a portion of it is, but technically the dog as such is not in the room. Therefore, this statement is false and its opposite (the dog is not in the room) is true. Second, in order for a statement to be true, it must fully and accurately represent the situation of reality. Since this statement does not fully represent reality, it is a false statement. Let's test a more accurate statement of the situation: "The dog is partially in the room and partially outside the room." Now, this statement is either true or false. It is clearly true, thus its opposite ("The dog is not partially in the room and not partially outside the room.") is not true and the law of the excluded middle is upheld. Although somewhat controversial, this principle still holds true and is useful in analyzing truth claims. To prove a statement to be true, take the opposite claim and demonstrate that it is contradictory or absurd and then demonstrate that there is no evident middle ground, and you have thus proven the original claim to be true by falsifying the opposite and excluding the middle.

Principle of Identity

The principle of identity asserts that a thing must be identical to itself, because if it is not then it is not itself. This is quite obvious. This principle can be applied to truth claims: if something is true, then it is true indeed, and if something is false, then it is false indeed. For the most part, this principle is not hotly debated or refuted. However, it is an important principle to keep in mind as we are thinking through issues and developing arguments. If a thing is identical to itself, then we want to make sure we are accurately representing that thing in our statements and arguments. We do not want to inadvertently change the meaning of something or shift our focus to something else but still claim we are referring to the original thing. In such a case, the thing discussed is no longer identical to itself and thus it is no longer truly part of the discussion.

When we start with one meaning of something and then shift or modify that meaning (knowingly or not) and then draw conclusions about the thing based upon the new or shifted meaning and apply that conclusion to the original thing, we have committed the logical error known as equivocation. For example, some may try to prove the truth of evolution (molecules-to-man evolution or macroevolution) by pointing to evidence of mutations and changes within a species. For example, take a strain of bacteria that becomes resistant to antibiotics. Those who defend Darwinism argue that the bacteria changed, it evolved, and therefore Darwinian evolution is true. This is equivocation and a violation of the principle of identity. The evolution or change demonstrated by the bacteria is microevolution and is not identical to macroevolution. Thus, the fact that bacteria change and become resistant is only proof that bacteria become resistant and is not proof of the original claim of macroevolution. The bacteria is still the same bacteria that has adapted to a changed environment.

When we are making complex arguments, we must make sure that our terms remain consistent throughout and that we do not violate the principle of identity by changing the definition or identity of a word or concept in the middle of our argument. Similarly, the principle of identity helps us to point out and avoid reductive arguments. A reductive argument is one that incorrectly identifies one thing with another and says that A is nothing but B. For example, some say that (immaterial) mind is nothing but (material) brain. This is a false reduction. To refute this reduction, you simply need to show that the two items are not identical. For example, a state of my material brain (condition A) can be characterized by electrical activity, tissue weight, and chemical composition; however, a state of my immaterial mind (condition B), say an emotion or a thought, has no weight, chemical composition, or electrical components. Therefore, we cannot say that condition A is identical to condition B; thus it is not true that the mind is nothing but brain.

Principle of Rational Inference

This general principle of logic is the cornerstone of rational thought, and it basically says that given sound principles, true presuppositions, and adequate evidence, we can arrive at a reasonable conclusion or course of action. To infer means to draw a conclusion or to reach a decision by reasoning from known information, facts, or evidence. For example, if you go to a friend's house, and he opens the door and you hear cheering burst from a room in the back of the house, you can infer celebration is going on, but you do not know exactly what kind of celebration or why people are celebrating. As you walk toward the room, you hear some familiar voices shouting and cheering about a goal being scored. Because a goal or a score is mentioned, you can conclude the celebration involves sports, and since the room is small, you can infer that they are not themselves playing a sport. Possibly, they are watching a game on television, or playing a video game. As you get closer, you hear an announcer's voice and people in the room talking about players on the team, so you infer they are watching a game on television, but is it soccer or basketball? Then, you hear the announcer talking about David Becham, and you hear the announcer shout, "Scooooooooore!" From all of the evidence, before actually entering the room, you can conclude that they are watching soccer (or what the rest of the world calls football) on television. We infer conclusions all the time, and rational inference is a necessary part of good thinking.

Principle of Causality

The last principle we will discuss is the principle of causality, which states that something cannot come from nothing, that nothing comes from nothing, and that something can only come into existence by a causal agent. Another way to phrase this law is to say that everything that has a beginning has a cause, or everything that has come into being has a cause. The principle of causality is the central law of logic for science, because science is the search for causes, be they natural or intelligent. Searching for causes is foundational to medicine (we need to know what causes an illness in order to prevent and/or treat it), to law (we need to know who committed the crime—the causal agent—in order pursue justice), to weather reporting (it is quite helpful to know the mechanisms by which the clash of cold and warm fronts produce tornadoes), to engineering (the causes of certain stresses on different building materials), and to many other disciplines.

The principle of causality is also vitally important to making convincing arguments, because if you can clearly demonstrate that action A causes effect B, then you can definitively argue for or against certain courses of action. For example, for many years doctors and scientists could not prove a direct causal relationship between smoking and poor health. However, once conclusive medical evidence was found to link smoking as a causal agent for heart disease, different forms of cancer, hypertension, and many other health conditions, then specific arguments could be made about the clear health risks of smoking, and various policies and regulations could be reasonably justified. On the other hand, we should also appreciate that it is not always easy to establish clear causes for certain effects. Note, I am not saying, as some try to claim these days, that we can never know the causes for effects (this is an extreme form of skepticism that is ultimately self-defeating and not supported by empirical evidence and everyday experience). However, I am saying that in some cases it is extremely difficult to identify causes (a cause exists, but we may not be able to identify it adequately). In these situations, we must be extra careful about the claims we make and the conclusions we draw based upon the strength or weakness of the evidence we have to support our causal arguments.

There are other such fundamental principles or laws of logic, but these five are the most important ones for us to keep in mind as we develop our critical thinking and writing skills. Remember, good writing depends upon good thinking, and good thinking depends upon understanding and properly applying these first principles of logic. Review them periodically and reflect upon them as you think through various issues, as you examine your beliefs and values, as you contemplate what is true and how we can know the truth, and as you express your views in writing.

Writing Tips:

1. As you are drafting your essays in your composition class, writing papers for other classes, or discussing issues with your friends and classmates, keep these principles in mind and practice them as you write and discuss.

2. As you read articles and books on various issues and topics, start to identify how the writers are using and/or violating these basic principles of logic.

FORMING AND EVALUATING BASIC LOGICAL ARGUMENTS

Many of us associate the word *argument* with heated disagreements or impassioned verbal fighting. How many times have we gotten into arguments with our parents or close friends? This negative understanding of argument makes it difficult to see how logic is fundamental to good argumentation. In the academic world, an argument is simply a well-reasoned position on an issue. A good argument is grounded in sound logic. Traditionally speaking, an argument is a group of statements, premises, or presuppositions that work together to sustain a conclusion. When we formulate an argument, we arrange ideas and evidence in a logical manner to present the strongest possible case for our conclusions. In our academic, professional, and personal lives, we should resist the temptation to be contentiously argumentative, and instead strive to present reasonable arguments for our beliefs and convictions.

There are two main types of arguments: inductive and deductive. An inductive argument starts by considering a series of observations and various lines of evidence dealing with a particular issue or question. Then, a general conclusion is drawn from these particular facts. For the most part, science operates from inductive methodologies. Scientists pose a question, propose a hypothesis, design an experiment to test the hypothesis, run a series of experiments, collect vast amounts of empirical data, analyze the results, and then draw a general conclusion based upon the collected data. A conclusion based upon inductive reasoning is only as good as the evidence explored and the analytical methods used. Usually, a conclusion will be strong and relevant if a wide variety of evidence is properly and carefully analyzed. That is why, for example, opinion polls try to survey as many different types of people as possible so that the conclusions drawn will be as valid as possible.

Whereas inductive reasoning works from the specific to the general (drawing a general conclusion from many specific facts), a deductive argument applies an already accepted premise to a specific case. For example, the principle of gravity has been well established through inductive scientific reasoning and common experience. If you bump your laptop computer off your desk and it crashes to the floor, you can deduce that gravity pulled it toward the center of the earth and the floor stopped it abruptly. You do not have to run several tests (like repeatedly dropping your laptop on the floor) to reach this conclusion. You can simply deduce from the premise of the law of gravity that gravity is responsible for pulling the laptop to the floor.

Clearly, inductive and deductive reasoning work in different ways: inductive arguments move from specific examples to reach a general conclusion, and deductive arguments move from general premises to reach a specific conclusion about a specific case. However, inductive reasoning and deductive reasoning work together in some cases. In the laptop example the law of gravity served as a premise in the deductive reasoning process. Prior to this instance of deduction, induction was used (several centuries ago by Newton) to establish the law of gravity. Often, conclusions reached by good inductive reasoning that are proven over time to be true are then used as key premises or lines of reasoning in deductive arguments. However, just as inductive arguments are only as strong as the lines of evidence analyzed to reach the general conclusion, a deductive argument is only as good as the premises used to support the conclusion.

Deductive arguments are often presented in the form of syllogisms. Traditionally, a syllogism is a three-step argument in which a major premise is presented, a minor premise or condition or instance is given, and then a conclusion is drawn. For example, all humans are mortal (major premise), I am a human (specific instance), therefore I am mortal (conclusion). Rarely are deductive arguments presented so rigidly, but underneath most deductive arguments is some sort of syllogistic pattern. For example, because smoking has been found to cause so many health problems, an argument could be made to ban smoking in public spaces. The implied syllogism here is: smoking endangers the health of those smoking and those exposed to smoke (major premise), smoking in public exposes people to hazardous smoke (minor premise), therefore to protect public health smoking, should be banned in public places (conclusion). Although syllogisms when traditionally formulated appear to be too rigid to apply to complex issues or problems, in actuality, syllogisms are frequently used to structure and support a larger argument, because they are powerfully convincing when used appropriately and when supported by undeniable premises and irrefutable evidence.

There are several types of syllogisms, but the three most frequently used are *modus ponens* (MP) which affirms a position, *modus tollens* (MT) which denies a condition, and disjunctive which decides between an either/or position. The basic structure of an MP syllogism is if premise, then conclusion; the premise exists or is affirmed to be true; therefore, conclusion. Here is an example of an MP syllogism:

Major premise: If the universe had a beginning then it had a cause.

Minor premise: The universe had a beginning.

Conclusion: The universe had a cause.

The major premise is clearly established by the first principle of causality (all things that came into being were caused). Several lines of scientific evidence prove the minor premise to be true beyond a reasonable doubt (for example, the Second Law of Thermodynamics, the fact that the universe is expanding, evidence of radiation from the Big Bang, the existence of galaxy seeds resulting from the Big Bang, and Einstein's General Theory of Relativity collectively sustain the premise that the universe had a beginning). Therefore, there is a strong deductive case for the truthfulness of the conclusion (the universe had a cause), and thus larger metaphysical issues can be further explored (like who or what caused the universe).

The structure of an MT syllogism is: if premise then conclusion; deny or disprove the conclusion; therefore the premise is not true. Here is an example of an MT syllogism:

Major premise: If there is no absolute moral law and no moral law giver, then morality is relative.

Minor premise: Morality is not relative.

Conclusion: Therefore, there is absolute moral law and a moral law giver (i.e., it is not the case that there is no absolute moral law and no moral law giver).

In this MT syllogism, the burden of proof is on demonstrating the minor premise (the claim that morality is not relative). There are several proofs and evidences to suggest that morality is not relative but, in fact, absolute. Here are just a few. First, the theory of moral relativity is grounded in self-defeating or self-refuting presuppositions that are ultimately false because they contradict their own claims (for example, the claim that there is no absolute is itself an absolute claim, and the claim that there is no absolute truth is itself an absolute truth claim). Second, moral laws cannot be infinitely relative, and we must ask, "Relative to what?" Ultimately, there is an absolute standard against which all moral laws are compared. Third, moral relativists claim to know that some morals are better or worse than others, but without an absolute moral standard we cannot measure better or worse. How can we ever know a society is getting morally better unless we know what is best? (The absolute moral law tells us what is best.) Fourth, without an absolute moral law, we could never have meaningful moral disagreement, and everything would degenerate into statements of taste or opinion. Fifth, without an absolute moral law, we could not have true justice and we could never say that Hitler, for example, was wrong for what he did to Europe, Jews, gypsies, and others. Sixth, it is fairly clear by comparing civilizations across time and geography that there are some things that all people consider to be good and that all people consider to be evil. Since the preponderance of this evidence suggests that morality is not relative but is, instead, absolute, then the conclusion stands in this syllogism: there is absolute moral law and thus a moral law giver. The larger metaphysical question becomes exactly who or what is this moral law giver.

Finally, the structure for the basic disjunctive syllogism is as follows: either A or B; not A; therefore, B (or, not B therefore A). In a disjunctive syllogism, the argument establishes two contrasting possibilities, and then disproves one of the possibilities in order to affirm the other possibility.

For example:

Major premise: Biological life either arose spontaneously on its own from unintelligent natural causes alone or biological life is intelligently designed.

Minor premise: Biological life could not have arisen spontaneously on its own from natural causes alone.

Conclusion: Biological life is intelligently designed.

The major challenge for disjunctive syllogisms is to avoid the either/or logical fallacy of reducing a complex issue down to an either/or proposition when there are other reasonable possibilities. Note, this does not mean that there are never any either/or scenarios; rather, this simply means that we must be careful not to reduce an issue unjustifiably to an either/or scenario. In our example, some may object to this either/or proposition and may propose that biological life has always been in existence or that the building blocks of biological life have always been around. However, this opinion is not supported by the vast amount of scientific evidence available to us presently. At best, this view is an unsupported presupposition that is assumed to be true without sufficient proof. So, for this example about the origin of biological life, it is reasonable to formulate the major premise that biological life either arose spontaneously on its own by natural causes or it is intelligently designed.

The burden in this disjunctive syllogism is to prove the minor premise, which claims unintelligent natural causes are not responsible for the origin of biological life. There are many points to support this premise, and only a few of them will be discussed briefly here by way of example. First, it is nonsensical to suggest that life can come from nonlife spontaneously on its own. This point is supported by the fundamental principle of logic that states effects (in this case, life) cannot be greater than their causes (in this case, nonlife or nonliving chemicals and unintelligent natural forces). Just as it is unreasonable to think that something can come from nothing on its own or that something can give rise to itself out of nothing, it is equally unreasonable to conclude that life can come from nonlife on its own.

Second, biological life is indeed made up of chemicals, but it is more than mere chemicals. The simplest DNA molecule, for example, contains vast amounts of specific information detailing complex instructions for gathering amino acids and organizing them in particular arrangements with unique shapes to build proteins. We would never conclude that the arrangements of letters in a bowl of alphabet soup such as ENJOY YOUR SOUP LOVE MOM arose by natural causes (like convection currents in the soup). The complex instructions for building proteins in the DNA molecule of the simplest single-celled organism are exponentially more sophisticated than this simple sentence. If we would never conclude that this soup-sentence arose naturally without the aide of intelligent causes (mom arranging the letters in the soup to express an intention that originated in her mind), then why must we conclude that DNA, with its volumes of information and complex instructions for building components of cells, arose naturally on its own without any involvement by intelligent causes?

Third, there are several irreducibly complex molecular machines (for lack of a better term) within the simplest of single-celled organisms, each of which are clearly designed with instructions in the DNA for their production. It is inconceivable for even one such molecular machine to arise by unintelligent natural causes, let alone the dozens of other cellular machines which then had to be arranged within the cell, yet placed outside of the nucleus (which also had to be designed and constructed with its own complex of internal protein machines), and all contained by a cellular wall which itself shows clear signs of a complex design. There are many more such lines of evidence, but the point, I think, is clearly made here that there is plenty of evidence to prove that the minor premise in our disjunctive syllogism is true (the claim that biological life could not have arisen spontaneously by natural causes alone). Therefore, it is reasonable to conclude, from this syllogism, that biological life is intelligently designed.

When carefully constructed and properly utilized, syllogisms can be used to create powerfully convincing arguments. Remember, the basic idea is to present a solid premise, then present and defend or explain a reasonable minor premise, and then discuss the relationship between these premises that leads to the logical conclusion. In addition to inductive reasoning, deductive arguments, and deductive syllogisms, another commonly used mode of logical argument is abductive reasoning, otherwise known as inference to the best explanation. In abductive reasoning, you start with a series of possible premises to explain a situation or set of data. You analyze the various possible explanations, ruling out each insufficient explanation one by one until you are left with the most reasonable of the available explanations. We see this method of analysis and argumentation in science all of the time.

C. S. Lewis, in his classic fantasy tale *The Lion, the Witch, and the Wardrobe,* presents readers with a charming example of abductive reasoning when Professor Kirk helps Peter and Susan figure out whether Lucy or Edmund is telling the truth about the existence or nonexistence of Narnia. Lucy claims it exists and Edmund denies it is real (although the readers know that he is lying). Professor Kirk walks Peter and Susan through the possible explanations: Lucy is not crazy based upon her other actions, so it is not reasonable to conclude she is delusional; Lucy usually does not tell lies, so it is not reasonable to assume she is lying in this instance; and Edmund is known to be mischievous and to lie far more frequently than Lucy. Given these facts, it is reasonable to conclude, until more evidence presents itself, that Lucy is telling the truth, that Edmund is lying, and that Narnia, therefore, is somehow real. Such a conclusion shocks the children, because they would not think an adult would ever conclude that Narnia, the fantastical realm of magic and myth, is real. However, in this case, abductive reasoning strongly suggests the most likely possibility is that Narnia indeed exists, and as the story progresses, this truth is confirmed. Abductive reasoning is yet another useful strategy for building logical arguments to support your positions or conclusions.

Writing Tips:

1. When reading articles and essays, especially editorials and opinion pieces, try to identify and analyze the different logical arguments advanced by the writers. What kind of arguments are they, how are they arranged, and are they effective and why?

2. As you draft your essays that call for taking a position and proving your point of view, consider how you can use different types of logical arguments to build your case.

Avoiding Logical and Emotional Fallacies

As we develop strong arguments for our various positions and points of view, we should avoid logical and emotional fallacies. Logical fallacies are errors in formulating arguments, and emotional fallacies are inappropriate manipulations of readers' emotional responses to certain issues. Sometimes we may decide to supplement our logical arguments by making appeals to emotion (see chapter 10, "Argumentation and Persuasive Writing," for more information on emotional appeals). However, if we try to manipulate the readers' feelings by making unfair or exaggerated emotional appeals, we are committing emotional fallacies. When we commit errors in logic or try to overpower a person's rational judgment by inappropriate appeals to emotion, we diminish the persuasiveness of our arguments, risk alienating our audience, and thus undermine our very purpose for writing the essay in the first place. Avoid the following common logical fallacies.

Affirming the Consequent

This fallacy results from an improper construction of the *modus ponens* syllogism. Recall that the MP syllogism basically says, if A then B; A is affirmed; therefore B. Affirming the consequent occurs when you say, If A then B; B is affirmed; therefore A. Note how this affirms the conclusion to prove the premise instead of affirming the premise in order to reach the conclusion. Also, in such a case, the premises could be true, but the conclusion can still be false. For example, if the oven is hot, then the oven is on; the oven is on; therefore, the oven is hot. The premises are true, but the conclusion (the oven is hot) reached by affirming the consequent (that the oven is on) is not necessarily true, because the oven could be on but not necessarily hot. When making an MP syllogism, just stick to the basic pattern: if A then B; A is affirmed; therefore B.

Denying the Antecedent

This fallacy involves an error in reasoning in the *modus tollens* syllogism. Recall that the MT syllogism states, if A then B; not B; therefore not A. Denying the antecedent occurs when you say, if A then B; not A; therefore not B. Note that instead of denying the consequent (the then statement), this fallacy denies the antecedent (the if statement). The premises may be correct, but the conclusion will not necessarily be true. For example, if Sam did well on the test, then he studied; Sam did not do well on the test; therefore, he did not study. The premises are true, but the conclusion (Sam did not study) reached by denying the antecedent (that he did not do well) is not necessarily true, because Sam could have studied but still have done poorly, due to other reasons (like test anxiety). When making an MT syllogism, just stick to the basic pattern: if A then B; not B; therefore not A.

Ad Hominem Attacks

When we formulate arguments, we should focus primarily upon the issues; however, there are times when some people choose to attack the person holding a view instead of analyzing the arguments behind the point of view. This is known as the fallacy of *ad hominem,* which means "to the man." Basically, you are criticizing the person instead of analyzing the argument. Here is an *ad hominem* argument: only a racist and sexist bigot would be opposed to affirmative action. Notice that in this statement there are no reasons given as to why affirmative action is necessary or beneficial or why it is wrong to oppose affirmative action; rather, persons who argue against affirmative action are simply labeled bigots. This is nothing short of school-yard name calling, which is itself a form of bigotry and has no place in serious discussions. There are, in fact, many prominent African Americans, immigrants, and women, as well as European Americans and men, who oppose various types of affirmative action, and they have reasonable arguments to support their position. People who disagree should address these reasons instead of attacking their opponent's character. When engaging in debate or academic discussions, we should avoid merely attacking our opposition with inflammatory names and, instead, focus on analyzing and refuting our opposition as well as building strong arguments to support our positions.

Guilt by Association

The fallacy of guilt by association is closely related to *ad hominem* attacks in that it makes an implied argument against the position by criticizing the character of the person holding the view. However, where *ad hominem* directly attacks the person, guilt by association indirectly attacks the person by associating the person with another person or group that has behaved questionably or that has expressed problematic, abusive, or unpopular statements. For example, in various types of confirmation hearings in the Senate, some senators try to discredit the candidate by associating him or her with a professional or political group that has expressed unpopular or extreme political views. The suggestion is that because the candidate is also a member of this organization, then he or she must also hold these questionable views and therefore should not be confirmed. Such an argument avoids dealing with the core issues of the debate and ignores the actual views of the candidate. As we construct arguments in support of our position or when we critique the views of our opponents, we should focus on the appropriate issues and avoid making fallacious arguments that merely attack the character of our opposition through either *ad hominem* attacks or guilt by association allegations.

Genetic Fallacy

When someone confuses the origins of an idea with the reasons for believing the idea, he or she is committing the genetic fallacy (*genetic* here pertains to the origins or genesis of the idea). Usually, this confusion of origins with reasons for belief is followed by a dismissal of the idea simply because of where the idea comes from instead of a careful analysis of the rationale for the belief. Another way of thinking about this fallacy is to recognize the difference between a "psychological why" and a "rational why": the psychological deals with the motive of a belief while the rational deals with the logic of the belief. For example, some argue against the existence of God by saying primitive man came up with the idea of God because of an innate fear of the dark and of the dangers of the unknown; therefore, there is no good reason for us to believe in God now. Actually, fear of the dark or of dangers is not the primary origin of the idea of God, but even if it were, this only speaks to the psychological reason or the motive behind the belief but says absolutely nothing about if the belief is true or not. That is, regardless of how one comes to believe in God, the questions of God's existence and if it is reasonable for humans to believe in God still remain.

Some people make a similar mistake when speaking about morality. They claim that morality is a relative social construct, and they support this view by arguing that people believe in a particular moral system simply because their parents taught them or because they grew up in a particular culture. This point merely addresses the origin of the belief, not if the belief is valid or true. It does not matter how one learned that murder is wrong, but it does matter very much whether or not it is actually true that murder is wrong. Avoid ignoring the reasons for a belief by simply attacking what you think is the origin of a belief. Regardless of the origin of a belief, good argumentation seeks to determine if the belief is reasonable or not or if the claim is true or false. The origin of a claim or belief is not to be confused with the truthfulness of the claim.

Straw Man Attacks

In a straw man attack, the arguer misrepresents the opposition's argument to make it easier to refute. Or, the arguer sets up the weakest argument of the opposition as the main argument and then refutes it, concluding that the whole position of the opposition is destroyed and should be rejected. We often see the straw man fallacy in debates over an originalist or constructivist interpretation of the Constitution versus the living document view. Living document adherents claim that originalists want to turn the hands of time back to the eighteenth century when the Constitution was first written and thus ignore the new issues of contemporary America. The charge is made that an originalist view is rigid and inflexible, rendering the Constitution irrelevant to address social issues of today. Some living document adherents even suggest that originalists are bigoted and against social justice (which amounts to an inaccurate *ad hominem* attack). For these reasons, they claim, the originalist view should be rejected. Of course, this is an unfair misrepresentation of the originalist view, which amounts to a simplistic straw man attack. Actually, the originalist or constructivist view was the dominant interpretive perspective of the Constitution for the first 170 years of its existence, and due to careful originalist interpretations of the Constitution and its underlying principles, numerous amendments were passed and several advances in social justice were accomplished (including abolishing slavery, establishing civil rights, and securing voting rights for African Americans and women). Straw man attacks ultimately reveal the weakness of the arguer who resorts to such tactics and do little to refute the other side.

Red Herring

Advancing a red herring argument means sending your readers on misleading tangents that conveniently avoid the main issues. Instead of dealing with relevant facts and arguments, the arguer raises irrelevant points, inappropriately applied analogies, or dubious historical connections to distract the audience from the main issues. Then, the arguer draws conclusions about the side issues as if they prove the main point. Ultimately, the arguer has argued around the issue and has not adequately supported the main conclusion.

For example, when discussing church-state issues some people will claim that we should heighten and strengthen the so-called wall of separation between the church and state, because if we do not the country will become a theocracy and will perpetrate similar horrors as those committed in the days of the Inquisition, the Crusades, and the Salem Witch Trials. This argument establishes the position or conclusion to be supported but then gets carried away in historical red herrings that are not directly relevant to the issue. Not only does it oversimplify this history, it inappropriately applies it to the situation or issue being discussed (separation of church and state) and avoids presenting any solid arguments for its position. The United States could never become a theocracy or even an approximate one for two main reasons: (1) the Establishment Clause of the First Amendment makes it impossible, and (2) the United States is a constitutional democracy. Also, although these historical events were associated with Christianity, they are not the logical expression of core Christian teachings and truths, and the atrocities of these historical events were ultimately ended by conscientious Christians. Christianity does not logically nor necessarily lead to these atrocities; rather, a false understanding of Christian doctrine, combined with zealous political ends, led to these atrocities. This red herring argument clearly fails. A good argument avoids such red herring tactics.

Begging the Question

This fallacy in argumentation amounts to arguing in a circle. Essentially, the arguer asserts the conclusion (what needs to be defended and proven) as a premise and then uses that premise to prove the conclusion. It is not obvious, sometimes, that someone is begging the question because the conclusion, when presented as the premise, may be phrased differently such that it is not easily recognized as the conclusion. Here is an example of an argument that begs the question: Capital punishment is wrong because the state should not take someone's life. Notice that the phrase "the state should not take someone's life" is simply another way of saying "capital punishment is wrong." Therefore, what this statement is *really* saying is this: Capital punishment is wrong because capital punishment is wrong. This argument simply asserts the conclusion (capital punishment is wrong) as its main premise (the state should not take someone's life) in order to prove itself. This is arguing in a circle. A good argument progresses linearly from sound premises to a good conclusion, not recursively from the conclusion to the conclusion.

Non Sequitur

A non sequitur is simply an argument that does not follow from the evidence or reasons given, because the logic attempts to link or associate ideas or facts that are unrelated. The following argument is a non sequitur: If we elect conservative Christian politicians into office, they will turn America into a Taliban-style oppressive regime. This argument attempts to identify conservative Christian politicians with oppressive Taliban officials by inaccurately equating orthodox Christianity with the Islamic fundamentalism practiced by the Taliban. The values are different, the beliefs are different, the practices are different, and the expressions of the beliefs in society are different. One system of belief and practice has absolutely nothing to do with the other, and such an argument fails because it is a fallacious non sequitur. When forming arguments, make sure the ideas, concepts, and assertions are reasonably and properly related.

Oversimplification

This fallacy occurs when we draw overly simplistic conclusions from the evidence, or if we oversimplify the relationship between causes and effects. Oversimplification is also called the nothing but fallacy or the reductive fallacy, because the fallacious argument reduces a complex issue down to a "nothing but" statement. Consider the following example: If we just pay teachers more money we will improve education in this country. This argument is basically saying that the education crisis is nothing but a salary issue. Indeed, it would be nice if teachers were paid more money, and there are some teachers who are grossly underpaid and need higher salaries. Conversely, there are some educators who are overpaid for what they do as compared to what some underpaid teachers must face in their classrooms each day. Basically, this salary solution oversimplifies the matter. It will make no difference to the quality of education if, for example, we pay unqualified teachers more money, or if we give teachers higher salaries but do not provide resources to the schools, or if we increase teacher pay but do not improve the teacher-to-student ratios, or if we increase teacher salaries but do not provide incentives for families to participate in the education process of children, and so on. Better salaries are needed in many school districts, but this is not the only solution, nor is it necessarily the main solution to our education crisis. When making your own points or analyzing the positions of your opposition, avoid oversimplifying the issues.

Either-Or Fallacy

The either-or fallacy is related to oversimplification in that it seeks inappropriately to reduce a complex situation down to an either-or situation (either we do X or we do Y) and then concludes that the one option must be pursued because the other is flawed or too problematic. Indeed, there are valid arguments in which the conclusion is either one or the other of two options: I exist or I do not; I am alive or I am dead; God exists or He does not; you are reading this book right now or you are not (or someone is reading it to you right now or someone is not); we should elect candidate A or candidate B (in a two-party election), and so on. However, there are many cases in which it is invalid to reduce the argument to an either-or proposition. The following is an example of the either-or fallacy: Abortion should be legal, because if we prohibit it, women will be forced to undergo dangerous, illegal, back-alley abortions. The way this argument is framed suggests that there are only two possibilities, either safe legal abortions or unsafe illegal abortions. This fails to consider the possibility of no abortions (sure, an unlikely state of affairs but a possible one), adoption, or caring for and loving the child within an extended family, among other possible arrangements. Also, this argument falsely characterizes legal abortions as safe. Sure, in most cases, legal abortions are *safer* than illegal abortions, but in no way is it medically accurate to present legalized abortion as *safe* for the woman (and, obviously, it is not safe for the unborn child for whom it is literally deadly). Finally, this argument completely ignores the medical ethics issues by reducing ethics to a matter of legality—if it is legal then it is ethical. In our complex world, this is simply not true. When structuring your arguments, be careful not to formulate unwarranted either/or positions.

Hasty Generalization

When an arguer draws a broad conclusion based upon too little evidence, we call this a hasty generalization. Consider the following argument: Hurricane Katrina devastated New Orleans, and the citizens should not try to rebuild that historic city to its former glory, because there will be even worse hurricanes in the next few years due to global warming. This is a hasty generalization based upon too little information and a misunderstanding of current data. While some politicians and political activist groups believe in global warming, the scientific community has not settled this issue, and more evidence is coming out to suggest that the entire planet as a whole is not actually warming up but that portions of the planet alternate through cycles of climate change. Moreover, water temperatures have a complex effect on hurricane development and trajectory, and we simply have no scientific or historical basis for concluding that there will necessarily be even more huge hurricanes smashing into New Orleans in the coming years than there were previously. It is sometimes tempting to make grand claims based upon little evidence; avoid this temptation when building arguments for your position.

In addition to avoiding these errors in logic, we should also avoid inappropriate appeals to emotion when we create arguments in defense of a position or point of view. The following are common emotional fallacies to avoid.

Appeal to Pity

Instead of providing a reasonable logical argument, the writer evokes pity in readers to manipulate them toward the desired conclusion. For example, in a moral argument regarding abortion, one may argue that if abortions are made illegal in the United States, then rich women will be able to go to another country that permits abortions while poor women will be forced to have children they are not financially capable of raising and thus add more strain in the welfare system, or they will risk serious injury or even death by resorting to back-alley, illegal abortions. Such an argument relies totally on an irrelevant and misdirected emotional response to conclude that it is morally permissible to abort a fetus. This emotional appeal completely avoids the moral issue of abortion and ignores the moral status of the fetus. Instead of dealing with clear moral arguments, this emotional appeal focuses upon the readers' emotional responses to the poor and a sense of unfairness that the wealthy would have options not available to the poor. (If any individual is to be pitied here, it is the unborn child whose life is being unjustly terminated for purely economic reasons.) Pity can be a very noble emotion that motivates us toward ethical behavior and responsible social action. However, avoid manipulating your audience's sense of pity when constructing arguments.

Flattery

When trying to convince readers of your position, avoid making strong appeals to their vanity or self-esteem; that is, do not try to suggest that by adopting your position they will be somehow cool, interesting, intelligent, or perceptive. Such appeals are pure flattery and provide no good reasons to accept your conclusions. Advertisers use this appeal all the time (you are cool if you drink our soft drink), but it will not work for serious thinkers who are looking for reasons and good arguments instead of flattery. For example, it is sometimes asserted that truly wise people are against war. But what, exactly, is so enlightened about being against war? Indeed, war is horrible, and few people want war, but it is rather unenlightened to think that peace is merely the absence of war, and it is incredibly naïve to think that war is not sometimes necessary to stop aggressive evil, to bring about justice, and to achieve a lasting peace. Flattery is wonderful for your girlfriend, boyfriend, or spouse, but it has no valid place in academic discourse.

In-Crowd Appeal

This fallacy appeals to a reader's emotional desire to belong, to be associated with what is popular, or to be identified with a certain group of people who accept a certain point of view. Such appeals strongly suggest that if you agree with a certain position, then you are "in the know" or are a part of the knowledgeable crowd. For example, it is sometimes suggested that truly compassionate and caring people are in favor of various government entitlement programs. Most people want to be compassionate (or at least thought of by others as being compassionate). This emotional appeal states that you had better support these social welfare programs or you will be considered an uncaring ogre. However, in such an emotional appeal, no logical arguments are given as to why entitlement programs are particularly valuable or why they are necessarily compassionate. A very good case can be made that it is the height of insensitivity and callousness to make someone dependent upon government, and that it is far more compassionate and reasonable to equip someone to care for themselves and to teach them to be independent of government. Also, forced compassion through taxation and government spending on social welfare is not true compassion. True compassion is expressed through a freewill choice to be charitable to those in need. We all have a powerful need to belong, but good argumentation avoids exploiting this deep human longing.

Bandwagon Appeal

The bandwagon appeal is related to flattery and the in-crowd appeal, and it basically says that since everyone else is doing it, so should you. Jump on the bandwagon and agree with all the other people onboard. I distinctly remember such arguments not working with my parents, because they would simply reply, "Well, if Johnny and all his friends were jumping off the cliff, should you jump as well?" Indignantly I would say, "Yes!" But, deep down I understood what they were saying. Instead of providing sound reasons for adopting a view or agreeing with a decision, the bandwagon appeal makes the readers feel as though they are somehow missing out by not agreeing with the other people, or that they are a fool or an outsider for not adopting this position. Unfortunately, this emotional fallacy is used too frequently in academia, and more reports are coming out each year demonstrating how professors make bandwagon appeals in lectures and presentations regarding certain views on religion, politics, philosophy, science, culture, and faith. For example, it is not uncommon for a philosophy professor to remark that only unthinking, uneducated people believe the Bible; or for a biology professor to claim that if students want to be serious about their scientific education then they must dismiss intelligent design and embrace neo-Darwinian evolution; or for a sociologist to proclaim that enlightened people agree that abstinence sex education programs in schools simply do not work and should never be advocated. Notice what is subtly done in such statements: no evidence is presented or logical arguments provided to sustain the claims; they are merely asserted as true and those who disagree are made to feel like ignorant outsiders. This is emotional manipulation, not enlightened educational discourse.

Veiled Threats

The veiled threat basically makes the readers feel that if they do not agree with the position being advocated, then they will be individually responsible for some negative outcome, or they will suffer some horrible consequence. Again, such a line of argumentation is not a reasoned position but merely an emotional manipulation (a scare tactic). For example, it is sometimes argued that if you subscribe to conservative political views or orthodox religious teachings, then you will be responsible for plunging the United States into the dark ages of racism, sexism, homophobia, and social injustice. This argument insults the reader's intelligence and degrades those thoughtful individuals who hold to political conservatism and religious orthodoxy. Moreover, this argument also commits the logical fallacy of hasty generalization by stereotyping groups of people and drawing unfair generalizations about them, and it levels a reductive ad hominem attack against the opposition, suggesting that conservatives and religious people are nothing but bigoted social tyrants. Avoid such arguments that offer little more than veiled threats, and especially avoid constructing arguments that commit several logical and emotional fallacies simultaneously.

False Analogies

False analogies draw inappropriate or unfounded comparisons between items or situations that are fundamentally unrelated. Usually, we use an analogy (a comparison between two things) in order to create certain emotional responses that help us make our point more vividly. Analogies can be effective tools in argumentation. However, if we draw false analogies, the readers will recognize that we are trying to manipulate them emotionally and will be distanced from our argument. Also, false analogies suggest that the arguer really does not understand the situation or the facts well enough to draw more appropriate comparisons. The following is an example of a false analogy: We should not be fighting a war in Iraq because our troops are getting bogged down, and it is becoming an unwinnable quagmire like Vietnam. Indeed, war is tragic and nobody really wants to be at war. However, there is very little similarity between the Vietnam War and the Iraq War, except both are wars. This argument is largely an emotional attempt to evoke outrage associated with the horrible tragedies of the Vietnam War and to project them onto the Iraq War. These two situations are entirely different historically and procedurally, and it constitutes a false analogy to compare the two merely for emotional effect. It is easy to make an analogy, but it is more challenging to make relevant and effective analogies. Be very careful when you use analogies to enhance your arguments.

Writing Tips:

1. Learning how to think logically and to present good arguments takes study, time, and practice. One way to develop good thinking skills is to study how other writers construct sound arguments. Carefully review the argumentative strategies of the writers you read and try to incorporate these strategies into your own writing.

2. In our zeal to make a good argument, we can sometimes inadvertently commit logical and emotional fallacies that do more harm to our argument than good. During the drafting phase of writing, be sure to evaluate your arguments carefully to make sure you are avoiding some of the common fallacies discussed above.

CONCLUSION

Logic is an expansive academic subject, and our discussion here merely scratches the surface. Much more has been said about this issue. Entire books are written on logic, and people spend their entire lives studying the intricacies of logical thought. The purpose of this chapter is to give you a brief introduction to the major topics of logic and to provide a foundation upon which to build and strengthen your critical thinking skills. Critical thinking is itself a large subject, but whatever perspective we take on it, we must begin with a solid foundation in logic.

After finishing this chapter, you may have noticed that you probably are already a rather logical person. Let's face it. The world would be incredibly chaotic were it not for logic. Without basic logical thought, we would be a sorry bunch of confused individuals. Just imagine what it would be like to live in a world in which no one realized or followed the law of noncontradiction. Arguably, such a world would be highly unlikely if not completely impossible. Ignoring the law of noncontradiction and the basics of logical thought is simply unlivable. Sure, you may not have been aware of many of these terms and principles of logic before reading this chapter, but if you really think about it, you probably have already conducted your thought processes according to many of them, and you expect others to do the same. While you do not have to be an expert in logic, it is vitally important that you understand the basic principles of logical thought so that you can become a capable critical thinker and an effective academic writer.

DISCUSSION QUESTIONS

1. What are first principles of logic and why are they important to good critical thinking?

2. What are syllogisms and how do they function in constructing arguments? What are the three main types of syllogisms? Come up with your own examples for each type of syllogism.

3. What is a logical fallacy and why is it important for good thinkers to avoid them? Give some examples of logical fallacies to be avoided.

4. What is an emotional fallacy and why should it be avoided in our thinking and writing? Give some examples of emotional fallacies that should be avoided.

GROUP ACTIVITIES

1. Share in your group some ideas from the chapter that you found confusing or challenging. Help each other come to a deeper understanding of logical thinking and how it relates to your writing.

2. Pick an article from the collection of articles in the back of the book or one that has been assigned by your instructor. Read that article carefully, and as a group discuss points of logic demonstrated in the article. Point out examples of some first principles of logic and explain how these principles strengthen the essay. Point out any errors, misuses, violations, or denials of first principles of logic.

3. Pick an article from the collection of articles in the back of the book or one that has been assigned by your instructor. Read that article carefully, and as a group identify any logical and/or emotional fallacies. Discuss how these fallacies detract from the effectiveness of the article.

WRITING ACTIVITIES

1. Write a brief essay on what logic means to you. Discuss how you use logic in your daily life, studies, work, and leisure. Discuss what you learned about logic and argumentation from this chapter and explain how you will use this new knowledge in your educational experiences. Explain why you think it is important for people to be logical.

2. If your class has a blog or an online discussion board, post a message about the importance of logic in the life of a writer and a thinker. Why is logic important?

3. Write a brief essay or an online posting (in a blog or discussion board for your class) in which you speculate what it would be like to live in a world that denies or rejects the fundamentals of logic. This essay could take the shape of a basic expository essay or a narrative essay. Or, try writing a story about a world devoid of logic.

5

Steps for Effective Critical Thinking

QUESTIONS TO CONSIDER BEFORE READING

1. How do you think critically about an idea or issue?

2. Why is understanding important to good critical thinking?

3. What does it mean to be open-minded and how does it relate to critical thinking?

4. What is the relationship between good critical thinking and academic writing?

INTRODUCTION

IN THE PREVIOUS CHAPTER we discussed the fundamentals of logic and how to construct different types of arguments while avoiding logical and emotional fallacies. Clearly, we cannot be critical thinkers if we do not understand the basics of logical thinking. However, in addition to using logic well, critical thinking also involves identifying and evaluating other people's arguments. How do we know what views to accept and which to reject? How can we tell if someone is presenting a reasonable argument? How do we know if our own views are reasonable? How do we know if what we believe is true or not? What is truth and why is it important that we understand the rational aspects of truth? Opinion and conviction differ significantly, and critical thinking allows us to distinguish between them. We must learn to evaluate the strengths and weaknesses of arguments, and we must learn how to formulate a clear position so that our beliefs move beyond the realm of mere subjective opinion into the realm of substantiated conviction.

In an academic discussion, it is not enough to assert a mere opinion or to express our point of view while avoiding analysis and debate. Contrary to what you may think or have been taught, beliefs, points of view, and truth claims are more than mere personal opinion. An opinion is a point of view grounded simply and sometimes arbitrarily in taste. A taste is a preference based upon superficial likes and dislikes that really cannot be argued, defended, or disputed. Tastes are often subjectively idiosyncratic or culturally specific, and sometimes they are random and arbitrary. For example, I happen to prefer mocha chocolate chip ice cream, but you may prefer rocky road. One person may like mango kulfi (a type of ice cream from India), whereas someone else may prefer plain kulfi (like vanilla ice cream but with a delicious, creamy cardamom flavor). But these are simply different tastes. It would be unreasonable for anyone to get into a heated debate over what flavor of ice cream or kulfi is the best. This is a matter of opinion grounded merely in taste or preference.

On the other hand, deciding what political party to join, or what candidate to vote for, or what worldview to follow, or what religion to believe are matters that transcend opinion. Some people try to present them as mere opinions, but this is not completely accurate or fully reasonable. Surely, one should resort to more than mere taste when making such a decision as what worldview to follow—a commitment to thought and ideology that has a profound consequence on the way you understand the world, your place and purpose in the world, and the meaning of life and death. Clearly, this is something on a scale far greater than deciding what flavor kulfi to have after the chicken tikka masala you ate with nan bread and rice. Indeed, considering a worldview, a religious perspective, an ethical decision, or a political position is a matter of conviction that is grounded in truth and sound argumentation, not a mere opinion grounded in taste. The question, then, becomes how can we know the truth and how can we decide what is a sound and truthful argument and what is not. Critical thinking helps us sort through various ideas and positions and to establish profound convictions that we can believe deeply in our hearts, because they are substantiated by logical arguments that make good sense in our minds.

Using the fundamental principles of logic that we learned in the previous chapter, we can develop a basic process for effective critical thinking. The basic concept of critical thinking can be understood by contemplating the two words *critical* and *thinking*. Critical refers to understanding, analysis, and evaluation. Thinking refers to the process of logical thought. When you put these ideas together, you have the foundations for effective critical thinking: the logical process by which we (1) understand an idea and its principles and assumptions, (2) analyze the strengths and weaknesses of these principles and assumptions, (3) evaluate the evidence supporting the claim, (4) arrive at our own views on the idea or claim, and (5) apply our view to lived experience. This form of critical thinking can be conceptualized as a basic three-step process that is easily remembered by these three terms: understanding, overstanding, and standing. Understanding involves getting to know the idea on its own terms. Overstanding is the process of critically evaluating the strength and weaknesses of the idea. Standing is the articulation of your own point of view. The sequence of this process is cumulative: we should not formulate nor articulate our position until we first understand and evaluate various principles, assumptions, logic, and evidence associated with different views on the issue.

STEP 1: UNDERSTANDING WHAT IS BEING SAID

The first step in critical thinking is to understand the position, argument, or point of view under consideration. We should learn as completely as possible the key elements making up the idea or argument. At this point, we are not evaluating or commenting on the idea but simply trying to understand it on its own terms. When we first consider an argument, it is sometimes difficult to resist evaluating it, commenting on its strengths and weaknesses, and determining if we agree with it or not. Indeed, we often have already made up our minds about an issue in advance, but we should try our best not to let our preconceptions cloud our critical thinking about the issue or topic. As academic writers and good thinkers, we want to be as fair and objective as possible, and we should start by letting the argument speak for itself and to learn as much about it as we can before we critically evaluate it. Understanding something as objectively as we can involves *open-mindedness* and *tolerance*. Then, with as much of an unbiased mind as possible, we *analyze* and *summarize* the idea in an attempt to thoroughly understand it. Let's examine these concepts in more detail to see how they relate to this first step in critical thinking.

Open-Mindedness and Tolerance

Thinking critically about an issue or critically evaluating a particular point of view must begin with an open-minded process. You must understand something fully and fairly before you can ever evaluate or critique it. Let's say your friend, Frank, told you that the movie you really want to see is not that good and that you should not see it. Now, what would you think of his point of view if you were to discover that he has not yet even seen the film? You would probably not take it very seriously, since he may not really understand what the movie is all about because he has not even seen it himself. He may have simply heard what some other friends thought, or maybe he read some reviews. But, does he have a sound case for arguing that you should not see this film? Probably not. Indeed, it would be reasonable for him to say that that many critics have pointed out various problems with this movie, that it may not be as good as you were hoping, and that you may not want to spend $10 on it. But, it is not reasonable or fair to argue confidently that you should not see it because it is supposedly a bad movie, even though he has not seen it himself or does not fully understand the film.

When we critically evaluate something, we have to start from a position of open-mindedness and tolerance. These concepts are sometimes misunderstood these days and have come to mean something entirely different than what they truly mean. Many people think that being open-minded and tolerant means accepting everything as equally valid and true, and that if you disagree with something then you are somehow closed-minded and intolerant. (Ironically, those who claim you are being intolerant because you disagree with them are themselves disagreeing with you and not accepting your position as true, so they too must be close-minded and intolerant according to their own definition.)

What they fail to fully realize is that in a rational world governed by the first principles of logic, namely the law of noncontradiction all things simply are not equally valid or true, particularly views that directly contradict each other. Remember, the law of noncontradiction states that an idea and its opposite cannot both be true or correct at the same time in the same way. Therefore, two contradictory or opposite views cannot both be true. So, if some things are right, then some things must be wrong. Tolerance, properly understood, means putting up with error. When you are tolerant of something, you understand that it is wrong or problematic, but you put up with it anyway. When most people speak of "tolerance" today, they really mean "acceptance." However, the rational, discerning mind understands that we should not accept, nor are we compelled to accept, all things as equally valid or true. Some things are to be accepted and some things are not. Critical thinking helps us determine with a reasonable degree of certainty what is true and what is not, what is valid and what is not, and, therefore, what is to be accepted and what is not.

The important first requirement of good critical thinking is not necessarily tolerance (properly understood), because the decision to tolerate something or not comes at the end of the critical thinking process. Once you have critically analyzed the concept, idea, or point of view, then you can decide if it should be tolerated or not, or if you should accept that view or not.

Please note that just because we decide that something is not acceptable and not to be tolerated does not give us the right to be cruel, rude, or condescending. These qualities are not proper characteristics of good critical thinking or the discerning mind. We should accept truth with humility and reject faulty ideas or problematic points of view with grace and kindness. However, before we ever get to the point of accepting or rejecting an idea, we still have to analyze it, and before we can analyze it we have to understand it, and in order to understand it properly, we have to be open-minded enough to review it carefully. Being open-minded does not require us to agree with all views, as some people seem to think. Such people equate open-mindedness with agreement in the same way they incorrectly identify tolerance with acceptance. Actually, being open-minded simply means being willing to listen to the idea and to consider it carefully. When we are trying to understand something, we have to learn about it with an open mind, and we have to be willing to hear the idea out in its fullest form. We must try to understand it on its own terms without evaluating or judging it, yet. Note the important qualifier "yet." Critical thinking begins with open-minded understanding, but it does not stop there. We start by listening to the ideas, the views, the arguments, and the evidence. So, being open-minded simply means listening to and considering different points of view.

Analysis

Effective understanding can be accomplished through careful analysis. To analyze something means to break it down into its component parts so that we can study each part and discover how they relate to each other in making up the whole. Analysis is a process of inquiry by which we come to a fuller, if not complete, understanding of something. Sure, since we are finite human beings, our understanding of things will be necessarily finite or limited as well. But, this does not mean that we can never come to a reasonably complete understanding of something. (The skeptic claims that we cannot know or understand something, yet he or she seems to know or claims to understand that we cannot know or understand things. See the self-contradictory irony?) Analysis helps us sufficiently know things. For example, scientists use analysis when studying a natural process, like photosynthesis. They study the various steps by which a plant cell can synthesize carbohydrates from sunlight, water, and carbon dioxide. This method of investigation is called process analysis.

Not only can scientists analyze processes, but we can analyze arguments in much the same way, by breaking the argument down into its component parts. The main things to identify when analyzing an argument are *presuppositions, principles, assumptions, premises* or supporting arguments, and lines of *evidence.*

A *presupposition* is a belief that is assumed to be true, and presuppositions are used as starting points in an argument. For example, many scientists who follow the scientific model known as methodological naturalism presume or presuppose that all observable phenomena can only have natural causes. *Principles* are concepts or theories used as the foundation for an argument. For example, the principle of materialism (the belief that the universe is made up of only matter and energy and that there is no such thing as soul, spirit, or metaphysical reality) is a major principle for scientific naturalism. Principles are often explicitly stated or explained in the development of an argument.

Assumptions are unstated principles that are assumed to be true. An assumption is a principle, concept, or idea that is simply asserted as true without any explanation or proof. Often, assumptions are just unspoken givens in an argument. For example, most naturalists assume macroevolution to be a true fact instead of treating it as a theory with clear limitations and challenges. *Premises* are supporting arguments or lines of reasoning used to make a series of arguments in support of the overall main point or main argument. Usually, a point of view or a main argument is made up of smaller arguments, and analyzing an argument involves identifying these supporting arguments.

Finally, lines of *evidence* are facts, statistics, empirical data, anecdotes, personal testimony, expert testimony, historical facts or events, and other forms of information used to support an argument or to provide examples in support of a claim. Once we have identified these major components of an argument, we can then examine how they relate to each other so that we can understand the argument as completely as possible. Remember that at this point in the critical thinking process, we are not yet concerned with evaluating the point of view; rather, we are simply trying to learn what the writer is trying to say by analyzing the main argument.

Summary

Summary is the process of explaining in your own words what another writer is trying to say, and it is a significant tool for learning and demonstrating knowledge of a topic. For example, if you are having a difficult time explaining a theory or concept to your friend without repeatedly referring to your notes or textbook, then you do not yet fully know the material. However, if you can accurately summarize the information in your own words without checking your notes, then you can be fairly sure that you have a good understanding of the information. The same is true for trying to understand an argument or point of view. After analyzing an argument, try to summarize the person's view in your own words. Write out the main point of the argument, the various minor points or arguments being made, the principles and assumptions of these minor points, and the key pieces of evidence or examples used to illustrate the points.

Remember, the objective is first to come to a complete understanding of the idea before you begin to evaluate it. Analysis followed by summary is an excellent strategy for accomplishing the first step in the critical thinking process, that of understanding the point of view under consideration.

STEP 2: EVALUATING WHAT IS BEING SAID

Once we have come to a comprehensive understanding of an idea, concept, or argument, we then evaluate its strengths and weaknesses. In this second step of critical thinking, we are trying to determine the validity of the argument and to decide if we should believe it or not. The first step involves *understanding*, which literally means to stand under the idea. Obviously, this does not mean standing proximately or spatially underneath the argument, for this is impossible. Rather, this simply means that we are bowing to the idea in respect as we learn about it; or, we are figuratively standing underneath the idea, looking up at it and studying it in order to figure out what it is all about.

Observationally, we are getting to the root of the idea, and we are peering underneath it in order to learn everything we can about it. Once we do that, we can then take the next step of critically evaluating the idea. Think of this step as *overstanding*. No, this is not a real word, but it follows conceptually from the process of understanding. First we stand under the idea in order to learn about it on its own terms, and next we stand over it in order to critically evaluate it according to objective standards for testing truth claims. Since evaluation is the fundamental thinking strategy in this second step of the critical thinking process, let's take a close look at what it means to evaluate something.

Evaluation

Evaluation is the process of determining value. To evaluate something means to judge it according to a set of criteria, expectations, or a standard of measure. We are often told these days that we ought not judge, but we judge all the time. You made judgments when you decided what clothes to wear today. You made judgments when you chose to eat whatever you ate today for breakfast. And if you decided not to eat breakfast, a judgment was required to make that decision. We simply cannot avoid making judgments.

However, we must distinguish between *making judgments* and *being judgmental*. Making a judgment means simply evaluating a situation and making the correct decision on a course of action or offering the best evaluation of something based upon the available information. However, being judgmental carries the negative connotation of looking down upon someone, being arrogant, or acting rudely dismissive of others with whom we disagree. We ought not to be judgmental in this negative sense, but we should not abstain from making judgments when necessary. Deciding between right and wrong requires judgment, deciding what movie to see involves making a judgment, and evaluating the quality of a new dish at your favorite restaurant necessitates judgment. (By the way, determining your favorite restaurant also requires judgment.) So, it's fine (and necessary) to make judgments, but we should avoid being judgmental. Evaluation and making rational judgments are crucial parts of critical thinking. Not only must we understand the argument or idea, but we must also critically evaluate its strengths and weaknesses.

Evaluating Arguments, Presuppositions, Principles, and Assumptions

Once we analyze an argument and identify its component parts, how do we critically evaluate it? Use the following evaluative criteria to determine the strengths and weaknesses of an argument and the presuppositions, principles, assumptions, premises, and evidence comprising the argument. Sometimes these criteria are called tests for truth, because they are rational ways of determining if a claim is true or false.

Test 1: Logical Consistency

Analyze the idea or truth claim and identify the logical arguments supporting the claim. Then, evaluate the premises and lines of reasoning to make sure they make logical sense, they do not violate principles of good logical argumentation, and they do not commit logical fallacies. A sound argument will not contradict itself or be self-refuting. A self-refuting or self-defeating statement is a statement that does not satisfy the conditions of its own claim. A statement that contradicts itself is usually unreasonable and generally false. There is no compelling logical reason to believe a self-defeating statement is true. Here are some examples of self-refuting or self-defeating claims:

- "I cannot write a word of English." Note that this sentence is written in English and therefore contradicts itself and is false.

- "I do not exist." I actually have to exist in order to think, let alone utter, this claim. The fact that I am writing or speaking this statement requires that I exist. I must exist to even make the claim that I do not exist. Therefore, this statement is self-defeating and thus false.

- "There is no absolute truth." This statement clearly refutes itself because the claim that there is no absolute truth presumes that this claim is itself absolutely true. This claim proves itself to be false.

- "There may be truth, but we cannot know for sure what is true." This sentence is self-defeating because while it claims not to be able to know what is true, it seems to know that it is true that we cannot know what is true. The person may not know anything else to be true, but by uttering this statement, he or she is claiming to know with certainty that the statement is itself true. This statement demonstrates that we can know some things are actually true and therefore the claim is false.

Statements that contradict themselves are illogical, and their truth, validity, and explanatory power must be questioned if not completely rejected. Some may try to claim that such self-defeating statements are true for all cases except when applied to themselves, but this commits the self-excepting error. It is intellectually dubious to excuse or except the statement itself from the conditions of its own claims. If a statement cannot stand up under the weight of its own claims, then it is a false claim.

In addition to passing the test of logical consistency (that statements should not be self-refuting or self-defeating), logical arguments should also avoid problematic logical and emotional fallacies. Study and memorize the various fallacies listed in chapter 4 and look out for them when you are analyzing arguments, positions, claims, and points of view. A fallacious argument is weak, and there is no compelling reason to agree with a conclusion drawn from arguments that demonstrate errors in logical reasoning. Moreover, if an argument is comprised of mainly fallacious emotional appeals, then there is little rational thought behind the position, and in the absence of sound logical reasoning, it is unreasonable to accept the position as presented. (Note: You may encounter a position on an issue with which you agree but that is not supported by good reasoning. It is up to you to fill in the logical gaps and to discover a good rationale to support the claim.) When you are evaluating the logic, premises, presuppositions, and assumptions of an argument, look to see whether or not they are logically consistent and if there are any logical and/or emotional fallacies present in the lines of argumentation.

Test 2: Empirical Adequacy

Not only must the logic of an argument be valid, but appropriate evidence should be supplied in support of the position. Check to see if there is any evidence to back up the claim. If there is no evidence given, then there is no rationally compelling reason why you should view the position as valid or believe it to be true. Whenever we advance an argument, it is our job to prove it with evidence. A strong argument will pass the test of empirical adequacy, meaning it will present adequate empirical evidence to prove the claims. However, it is not enough just to present evidence; the evidence must be relevant to the claims being made, and it must actually support the point of view. Recall the logical fallacy of red herring argumentation, which presents a line of reasoning that directs readers away from the main point being made. Sometimes offering unrelated or irrelevant evidence is a form of red herring. Carefully consider the evidence presented and make sure it is relevant to the argument.

Also, make sure the writer is discussing the evidence accurately and fairly. Sometimes a writer will make too much of evidence (hasty generalization), or will misrepresent the evidence, or will provide false or inaccurate evidence. Just because there is evidence does not mean it is correct. Carefully evaluate the nature of the evidence, how it is being presented, how it is being used, and how it is being interpreted. Remember: facts do not interpret themselves. Facts, evidence, and information can be misused or misrepresented in service of the argument. Carefully evaluate the evidence and determine if the conclusions are legitimate and warranted.

Test 3: Experiential Relevance

This evaluative criterion or test for truth seeks to consider the relationship of the claim to lived experience. We should be careful to note that just because an idea does not directly relate to our own experience does not necessarily mean that the idea is false. We must understand that truth transcends the self and is not solely determined by our own subjective experience. Truth is not subjectively determined by our own experiences nor constructed by our points of view (this idea is an example of relativism, which is a self-defeating concept). However, we should not completely ignore our own experience or the general experience of others. One way to evaluate the legitimacy of a claim about life is to consider the claim in relation to our own experience and to that of others who regularly have experiences relevant to the claims being made. If many of your own life experiences or the testimony of other people's experiences clearly and consistently contradict the claims being made by the argument, then you have good reason to doubt the veracity of the claim. It is irrational to accept an idea that asks you to doubt and reject your own valid experiences.

STEP 3: ESTABLISHING YOUR CRITICAL POSITION

In step 1 of the critical thinking process, we attempt to understanding the argument, and in step 2 we evaluate the principles, assumptions, premises, and lines of evidence supporting the argument. In step 3 we finally establish our critical position by "standing" on the conclusions of our critical thinking process. Thus, we move from understanding, to overstanding, to standing. By the time we get to step three, most of the work of critical thinking as been completed. Once we fully understand the ins and outs of an idea or argument, we can then evaluate it to see how well it stands up to critical scrutiny. After we have analyzed and critically evaluated the argument, then we are in a good position to comment on the legitimacy of the argument, and thus to accept, reject, or modify it. The ultimate goal is not simply to comment on the argument being explored but also to establish and substantiate our own view on the subject. As critical thinkers, we must not unthinkingly accept anything and everything that is presented to us. Rather, we must come to specific conclusions about various issues.

However, our conclusions should be more than simple opinion supported only by subjective taste or preference. Critical thinking allows us to examine a position, evaluate the reasons supporting it, and then to arrive at our own conclusions that are logically consistent, supported by good evidence, and relevant to lived experience. Whether you agree with an idea, disagree with it, or form a mediate or in-between position, your conclusion should be grounded in good logical reasons, not mere opinion. Critical thinking allows us to shift from vague taste and opinion to deeply held conviction grounded in truth and rigorous argumentation. If we use critical thinking in our dialoging with people who hold different points of view, we will have more constructive and meaningful exchanges. Instead of merely butting heads and making dead-end declarative statements of taste or preference, we will engage in truly meaningful dialog in which ideas are presented, points of views analyzed, and arguments evaluated.

Writing Tips:

1. After some practice, critical thinking will become second nature. Start practicing these strategies by applying them in your everyday life. As you watch television programs or news reports, try to analyze and evaluate the ideas presented.

2. Keep a critical thinking journal. As you read articles and study information for your classes, record your impressions and observations in a journal in which you practice the three steps of critical thinking: summarize the idea (understand), evaluate the supporting logic and information (overstand), and then establish your position on the issue (stand).

Examining an Example: Moral Relativism

Critical thinking is a complex process of logical reasoning that is difficult to understand fully in the abstract. Let's look at a specific example of how we can use critical thinking to evaluate the legitimacy of an idea. The following is a belief that many people today consider to be true: morality is relative, not absolute, and we ought not to judge others if their moral decisions or ethical behavior differ from our own. How might we examine this belief from a critical thinking perspective?

1. Understand the Statement

It helps to understand a belief or truth claim by restating its basic principles, assumptions, and presuppositions. Moral relativity presupposes that there are no absolute truths, that truth is relative to the individual and culture in history, and that truth changes over time. From this presupposition, the claim assumes that morality is a code of behavior based simply in personal preference, a subjective choice that each individual makes. A guiding principle is that any notion of a universal absolute is necessarily false. This view asserts that what we think of as an absolute moral code is nothing more than a product of culture or society or a political institution that has lasted for a significant amount of time, thus giving the impression of being universal and absolute. Finally, a central premise supporting this view claims that there are many different moral systems and moral values, and each is equally valid such that one is not superior to another. From these presuppositions and principles, moral relativism concludes that when a person makes a different moral decision than what we might make, we ought not judge that person because there are different moral systems, each with their own legitimacy.

2. Critically Evaluate the Argument

Now that we understand the arguments, principles, and assumptions supporting the claim, we can then critically evaluate it with the tests of logical consistency, empirical adequacy, and experiential relevance.

Logical Consistency

This argument is self-defeating on many levels. It claims there are no absolutes, yet makes an absolute claim to this fact. It assumes there are no absolute truths, yet it assumes that it is absolutely true that there are no absolute truths. It also claims that morality is not absolute, yet this is itself an absolute moral claim. The "ought not" phrase is a moral demand not to do something. This "ought not" statement is assumed to be applicable to everyone, because those who subscribe to this idea believe that it is wrong for anyone at any time to judge another person's moral values. This is an absolute moral claim, thus violating its own claim that morality is not absolute. This position does not pass the test of logical consistency, and we could conclude at this point that there is no good logical reason to believe this statement to be true. But, for the sake of illustration, let's continue the evaluation.

Empirical Adequacy

The statement as presented does not provide any specific evidence for our analysis; however, there are several lines of evidence that can be given to support the claim that morality is relative and not absolute. Let's evaluate some of this evidence. For example, some moral relativists note that people in different countries or societies act differently, thus proving that morality is relative. If people in different cultures behave in different ways, then morality must be tied to culture, because as cultures differ so too do behavior and morality. *Evaluation:* Indeed people act differently, but this point confuses a fact with a moral value; that is, it confuses what is (fact) with what ought to be (a moral value). Just because a culture acts a certain way does not make it right. In this case, relativists are confusing sociology (descriptive of society) with morality (prescriptive of how society ought to act). Just because people act differently does not mean that all people are acting correctly, nor should we conclude from the fact that there are different behaviors that morality is thus relative. This fact only proves that there are different behaviors, but this fact proves nothing about the moral correctness of the different behaviors.

Another piece of evidence moral relativists present in support of their position is that moral values have changed over time; therefore, morality is relative to history. *Evaluation:* This is a compelling piece of empirical evidence; however, the reasoning misunderstands the difference between a moral value and the expression of that moral value over time. For example, at one time witches were sentenced as murders, yet now they are not. However, this historical change does not prove moral relativism, because the basic moral value that murder is wrong remains absolute and unchanged. What has changed, though, is our understanding of witches. We no longer believe witches are killing people with their curses; therefore, we are not rounding them up and charging them with murder. If a self-proclaimed witch did in fact murder someone, then we would arrest her and try her not because she is a witch but because she has committed the crime of murder.

We should also note that change in moral behavior over time does not prove that morality is relative. Instead, these shifts in behavior demonstrate that our understanding of morality changes. In some cases our moral understanding increases and we become more morally aware, and at other times our moral understanding diminishes and we become less morally aware. Morality is a knowledge that can be gained or lost. Variance in morality between individuals, between groups of people, or across historical time periods is a result of differences in the level of moral knowledge; moral variation is not due to morality being relative.

Finally, moral relativists claim that because different cultures exhibit different moral behaviors and moral codes, morality must be relative. *Evaluation:* The apparent cultural differences in behavior are usually nothing more than cultural differences in expressing an absolute moral value. For example, in some cultures, people kiss when they meet, in other cultures people shake hands, in others people bow, while in still others people politely nod. All cultures have a concept of what is proper when greeting someone else. What should be done is common (greet the person with respect), but how that is done may differ. Such difference is merely a variation in expression, but the underlying moral value (greeting the person with respect) is universal. There are other points to be made here, but this more than sufficiently evaluates the weaknesses in the empirical evidence often presented in support of the belief that morality is relative. Note in this example, the main problem is not so much with the empirical evidence as with how the evidence is interpreted.

Experiential Relevance

What happens if we put this notion of moral relativism to the test in the everyday lives of ordinary people? Does it make sense in relation to lived experience? Say you go out to the parking lot after one of your classes and you see a man driving away in your car. Has any immoral act been committed? "Sure," you say, "my car has been stolen. Stealing is wrong." But wait a minute. Moral relativism assumes truth is relative. Maybe it is not true that your car was stolen. Or, maybe for you the car was stolen, but for the person driving the car it was not stolen at all. He is just driving a car that he found. What is the truth here? Has your car been stolen or not? Logical thinking clearly has an answer here (the principle of excluded middle holds that the car was either stolen or it was not), but relativism offers no clear answer, other than "it depends." Relativism claims that for some observers it is true the car was stolen, but for others it is true the car was not stolen. Thank you very much, that's really helpful. However, we can prove that you own the car, and the person who drove away in it without your expressed permission has in fact and in truth stolen the car.

So, the car was indeed stolen, but why are you so upset? Moral relativism does not justify or explain your anger, because it does not allow you to claim definitively that stealing your car is wrong. Maybe for you stealing is wrong, but for the person who stole your car, maybe stealing is not wrong. We know in our gut that this is ludicrous. Your own outrage at having been wronged by the theft experientially suggests that something more than a mere law has been broken. You are upset that your car was stolen because you know you have been fundamentally wronged and violated, and you know this because there is an absolute moral law that has been violated, and you are the victim. Notice that by making the situation real, we can see how unreasonable and unlivable moral relativism is.

But, some moral relativists may object and claim there are social contracts and civil laws that determine right and wrong for each society. So, any "wrong" that is felt is merely due to a crime being committed, which is a violation of the laws of the social contract and nothing more. No absolute moral law has been broken. You feel bad because your society has taught you to feel bad when your legal rights are violated. Indeed, it is true that there are civil laws, but there is a distinction between legality and morality. In an ideal world, what is legal will also be what is moral. Good civil law is rooted in natural law or absolute moral law. However, that is not always the case. For example, abortion is legal in this country, but it is hardly moral to kill an unborn human being. Also, resorting to social contracts within the realm of moral relativism does not really help us on the experiential level. What if the person driving away in your car decides not to accept the moral contract? That person who stole your car has technically done nothing wrong (and, by the way, we cannot say he has "stolen" your car, but that he is simply driving away in it). Similarly, if the person is never caught, then technically he has done nothing wrong, for there is no affirmation of the social contract being broken. But, we know in our gut that even if he is not caught, he has still done something wrong. Why? Because he has broken an absolute moral law, regardless if he is caught or not and regardless if he thinks he has done something wrong or not.

Another problem with the social contract view of morality involves conflicts between societies with different and contradictory social contracts. Whose contract takes precedence if there is a conflict between citizens of those countries? Also, what about justice? Without an absolute moral law that stands objectively outside all societies, there is no way to determine when a society is morally right in its actions and when a society is morally wrong. For example, without an objective moral law we cannot say that Hitler's genocidal policies were wrong, and we could not justify the allied countries' actions against him. Nor can we say that the Japanese soldiers following orders from the Japanese government did anything wrong when they slaughtered over 300,000 unarmed Chinese soldiers and civilian men, women, and children during the horrific rape of Nanjing in 1937. Clearly, on an experiential level, moral relativism is severely problematic and completely inadequate as a viable, practical worldview.

3. Establish Your Position

Having understood and thoroughly evaluated moral relativism, its arguments, its principles, its assumptions, its evidence, its conclusions, and its practical applications, we are ready to establish our view. Since the idea does not pass the three basic evaluative tests or criteria for a sound argument (logical consistency, empirical adequacy, and experiential relevance), there is no rational justification for believing the statement that says, "Morality is relative, not absolute, and we ought not to judge others if their moral decisions or ethical behavior differ from our own." If this statement is false (as we have clearly demonstrated), then we can conclude from the law of noncontradiction that the opposite is true, namely that morality is absolute and that we can make moral judgments.

Of course, we are not to be arrogantly judgmental and condescending to others (for, indeed, who among us has not done something wrong), and we are not to mistreat others because of their immoral behaviors (note that proper and legal punishment is justice and is not to be considered mistreatment, unless the punishment is cruel and unusual). However, we have every right (and duty) to judge between moral and immoral behavior, so that we can learn to lead moral lives ourselves and to encourage others toward a greater awareness of morality. Contrary to what some people say, we can, in fact, love and care for the person while still judging the behavior to be immoral. To believe otherwise is to commit the nothing-but fallacy (also called the reductive fallacy), reducing the person to nothing but behavior, such that a judgment against the behavior is necessarily a judgment against the person. We must be careful not to reduce a person to mere behavior and always remember that a person is a living soul who is far more than just matter or behavior.

CRITICALLY EVALUATING YOUR OWN WRITING

In addition to evaluating the legitimacy of another writer's argument, position, or point of view, critical thinking should also be used to determine the strengths and weaknesses of our own arguments. During the revision phase of writing, we can use these critical thinking steps to determine if we are creating sound arguments, if we are committing any logical or emotional fallacies, if we are basing our views on self-defeating statements or self-refuting presuppositions, if we are providing enough evidence or not, if we are interpreting the evidence correctly, if the evidence we present is relevant to our arguments, and if our arguments make sense to lived experiences, not just our own but those of other people as well. By critically evaluating our own positions, we will strengthen them and thus make them more authoritative and convincing to our readers. Our critical evaluation allows us to discover serious weaknesses in our point of view and then encourages us to seek ways to strengthen the argument. Occasionally, the process of critically examining our arguments leads us to change our minds about our positions. Writing is a process of learning and discovery, and sometimes we discover in the process of writing and revising that our initial position was wrong and that we need to change our minds and develop a new position that is logically sound, supported by the available evidence, and relevant to our lives and the lives of our readers. This is the mark of a good thinker, an honest writer, and a humbly open-minded person.

> *Writing Tip:*
> During the revision stage of writing, use these critical thinking strategies to evaluate the strengths and weaknesses of your own ideas and arguments.

CHECKLIST FOR CRITICAL THINKING

- ✓ Study the argument, concept, or idea thoroughly. Use analysis and summary to understand the position as fairly and completely as possible. Identify presuppositions, principles, assumptions, premises or supporting arguments, and lines of evidence.

- ✓ Critically evaluate the various aspects of the argument discovered through the processes of analysis and summary. Test the claims for logical consistency, empirical adequacy, and experiential relevance. Does the argument make logical sense? Is there evidence to support the claim, and does the evidence actually support the claim being made? Does the claim correspond to lived experience?

- ✓ Carefully establish your own point of view based upon your analysis of the arguments, and then clearly articulate your informed position, making sure that your own view is logical, supported by evidence, and relevant to lived experience.

Conclusion

Critical thinking is not easy, but it is the calling of a good writer and the foundation of academic success. Moreover, it is the cornerstone of living a thoughtful and meaningful life. It is easy to believe what we want to believe and to live our lives according to our subjective desires. But, it is far more challenging, meaningful, glorious, and fulfilling to live a life in pursuit of truth and to be motivated by that which is good, as understood universally in the absolute. As Socrates noted nearly two and a half millennia ago, the unexamined life is not worth living. This idea is not unique to Socrates, for thoughtful men and women have believed this axiom and lived by it in one way or another since the beginning of humanity. Life is a blessing, a gift not of ourselves. Therefore, living entails duty and responsibility. We are responsible for what we do with this precious gift of life, and responsible living starts with good critical thinking. Avoid living unexamined lives. Learn how to think critically and pursue a life not of quiet desperation but, rather, one that proactively seeks purpose, meaning, and truth.

Discussion Questions

1. Explain what critical thinking is and what it is not. Provide some examples to illustrate your observations.

2. What are the three main steps in critical thinking?

3. What are the three main evaluative tests for truth or for the legitimacy of an argument or point of view?

Group Activities

1. In your group, discuss what critical thinking means to you. Share with each other what you learned from reading this chapter.

2. Pick a controversial issue and individually conduct research to discover various views on this issue. Share your research in your group and discuss the strengths and weaknesses of the different

points of view. Try to decide as a group what you think is the most reasonable position to take on the issue, and provide clear justifications for your position.

3. Pick an article from the collection of articles in the back of the book or one that has been assigned by your instructor. Read that article and critically evaluate it. Assign roles for each person in the group (summary, evaluation of specific points, etc.), and then collectively write a 1–2 page critical evaluation of the article.

4. In your next peer review or editing session, use critical thinking strategies to evaluate your partner's draft and to suggest meaningful revisions.

WRITING ACTIVITIES

1. Write an essay in which you critically evaluate an article either from the book or one that you find on your own. Be sure to use the critical thinking model presented in this chapter: understanding, analysis and evaluation, and declaration of your point of view.

2. If your class has a blog or a discussion board, practice your critical thinking skills by composing thoughtful responses in which you use the three key steps to critical thinking.

3. If you write for a blog or post on several blogs, try to use critical thinking strategies in your postings. Do you see a difference in the quality of your thinking and writing? How does critical thinking help you write more substantive and thoughtful blog entries?

6

Voice in Academic Writing

QUESTIONS TO CONSIDER BEFORE READING

1. What is voice in writing?

2. How does voice relate to the rhetorical situation of writing (purpose, message, and audience)?

3. What are some key ways to express voice through writing?

4. How does grammar and syntax establish voice in writing?

INTRODUCTION

HAVE YOU EVER BEEN walking along and suddenly found yourself humming a familiar tune for no apparent reason? Why does your spirit lift when a favorite song plays on the radio? Have you ever teared up in a movie during a tender scene, especially when the music starts to swell? (Come on, admit it.) Why does music affect us so deeply? Could it be that our hearts and souls are tuned to certain sounds that evoke strong emotion? Isn't it interesting that music has a voice, that it expresses certain feelings, moods, attitudes, and emotions? The voice of music extends beyond a singer's words. Sure, it is easy to identify the voice of a lyrical song. But, instrumental music has a voice as well, and it communicates a particular emotional message. A screaming guitar solo in a rock song may express power or anger. A soft violin melody in a concerto may whisper a longing plea to the listener. And a sultry saxophone may coyly tease the audience. Even though no words are expressed in these instrumental examples, there is a clear voice. Something is being communicated, usually a powerful emotion that becomes the central focus of the larger message expressed by the whole instrumental song. Voice in music helps express meaning.

You may not have realized it, but writing expresses voice as well. Sure, there are words that communicate a specific message with a clear meaning. However, these words on the page are more than mere symbolic marks. These often unspoken words written on a seemingly lifeless page actually express a vital voice. Writing can be bland and dead, but good writers breathe life into their words and express more than a thought through language. Good writing also expresses tone, mood, and feeling. Good writing has voice. It is important for us to realize that through the voice of our writing, we can express many different moods, and these moods help us sharpen the meaning of our words. Think for a moment about how we speak the words and sentences that appear in our minds. We can say the same sentence in different ways by placing emphasis on different words, by using different inflections, and by modulating the pace or volume of the spoken words. As a result of saying the same sentence in different ways, we can actually express completely different meanings. "He*llo* there" is very different from "hel*lo* there," which can be distinguished from *"Hello there!"* How we say something is expressive of our voice, and like music or a song, our voice expresses certain moods and feelings and helps specify the particular meaning of our expression. Voice and tone are powerful communication tools that are important aspects of writing.

WHAT IS VOICE?

Voice is the quality in writing that associates a person with the writing. Voice is that which provides personality or a persona behind the writing. It is that quality which makes the writing seem alive or to be expressive of a living agent. We have discussed that humans have minds and souls, that we are more than a physical body, that to reduce the mind to mere brain or to say that the human being is nothing but an expression of a complex mechanistic arrangement of cells and tissue is to commit the reductive fallacy. If we are nothing but body and have no mind or other metaphysical component that distinguishes our mental, emotional, intellectual, and spiritual states of being from another person's state of being, then it would be very difficult to explain why it is we have different voices. Sure, we could say that the physical structures of the larynx differ between individuals, thus rendering different sounds as the air passes over the vocal cords, giving rise to differences in audible voice. However, this merely accounts for the different mechanical sounds emanating from an individual and offers no explanation for the mental, emotional, and spiritual motivations for the speaking that give unique personality to the expression. What about those who cannot speak, like Stephen Hawking? Doesn't he have a voice? If you have read any of his books, you will know that indeed he does have a unique voice, and this voice has nothing to do with his physical body.

Voice is an expression of the person, not merely the body. Voice is unique to the person, because the person is a unique being with thoughts, emotions, opinions, views, and spiritual reactions that transcend the physical body and material brain. Our voice is an expression of our personality and our humanity. Our voice is part of our identity as a human being, and it gives individuality to our writing. Voice makes our writing our own.

As we all know, we have different moods and express different feelings at different times. We are not different people at different times, but we certainly act in different ways depending upon the social or professional context, and in these various circumstances, we seem to have alternate personas. If we are too different in various situations, some people may question our sincerity and may consider us to be disingenuous or phony. But for the most part, it is true that we behave and speak in different ways depending upon the occasion. The same is true of our writing. Remember the rhetorical situation? When we develop ideas and plan our document, we have to consider the purpose of writing, the message being communicated, and the audience to whom that message is expressed. By contemplating the rhetorical situation, we can also make better decisions on what kind of voice or persona we wish to express. We want to make sure that we use the most appropriate voice for a particular writing task. Often, this is a very challenging thing to do, for we do not always know the best voice to use, and if we are not careful, we may use an inappropriate voice without even realizing it.

There are two main types of voice in our writing: informal and formal. Both have specific characteristics and are used in particular situations to achieve certain goals. The informal voice is by far more frequently used, and it is generally familiar, chatty, and casual. For example, when writing to a close friend, a family member, a peer, or a colleague, we generally use the informal voice. However, within this category, there are many degrees of informality. An e-mail to a friend is apt to be rather chatty, and it will probably have a relaxed tone and contain some slang and possibly sarcasm, depending upon your relationship. A letter to your mother will be conversational and relaxed, but it probably will use Standard English, will be more respectful (at least it should be), and will use less slang. And, if you are asking your mother for money, your voice will probably be even more respectful and proper, yet still familiar and informal. In an e-mail exchange with a peer editing partner who is a new acquaintance from your college composition class, you may have a more professional tone, but your writing will probably still be somewhat informal and chatty. Note that we can be informal without being unprofessional. Overall, the informal voice is more natural and conversational.

On the other hand, the formal voice is much more rigid, professional, and measured. The informal voice expresses familiarity and identification with the reader, whereas the formal voice expresses respect, objective distancing, and professional courtesy. You may speak to your friend in an informal voice, but you probably talk more respectfully to his or her parents, depending upon the type of relationship you have with them. The formal voice is far less conversational than the informal voice, and it usually follows certain writing conventions and fulfills specific reader expectations. For example, an e-mail to your professor regarding a change of grade will adopt a level of formality that you generally would not use when writing to your friend about the grade you earned on your last essay. Similarly, a letter written to your senator regarding a proposed law will be respectful, factual, and logical, expressing a more formal tone than an instant message (IM) chat session with your classmates regarding your political views on the law being considered.

Generally speaking, the formal voice adopts the stance of a respectful member of the community to which your audience belongs, be it academic, professional, or political. As a member of that community, you then follow the rules and adhere as best you can to the expectations of word usage and writing conventions of that community. Specific groups of people that have particular writing conventions and communication expectations are called discursive communities. When adopting a more formal voice, it is helpful to understand some of the writing conventions and language expectations of that discursive community so that you can strike an appropriately formal tone. However, you can overdo the formal voice, becoming too rigid, stuffy, or stilted. When trying to be formal, avoid using unnecessary jargon and overly complicated sentence structures. Avoid forcing a formal voice at the expense of clarity.

It is sometimes difficult to know what kind of voice to express in our writing. If we are too formal, we risk being too wooden and dry, and our readers may think us pretentious or condescending. If we are too informal, we may come across as irreverent and disrespectful, thus alienating our audience. There are also cultural issues to consider, particularly if we are writing to an international audience or to a mixed audience with members from various cultures including our own. Some cultures expect a high level of formality in writing, while other cultures desire more personality or emotional connectedness in the writing. If we do not strike just the right tone in our writing, we may inadvertently offend our audience and thus not effectively communicate our message nor achieve our purpose for writing in the first place. Adopting the right voice is vital to the effectiveness of our writing, but how do we determine the appropriate voice for a piece of writing?

This is where analyzing the rhetorical situation is so important. Carefully reflect on the message and purpose of the writing task, and then study the audience you are trying reach. When trying to decide what voice to use in a piece of writing, it is particularly important to fully understand your audience. If you do not know much about your readers and their expectations, then find out. Talk to others who may know about that audience, or talk to representatives of your audience. Try as best you can to find out their expectations of tone, formality, and language. By understanding your purpose, message, and audience, you will make better decisions about the appropriate voice to use in the writing. Sometimes the tone will be dictated by the genre of writing—academic reports, professional documents, research reports, and business letters generally require a more formal, professional voice. On the other hand, personal letters, memos to colleagues, informal e-mail responses, personal narratives, or opinion pieces can take a more informal (though not necessarily unprofessional) voice.

Remember, you are a living human being, with a mind, heart, and soul. This humanity should show in your writing. Your task as writer is to figure out how to reveal appropriate and relevant aspects of your humanity in your writing.

Writing Tips:

1. Start paying more attention to your own voice when you are talking. What are the distinguishing characteristics of your voice? Start thinking about how you can replicate your speaking voice in your writing.

2. As you write different types of documents for different types of audiences, pay more attention to how you express voice and personality. Consider how you can modify your voice in different writing situations to be more effective and appropriate.

WHY IS VOICE IMPORTANT?

Voice is a fundamental component of good writing, one that is too often neglected. Many times we are just in too much of a hurry to worry about our voice, or we simply forget about our tone in our rush to finish the document. For example, most of us neglect our voice in e-mail correspondence. How many times have you read an e-mail from a friend or classmate and have quickly fired off a response, only to discover later that you have offended the recipient of your message? You may not have intended to offend, but you did all the same and now you are trying to make amends for the hurt feelings. Had you just taken the time to read over your e-mail response with an ear for tone, you may have noticed that you sounded a bit curt. You could have made some quick changes and avoided a big mess.

Voice is important because it is the most human element of writing. As such, it is the most precarious or volatile, because it involves the personal and the emotional. Voice helps establish the human connection in your writing, and thus should be considered with great care. Voice is also important because the writing often stands in for the writer. Think about that for a moment. In some cases, the only interaction you may have with other people is through writing (like in an online class, for instance). You will not necessarily be physically present to express your personality, to clarify ideas, and to explain statements. You are represented by marks on a page or computer screen. Those marks can be either dull and lifeless, or they can express your message with life and personality appropriate to the writing context. Voice reveals the living person behind the nonliving writing. If you want to present yourself accurately and honestly in your writing, be attentive to the voice you use to express your thoughts and feelings.

In addition to revealing our personality, voice also enhances the effectiveness of our writing. If we use voice effectively, we can highlight content and make arguments more memorable. Winston Churchill, prime minister of England during World War II, was a master in this regard. With the power of his voice, he instilled confidence in the British people and emphasized his point of view, searing his arguments in the minds of his listeners and readers with his distinctive and commanding voice.

A confident, authoritative voice can also build trust with an audience. Who are you more likely to believe, a writer who asserts positions with confidence or the writer who is tentative and timid? The confident writer commands more authority, is usually trusted, and often is more successful in convincing readers. Furthermore, voice can enhance the expression of the meaning of our writing by striking a particular emotional tone. Language is inherently musical, and a good writer will use language, style, and rhythm to provide a musical or lyrical dimension. This lyrical quality can emphasize a point, or it may express a specific tone (outrage, humor, disgust, joy) that clarifies your meaning.

Remember, the goal of writing is to communicate, and communication is an interaction between people, between human beings, between a real writer and a real reader. Your voice expresses your persona to that real reader, thus allowing for true communication, an exchange of ideas between people.

Writing Tips:

1. As you are reading essays, articles, and books, take note of how different writers' voices are unique. What makes their voices distinctive? How can you make your own writing more unique while still meeting the requirements of the particular rhetorical situation?

2. Keep a journal of model writers whose voices you admire. Try to learn how to develop your own writer's voice by studying the voice of these model writers.

HOW TO ESTABLISH VOICE IN YOUR WRITING

It may be confusing to use a term like *voice* to describe tone, feeling, and personality in writing. The concept of voice directly implies a speaker whose voice is heard; however, when we read, there is no audible voice, unless we are reading out loud or listening to someone else read. But let's not forget that writing is basically a symbolic system that stands in for the speaking voice. In some respects, we must speak, either out loud or in our minds, before we can write. The term *voice* reminds us that writing is directly related to speech and sound, and it encourages us to contemplate the sound qualities of our writing and to view writing as a vocal endeavor. As I am writing this sentence, I literally hear myself, my voice, in my head. Do you experience this phenomenon, or am I just crazy? As I am writing, I am really listening to myself. I hear the pauses, I notice when I slow down and speed up, I listen to the emphasis, I smile at the sarcasm, and I ponder the seriousness. In other words, I am aware of the tone I am trying to express, and I listen for it in my "voice" as I am thinking about my ideas and forming sentences in my mind. Then, I try to craft my sentences—using grammatical and structural elements—to reflect what I am hearing in my head. There is a rhythm and style to our speech that is related to our personality, and we should try to recreate that style, that rhythm, that lyricism in our writing.

Voice is a difficult concept to teach. Principles of design, theories of composition, and techniques of painting can be taught, but the inspiration and creative eye behind good art cannot be taught. Voice in writing is similar to creativity in art. However, unlike art in which some people have talent and others do not, everyone has a voice. If you are a living, thinking, feeling individual, then you have a voice. It may not be as dynamic, compelling, commanding, or noticeable as someone else's voice, but you do have a unique voice. Your task as a writer and thinker will be to discover your voice, develop it, shape it, and give expression to it. As you write, start listening for your voice. It may be hard to hear at first, but keep trying and keep searching. The more you listen for it, the more you will start to notice it, and then you will be able to develop it and modify it for different purposes in different writing situations. Try some of the following strategies to reflect your voice and speech patterns in your writing.

Diction

Vocabulary and word choice (diction) are indeed important to establishing voice in your writing. A writer's diction establishes the degree of formality or informality to the piece of writing, and good writers try to use appropriate words and language for the particular writing context. In an informal situation, slang or common language helps establish a more casual voice. A eulogy, on the other hand, requires a more somber and reverent tone and thus necessitates a formal and possibly religious vocabulary. An academic essay should have an authoritative and scholarly voice, and the writer may use the more specialized language of an academic discipline. Use the appropriate vocabulary to establish the desired tone that best reaches your intended audience with your clear message. In the following passage I wrote about the novel *Dracula*, notice how certain scholarly words are used to express an academic voice:

> In Bram Stoker's *fin de siecle* Gothic novel *Dracula*, the vampire represents an epistemological inversion of dominant Victorian worldviews. Count Dracula is the embodiment of cultural deviance and metaphysical defiance whose very existence could destroy an increasingly destabilized Victorian reality. Unfortunately, the predominant methodological naturalism of the Victorian period as represented in the novel is incapable of identifying and dealing with Dracula's epistemological and, ultimately, ontological threats.

If the basic meaning of this same passage were to be communicated in a less formal voice to a general, nonscholarly audience, then the diction would have to be revised. Notice the different voice in the following revision:

> The vampire in Bram Stoker's late nineteenth-century novel *Dracula* turns Victorian values upside down. English Victorian culture was unstable enough as it was without a moral and spiritual freak like Dracula showing up to make matters worse. However, the Victorian scientific mindset as depicted in the novel was incapable of identifying Dracula as a clear danger to their understanding of reality and, thus, as a true threat to their very existence.

Just by changing your vocabulary, you can express the same message in an entirely different voice.

Tone

Most writing expresses some kind of feeling, mood, or attitude, otherwise known as tone. Writers often use a predominant tone to establish voice in their writing. Some people who are generally known to be quite funny will express a humorous or sarcastic tone. If a person wants to express outrage, he or she may create an angry tone. Conversely, if a writer wants to emphasize enthusiasm or joy, he or she may express a happy or light-hearted tone. In the following example, C. S. Lewis adopts a very serious and authoritative tone, because he is discussing a complex philosophical issue and seeks to substantiate his position with a scholarly, knowledge-able voice:

> All the human beings that history has heard of acknowledge some kind of morality; that is, they feel towards certain proposed actions the experiences expressed by the words "I ought" or "I ought not." These experiences resemble awe in one respect, namely that they cannot be logically deduced from the environment and physical experiences of the man who undergoes them.[1]

In addition to expressing a serious, scholarly tone, Lewis adopts a witty tone when he writes satire to critique the follies of human nature. The following excerpt comes from a satirical story in which a demon named Screwtape is instructing his nephew, Wormwood, how to ruin a human being:

> It sounds as if you supposed that *argument* was the way to keep him out of the Enemy's [God's] clutches. That might have been so if he had lived a few centuries earlier. At that time the humans still knew pretty well when a thing was proved and when it was not; and if it was proved they really believed it. They still connected thinking with doing and were prepared to alter their way of life as a result of a chain of reasoning. But what with the weekly press and other such weapons we have largely altered that. Your man has been accustomed, ever since he was a boy, to have a dozen incompatible philosophies dancing about together inside his head. He doesn't think of doctrines as primarily "true" or "false," but as "academic" or "practical," "outworn" or "contemporary," "conventional" or "ruthless." Jargon, not argument, is your best ally in keeping him from the Church.[2]

1. Lewis, *The Problem of Pain*, 10.
2. Lewis, *The Screwtape Letters*, 1.

Satire is an effective method of analyzing and critiquing society, and Lewis effectively creates a witty, satirical voice in the persona of Screwtape, through whom he levels many pointed observations about the follies and foibles of modern humanity. Here, he notes how the contemporary mind has rejected sound logic and has glutted itself upon vacuous jargon and contradictory premises.

The following excerpt is a final example of how tone can establish a clear voice in a piece of writing. Notice how Malcolm Muggeridge uses an ironic tone to express his harsh criticism of the way the media contributes to human barbarism even as it claims to be merely reporting it:

> The most horrifying example I know of the camera's power and authority, which will surely be in the history books as an example of the degradation our servitude to it can involve, occurred in Nigeria at the time of the Biafran War. A prisoner was to be executed by a firing squad, and the cameras turned up in force to photograph and film the scene. Just as the command to fire was about to be given, one of the cameramen shouted "Cut!"; his battery had gone dead, and needed to be replaced. Until this was done, the execution stood suspended. Then, with his battery working again, he shouted "Action!," and bang, bang, the prisoner fell to the ground, his death duly recorded, to be shown in millions of sitting rooms throughout the so-called civilized world. Some future historian may speculate as to where lay the greatest barbarism, on the part of the viewers, the executioners, or the cameras. I think myself that he would plump for the cameras.[3]

The irony is expressed in the unexpected turn of events in which the cameraman usurped the executioner's authority and determined the course of the execution. The other irony comes at the end, when the writer unexpectedly yet poignantly suggests that the cameramen, in their desire to capture the sensationalism of this execution, instead of registering its true tragedy and horror were ultimately more barbaric than the actual executioners. Muggeridge's irony establishes an authoritative voice, making his critique all the more convincing.

Creative Comma Usage

This grammatical suggestion may be misleading, so let's clarify something first: comma usage should always be governed by proper grammatical

3. Muggeridge, *Christ and the Media*, 64.

rules and principles. The use of the word *creative* in *creative comma usage* does not mean using commas your own way or that the writer has artistic license to use commas as he or she sees fit. However, we can use commas in carefully planned and grammatical ways in order to provide a sense of personality. Listen to how different people talk, and you will notice that they pause in different places in their sentences. There is a rhythm or cadence to their speaking. This variation creates a distinctive voice, and you can do the same thing in your writing through effective comma usage. For example, you can use commas to set apart important supporting details in your sentences through the use of dependent clauses and nonrestrictive elements (review your grammar handbook for these types of clauses and phrases). Or, you can use commas to set off introductory phrases in your sentences. And don't forget that we use commas in lists. Such uses of commas, though governed by proper grammatical rules, have the effect of breaking up the sentence, creating rhythm, and thus establishing voice. Let's analyze the voice in the previous sentence by imagining it is being spoken or read out loud:

> [Normal pitch] Such uses of commas, [lower pitch] though governed by proper grammatical rules, [normal pitch] have the effect of breaking up the sentence, [pause] creating rhythm, [pause] and thus establishing voice.

Notice how the grammatical use of commas—a dependent clause and a list or series of phrases—created a modulation in pitch and rhythm, thus giving the sentence a dynamic nature, a voice. There is clear agency, purpose, and personality behind that sentence—voice—and this voice is established through the use of commas, clauses, and a series or list. Read the following passage with an eye for how voice is established by effective uses of commas and semicolons to set apart introductory phrases, dependent clauses, independent clauses, and lists of words. Try even reading it out loud to notice how your own voice modulates in pitch and rhythm:

> A little girl, now a very normal and cheerful young lady, had an insomnia of insane terror entirely arising from the lyric of "Little Bo-Peep." After an inquisition like that of the confessor or the psychoanalyst, it was found that the word "bleating" had some obscure connection in her mind with the word "bleeding." There was thus perhaps an added horror in the phrase "heard"; in hearing rather than seeing the flowing of blood. Nobody could possibly provide against that sort of mistake. Nobody could prevent the little girl

from hearing about sheep, any more than the little boy from hearing about cows. We might abolish all nursery rhymes; and as they are happy and popular and used with universal success, it is very likely that we shall. But the whole point of the mistake about the phrase is that it might have been a mistake about any phrase. We cannot foresee all the fancies that might arise, not only out of what we say, but of what we do not say. We cannot avoid promising a child a caramel lest he should think we say cannibal, or conceal the very word "hill" lest it should sound like "hell."[4]

Creative Use of Punctuation

Again, let's be clear that by "creative" we do not mean unrestrictive artistic license to use punctuation any way we see fit. Rather, we must abide by proper grammatical rules of punctuation usage; however, as thoughtful writers, we can construct sentences in such a way that we use proper punctuation—like commas, dashes, and semicolons—to break up the flow of sentences, to add emphasis, and to establish rhythm. In this way, we add a sense of individuality, personality, and voice to our writing. Let's analyze the rather long sentence you just read and point out how voice is expressed through punctuation:

> Rather, [short pause] we must abide by proper grammatical rules of punctuation usage; [long pause] however, [short pause] [lower pitch] as thoughtful writers, [normal pitch] we can construct sentences in such a way that we use proper punctuation—[long pause] [lower pitch] like commas, [short pause] dashes, [short pause] and semicolons—[long pause] [normal pitch] to break up the flow of sentences, [short pause] to add emphasis, [short pause] and to establish rhythm.

As you are composing sentences, try to hear them in your head and use punctuation to recreate the voice, pitch modulations, and pauses you hear in your head. Allow your readers to "hear" your voice by the way you construct your sentences on the page. Read the following passage from philosopher Dallas Willard and notice how he uses punctuation to reveal his own voice and that of others he is writing about:

> Professor Robert Coles' essay was occasioned by an encounter with one of his students over the moral insensitivity—is it hard for him

4. Chesterton, "The Fear of the Film," 228.

to say "immoral behavior"?—of other students, some of the best and brightest at Harvard. This student was a young woman of "a Midwestern, working class background" where, as is well known, things like "right answers" and "ideology" remain strong. She cleaned student rooms to help pay her way through the university

Again and again, she reported to Coles, people who were in classes with her treated her ungraciously because of her lower economic position, without simple courtesy and respect, and often were rude and sometimes crude to her. She was repeatedly propositioned for sex by one young student in particular as she went about her work. He was a man with whom she had had two "moral reasoning" courses, in which he excelled and received the highest of grades.

This pattern of treatment led her to quit her job and leave school—and to something like an exit interview with Coles. After going over not only the behavior of her fellow students, but also the long list of highly educated people who have perpetrated the atrocities for which the twentieth century is famous, she concluded by saying to him, "I've been taking all these philosophy courses, and we talk about what's true, what's important, what's *good*. Well, how do you teach people to *be* good?" And, she added, "What's the point of *knowing* good if you don't keep trying to *become* a good person?"[5]

Vary Sentence Structure and Length

An effective strategy for expressing voice in your writing is to vary the length and structure of sentences. When we speak, rarely is each of our sentences equal in length. If that were the case, our speaking would sound rather robotic and artificial. Pay careful attention to the sentences as you write them and try to create different types of sentences (simple, compound, complex, compound-complex) and to vary the lengths of your sentences. One of my favorite strategies is to use a series of longer sentences or to link several phrases and ideas together into a rather long, albeit grammatically correct, sentence, and then follow up with a single, short statement as a way to emphasize a point. I did so just now. The short sentence after a really long one is thus highlighted, and readers pay attention to it. Also, such variance in sentence structure and length creates a rhythm and thus breathes life, personality, and voice into your writing.

5. Willard, *The Divine Conspiracy*, 4.

You can use shorter sentences to create a hurried, choppy effect. You can use longer sentences to create a sense of flow, carrying the readers through the logic of your message. However, you do not want to use the same pattern too frequently, because you will create a repetitious, sing-songy quality that is not very interesting. Read the following passage from G. K. Chesterton, a master writer and an engaging one. Note how he uses different sentence structures and lengths to provide a distinct personality behind the writing. This is not a dry or lifeless laundry list of ideas and observations; rather, Chesterton presents a keen philosophical argument with pointed wit and interesting illustrations. There is a person behind the writing, and that persona comes through in the way he structures his sentences:

> But this notion of something smooth and slow, like the ascent of a slope, is a great part of the illusion. It is an illogicality as well as an illusion; for slowness has really nothing to do with the question. An event is not any more intrinsically intelligible or unintelligible because of the pace at which it moves. For a man who does not believe in a miracle, a slow miracle would be just as incredible as a swift one. The Greek witch may have turned sailors to swine with a stroke of the wand. But to see a naval gentleman of our acquaintance looking a little more like a pug every day, till he ended with four trotters and a curly tail, would not be any more soothing. It might be rather more creepy and uncanny. The medieval wizard may have flown through the air from the top of a tower; but to see an old gentleman walking through the air, in a leisurely and lounging manner, would still seem to call for some explanation. Yet there runs through all the rationalistic treatment of history this curious and confused idea that difficulty is avoided, or even mystery eliminated, by dwelling on mere delay or on something dilatory in the process of things.[6]

You may have noticed that these strategies for discovering and expressing voice are closely related to grammar and style. After all, we often refer to the writer's style as that artistic or aesthetic quality that distinguishes one writer from another. Think of your favorite author. Isn't it true that as you become more familiar with a writer's style, you can usually pick up a book, without knowing who wrote it, and notice pretty quickly that the style of writing is similar to that of your favorite author and that you can guess with a high degree of certainty the identity of the author, just

6. Chesterton, *The Everlasting Man*, 25.

from the style of writing? (Or, think of your favorite musical group. You can usually identify one of their songs just from a few notes or opening phrases.) That is because through style, the author has successfully communicated his or her voice. There is a direct relationship between style and voice, and a good writer will use diction, tone, grammar, and sentence structure to express voice and thus bring his or her writing to life.

Writing Tips:

1. Review your own writing and see what kind of style you have. Does your voice come through in your writing? Consider how you might use some of these strategies (diction, tone, comma usage, grammar, and sentence length) for revealing the person behind your writing.

2. As you read other people's writing, look for how these writers use diction, tone, grammar, and sentence structure to create a distinct style and to express voice. Are there strategies and patterns these writers use that you can incorporate into your own writing to help you reveal your own unique voice?

3. Read your drafts out loud and listen for your own voice. Consider how you might revise your sentences to sound more like your own natural voice.

Voice and Academic Writing

In college, you will be asked to write many different kinds of papers, essays, reports, and documents. Generally speaking, the style of writing required in college is called academic discourse. What immediately comes to mind when you think of academic writing? Maybe such words as *dull, boring, dry, tedious,* or *pretentious?* Indeed, too often this is the case for much academic writing. How interesting is your chemistry or physics textbook? Would you consider your C++ computer programming textbook engaging reading? Probably not. Sure, these texts are important and even interesting for many people, but they are hardly gripping or engaging books. They are generally very factual and formal.

However, not all academic writing need be dull, boring, and repressively formal. Academic writing, in appropriate circumstances, can express a very unique and lively voice, if the rhetorical situation warrants it. For example, you may be asked to write a personal narrative essay in which you describe a significant event that happened to you and then discuss its significance. This form of academic writing calls for your voice to come through clearly. You may be asked to write a persuasive essay on some social or political issue about which you have deeply held convictions. In such a paper, you are detailing your point of view, and so it is to be expected that you express your voice. On the other hand, you may have to write a research paper, say on the immigrant experience in America, for your American history class. In this case, your voice will be more formal and objective, presenting and discussing the significance of relevant facts. However, if you choose to provide some anecdotes from your own personal experience as an immigrant or some experiences of your immigrant parents or grandparents, then you have an opportunity to express voice in those sections of your research paper.

Therefore, just because you are writing an academic paper does not mean you have to strip your writing of your unique voice. In each field of study, there are well-known scholars who write books and articles, and their writing is very distinct. Just talk to your professors about the writers and scholars they read and ask them if these scholars have identifiable voices. More often than not, the big names in a given field have carved out a specialty niche, and their personas do come through in the voice of their writing.

As you learn how to write academic papers for your different classes, be mindful of your voice. Try to express your personality, but do not forget about the necessary language conventions of the discipline for which you are writing. You must still keep the rhetorical situation in mind—the purpose for writing, the message of your document, and the target audience. But try not to lose yourself in the writing, and be sure to experiment with effective and appropriate ways of enhancing your academic writing through a measured expression of your voice.

CONCLUSION

Voice is a crucial component for successful writing; however, it is not a simple concept, nor is it easy to express voice in writing. Remember that voice is the soul of writing, it is the animating principle of discourse, and it is that which reveals the person behind the words on the page. Think of voice as your chance to express your unique personality through writing, and just as your personality is multifaceted, so too should be your expression of voice. You present yourself one way to your professors and another way to your peers. You act one way toward your closest friend and a different way to a stranger you are meeting for the first time. You behave differently when you are sad than when you are happy. Yet, you are still one person. The same is true for your writing. You are the same person writing the different documents, and you can express different aspects of yourself by using different voices, depending upon the message you are trying to convey and the audience you are trying to reach.

Discussion Questions

1. What is the writer's voice and how does it function in writing?

2. How does considering the rhetorical situation of a writing task help you determine the appropriate voice for a particular document?

3. Describe the various ways writers can express voice in their writing.

4. How can voice be used in academic writing? Is there a place for voice in academic writing? Explain.

Group Activities

1. As a group, pick an essay from the book (or one assigned by your instructor) and read it through with an ear for voice. Discuss in your group what kind of voice comes through in the writing and point out specific ways you see the writer expressing his or her voice through such things as diction, tone, grammatical structures, sentence structure, and style.

2. As a group, pick a topic. Then each person in the group should pick a different tone or mood in which to write (negative, positive, witty, humorous, ironic, etc.), but do not tell others in the group what tone you are using. Each person should start writing about that topic and use voice to express your particular mood or tone. After a few minutes, exchange papers with someone in the group.

Read through what has been written, and try to decide what voice was used, and then continue writing in that same tone. Exchange papers a few times and repeat this activity of trying to identify and maintain the proper voice. Return the paper to the original student writer, and then discuss the degree to which the voice was maintained by the other writers. Discuss how you tried to express the voice in the writing.

Writing Activities

1. Pick a topic and write a few paragraphs using a specific voice. Then, write on that same topic using a different voice. Note what strategies you used to express different voices.

2. Choose an article from the book (or one assigned by your instructor) and write a brief response to the article in which you identify the writer's voice. Explain the strategies used by the writer to express that voice and discuss the degree to which this voice enhanced the effectiveness of the article.

3. As you are revising one of your essays, pay attention to your voice. Revise your sentence structure, grammar, word choice, and style in order to better reveal the intended voice.

PART TWO

Academic Modes of Writing

7

What Does an Essay Look Like?

QUESTIONS TO CONSIDER BEFORE READING

1. What is an academic essay?
2. What is the relationship between form and meaning?
3. What are the key components of an effective academic essay?
4. Why are introductions and conclusions so important for the success of an essay?

INTRODUCTION

THUS FAR, WE HAVE spent a great deal of time exploring the basics of composition, rhetoric, and critical thinking. We have made a sound case for the importance of developing good writing habits, learning how to use language to achieve certain academic goals, and building constructive critical thinking strategies. Without these various skills, we simply cannot succeed as academic thinkers and writers. However, this begs the larger question: what is academic writing? It is assumed that students will do quite a bit of writing in colleges and universities, and because of this reality, you are reading this book and taking a writing or composition course. But, what kinds of writing will you do in your academic career? What will this writing look like? What different forms will it take? These are some of the questions that we will explore in the next few chapters. However, before we answer these questions or even the question of this chapter—what does an essay look like?—it may be helpful to know what an essay is. This may seem a bit unnecessary; after all, doesn't everyone basically know what an essay is? If you have gone through at least twelve years of schooling before reaching the university, you have probably already encountered an essay and are quite sure what it is. All the same, let's not make any unwarranted assumptions.

An essay is a piece of writing on some focused subject that expresses the writer's personal point of view on some issue. Generally, an essay is a piece of nonfiction prose that does not follow a poetic or metrical or verse pattern. One goal of higher education is to teach individuals how to think critically and how to express specific perspectives in concise, clear, interesting, and intelligent ways. The essay is an ideal educational tool by which to develop these higher thinking and communicative skills. Although you may not find yourself writing too many essays once you leave college (unless you become an essay writer or an academic), the practice of writing essays in college will develop your ability to think critically and to communicate your thoughts clearly and carefully to others. And these skills will serve you well in your professional and personal lives. As you take various courses in your college career, you will undoubtedly be asked to write numerous essays, and it is important that you learn what they are, what they look like, what types there are, and how to write them effectively. Everything we have discussed up to this point has been in preparation for learning how to write academic essays. So, let's get started.

FORM, FUNCTION, AND MEANING

There is no such thing as an academic essay. Rather, there are many types of academic essays. This chapter provides a general overview of the basic essay structure, and subsequent chapters examine the main types of academic essays commonly written in university courses.

You may be asking yourself why there are different types of academic essays, and this is a reasonable question. The answer can be found in a fundamental concept of basic communication: form is directly related to function and thereby communicates meaning. When we write, we are communicating an idea or point of view to a particular audience. We are expressing meaning. Our writing serves a function. It has a purpose. Because writers have intentions and write to achieve a purpose, their writing has functionality, and the specific form or shape of the writing helps the document function properly to communicate a desired meaning.

Architecture provides a helpful analogy for understanding the relationship between form, function, and meaning. Architects carefully consider shape, space, and form, because they recognize that structural shape expresses a message, and that the form of a building contributes to its function. For example, gas stations look very different from residential homes, because these two buildings serve very different functions. A museum (at least a more traditional one) looks different than a supermarket—again, because these two buildings have very different purposes. They establish fixed spaces (rooms) and relationships between spaces very differently.

The same is true for writing. There are different genres or categories of writing, and these different genres take on different shapes. The shapes of these documents help determine a specific message and its expression. For example, a poem looks very different than a short story, which itself looks different than a resume, which just so happens to look very different from a recommendation report, which in turn looks different than an academic essay. Each of these documents has a specific form that helps it do its job of expressing meaning in a particular way to an audience that has certain expectations prompted by the very form of the document.

Moreover, there are different forms of academic essays. At first glance, all academic essays may seem to look very much alike. However, upon closer examination, as we will see in the following chapters, there are different forms that academic essays take, and they arrange information and achieve their communication goals differently. But before we start distinguishing different types of academic essays, it is important first to recognize that an essay has a general shape or form designed to achieve its specific academic purpose.

Writing Tips:

1. As you read various academic essays for your different college courses, study their message and content as well as their format and organization. What makes them academic essays? What elements and features do they have in common? What do you like about them? What don't you like about them? What features can you try to emulate in your own academic writing?

> 2. Compare essays in different disciplines. How is a history essay different than a philosophy essay? How does an article that analyzes a piece of literature differ from a psychology essay? What do these various essays and articles have in common? How can you develop your own academic essay writing skills by studying these examples and modeling your own writing after them?

IS THE WHOLE A SUM OF ITS PARTS?

The purpose of an academic essay is to explore the depths of some subject, be it a contemporary issue, a literary theme, a current event, scientific data, or political opinion. Generally speaking, the academic essay is written for academic audiences, which include scholars, professors, academics, students, or anyone else who is interested in intellectual issues. Because of this scholarly purpose and audience, the academic essay has a particular shape or form that helps it achieve its scholarly purposes and to reach its academic audience. Readers expect to encounter certain elements or features in an essay, so we need to understand what these expectations are so as to reach the intended audience most effectively. Most academic readers expect to encounter the following elements in an essay: title, introduction, thesis statement, logically organized and clearly discussed evidence in well-focused paragraphs, clear transitions between paragraphs, and a satisfying conclusion. Let's look at each of these elements.

Title

Titles are crucial to the success of an essay. The title is the first thing the readers usually encounter, and it is the one thing that can grab or alienate your readers the quickest. The title is like a hook, and you have to become skilled at using this hook to snag your readers and to encourage them to read your essay. Think about whom you are trying to reach with your essay and what your overall focus or message is. Then, write a catchy (but appropriate) title that will intrigue the reader, give them enough information about the focus of the essay, and encourage them to read further. A title is like a commercial—it is a marketing tool for your essay. Use it to make your readers want to read your essay.

Some writers try to write several different possible titles during the invention phase of the writing process as a way to help them narrow their topic and to establish a working focus for the essay. If you can write a title, then you have a good idea what you really want to say. However, do not worry if you cannot write a title ~~~~y on in the writing process. You can ⋯ he process, when you finally know

⋯ riptive, and interesting. Avoid titles ⋯ gnment or provide a vague, general ⋯ eresting titles:

⋯ e Essay"
⋯ Vacation"
⋯ Pro-Abortion"
⋯ Goodman Brown'"
⋯ fare State?"

⋯ hey are not catchy, they do not grab ⋯ rage you to read further. Now, let's ⋯ published essays:

⋯ 101" (Michelle Malkin)
⋯ s" (Clifford D. May)
⋯ litical Soapbox" (Star Parker)
⋯ (William F. Buckley, Jr.)
⋯ " (Michael Medved)
⋯ (Charles Krauthammer)
⋯ en We Forget What Sex Is For"
⋯ vski)

⋯ interesting and compelling than ⋯ , they all may not appeal to you (a writer cannot please everyone all of the time), but we can see how they seek to create intrigue, pique interest, and cause longing in the reader to find out more specifically what the writer is driving at. Take "AWOL in the War of Ideas": "AWOL" and "War" are conceptually linked, but the reader wonders what is this war of ideas, who is AWOL in such a war, and what is the consequence of being AWOL in this war? Only by reading the article can the reader find out. "Of Headless Mice . . . and Men" is a clever play on the classic John Steinbeck novel *Of Mice and Men*, but the reader wants to know what the "Headless" refers to and must read the essay to find out.

Introduction

If the title's main function is to grab the reader's attention, then the introduction invites an attentive reader into the essay. Think of the introduction as a greeting and an invitation to explore your subject matter—it embraces your readers and gradually brings them into your discussion. Imagine an embrace or a hug. You approach the individual with your arms wide open, and as you draw near you gently wrap your arms around the person and hug him or her close. This is exactly what an introduction seeks to do; it reaches out to your readers and draws them in near to your heart and mind. When you have their attention and have welcomed them into the proximity of your mind, you can then start sharing your thoughts, ideas, positions, and views, conversing with them through the rest of your essay.

You might also think of an introduction as a type of prose funnel. A funnel is shaped to gather a lot of material and channel it into a focused area, and this is exactly what your introduction does. A good introduction starts with a catchy phrase, statement, or question to grab the reader's attention. Next it broadly announces the subject matter of the essay, narrowing the focus and specifying the scope of the discussion. Then it presents the readers with the one main idea of the essay, which is articulated in the thesis statement that usually comes near the end of the introductory paragraph.

There are many ways to introduce an essay, and writers choose different strategies depending upon the topic, the audience, the purpose of the essay, and the tone of the writing. Consider the following strategies for writing introductions.

Start with an Anecdote

An anecdote is a story or brief narrative. You can start an essay by telling a short anecdote that illustrates the main focus of your essay. This anecdote can be a personal story, a narrative about some relevant current or historical event, or a description of an imagined event. Here is an example of a narrative or anecdotal introduction:

> I hesitated briefly as I entered the large, inhospitable lecture hall to which my beginning class in theology had been assigned. My hesitation had little to do with the room, though that does leave something to be desired. Not only is the professor's desk remote from the students, who are banked away in ascending tiers to the point of dim visibility at the back, but the heating system often goes into reverse. From time to time in winter, the bonhomie is rudely broken, with little warning and less reason, by a merciless, icy blast as this rogue system suddenly begins to suck air in from the outside instead of warming and circulating it from within. Here, indeed, is a parable of modern existence: a machine that no one can tame, intended for the comforting of human life, working its wreckage on the best laid plans of the institution.[1]

Start with a Quote

Sometimes, readers can be intrigued by an interesting or curious quote. If you use a quote, be sure it is relevant to the topic of your essay and that it logically leads your readers into your main focus. Notice how the following sample introduction uses a quote to establish the focus for the rest of the discussion:

> "It really does matter, and matter very much, how we think about the cosmos," says historian and college president George Roche. If the universe is simply uncreated, eternally self-existent or randomly self-assembled, then it has no purpose and consequently we have no purpose. Determinism rules. Morality and religion are ultimately irrelevant, and there is no objective meaning to life. On the other hand, if the Creator is personal, then love, compassion, care, beauty, self-sacrifice, mercy and justice could be real and meaningful.[2]

Start with a Question

Essays very often are extended answers to a significant question; therefore, it makes sense sometimes to introduce an essay with a relevant question that grabs the reader's attention and that suggests the main

---

1. Wells, *No Place for Truth*, 1.
2. Ross, "Astronomical Evidences," 141.

focus of the essay. Avoid writing too many questions in the introduction, which can become distracting and tedious. The question should invite readers and pique their curiosity. Notice how questions in the following introduction to one of my papers lead readers deeper into the main topic of discussion:

> Have you ever wondered if maybe Bram Stoker's Gothic classic *Dracula* is less a horror story and more a science fiction tale? Wait a minute, you say to yourself, aren't there vampires and undead creatures, along with some creepy trans-species morphing with the requisite supernatural mysticism that give this novel its Gothic appeal? Sure, you have the fear, the horror, the mysterious vampire, the threatening succubae, the Gothic castle, and Eastern superstition. Yes, *Dracula* is a Gothic novel. However, what is to be made of the curious Van Helsing character? He is a learned scientist who is also a philosopher, metaphysician, and theologian. Because of his multifaceted system of knowledge, Van Helsing comprehends reality in all of its physical and spiritual complexity, and since he does not uncritically dismiss metaphysical truth through a narrow embracing of pure empiricism, Van Helsing is able to solve the mystery of the vampire's threat and thus save an unbelieving Victorian culture that is too dependent upon scientific naturalism to recognize the various supernatural dangers threatening its very soul and physical existence.

Start by Explaining the Main Issue or Problem

Essays often discuss an issue or problem and then recommend solutions. One way to begin an essay is simply to describe the main issue or problem. However, this strategy can sometimes be dull and dry, running the risk of losing your reader's interest. If you are going to start an essay by establishing the problem, consider how you can do so in an engaging way, as in the following example:

> *Midnight.* Shelly is getting herself drunk so that she can bring herself to go home with the strange man seated next to her at the bar. *One o'clock.* Steven is busy downloading pornographic images of children from Internet bulletin boards. *Two o'clock.* Marjorie, who used to spend every Friday night in bed with a different man, has been binging and purging since eleven. *Three o'clock.* Pablo stares through the darkness at the ceiling, wondering how to convince his girlfriend to have an abortion. *Four o'clock.* After partying all night, Jesse takes another man home,

not mentioning that he tests positive for an incurable STD. *Five o'clock.* Lisa is in the bathroom, cutting herself delicately with a razor. This isn't what my generation expected when it invented the sexual revolution. The game isn't fun anymore. Even some of the diehard proponents of that enslaving liberation have begun to show signs of fatigue and confusion.[3]

Start with a Surprising Illustration, Concept, or Idea

Few things intrigue the imagination like a surprising illustration, a shocking concept, or a novel idea. The unexpected can serve as an effective introduction; however, be careful not to disturb, horrify, or offend your readers. Note how the writer in the following example uses a surprising anecdotal illustration to introduce his subject:

> Recently a pilot was practicing high-speed maneuvers in a jet fighter. She turned the controls for what she thought was a steep ascent—and flew straight into the ground. She was unaware that she had been flying upside down.
>
> This is a parable of human existence in our times—not exactly that everyone is crashing, though there is enough of that—but most of us as individuals, and world society as a whole, live at high-speed, and often with no clue to whether we are flying upside down or right-side up. Indeed, we are haunted by a strong suspicion that there may be no difference—or at least that it is unknown or irrelevant.[4]

Use a Combination of These Strategies

Creative writers will sometimes combine these strategies to write a special introduction unique to their purposes and goals. Read the following example and look for the combined strategies:

> On August 7, 1961, twenty-six-year-old Major Gherman Titov became the second Soviet cosmonaut to orbit the earth and return safely, climaxing a monumental feat for humankind. Some time later, speaking at the World's Fair and savoring his moment of glory, he recounted this experience, vouchsafed to a privileged few. Under a triumphant pretext, he let it be known that, on his excursion into space, he hadn't seen God. Upon hearing of this exuber-

3. Budziszewski, "Designed for Sex," 22.
4. Willard, *The Divine Conspiracy,* 1–2.

ant argument from silence, someone quipped, "Had he stepped out of his space-suit he would have!" Evidently reluctant to restrict the immediate gains of the moment to the disciplines directly involved in that endeavor, Titov attempted to draw theological blood. Thus, one great step for science became, for him, an immensely greater leap in philosophy.[5]

Thesis Statement

In addition to having an introduction, a good academic essay also presents a thesis statement, usually toward the end of the introduction. Note that not all essays need to have an explicit thesis statement—you can have a narrative essay or an informative essay that does not require a specific thesis statement, as is true in a lot of journalistic or informational writing. In such cases, the focus of the essay may be implied by the introduction or suggested by a question near the end of the introduction. However, when you are writing academic essays, the thesis is a crucial and necessary element that should be clearly presented in the introduction.

A good thesis does two things. First, it guides the writer during the drafting and revision stages. When you have a working thesis in mind, it is easier to draft your essay, keeping the discussions focused around what you are trying to accomplish in the essay. The thesis can serve as a basic road map that guides, directs, and focuses the writer. However, during the writing process, the focus may develop or shift away from the original idea. In such cases, the writer simply revises the thesis and continues writing accordingly.

Second, the thesis establishes the essay's scope and purpose, thus guiding readers through your essay toward your conclusion. The thesis thus serves as a guiding light or conceptual principle that establishes your readers' expectations and focuses their attention upon the main arguments, lines of reasoning, and pieces of evidence presented in your essay. The thesis, therefore, is a road map of sorts for both the writer and the reader.

A good thesis has two components: a subject and a comment. The subject is the "what" you are writing about, the general topic of your essay. The comment is your perspective on the subject. In addition to expressing a subject and a comment, a good thesis should be specific and focused.

5. Zacharias, *The Real Face of Atheism*, 19–20.

For example: "Peter Jackson's *The Lord of the Rings* is a great film series." This statement has a subject (*The Lord of the Rings* movies) and a comment (they are great); however, this thesis is vague and uninteresting. Contrast that weak thesis with the following example: "Peter Jackson's *The Lord of the Rings* is a compelling film series that recaptures the majesty of Tolkien's fantasy novels and explores the depths of human nobility, reminding us that even the seemingly insignificant individual can play a monumental role in the history and destiny of civilization." The subject of this thesis is the film series, and the comment is the positive evaluation and the specific interpretation stated in the rest of the thesis. Notice how this thesis is very specific and focused. This thesis sets up concrete expectations, and readers have a good idea what the rest of the essay is going to examine. The thesis should be specific and clear—remember that you are establishing the focus and scope of the essay, articulating your unique perspective on an issue.

Writing Tips:

1. Introductions are as unique and varied as the personalities of the different people writing them. Read different articles, essays, and book chapters and note how the writers choose to introduce their subject. Jot down your observations in a writing journal and create a catalog of introduction strategies. Experiment with these strategies as you draft and revise your own essays.

2. Introductions and thesis statements are obviously related writing elements. As you read different pieces of writing, look for thesis statements and note which ones work well and which ones do not, and try to figure out why they work or fail. Use what you learn from such observations to develop your own skill at writing effective thesis statements.

Body Paragraphs

Once you establish your main subject in your introduction and articulate your specific focus in a carefully worded thesis statement, you then have to accomplish your purpose in the body of your essay. That is, you now have to prove your thesis by developing a logical argument and discussing various lines of evidence supporting your various claims. In chapter 3 we discussed how to write, organize, and develop paragraphs. It is one thing to write an individual paragraph that is unified, coherent, and detailed. It is quite another to write several good paragraphs making up a unified, coherent, and detailed essay. When you are drafting an academic essay, you need to consider what main points you will make, what data and evidence you will examine, and how you will present your information in a logically organized way. Each paragraph must serve a specific function within the larger purpose of the essay. There is no one formula for organizing paragraphs. The arrangement of information depends upon your main purpose, message, thesis, and audience. In the next few chapters, we will examine specific types of academic essays and how to organize them. At this stage in our discussion we need to understand that the paragraphs of an essay should be unified, coherent, and detailed, and they should be arranged in such a way that smoothly moves your readers from your introduction through the logic of your argument to a satisfying conclusion.

Some of you may be familiar with the five-paragraph theme, which is a generic model for organizing short essays: introductory paragraph, three supporting paragraphs, and a concluding paragraph. Many students learn this basic essay model in high school, and it is a good model for writing shorter essays. In college, the five-paragraph theme is a useful model for writing in-class essay exams. However, the five-paragraph theme is usually not sufficient for writing college-level academic essays, because it is too restrictive. A complex academic topic cannot be thoroughly treated in five paragraphs.

If you are wondering how many paragraphs you should write in an academic essay, a good rule of thumb is to write as many paragraphs as it takes to achieve your purpose. Your professors may give you a page requirement or a word limit. Always be sure you fully understand the nature and scope of the assignment, and discuss any questions you may have with your professors. When considering the length of your essay, plan to write as many paragraphs as is necessary to achieve your writing goals, and be sure to follow all assignment guidelines and expectations provided by your professors.

Transitions

Paragraphs serve as supporting structures to the thesis and as steps in the logical progression of the argument. In order for the paragraphs to function properly in an academic essay, they should flow smoothly from one to the next. When writers refer to the flow of an essay, they are talking about the overall movement of the piece. This may seem like a strange idea, because an essay is an inanimate object. How can it have movement? Indeed, the essay does not move spatially, but the reader moves rationally and imaginatively through the essay. If there is a good flow to the essay, the reader will glide effortlessly from one section to the next, from one paragraph to the next, gleaning information along the way and enjoying a satisfying reading experience. On the other hand, if the essay does not have an effective flow, then the reader will trudge along, bumping from one paragraph to the next or tumbling in several different directions, in a circle, or toward no particular destination at all.

It is the writer's responsibility to craft the essay so that the reader moves smoothly from beginning to end. The writer's responsibility is to take readers on an intellectual journey, and the writer has to be there with the readers throughout the journey, leading and guiding them along the way. Transitions are effective tools by which writers lead readers through the essay. A transition is simply a phrase or sentence that moves the reader from one point in the essay to the next. Think of it as a signpost that indicates where the reader has been (previous paragraph) and where he or she is going (next paragraph). Usually, the transition occurs at the very beginning of the paragraph, and it provides a satisfying bridge between the new paragraph and the previous one. For more information on transitions and transitional phrases between paragraphs, please review chapter 3, the section titled "Transitions between Paragraphs."

Conclusion

The conclusion is the final section of your essay (usually one or two paragraphs). It provides a satisfying closing to the discussion by articulating the main idea or thought that you want your readers to consider. Avoid formulaic statements like, "In conclusion..." or "In closing..." These statements are not needed in shorter essays that range from four to six pages. Longer documents, like research reports or term papers, may have a clearer indicator for the conclusion (like a section heading or the phrase "In conclusion"), but in shorter essays you do not need to announce the conclusion. The objective is to provide a satisfying sense of closure without directly stating, "Okay, folks, I'm ending this thing now." Think of the conclusion as tying up all the threads of your essay in a nice neat bow and providing a clear indication that the essay is now finished. The test of a good conclusion is that if it were to end at the bottom of the page, the reader should not feel a need to turn the page. The reader should come to the last sentence and know that the essay is finished.

Effectively concluding an essay without directly announcing that the essay is finished is a challenging task. There are many different strategies for concluding an academic essay. Review the following suggestions and experiment with different types of conclusions when you are drafting and revising your essays.

End with a Surprising Concept or Idea

The conclusion seeks to pull the various concepts and ideas together at the end of the essay and to make a lasting impression on the reader, one that drives home the main point in a memorable way. Some writers accomplish this goal by ending with an interesting idea that the reader did not expect. The surprising or unexpected idea causes an "Aha!" moment within the reader's mind, thus reinforcing the main idea of the essay. Note how the writer of the following example provides a series of ideas and observations, all leading up to an unexpected yet profound idea:

> Joy, which was the small publicity of the pagan, is the gigantic secret of the Christian. And as I close this chaotic volume I open again the strange small book from which all Christianity came; and I am again haunted by a kind of confirmation. The tremendous figure which fills the Gospels towers in this respect, as in every other, above all the thinkers who ever thought themselves tall. His pathos was natural, almost casual. The Stoics, ancient and modern, were proud of concealing their tears. He never concealed His tears; He showed them plainly on His open face at any daily sight, such as the far sight of His native city. Yet He concealed something. Solemn supermen and imperial diplomatists are proud of restraining their anger. He never restrained His anger. He flung furniture down the front steps of the Temple, and asked men how they expected to escape the damnation of Hell. Yet He restrained something. I say it with reverence; there was in that shattered personality a thread that must be called shyness. There was something that He hid from all men when He went up a mountain to pray. There was something that He covered constantly by abrupt silence or impetuous isolation. There was some one thing that was too great for God to

show us when He walked upon our earth; and I have sometimes fancied that it was His mirth.[6]

End with a Question

An effective way to tie your ideas together and to provide a definite sense of closure is to pose a final question and then briefly present your answer. This strategy is a bit tricky, because if you are not careful, you can open up a whole new topic and introduce another discussion instead of concluding the essay. Consider revisiting a question you posed at the beginning of the essay by rephrasing it and providing an answer that synthesizes your main points from the essay, as in the following example:

> So who has a natural right to a child, a right that the state should recognize and support? The most compelling candidate is the child's pair of biological parents, who have committed themselves to creating a common life together for the sake of their child as well as themselves. In other words, married couples. They may be said to have a right to a child (though not one that gives them a right to the aid of others or of technologies like artificial insemination), but no one else.[7]

End with a Synthesizing Summation

Summary is an excellent strategy for concluding an essay, particularly if you have just written a very long term paper, an essay that develops a complicated argument, or a complex technical report or scientific paper. The summary strategy reminds readers of the main points and how they all fit together to prove your larger point. However, avoid simply repeating in a laundry-list fashion each of your main points. In the following example, notice how the writer uses italics to indicate a summary of the main concepts covered in the scientific report:

> If intelligent design were the only source of biological complexity and innovation, then the *absence of nascent organs* would be explained, as it is not in evolutionary theory. Similar organisms' migrating together into similar environments and postcreation diversification within created groups may explain *biogeographic evidences for macroevolution.* A global deluge that gradually buried

6. Chesterton, *Orthodoxy*, 167–68.
7. Morse, "First Comes Marriage," 14.

organisms already filling a well-integrated biosphere explains the *general water-to-land fossil order* as well as *stratomorphic intermediates* among the plants and vertebrates, often used as evidence for evolution. At the same time, it explains the *general nonevolutionary order of higher group appearance*, the *rarity of stratomorphic intermediates* and *higher group stasis*, which are not explained by evolutionary theory. The high level of intelligence of the Creator explains the high level of life's *complexity* and *integration of complexity*, unexplained by evolutionary theory. Finally, the aesthetic nature of the Creator explains the *strong aesthetic components* of life, which again cannot be explained by evolutionary theory.[8]

End with a Proposed Solution or a Call to Action

This particular strategy is most frequently used in persuasive essays, argumentative pieces, or editorials. After arguing for a particular position on an issue, an effective way to conclude is to challenge your readers to act upon certain convictions. Notice how in the following example, the writer poses a direct challenge to the scientific community to examine its own practices and presuppositions, become more academically honest, and allow for true scientific progress as new ideas are discovered and disseminated:

> With the publication of The Origin of Species, Darwin produced a stack of promissory notes for future theories. This stack, dusty and yellowing with age, has lain undisturbed and unredeemed for nearly 150 years. The time is past due for an independent audit of the Darwinian enterprise, one that can write off irredeemable debt and rebalance the ledger books, cutting through the self-serving boosterism of its official spokesmen. Are there still grounds, as there were in 1859, for hoping that Darwin's ideas might one day engender a genuinely scientific explanation of the apparent design of the biological world? These hopes are fading, but progress will be absolutely beyond reach so long as the leaders of the evolutionary community continue to exaggerate the status they have so far achieved, and so long as the resulting dogmatism arbitrarily limits the range of theoretical options.[9]

8. Wise, "The Origin of Life's Major Groups," 233.
9. Koons, "The Check Is in the Mail," 22.

Writing Tips:

1. There is no magic formula for writing effective conclusions. As you are drafting your conclusions, try writing two or three different versions of your ending and test them on different readers.

2. Keep a reading journal in which you record sample conclusions that you think are particularly effective. Summarize why you think the example is a successful conclusion, making note of particular features or strategies you see the writer using. Draw from these sample conclusions as you write and revise your papers.

ANNOTATED STUDENT ESSAY

Brandon Kubik

Dr. Hogsette

WRIT 101-WH8

November 10, 2005

American Generosity

J. Randy Forbes, Republican representative from Virginia, once said, "As Americans, we have always had a strong willingness to stand hand in hand when times are tough" (Forbes). Throughout the history of the United States, not only have we had to confront disastrous times in our own country, but in all parts of the world as well. With the recent terrorist attacks, wars, and natu-

MLA citation of electronic source without page numbers.

ral disasters, it may seem like we are going through a dark and dismal period in our
history and that there is no hope for our
future. However, in our bleakest hours the
American people come together and take care
not only of our own, but also the rest of the

Specific and clear thesis statement. world. Through charities, federal and local
relief efforts, and the generosity of the
American people, America creates a ray of
hope in an otherwise dark time.

On September 11, 2001, terrorists struck
New York City destroying the World Trade

Discussion of a significant historical event to illustrate thesis. The paragraph is developed with specific examples. Center's Twin Towers and murdering thousands
of people. In this bleak time, New York's
police and fire departments mobilized as
many units as they could to assist with the
situation. Many of the people sent to rescue the survivors wound up losing their own
lives. After an extensive search and rescue
process, many realized that a rescue was no
longer possible, and the job turned to salvage and clean up. This is when the American
people started to shine. The people of the
United States sent supplies to the workers;
donated blood, money, food, and anything
else that was needed; established charities

Kubik 3

for the victims and their families; and did whatever else they could to help. No matter the economic situation, religion, or ethnic background, people from all levels of society donated what they could. Even celebrities joined in the cause and held concerts and benefits, where all the money raised was sent to various funds to help those in need.

This sense of American generosity is fueled by the country's sense of shared standard of living. In the essay "Why I Am Optimistic about America," the noted historian Robert J. Boorstin wrote, "Wealth is what someone possesses, but a standard of living is what people share" (169). Even though the American citizens had wealth they could use to assist, it was their need to restore their standard of living for everyone in the country that made them truly want to help. Although the tragedy will leave a sad spot on our country's history, we will always remember those who were lost as well as those who rose up to help their fellow humans in a time of need.

After the events of September 11, America declared war on terrorists and states sup-

Effective transition and clear topic sentence.

Transition into next main point: America's generous foreign policy. While waging a war against terrorism, the US policy is to provide for the needs of the soldiers but also the civilians and communities affected by the war.

porting terrorism. This was no ordinary war; it was an unprecedented war on terrorism. Under the leadership of President George W. Bush, U.S. troops were sent into the Middle East to eradicate the threat of terror- ism and to spread Democracy to those who did not have it. As the fighting continued, the American people came through again to help their own, as well as those civilians suf- fering from the war. We sent supplies and comfort items from home to our soldiers, and through federal programs and private organi- zations, we sent food, medical supplies, and help to the people of the war torn countries. One such program, set up by President Bush, showed that even the youngest citizens did what they could to help. He asked the chil- dren of America to send one dollar to help out the children in Afghanistan. Clearly, the American people not only care about their own, but they also care enough about the oth- er people of the world to help them in their time of need. Dinesh D'Souza, a syndicated writer, wrote an article entitled "10 Great Things about America" in which he describes his views on America and what he feels makes

Kubik   5

America such a great country. One of the
points he brings up in his article is that
"America has the kindest, gentlest foreign
policy of any great power in world history"
(D'Souza). Such foreign policy is evident
through the actions America is taking in the
Middle East. Although we went there with military force, we are still looking out for the
civilians who were not involved in the war by
providing food, supplies, and medical attention. Many foreign countries view the United
States as an evil country, which selfishly
cares only for its own well being. However,
such acts of kindness and brotherhood in the
war zones of the Middle East prove this claim
is false.

Use of outside source to substantiate main point of the paragraph. MLA citation of electronic source without page numbers.

Most recently, the Gulf Coast of the
United States has been devastated by numerous
hurricanes, with the two most prominent being Katrina and Rita. When these hurricanes
made landfall, the natural devastation was
the greatest in United States history. The
storms left entire cities flooded. People
were trapped in their homes or other structures, and tens of thousands were left without food, water, or power. Worse, thousands

Transition and topic sentence for next main point: the generosity of the American people during disaster.

Kubik   6

died in the storms. The Red Cross, FEMA, the
National Guard, and several other private organizations and government agencies went to
aid the victims. Again, the American people
responded from their hearts. They sent supplies, food, money, and human resources to
help in the evacuation and recovery process.
State and local governments sent convoys of
trucks loaded with supplies to the areas affected by the storms. The American people
responded generously to the recent disasters
that America has faced, setting up charities
and organizations to help, holding benefit
concerts and fundraisers, and doing whatever else they could in the country's time of
need.

A brief   As is evident from the recent events
conclusion that
uses the   in America as well as around the world,
summary/   Americans have played a major role in the
synthesis
approach and   relief efforts for many of the disasters
restates the   the world has recently experienced. In the
major point of
the essay.   face of these tragedies, the American people
stood up and did their part to help their
neighbors in America, as well as their
neighbors in the global community.

Kubik 7

Works Cited

Boorstin, Daniel J. "Why I Am Optimistic about America." American Voices: Culture and Community, 5th ed. Eds. Dolores LaGuardia and Hans P. Guth. New York: McGraw Hill, 2003. 165–71.

D'Souza, Dinesh. "10 Great Things about America." The San Diego Union Tribune 6 July 2003: G1. ProQuest 9 Sept. 2004 <http://proquest.umi.com.arktos.nyit.edu>.

Forbes, J. Randy. "J. Randy Forbes Quotes." BrainyQuote. 1 Nov. 2005 <http://www. brainyquote.com/quotes/authors/j/j_randy_ forbes.html>.

Works Cited using the MLA format for print and electronic sources.

CONCLUSION

Writing academic essays can be very challenging; however, if you understand the basic components and processes, you will be better equipped to succeed. By studying the building blocks of an essay, you will be able to write different types of essays effectively and with confidence. Not every essay is exactly the same, so try not to assume that the main points in this chapter are merely a formula into which you can just plug some ideas and phrases to get a nice essay. You will still have to do a lot of planning, thinking, writing, and revising. You will have to adapt this model to each writing task. But with these building blocks in mind, you should be able to write good academic essays that accomplish your rhetorical goals.

DISCUSSION QUESTIONS

1. Explain how your understanding of an academic essay has been enhanced by reading this chapter.

2. What is the purpose of an introduction? Explain some strategies for writing effective introductions.

3. What is the purpose of a conclusion? Describe some strategies for writing effective conclusions.

4. Why is the five-paragraph theme not generally recommended for academic writing? When is it appropriate for academic assignments?

GROUP ACTIVITIES

1. In your group, decide on a topic for an essay and write an outline. Discuss what strategies you will use for the introduction, body paragraphs, and conclusion.

2. As a group, pick a topic for an essay. Have each person in the group write his/her own introduction and thesis statement for that topic. Share and discuss each of your introductions and explain your writing choices.

3. Form peer revising groups and exchange copies of an essay you are currently drafting. Rewrite the introduction and conclusion of one peer's paper and then discuss your revision choices.

4. As a group pick one essay from the collection of essays at the end of this book. Analyze the essay and explain how and why it is effective or not. Be sure to discuss the introduction, the thesis statement, the organization and development of the body paragraphs, transitions between paragraphs, and the conclusion. Be prepared to present your analysis to the class.

WRITING ACTIVITIES

1. Choose a professional essay from the back of the book and analyze its introduction. What strategy (or strategies) does it use? What is the thesis? Is the introduction effective for that essay? Why or why not?

2. Choose a professional essay from the back of the book and analyze its conclusion. What strategy (or strategies) does it use? Is the conclusion effective for that essay? Why or why not?

3. Take an essay you are currently drafting and write three versions of the introduction and conclusion. Analyze them and pick the introduction and conclusion that you plan to use in the final draft.

8

Informative Writing and Reporting

Questions to Consider Before Reading

1. What is expository writing?

2. What are some examples of informative writing that you can expect to encounter in your college courses?

3. What rhetorical strategies are useful for writing informative essays and reports?

4. What is the main purpose of informative writing?

Introduction

MANY SOCIAL HISTORIANS AND cultural commentators say that we have entered the information age. Of course, as far back as recorded history can take us, it is clear that human civilizations and cultures have always developed and exchanged information. That we are currently in "the information age" simply means that due to advances in communications technology, more people have access to more information than ever before. We are inundated with information. Information is on our herbal tea packages. Information is printed underneath bottle caps. Information comes on bumper stickers (some are more incendiary than insightful). Information flashes on electronic road signs. Information blinks at us on Web page banners. Information zips across our cell phones and blackberries. Information is on some people's bodies in the form of tattoos. And information (lots of it) is even inside all our bodies in our DNA. We cannot escape information. When readers read an academic essay, they want to learn something. They want information. The first, major type of academic essay we will explore in this chapter is the informative essay or report.

WHAT IS EXPOSITORY WRITING?

Academic writing is primarily about sharing information. Scholars study particular subjects, conduct various forms of research, and then write different types of documents in order to explain what they have learned. Academics discover new information and share it with the academic community and with the public. One main function of academic writing, then, is to inform audiences through informative essays and reports. This type of academic writing is generally called expository writing, which simply means to explain what something means or to provide information about an issue or topic. The term "expository" means to expound or to provide an exposition. Simply put, it means to expose. As a writer of an expository essay, you are exposing a perspective or explaining what something means. The expository essay provides information and thus satisfies the academic reader's primary goal of understanding a topic.

Expository writing comes in various forms. As a college student, you may be asked to write an in-class essay (as in an exam situation) about the successes and failures of the French Revolution. Or, your literature professor may ask you to write a biographical sketch of a certain author and to explain some of the major features of his or her writing style. Your physics professor may ask you to write a research report on the history of how theories of black holes were developed. In an architecture class, you may be asked to write a brief essay defining the American Gothic revival and how it influenced domestic architecture in the South. And in your organic chemistry class, you may be asked to write up research reports for the different synthesis experiments completed in the lab portion of the course. In each of these examples, the main purpose is to inform, to explain, or to reveal—in other words, to share information.

Unfortunately, there is no magic formula for writing an expository essay. Each informative document will be unique, and the distinguishing features of different types of informative essays depend largely upon the expectations of the different academic disciplines. History papers have certain requirements that differ from literature papers, which differ from chemistry reports. As you learn more about various disciplines, you will learn about the document requirements for your classes. If you are ever in doubt, speak to your professor about the requirements of any writing assignment. Although there are differences between the various types of academic papers you will write in college, there are some strategies that you can keep in mind as you plan and draft your papers. Remember that rhetoric, generally speaking, is the use of language to achieve some end, goal, or purpose. In the case of writing expository documents or informative papers, your main rhetorical goal is to inform, to share information, to reveal truth, or to expose meaning. Consider using the following rhetorical strategies to develop and organize your informative papers (review chapter 2, "Rhetorical Strategies," for detailed discussions of these strategies):

- *Definition*: to explain what something means

- *Description*: to paint a vivid mental picture of something by appealing to the main empirical senses of sight, sound, touch, taste, and smell; to explain the physical characteristics of something

- *Narration*: to retell the details of an event, generally in chronological order. Narration can be used to share anecdotal evidence or personal experience

- *Summary*: to explain a complex idea in your own words and to reduce it to its major points or features

- *Process Description*: to explain how something functions or to explain how to perform a task

- *Comparison/Contrast*: to explain what something is by describing it in relation to something else; to point out the similarities and differences between two or more items in order to come to a deeper understanding of the items

Consider how you can use these strategies to develop and present information in a logical way so that your readers can gain valuable and meaningful information from your essay.

CRITICALLY THINKING ABOUT YOUR INFORMATION

Since the main purpose of an expository essay is to share information, one of your main responsibilities as an effective writer is to make sure your information is valuable, accurate, and credible. Your information will come from various sources: your own observations, your own experiences, firsthand testimonies from other observers, library and online database research, and interviews with experts. Regardless of where you get your information, you will want to make sure that it is valid. If you do not provide accurate information, you are first and foremost hurting your readers by giving them misinformation. Moreover, if readers find out about your misinformation, your credibility as a writer is undermined, and your readers will not respect you or value your point of view.

Review chapters 4 and 5 on critical thinking, and use the strategies to test the quality of your information. The following summary of how to apply critical thinking to information acquisition should be helpful. Consider the logical consistency of the information, the empirical adequacy of the facts, and the experiential relevance of the personal experiences and testimonies that you gather. The information must make logical sense and not violate major principles of rational thinking. The information must correspond to reality and thus be factually accurate. Moreover, the facts must be accurately interpreted (remember, facts do not interpret themselves), and statistics should be understood from an appropriate context. Avoid using information to mislead your readers, and avoid using information that has been used by other writers to deceive their readers. Finally, the information must make sense to lived experience. Ask yourself if the observations, claims, and facts presented in your research correspond with what you and with what any other rational person would know to be true from general experience. Or, make sure that the information you use coincides with what most other experts you have researched seem to be observing. Their conclusions may differ, but the information should be consistent or at least corroborated by other experts. As responsible expository writers, we should critically evaluate our information and only use that which is reasonable, valuable, and credible, as determined to the best of our rational abilities, using basic critical thinking principles.

Writing Tips:

1. As you read various essays, chapters, and books for your different classes, take note how information is presented in different types of documents from different disciplines. Familiarize yourself with the main conventions of writing in the different disciplines.

2. When you read information, practice critically evaluating that information using critical thinking strategies. The more you practice assessing information, the easier it will become to evaluate the legitimacy of the information you encounter. Model your own writing after the examples in which you see information being used in responsible, rational, and reasonable ways.

WRITING THE EXPOSITORY ESSAY OR INFORMATIONAL REPORT

When facing a writing assignment, consider the various steps of the writing process and adapt it to the specific writing task (review chapter 1 on the writing process). The following are some suggested steps for successfully writing expository or informative documents:

1. *Invention or discovering what you already know*: Make sure you understand the purpose of the writing task and that you know your intended audience. Start by discovering all that you already know about the topic. Consider using such invention strategies as brainstorming, freewriting, or clustering.

2. *Gathering information*: Depending upon the requirements of the assignment, you may need to conduct some research to gather more information (clarify the requirements with your professor). Research comes in various forms. You may need to do your own field research in which you observe and take notes on a particular event. You may want to consider interviewing relevant individuals and talk to experts. You may also need to conduct library or online database research. Be sure to take detailed notes and to organize them carefully. For field research, consider using a video camera,

digital camera, and/or audio recorder. Always inform your subjects of any recording you do and seek their permission. Consider speaking to your professors about using recording devices for collecting information.

3. *Review and organize your information*: Read through your information and start looking for patterns connecting the various facts and pieces of information. Examine your topic, identify a focus, and consider how to organize your information. What content is clearly relevant to your topic? What information seems less important? What do you think your readers will really want to learn more about? What should be included in your paper? What could reasonably be left out?

4. *Write a working thesis statement*: Consider your main question, issue, or problem. What is your main focus? What are you trying to say? Formulate your main point as a working thesis statement that expresses the main subject and your comment or perspective on the topic. (Review how to write thesis statements in chapter 7, "What Does an Essay Look Like?") Note: Do not worry too much about the thesis statement at this point, because it may change a bit as you draft and revise. However, try to get as specific and focused a working thesis statement as you can to help guide your writing. Consider it a "working" thesis statement, because you are still working on it, and you may modify it as you are writing, drafting, and revising.

5. *Create a working outline*: Given your purpose, audience, topic, information, and working thesis, develop a plan or basic outline for your informative paper. Consider organizing your paper from the least interesting points to the most engaging information. Or, you may need to organize the paper chronologically if it is primarily a narrative paper. Or, you may need to structure the paper according to the sequence of a process if you are writing a process analysis or set of instructions (the basic "how to" paper). Whatever your writing situation, create a working outline that will help you draft an organized paper. Consider it a working outline, as you may need to modify it slightly during the process of drafting and revising.

6. *Draft your paper*: Write a solid draft of your informative paper, using your plan or working outline. Be sure to include an interesting introduction with a clear thesis. Reveal your information in an organized, focused manner, using unified and well-developed paragraphs. Provide clear topic sentences and nice transitions between the paragraphs. End the draft with an effective conclusion. If you are using research sources, be sure to include the proper in-text citations and bibliography (review chapter 13 on information literacy and research writing). Clarify citation requirements with your professor.

7. *Revise and edit your draft*: Leave enough time to revise at least once. When revising, look for the global issues: Is your introduction engaging? Do you have a clear and specific thesis? Do you have compelling information and details? Are you using the information to prove your points? Is your conclusion effective? Revise your paper as many times as you can. Then, edit the paper for grammar, punctuation, spelling, and sentence clarity. Submit your paper by the due date as assigned by your professor.

PROFESSIONAL EXAMPLE

New Symbols for an Old Season
By Paula R. Stern
FrontPageMagazine.com | May 6, 2005

Paula R. Stern is a freelance journalist whose articles have appeared in newspapers, magazines, and journals in the United States and Israel. Her columns are also published on various Web sites. She now lives with her family in Ma'aleh Adumim, just east of Jerusalem in the Jordan Valley. She is also the founder and documentation manager of WritePoint, a technical writing consulting firm.

Even before the Passover holiday ends, people in Israel rush to bring out the flags, the symbol of the days ahead. The flags bring color and comfort in these unsettled times, a reminder that there are powers greater than those we elect, to guard our people. It is an emotional rollercoaster that begins in despair and sorrow and usually ends in the joy of the rebirth of our nation.

> *The land of Israel was the birthplace of the Jewish people. Here their spiritual, religious and national identity was formed. Here they achieved independence and created a culture of national and universal significance. Here they wrote and gave the Bible to the world.*
> (Israel Declaration of Independence, May 1948)

This week, we will commemorate Yom HaShoah, during which we remember the victims of the Holocaust. It is a tragedy that binds us to who we are, who we were, and reminds us of what our enemies can do to us, if we let them.

On the morning of Yom HaShoah in Israel, all over the land, a siren is sounded. For two minutes it will wail and all of Israel will stop. Cars, buses, people in the middle of their day, shopping, walking, eating, everything stops. A world suddenly frozen in grief, while a nation stops to remember and to mourn.

Then, when the siren stops, we get back into our cars, go back to our coffee, our shopping, our newspapers. We do not forget, but we live on. Stronger for having remembered, better for having survived.

> *The Nazi holocaust, which engulfed millions of Jews in Europe, proved anew the urgency of the re-establishment of the Jewish state, which would solve the problem of Jewish homelessness by opening the gates to all Jews and lifting the Jewish people to equality in the family of nations. The survivors of the European catastrophe, as well as Jews from other lands, proclaiming their right to a life of dignity, freedom and labor, and undeterred by hazards, hardships and obstacles, have tried unceasingly to enter Palestine.* (Israel Declaration of Independence, May 1948)

Yom HaShoah is followed by Yom HaZikaron, Israel's Memorial Day. We remember those who fought so that this nation could live. If not for the sacrifices of the brave soldiers of Israel, our nation would not have survived the endless wars and terrorist attacks that have plagued us for all of our existence.

> *"Beloved and pleasant in their life, And in their death they were not parted; They were swifter than eagles, they were stronger than lions."*
> (Book of Samuel II)

Yom HaShoah is a day of mourning as a people, for a crime commit-ted against an entire religion. Yom HaZikaron is something even more personal. We mourn as a nation, pull into ourselves for a day in which we remember the strongest, the bravest, the finest who fell. It is a day that breaks your heart over and over again. They died too young, too soon. Each year, as the names scroll over a 24 hour period, they move just that much faster because this year there are more names to display, more soldiers to mourn, more sons and daughters, fathers and husbands to remember.

And before the mourning ends, before the grief lessens, dusk falls over the land and almost without warning, we are reminded that they died to ensure our freedom. The sun sets, and the eve of our indepen-dence day, Yom Ha'atzmaut, begins.

> *In the midst of wanton aggression, we yet call upon the Arab inhabit-ants of the State of Israel to return to the ways of peace and play their part in the development of the State, with full and equal citizenship and due representation in its bodies and institutions—provisional or permanent. We offer peace and unity to all the neighboring states and their peoples, and invite them to cooperate with the independent Jewish nation for the common good of all.* (Israel Declaration of Independence, May 1948)

It is for this day that we have been hanging flags around the country. From the rooftops and in the streets, from the windows and attached to so many cars. Every year, the land is covered with blue and white. But this year, the symbol has changed for many because the country has changed. We are divided, as we have not been for many years.

What four years of Palestinian terrorism succeeded in achieving, months of Sharon's expulsion plan has destroyed. United we began this year, and divided we will finish it. The symbols have changed, as have the colors. My car flies two flags, as it has for almost all of the years I have lived here. It is the flag of Israel, proudly displaying the Star of David at its center on both sides of the car. One flag never seemed enough to contain my joy of living here and four seemed slightly ostentatious, so I settled for two.

But this year, an orange strip will fly on each flag, attached to the base, as the settlers of Gaza, Judah and Shomron are attached to Israel. A symbol that should unite us in pride, will instead symbolize the great divide.

I am a settler, as are my children. Had I chosen some place other than Maaleh Adumim to live, I would still be a settler. It is what I have dreamed of doing since the age of 13, settling in the land of Israel. It is what those who died in the Holocaust wished to do, and those who died in Israel's wars fought to defend. The right to settle the land of Israel is an inalienable right of the Jewish people and when we deny that right, we deny our future.

> *Our call goes out to the Jewish people all over the world to rally to our side in the task of immigration and development and to stand by us in the great struggle for the fulfillment of the dream of generations—the redemption of Israel.* (Israel Declaration of Independence, May 1948)

This year, the struggle for the fulfillment of the dream of generations, the redemption of Israel, seems very far away. We are not on the brink of peace and security. There will be no peace agreement when Sharon breaks his own declarations not to withdraw under fire, when he betrays those who voted for him and divides the nation in a way no one has ever succeeded in doing before. Worst of all, the ones who order Jews to be torn from their homes, destroy synagogues, and desecrate the resting places in Jewish cemeteries will be those who live in this country by virtue of the sacrifices of those we mourn on Yom HaShoah and Yom HaZikaron.

Each year, our sadness has given way to joy and celebrations. This year, I wonder how we can celebrate when the expulsion of Jews from their homes comes closer and closer, and Sharon continues to ignore the right of the people to decide.

Questions for Analysis

1. How effective is the title? Explain.

2. List and discuss some of the expository rhetorical strategies the writer uses.

3. Is there a direct thesis statement? What is the larger focus of the essay? Explain.

4. Discuss the effectiveness of interspersing personal observations with portions of the Israeli Declaration of Independence.

5. As an expository or informational essay, what does the writer want her readers to learn and discover? What did you as an individual reader learn from this essay?

STUDENT EXAMPLE

Kathie Bostanian

Dr. Hogsette

WRIT 101-WH8

October 6, 2005

Bias—Is It Really Two Sided?

The question of whether there is bias in our media has been asked for many years. A majority of people do believe that there is some political slant in the news media. Whether they are listening to the news on the radio, watching television reports, or reading the newspapers, consumers of news strongly believe that the reporter has either a liberal or a conservative bias. What is even more surprising, however, is that more and more people today believe that there is a much greater amount of liberal bias in the media than conservative. In addition, the bias does not stop in the media. There is a significant amount of liberal bias in our educational systems as well. Many people have often suspected the presence of bias in our

media and education, but only recently has it
been proven through surveys and research that
this bias favors liberal views.

Within this past year, many authors have
researched this idea of strong liberal bias
in our media. Some interesting surveys prove
that many news viewers believe that there is
a greater amount of liberal bias in the media than conservative bias. What is even more
shocking still is that there are many liberals who believe this as well. Ted J. Smith
III, author of "Public Sees Media Bias,"
conducted a survey with remarkable results.
Smith commissioned a study of public attitudes about the press and found out that
"[a]mong the whole public, a plurality of
43 percent described the news media as very
or somewhat liberal" (Smith). One would assume that the awareness of political bias in
the media would be based on the perception
of each individual person. For example, a
conservative person may be watching the news
and immediately assumes that the reporter is
speaking with a liberal slant. In the same
way, a strongly liberal person can be reading an article in a newspaper or magazine

and feel that the reporting favors the conservative view. Smith's findings prove that
identifying bias in the media is not based on
personal perception. Rather, people clearly
recognize that bias in the mainstream news
media is predominantly liberal.

Not only does the mainstream press exhibit
a liberal bias, but so too do many schools
and colleges. For example, in American universities, only 15% of professors identify
themselves as conservative, while over 70%
of professors identify themselves as liberal
(Rothman et al.). This general trend toward
liberal bias is also seen in high schools
across America. Such liberal bias in education must affect the way students are learning. If teachers or professors happen to
feel strongly about a particular issue or
point of view, they will generally include
their own beliefs in what they are teaching. Since liberal teachers and professors
greatly outnumber conservative teachers and
professors, students are generally being
taught from a liberal point of view. It is
not right that students are generally getting a one-sided view on various subjects.

These students are not learning how to think
for themselves. Instead, most of them will
just believe what their teachers tell them is
true. In an article titled "Conservatives See
Liberal Bias in Class—And Mobilize," Jeffrey
MacDonald discusses his concern that public
schools are becoming "sites of liberal indoctrination" (MacDonald). He explains that
younger students, especially, are much more
impressionable than the average person. These
students are very likely to take what their
teachers and professors teach them as truth
(MacDonald).

The increase in liberal bias in American
mainstream press and school systems is a very
real trend. It is difficult to come across
any piece of news today and truly get an unbiased description of the events. Although
this may seem like a bad thing for conservatives who want to hear unbiased news or even
for the average person who would like to
know the truth without the personal opinions
of the reporter, there are some steps being
taken to overcome this bias, especially in
education. According to MacDonald, many legislatures have thought about passing bills

aimed at college professors that would restrict them from speaking with any sort of
bias (MacDonald). To counter the liberal bias
in the news media, more alternative outlets
are being created. Some cable news channels
provide a more balanced presentation of the
news from both liberal and conservative perspectives. There are more conservative newspapers and magazines being published online.
And, there is news talk radio that is generally more conservative than liberal.

Now that we know how prevalent liberal
bias is in the news media and education, we
are more likely to take what we hear and read
with a grain of salt. We must be aware that
reporters will most likely add their own beliefs to the news, and because of this we
have to be able to understand the difference
between the opinions of the reporters and the
general content of the news itself. Also,
students should be more aware of the fact
that what their teachers are saying is not
necessarily the final word on the issue being presented and discussed in the classroom.
Students can still learn from what their
teachers tell them, but students should also

Bostanian   6

be encouraged to research and learn on their
own. Now that we are more aware of the extent
of the bias, we can be more prepared for how
to deal with it.

Bostanian   7

Works Cited

MacDonald, G. Jeffrey. "Conservatives See
   Liberal Bias in Class—and Mobilize." *The
   Christian Science Monitor* 6 June 2005. 14
   Sept. 2005 <http://www.csmonitor
   .com/2005/0606/p01s03-legn.htm>.

Rothman, Stanley, S. Robert Lichter, and
   Neil Nevitte. "Politics and Professional
   Advancement Among College Faculty." *The
   Forum* 3.1 (2005). *Bepress.com.* 25 Nov.
   2005 <http://www.bepress.com/forum/vol3/
   iss1/art2/>.

Smith III, Ted J. "Public Sees Media Bias."
   The American Enterprise 13.5 (2002):
   11-12. *ProQuest* 14 Sept. 2005 <http://
   proquest.umi.com.arktos.nyit.edu>.

CHECKLIST FOR WRITING THE EXPOSITORY ESSAY OR INFORMATIONAL REPORT

✓   Write a catchy title that clearly indicates the topic and focus of the essay.

✓   Attract the reader's attention with an interesting introduction that establishes the general topic or subject, gradually directs the reader to your focus, and provides a specific, clear, and focused thesis.

✓   Organize your essay into unified, focused, well-developed paragraphs. Each paragraph should deal with a specific issue, point, or piece of information. Provide credible information—avoid vague generalities. Develop with relevant details.

✓   Organize the paragraphs appropriately, depending upon the type of paper you are writing. Consider such patterns as chronological, sequential, or relative importance (arranging information from least important to most significant and interesting).

✓   Write a satisfying conclusion that provides a clear sense of closure, reminds readers of the main point, and establishes the overall relevance or significance of the topic.

✓   Format the final draft according to your professor's requirements.

✓   Include appropriate citation and documentation, according to your professor's requirements.

CONCLUSION

Why do most people read an essay? Usually it is to gain information. Sure, some people are entertained by reading essays, but even these readers expect to receive some information with their enjoyment. Expository writing exposes things, brings truth to light, explains issues, and relays specific information about a particular topic. Informational essays and reports are the mainstay of the academic world. Through reading expository writing, we share information with each other and we develop our knowledge. We learn by reading expository writing. However, we should understand that we also learn by writing expository essays. Through the process of discovering a topic, generating material, researching information, interviewing experts, organizing our information, formulating a thesis, and drafting and revising the essay, we gain knowledge. As you prepare to write your various expository essays, try to view them as more than mere busy work or academic writing tasks; rather, view them as opportunities to learn about a topic and to discover information and truths that otherwise you may have never discovered.

DISCUSSION QUESTIONS

1. Define expository writing in your own terms and describe some examples.

2. What is the main purpose or goal of expository writing?

3. What do you think is the most challenging part of expository writing? Explain.

4. Explain how expository writing educates or informs both the reader and the writer.

GROUP ACTIVITIES

1. In your group, discuss the strengths and weaknesses of the professional sample essay included in this chapter. What elements worked for you as a reader? What elements did not work? Explain.

2. In your group, discuss the strengths and weaknesses of the student sample informational essay. What did you learn from that essay that you can apply to your own writing?

3. As a group, pick one expository essay from the collection of essays at the end of this book. Read it and then analyze it as an example of expository writing. Discuss the introduction, the thesis, the organization, the quality of the details and information, and the conclusion. What do you learn about expository writing from this essay?

WRITING ACTIVITIES

1. Review the student sample expository essay above. Write a short essay in which you summarize the main points of the essay and then analyze the strengths and weaknesses of the organizational strategies used by the student writer. Conclude by explaining what you learned about writing expository essays through analyzing

this sample. If your class has an online discussion board, post your essay and discuss your assessment with other students by posting threaded responses.

2. Pick a topic about which you are interested or get a topic from your professor and write a brief, in-class expository essay. Be sure to use the key features of expository writing. Consider using the checklist above to help you write the short essay.

3. If your class has an online discussion board, analyze an expository essay that your professor assigned you to read this week. Discuss the strengths and weaknesses of the essay as an example of expository writing. Post your analysis in the discussion board and respond to at least two other student postings.

9

Critical Evaluation

QUESTIONS TO CONSIDER BEFORE READING

1. What is evaluation and critical writing?

2. What are some examples of evaluative writing that you can expect to encounter in your college courses?

3. What rhetorical strategies are useful for writing critical evaluation essays?

4. What is the main purpose of evaluative writing?

INTRODUCTION

Do you realize that we make evaluations and judgments every day? What did you eat for lunch yesterday, and why did you choose that particular food item? Did you enjoy it? Why or why not? What movie do you plan to watch this weekend? Or, if you do not want to watch a movie, why not? Has your favorite musical artist or band released a new compact disc (CD) lately? Did you like it? Why or why not? Do you have a friend, acquaintance, or family member who disagrees with you on some important social or political issue? What are the strengths and weaknesses of that person's point of view? What are the strengths and weaknesses of your point of view? Think about all the decisions you make in a single day, from the mundane (choice of clothing to put on in the morning) to the vitally important (choice of academic major or career path).

We simply cannot go through a single day without evaluating information, formulating judgments, and making decisions. We must be critical evaluators, or we run the risk of making uninformed and thought-less choices that could seriously impact our lives and the lives of those around us. Moreover, critical evaluation is not limited to our daily private and professional lives. Critical evaluation is also an important part of a college education, and it forms the backbone of any legitimate academic experience. From the student to the scholar, all members of the academic community must learn how to think critically, evaluate information, analyze positions, examine arguments, and articulate points of view. In this chapter, we discuss what critical evaluation is and how to write an evaluative essay.

WHAT IS CRITICAL EVALUATION?

What immediately comes to mind when you think of "critical evaluation"? What if we consider the words separately? What comes to mind when you think of "critical"? I'm guessing negative associations: harsh criticism, attacking an idea, trashing a plan, objecting to a point of view, explaining why something cannot be done, and so on. What about "evaluation"? I'm guessing that equally negative thoughts come to mind here too: judging, being judgmental, harsh grading, idea bashing, and the like. Put these two words together, and it seems we get a double whammy of negativity.

Indeed, you will encounter some pretty heavy negativity in the realm of critical evaluation, but that is not what critical evaluation necessarily is or should be. As we saw in chapter 4, being critical does not simply mean negatively criticizing things; rather, we discovered that to be critical mainly means to be analytical. We ask various questions about a topic, subject, thought, or idea in order to better understand it. What does evaluation mean? To evaluate something. Great, that really helps. What does evaluate mean? To determine the value or quality of something based upon specific guidelines or criteria. Okay, now we are getting somewhere. With these concepts in mind, we can understand that critical evaluation involves carefully analyzing something (breaking it down into its various components) and then determining its value based upon certain expectations, guidelines, or criteria.

How does critical evaluation relate to academic writing? Good question. In the previous chapter we learned that academic writing involves the discovery, explanation, and dissemination of information. One major purpose of the academic community is to discover knowledge and to explain it clearly to other academics and to lay people or those outside of the hallowed halls of academia. But this raises some larger questions. What is the quality of this information? Is the information valid? Are the conclusions true? What are the ramifications of this information? What are the consequences of a new idea? Should we accept this information? If so, why, and if not, then why not? In the academic world, not only do we search for knowledge and information, but we should also critically evaluate our discoveries. This is where critical evaluation comes into play, and that is why we as academic writers should learn how to write critical evaluation essays.

You will encounter critical evaluation in your different courses, but it will present itself in various guises. On an art history exam you may be asked to write an essay in which you analyze the effects of the Enlightenment upon Western art of the eighteenth century. In a political science course, the professor may ask you to write an essay in which you critically evaluate communism and discuss its various failures and its devastating effects on personal liberty and human rights throughout the world. Your literature professor may ask you to share your interpretations of a story in a small group and then to evaluate the strengths and weaknesses of the various interpretations you discussed. In a philosophy class, you may be asked to write an assessment of a philosopher's treatment of some philosophical question and to compare his or her conclusions to what some other philosophers have argued about that same issue. In a film studies course, your professor may ask you to watch an independent film and then to write a review based upon certain principles of filmmaking that you are studying in the course. Notice that in each of these writing examples, the main purpose is to critically evaluate a particular idea or point of view.

Because critical evaluation in the academic community comes in different forms, there is no single formulaic way to write an evaluative essay. As an academic writer, it is your responsibility to learn about the various expectations and criteria for writing in the various disciplines (also known as conventions of academic writing). No one is born knowing these conventions, obviously, so do not feel self-conscious if you do not know them. Ask. The only stupid question is the one not asked. So, if you are not sure how to complete a particular critical evaluation assignment, then get help. Ask the professor who has assigned the writing task. Speak with other students who have written such essays. Go to your college's writing center and discuss the assignment with writing tutors.

Although evaluative essays in different disciplines will have slightly different writing requirements, there are some basic rhetorical ideas that are common to all forms of critical evaluation. Remember that rhetoric is the use of language to achieve some end or goal. The goal or purpose of the critical evaluation is to analyze something (an idea, a principle, a thought, a premise, a theory, a point of view, an artifact, an historical event) and to discuss its value, strengths, and weaknesses according to some set of criteria or expectations. As you develop information, plan and organize your thoughts, and draft your evaluative paper, keep the following rhetorical strategies in mind and think about how you can use them to develop and organize your paper (review chapter 2, "Rhetorical Strategies"):

- *Definition*: Critical evaluation may require defining certain terms and explaining criteria used in making an evaluation.

- *Description*: Objects and events often must be described in detail before they are evaluated.

- *Narration*: Narration may be used to describe an event (current event or historical) that is being evaluated; narration may also be used to organize an evaluation of architecture and other spaces in which the writer narrates his or her experience of moving through the space or building as evaluative comments are presented. Food critics also use narration as a major organizing and development strategy for writing restaurant reviews.

- *Quotation/Summary/Paraphrase*: Evaluating concepts, ideas, theories, and principles may involve quoting, summarizing, or paraphrasing specialized information first and then offering critical evaluations.

- *Process Description*: If a process or mechanism is to be analyzed and evaluated, then the writer may have to describe that process or mechanism first before presenting the evaluation.

- *Comparison/Contrast*: Some things are effectively evaluated by comparing or contrasting them to a different yet related item; comparison/contrast can also be an organizing principle for an evaluative essay.

- *Analysis*: Before an item, object, theory, or idea can be evaluated, it first must be described and explained; analysis, or the process of breaking something down into its component parts, is an effective way to describe the item before evaluating it; analysis can also be an organizing principle in which the writer organizes the evaluation point by point, describing an element and evaluating it and then moving to the next element to be described and evaluated.

- *Evaluation*: As already described, evaluation involves determining the value of something according to a set of criteria or expectations; this is a major rhetorical strategy central to critical evaluation essays; be sure to use clear and relevant criteria when evaluating.

Carefully consider how you might use these various rhetorical strategies when planning and drafting your critical evaluative essays. You will not necessarily use each of them; however, you should examine your purpose and focus for the evaluation and then use the appropriate rhetorical strategies to help you achieve your writing goals.

EVALUATION AND CRITICAL THINKING

Obviously, critical thinking is essential to good evaluation. You simply cannot write a successful critical evaluation without engaging in critical thinking. In chapter 5 we discussed the basic steps of critical thinking, and these same steps form the foundation for critical evaluation. Recall the critical thinking steps:

1. Understanding what is being said: determine what something is all about.

2. Evaluating what is being said: test the various claims and ideas and determine the strengths and weaknesses of the ideas presented.

3. Establishing your critical position: draw conclusions about the idea or point of view and then present your own point of view based upon the discoveries you made by critically examining the strengths and weaknesses of various points of view.

Critical evaluation involves very similar steps:

1. Understanding: Study and examine the idea, thought, principle, object, or artifact being evaluated; analyze it or break it down into its component parts; understand it on its own terms.

2. Critical evaluation: Determine your criteria for evaluation and then evaluate the various aspects of the thought, idea, principle, object, or artifact being critically examined.

3. Present your evaluative conclusions: Discuss and explain your assessment or evaluation of the item, thought, idea, artifact, or object being critically evaluated; support your claims from the information generated in the first two steps.

Writing Tips:

1. Critical evaluation does not come naturally; we have to practice it. Our current culture does not encourage critical evaluation, particularly mass media and television. Use the principles of critical evaluation and practice critical thinking and evaluation when you read the newspaper, watch the television, or see a movie. Consider jotting your evaluative thoughts down in a writing journal.

2. As you read textbooks, essays, and articles, look for examples of critical evaluation. Study these examples and incorporate the writer's strategies into your own writing.

WRITING THE CRITICAL EVALUATION

As with any writing assignment, consider the various steps of the writing process and adapt it to the specific writing task (review chapter 1 on the writing process). The following are some suggested steps for successfully writing the critical evaluation essay.

1. *Observe the subject*: Critical evaluation starts with a thorough understanding of the subject. The invention phase of writing a critical evaluation involves careful observation and analysis. Take careful

notes as you study the topic and attempt to come to a better understanding of it on its own terms.

2. *Determine the criteria*: Evaluation must be carried out according to appropriate criteria or expectations. You cannot evaluate a dramatic performance the same way you critique a philosophical approach to the problem of pain and suffering in lived experience. These are two different subjects that require different criteria. Avoid comparing apples with oranges, so to speak. Establish appropriate and relevant criteria and then take careful notes as you evaluate the strengths and weaknesses of your subject according to the criteria. If you are analyzing the strengths and weaknesses of an argument, a position on a social issue, or philosophical truth claims, then consider using the tests for truth outlined in chapter 5 (logical consistency, empirical adequacy, and experiential relevance).

3. *Consider research information*: Depending upon the requirements of the assignment, you may want to consult other experts and thinkers who have critically examined the subject. Be sure to record the bibliographic information accurately so that you can provide proper citations in your paper.

4. *Review and organize your information*: Read back through all of your notes and observations and look for common threads. Consider how you can group the information and how you might organize your evaluation. Point-by-point is a common structure in which you present a description and evaluation of each main aspect of the subject. This organizing strategy is used especially for critically evaluating arguments or perspectives on issues. In a point-by-point analysis, each main point of the argument or perspective is described and evaluated.

5. *Write a working evaluative thesis*: An effective critical evaluation contains an evaluative thesis. Remember that thesis statements provide the main focus for the essay. A good thesis is concrete and establishes the subject of the essay and a comment or perspective on that subject. In a critical evaluation thesis, the subject is the item being evaluated and the comment is the overall assessment or evaluation of the item. Here is an example of a weak and vague evaluative thesis: "I disagree with the pro-abortion position." The

following revision presents a stronger, more focused evaluative thesis: "The pro-abortion stance ultimately fails as a viable political and ethical position because it presents contradictory views of choice, fails to address the issue of responsibility that accompanies choices, and fails to understand that the unborn child is a unique human being that is separate from yet dependent upon the mother." Remember that early in the writing process your thesis is still in process and may be changed and sharpened as you draft and revise the paper.

6. *Create a working outline*: Based upon the working thesis and the information discovered during the invention phase, write a general working outline to serve as a road map for drafting the essay. One way to organize an evaluation essay is point-by-point: describe one element of the subject and then evaluate it; present the next element and evaluate it; and so on. Comparison/contrast could be an organizing structure as well, in which you evaluate something by comparing (or contrasting) it to a known item. Culinary and music reviews often use this strategy. Chronological organization can be used for evaluating an event (either current or historical). Sequential organization can be used when describing how something works and evaluating the effectiveness of the process, procedure, or mechanism. Spatial organization can be used for evaluating art or architecture in which you describe and evaluate one element of the artifact and then move spatially to the next major element to be described and evaluated.

7. *Draft your paper*: Write a solid draft of your critical evaluation paper, using your plan or working outline. Be sure to include an interesting introduction with a clear evaluative thesis. Present your descriptions and evaluations in an organized, focused manner, using unified and well-developed paragraphs. Provide clear topic sentences and effective transitions between the paragraphs. End the draft with an engaging conclusion. If you are using research sources, be sure to include the proper in-text citations and bibliography (review chapter 13 on information literacy and research writing). Clarify citation requirements with your professor.

8. *Revise and edit your draft*: Leave enough time to revise at least one time. When revising, look for the global issues. Is your introduction

engaging? Do you have a clear and specific evaluative thesis? Do you have compelling information and details? Are you using the information to prove your points? Is your conclusion effective? Revise your paper as many times as you can. Then, edit the paper for grammar, punctuation, spelling, and sentence clarity. Submit your paper by the due date as assigned by your professor.

PROFESSIONAL EXAMPLE

Turning a Funeral Pulpit into a Political Soapbox
By Star Parker
February 13, 2006 | Townhall.com

Star Parker is an African American who founded and is the president of the not-for-profit organization Coalition on Urban Renewal and Education. This organization engages in national dialog pertaining to issues of race, poverty, the family, and faith. She is a regular commentator on CNN, MSNBC, and Fox News, and she regularly lectures at colleges and churches across the nation, speaking about the relationship between her Christian faith and social activism. Her articles and columns appear in such publications as USA Today, Washington Times, Christianity Today, *and* World Magazine.

It's sad to say but it must be said. It should be clear to anyone who watched the tasteless politicization of Coretta Scott King's funeral by a black minister and by a former president why the black community remains, after all these years, as troubled as it is.

Children of the civil rights movement of the '60s are grandparents today. Babies born after the Civil Rights Act are now parents. Yet, despite the passing of generations, not only do many of the problems in the black community persist, but by many important measures, we're much worse off than we were 50 years ago.

Why do things go on with so little change? Why do they get worse?

One big reason, as the Rev. Joseph Lowery so aptly demonstrated at Mrs. King's funeral, is that those who have exercised leadership in our community since those days in the 1960s, those whom black citizens have listened to and heeded, have never understood, or never wanted to understand, when it's time to turn off the politics and the show business.

Is the pulpit at a funeral, any funeral, the place to be talking about the politics of the war in Iraq?

Aside from the question of propriety, what about the message? "For war, billions more, but no more for the poor?"

Does Lowery really believe that blacks are suffering today because they are not getting enough government money?

As I, and others, have pointed out, time and again, incomes of intact black families, those with a married father and mother living at home with their children, are in line with those of all Americans.

The glaring pockets of poverty in the black community are in the broken families, the single parent homes. The incidence of these broken families is three times higher today than they were in the 1960's when Lowery was marching with Dr. King.

If personal responsibility, and really trying to solve problems, were Lowery's game, he'd be trying to understand what happened.

If he thought about it, and wanted to be honest about it, he might appreciate that because he and his colleagues couldn't get off the soapbox after the work was done in 1965, just as he couldn't get off the soapbox at Mrs. King's funeral, they helped lead a community that was breaking out of the shackles of oppression into a new slavery of dependence.

These black leaders helped build a culture built on the assumption that freedom and justice were always one new government program away. The behavioral problems that have besieged our community since the 1960s—family collapse, promiscuity, drugs, crime, disrespect for education—directly result from this.

I'm sure Lowery must have some way to blame President Bush for the fact that although blacks constitute 13.5 percent of the U.S. population, they account for 47 percent of the million Americans with HIV infection. Or to point to Republicans as the cause of HIV/AIDS rates being 19 times higher among black women than among white women and seven times higher among black men than among white men.

Surely Lowery must believe that if the United States didn't invade Iraq, black women today would not be aborting as many babies as they are birthing.

Certainly, in the good reverend's mind, if it weren't for Republicans, the majority of black men would marry the women they impregnate and seven out of 10 black children wouldn't be in homes without fathers.

President Carter also did his part to get the word out about what the problems are in black America.

"We only have to recall the color of the faces of those in Louisiana, Alabama, and Mississippi, those who were most devastated by Katrina, to know that there are not yet equal opportunities for all Americans."

I guess it must have been a freak of nature that opened the door for Condoleezza Rice to emerge out of the backwaters of Alabama to become provost of Stanford University and make her way to become our secretary of state.

The good news is that as I travel around the country, I have a sense that increasing numbers of blacks are getting the message that they don't need government. They're discovering that opportunity in America is there for everyone. But that success reflects the values that individuals, regardless of color, adopt today and the choices they make.

It's sad that today blacks still have to hear from a minister who worked with Dr. King and from a former president of the United States that they suffer because America is racist and because the government doesn't spend enough money. But, as was once said, we shall overcome.

Questions for Analysis

1. What is the main evaluative question in this column? What is Parker's answer?

2. Discuss the organization of the column. What is the main structural pattern?

3. This article follows the journalistic model for column writing. What writing elements and structures does she use that are usually not found in more formal academic writing?

4. What rhetorical strategies does Parker use to develop her point of view?

5. What main points of view expressed by Rev. Joseph Lowry and former President Jimmy Carter does Parker critique? What do you think of her assessments?

6. In the 1960s what did the expression "we shall overcome" signify? How does Parker use that phrase in her conclusion? What, in her opinion, will be overcome?

EXAMPLE CRITICAL EVALUATION ESSAY

Article to Be Evaluated

Human Cloning?: Don't Just Say No

By Ruth Macklin

March 10, 1997 | *U.S. News & World Report*

Last week's news that scientists had cloned a sheep sent academics and the public into a panic at the prospect that humans might be next. That's an understandable reaction. Cloning is a radical challenge to the most fundamental laws of biology, so it's not unreasonable to be concerned that it might threaten human society and dignity. Yet much of the ethical opposition seems also to grow out of an unthinking disgust—a sort of "yuk factor." And that makes it hard for even trained scientists and ethicists to see the matter clearly. While human cloning might not offer great benefits to humanity, no one has yet made a persuasive case that it would do any real harm, either.

Theologians contend that to clone a human would violate human dignity. That would surely be true if a cloned individual were treated as a lesser being, with fewer rights or lower stature. But why suppose that cloned persons wouldn't share the same rights and dignity as the rest of us? A leading lawyer-ethicist has suggested that cloning would violate the "right to genetic identity." Where did he come up with such a right? It makes perfect sense to say that adult persons have a right not to be cloned without their voluntary, informed consent. But if such consent is given, whose "right" to genetic identity would be violated? Many of the science-fiction scenarios prompted by the prospect of human cloning turn out, upon reflection, to be absurdly improbable. There's the fear, for instance, that parents might clone a child to have "spare parts" in case the original child needs an organ transplant. But parents of identical twins don't view one child as an organ farm for the other. Why should cloned children's parents be any different?

Another disturbing thought is that cloning will lead to efforts to breed individuals with genetic qualities perceived as exceptional (math geniuses, basketball players). Such ideas are repulsive, not only because of the "yuk factor" but also because of the horrors perpetrated by the Nazis in the name of eugenics. But there's a vast difference between "selective breeding" as practiced by totalitarian regimes (where the urge to propagate certain types of people leads to efforts to eradicate other types) and the immeasurably more benign forms already practiced in democratic societies (where, say, lawyers freely choose to marry other lawyers). Banks stocked with the frozen sperm of geniuses already exist. They haven't created a master race because only a tiny number of women have wanted to impregnate themselves this way. Why think it will be different if human cloning becomes available? So who will likely take advantage of cloning? Perhaps a grieving couple whose child is dying. This might seem psychologically twisted. But a cloned child born to such dubious parents stands no greater or lesser chance of being loved, or rejected, or warped than a child normally conceived. Infertile couples are also likely to seek out cloning. That such couples have other options (in vitro fertilization or adoption) is not an argument for denying them the right to clone. Or consider an example raised by Judge Richard Posner: a couple in which the husband has some tragic genetic defect.

Currently, if this couple wants a genetically related child, they have four not altogether pleasant options. They can reproduce naturally and risk passing on the disease to the child. They can go to a sperm bank and take a chance on unknown genes. They can try in vitro fertilization and dispose of any afflicted embryo—though that might be objectionable, too. Or they can get a male relative of the father to donate sperm, if such a relative exists. This is one case where even people unnerved by cloning might see it as not the worst option.

Even if human cloning offers no obvious benefits to humanity, why ban it? In a democratic society we don't usually pass laws outlawing something before there is actual or probable evidence of harm. A moratorium on further research into human cloning might make sense, in order to consider calmly the grave questions it raises. If the moratorium is then lifted, human cloning should remain a research activity for an extended period. And if it is ever attempted, it should—and no doubt will—take place only with careful scrutiny and layers of legal oversight. Most important, human cloning should be governed by the same laws that now protect human rights. A world not safe for cloned humans would be a world not safe for the rest of us.

Critical Evaluation Essay of "Human Cloning?:
Don't Just Say No"

Saying No to Human Cloning Is the Morally Right Decision: A Critique of Ruth Macklin's "Human Cloning?: Don't Just Say No"

By David S. Hogsette

The idea of human cloning strikes fear in the heart of some, while for others it seems to promise the hope of a better future in which many human diseases will be eradicated and the lives of many greatly improved. No matter what people think about the possibilities (or even inevitability) of human cloning, most agree that this not-so-futuristic medical science raises a number of bioethical questions, most of which are not easily answered. Ruth Macklin, a professor of bioethics, cautions everyone in her article "Human Cloning?: Just Don't Say No" to take a deep breath, to step back from the immediacy of apparent horrors, and to reason carefully through the issues before simply banning human cloning research and development. Her main argument is that we should not abandon research into human cloning because, although no real benefits have been suggested, no one has yet demonstrated that it would do any real harm. At first, this seems like a reasonable position to take; however, upon closer examination, this central thesis is seriously flawed. Macklin misrepresents the issues raised by her opposition, presents thinly veiled *ad hominem* attacks against her opposition, and ultimately provides no compelling reasons to pursue human cloning, beyond the vague suggestion that no one has yet presented any good reasons not to pursue human cloning. This claim is simply untrue, and the apparent no-harm claim is a philosophically weak ethical position upon which to base public policy.

Effective arguments generally begin by establishing a common ground among the various positions. Macklin does an admirable job in the opening paragraph of raising the ethical specter of human cloning in the wake of Ian Wilmut's successful cloning of the sheep named Dolly. Macklin rightly notes that because cloning represents a scientific challenge to fundamental principles of natural law, many people are thus reasonably concerned about the moral ramifications of such new technology. However, in the very next sentence, she destroys this common ground by alienating most of her opposition, dismissing them as unthinking simpletons who are supposedly merely reacting by saying, "Yuk, that's gross; therefore we shouldn't do it." She further notes that such unthinking reactions make it harder for thinking people to sort through the issues. Basically, Macklin undermines her position by insulting most of her opposition. Instead of truly establishing common ground, she has hurled that ground at her opposition. When you sling mud at your opposition, generally you both get dirty and you lose a lot of ground.

The main target of this thinly veiled mud-slinging are theologians, and by extension anyone who expresses theistic views and who shares the objections of these theologians. Knowingly or not, Macklin throws up an artificial wall of separation between science and theology, identifying science as the thoughtful camp trying to sort out the issues and theology as the mindless camp that simply says, "Eew, yuk, that's gross." I'm not sure how much real theology Macklin has actually read or studied, but even a cursory reading demonstrates that theology is far from simplistic or mindless. She then dismisses the concern that clones may not be afforded the same status as the host human, suggesting that there is no reason to assume the clone would not be viewed as equal. However, she gives no reason why we should make this assumption. This is not a point to be glossed over, because many horrors in recent human history (slavery, eugenics, and abortion, just to name a few) have been justified by viewing the victim as either non-human or significantly less-than-human. Theology offers valuable insights to the issue of human identity and intrinsic human value that secular science simply cannot offer. We would do well to consider the contributions of theology to this question of the status of the cloned human agent.

Macklin further misrepresents the questions about genetic identity that human cloning raises; thus her rebuttals are irrelevant to the real issues. Indeed, the right to genetic identity of the original human is not violated if he or she consents to being cloned. However, the host is not the only person under consideration—what about the right to genetic identity of the cloned agent? That person was not consulted (because he or she did not yet exist), and upon birth, the clone cannot claim exclusive genetic identity. More to the point, the cloned agent can never claim exclusive genetic identity because he or she is intrinsically a copy. Since this new person was cloned at the request of the original human, there is a sense in which the derivative clone is contingent upon the original, if not the sole property of the original, thus diminishing and possibly even eradicating the clone's identity rights. Is that clone truly free to do as he or she pleases with the cloned body and resulting life? Won't his or her actions necessarily reflect upon the nature and status of the original, thus limiting the degrees of freedom enjoyed by the clone? The answers to these questions are not as obvious as Macklin seems to think.

In a related point, Macklin dismisses as improbable science fiction the concern that clones would be created for spare parts. We must not forget that science fiction, as with all good literature, is created not just to entertain but also to instruct, to inform, to raise questions, and to encourage debate about important issues. This science fiction scenario allows us to sort through the questions theoretically before we may have to deal with them in reality. Science has come to the point that we must deal with this question, and it is not improbable science fiction. Suggestions have been made that human cloning be used for providing organ transplants that the body will not reject. Moreover, there are cases in which couples have used fertility procedures in order to create and choose a fetus with the right genetic makeup so as to produce a child who will serve as a bone marrow donor for a sick sibling. (Consider the Molly Nash case or the Hailey Kent case.) In such cases, the subsequent child is fashioned, chosen, and born for the main purpose of treating the sibling. The child is reduced to a medical treatment. Indeed, the parents may love that child, but the inescapable truth is that the child's primary purpose was to provide a medical treatment for the sibling, thus diminishing her in the eyes of the family, making her subservient to, not co-equal with, the sibling. So much for improbable science fiction scenarios.

Macklin continues trying to debunk supposed SF "yuk-factor" objections to human cloning, but her arguments fail because she makes faulty analogies. She correctly notes that totalitarian regimes who have practiced eugenics have failed, but she misses the point that in these societies they did try to create master races and to purify the human race through selective breeding and prescriptive abortion. These societies failed not because they realized the ethical problems with eugenics but because moral civilizations stood up against these regimes and defeated them and their evil ideologies. Also, professionals who marry others of the same profession are not practicing a benign form of selective breeding or trying purposefully to propagate a superior race. Such professionals generally marry because of compatibility and true complementarity. Her analogy to justify cloning simply fails here.

Macklin then discusses three types of couples who may be inclined to use cloning. First is the grieving couple who has lost a child. Macklin claims the cloned child has just the same likelihood of being loved as a child naturally conceived. Again, she misses the point and is actually wrong. Here the human dignity and genetic identity argument is applicable. The cloned child is created not because the parents want it to be its own person but because they want a replacement of the lost child. The clone's identity is predetermined by the expectations that it will be like the lost child, which is impossible. The clone would be pressured to be someone he or she simply cannot be, and this is unfair and abusive to the clone. Moreover, the inevitable frustration experienced by the parents at the clone not being like the lost child will produce resentment and thus decrease the likelihood of the clone being properly loved.

Macklin briefly mentions a second use for human cloning: it could be a way to solve infertility in couples who cannot have children naturally. She doesn't seem to realize or acknowledge that cloning one of the partners is not procreation; it is duplication, and the child becomes the twin of one of the parents. What happens when that child grows up and looks physically like the parent, and the spouse is thus parent to a person who looks like the person he or she originally married? Macklin then contradicts herself, claiming the infertile couple's right to clone should not be denied. But, earlier in her essay Macklin claims there is no such thing as a right to genetic identity and argues that opponents of human cloning should not base an argument on a fictitious or nonexistent right. Well, where does the supposed right to cloning come from? Macklin also should not base an argument upon a nonexistent right, or she should at least explain where this supposed right originates.

The third use of human cloning, according to Macklin, is to provide a way for a couple in which the husband has a tragic genetic disease to reproduce safely. She suggests that cloning would be a way for the couple to have a genetically related child and thus avoid the unpleasantness of the alternatives (risking the deformity in a natural offspring, artificial insemination from unknown donor, artificial insemination from a male relative, or in vitro fertilization in which infected embryos are discarded and the healthy one chosen). Interesting that she acknowledges the last option may by objectionable. But if this is so, and I agree, then she must also consider human cloning objectionable, because in order to perfect the process of human cloning thousands of embryos of failed attempts will have to be destroyed before the process is ever perfected (assuming it could be perfected). That too, by Macklin's own logic, must be considered objectionable. Furthermore, why must the couple choose any of these options? Why must they be compelled to clone? Why not adopt?

Macklin's final argument against banning cloning is her most problematic and irrational position. She claims that democratic societies do not (and by implication should not) pass laws banning anything until a clear harm is demonstrated. This is a highly flawed ethical position. First, we can know some things are harmful without first empirically experiencing the harm. Creating lane violation laws for driving did not first require a series of head-on collisions before society realized such collisions would be harmful. Second, it is known, contrary to Macklin's claim, that human cloning will cause great harm to the cloned fetus, especially in the early phases of perfecting the process. It took hundreds of trials before producing Dolly, and in those failed trials, the clones experienced the harms of deformity, pain, suffering, and death. Thousands or more human subjects will suffer these harms before the process in humans is perfected. Moreover, the one successful sheep clone was not completely satisfactory, as its biological clock was not reset upon "conception." Even though it was born a baby, the cells were the age of an adult sheep, and thus the sheep did not live a full life of a normal sheep. Until that complicated design element in biological life is figured out, any cloned human that actually survived its birth will live only a fraction of a full lifespan. Finally, civil law, moral law, and ethical principles are not determined solely by what is harmful or what is helpful. Civil law is (or at least should be) based upon absolute moral law which is founded in universal principles, not subjective notions of what is harmful or what is helpful.

Indeed, human cloning is a very important contemporary issue, one that deserves far more careful attention than that given to it in Macklin's article "Human Cloning?: Don't Just Say No." Those thoughtful bioethicists who are objecting to human cloning are not just saying no for no apparent reason. Nor are such objections based on uncritical "yuk factor" responses. Sure, there are those in society who hear human cloning and say, "Yuk, that's gross; let's not do it." But to argue against such proclamations as a way to justify human cloning is to commit the straw man fallacy. There are legitimate moral reasons to oppose human cloning, ranging from the scientific to the theological. These objections should be treated with respect and analyzed fairly and thoughtfully. Macklin's article fails precisely because she does not give her opposition a fair hearing. Furthermore, she does not give any reasonable arguments in favor of pursuing human cloning. Therefore, we should say no to human cloning, not because it's gross, but because it is fundamentally immoral. Its various possible applications violate fundamental human dignity (for both the host and the clone), the process of perfecting the process violates the basic right to life of the fetuses that will need to be aborted along the way, and the process of perfecting the process knowingly visits the indefensible evil of pain, suffering, and deformity upon the failed clones that will experience some degree of horrific life before they naturally die or are terminated. It is simply wrong to subject human beings knowingly and willingly to such suffering.

CHECKLIST FOR WRITING THE CRITICAL EVALUATION

✓   Write a catchy title that clearly indicates the topic and evaluative focus of the essay.

✓   Attract the reader's attention with an interesting introduction that establishes the general topic or subject, gradually directs the reader to your focus, and then provides a specific, clear, and focused evaluative thesis. Remember your purpose in this type of essay is to evaluate, not simply to describe or to inform.

✓   Organize your essay into unified, focused, well-developed paragraphs. Each paragraph should deal with a specific issue, point, or element being described and evaluated. Note that sometimes you can describe an element in one paragraph and then evaluate it in the next. Other times, you can describe and evaluate in a single paragraph. Avoid vague generalities and develop with relevant details and specific evaluations of the details.

✓   Organize the paragraphs appropriately, depending upon the type of paper you are writing. Consider such patterns as point-by-point (for evaluating essays, arguments, or points of view), chronological (for evaluating events), sequential (for evaluating processes or mechanisms), or spatial (for evaluating art and architecture).

✓   Write a satisfying conclusion that provides a clear sense of closure, reminds readers of the main point, and establishes the overall relevance or significance of the topic.

✓   Format the final draft according to your professor's requirements.

✓   Include appropriate citation and documentation, according to your professor's requirements.

CONCLUSION

Academic writing is not only about informing our readers. A learned person should also be able to evaluate information critically. The larger goal of a university education is not merely to prepare you for a job or to train students for a profession (that is the legitimate function of a trade school). In addition to learning the fundamentals of a particular discipline or professional area, higher education also teaches us how to think about that field, the work performed in that discipline, and the types of knowledge and information generated and used in that field. Being an educated person is not primarily about stuffing your brain with information—facts, figures, theories, and principles. We should also develop the ability to think critically about that information.

A learned person is a critical evaluator. A great potential for disaster exists if we simply stockpile information without critically evaluating that which we accept as true or right. That is why critical evaluation is a fundamental component of higher learning. Moreover, critical evaluation is a crucial method for learning and discovering knowledge and truth for both the reader and the writer. When we read critical evaluations, we gain perspectives on truth from other thinkers. However, when we write critical evaluations we first must go through the process of learning about something and then determining what we individually think about that subject. This process involves serious and true learning. Avoid being passive recipients of information, and learn to be a critical evaluator of information and truth claims.

DISCUSSION QUESTIONS

1.   Define evaluation in your own terms and describe some examples.

2.   What is the main purpose or goal of evaluative writing?

3.   What do you think is the most challenging part of evaluative writing? Explain.

4.   What is the relationship between critical thinking and evaluation?

GROUP ACTIVITIES

1. In your group, discuss the strengths and weaknesses of the professional sample critical evaluation essay. What elements worked for you as a reader? What elements did not work? Explain.

2. In your group, discuss the strengths and weaknesses of the sample critical evaluation essay. What did you learn from that essay that you can apply to your own writing?

3. As a group, pick one critical evaluation essay from the collection of essays at the end of this book. Read it and then analyze it as an example of critical writing. Discuss the introduction, the thesis, the organization, the quality of the details and information, and the conclusion. What do you learn about critical writing from this essay?

WRITING ACTIVITIES

1. Review the sample critical evaluation essay above. Write a short essay in which you summarize the main points of the essay and then analyze the strengths and weaknesses of the organizational strategies used by the writer. Conclude by explaining what you learned about writing evaluative essays by analyzing this sample. If your class has an online discussion board, post your essay and discuss your assessment with other students by posting threaded responses.

2. Pick an essay from the collection of essays at the end of this book and read it carefully. Write a brief outline for a critical evaluation of that essay. Be sure to formulate an evaluative thesis for your evaluation.

3. If your class has an online discussion board, analyze an evaluative essay that your professor assigned you to read this week. Discuss the strengths and weaknesses of the essay as an example of critical writing. Post your analysis in the discussion board and respond to at least two other student postings.

10

Argumentation and Persuasive Writing

QUESTIONS TO CONSIDER BEFORE READING

1. What is argumentation?

2. What are the purposes of argumentation?

3. What are the two main ways to organize an argument?

4. Why is it important to assess and critically evaluate your opposition?

INTRODUCTION

WHAT GENERALLY COMES TO mind when you hear the word *argument*? Maybe you think of two people yelling at each other in anger. Or, maybe you think of a lively exchange of ideas. Possibly, the image of a formal debate pops into your head. In the popular view, "getting into an argument" generally involves anger and hurt feelings. However, in the classical philosophical view, an argument is a reasoned position on an issue. When presenting an argument, you are revealing and explaining certain reasons why you believe something to be true. In the Greek, the word *apologia* is related to argumentation. An *apologia* simply means to give an explanation, an answer, or a reason for what you believe. We derive the English word *apology* from *apologia*, but in English this word has also taken on the meaning of contrition or feeling sorry for an action, deed, or idea. When we apologize, we are explaining why we did something, expressing sorrow or regret, and generally asking forgiveness of the hurt person or party. Traditionally speaking, however, to give an *apologia* is to give a reasoned answer to a question or to provide a rational explanation for your beliefs.

An argument in an academic setting pertains to this traditional notion of *apologia*. To present an argument in the classroom or in an academic paper means to lay out your best reasoned case or explanation for your point of view. It is like a lawyer who must argue a case before a judge and jury. An argument involves outlining the various logical reasons for a point of view and then explaining the evidence supporting those reasons. Persuasion, a rhetorical concept associated with argumentation, means to encourage another person to agree with your own position on an issue.

It is one thing to argue, and generally speaking it is rather easy to argue. It is easy to present an argument, once you learn the basic requirements for and strategies of argumentation. However, it is quite another thing altogether to persuade. It is very difficult to convince someone that his or her position is insufficient and that he or she should embrace your point of view. Whereas argumentation involves the mental faculty of reason, a human being is not comprised of reason only. We have feelings and a will. Persuasion involves the reason, the emotions, and the will. It is a monumental challenge to change people's minds, because you have to appeal to reason and emotion and then influence their wills. Most humans are quite willful, and you will soon discover that many people hold various beliefs not because they are indisputably true or because they are supported by sound logic and clear evidence but, rather, because they want the beliefs to be true. Many people hold on to their views by sheer strength of will and not strength of reason or evidence. Therefore, persuasion is a much more delicate art. In this chapter we will focus mainly on argumentation, learning how to structure arguments and how to organize argumentative papers. As you practice your argumentative skills and interact with more people inside and outside the academy, you will learn how to develop the art of persuasion. It is enough to learn at this stage that effective persuasion begins with careful argumentation.

PURPOSES OF ARGUMENTATION

The following are the major reasons we might engage in argumentation, especially in relation to academic work and writing:

To Win the Debate

Traditional argumentation is a debate between two or more individuals advocating discrete positions. For example, we see various academic debates in the scientific community over the best explanation for the existence of the universe and the origin of life. Some scientists believe the universe has always existed and that life arose by accident from nonliving materials purely through unintelligent, unguided natural forces. Other scientists believe that the universe had a beginning and was thus designed through intelligent agency; hence life was designed and brought into being by a living, personal intelligent designer. Both sides present their best arguments and most compelling data in order to win the debate. The objective is to present the strongest argument. Persuasion is a secondary matter. Often in such debates, one side will clearly win, but both sides will leave the debate still believing in their respective positions just as strongly, if not more strongly, than when they entered the debate. Winning a debate can be exciting and personally rewarding; however, remember that even though you win a debate, you may still have not won the heart and mind of your opposition.

To Convince or to Persuade

In addition to trying to win a debate, we may engage in argumentation in order to convince someone that our position is correct, or at least more valid than the position the other person happens to hold. Argumentation in this case is used to persuade the opposing side to reconsider their views, to reject them as flawed or false, and to embrace a different point of view. Persuasion is very difficult, because changing one's mind not only involves reexamining opinions that reflect mere taste or personal preference, but it also requires reconsidering deeply held convictions that are rooted in conscience. To change a conviction requires a struggle of both intellect and conscience, and such a struggle can be very tough going. Persuasion is thus the most challenging and demanding purpose for argumentation.

To Reach a Decision

Argumentation is sometimes used within one's own mind to reach a decision on some important issue or course of action. For example, deciding what college to attend and what major course of study to pursue are not easy decisions to make. You have to look at the various options, examine the pros and cons of the various choices, construct arguments for and against the various options, argue the case with yourself, talk with other people, and then reach a final decision. Argumentation—the laying out of careful reasons based upon logic and evidence—is fundamental to making well-informed decisions.

To Call to Action

Related to reaching a decision is the call to action. On the one hand, decision making is often personal, or you may help another person make an individual decision using argumentation. On the other hand, a call to action is usually directed at larger numbers of people, like a committee, a community, or a governmental body. In calls to action, argumentation is used to present a particular point of view and then to defend a recommended course of action. Political action groups often present position briefs (statements arguing a particular point of view on a political issue) and then use the arguments in the brief to justify a specific course of action. A call to action is an effective way to conclude some argumentative essays.

To Meditate On an Issue

Sometimes when we contemplate an issue, we simply do not know what to think or what position to take. Argumentation can be used to examine the various points of view and to learn more about the issue. We become more informed about an issue by studying the different points of view, and through this meditative process we ultimately can determine our own point of view on the issue. Argumentation in this case is used mainly as a learning or meditative process, helping us come to our own position. This meditative process can also be used as a way to structure an argumentative essay: the essay begins with an open-ended question on some issue, arguments for various positions are summarized and evaluated, and then a conclusion is reached as to the most reasonable position to adopt. Note that this meditative process is very similar to the basic process of critical thinking (understand the issue, examine the points of view, determine your own point of view).

Writing the Persuasive Essay

Persuasive essays and assignments come in various forms, depending upon the topic and the course of study. In a history class you may write a paper arguing that European appeasement policies toward Hitler emboldened him and made it that much harder to defeat him later. In a speech class you may present a cogent defense of the death penalty. In a literature course you may argue that Flannery O'Connor presents an effective theistic argument against the spiritual bankruptcy of existentialism in her story "A Good Man Is Hard to Find." Or, in a political science class, you may discuss the strengths and weaknesses of different perspectives on interpreting the Constitution, ultimately arguing for the superiority of the originalist model over the living document model.

Whatever the specific purpose of the persuasive assignment, it is important that you (1) choose a controversial topic and that you (2) have a clear argumentative thesis. Remember that controversial does not mean wild and outlandish; rather, it simply means that there are various (at least two) reasonable yet different, even opposing, perspectives on the issue. You should try to argue for a specific point of view on the issue. The argumentative thesis will be your claim, point of view, or position on the controversial issue. The thesis should have a subject (main topic or issue) and a comment (your point of view), and it should be specific. "Abortion is wrong" is too vague to be an effective argumentative thesis. Consider this more specific statement: "Life is the most fundamental inalienable right given to all human beings, without which no other rights are even relevant or meaningful and out of which all other rights have their expression. Therefore, the supposed right to an abortion is a contradiction in terms and abortion, except in the rare case when the mother's life is threatened, should be banned." In this thesis, a controversial claim is presented (there are at least two opposing views), a clear position is articulated (abortion should be banned), and the point of view is specifically focused (reasons are given that must be discussed).

There are two main models or organizational structures one can use to formulate an argument and to write a persuasive essay: (1) the Toulmin Model, named after the philosopher Stephen Toulmin, and (2) the Classical Model, a system originally used by ancient Greek and Roman orators that is still prevalent today.

Toulmin Model

The Toulmin model for presenting an argument has seven basic components:

1. State your main claim or position in your introduction.

2. Qualify and focus the claim by articulating any limitations in scope or clarifying reasonable exceptions to your main claim.

3. Present and discuss reasons to support your claim.

4. Discuss and explain the *warrant,* that is, any underlying principles and assumptions that connect your reasons to your main claim or that help your readers understand why your reasons support your main claim.

5. Offer and explain grounds or backing to support your claims and to clarify the principles and assumptions underlying your claim (statistics, data, facts, testimony, precedents, logical appeals, emotional appeals).

6. Discuss and refute possible counterclaims or counterarguments.

7. Present your main conclusion.

Let's illustrate with an example. Suppose you were writing an essay in favor of the pro-life position against abortion.

1. Your main claim or position is that abortions should be banned.

2. You qualify your position by establishing an exception for the rare case when the mother's life is at risk. You may also wish to consider exceptions for rape and incest (but for these exceptions, you will want to explain why the unborn child should pay with its own life for the crimes of someone else).

3. You could present such reasons as the following to support your claim:

    *   from conception the unborn child is clearly a human being that is physically separate and genetically distinct from the mother;

    *   killing an innocent human being, regardless of its stage of development, is murder and thus legally and morally wrong;

- the abortion procedure not only kills a human being (the innocent, unborn child) but it also threatens the health, future fertility, and in some cases even the very life of the mother.

4. Some warrants or underlying principles of these reasons include:

- at conception the fetus is a genetic human being, not mere tissue or an indescribable clump of unidentifiable molecules (factual, biological premise);

- the mother's right over her own body does not extend to and ought not impose upon the separate body of the unborn child (legal premise);

- the mother is not the only person contributing to the genetic makeup of the unborn human being, and certain rights of the biological father must be considered as well (factual, biological premise);

- the right to life is the most fundamental right that is inalienable to the unborn human being and that must be preserved as a foundational right necessary for all other rights to apply (legal premise);

- a vague right to privacy (which is not clearly established in the Constitution) does not trump the fundamental and explicit right to life (which is specifically established in the Declaration of Independence and in the Constitution) of the unborn human being (legal and constitutional premise);

- the unborn human being is vulnerable and dependent upon the mother and thus deserves care, not death (factual premise);

- an individual's rights and exercise thereof are limited by the rights of other individuals regardless of how small or dependent that individual may be (legal premise);

- a civilized society ought not to be wantonly destroying unborn human beings (moral premise);

- a civilized society is necessarily damaged and scarred by allowing, embracing, and encouraging the wanton destruction of innocent human life, be it that of the unborn child, the mentally impaired, or the terminally ill (social premise).

5. Various statistical data can be presented as grounds supporting the claims and backing the warrants, including:

   - the alarmingly high number of abortions performed each year in the United States alone;

   - data on complications to the mother's health, fertility, and life resulting from abortion procedures;

   - data on the traumatic emotional ramifications of abortion upon the woman, her spouse (or the biological father), and extended family;

   - medical evidence revealing the level of pain experienced by the unborn human being when aborted at various stages of development;

   - scientific evidence such as genetic analysis and microphotography of the unborn human being proving that the unborn baby is in fact a human being that is separate from the mother and unique in identity.

6. Counter claims can then be directly refuted, like:

   - the argument that the mother's right to her own body extends to the body of the unborn baby;

   - the mother's sovereignty over her own body trumps the life right of the unborn human being;

   - the unborn human being is not really a human being;

   - the unborn human being is not really a person deserving a right to life.

7. Finally, your conclusion can be presented, clearly establishing the legitimacy of your main claim and, in this case, calling for specific action—that abortion be banned (except in the rare cases when the mother's life is at risk).

Classical Model

The basic classical model for constructing an argument can be outlined as follows:

1. Introduction

    -   Establishes the main topic or issue.

    -   Gradually brings readers into the discussion.

    -   Establishes common ground that brings audiences of different views together.

    -   Presents a clear and specific argumentative thesis.

2. Background information

    -   Provides any necessary historical, theoretical, philosophical, theological, political, or other such information that helps readers better understand your position.

3. Discussion of main opposing views

    -   Some writers discuss the opposition after first presenting their main case—consider addressing the opposition first, which defuses their views and expectations and prepares them to focus on your views.

    -   Sometimes you can structure your whole paper as a point-by-point refutation of your opposition, ending with your strongest, main argument.

    -   Summarizes the main points of the opposition fairly, honestly, and accurately.

    -   Discusses the strengths and weaknesses of the opposition.

    -   Concedes undeniable or irrefutable points of the opposition.

    -   Refutes the remaining points in an honest, fair, and respectful manner.

4. Presentation of main lines of reasoning

    -   Presents and explains the reasons and arguments supporting your position, generally organized from the weakest point to the strongest.

- Presents logical appeals and appropriate emotional appeals.

- Presents precedent, data, statistics, and other evidence to support the reasons.

- Explains how and why these points support the main claim.

5. Conclusion

- Summarizes the main point (especially in a longer essay or an essay that presents a complex argument).

- Explains what you want your readers to think and believe.

- Explains why this position is important or significant.

- May present a call to action.

- May present a compelling and relevant ethical or emotional appeal.

See the professional and student sample essays below for examples of how to structure persuasive essays using the classical model.

Using Outside Sources

Depending upon the requirements of the argumentative assignment and your own knowledge of the issues, you may need to do some research and incorporate outside sources into your argument. (See chapter 13 for more information on research and information literacy.) Your research may involve examining library books, journals, and magazines; browsing online library databases; and interviewing experts or other individuals with specific and credible knowledge pertaining to your issue (interviews can be conducted in person, over the phone, or electronically through e-mail, instant message (IM) chat, blogs, or other discussion board environments). Consider the following key reasons for using outside research when writing argumentative essays:

1. To understand the opposition: We often do not know what our opposition thinks, feels, and believes, and research can help us better understand our opposition and thus to strengthen our analysis and refutation of their views.

2. To strengthen arguments: We may have strong views and good arguments to support them, but usually our points of view can be

strengthened even further by reading what others have to say in support of our position. There may be other compelling arguments that we haven't thought of that can be learned and incorporated by conducting some research.

3. To find supporting data and evidence: Our claims, arguments, and reasons should be supported by evidence, data, statistics, precedent, and other corroborating information. Research helps us discover evidence and information to strengthen our arguments.

4. To enhance our authority as writers: When trying to persuade our opposition, we have to anticipate the reasonable question, "Who says?" Most of us are not experts on the issues, so we cannot expect our opposition simply to accept what we say. We have to establish our authority as a writer if people are to believe us, and if we are not experts ourselves then we should conduct research to present expert testimony, evidence, and arguments.

5. To enhance our credibility as writers: Credibility is simply our believability, or the degree to which people are willing to believe what we say is true. Credibility is directly related to the issue of the authority of the writer. Usually, the greater our authority, the more likely it is that our readers will believe us. But more important is that our readers trust us, and the best way to gain the readers' trust is to present detailed information honestly and accurately and to discuss it clearly and fairly. Researching credible sources and using credible information lend greater credibility to our views and increases the chance of persuading our audience.

CRITICAL THINKING AND THE PERSUASIVE PAPER

Critical thinking is essential to effective argumentative writing, and it is particularly crucial to persuasive writing. Remember, presenting an argument is one thing, but persuading your opposition that your argument is true and that they should abandon their view and adopt your own is very difficult. Critical thinking strengthens your arguments and enhances your persuasiveness by (1) helping you assess your opposition's views and (2) allowing you to analyze and strengthen your own arguments.

Assessing and Refuting Your Opposition

Remember that a major strategy for good argumentative and persuasive writing is to understand and refute your opposition's views. Critical thinking strategies help you in this assessment and refutation process. Once you identify your opposition's main arguments, critically analyze them by first understanding them fully, completely, and fairly. Then, evaluate the strengths and weaknesses of their arguments, looking for logical inconsistencies, logical fallacies, and emotional fallacies. Evaluate the lines of evidence and the data used to support the arguments—is the evidence adequate and relevant, is the evidence used properly and fairly, and does the evidence prove what your opposition claims it proves? Also, consider comparing their claims with your own lived experience and that of other individuals who have had similar experiences as those described by your opposition. Once you have fully understood and evaluated the views of your opposition, you will be in a better position to summarize them, assess them, and then refute them (where possible).

Analyzing and Strengthening Your Position

In addition to evaluating the views of your opposition, you can also use critical thinking to analyze and strengthen your own arguments. Use the same critical thinking strategy outlined above to analyze your own arguments and evidence. Where you find any weaknesses, holes, inconsistencies, or ineffective arguments, make revisions to strengthen your position. In some cases, you may wish to exclude certain arguments that are too weak and that do not serve the best interests of your argument. If you can refute one of your own claims, then your opposition can too. Use critical thinking strategies to review and strengthen your arguments and evidence.

MAKING LOGICAL APPEALS

As we have discussed, arguments are lines of reasoning supporting a point of view. When we present reasons, we can make appeals to logic or appeals to emotion. In academic persuasive writing, you should concentrate more on logical appeals, because if you rely too heavily upon emotional appeals, your academic audience may conclude that you are simply trying to manipulate them emotionally instead of presenting sound logical reasons for your position. There is a place for emotional appeals (see below), but in academic writing, your main lines of reasoning should appeal to the logical sensibilities of your readers. There are three major types of logical approaches: inductive reasoning, deductive reasoning, and abductive reasoning. (Review chapter 4 for a more in-depth discussion of modes of logical thinking.)

Inductive Reasoning

Induction begins by considering a series of observations and many different lines of evidence regarding some phenomenon or point of view. Reasonable conclusions are then drawn from the wealth of evidence observed and analyzed. Generalizations or basic principles are drawn from the careful consideration of specific facts (working from the specific to the general). Science often uses inductive reasoning as a main operating principle. Say, for example, you allowed several groups of young boys to watch violent television programs and then sent them outside to play. If you consistently observe that a vast majority of the boys in each of the groups played more violently after watching the violent programming than did other young boys who did not watch violent programs before playing, then you could inductively conclude that violent television programs influenced how the boys played. Note that inductive conclusions are only as good as the evidence upon which they are based.

Deductive Reasoning

Deduction begins by applying a general principle to a specific situation in order to explain or understand that specific situation. For example, you watch an episode of Power Rangers with your young nephew, and then take him to a local park to play. If you notice that he is playing rough with the other children, then according to the general principle that watching violent television program influences the manner of play in young boys, you could deduce that your nephew is playing rough (throwing side kicks and karate chops at the other children) because he is acting out the violent behavior he watched on television just a few moments prior to going to the park. Note that deductive conclusions are only as valid as the general principle upon which the deduction is based. Effective inductive procedures will generally result in valid general principles that can then be successfully used to draw sound deductive conclusions.

Abductive Reasoning

Abductive reasoning is also known as an inference to the best explanation. In abductive reasoning, you consider the various possible conclusions and rule out the ones that are least reasonable, until you are left with the most reasonable conclusion. For example, you take your nephew to the park and he starts playing roughly with the other children. Possible explanations you consider: he is hyperactive, he had too much sugar at lunch, he is emotionally disturbed, or he is acting out scenes from a recent episode of Power Rangers. After analyzing each possible explanation, you note that your nephew is not normally hyperactive, you recall that he did not eat more sugar than he normally has at lunch, and you recognize that your nephew is not emotionally disturbed. Then, you remember that you watched Power Rangers with him before going to the park, and you abductively conclude that the best explanation is that your nephew is acting out scenes from the television show. Note that abductive reasoning is effective and persuasive, but it assumes that you have considered and ruled out all the major possible explanations before reaching your conclusion. There may indeed be other possible explanations that you have not yet considered that truly explain the situation. When reasoning abductively, you must try very hard to consider the best possible explanations.

These are the three major logical approaches generally used in academic writing. Rarely will you use only one of these approaches. As you develop your arguments and structure your paper, consider how you can develop your logical appeals by combining inductive, deductive, and abductive reasoning.

Avoiding Logical Fallacies

When formulating sound logical arguments, be sure to avoid logical fallacies (errors in logic), which undermine the legitimacy of your position and diminish your authority as writer and credibility as thinker. Review chapter 4 for a full list and explanation of logical fallacies. Below is a shorter list of the most common logical fallacies that should be avoided in academic writing:

Ad hominem attacks: Attacking the person's character or calling your opponent a harsh name instead of dealing with the issues and arguments at hand. Also known as character assassination.

Guilt by association: Trying to discredit the person by unfairly associating him/her with someone else known to be guilty of a crime or some immoral act. This fallacy avoids the issues by trying to smear the person's character.

Straw man attacks: Misrepresenting your opposition's main point in order to make it easier to refute; or presenting your opposition's weakest point as if it were the main point, refuting the weak point, and then claiming your opposition's position has been soundly undermined.

Red herring: Raising and discussing irrelevant points in an attempt to distract the opponent from the main issues.

Non sequitur: An argument or conclusion that simply does not follow from the evidence or reasons given, because the logic attempts to associate ideas or facts that are logically unrelated.

Either-or fallacy: Inappropriately reducing a complex situation into an either-or situation and then arguing that since one option is false, the other must be true. Note that there are times when you can present an either-or situation: God either exists or He does not; I am either alive or dead; you are either reading this book right now or you are not. However, many issues are quite complex and cannot be reduced to an overly simplistic either-or scenario.

Hasty generalization: Drawing too grand a conclusion based upon too little evidence.

Oversimplification: Drawing overly simplistic conclusions from complex situations. This fallacy is sometimes called the nothing but fallacy or the reductive fallacy.

MAKING EMOTIONAL APPEALS

In addition to using logic when formulating sound arguments, we can also appeal to our readers' emotions. However, we have to be careful that we not rely too heavily upon emotional appeals, particularly when writing to an academic audience. Academics like to think about issues and to consider logical arguments and sound evidence, and they do not like to have their emotions unduly manipulated. If you rely too heavily upon emotional appeals, you run the risk of alienating your academic audience. That said, we can use carefully constructed emotional appeals successfully in academic writing. Keep the following concepts in mind when formulating emotional appeals in your academic papers:

Crafting Language

Making emotional appeals requires that you use language in a creative way so as to evoke an emotional response in your reader. Your language should be specific, concrete, and descriptive. Consider using figurative language, which describes one thing in terms of something else. It is expressive and imaginative language that creates a vivid emotional response or creates a vivid image in the minds of your readers. Analogies, metaphors, and similes are examples of figurative speech. An analogy compares an unknown or unfamiliar item or process with one that is generally known. Metaphors and similes are two ways of creating an analogy. The metaphor directly compares two things; for example, writing persuasive papers is a bear. The simile indirectly compares two things using "like" or "as" in the comparative statement; for example, writing persuasive papers is as daunting as wrestling with a bear. Obviously, these statements are not meant to be taken literally, for that would be absurd. Instead, the comparisons attempt to communicate in a creative way the difficulty of writing an argumentative paper. Good writers can create powerful analogies that communicate the main message through evoking strong emotion.

Appealing to Specific Audiences

In order to create an effective emotional appeal, you must know your audience. Not everyone reacts to emotional appeals in the same way. Carefully consider your audience and try to discover their interests, concerns, needs, fears, likes, and dislikes. Then, try to use concrete and descriptive figurative language to appeal to their emotions in meaningful ways. If you are writing to parents, then addressing issues related to children will evoke certain emotions. If you are writing to college students, then raising issues about the uncertainties of the future will evoke other types of emotions. Get to know your audience and then craft emotional appeals that are directed at that specific audience.

Avoiding Emotional Fallacies

When you are making emotional appeals, be sure to avoid committing emotional fallacies or inappropriate manipulations of your readers' emotions. If you try to tug at your readers' heartstrings a bit too much or if you come across as being too emotionally sappy, then your readers (particularly academic ones) will not take your arguments very seriously, and some readers may even become resentful. Emotional fallacies diminish your credibility as a thinker and writer and thus undermine your attempt at argumentation and persuasion. Review chapter 4 for a more complete list and description of emotional fallacies. The following is a brief list of the common ones to avoid when writing academic persuasive papers:

Appeal to pity: Evoking undue pity in your readers instead of presenting logical reasons for agreeing with a certain position.

Bandwagon appeal: This is the everyone-is-doing-it appeal. Rather than provide a good reason to adopt a position or to pursue a course of action, bandwagon appeal argues that since most people agree or are doing it, then so should you.

Flattery: Making the person feel good, cool, or smart for agreeing with your position. This emotional fallacy appeals to the vanity or pride of the reader instead of offering sound reasons for your position.

Veiled threats: Making the person feel threatened, afraid, or insecure for not agreeing with your position. This tactic preys on the reader's insecurities instead of appealing to sound reason.

False analogies: Drawing inappropriate or unfounded comparisons between two items that are fundamentally unrelated. Analogies can be powerful emotional appeals, but if the analogy is inappropriate or unfounded, then your credibility can be questioned because it will seem that you really do not know or understand the issues you are discussing.

ESTABLISHING CREDIBILITY

Your credibility as a writer is the degree to which readers believe what you say. Credibility is an essential quality to establish and maintain throughout the paper, because without credibility, you cannot achieve your purposes for argumentation. The following are some important strategies for establishing credibility:

Establishing Common Ground

Most controversial issues are very complex, and different people hold different positions. When you argue for your position and try to convince your opposition that your views are correct and more reasonable than their view, you have to work very hard just to get them to hear you out. How do you get them to even listen to you, let alone to accept your point of view? Try establishing common ground early in your paper, either in the introduction or in the first paragraph after the introduction. Common ground simply refers to a general understanding of an issue with which all people can agree. First, explain the issues that most people agree with, and then discuss the key elements of your point of view that differ from your opposition. For example, in a persuasive essay dealing with the Arab-Israeli conflict, it would be important to first establish that many on both sides have experienced pain, loss, and suffering, that there is a complex history to the conflict dating back several thousands of years, and that everyone can agree that something specific must be done to achieve peace in the region. This is a common ground that everyone can agree with, and it is an effective starting point for a discussion of whatever point of view your paper argues. By establishing a common ground, you communicate to your readers that you understand the complexity of the problem, and you communicate a willingness to consider various points of view. Your readers will view you as a reasonable person and will acknowledge you as a credible writer.

Demonstrating Knowledge

Credibility can also be established by demonstrating that you know what you are talking about. How do you communicate your expertise? By demonstrating knowledge of the issues. If you just blurt out an opinion and support it with some vague points, then you appear unknowledgeable. Very few people are persuaded by people they perceive to be unknowledgeable. By demonstrating knowledge, you establish a degree of credibility in the minds of your readers, and they are more likely to take your positions and arguments seriously. They may not totally agree, but they will not dismiss you as an ignoramus. You demonstrate knowledge by formulating a specifically focused argumentative thesis; by providing necessary background information; by outlining in detail your various arguments; by supporting your claims with precedent, evidence, data, and other supporting information; and by addressing your opposition's point of view. You may have to conduct some outside research in order to gain the necessary information to demonstrate effectively that you are knowledgeable.

Demonstrating Fairness

Generally, people do not appreciate being treated unfairly. We do not like being conned, cheated, manipulated, or deceived. If someone treats us unfairly in some way, we usually do not trust that person; it is a natural and reasonable reaction. The same is true for writers. If you are not fair and honest in how you represent yourself, how you discuss information, how you craft your arguments, how you use evidence, and how you treat your opposition, then your readers will not consider you a fair and honest writer. As a result, your credibility will be diminished, and your readers will be unwilling to believe you or to accept your position as true. Be fair and honest in your persuasive paper, and your readers will at least be more likely to believe you and to take you seriously, and they may even eventually agree with your position.

Avoiding Logical and Emotional Fallacies

One of the best ways to establish and to maintain your credibility as a thinker and a writer is to avoid logical and emotional fallacies, as discussed in detail above and in chapter 4. Errors in logic reveal sloppiness in thinking, and manipulative emotional appeals suggest shallowness in your arguments. Few things will destroy your credibility and the effectiveness of your argument quite like committing logical and emotional fallacies.

Writing Tips:

1. Look for examples of argumentation and persuasion in the various articles, chapters, and books you are assigned to read in your classes. Take notes on what works and does not work as effective argumentation.

2. As you read various writers, take note of how different authors establish their authority.

3. Do you notice any logical or emotional fallacies being committed by the authors you are reading? Consider how you can avoid similar fallacies in your own writing.

PROFESSIONAL EXAMPLE

The Meaning of Meaning: The Politics of Reader-Centered Interpretation

By Michael Bauman

2005 | TrueU.com

Michael Bauman, PhD, is professor of theology and culture and the director of Christian studies at Hillsdale College. He is a former member of the editorial staff of Newsweek *magazine; he has written, edited, and coauthored approximately 20 books; and he has written around 50 articles. He writes on theology, culture, politics, economics, literature, and sports.*

Intention? Who Needs It?

Though, like all things human, it is deeply flawed, Western tradition—the culture that arose from the triple pillars of Greek philosophy, Roman law, and biblical religion—is the greatest human achievement of all time. From it has risen sustained rational analysis, representative government, freedom under law, unimaginable prosperity, scientific progress beyond our greatest dreams, and an unprecedented and unequaled spread of human rights, and human liberation.

Western tradition is the fertile soil that gave rise to the encyclopedic artistry and intellect of Dante, the soaring spirituality of Bonaventure, the unflinching and penetrating human insight of Augustine, the unparalleled natural genius of Shakespeare, the undaunted, indeed undauntable, heroism of Milton, and the haunting, chiaroscuro craftsmanship of Rembrandt. To be an heir of Western tradition is to inherit the greatest human legacy the world has seen.

But Western tradition has its sworn enemies, not just its grateful heirs and defenders. Sometimes those who hate the West do so overtly. They fly jetliners into the nerve center of Western commerce in New York City and into the heart of Western military defense in Washington. They detonate bombs in the transportation systems of European capitals. Their intentions are obvious.

Not all the West's most resolute enemies, however, are so overt. Some are more subtle, though no less intent. Like their more militant counterparts, they name the West as the chief source of what they oppose, as the fountain of multiform oppression: chauvinism, colonialism and racism, to name a few.

These detractors of the West know that much of the substance of the culture they so despise resides in what are known as the great books of the Western world. They despise those books because they despise the ideas those books preserve and advance. While these detractors don't destroy libraries and burn books (the way some of them did when they were college students in the 1960s), they target the books nevertheless.

They seek to empty the great books of their content by means of hermeneutics, or the rules of interpretation. They purposely intend to evacuate the great books of their author-given meaning because they hate both those writers and their ideas. They denigrate the biblicism of Milton, the hierarchicalism of Chaucer, the conservatism of Burke, and the piety of Spenser, and they seek to rid the world of it all—hermeneutically.

They know they can silence the great authors—the much-hated Dead, White, European Males (DWEMS)—simply by insisting that meaning equals interpretation, that a text means whatever the reader says it means, not what its author intends it to mean. That way, the meaning of *Paradise Lost* is not tied to John Milton's intention for his poem, or to the words and word sequence he so carefully selected in constructing it, but to the (for instance) postmodern, feminist readers who want to silence him and his patriarchal notions.

That's Not What I Meant!

Here's how it works: If meaning is the reader's prerogative and not the author's—if the meaning of a text is tied to the reader's response and not to the author's intention—then a text has no meaning until a reader gives it one. Because there are many possible readers, all with potentially different interpretations of the text, then there are many possible meanings of any given text, none of which is subjected to the author's intention.

Philip Sidney cannot complain that the meaning a modern reader gives to the sonnets in his *Astrophil and Stella* is nothing like his intention for them because his texts mean what the reader says they mean, not what Sidney intended. By this leftist-inspired, hermeneutical sleight-of-hand, Sidney is silenced and the meaning of his texts is evacuated. And what is done to Sidney and his texts can be done to any author and text, whether it be the Constitution of the American founders or the letters of the Apostle Paul—texts whose traditional interpretation and application the postmodern left hates.

Without this radical and revolutionary way of reading, neither abortion nor evangelical feminism, for example, could or would find any basis at all in our foundational documents, a basis the left is intent to manufacture *ad hoc*. Armed with this hermeneutic, all things are possible. Tied to authorial intention, they are not.

But, of course, this hermeneutic is utterly indefensible. It will never do. Let me illustrate.

While I was a National Endowment for the Humanities scholar at Princeton, I debated a feminist literary critic on the nature of meaning. She spoke first, explaining why she thought that meaning ought to equal the reader's interpretation, not the author's intention. When her 10-minute introductory remarks were completed, she sat down.

I walked to the podium, turned directly to her and said, "Thank you, Professor X, for agreeing with me that meaning equals the author's intention."

"That's not what I meant," she insisted loudly and forcefully enough for all to hear.

I paused to let the point sink in, and then said again, "Thank you, Professor X, for agreeing with me that meaning equals the author's intention."

She was speechless. She could not argue that I was wrong unless she first agreed that I was right. I had silenced her by precisely the same means she had tried to silence Shakespeare and Spenser, and she didn't like it. She wanted to privilege her words and meaning, by excluding them from the evacuative grid through which she intended to pull Chaucer's or Wordsworth's.

I proceeded.

"Professor X, if you are correct, rape is impossible. Rape is impossible because 'no' does not mean 'no.' It means whatever the interpreter of the victim's words says it means. If you are right, when a woman in danger shouts this word in fear or in great distress, her word has no meaning until the rapist gives it one. You and I know what meaning will be given to it. So, I ask you, is rape possible or impossible? If your hermeneutic is correct, rape is impossible. But if rape is possible, if 'no' means 'no,' then you must give up your hermeneutic. If her 'no' means 'no,' so does Dante's. Which do you choose?"

Silence.

Drenched Deconstructionism

With Professor X's silence still hanging in the air, I began the following story: In my view, Maurice Kelley is probably the 20th century's greatest American Miltonist. Back in the 1930s, when he was still a young man, Kelley got the chance to go to England to work firsthand with Milton's manuscripts, a lifelong dream. As a young cultural liberal who was hoping to make his way up the ladder of academic success, he had uncritically accepted the notion of most of his superiors and peers that meaning equals the reader's interpretation.

At the end of his first day in the British Museum, Kelley and all the other hard-working scholars in the place were hustled out the front door. It was raining, and in the rush to get his things together and to leave in a timely fashion, Kelley had somehow misplaced his umbrella. As he fought his way manfully toward the apartment he had rented, he was soaked to the bone, cursing his fate. Suddenly, on an overhead shop sign he spied the words "Umbrella Recovered."

"Good," he thought, "perhaps this man can help me recover mine."

A moment's reflection revealed his folly: "Recovered" meant "repaired" or "refurbished," not "retrieved," he realized, and nothing he could do would change that fact. The meaning of the word was the one given it by the shopkeeper who put up the sign, not the one given it by the drenched pedestrian who was reading it. No matter how badly Kelley wanted the word to mean something different, it did not.

"At that moment," he later explained to me, "I stopped being a liberal because I figured out how words really work."

Questions for Analysis

1. What is Bauman's argumentative thesis? Is it controversial? Why or why not? Is it clear and specific?

2. How does Bauman use evidence to support his claims that post-modern ideologies ultimately seek to undermine certain foundations of Western civilization?

3. Discuss how Bauman uses the law of noncontradiction to refute "Professor X's" view that meaning lies with the reader.

4. Do you think Bauman's position is convincing? Why or why not?

5. Discuss Bauman's use of the debate structure in this essay. Is it successful? Why or why not?

6. Discuss how Bauman engages his opposition.

STUDENT EXAMPLE

Daniel Salerno

Dr. Hogsette

WRIT 101-WH8

December 8, 2005

Hydrogen Powered Automobiles

The search for an alternative fuel for automobiles has been a major issue for every automotive company in the world. Over the past several years, automotive companies have come out with hybrid cars that combine electricity with gasoline. However, the push for non-gasoline cars has led multiple automobile companies to hydrogen fuel cells. Those who fear global warming and a shortage of petroleum have been calling for the introduction of hydrogen cars. Unfortunately, most people do not realize that the use of hydrogen to power automobiles has many drawbacks. Replacing gasoline with hydrogen fuel systems will not have the benefits that most people think; therefore, the change to hydrogen fuel systems should not be made at this time.

Hydrogen, the most abundant element in the universe, exits only as a gas at standard temperature and pressure. Hydrogen is found in water, all organic compounds, and all living organisms, but it is rarely found as a free gas. There are two ways that hydrogen can be used to power automobiles. Similar to gasoline, hydrogen can be used in internal combustion engines. The hydrogen is burned in essentially the same way gasoline is burned; however, only water vapor is given off as exhaust. The use of hydrogen in this manner would make for an easy conversion for

most automobiles already in production. With
simple modifications, gasoline engines can be
altered to run on hydrogen. Alternatively,
hydrogen fuel cells present a more efficient
way to use hydrogen in automobiles. In fuel
cells, the hydrogen is turned into electricity, which then powers electric motors.
Similar to the combustion method, water is
the only byproduct of the fuel cell process.
Both processes for using hydrogen as a fuel
source have been tested in concept vehicles.
BMW has mastered the use of the hydrogen combustion engine in its HR2 concept vehicle.
The car sports the 7-series body styling and
is powered by a 282-hp, 6.0-liter V-12 hydrogen combustion engine. Similarly, General
Motors has introduced a hydrogen fuel cell
powered automobile that places all of the
vehicle's mechanical and electrical parts in
a foot-thick platform at the bottom of the
vehicle and covers it with either a truck or
car body (Bedard, "If We Have a Problem").
Automobile companies have already created hydrogen vehicles, but several questions still
remain. Will hydrogen cars benefit the environment? Will hydrogen cars be too expensive

for mass production? Is there enough hydrogen in the environment to fuel an entire fleet of vehicles? Will hydrogen vehicles be as efficient as conventional vehicles?

Without considering the negatives, using hydrogen to power automobiles rather than gasoline seems advantageous. In 2000, gasoline consumption in the United States averaged 8.47 million barrels a day and has only gone up. The price of gasoline has also increased significantly over the past 5 years (Bedard, "The Case for Nuke Cars"). Using hydrogen to power vehicles would cut down on the United States' dependence on foreign oil. In his 2003 State of the Union Address, President George W. Bush announced a $1.2 billion hydrogen fuel initiative to cut down on America's dependence on foreign oil. President Bush also stated that through the hydrogen fuel initiative it would be practical and cost-effective for a large number of people to use clean, hydrogen fuel by the year 2020. The program is designed to not only reduce the need for imported oil but also to help clean our air and reduce greenhouse gas emissions (Bush). Producing

only water vapor as a byproduct, the use of
hydrogen fuel would cut down on pollution
in the environment and help to slow global
warming. According to Anthony Eggert, the associate director of research in the "Hydrogen
Pathways" program at UC Davis, a switchover
to hydrogen fuel would result in the nation's
total emission of greenhouse gases declining
between 10 and 50 percent (Davidson). The use
of hydrogen fuel instead of gasoline looks as
if it would benefit both the economy and the
environment.

   While the advantages of an all hydrogen
vehicle fleet seem outstanding, there are a
number of problems that car companies and
President Bush have overlooked. According to
the American Geophysical Union conference
held in San Francisco, hydrogen is a very
leaky gas that could escape from cars and hydrogen plants into the atmosphere. This could
set off chemical reactions that contribute to
atmospheric warming (Davidson). Additionally,
hydrogen fuel is very hard to store. Because
hydrogen is a gas it needs to be either compressed or liquefied in order to be stored in
automobiles. BMW uses liquefied hydrogen in

its concept vehicle while General Motors used compressed hydrogen. The BMW H2R concept vehicle carries 24 pounds of hydrogen in liquid form in a big super-thermos. Unfortunately, the insulated tanks required to hold hydrogen at 423 degrees below zero are heavy and bulky. Moreover, it takes roughly six-kilowatt hours of electricity to liquefy each pound of hydrogen. Generated in a coal-fired plant, that quantity of electrical energy creates the same amount of carbon dioxide as burning half a gallon of gasoline (Csere). On the other hand, General Motors stored the hydrogen fuel in three large cylinders that were about five feet long and 10 inches in diameter. Pressurized to 10,000 psi, they held just 18 pounds of hydrogen. Compressing hydrogen to 10,000 psi requires about a third of the energy that liquefying it does, but the ultra-pressure tanks are large and expensive (Csere). Furthermore, hydrogen gas containing the same energy as a gallon of gasoline takes up 3107 gallons of space. A full tank of hydrogen would only last between 150 and 180 miles (Bedard, "The Case for Nuke Cars). Since hydrogen fill stations are

very scarce, hydrogen vehicles are not very
practical.

   The storage and use of hydrogen fuel
is both expensive and inefficient, but the
largest problem lies in actually obtaining
the hydrogen. Two possible ways of obtaining hydrogen gas are either extracting it
from methane or extracting it from water via
electrolysis. In order to extract hydrogen
from methane, the methane must be decomposed,
which produces carbon dioxide, a greenhouse
gas. Electrolysis, the splitting of water
and hydrogen molecules using electricity,
requires enormous sources of energy (Bedard,
"The Case for Nuke Cars"). Donald Anthrop, a
professor at San Jose University, estimates
that the hydrogen fuel cell power needed to
travel the to 2.5 billion miles driven in the
United States in the year 2000 would be twice
the actual amount of energy consumed in 2000.
Anthrop also states that the use of coal to
create electricity for the electrolysis process would produce a 2.7 fold increase in
carbon emissions. The United States' consumption of gas would have to increase 66 percent
in order to create enough hydrogen to replace

gasoline. Environmentalists argue that green
electricity such as hydro-electricity and
wind power can be used to create the electricity for electrolysis. However, Anthrop
points out that it would take 15 times the
current amount of green electricity to power
an all hydrogen vehicle fleet (Bedard, "The
Case for Nuke Cars"). Producing enough hydrogen to power the entire vehicle fleet of the
United States would increase both oil consumption and pollution.

While most people believe that the introduction of hydrogen fuel will save the environment and cut back on America's dependence
on foreign oil, they are wrong. Leakage of
hydrogen into the environment and pollution
from the production of hydrogen fuel would
be worse for the environment then the use
of gasoline fuel. Additionally, the use of
hydrogen instead of gasoline would increase
America's oil usage. The two current storage methods use a large amount of energy and
can only hold a small amount of hydrogen. The
storage problems and the lack of hydrogen
fuel stations combine to make the mass use
of hydrogen automobiles highly impractical.

Salerno   9

Changing over the entire automotive fleet of the United States to hydrogen fuel may one day occur. At this point in time the switch from gasoline fuel to hydrogen fuel would be detrimental to American society and should not be made.

Salerno   10

Works Cited

Bedard, Patrick. "The Case for Nuke Cars—It's Called 'Hydrogen.'" *Car and Driver.com* Oct. 2005. 1 Dec. 2005 <http://www.caranddriver.com/article. asp?section_id=27&article_id=9978>.

———. "*If* We Had a Problem, *Maybe* the Solution is H2." *Car and Driver.com* Nov. 2001. 1 Dec. 2005 <http://www.caranddriver .com/article.asp?section_id=27&article_id= 3599>.

Bush, George W. "State of the Union." *Whitehouse.gov* 28 Jan. 2003. 1 Dec. 2005 <http://www.whitehouse.gov/news/releas- es/2003/01/20030128-19.html>.

Csere, Csaba. "The Season for Powertrains
    of the Future." *Car and Driver.*
    com Apr. 2005. 1 Dec. 2005 <http://
    www.caranddriver.com/article.
    asp?section_id=27&article_id=9282>.

Davidson, Keay. "Road to Hydrogen Cars May
    Not Be So Clean: Environmental Peril in
    Making, Containing Fuel." *San Francisco
    Chronicle* 20 Dec. 2004. 1 Dec. 2005
    <http://www.sfgate.com/cgi-bin/article.
    cgi?file=/c/a/2004/12/20/HCAR.TMP>.

CHECKLIST FOR WRITING THE PERSUASIVE PAPER

✓ Write a catchy title that clearly indicates the topic and persuasive focus of the essay.

✓ Attract the reader's attention with an interesting introduction that establishes the general topic or subject, establishes a common ground, gradually directs the reader to your perspective on the issue, and then provides a specific, clear, and focused argumentative thesis. Make sure your topic and thesis are controversial in the sense that there is reasonable opposition to your point of view. Remember your purpose in this type of essay is to argue a point, not simply to describe or to inform.

✓ Organize your essay into unified, focused, well-developed paragraphs. Each paragraph should deal with a specific step in your larger argument. Discuss your arguments and provide background information, warrants, and evidence to prove your points.

✓   Organize the paragraphs appropriately, depending upon the type of argument you are making. Consider organizing your paper according to the Toulmin model or the classical argument model.

✓   Be sure to address opposing arguments effectively. Concede strong points, but refute opposing arguments where possible. Refute by analyzing your opponent's logic, premises and assumptions, use of evidence, and application of the arguments to real-life experiences. Be sure to discuss any logical and emotional fallacies in your opponents' arguments.

✓   Critically examine your own position and avoid logical and ethical fallacies.

✓   Write a satisfying conclusion that provides a clear sense of closure, reminds readers of the main point, and establishes the overall relevance or significance of the topic. Consider a call to action if appropriate to your persuasive topic.

✓   Format the final draft according to your professor's requirements.

✓   Include appropriate citation and documentation, according to your professor's requirements.

CONCLUSION

Argumentative and persuasive writing is a significant form of writing in academic settings. You have to present your position, inform your readers of your various arguments, evaluate data and evidence, use the evidence to prove your points, assess the points of your opposition, and then refute their main arguments. In most academic rhetorical situations, the main purpose of argumentation is to present the most compelling case in order to win the debate. However, there are times when argumentation can be used to convince others to adopt your point of view, to reach a decision, to call people to action, or simply to meditate on an issue and to make up your own mind as to the most reasonable conclusion. Persuasion is everywhere, in your classes, on the television, on the radio, in magazine and journal articles, in the news, and in your personal relationships. People are trying to persuade you and you are trying to persuade others—the question becomes what is the purpose of the persuasion and is it reasonable or not to be persuaded to agree with the idea or position being presented? Indeed, there are many different points of view, but as critical thinking demonstrates, not all views are equally valid and not every opinion is equally true. As you learn more about persuasive writing and forming arguments, you will also become a better critical reviewer of the various arguments you may encounter.

Discussion Questions

1. What is argumentation and how is it used in academic writing?

2. What are the main purposes for argumentation?

3. What do you think is the most challenging part of persuasive writing? Explain.

4. What is the relationship between critical thinking and persuasive writing?

Group Activities

1. In your group, discuss the strengths and weaknesses of the professional sample persuasive essay. What elements worked for you as a reader? What elements did not work? Was the essay persuasive? Explain.

2. In your group, discuss the strengths and weaknesses of the student sample argumentative essay. What did you learn from that essay about argumentation that you can apply to your own writing?

3. As a group, pick one persuasive essay from the collection of essays at the back of this book. Read and analyze it as an example of persuasive writing. Discuss the introduction, the thesis, the organization, the quality of the details and information, and the conclusion. What do you learn about persuasive writing from this essay?

Writing Activities

1. Review the student sample persuasive essay above. Write a short essay in which you summarize the main points of the essay and then analyze the strengths and weaknesses of the organizational strategies used by the student writer. Conclude by explaining what you learned about writing persuasive essays by analyzing

this sample. If your class has an online discussion board, post your essay and discuss your assessment with other students by posting threaded responses.

2. Pick an essay from the collection of essays at the back of this book and read it carefully. Write a brief outline for a persuasive essay on that same topic. If you agree with the position in the article, create an outline for an essay in which you articulate your own views in your own way. If you disagree, create an outline in which you refute the position of that article. Be sure to formulate a persuasive thesis articulating your own position on that issue.

3. If your class has an online discussion board, analyze a persuasive essay that your professor assigned you to read this week. Discuss the strengths and weaknesses of the essay as an example of persuasive writing. Post your analysis in the discussion board and respond to at least two other student postings.

11

Synthesis and Discovery

QUESTIONS TO CONSIDER BEFORE READING

1. What is synthesis?

2. How is synthesis a form of academic discovery?

3. Why is it important to integrate other writers' ideas into your own writing?

4. What is the relationship between critical thinking and synthesis writing?

INTRODUCTION

WHAT GENERALLY COMES TO mind when you think of synthesis? I imagine English composition is not the first thing that pops into your head. Maybe you think of a scientist in a lab, mixing chemicals to create some new compound. Or, maybe you think of a synthesizer or electronic keyboard that combines various simple waveform sounds to generate more complex sounds. Synthesis is the act of producing something different, unique, original, or new by combining different components. Synthesis is an important aspect of exploratory science in which new concepts or theories are created by combining traditional views in nontraditional ways to produce something unexpected yet interestingly meaningful. Such theoretical synthesis has practical application in the field of medicine and pharmacology. Researchers synthesize new medications by combining different chemical compounds in innovative ways to create new treatments for age-old ailments. Synthesis is also important in the artistic fields. Artists explore their imaginations, worlds, and experiences, along with the materials of their craft, searching for creative new ways to express what develops in their hearts and minds. The imagination is primarily a synthesizing agent—its main purpose is to take discordant aspects of reality and lived experience and give them meaningful expression in some tangible medium, be it music, painting, sculpturing, fiction, or filmmaking.

As such, synthesis is all about discovery. Through the process of synthesis, we examine the known so as to give shape to that which was previously unknown. We discover truth and come to a deeper understanding of this truth through synthesis. Therefore, synthesis writing is a form of discovery and is an important aspect of academic writing. It is a fundamental method of advanced learning. A synthesis paper brings together various points of view, different kinds of information, and different voices (other writers), integrating these elements with your own voice and ideas to generate your own unique approach to the issue or topic.

DISCOVERING YOUR FOCUS AND VOICE

When chemists synthesize new chemical compounds, they must start with preexisting theories, concepts, procedures, elements, and materials. Through the synthesizing process, new ideas are formed, new procedures are developed, new scientific truths are discovered, and, hopefully, new chemical compounds are created. Similarly, when we grapple with an idea, issue, or problem, we must start with preexisting thoughts, experiences, concepts, and solutions. However, if we engage our critical minds and think about the preexisting information in creative ways, then we may be able to synthesize a new approach to the issue or discover a new solution to the problem. Synthesis writing starts with an issue, a problem, or a question—a topic. Then you explore your own thoughts on the topic. What do you already know? What do you think about the issue? What is your position? What do you think is the best solution? In the invention phase of writing a synthesis paper, begin exploring your own views so as to discover your focus and your voice. How will you approach the issue? What will your angle be? What do you want to say about it? What is your own unique contribution to the issue? What do you want to bring to the conversation or discussion? The main objective early on in the writing phase is to discover your position and your voice. As you continue through the thinking and writing process, you will most likely refine your position and possibly modify your voice. This is perfectly normal and to be expected, as long as you do not lose your own voice in the process.

INTEGRATING OTHER VOICES INTO YOUR WORK

Because synthesis writing, by definition, involves integrating various points of view and pieces of information into your own writing, at some point you have to move beyond yourself and investigate what other people think about the issue or topic. Indeed, it is important to establish your topic and focus and to figure out what you think about the issue and to clarify your own voice, but you also need to place your own voice in relation to other voices. Contrary to what some may think and how others may behave, we are not alone on this planet. The individual self is not the center of the universe, and we do not subjectively create reality from our own experience. Rather, we are participants in a larger reality beyond ourselves. We contribute to and interact with this larger reality, but we are not its creator. There are other thinking human beings in the world, some who are contemporary to our own lives, some who have lived before us, and some (hopefully) who will live after us. Many of these other people have thought, are thinking, and will think about the same issues we are discussing in a given synthesis paper. As synthesis writers, it is our obligation to seek out these other voices (past and present), integrate them into our own writing, and then contribute to the ongoing conversation in the present that will, hopefully, also influence our contemporaries and others who come after us.

In other words, a synthesis paper is not a monolog; rather, it is a dialog. The purpose of synthesis writing is to dialog with other minds and to engage in academic conversation with other thinkers and writers. Instead of merely proclaiming your own view as from on high, you are first listening to and examining what others have said and are saying on the issue, integrating these ideas into your own views. Then, you are presenting a synthesized perspective that is an amalgam of many voices and your own. The important point to remember here is that a synthesis is not a report of what others have said. Such a report is expository writing (review chapter 8, "Informative Writing and Reporting"). Instead, synthesis writing presents a new thought, or at least a unique thought, that involves other people's ideas but which is not dominated by them.

What, then, makes the synthesis unique? Your own voice. Instead of merely reporting information, a synthesis examines the information, combines it with your thoughts, and then presents a new idea that is unique due to your individual perspective. It is easy to report information, but it is much more challenging to shape the information and to present your own views as enhanced by and, in some cases, shaped by the information you analyze. The goal is to integrate the voice of others into your own writing without losing your own voice. A synthesis depends upon the necessary voice of the writer. In a synthesis, it is not enough to state what someone else has said; you must also comment upon it, explain it, discuss its merits, reveal its shortcomings, and then explain what you think it all means in relation to the larger point you are trying to make.

CRITICAL THINKING AND SYNTHESIS

If you are to write an effective synthesis essay in which you integrate other people's views into your own discussion, comment upon that information, and then use it to make your own point, then you must use critical thinking strategies. Good synthesis writing depends upon good critical thinking. You must critically examine the topic itself, identifying the crucial elements of the issue and disregarding the superfluous issues or red herrings. You must find compelling thinkers who are writing about the topic and then determine what is interesting and important and what is frivolous and irrelevant to your discussion. You must be able to read and understand what others are saying about the topic and then critically examine their thoughts, points, arguments, and conclusions: Do their points make logical sense or are there contradictory thoughts; is there sufficient evidence to support their claims; have they fairly and honestly treated the evidence; have they ignored certain pieces of evidence; do their thoughts make sense to lived experience; do their ideas correspond to reality as most people experience it? These are the types of questions you must ask of the materials that you read, and such questions are at the heart of critical thinking. (Review chapter 5, "Steps for Effective Critical Thinking.")

Critical thinking not only helps you examine the other voices that you encounter, but it also helps you determine how to integrate them into your own voice. As you critically review the information, you will begin to see the strengths and weaknesses of certain ideas and points of view. You will begin to discover what ideas are relevant to your point of view and which ones are not. You will find ideas that challenge your point of view, and this material should encourage you to reexamine your position.

Note, I said *reexamine* your position, not necessarily *change* it. Critical thinking teaches you not to back down at the first sign of a challenge. Instead, a good critical thinker will accept the challenge presented and then go back to the basis of the thought, idea, or argument. Critically examining the thoughts of others should, at some point, lead you back to a critical examination of your own thoughts and arguments. A direct challenge from another thinker should encourage you to dig deeper, to investigate the merits of the challenging thought, to seek out the strengths and weaknesses of that thought, to review the strengths and weaknesses of your own views, and then to develop your own thought in the essay. This development can be a strengthening of your view by integrating other materials you had not considered, a modification of your view, or, in some cases, a radical change or revision of your view. Critical thinking is vitally important to an effective synthesis essay, because it helps you examine the materials you are reading, and it encourages you to review your own thoughts. Critical thinking is the primary cognitive procedure for good synthesis writing.

Writing Tips:

1. Synthesis writing is not easy, especially since much of your education may have asked you mainly to report information. Try to think of synthesis writing as engaging a conversation with the other writers.

2. Practice synthesis approaches to writing by using synthesis in your speech and conversations with your professors and your peers. Integrate the professor's lecture material, course readings, and other students' ideas into your discussion. Reference other people's ideas with phrases such as, "According to the professor . . ." or "In the article we read for today the author notes that . . ." or "Last week Jane from our discussion group explained that . . ." After bringing in such information, discuss it, analyze it, and use it to make your own points. You may agree or disagree, but practice integrating the ideas and thoughts of others into your thinking and speaking. Once this kind of synthesis becomes second nature in your speaking, it will be easier to use synthesis in your writing.

WRITING THE SYNTHESIS ESSAY

The synthesis essay is itself a synthesis of other writing modes, combining expository, evaluative, and argumentative writing. Synthesis writing is an act of discovery that involves several (if not all) of the major rhetorical strategies (review chapter 2, "Rhetorical Strategies"):

- *Definition*: As you integrate information from various sources and voices, you may need to define certain terms and concepts for your readers, depending upon their knowledge level.

- *Description*: Descriptive details may be important when integrating your own personal experiences or when using the experiences of others as evidence for your main point.

- *Narration*: When your own personal experiences or other people's personal testimony is relevant to your focus, you can narrate this evidence (called anecdotal evidence). You should not rely exclusively on anecdotal evidence, because your readers may consider it too subjective. However, depending upon your topic and focus, such evidence (when supplemented by other forms of evidence and examples) can be very effective, and narration allows you to present such information in interesting ways.

- *Summary, Quotation, Paraphrase*: These rhetorical strategies are foundational to effective synthesis writing. When you integrate information from other sources or incorporate the views of other writers, you may summarize information, provide direct quotes, or paraphrase the information in your own words. Remember, whenever you present research information or the views of others through summary, quotation, or paraphrase, you must provide the proper citation. Follow your instructor's guidelines to avoid plagiarism. (Review chapter 13, "Introduction to Information Literacy and Research Writing.")

- *Cause and Effect/Causal Analysis*: Depending upon the type of information you are integrating into your discussion, you may need to use causal analysis, particularly if you are examining different causal arguments or discussing technical, scientific, or medical information, which is often causal in nature.

- *Comparison and Contrast*: Synthesis essays generally discuss various points of view and different kinds of evidence, discussing the strengths and weaknesses of the arguments as a means to synthesize the main conclusion. Such writing necessarily involves comparison and contrast, because the different views are discussed in relation to each other.

- *Analysis*: When writing a synthesis essay, you will have to analyze various points of view, breaking them down into their main points, arguments, and lines of evidence. Such analysis allows you to critically examine the information and to discuss it appropriately.

- *Evaluation*: After analyzing the information, you then have to evaluate it to determine its strengths and weaknesses and to decide which views to integrate into your writing and which views to refute or simply to disregard.

There is no standard formula for writing a synthesis essay, and the structure of your essay will be determined by the subject matter, your focus, and your audience. However, there are some basic concepts to consider as you are writing, developing, and revising your synthesis essay:

1. *Reflect upon the topic*: Spend some time brainstorming or freewriting about the topic. What do you know about it? What are your views? What arguments do you already know that sustain your views? What evidence do you already know that supports your views?

2. *Research what others have to say*: After reflecting upon the topic, you should have a better grasp on your focus. Next, start conducting some research (follow your instructor's guidelines). Find books, journal articles, magazine articles, news stories, and other sources in the library or online databases. Avoid using nonacademic Web sites and articles that are not published in refereed sources (a refereed source is one that has an editorial board that reviews and approves articles for publication). You may also want to interview experts or individuals who have authoritative knowledge or first-hand experience with the subject you are investigating. Take careful notes on what other people are saying: their views, arguments, principles, assumptions, and lines of evidence.

3. *Reflect upon the thoughts of others in relation to your own*: Review your own ideas in relation to the ideas and information you found in your research. Which views do you agree with and why? Which ideas do you disagree with and why? What new thoughts and arguments have you discovered? How do they impact your views? What new information have you discovered? How does it impact your views? Critically examine the information and start thinking about what it all means and what you now want to say after having examined this information.

4. *Establish your focus and thesis*: A synthesis essay is not merely a report of ideas and information; it has a point of view, a new idea, or a unique perspective (your own). Communicate this focus in a specific and clearly stated thesis. Remember that a good thesis is concrete, not vague, and it has two main components: a subject (the main topic or issue) and a comment (the perspective or point of view about the topic being expressed).

5. *Develop a working outline*: A synthesis essay can take on various shapes and organizational patterns depending upon the focus. If the essay is ultimately arguing a point of view, then the classical argument model or Toulmin model can be used. Or, a point-by-point organization can be used, presenting the various arguments, discussing them, and leading toward a conclusion. If the essay analyzes a few key pieces of information and then reaches a final conclusion, then a comparison/contrast model can be used. There is the block method in which each point of view is fully explained separately (in chunks or blocks of text, usually separate para-graphs) and then discussed at the end. And, there is the alternating method in which one point is discussed from each position, and then the next point is discussed from each position, and so on until all of the main points have been discussed from each point of view. Whatever organizational strategy you choose, be sure to develop a clear outline to guide you through the drafting process.

6. *Draft your paper*: Write a solid draft of your synthesis paper, using your plan or working outline. Be sure to include an interesting introduction with a clear thesis. Present your information and discussions in an organized, focused manner, using unified and well-developed paragraphs. Provide clear topic sentences for each

paragraph and nice transitions between the paragraphs. End the draft with an effective conclusion. Be sure to include the proper in-text citations and bibliography for your researched sources (review chapter 13 on information literacy and research writing). Clarify citation requirements with your professor.

7. *Revise and edit your draft*: Leave enough time to revise at least one time. When revising, look for the global issues. Is your introduction engaging? Do you have a clear and specific thesis? Do you have compelling information and details? Are you using the information to prove your points? Are you discussing the information? Are your voice and perspective coming through, or is this merely a report? Is your conclusion effective? Revise your paper as many times as you can. Consider discussing a draft with your professor and/or with a peer review group. Then, edit the paper for grammar, punctuation, spelling, and sentence clarity. Submit your paper by the due date as assigned by your professor.

PROFESSIONAL EXAMPLE

The Privileged Planet

An excerpt from Guillermo Gonzalez and Jay W. Richards' groundbreaking book, The Privileged Planet *published in 2006, on the ways in which our place in the cosmos is designed for discovery.*

> *Discovery is seeing what everyone else saw and thinking what no one thought.*
>
> —Albert von Szent-Györgyi

On Christmas Eve, 1968, the Apollo 8 astronauts—Frank Borman, James Lovell, and William Anders—became the first human beings to see the far side of the Moon. The moment was as historic as it was perilous: they had been wrested from Earth's gravity and hurled into space by the massive, barely tested Saturn V rocket. Although one of their primary tasks was to take pictures of the Moon in search of future landing sites—the first lunar landing would take place just seven months later—many associate their mission with a different photograph, commonly known as Earthrise.

Emerging from the Moon's far side during their fourth orbit, the astronauts were suddenly transfixed by their vision of Earth, a delicate, gleaming swirl of blue and white, contrasting with the monochromatic, barren lunar horizon. Earth had never appeared so small to human eyes, yet was never more the center of attention.

To mark the event's significance and its occurrence on Christmas Eve, the crew had decided, after much deliberation, to read the opening words of Genesis: "In the beginning, God created the heavens and the Earth. . . ." The reading, and the reverent silence that followed, went out over a live telecast to an estimated one billion viewers, the largest single audience in television history.

In his recent book about the Apollo 8 mission, Robert Zimmerman notes that the astronauts had not chosen the words as parochial religious expression but rather "to include the feelings and beliefs of as many people as possible." Indeed, when the majority of Earth's citizens look out at the wonders of nature or Apollo 8's awe-inspiring Earthrise image, they see the majesty of a grand design. But a very different opinion holds that our Earthly existence is not only rather ordinary but in fact insignificant and purposeless. In his book *Pale Blue Dot*, the late astronomer Carl Sagan typifies this view while reflecting on another image of Earth, this one taken by Voyager 1 in 1990 from some four billion miles away:

> Because of the reflection of sunlight . . . Earth seems to be sitting in a beam of light, as if there were some special significance to this small world. But it's just an accident of geometry and optics. . . . Our posturings, our imagined self-importance, the delusion that we have some privileged position in the Universe, are challenged by this point of pale light. Our planet is a lonely speck in the great enveloping cosmic dark. In our obscurity, in all this vastness, there is no hint that help will come from elsewhere to save us from ourselves.

But perhaps this melancholy assumption, despite its heroic pretense, is mistaken. Perhaps the unprecedented scientific knowledge acquired in the last century, enabled by equally unprecedented technological achievements, should, when properly interpreted, contribute to a deeper appreciation of our place in the cosmos. Indeed, we hope to substantiate that possibility by means of a striking feature of the natural world, one as widely grounded in the evidence of nature as it is wide-ranging in its implications. Simply stated, the conditions allowing for intelligent life on

Earth also make our planet strangely well suited for viewing and analyzing the universe.

The fact that our atmosphere is clear; that our moon is just the right size and distance from Earth, and that its gravity stabilizes Earth's rotation; that our position in our galaxy is just so; that our sun is its precise mass and composition—all of these facts and many more not only are necessary for Earth's habitability but also have been surprisingly crucial to the discovery and measurement of the universe by scientists. Mankind is unusually well positioned to decipher the cosmos. Were we merely lucky in this regard? Scrutinize the universe with the best tools of modern science and you'll find that a place with the proper conditions for intelligent life will also afford its inhabitants an exceptionally clear view of the universe. Such so-called habitable zones are rare in the universe, and even these may be devoid of life. But if there is another civilization out there, it will also enjoy a clear vantage point for searching the cosmos, and maybe even for finding us.

To put it both more technically and more generally, "measurability" seems to correlate with "habitability." Is this correlation simply a strange coincidence? And even if it has some explanation, is it significant? We think it is, not least because this evidence contradicts a popular idea called the Copernican Principle, or the Principle of Mediocrity. This principle is far more than the simple observation that the cosmos doesn't literally revolve around Earth. For many, it is a metaphysical extension of that claim. According to this principle, modern science since Copernicus has persistently displaced human beings from the "center" of the cosmos, and demonstrated that life and the conditions required for it are unremarkable and certainly unintended. In short, it requires scientists to assume that our location, both physical and metaphysical, is unexceptional. And it usually expresses what philosophers call naturalism or materialism—the view that the material world is "all that is, or ever was, or ever will be," as Carl Sagan famously put it.

Following the Copernican Principle, most scientists have supposed that our Solar System is ordinary and that the emergence of life in some form somewhere other than Earth must be quite likely, given the vast size and great age of the universe. Accordingly, most have assumed that the universe is probably teeming with life. For example, in the early 1960s, astronomer Frank Drake proposed what later became known as the Drake Equation, in which he attempted to list the factors necessary for the existence of extraterrestrial civilizations that could use radio signals to communicate. Three of those factors were astronomical, two were biological, and two were social. They ranged from the rate of star formation to the likely age of civilizations prone to communicating with civilizations on other planets. Though highly speculative, the Drake Equation has helped focus the debate, and has become a part of every learned discussion about the possibility of extraterrestrial life. Ten years later, using the Drake Equation, Drake's colleague Carl Sagan optimistically conjectured that our Milky Way galaxy alone might contain as many as one million advanced civilizations.

This optimism found its practical expression in the Search for Extraterrestrial Intelligence, or SETI, a project that scans the skies for radio transmissions containing the "signatures" of extraterrestrial intelligence. SETI seeks real evidence, which, if detected, would persuade most open-minded people of the existence of extraterrestrial intelligence. In contrast, some advocates (and critics) of extraterrestrial intelligence rely primarily on speculative calculations. For instance, probability theorist Amir Aczel recently argued that intelligent life elsewhere in the universe is a virtual certainty. He is so sure, in fact, that he titled his book *Probability One: Why There Must Be Intelligent Life in the Universe.*

Although attractive to those of us nurtured on *Star Trek* and other fascinating interstellar science fiction, such certainty is misplaced. Recent discoveries from a variety of fields and from the new discipline of astrobiology have undermined this sanguine enthusiasm for extraterrestrials. Mounting evidence suggests that the conditions necessary for complex life are exceedingly rare, and that the probability of them all converging at the same place and time is minute. A few scientists have begun to take these facts seriously. For instance, in 1998 Australian planetary scientist Stuart Ross Taylor challenged the popular view that complex life was common in the universe. He emphasized the importance of the rare, chance events that formed our Solar System, with Earth nestled fortuitously in its narrow habitable zone. Contrary to the expectations of most astronomers, he argued that we should not assume that other planetary systems are basically like ours.

Similarly, in their important book *Rare Earth: Why Complex Life Is Uncommon in the Universe*, paleontologist Peter Ward and astronomer Donald Brownlee, both of the University of Washington, have moved the discussion of these facts from the narrow confines of astrobiology to the wider educated public. Ward and Brownlee focus on the many improbable astronomical and geological factors that united to give complex life a chance on Earth.

These views clearly challenge the Copernican Principle. But while challenging the letter of the principle, Taylor, Ward, and Brownlee have followed its spirit. They still assume, for instance, that the origin of life is basically a matter of getting liquid water in one place for a few million years. As a consequence, they continue to expect "simple" microbial life to be common in the universe. More significant, they all keep faith with the broader perspective that undergirds the Copernican Principle in its most expansive form. They argue that although Earth's complex life and the rare conditions that allow for it are highly improbable, perhaps even unique, these conditions are still nothing more than an unintended fluke. In a lecture after the publication of *Rare Earth*, Peter Ward remarked, "We are just incredibly lucky. Somebody had to win the big lottery, and we were it."

But we believe there is a better explanation. To see this, we have to consider these recent insights about habitability—the conditions necessary for complex life—in tandem with those concerning measurability. Measurability refers to those features of the universe as a whole, and especially to our particular location in it—in both space and time—that allow us to detect, observe, discover, and determine the size, age, history, laws, and other properties of the physical universe. It's what makes scientific discovery possible. Although scientists don't often discuss it, the degree to which we can "measure" the wider universe—not just our immediate surroundings—is surprising. Most scientists presuppose the measurability of the physical realm: it's measurable because scientists have found ways to measure it. Read any book on the history of scientific discovery and you'll find magnificent tales of human ingenuity, persistence, and dumb luck. What you probably won't see is any discussion of the conditions necessary for such feats, conditions so improbably fine-tuned to allow scientific discoveries that they beg for a better explanation than mere chance.

Our argument is subtle, however, and requires a bit of explanation. First, we aren't arguing that every condition for measurability is uniquely and individually optimized on Earth's surface. Nor are we saying that it's always easy to measure and make scientific discoveries. Our claim is that Earth's conditions allow for a stunning diversity of measurements, from cosmology and galactic astronomy to stellar astrophysics and geophysics;

they allow for this rich diversity of measurement much more so than if Earth were ideally suited for, say, just one of these sorts of measurement.

For instance, intergalactic space, far removed from any star, might be a better spot for measuring certain distant astronomical phenomena than the surface of any planet with an atmosphere, since it would contain less light and atmosphere pollution. But its value for learning about the details of star formation and stellar structure, or for discovering the laws of celestial mechanics, would be virtually worthless. Likewise, a planet in a giant molecular cloud in a spiral arm might be a great place to learn about star formation and interstellar chemistry, but observers there would find the distant universe to be hidden from view. In contrast, Earth offers surprisingly good views of the distant and nearby universe while providing an effective platform for discovering the laws of physics.

When we say that habitable locations are "optimal" for making scientific discoveries, we have in mind an optimal balance of competing conditions. Engineer and historian Henry Petroski calls this constrained optimization in his illuminating book *Invention by Design*: "All design involves conflicting objectives and hence compromise, and the best designs will always be those that come up with the best compromise." To take a familiar example, think of the laptop computer. Computer engineers seek to design laptops that have the best overall compromise among various conflicting factors. Large screens and keyboards, all things being equal, are preferable to small ones. But in a laptop, all things aren't equal. The engineer has to compromise between such matters as CPU speed, hard drive capacity, peripherals, size, weight, screen resolution, cost, aesthetics, durability, ease of production, and the like. The best design will be the best compromise. Similarly, if we are to make discoveries in a variety of fields from geology to cosmology, our physical environment must be a good compromise of competing factors, an environment where a whole host of "thresholds" for discovery are met or exceeded.

For instance, a threshold must be met for detecting the cosmic background radiation that permeates the universe as a result of the Big Bang. (Detecting something is, of course, a necessary condition for measuring it.) If our atmosphere or Solar System blocked this radiation, or if we lived at a future time when the background radiation had completely disappeared, our environment would not reach the threshold needed to discover and measure it. As it is, however, our planetary environment meets this requirement. At the same time, intergalactic space might give us a slightly better "view" of the cosmic background radiation, but the improvement would be drastically offset by the loss of other phenomena that can't be measured from deep space, such as the information-rich layering processes on the surface of a terrestrial planet. An optimal location for measurability, then, will be one that meets a large and diverse number of such thresholds for measurability, and which combines a large and diverse number of items that need measuring. This is the sense in which we think our local environment is optimal for making scientific discoveries. In a very real sense the cosmos, our Solar System, and our exceptional planet are themselves a laboratory, and Earth is the best bench in the lab.

Even more mysterious than the fact that our location is so congenial to diverse measurement and discovery is that these same conditions appear to correlate with habitability. This is strange, because there's no obvious reason to assume that the very same rare properties that allow for our existence would also provide the best overall setting to make discoveries about the world around us. We don't think this is merely coincidental. It cries out for another explanation, an explanation that suggests there's more to the cosmos than we have been willing to entertain or even imagine.

Questions for Analysis

1. What key features or characteristics make this a synthesis essay?

2. What is the main focus of the essay? How is it asserted in the introduction and confirmed in the conclusion?

3. The authors present a lot of information from different sources and writers. After they present information, what do the writers do with the information?

4. Does the main collaborative voice of these two writers get lost in all the other voices of the essay? Why or why not?

5. Identify and discuss some of the rhetorical strategies used in the essay.

6. What would you say is the main organizational pattern of the essay? Explain.

STUDENT EXAMPLE

Mohanlall Narine

Dr. David S. Hogsette

WRIT 101-WH8

October 21, 2005

The Greatness of America

Before the establishment of the United
States of America, there were a mere thirteen colonies under British control in the
North American continent. After the American
Revolution that occurred in the late eighteenth century, the colonies declared themselves to be the United States of America.
The country gradually expanded and now has a
total of fifty states. Its reputation stands
as one of the greatest countries in the
world. Many people, however, tend to think
the contrary. They exhibit hatred for America
and often criticize it in the harshest of
terms. Yet, the United States is a country
that is far greater than any other in terms
of what it offers. It is the land where any
immigrant can arrive penniless and achieve
the status of middle class or even upper
class. It is a secular country and does not
govern according to any religious belief. The

opportunities that America offers are seemingly limitless. Educational and economic opportunities abound. This country also offers religious freedom and democracy to all residing here. Why is it, then, that despite these realities, there are still some who express such an extreme degree of animosity towards the United States?

During the latter part of the twentieth century and to the present, America has been and still is the victim of terrorist attacks. These attacks were primarily carried out by Islamic terror groups that believe the American way of life is filled with immorality and numerous sins. In order to stop the spread of American ideology to Islamic nations, these terrorists feel the need to kill many innocent lives to force the United States to withdraw from the international community. They seem to hate America for the very reasons that make it so great and appealing to their citizens. Freedom of speech, the freedom to practice one's own religion, educational opportunities, ethnic equality, and the opportunity for success are all aspects of greatness in America. Medical ad-

vances that improve the overall health of
our bodies are not as common in some other
countries as they are in America. The curious irony is that those who hate America
seek to "protect" their people from exactly
that which they seek—freedom, liberty, and
opportunity.

The most appealing trait in America is
its open-market economy that allows for great
opportunities. My family migrated to this
country over fifteen years ago. When we first
arrived, of course, things were difficult.
All hopes of owning a home at the time were
unrealistic. My father was unemployed for six
months, which was challenging for all of us,
since he was the sole provider of the family.
Eventually, we went from being financially
challenged to being financially stable. My
father soon learned that in America, all it
takes is a little will and persistence for
anyone to be able to make a living to support
a family. Many poor foreigners recognize this
fact, and Dinesh D'Souza makes this point
clear in his article "10 Great Things about
America," published in *The San Diego Union-
Tribune*. In his second point, he states that

America, out of all other countries, offers
the most opportunity and social mobility.
It has created a population of "self-made
tycoons," of people who at first had virtually nothing, and after years of hard work
have become prosperous in different professional fields (D'Souza). Pierre Omidyar and
Vinod Khosla are prime examples of such success. Both are immigrants who have settled
in America. Pierre Omidyar grew up in Paris
and today is recognized as the founder of
the auction company eBay, which is used by
millions of people around the world. Vinod
Khosla, from India, is one of the leading
venture capitalists today, and is now a bil-
lionaire. Their accomplishments are reminders
of what we are able to achieve once persistence and determination is present within
us. Such opportunities for social mobility
and economic success are often denied to the
residents of other countries, and some these
people express their frustration as envy and
hatred of America. Others choose to share in
the opportunities of the United States and do
all they can to immigrate.

Another remarkable feature of America is the educational opportunity it offers to all people that come here. As a youth in America, I can testify to how the education I am receiving here continues to help me achieve my life goals. A free public education is not always offered in other nations, especially in third-world nations. Only those who can afford it go to school. This factor is the main cause of the substantial amount of poverty in some of these nations. Due to a lack of academic knowledge, some people are limited as to how successful they can be. India has one of the largest populations that suffer from extreme poverty. The United States, on the other hand, gives everyone the equal opportunity to achieve an education. In fact the parents or guardians who fail to take the responsibility of sending their child to school are breaking the law and will be punished accordingly; they might even serve time in prison. Yet there are still those who do not make it far with their knowledge. Language barriers, lack of focus, or reluctance to learn are possible reasons. In many cases, those who don't go far in their education are the ones who end up taking the lower paying jobs. They are the ones the American society views as poor, but to a foreigner, to be poor in America is considered a blessing. D'Souza mentions how America provides a great life for the ordinary guy, describing an acquaintance of his from India, who is continuing to try to immigrate here primarily because he wants to "live in a country where the poor people are fat" (D'Souza).

Perhaps the number one reason why some foreigners hate America so much is because of the most attractive characteristics of freedom of religion and the right to vote. Unlike some other countries, the United States is one of the most tolerant of religious freedom to date. Admittedly, over the recent years there have been some prejudices towards some religions by Americans, especially Islam. The law has punished such acts of discrimination, at the same time, keeping the freedom of the Muslims intact to continue to practice their religious belief. Yet in Muslim countries, the same cannot be said of religious tolerance, and people of other faiths, especially Christians and Jews, are harshly

persecuted. In Venezuela, the country where
I was born and raised for the first four
years of my life, there is discrimination
towards any religion other than Catholicism
or Christianity. My family and I found it
extremely difficult to practice our Hindu
faith and often times were led to discreetly
practicing our religion. The Pilgrims originally came to America to flee religious oppression. They, like my entire family, were
able to migrate to America to escape the wars
fought over their own beliefs. America, up to
this day, has never experienced a religious
war, as Daniel J. Boorstin discusses in his
article "Why I am Optimistic about America,"
making this country distinct from most other
nations of the world.

   Along with religious freedom, the ability to participate in truly democratic elec-
tions is another primary reason for the
anti-American hatred. Many Islamic countries
use propaganda techniques to force their
citizens into thinking that voting and freedom encourage sinful activities and that in
order to attain enlightenment, they must
obey the radical rules that their religion

teaches. However, many of the citizens of Middle Eastern Islamic nations are now seeing the benefits that come with voting. They are witnessing this through their neighboring country, Iraq, which, because of America, has been freed from the tyrannical rule of their leader, Saddam Hussein. This year I will be privileged to vote for who I think should be the mayor of New York City. What I am able to do is what the majority of those in most Islamic nations cannot. Understandably, they yearn for democracy that would allow them the opportunity to vote and to determine their own government.

There are many ups and downs that America has faced. What is so great about this country is how it has been able to rise above its political and social problems. The striving to be prosperous never ends and the constant effort to make all that come here feel welcomed and free from all conflicts is what is so great about America. With my family, I have witnessed all of the turmoil, prejudice, and oppression that one country had to offer its citizens. It wasn't until after migrating to the "land of the free and home of the

Narine   9

brave" that we became aware of the extent of
American opportunity. The fact that Americans
are able to freely practice their religion,
become successful, climb up the ladder of
social mobility, experience educational opportunities, and of course participate in
democracy continues to appeal to many who
reside outside of America. As we continue to
prosper, the jealousy and envy on the part
of some will increase. However, so too will
the desire to experience these same free-
doms, either by immigrating to America or by
refashioning their own countries into new
democracies.

Narine   10

Works Cited

Boorstin, Daniel J. "Why I Am Optimistic
        about America." *American Voices: Culture
        and Community*, 5th ed. Eds. Dolores
        LaGuardia and Hans P. Guth. New York:
        McGraw Hill, 2003. 165-71.

D'Souza, Dinesh. "10 Great Things about
    America." *The San Diego Union Tribune*
    6 July 2003: G1. *ProQuest* 9 Sept. 2004
    <http://proquest.umi.com.arktos.nyit.edu>.

CHECKLIST FOR WRITING THE SYNTHESIS ESSAY

✓ Write a catchy title that clearly indicates the topic and focus of the essay.

✓ Attract the reader's attention with an interesting introduction that establishes the general topic or subject, gradually directs the reader to your focus, and then provides a specific, clear, and focused thesis. Remember your purpose in this type of essay is to present a unique or compelling perspective on an issue, not simply to describe or to inform.

✓ Organize your essay into unified, focused, well developed paragraphs. Each paragraph should deal with a specific issue, point, or element being discussed. Provide details and specific discussions of concrete information and points of view—avoid vague generalities. Be sure to present and discuss information and points of view from other writers. A synthesis is a conversation with other writers, not merely a presentation of information.

✓ Organize the paragraphs appropriately, depending upon the type of paper you are writing. Consider such patterns as classical or Toulmin models (for persuasive synthesis essays), point-by-point, or comparison/contrast.

✓ Write a satisfying conclusion that provides a clear sense of closure, reminds readers of the main point, and establishes the overall relevance or significance of your unique perspective.

✓ Format the final draft according to your professor's requirements.

✓ Include appropriate citation and documentation, according to your professor's requirements.

CONCLUSION

The synthesis essay is one of the most challenging types of academic papers to write, but it is also the most rewarding. When you prepare a synthesis essay, not only are you exploring your own thoughts and points of view, but you also have the opportunity to investigate what many other thinkers and writers have to say about your topic. The process of writing the synthesis essay is a true learning experience that develops your knowledge of the subject matter and enhances your writing and thinking skills. Obviously, you learn a great deal just from the process of searching, finding, reading, and studying different people's points of view. Beyond learning the content, you must also utilize critical thinking strategies to review, analyze, and evaluate the information to be discussed in the paper. You must carefully consider which rhetorical strategies to choose, and then use them constructively to express your point and to achieve your purpose for writing. Then, you have to examine your own thoughts and views, make revisions where warranted, and sharpen your view with the information you gathered from your research. Finally, you must synthesize this information into a unified and well-organized discussion of your point of view. In many ways, the synthesis essay is the culmination of all that you will have learned in your writing class, and it is the one type of paper that will best prepare you to meet the many challenges of academic writing and intellectual exchange.

DISCUSSION QUESTIONS

1. What is synthesis and how is it used in academic writing?

2. What are the main purposes for synthesis writing?

3. What do you think is the most challenging part of writing a synthesis essay? Explain.

4. What is the relationship between critical thinking and synthesis writing?

GROUP ACTIVITIES

1. In your group, discuss the strengths and weaknesses of the professional sample synthesis essay. What elements worked for you as a reader? What elements did not work? Explain.

2. In your group, discuss the strengths and weaknesses of the student sample synthesis essay. What did you learn from that essay that you can apply to your own writing?

3. As a group, pick one synthesis essay from the collection of essays at the back of the book. Read it and then analyze it as an example of synthesis writing. Discuss the introduction, the thesis, the organization, the quality of the details and information, and the conclusion. What do you learn about synthesis writing from this essay?

WRITING ACTIVITIES

1. Review the student sample synthesis essay above. Write a short essay in which you summarize the main points of the essay and then analyze the strengths and weaknesses of the organizational strategies used by the student writer. Conclude by explaining what you learned about writing synthesis essays by analyzing this sample. If your class has an online discussion board, post your essay and discuss your assessment with other students by posting threaded responses.

2. Pick and carefully read one essay from the collection of essays at the back the book. Write a brief outline for a synthesis essay on that same topic. Consider using in your outline some evidence and ideas from the essay you read.

3. If your class has an online discussion board, analyze a synthesis essay that your professor assigned you to read this week. Discuss the strengths and weaknesses of this synthesis essay and explain what you learn about synthesis writing by analyzing this essay. Post your analysis in the discussion board and respond to at least two other student postings.

12

Collaborative Writing Projects

Questions to Consider Before Reading

1. What is collaboration?

2. How might collaboration be used in writing courses?

3. What kinds of collaborative projects might you encounter in other courses?

4. What are the benefits and potential drawbacks of collaboration?

Introduction

COLLABORATION IS THE ACT of working together with other people to accomplish a particular complex task or shared goal. Collaboration is a cooperative activity in which the skills, knowledge, and expertise of different individuals are pooled and used constructively for the good of the group. We see examples of collaboration throughout the world, from the smallest of ant colonies in our backyards to the largest of corporate project groups in the most complex cities on the planet.

Most people recognize that cooperation is a wonderful work strategy that is both pragmatic (it helps us achieve certain goals or projects that normally could not be accomplished individually) and virtuous. Collaboration has a moral component in the sense that those who agree to collaborate generally do so because they seek the greater good of the group. (Admittedly, though, some people may work collaboratively from purely selfish motivations.) Precisely because collaboration in its intended design is a virtuous enterprise, it is thus one of the most difficult things to do well. We have to learn to be cooperative, we have to learn to share, and we have to learn to collaborate. (Note that we generally do not have to teach a child to be selfish, but we do have to teach him or her to share or to cooperate.)

Curiously, though, you may not encounter collaboration very frequently in your academic studies. It depends upon the nature of the disciplines and the teaching practices of the professors at your college or university—some professors use collaboration quite a bit and others not at all. Generally speaking, you will probably spend most of your time completing individual assignments and demonstrating your mastery of various subjects. Moreover, writing is very often a lonely activity: you contemplate an idea, figure out your position, conduct some research (maybe), plan your essay, draft it, revise it, edit it, and submit it for a grade—all on your own. Sure, you may talk with your professor about the paper, and you may share a draft with friends and classmates, but for the most part you complete your thinking and writing individually on your own. However, there will be times in your college experience when you will be asked to participate in collaborative writing, and there will definitely be times in your professional career when you will be required to work in project groups. Therefore, it is important that you learn something about how to participate effectively in collaborative writing situations.

TYPES OF COLLABORATION

Just as there are different types of writing, there are also many different types of collaboration. In a science class you may be asked to collaborate in a lab group; in an art history class you may be asked to go to a local museum in a small group to write a review of a famous painting; in your journalism class you may be asked to work with a few other students as a correspondent team covering some local event; your drama professor may put you into acting groups to perform short scenes from the plays you are reading in class; and your writing instructor may form peer editing groups. Collaborative projects come in many shapes and sizes, but they can be classified generally into two main types: groups that create a single document or project and peer editing groups.

Producing a Single Document or Project

Some groups are formed for the purposes of putting several people together to complete a single task. The working principle here is that two or more heads are better than one. Of course, this principle assumes that the heads being assembled are thoughtful, reasonable heads that are willing to work on the project (see "Strategies for Effective Collaboration" below). Such project groups are usually assembled because the assigned task is too great for any single person to complete individually. The individuals in the group must figure out how best to work together as a team to finish the task and to produce the final product, be it a written document, a group oral presentation, a Web site, or some other document or project.

Generally, the team selects a project manager or group leader who then directs the group. The project is broken into smaller tasks and assigned to group members, who work on separate tasks and then piece them together to produce the final product. Often team members also serve as editing partners, helping each other polish their own sections of the project and to combine them into the single document. A particular challenge in this kind of project is to produce a final document that has a unified voice. However, depending upon the nature of the assignment or project, sometimes a unified voice is not expected or desired.

Peer Review/Editing

The other main type of collaborative group is the peer review or editing team. We mainly see this in college writing courses, but you may also encounter it in the professional world. Your professor may assign you to a peer review team and expect you to share drafts of your essays with team members. For many people, this is a very uncomfortable arrangement, because they may not be used to sharing their writing with other people or they may not like the idea of others seeing their work in progress. For this reason, peer review teams may seem awkward at first, but as people get to know each other better, the team should begin working together more smoothly.

Another hindrance to peer review groups is the fear of offending others in the group with constructive criticism. Remember, there is a difference between good, constructive criticism and negative slamming of the person's writing and ideas. (See "Strategies for Effective Collaboration" below.) The main objective of peer editing groups is to help each other produce better final products. Unreasonable or unduly personal competitiveness is counterproductive in such groups. Similarly, being overly accommodating to the point of not giving any constructive feedback is equally counterproductive. Comments like "very good" or "loved it" or "I wouldn't change a thing" do not help the writer one bit. You should provide specific and constructive feedback.

Recall that there is a difference between revision (larger, global issues like focus, content, and organization) and editing (smaller, local issues like spelling, grammar, and sentence clarity). If you are conducting a peer revision session, consider using the revision criteria questions outlined in chapter 1, "Writing as Process," or use revision criteria provided by your professor. Review and comment on the thesis, paragraph order, and development of information. If you are conducting a peer editing session, then focus on the sentence level issues of grammar, spelling, mechanics, punctuation, and sentence structure. The point to peer review teams and editing groups is to help each other write good, successful essays.

Strategies for Effective Collaboration

We are not born knowing how to collaborate, because by nature most of us are rather self-centered. Clearly, some of us are far more egocentric than others, but each of us must overcome to one degree or another some level of selfishness if we want to be effective collaborators. Consider the following guidelines for effective collaboration.

Commit to Collaboration

Collaborative work succeeds or fails depending upon the team members' level of commitment to collaboration. If your team is not interested in collaborating or thinks it is not a valuable exercise, then the team will fail. Consider signing a collaboration agreement in which everyone in the group agrees to work for the good of the team and vows to complete his or her own work in a timely manner. Ask your professor for example team contracts.

Be Rationally Open-Minded

Collaboration will not work if group members do not think they can learn from each other. Individuals must be open to other people's ideas, and they must accept that sometimes other people have better ideas or that their own ideas may be wrong and someone else's idea may be right. In our pluralistic age, such language of right and wrong is often avoided. But let's think about it this way: if no one is ever right and no one is ever wrong, then why listen to anyone else at all? The agreement to learn from other people presupposes that there is actually something to be learned from others, that you may be wrong, that you may not know all the answers, and that you may not have the solutions while other people do.

The whole point of collaboration is to draw from each other's strengths and to minimize weaknesses. It is irrational (and unproductive) to believe everyone is right and no one is ever wrong. The rational person recognizes that the law of noncontradiction operates even in group work. Be honestly and rationally open-minded: if someone else has a better idea or a more efficient solution or a correct bit of knowledge, then concede to that better or correct idea for your own personal growth and for the good of the group. However, do not be so open-minded that your brain falls out. Don't accept anything and everything others in the group say: analyze and evaluate everyone's ideas and then rationally choose the best ideas and the soundest suggestions.

Solve Conflicts Early

People are people no matter where you go and no matter what you do. In any group made up of people there will most probably be conflict. Be thankful if you have conflict-free group experiences. However, be realistic and understand that this is not the norm: do not be surprised, shocked, or outraged if your group experiences some personal bumps along the way. That is just part of being a person working with other people in this world.

If conflicts arise, be mature enough to acknowledge them and to address them as soon as possible so that it does not negatively affect the project outcome. Resolve all conflicts as soon as you can. Sometimes a conflict can be quickly resolved by one or two people in the group, and sometimes the whole group must intervene to solve the problem. At other times, the group may need to bring the issue to the professor's attention. Whatever the case may be, address and resolve the conflict as soon as soon as possible for the sake of the project (and for the sake of everyone's sanity).

Be a Team Player

Collaboration involves different people working together as a team. Please realize that there is no such thing as a team of one. This is like trying to say there are such things as round triangles—it is definitionally impossible. Commit to the team and work your hardest to complete your team task. Contribute in productive ways to the team effort. Do not sit back and let others do all the work and then expect to get the same grade as everyone else. Why should you, if you did not contribute significantly to the group project? Do your work and encourage others to do their work too—be a true team player.

Do Your Work and Keep Deadlines

Part of being a team player is doing the work assigned to you and completing the work on time. Each group has a final deadline—the date the assignment is due. However, before the group can reach that deadline, everyone else in the group must do his or her job by certain intermediary deadlines so that all of the work can be assembled into the final product. Consider establishing internal group deadlines for various portions of the project to keep the project on schedule, and be sure to leave time for assembling the individual portions and for revising and editing the final product.

Communicate, Communicate, Communicate

Collaboration is just like any other complex relationship between people—it requires clear and open communication to succeed. A marriage will not work if a husband and wife do not communicate. You cannot learn from your professor if he or she never communicates with you or vice versa. Friendships do not last if there is no communication. Communication is the key to community. A collaborative group is a small community, and it requires communication to succeed.

Resolve to be a clear, fair, honest, sensitive, and sensible communicator in your team. If you have questions, ask. If you disagree, rationally and politely voice your opinion. If you have a problem or a conflict, express your concerns sensibly and then offer recommended solutions (do not just gripe or complain while offering no solutions). If you need to miss a meeting, let your team know and give a reasonable explanation or excuse. If you are going to be late on completing your part of the task, let your team know as soon as you can. If you have a good idea or an innovative recommendation, offer it as soon as you can. Do not let the group work away at a bad idea and then offer the solution a few days or weeks later. Your hesitation will only waste the group valuable time.

Most conflicts or problems in a group are caused by a lack of communication. We are social beings, so be communicative in your group. There is little excuse these days for not keeping in touch with your team: consider exchanging phone numbers, cell phone numbers, email addresses, and instant message (IM) chat names. Also, your professor may put you into electronic teams in online environments like Blackboard or WebCT. These programs have excellent collaboration tools—use them to communicate with your team members.

Set the Ground Rules

Anarchy and nonconformist attitudes may sound hip, cool, and avant-garde in theory or when romanticized by nostalgic professors, but such notions are naïve, irrational, and ultimately destructive to a project group. Counterculture in professional and academic collaborative contexts is counterproductive. Project groups, just like families, relationships, friendships, organizations, companies, and nations, require reasonable ground rules to function properly. Immediately after your group is formed, get together and work out your team's purpose, clarify the requirements of the assignment, and establish reasonable expectations for working as individuals toward the good of the team. You may want to consider drafting and having each member sign a team contract or agreement, establishing team accountability (the consequences of not doing your share of the work), and acknowledging that everyone knows and understands the team expectations.

Consider Team Leaders

Some projects may be so complex that it requires a large team (of five or more members). In such cases, you may want to assign a team leader or project manager who will help make sure that everyone is on target and completing his/her respective portions of the project. If your team will be completing several large projects over the course of the semester, consider rotating the role of team leader. Team leaders provide unity to a group, and in some cases they may even be helpful in spotting and resolving conflict early, before it becomes disruptive.

Team Assessment

One method of accomplishing team accountability is for each team member to assess himself/herself and the other team members. Establish early on if you will be completing team assessments or not—this accountability strategy only works if everyone realizes from the beginning that they will be evaluated by others in the group. Consider submitting the assessments to your professor with the final team project. In some cases, your professor may require team assessments and will provide each team with assessment forms. When assessing team members, consider such criteria as: keeping up with the team activities; submitting tasks on time; participating in group meetings; remaining focused in the group meetings; contributing helpful suggestions and information; attending scheduled meetings; and demonstrating respect to other members (note, disagreement is not necessarily disrespect; we can disagree in respectful ways).

Working in Online Collaborative Groups

In some cases, you may be required to work in online collaborative groups. If you take an online class, if you take an online hybrid course (part of the time is spent in a traditional classroom and part of the course meets online), or if your professor makes use of an online environment to supplement your traditional face-to-face course (sometimes called an online enhanced course), you may be required to work in virtual teams in online environments like Blackboard or WebCT. These online team environments are very convenient, because you can meet outside of class any time of the day, and you do not have to come to campus to hold a team meeting. These online programs have group discussion boards where you can submit drafts of your work and post replies and comments; chat rooms where you can hold virtual team meetings and discuss the progress of your team work; and email systems that allow you to send email to individual team members or to the whole team (including your professor).

Online collaborative groups are excellent ways to conduct team projects in online classes or to supplement group work in traditional classes. However, we must remember that teamwork is still teamwork, whether it is held online or face to face. When working in online teams, remember the above general strategies for effective collaboration and consider the following suggestions for effective online teamwork.

Get to Know the Team Members

In online courses it is difficult to get to know the other team members. Consider holding an initial chat session as a group social event in which people introduce themselves and get to know each other better. Also, consider posting brief personal introductions in the team discussion board. However, do not socialize for more than one or two sessions when the team is first formed, as you do not want to divert time away from the team's primary academic task. Once everyone has basically met each other, move forward with your team tasks.

Clarify the Assignment

In online courses, it is easier for different people to have slightly (or sometimes significantly) different understandings of the team assignment. Make sure everyone in the group understands what the group is supposed to be doing and that everyone knows what the assignment is, what the requirements are, and when the project is due.

Make Sure Everyone Knows His/Her Role

For most team projects (either online or traditional), specific tasks will need to be assigned to different people in the group. Since online teams do not meet face-to-face in a room together, it is easier to become confused as to who is doing what. Make sure everyone in the group understands his or her individual role. Consider holding a chat session or a discussion board meeting in which team members discuss their strengths and weaknesses and volunteer to complete certain tasks. If your team has a team leader, he/she should post an assignment message listing each team member's respective duty or task.

Determine a Team Leader

Working online can be chaotic enough, and you do not need to compound the confusion with a directionless or leaderless group. Team leaders are a great help to traditional groups, and they are essential to successful online teams. The team should choose a team leader early on, within the first or second virtual meeting. The team leader clarifies the assignment, helps establish everyone's role and duty, makes sure everyone is staying on target, and then pulls the project together at the end. If your team will be working on multiple projects, consider rotating team leaders. However, some online teams prefer to keep a single team leader for continuity. Each team should decide its own team leader practices.

Stay Focused in Online Chat Sessions

Collaborating online can be very productive, but online distraction is its main enemy. When you are working with your team, especially in an online virtual chat, stay focused on the teamwork. Friendly chit-chat at the very beginning of a session is fine, but avoid indulging idle conversation for too long. It is easy to start chatting about everything except the assignment. Stay focused on the task at hand. Also, close all unrelated Internet browser windows and close all unrelated IM chat sessions. We may think of ourselves as great multitaskers, but the truth is that few of us can multitask effectively. When working in an online group, minimize all possible distractions and focus on the group work.

Clarify Technology Usage

If you are working in a comprehensive online environment like Blackboard or WebCT, then you do not have to worry so much about the technology, because everything is self-contained within the program. However, if your group decides to use secondary technologies (like other chat programs or meeting spaces), make sure that everyone in the group has equal access to the different technologies. You should also standardize your word processing format, because when you are creating collaborative projects, each individual piece must fit together into a single document at the end of the process. It is important that everyone submit their work to the group in the same word processing format. If people are using different word processors, then agree upon a standard format, like Rich Text. Your college or professor may require that everyone use the same word processing program; if this is the case, make sure you understand and abide by these requirements.

Consider Time Zone Differences

In many online courses and online hybrid courses, students are located in different time zones, thus making synchronous online team meetings difficult if not impossible. As you are getting to know your team members, learn where people reside and be sensitive to the challenges that different time zones bring to the online learning experience. If most of the group live within two to three time zones of each other, then holding synchronous online chat sessions should not present any major problems. However, if some team members live on the east coast of the United States and other team members live in New Zealand, then holding synchronous chat sessions may not be feasible. In such cases, you will probably rely more on the asynchronous discussion board to communicate and share work.

CONCLUSION

Even though collaboration does not come naturally to most people, it is a skill than can be strengthened and perfected with practice. The more you work at collaboration, as with most things, the more second nature it becomes. You may have some horrible collaborative experiences, but you will also have some fantastic ones. If you have had bad experiences with teamwork in the past, try not to roll your eyes in disgust if your professor announces a collaborative project. Believe me—you will survive it. And who knows, you may even have a truly wonderful experience, and you may meet and work with some truly interesting people whom you otherwise would have never met. Moreover, when you go into the professional world, whatever your chosen career may be, you will have to engage collaborative work in one form or another, be it a basic professional meeting or an actual project group with a real project manager and other employees. Collaboration is not always easy, but it can be very rewarding, and if you follow some basic strategies for effective collaboration, then your collaborative experience can in the very least be quite successful if not actually fulfilling.

DISCUSSION QUESTIONS

1. What is collaboration and how is it related to academic writing?

2. Why do we collaborate in educational and professional situations?

3. What are some important strategies for effective collaboration?

4. What are some unique online challenges that can complicate collaboration?

GROUP ACTIVITIES

1. In your group, decide upon a topic, narrow it to a focus, and collaborate on an outline for a possible paper on this topic. Discuss your experience—was it challenging to complete this assignment as a group? Why or why not? What strategies for effective collaboration did you use and why?

2. As a group, discuss the value of team assessment. Do you think it is a good idea for team members to be assessed by other team members? Why or why not? What types of criteria should be used when assessing other team members?

3. As a group, discuss the merits of peer review/editing groups. In what ways are they helpful? What are some recommendations for effective peer review/editing groups?

COLLABORATIVE WRITING ACTIVITY

As a group, pick a topic that the group finds interesting, and then plan to write a single collaborative synthesis essay on that topic. Brainstorm as a team and develop the focus, thesis, and a basic outline for the paper. Assign different sections of the paper to different people in the group. Each member should conduct his/her own research and write drafts of his/her own section of the paper. Then, the team should assemble the sections and compose an introduction and conclusion to the paper. As a team, revise the draft and try to even out the different sections such that it has as unified a voice as possible. (Note, there are some collaborative papers that do not require a unified voice; follow your professor's instructions regarding unity of voice in the paper.) Each team member should contribute to editing the whole paper.

13

Introduction to Information Literacy and Research Writing

QUESTIONS TO CONSIDER BEFORE READING

1. What is research writing?

2. Can we have true academic writing without research writing?

3. What is information literacy?

4. How are information literacy and research writing related to life-long learning?

INTRODUCTION

OFTEN WHEN I MENTION research papers to students, the initial responses range from mild annoyance ("Ugh! We have to go to the library?"), to frustration ("Not this class, too! I simply don't have enough time this term."), to sheer panic ("You're kidding! I've never written a research paper before, and I haven't a clue how, where, or when to begin!"). If you react like this when your professors assign research papers, then don't worry—it's perfectly normal. If you are one of the few students who say, "Oh goody, a research paper!" then you are a rare bird indeed.

Most of us fear and loathe research writing. I'm convinced it's because we have not been taught how to conduct research effectively, nor have we come to appreciate how research writing enriches us intellectually and spiritually. No, I am not crazy (though I must admit the thought did occur to me as I wrote that sentence). I think we can agree that, if nothing else, research indeed can develop our intellectual lives. How can it not?

Even the act of looking up information without actually finding anything can teach us something. Irrelevant information is still information, and though it may not pertain to our topic or research focus, it pertains to something, and as such is meaningful.

But what does research have to do with our spiritual development? Note that in this context, "spiritual" does not necessarily mean something religious or theological. Rather, I am referring to the metaphysical or soulish nature of our very being. When we discover an interesting topic, develop a compelling question, struggle through finding and exploring information on that topic, formulate answers to the question, and then present our findings in such a way that helps us demonstrate our new mastery or understanding of the topic to our readers, we are fulfilled deep within.

Unfortunately, the structured academic setting sometimes strips us of that experience, because we view the research paper as just another exercise we have to write for our classes. We do the work, get the grade, and we are off worrying about the next assignment. Try as hard as you can to avoid falling into that academic treadmill. Sincere learning satisfies the mind and the soul. There is nothing more engaging than completing a research project in which you are deeply invested.

The educational experiences I remember most from my college and graduate school days are the research papers in which I was able to identify the topic, explore my own answers to that issue, and then present my findings in the form of a well-written, well-researched, and well-documented paper. You may not ever fall in love with research writing. However, I hope that you will learn to view it as more than just another academic exercise. And, I hope that you come to experience the deep satisfaction that can emerge from challenging yourself intellectually to discover knowledge and truth that impacts your whole being.

WHAT IS INFORMATION LITERACY?

Effective research writing actually begins with developing information literacy. This may be a new term to many of you, so let's look at what it means. Information is another term for knowledge—facts, figures, statistics, data, and other forms of meaningful expression or communication about things, concepts, ideas, persons, and historical events. Literacy is usually associated with the ability to read and write, but it also means having expertise in something or being knowledgeable about some issue or topic. Information literacy, then, means quite simply being knowledgeable about knowledge.

Great, but what does that mean? Basically, information literacy involves (1) having the necessary skills to recognize when you do not have adequate knowledge of a subject, (2) acknowledging the need to discover knowledge, (3) possessing the skills to search for information, (4) understanding how to assess the information (this is where evaluation and critical thinking comes into play), and (5) being able to use that information in creative and meaningful ways to supplement your knowledge and to apply it to specific contexts. Put more simply, information literacy is the ability to recognize a need for information, to search out information, to assess the information, and to use the information. To be an effective research writer, you must develop a comprehensive literacy in information. Good academic writers are usually information literate; they are knowledgeable about the acquisition, evaluation, and integration of knowledge.

Why Research?

Probably the first question you ponder when you are given a research project or assignment is, "Why me?!?" Once the shock of the assignment finally sinks in, you may next wonder, "Why do I have to do a research paper?" This is a fair question. In our contemporary age, we are frequently encouraged to think quite highly of ourselves. Self-discovery and self-expression are all the rage these days; of course, these activities presuppose that the self as such is worthy of discovery and expression. Don't get me wrong—the human subject is valuable and important, but too often we focus on the self to the exclusion of the other such that the self becomes the center of the universe in our minds. We lose sight of the fact that we are unique and valuable beings in relationship with other unique and valuable beings.

Research, when performed properly, moves us beyond self-indulgence toward recognizing that we do not have all the answers and that there is much to be learned by searching out and critically examining what other minds have thought about various subjects. Research takes us out of ourselves toward contemplating ourselves in intellectual dialog with other minds. This is the mark of a true learner and committed intellectual.

In addition to enhancing the learning experience by allowing the individual to discover information from sources outside the self, research also plays a practical role in academic writing. Research contributes the following key elements to effective writing:

Information

Generally, readers want information, and they want to learn something from the essays they read. Writers can provide a lot of information from their own experiences and thoughts, but sometimes writers must move beyond the subjective and provide more objective perspectives and pieces of information.

Also, good information produces more lively writing, and research can help provide an abundance of information. Vague writing filled with generalities is dull and uneventful. Specific and detailed writing is interesting and engaging, especially if you can reveal knowledge that your readers did not know before encountering your essay. Conducting research helps the academic writer develop his or her thoughts more fully and to write detailed and interesting papers.

Audience Awareness

Good writers try to learn as much as they can about their audience or readers so that they can achieve their writing goals and share their messages effectively. Many times we do not know much about our readers, their expectations, their knowledge level, and their perspectives on the issues of our paper. Through research we can hope to learn something about our audience so that we can reach them.

For example, if you are trying to persuade your readers to adopt a certain point of view or to convince them to take a course of action, then you will need to know what your readers already think or believe so that you can effectively discuss and refute their claims and convince them to adopt your own views. Unless you have studied your readers or have debated representatives from your opposition, you simply will not be aware of your audience, and you will not know how to persuade them. Research can help you learn about your opponents' views and thus help you engage them more effectively in your persuasive essay.

Credibility

Good writers are credible, meaning they are believable. If you do not know what you are talking about and just toss out random thoughts or unsupported ideas, your readers will not find you very credible. Most likely, they will dismiss your point of view. By conducting research, you can increase your knowledge level, understand your audience, and present specific information in your paper.

In other words, research will help you build, establish, and maintain your credibility as a writer. If you are writing a persuasive essay, increased credibility usually improves your chances of convincing your opposition that they should accept your views. In the very least, research will encourage your readers to view your ideas as valuable and worthy of careful consideration. Research helps to establish your credibility as a writer.

Authority

Research also helps to establish your authority as a writer. Whenever you make a point or draw conclusions in your essays, the reader will probably think, "Who says?" In other words, readers usually do not want to take just anyone's word at face value, especially if the writer is virtually unknown. Even experts in a field conduct research and cite other authorities or experts in their writing. (How do you think they became experts themselves?)

Generally speaking, your professors and your classmates are not going to be fully convinced of your perspectives if you do not substantiate your thoughts with valuable information and credible expert testimony. Research helps you build a convincing case for your point of view by discovering new arguments and finding information to support your claims. Such information elevates your level of authority, because your readers become more convinced that you know what you are talking about. Also, your own authority as a writer is enhanced if you cite other experts and authorities to support your own claims.

We conduct research in the academy because we must learn what has been said about an issue. Then, we use that information to establish our own perspective and to express our views to others. This kind of writing is essential to college-level learning. Moreover, conducting research trains us to become life-long learners—individuals who continue to ask questions after graduation and to seek answers to those questions throughout their lives.

AVOIDING PLAGIARISM

Before we begin discussing the basic process of research writing and developing information literacy skills, we should first discuss the issue of plagiarism. As we have discovered, academic writing necessarily involves the integration of other people's ideas, thoughts, views, theories, arguments, and information into our own writing. There is a clear distinction between our own ideas and those of other people, and when we use information from other people in our own writing, we have to distinguish our thoughts from the thoughts of others. And, we must give appropriate credit to those from whom we have borrowed information. It is permissible and expected in academic writing to use other people's ideas, as long as we give appropriate credit. However, if we take other people's information and pass it off as our own work, then that is plagiarism, a form of academic dishonesty.

Plagiarism is basically intellectual property theft. Wait a minute, how can an idea be property that can be stolen? After all, it is not a physical or material item, so how can it be property? Legally and ethically the thoughts, ideas, views, concepts, theories, music, art, drawing, painting, computer code, or any other such product of intellectual activity is considered the property of the person who created that intellectual item or artifact. If you take it and present it as your own, you are basically stealing it and pretending that you created it.

In academic writing, there are three main ways of integrating other people's information into your own writing: directly copying or quoting, paraphrasing (restating the information in your own words), or summarizing (reducing the information down to its basic idea and explaining it in your own words). If you borrow information in any of these ways without giving proper credit or citation, then you have plagiarized.

Think about it this way: directly quoting without giving credit is like stealing your friend's car; paraphrasing without providing a citation is like stealing your friend's car and giving it a new paint job—it is still your friend's car but it only looks a little different; and summarizing without providing a citation is like stealing your friend's car and then stripping it down to its basic elements—it is still your friend's car but with some components missing.

You can use information from various sources, but make sure you credit the source or provide a proper citation (see the section below on the basics of citation). As a student, you can fail an assignment, fail the course, or even be dismissed from the university for plagiarism. Professional writers can lose their jobs or be sued over copyright violation and intellectual property theft. Plagiarism is no small matter, so please make sure you understand what it is, what it is not, and how to avoid it. Always speak to your professor if you have any questions about plagiarism before you submit an assignment.

BASICS OF THE RESEARCH PROCESS

A major aspect of academic writing involves seeking what others think about an issue or topic and then developing your own views in relation to the other views you discover. You can refute their views, engage in dialog or debate with other writers, use other people's ideas and information to corroborate your own views, or change your own view based upon new information you never before considered. Research helps you discover topics and to shape your point of view. The following are some basic elements in the research process, and coming to a practical understanding of these basics is an important step in developing information literacy.

Preliminary Research

Sometimes we simply do not know what we want to write about, and preliminary research can help us discover a topic. With the development of the Internet and various online library databases, preliminary research is easy, efficient, and effective. The main thing to remember is that preliminary research is exactly just that—preliminary. It is research conducted before you really get serious about your research.

For example, let's say you are interesting in writing about stem cell research, but you do not yet know what focus you want to pursue. Preliminary research can help you discover a more specific angle on the issue. You can do a Google or Yahoo Internet search on stem cell research and see what Web sites come up. You can browse through some of those sites to see what other people are talking about, and this may help you narrow your focus. Or, you can log in to your university library's online database system and search journals, magazines, and other periodicals on the topic of stem cell research. Browse the article titles and consider browsing through some of the full-text articles provided by your library system.

Please note that the objective here is not to locate and read all of these materials. Rather, you are merely browsing Web sites, skimming through article titles, and browsing a few articles here and there just to get a preliminary idea of what kinds of issues people are talking about in relation to your chosen topic. The purpose is to use preliminary research to get a general understanding of your topic and to narrow your focus.

Questions and Quests

Once you have a clearer understanding of your main topic and an idea of what your focus might be, you need to start formulating your project more specifically. A research project is basically a type of intellectual quest. It is an intense search for information, and this search starts with a guiding question. Notice the root word in "question" is "quest." A quest must be motivated by a question. In Arthurian quest narratives, there is always some problem in the kingdom that then generates a question (How do we solve the problem?), and then the valiant knight prepares for the quest, which is the treacherous search for an answer to the question that will then solve the problem.

J. R. R. Tolkien's *The Lord of the Rings* is an excellent example of a modern-day quest narrative. Problem: The evil Lord Sauron is regaining strength and threatening to conquer Middle Earth, and he seeks the master ring that will allow him to take physical form once again and rule Middle Earth. Question: How can Sauron be stopped and Middle Earth saved? Answer: Destroy the ring of power. Quest: Take the ring to Mount Doom, destroy it utterly, and defeat Sauron and the forces of evil once and for all.

Maybe not all research quests will be this exciting, but the basic idea is the same. As a researcher, you must identify an issue or problem, and then you must formulate a question. That question will guide your research strategies and practices, and your quest becomes the search for answers to that question. Once you have found your answers, you must then structure them into a coherent and engaging written document, the research paper. To extend the quest metaphor a bit further, the final research paper document is the holy relic or treasure (like the Holy Grail) that is presented to the king as the culmination of the quest adventure. Instead of presenting a relic to the king, you are preparing a research paper and submitting it to your professor.

Research Strategies

With your problem and question in mind, you must next start searching for information that will help you answer your main research question. It is pointless to begin serious research without a question in mind. Without a guiding question, you will most likely waste a lot of precious time. The question narrows your search and focuses your research efforts. As you search for information to answer your research question, consider the following research strategies.

Data Mining—Search Bibliographies in Books and Articles

Sometimes we fear research because we do not know where to begin, and we feel like we have to reinvent the wheel. Try not to panic when you are beginning your research—recognize that others have done a lot of research before you, and you can benefit from the work they have already done. Below I explain ways of finding information in your library, online, and in interviews. Keep in mind that the books and articles you find will also have bibliographies or lists of sources that the writers consulted in writing their documents. Use their research to your advantage. Read through their bibliographies and make a list of any sources that you think will be helpful to you. If you interview people (see below), consider asking them for suggestions on books and articles or research Web sites you should consult. The idea here is to mine the data that already exists (in this case, lists of sources).

Traditional Library Research

Although we are clearly in the electronic information age, we should not ignore traditional library research. Most university libraries and local community libraries have extensive book collections and periodical subscriptions. Start your research by discovering what your libraries have to offer. Learn how to use the electronic catalog system and conduct subject searches using important keywords associated with your research topic. Make friends with your local reference librarian, and learn important tips on how to conduct keyword searches. The electronic catalog searches will tell you what books and periodicals are available in that particular library. If your libraries have certain online services, these searches will link you to full-text online books and periodical articles.

You may also want to consider using various print bibliographies, which list books and articles available on various topics. Each major academic discipline has certain bibliographies devoted to topics in that area of study. Ask your professors and reference librarians which bibliographies to search for different subjects. Note that these print bibliographies will tell you what books and articles have been published on certain topics, but they will not tell you if your library has these books and articles. When using bibliographies, first write down the author, title, and publication information of the resource you are interested in finding. Then, check in your library catalog system to see if that resource is available in your library or not. If it is not, you may be able to use an interlibrary loan service to borrow the resource from another library. Speak to your reference librarian about such services.

Online Database Research

Most print bibliographies (see above) are now available in electronic format, and they are generally called online databases or indexes (indices). Just as with print bibliographies, online databases and electronic indexes exist for each of the major academic disciplines. Most libraries link to these databases from their Web site. If you are not familiar with your library databases, speak with your reference librarian and browse through the various database systems to learn how to use them effectively. Each database is slightly different, but many are becoming standardized in their functionality (mainly because the major research companies that provide these services are either consolidating or are forming research consortiums that use the same search portal systems).

These online databases and electronic indexes list what books and articles are available on various topics. As you search through these systems, create a list of resources you want to locate (note that most databases allow you to bookmark resources or create a list of resources that you can print out). Then try to find these resources in your library or through interlibrary loan. Some of these databases contain full-text materials or are linked to full-text material locators. Learn how to use these systems to download and/or print full-text articles and books.

Interviewing

In addition to traditional library research and online database searches, you may also want to find experts in the subject you are studying to conduct interviews. Some assignments like journalistic writing, or sociological studies, or anthropological ethnographies require the writer to conduct interviews of different people. Consider the following major methods of interviewing.

IN-PERSON. The most common type of interviewing is in-person. You should prepare a series of open-ended questions to ask during the personal interview. Review the journalistic method of invention (chapter 1) and formulate interesting questions starting with who, what, when, why, where, and how. Be sure to take careful notes during the interview, or record the interview. Always ask permission from your subject before recording the interview. You may also want to consider video recording the interview, but keep in mind that most people are very uncomfortable being video recorded.

TELEPHONE. You can also conduct interviews over the phone. Arrange a time in advance and make sure you and your subject can have a significant amount of uninterrupted time to conduct the interview. Prepare interesting questions in advance, and take careful notes during the interview or record the interview. Be sure to get your subject's permission before recording any phone interview.

E-MAIL. E-mail interviews are becoming much more common, mainly because of convenience. You can simply e-mail the questions to your subject, who can then take time to answer each question thoroughly and thoughtfully. The e-mailed response is basically a written transcript of your interview.

BASICS OF RESEARCH WRITING

Once you have discovered your topic, formulated your question, searched out answers to that question, and gathered research information, you are ready to begin writing. As with any other writing task, it helps to view research writing as a process. If we think mainly about the large research paper that is due at the end of the term, then most likely we will freak ourselves out, succumb to the paralyzing fear that is inherent to research writing, and either not finish the project or not do as well as we would have liked.

Okay, maybe that is a bit of an exaggeration, but there is a tendency in most writers to obsess about the final product, which generally does much more harm than good. However, if we break research writing down into its major stages and focus on accomplishing the tasks required at each stage, then we will eventually complete the research project to the best of our ability. As with the general writing process we examined in chapter 1, there really is no such thing as "the research writing process." However, there is a general model that we can examine. Different writers have their own way of engaging this model of research writing. And, the exact process may be slightly different in different writing contexts. Described below are some key phases of the research writing process. When preparing for a particular research writing project, adapt this general model accordingly.

Invention

Invention involves generating content for a paper. In research writing the invention process mainly involves conducting formal research (library research, online database research, and/or interviews as described above). Generally speaking, most of your time on a research writing project will be spent in the invention phase, searching for sources, evaluating sources, deciding which sources to uses, and taking notes. Avoid shortchanging yourself at this stage. The more time you spend in the invention phase of a research project the more material you will have to work with later, and the easier it will be to plan and write your research paper. The following are some strategies you can use to make your research paper invention process more efficient and productive.

Thinking Critically about Sources

A research project is only as good as the resources used. Good researchers know how to evaluate sources and how to select those sources that best suit the needs, purposes, and goals of the research project. Information literacy begins with learning how to think critically about the information you are selecting. We noted that it is fine to use general Web sites and Web site searches on Yahoo.com and Google.com for preliminary research. However, once you have focused your topic and have a narrow research question, you must move beyond general Web sites and search engines.

When writing an academic research project, you must use academic sources. If you are using Web sites, make sure the sites contain quality information. A good principle to follow is that you can usually trust Web sites that are part of a university library collection or research service. If the site has an academic editor or is created by a specialist in the field, then you can probably trust the site. If you are in doubt, then ask your professor before using such a site. (Note: Wikipedia is not a valuable academic resource. Avoid using it when writing college research papers.)

Information from a university library database is usually acceptable. Books and journal articles from your university library are also generally acceptable, because the library staff has purposefully purchased quality academic resources to be used for research purposes. A good way to evaluate a book resource is to see if the book has been published by a university press (for example, Cambridge University Press or Ohio State University Press) or another academic press. If you are not sure, ask your professor or librarian. A way to test a journal article is to make sure it is published in an academic journal with an editorial staff that reviews and approves articles before they are published (such journals are called refereed journals). If you are not sure of the quality of an article, ask your professor or librarian.

You should also consider the date of publication. Depending upon your topic, you may need to use more current information. Indeed, some ideas, concepts, and truths do not go out of date, and there are some classic or well-known studies that are important to the subject matter, which should not be ignored. Discuss with your professor any questions you have about how current the information you use in your paper should be.

Basically, you want to select and use the very best sources you can. Not all information is equally valid or valuable, so be selective and be smart about what you choose. To be information literate you need to learn how to choose quality information. Think critically about the sources (logic, evidence, relevance): Are the sources written by academics and experts in the field and do the ideas make logical sense? Do they present quality information in great detail and abundance? Do they treat the information accurately and fairly? Do they clearly relate to your project? And do they help you answer your research question?

Finding and Using Sources

Learning how to find, evaluate, and select your research materials is vitally important to any successful research project. Wasted effort impedes many good projects: often we waste much time working with inappropriate or irrelevant materials. Let's face it: we are all busy people, and rarely can we devote all our time to a research project. We have other things to do, and we cannot spend all our time reading through hundreds of books and articles. To be information literate, not only must we learn how to identify and assess quality information, but we must also learn how to use research resources efficiently.

As we have already established, we must have a clear topic and specific research question to guide our research. With this question in mind, start searching for books, articles, and other resources in your library stacks (collection of books and journals) and library online databases. Read the titles of the sources, and make a list of any material that seems relevant to your topic. If you are not sure, include it on your list (you can weed sources out later, and you never know when a seemingly irrelevant source may turn up lots of helpful information). Next, do your best to locate the items on your list. Most of them should be in your university and/or local library. You may have to retrieve other items through interlibrary loan services (consult your librarian for more information on such services). Once you have your various items, separate them into at least two separate piles: one for books and one for articles.

Next, determine which sources you will study in detail. Do not try to read all of your sources cover to cover just yet. Instead, categorize your items according to level of importance: essential to your project, moderately important, barely important, and irrelevant or useless. How to review and itemize books:

1. Review the table of contents and skim through the index (looking for keywords related to your topic) to see if there are major portions of the book that speak to your research question.

2. Read the preface and/or introduction to the book. These sections are usually short (10–20 pages) and provide a good overview of the book. There should be chapter summaries in the introduction that will give you a good idea if there are any chapters relevant to your topic.

3. Review chapters of interest by reading the first paragraph, skimming the body paragraphs (read the first and last sentences of each paragraph), and reading the last paragraph. This should give you a good idea if the chapter is important to your project or not.

How to review articles:

1. If there is an abstract, read it carefully. Well-written abstracts provide an overview of the subject, focus, and conclusions of the article, and they generally can tell you if the article is relevant to your topic or not. As a general rule, scientific, technical, and sociological articles usually have abstracts, while literary and other humanities articles often do not.

2. Read the introduction section or the first two paragraphs carefully to get a clear sense of the topic and focus of the article.

3. Skim the body paragraphs by reading the first and last sentence of each paragraph to get a general sense of the various topics and types of information discussed in the article.

4. Carefully read the last paragraph to discover the main conclusions of the article.

Remember, at this point you are not studying the resources; rather, you are reviewing them quickly to see which sources are useful and which are not. Based upon this preliminary review, organize your materials according to the degree of relative importance (essential to your project, moderately important, barely important, and irrelevant or useless). Spend more time reading and studying the really important resources, and as time permits read and study the remaining resources.

Critical Thinking and Taking Notes

Once you have the main resources you plan to use in your project, read them thoroughly and take careful notes. The reading part is relatively easy; note taking is usually the most challenging. Remember that you are not just reading these sources for delight—you are working on a research project. Your reading and study must be focused by the purposes of your project. You are on a quest to answer your research question; therefore, you should actively seek answers and search out clear evidence that you can use to answer your question and to support your conclusions.

Approach the information with your critical thinking glasses on. Continually keep your project in mind. As you read, ask yourself such questions as: What is the information all about? What is this writer trying to say? Do I agree or disagree and why? What can I use from this resource to answer my research question? How am I going to use this information in my paper? Does it support my claims? If so, how can I use it to strengthen my case? Does it refute my claims? If so, does it weaken my case and should I modify my case in some way? If yes, then how? If it does not weaken my case, then how can I refute the counter-claims? Keep such questions in mind as you read, and then write down answers to these questions as you take notes. Here are some tips on note taking for research projects:

1. Consider printing out full-text online sources (articles, book chapters, Web documents) and photocopying print materials. You can highlight and mark up these copies and keep them as long as you need. Please do not write on library print materials.

2. Avoid using note cards, as they are generally too small to write anything substantive or meaningful, and you end up using too many cards to keep organized. If you use cards successfully, then continue using them. If your professor requires them, then follow his or her instructions. Generally speaking, I do not recommend using note cards.

3. Write notes in a notebook, on a legal pad, or on a word processor (I recommend using a laptop computer and backing up your notes on USB flash drives or memory sticks.)

4. Write the full bibliographic information of the resource at the top of the page. This will be most helpful when writing your works cited or resource list. Make sure you get the complete bibliographic information of the resource.

5. Write your notes underneath the bibliographic information. Write the page number of the resource (if applicable—many electronic sources do not have page numbers) and then write your notes. If you have several notes to take from a single page in your resource, write them in separate sections, but still write the page number before each section of notes so that you do not get confused later about where that information comes from in your resource. You

need to keep track of the page numbers so that you can write accurate citations in your paper.

6. When taking notes, first accurately copy any information you want to use as direct quotes. Indicate in your notes that it is a direct quote. You should also paraphrase portions of important information (writing the content in your own words without changing the meaning) and summarize larger portions of information (reduce the content down to its basic point or message without changing the meaning of the content). Be sure to record the page number from the resource whenever you are quoting, paraphrasing, or summarizing.

7. In addition to recording information, you should also comment on the information. Jot down in your notes any reactions you have (why you agree or why you disagree). If it is a counter-claim, discuss it, critically examine it, and refute it in your notes. If it is supporting data, explain what the information means, what you think about it, and how it supports your claims. Note how you plan to use it in your paper.

8. Talk back to the information. Discuss it, dialog with the writers, and explain your thoughts and reactions. The more you write during the note-taking phase, the more material you will have to work with during the drafting phase. Sometimes you may write whole paragraphs or sections of your paper in your notes, and later all you have to do is copy/paste that material into your draft and then revise it. For this reason, you should consider taking notes on a word processor, as it can make the drafting phase less painful if not actually easier than working with handwritten material.

9. If taking notes on paper, staple pages of notes written about a single source. If writing notes on a word processor, save notes on a single source as a separate word processing document. Keep your note documents in a single folder on your computer, and be sure to back up copies of all your work on USB flash drives or memory sticks.

See the figure below for an example of notes taken on a word processor. This note-taking example is taken from a project analyzing the Van Helsing character in the Gothic novel *Dracula*. Notice the bibliographic information at the top, page numbers on the left, information recorded to the right of the page numbers, and then ideas and reflections on the information written underneath.

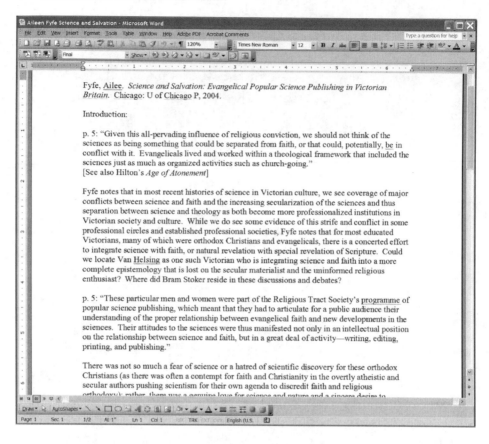

Figure 1: Taking Notes in a Word Processor

Planning

In the planning phase of writing you need to plan your time and plan your document. Be sure you know the deadline for the project and then work back from that time to create a plan for completing the different segments of your project. As mentioned above, most of your time will be spent in the invention phase identifying and locating sources and then studying them, taking careful notes to generate content for your paper. Leave plenty of time to complete your research. After you have finished compiling notes and information for your research project, you need to organize the information. If you have not yet already done so, formulate your thesis as clearly and specifically as you can. This will help you pick out key pieces of information from your notes that you can use to build your case and to prove your main points. Consider planning your information in two major stages: cataloging your notes and creating an outline.

Cataloging Your Notes

By the time you have finished reviewing your sources and taking notes, you should have a pretty good idea what you want to say. Now you need to organize your data. I recommend going back through your notes and cataloging them so that you can find information more easily when you begin writing. If you have taken notes on paper, read through the notes and write keywords in the right-hand margin of your notes that identify that main idea of the information. If you wrote notes in a word processor, then use the program's "sticky note" or comments feature to write marginal keywords identifying the main content or idea of the information. By cataloging your notes this way, it will be easier to go back through them when creating your outline or when trying to locate specific information to put in your paper. You only have to read the keywords in the margins instead of skimming your notes each time. Below is an example of marginal keywords within notes written in a word processor.

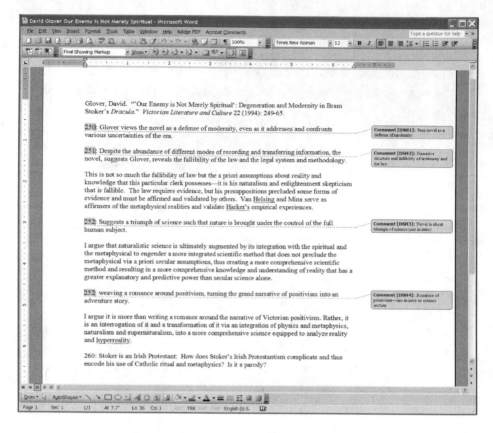

Figure 2: Cataloging Notes in a Word Processor

From Notes to Outline

After you have cataloged your notes, go back and skim through all of your notes and formulate a working thesis, if you have not already done so. This thesis will be your basic answer to your main research question. You started the research journey with a question, and you should now have your answer, or at least a tentative answer that you can sharpen as you draft and revise your document.

With this thesis or focus in mind, start grouping your content and decide how you want to present it in your paper. Consider various organizational patterns, depending upon the type of paper you are writing (an informational or expository report, an evaluation, a persuasive piece, an interpretation, or a synthesis). Write a general outline that will help guide you through the writing process. Avoid overly detailed outlines, as they may bog you down. Instead, outline the main sections of your paper, and then create a list of resources and ideas that you plan to discuss in each of the main sections.

I recommend writing an electronic outline in a word processor. As you write your draft, you may discover better ways to organize the information, and you can easily revise your outline as you are writing. Below is an example outline that is not overly structured or detailed but has enough structure and information to guide the writing of a draft. Notice that the Roman numerals indicate major sections of the document. Underneath each main section heading is a list of sources (by author's last name) and topic ideas to be discussed in that section of the paper.

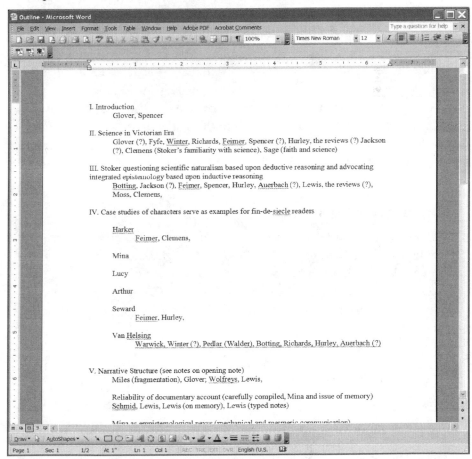

Figure 3: An Electronic Outline

Writing

If you have done your job well in the invention and planning phases of the research project, then writing the paper should not be all that difficult. Sure, it will be a challenge, but if you have lots of research material, clear notes, specific reactions to the information, and a good outline, then you should have relatively little difficulty producing a first draft. Depending upon how long the paper needs to be, you may have to spend a couple of days writing the first draft. Try to produce the first draft, complete with a beginning, a middle, and an end, as quickly as possible. However, do not sacrifice thoroughness for speed.

Follow your outline or plan, work from your notes, and write a complete and coherent draft. If you find that elements of your initial plan are not working out, then reorganize accordingly and keep plugging away. If you get bogged down or frustrated, as all writers do at some point, then take a break, clear your head, get something to eat, call a friend, shoot some hoops, do something to take your mind off the paper for a little bit. But do not stay away from the writing for too long. Avoid procrastinating. Get back to writing as soon as you can and finish the draft. I also recommend that you include your citations in the first draft. It is much easier to include the citations as you are writing from your notes on the first draft then to try to go back and fill in the citations later. The following are some constructive tips on successfully drafting your research paper.

Drafting from Your Notes

If you have taken detailed notes, it will be much easier to produce the first draft, because you have already thought through much of the material in your notes. All you have to do is copy portions of your notes into the appropriate section of your paper. If you have composed your notes in a word processing document, it is even easier, because you simply have to copy the content and paste it into the draft.

As you are pasting material from your notes or copying from handwritten notes, be sure to provide appropriate transitions between the portions of text inserted from your notes. Remember you are crafting a research document, and you need to lead your readers through your discussion of the material. If you merely insert chunks from your notes, your draft will be choppy and uneven. As you work from your notes, build your argument, provide introductory phrases to the material, explain the material, and make your points clear in each paragraph. Information literacy involves not only learning how to identify an issue and finding appropriate information, but it also involves learning how to use that information to achieve your writing goals.

Incorporating Sources

An effective research writer incorporates outside sources into the paper in constructive ways without losing sight of his or her own voice. It is easy to copy/paste a bunch of material into a paper, but it is much more difficult to craft a research essay. You must integrate outside sources and other people's ideas while maintaining your own voice and achieving your writing goals. This type of writing takes practice, and it helps to read as many sample research papers, essays, and articles as possible to become familiar with this type of academic writing. There are three main ways to incorporate other people's ideas and outside information into your writing: quotation, paraphrase, and summary.

QUOTATION. Quotation involves copying someone's words exactly as they appear in the original document. Usually, you should avoid too many direct quotes in your paper (use paraphrase instead—see below). You should only quote information that is particularly interesting, rather complex, or beautifully expressed. Only quote material that you want your readers to encounter in its original form. Generally your quotes should be a few sentences long; use large blocks of quoted text occasionally, and only when absolutely necessary. If your quote is four lines or fewer of your own typing, then put quotation marks around the quoted material. If your quote is five or more lines of your own typing, then block the whole quote by indenting it ten spaces or two tabs (use the increase indent feature of your word processor). Again, avoid including too many long quotes in your paper, as this gives the impression that you are merely presenting copies of other people's ideas without crafting your own perspective or argument.

When you are using quotes, avoid just dropping them into your sentences unannounced. Such quotations are awkward and sometimes confusing to your readers. Introduce the quote or set it up in some way so that your readers know it is coming and why it is there. It is usually a good idea to refer to the source of the quote in your introductory phrase. The first time you quote someone, use his or her full name and consider including qualification tags that give the readers some sense of the credibility of the person you are quoting. Here are some examples of direct quotes:

> Kathleen L. Spencer argues that when characters in Victorian Gothic novels are faced with such a metaphysical intrusion, a "method for dealing with the supernatural must be created, drawing on the most powerful and prestigious tools at their disposal: the methods of science, shaped by a secular world view—paradoxically, the very world view that was initially overthrown by the fantastic intrusion." (220)[1]

> According to Kathleen Le Spencer, a critic who writes extensively on the urban Gothic tale of the nineteenth century, when characters in Victorian Gothic novels are faced with the supernatural, a "method for dealing with the supernatural must be created, drawing on the most powerful and prestigious tools at their disposal: the methods of science, shaped by a secular world view—paradoxically, the very world view that was initially overthrown by the fantastic intrusion." (220)

Avoid using the same method for introducing a quote so that your writing remains engaging and fresh. Generally, use the present tense when introducing and setting up a quote (however, if you are using the APA format, use the past tense). Consider using such introductory or lead-in verbs as the following when introducing your quotes:

> analyzes, argues, acknowledges, cites, concludes, considers, demonstrates, defines, examines, explains, finds, formulates, identifies, indicates, lists, notes, reports, shows, summarizes.

When you are quoting material, make sure you copy it accurately. Do not change the meaning of the quote by removing it from its original context and using it to prove something that the author is not saying.

PARAPHRASE. Quotation copies the passage exactly word for word; a paraphrase presents the content and meaning of the information in your own words. Generally, you should use more paraphrases than quotations. When you paraphrase content, make sure you do not change the meaning of the original passage. Also, you must do more than just change a word or two; you must truly rephrase the information in your own language.

---

1. For the purposes of illustration, I am using MLA parenthetic citation. This quote is from Spencer, "Purity and Danger," 220.

Paraphrases are effective ways of bringing in outside information while maintaining your own voice, because you are restating the content in your own style and words. When paraphrasing, try not to look at the original passage too much, because you will end up copying more than paraphrasing. Read the information, and then restate it without looking at the passage; refer to the original as few times as possible when writing your paraphrase. You should use lead-in words to set up or to introduce the paraphrased information as you would a direct quote. And, you must provide proper citation for all paraphrases, as you would for a direct quote. Here are some example paraphrases:

> Original passage from Rosemary Jackson's book *Fantasy: The Literature of Subversion*: "The fantastic is predicated on the category of the 'real,' and it introduces areas which can be conceptualized only by negative terms according to the categories of nineteenth century realism: thus, the im-possible, the un-real, the nameless, formless, shapeless, un-known, in-visible."[2]

Two paraphrases:

> According to Rosemary Jackson the fantastic is that which breaks through the confines of the natural, giving shape, voice, and reality to the unreal, the unnatural, or the empirically unverifiable. (25–26)

> Fantastic elements, Rosemary Jackson argues, are those strange or unexpected occurrences that intrude into the natural world, making the supernatural or things that we assume to be unreal seem quite real and empirically verifiable. (25–26)

Consider using paraphrases in conjunction with direct quotes. You can paraphrase some content, provide a direct quote of a passage that is beautifully or compellingly worded, and then shift back to paraphrasing information. If you are paraphrasing information from different sources, make it clear in your writing that the information is coming from different sources by properly introducing the content and using proper citation. In the following example, note how the first source is quoted but the second source is paraphrased:

> Kathleen L. Spencer argues that when characters in Victorian Gothic novels are faced with such a metaphysical intrusion, a

2. Jackson, *Fantasy*, 25–26.

"method for dealing with the supernatural must be created, drawing on the most powerful and prestigious tools at their disposal: the methods of science, shaped by a secular world view—paradoxically, the very world view that was initially overthrown by the fantastic intrusion" (220). But what is the supernatural or the fantastic? According to Rosemary Jackson the fantastic is that which breaks through the confines of the natural, giving shape, voice, and reality to the unreal, the unnatural, or the empirically unverifiable. (25–26)

SUMMARY. Summary is used to present the main idea of a long passage or collection of information in a short amount of space. The challenge of a good summary is to capture the main focus or dominant idea of a long passage and to communicate it succinctly yet accurately in your own words. For example, you can summarize the main point of an article in just a few sentences. Or, you can reduce a lot of statistical data down to the main point the data proves. Or, you can sift through the complicated twists and turns of a complex argument and summarize in just a few words the main conclusion of that argument. Use summary to present ideas, observations, and conclusions made by other writers, and then discuss the significance of this information in relation to your main point in that paragraph or section of your paper.

Like quotations and paraphrases, summaries require a citation, and the main reason for citing the source, in addition to avoiding plagiarism, is to allow the reader to find and read the original information. When summarizing, be sure to reflect accurately the main idea of the original. Do not twist or distort the information. Read the original passage carefully and repeatedly to make sure you fully understand the main idea. Then, without looking at the original, explain the main idea of the passage or information in as few words as you can. Be sure to provide appropriate lead-in words to introduce or set up the summary, and provide the appropriate citation. Consider the following example:

> *Original:* On Saturday evening, September 15, 2001, I went to a chamber music concert. Most entertainment events for the weekend had been cancelled, since the country was in mourning. I was grateful that the musicians had decided to go on with the concert. Hearing the music (some popular opera arias, then Mozart's "Gran Partita" Serenade for winds), drawn into the performers' concentrated creative energy, I felt my spirits lifted for the first time since

September 11. I wasn't alone in this response. The somber audience was more than usually appreciative. Since then, when I've felt overwhelmed by news of horror upon horror, I've put on a CD of Chopin's Etudes or Messiaen's *Quartet for the End of Time*, or read a Sara Maitland novel or Adam Zagajewski's poetry, or sat with the paintings in *Sister Wendy's Book of Meditations*, a recent gift from a friend. Clearly I need the arts in time of war.[3]

Summary: Peggy Rosenthal observes that during a tumultuous time of war, listening to beautiful music, reading excellent literature, or appreciating a complex painting brings peace to the mind and restores balance to a disquieted soul, if only for a short time.

(Note: this is a summary of an online source without page numbers; therefore, since the author's name is used in the sentence, no in-text citation is necessary under the MLA format rules. Consult the appropriate citation style manual as per your professor's instructions.)

The main reasons for incorporating outside sources into your own writing are to supplement your voice, to build your case, to develop your ideas and writing, to accomplish specific rhetorical goals, to establish your authority as a writer, and to affirm your credibility as a writer. However, you must remember that you are the writer, and you should not allow outside material to speak for itself, unless the meaning or message of the material is perfectly obvious and incontrovertible. Generally, after you provide outside information, you should explain what it means and clarify your main point. Consider the following checklist for a good paragraph that incorporates outside material:

✓ Transitional phrase moving smoothly from previous paragraph to the next.

✓ Clear topic sentence that focuses the new paragraph.

✓ Explanation of issue or topic of the paragraph.

✓ Presentation of information (quotations, paraphrases, summaries), using proper citation.

✓ Discussion of the information in terms of the point you want to make in that paragraph.

✓ End by asserting the main point of the paragraph if necessary.

3. Rosenthal, "Why We Need," para. 1.

BASICS OF CITATION

Citation is a basic method by which you acknowledge the sources of your information to avoid plagiarism (the use and presentation of other people's ideas and information as if they were our own). However, citation also serves a basic research function as well: it helps direct your readers to your sources so that they can follow up on your research and conduct research of their own. Citation, then, serves two key functions: it helps writers avoid plagiarism, and it aids others in their own research process. (Keep this in mind as you are conducting research—read through other writers' bibliographies or works cited lists to find sources that you may wish to consider for your own paper.) There are many different citation systems, but the three most frequently used are journalistic attribution, MLA, and APA.

Journalistic Attribution

Journalistic attribution is mainly used in newspaper and popular magazine writing, and you will rarely see it in academic writing. However, in some introductory writing courses, your professor may teach journalistic attribution just to get you used to the concept of acknowledging your sources without worrying about the complexities of citation systems. (Of course, if you are a journalism major, you will learn more about attribution in your journalism courses.) In journalistic attribution, you are attributing the information to its source by naming the source in your sentence.

If you read newspapers and newsmagazines, how many times do you see footnotes, parenthetical citations, or a works cited list at the end of the article? Rarely, if ever. Instead, you will see the source acknowledged in the sentence without any citation. For example, a newspaper reporter may say something like: "According to the mayor, the budget for town sanitation will be increased next year." Or, you might see something like this: "Sources close to the university president's office report that a growing number of students are complaining that some professors are unfairly ridiculing students who hold conservative political values or who publicly discuss their Christian faith." When citing your sources using journalistic attribution, set up the information by using introductory words or phrases and then state the name of the source as specifically as you can, along with any affiliation that lends credibility to the source.

MLA

MLA is an acronym for the Modern Language Association, which has formalized the in-text citation format used in literary studies and other humanities disciplines. Basically, this citation system has two main components: a parenthetic in-text citation with minimal information, usually author last name and page number where applicable, and a works cited list at the end of the document. The two work in conjunction. The in-text citation lets the reader know what information has been borrowed, and it directs readers to the works cited list to get the complete bibliographic information. Interested readers can then use that information to locate the source. For more information on formatting MLA in-text citations and works cited pages (the bibliography), consult the latest edition of the *MLA Handbook*.

APA

The APA citation system has been established by the American Psychological Association, and it is used mainly in various social sciences classes. Like the MLA, it is an in-text citation system that has two main components: a parenthetic citation within the text of the paper, containing the author's name, the year of publication, and a page number (used only for direct quotes), and a reference list at the end of the document. Because social science theories, ideas, and data change so frequently, researchers are more interested in the date of the information used in a paper. That is why the APA system includes the author's name and the year of publication within the in-text citation. For more information on formatting APA in-text citations and references (the bibliography), consult the latest edition of the *Publication Manual of the American Psychological Association*.

SAMPLE STUDENT MLA RESEARCH PAPER

NOTE: Do not use a cover page for an MLA formatted research paper, unless otherwise instructed by your professor. On the very first page, include in the upper left-hand corner your name, your professor's name, the course number and section, and the assignment due date. Also, in the upper right-hand corner of each page, include a header with your last name and the page number. Use the insert header feature of your word processor.

Lotus Young

Dr. Hogsette

WRIT 151-W01

June 24, 2005

Madness from Oppression

For as long as anthropologists can trace the timeline, our societies have been mainly patriarchal. In the earliest days, women were oppressed, most remaining uneducated and many unable to express themselves through creative outlets. Back in the nineteenth century when Charlotte Perkins Gilman wrote, "The Yellow Wallpaper," male dominance was more overbearing and controlling than it is today. During that time, "the middle and upper class ideal of woman was that of an 'invalid' [and their] God-given role . . . was as wife and mother, keeper of the household" (Hartman). The main character, a woman who remains anonymous throughout the whole story, is driven to insanity as a result of that image and the dominance from the men in her life. Unable to assert her will, she slowly unravels into a downward spiral of madness from the restrictions forced on to her by John, the symbol of male oppression in society.

In the beginning of the story, the main character is taken to a grand estate in an attempt to cure her "temporary nervous depression" (Gilman 361). The treatment prescribed by both her husband and her brother is to restrain from any activity they construed as "work" (Gilman 361). Gilman relates this to her own experience of when she suffered from severe and continuous nervous breakdown. She sought the advice of a specialist for nervous diseases who consequently prescribed to her the rest cure and advised her to "'live as domestic a life as far as possible,' to 'have but two hours' intellectual life a day,' and 'never to touch pen, brush, or pencil again' as long as [she] lived" (Gilman, "Why I Wrote"). Gilman's own renowned physician, Dr. Weir Mitchell, was quoted as saying:

> American woman is, to speak plainly, too often physically unfit for her duties as woman, and is perhaps of all civilized females the least qualified to undertake those weightier tasks which tax so heavily the nervous system of man. She is not fairly up to what

nature asks from her as wife and mother. How will she sustain herself under
the pressure of those yet more exacting
duties which nowadays she is eager to
share with the man? (Thomas)

During the late nineteenth century, it
was the widely accepted "notion that by keeping a clean, neat, pious home and filling it
with warmth and inviting smells, women are
achieving their highest calling" (Hartman).
Gilman expresses her disapproval of these
concepts through the narrator of her story
who says, "Personally, I believe that congenial work, with excitement and change would
do me good" (Gilman 361). Thus, the narrator turns to writing, her only source of
stimulus. However, she is met with "heavy
opposition" (Gilman 361). She strains for a
channel for her thoughts and feelings but
finds it "discouraging not to have any advice
and companionship about [her] work" (Gilman
363). The narrator is clearly a writer who
feels the necessity for a creative outlet,
but writing in solitude exhausts and dis-
heartens her. She resorts to subversive means
of relieving her thoughts but doesn't find

pleasure in doing so. The inability to write causes the narrator to start obsessing on the grotesque wallpaper in her room, where she spends hours tracing the "bloated curves and flourishes" (Gilman 364). As a result of her husband preventing her from doing any work, she has nothing to keep herself occupied. The narrator's unhealthy fixation on the yellow wallpaper eventually leads to her complete madness. Similarly, the author comments that when she was restricted from her work, she "came so near the borderline of utter mental ruin that [she] could see over" (Gilman, "Why I Wrote").

Another instance of her husband's op-pression which ultimately caused her men-tal breakdown is apparent when the narrator states, "At first he meant to repaper the room, but afterwards he said that I was let-ting it get the better of me, and that noth-ing was worse for a nervous patient than to give way to such fancies" (Gilman 362). The husband had already intended on changing the wallpaper because it was truly unappealing. However, when the narrator complained, he felt that action would be giving way to her whims and she passively accepts his decision. This idea is supported by Lisa Spiro who states in her essay "A Tragic Triumph: A Look at Individuality in 'The Yellow Wallpaper,'" "her passive acceptance of his decision against her desires signifies another failure on her part to exert her own will. Because she is . . . trying to please her husband, she puts aside her irritation by the paper, and focuses on the view . . ."

Another example occurs in "Struggle for Power," in which Melissa Grosso remarks, "She is forced to live with the wallpaper no matter how repulsed by it she is. Similarly, she is forced to live in a society and with a man who suppresses her thoughts and ideas and from whom she is trying to break free. John, who acts as the defining power in the narrator's life, is the authority that is reflected in her interpretation of the wallpaper." Thus, the narrator is forced to focus on an object she originally abhors. However, as a result of her husband's obstinacy, her repulsion slowly mutates into fascination. Not long after her initial reaction, the narrator claims that she is "getting really

fond of the room in spite of the wallpaper.
Perhaps because of the wallpaper" (Gilman
364), showing her growing obsession with the
yellow wallpaper. Then the narrator begins to
see glimpses of a shape and finally a woman
behind the wallpaper (Gilman 364-67). The
wallpaper turns into bars in the moonlight
and "the woman behind it as plain as can be"
(Gilman 367). The patterns on the wallpaper
becoming bars symbolizes her own prison with
her trapped inside. The woman trapped behind
the wallpaper is the narrator. Her husband's
refusal to remove the wallpaper represents
his domination over her. If he had removed
the wallpaper when she requested, and in essence her bars, her vivid imagination would
never have led to her unraveling sanity. In
essence, "she [becomes] swallowed up by her
own imagination, projected onto a pervasive
yellow wallpaper" (Spiro).

Towards the end of the story, while the
narrator is still hanging on to her thin
threads of mental clarity, she makes one last
attempt to persuade her husband to allow her
to leave the room. He remains adamant that
she is recovering and that they should re-

main until the allotted time (Gilman 366).
The final act of her husband's refusal to
allow her volition shreds her last threads
of reality. After her failure to break away
from her husband's control, the figure of a
woman definitively appears before the narrator. She no longer wants to leave but starts
obsessing over the woman behind the wallpaper. Soon she creates not only one but many
women, portraying the larger picture of society's oppression on women as a whole. The
narrator sees these women in the wallpaper
who are trying desperately to break through
the pattern on the wall that restrains them,
as an attempt to break society's restraints.
Yet as hard as they try, they never succeed
in breaking out: "They get through, and then
the pattern strangles them off and turns them
upside down, and makes their eyes white!"
(Gilman 369). She feels that "they are both
locked away under authority—the narrator by
her husband and society and the woman by
the confines of the wallpaper" (Grosso).
The narrator identifies with the women and
wants to be the one who releases them. This
is expressed when she exclaims, "no person

touches this paper but me—not alive!" (Gilman 370). She soon becomes paranoid that other people will take her away or prevent her from releasing the woman from her imprisonment (Gilman 369). Thus when the narrator is in private, she quickly tears down the wallpaper and in effect, "[makes] a jail break from which she was held" (Grosso). Her husband's ultimate act of refusal causes her to attempt to free herself and the women, illustrating her fall into utter and complete insanity.

Sadly, the narrator of the story wasn't always mentally unwired. In the beginning, when she first arrived at the estate, she still retained her full faculties. However, under the control of her husband, she starts her unhealthy obsession with the wallpaper— an obsession that would not have cause to originate if he had allowed her to make her own decisions. The husband restricts her from her most basic creative desires and the wallpaper distorts in the vivid imagination of the narrator to become the bars behind which she is trapped. As the ultimate result of her husband's constant overbearing dominance, the narrator loses her insanity. Ironically, this

madness is the one place "where she can have
supreme control, and nothing will contest it"
(Spiro). In her attempt to rebel against her
husband's rule and society's shackles, the
narrator liberates herself by tearing down
the wallpaper, and symbolically, the chains
that bind her. By doing so, she has reached
the final point of insanity, driven there by
her husband, where she can finally be free.

Works Cited

Gilman, Charlotte Perkins. "Why I Wrote 'The
    Yellow Wallpaper.'" *The Forerunner*. Oct.
    1913. 10 June 2005 <http://www.kino-eye.
    com/yp/whyiwrote.html>.

———. "The Yellow Wallpaper." *An
    Introduction to Literature*. 13th ed. Eds.
    Sylvan Barnet, William Burto, and William
    E. Cain. New York: Longman, 2004. 360-71.

Grosso, Melissa. "Struggle for Power." *The Honors Review* (2000). Southern Connecticut State University. 10 June 2005. <http://www.southernct.edu/organizations/hcr/2000/nonfiction/astruggleforpower.htm>.

Hartman, Dorothy. "Women's Roles in the Late 19th Century." Conner Prairie Living History Museum. 10 June 2005. <http://www.connerprairie.org/HistoryOnline/1880wom.html>.

Spiro, Lisa M. "A Tragic Triumph: A Look at Individuality in 'The Yellow Wallpaper.'" 10 June 2005 <http://sparta.rice.edu/~lspiro/portfolio/wallpapr.htm>.

Thomas, Deborah. "The Changing Role of Womanhood: From True Woman to New Woman in Charlotte Perkins Gilman's 'The Yellow Wallpaper.'" American Literature and Research Web site. 10 June 2005. <http://itech.fgcu.edu/faculty/wohlpart/alra/gilman.htm>.

SAMPLE STUDENT APA RESEARCH REPORT

NOTE: When submitting an APA formatted research report, include a separate title page and center the following information: the title of the paper, your name, the professor's name, the course number and section, and the due date of the assignment. The next page should contain an abstract of your report of roughly 100–150 words. On the following page, include the title of your report (centered on the page) and then start your report. In the upper right-hand corner of each page of your report (in the header field of the page), include an abbreviated form of your report title and the page number. Use the insert header feature in your word processor.

```
Running Head: THE ACCEPTANCE OF OSTEOPATHY


        The Acceptance of Osteopathy
     as an Orthodox Form of Medicine
           Chandrika Balgobin


              WRIT 316-W01
        Dr. David S. Hogsette
           June 27, 2005
```

The Acceptance of Osteopathy   2

Abstract

This report discusses the acceptance of osteopathy as an orthodox form of medicine. It explores how osteopathy has developed from its inception in 1874 to the present. In addition, this report observes osteopathy's legal status across the United States and throughout the world. Challenges osteopaths faced in gaining acceptance are also noted. This report includes a background of osteopathic medicine, a brief history, its current legal status in the United States, its international legal status, and conclusions based on findings. Osteopathy continues to grow, but still faces a number of issues that challenge its growth.

The Acceptance of Osteopathy as an Orthodox
Form of Medicine

Introduction

This report is about osteopathy's quest
for acceptance as an orthodox form of medicine. Although it is a separate but equal
form of medicine compared to allopathic medicine, osteopathy is relatively new. As such,
many people are not familiar with it, or have
misconceptions regarding it. Osteopathic
medicine is a growing field, and can only
grow further as the public will allow it to.
If one does not feel that it is a legitimate form of medicine, he/she may not take
it seriously, or be hesitant to try it. This
report will discuss osteopathy, its overall
legal status, and its challenges in gaining
acceptance.

A Background of Osteopathic Medicine
An Overview of Osteopathic Medicine

Osteopathic medicine is a form of holistic medicine which emphasizes structural and
functional relationships in the body. It has,
as a guiding principle, the body's ability

The Acceptance of Osteopathy   4

to heal itself within the unity of the body,
mind, and spirit. Osteopathy places an emphasis on preventative medicine. This approach
to medicine offers decreased healing time
with preventative medicine, decreased side
effects with less emphasis on medication, and
more personal interactions between a patient
and a doctor.

Osteopathic Principles

The basis of the osteopathic approach
lies in its principles. The first principle
is the unity of the body, mind, and spirit
of a person. If there is a factor affecting
any of these, the others will be affected in
some form. The next principle is the inter-
relation of structure and function. If there
is a problem with either, the other will be
limited. The third principle of osteopathy is
the body's tendency towards homeostasis. The
body has a propensity to influence healing,
or restore homeostasis. However, it is necessary to note that if the body is unable to
resolve the problem by itself, the condition
may worsen.

Another perspective osteopathy places emphasis on is the role of the musculoskeletal system in influencing organ systems. As such, an aspect of osteopathy includes manipulative therapy, known as osteopathic manipulative treatment. Osteopathy also supports preventative medicine, or the lifestyles of its patient. This theory, which supports proper nutrition and exercise, enables a healthy lifestyle and promotes overall health. In doing so, it allows one to resist the chance of sickness (Collinge, 1997).

A Brief History of Osteopathy
The Need for a Change

Existing medicine in the United States in the nineteenth century was crude and few professionals based it on science. Medicine of the time was largely based on superstition. The focus of medicine was to treat symptoms, not alleviate the cause of the disease. According to Gevitz (2004), osteopathy began as a revolution against the pre-existing system of medicine.

Andrew Taylor Still

Andrew Taylor Still, a physician of that time, became disillusioned with the practice of medicine, due to the deaths of his wife and children from spinal meningitis. He went on to develop osteopathy in 1874, using structural and functional relationships as a key in understanding the human body and the means by which a disease may develop (Collinge, 1997).

Osteopathy has developed vastly from Andrew Taylor Still's day, with the inception of the first osteopathic school founded in 1892. According to the American Association of Colleges of Osteopathic Medicine (2005), there are twenty accredited osteopathic medical schools open across the United States of America.

Osteopathy's Current Legal Status in the United States

The AMA's Initial Response to Osteopathy

There has been a continuous battle over the acceptance of osteopathy as a valid form of medicine from the moment Andrew Taylor Still initiated the theory of osteopathy up

The Acceptance of Osteopathy   7

until now, over one hundred years after its
inception. According to Bob E. Jones (1978),
the American Medical Association (AMA) dismissed osteopathic medicine early on because
it did not think that these ideas would
survive in the long run. Contrary to this
belief, osteopathic medicine continues to develop into what it is today.

World War I and Osteopathy

At the beginning of World War I, Doctors
of Osteopathy offered their services to the
armed forces, but were denied this opportunity. The American Medical Association's
response to this offer was that they were
neither equipped nor prepared for such a duty
(Jones, 1978). Although legislative bodies
said it was shown that D.O.'s had completed
equivalent courses of study and their per-
formances on licensing exams were equal to
or better than that of M.D.'s, the AMA still
opposed them. D.O.'s were still not allowed
to serve in the armed forces as physicians
(Jones, 1978). At one point, the Surgeon
General William Crawford Gorgas said that if
D.O.'s were accepted by the armed forces,

The Acceptance of Osteopathy   8

then allopathic physicians would not enlist
(Jones, 1978). This is an example of the
challenges osteopathic physicians were given
to prevent them from being integrated into
the healthcare system as their allopathic
counterparts were.

World War II's Effect on Osteopathy's Growth

In World War II, osteopathic physicians
were once again denied entry into the armed
forces as physicians. However, this worked in
their favor this time. As many of the allopathic physicians were being enlisted in the
armed forces, this led to a decrease in the
amount of M.D.'s available for civilian use.
This shortage of M.D.'s gave the osteopathic
physicians an opportunity to work with civilians more so than before. In addition, civilians were given the opportunity to experience
osteopathy first hand. This opportunity allowed osteopaths to increase public awareness, in regards to osteopathic medicine.
After much trials and tribulations, the U.S.
government ordered the armed forces to accept
D.O.'s for military service in 1966. In 1973,

The Acceptance of Osteopathy   9

osteopathic physicians were granted full licensure in all the states (Jones, 1978).

Osteopathy's International Legal Status

How Osteopathy Is Acknowledged
Internationally

Though osteopathic physicians have come a long way, they still have not gained full acceptance as physicians that are acknowledged internationally. Not being able to practice as a physician on an international level gives people the impression that osteopathy is less valid than allopathic medicine. In Canada and America, osteopaths are recognized as physicians, whereas in Europe they are not.

European Osteopathic Diplomas

In Europe, according to the International Academy of Osteopathy (2005), one can follow a five year course of become a Diplomated Osteopath (D.O.), or obtain a Bachelor of Science with Honors in Osteopathy (B.Sc. [Hons] in Ost.). This discrepancy from one nation to another makes the field of osteopathy seem less valid, as accreditations for osteopaths are not uniform.

Osteopathy in Australia

The attempt to spread the osteopathic philosophy has resulted in an increase in the amount of osteopathic colleges on an international level. For example, there was an establishment of the Chiropractic and Osteopathic College of Australasia in Queensland, Australia, which serves to increase the osteopathic philosophy (Walker, 2005). However, its graduates are not considered physicians and are only allowed to use manipulation as their only form of therapy. Although this increases osteopathic awareness, it also makes the international view of osteopathy seem solely related to chiropractic and manipulation techniques. As such, the public may not realize that osteopathy is an orthodox form of medicine, which is separate but equal to allopathic medicine.

Conclusion

Osteopathy is a steadily growing field of medicine. Although osteopaths are consid-

The Acceptance of Osteopathy   11

ered equivalent to allopathic physicians in
the United States and Canada, the public is
not often aware of osteopathy and its phi-
losophies. This can be resolved by increasing public awareness of osteopathic medicine.
Osteopathy's status should be preserved as
separate, but equal to allopathic medicine.
The international status of osteopathy must
be further developed, in order for osteopathy
to grow as a field. Once this occurs, osteopaths should have a uniform international
accreditation. This will help citizens understand that osteopathy is an orthodox form of
medicine. In addition, osteopathy should not
be misconceived as equivalent to the practice
of chiropractors. Once these issues are recognized and resolved, osteopathy can further
grow in its own right.

The Acceptance of Osteopathy   12

References

American Association of Colleges of
    Osteopathic Medicine. (2005). *Colleges
    by geographic region*. Retrieved June 22,
    2005, from http://www.aacom.org/data/
    cib/16-geographic.asp.

Collinge, W. (1997). *The American Holistic
    Health Association complete guide to
    .alternative medicine*. New York: Warner
    Press.

Gevitz, N. (2004). *The D.O.'s: Osteopathic
    medicine in America (2nd ed.)*. Baltimore:
    Johns Hopkins University Press.

Jones, B. E. (1978). *The difference a D.O.
    makes: Osteopathic medicine in the twenti-
    eth century*. Oklahoma City: Times-Journal
    Publishing Company.

The International Academy of Osteopathy.
    (2005). *Diplomas*. Retrieved June 22, 2005,
    from http://www.iao.be/eng/diplomas.htm

Walker, B. F. (2005). The establishment of
    the Chiropractic & Osteopathic College of

The Acceptance of Osteopathy   13

Australasia in Queensland. *Chiropractic & Osteopathy, 13*(3). Retrieved June 22, 2005, from http://www.chiroandosteo.com/content/13/1/3.

CHECKLIST FOR WRITING THE RESEARCH PAPER

✓ Establish a clear idea of topic (consider preliminary research to identify topic and narrow focus).

✓ Develop specific research questions.

✓ Conduct careful search for appropriate resources based upon the objectives of your research questions.

✓ Critically evaluate your resources before studying them.

✓ Narrow your resources to the most appropriate for your topic.

✓ Carefully study and analyze your resources.

✓ Take detailed notes of your sources. Consider using a computer word processor when taking and organizing notes.

✓ Review your notes and establish your thesis (the main answer to your research question).

✓ Organize and catalog your notes based upon the main focus, purpose, and message of your research paper.

✓ Develop a general outline to guide you as you write your paper.

✓ Draft your research paper based upon your thesis and outline. Be open to making changes to your focus and organization as you are writing.

✓ Use the proper format (MLA or APA, for example), according to your professor's instruction.

✓   Cite your material properly to avoid plagiarism.

✓   Carefully revise your draft, looking to the larger issues of focus, thesis, organization, argument, content, discussion, and analysis.

✓   Carefully edit your paper, focusing on the sentence-level issues of proper citation, grammar, spelling, and sentence structure.

✓   Submit your paper by the due date according to your professor's instruction. If you are submitting the document in print, make sure it is a clean printing and bind it according to your professor's instruction. If you are submitting the document online (via e-mail or a learning environment like Blackboard or WebCT), make sure you have saved the document in the appropriate file format according to your professor's instruction (MS Word document, Rich Text, or PDF file, for example).

✓   Keep a backup copy of your paper.

CONCLUSION

The research paper is one of the most challenging writing assignments you will face in college. However, when written properly it can also be one of the most satisfying assignments of your college career. The research paper allows you to identify an issue or question that interests you or that truly captivates your imagination and then allows you the opportunity to investigate that topic thoroughly. Try not to view the research paper as just another academic chore that you must complete in order to get a grade or to pass a course. Instead, view the research paper assignment as an opportunity to learn, to grow, to develop your understanding of a topic, and to share your learning experience with others (namely your professor and other students).

Generally, we view *chores* as a negative task and we do what we can to get them done as quickly and painlessly as possible. On the other hand, we usually view *opportunities* as exciting tasks with unforeseen benefits, and we often do our very best to achieve success and to grasp the positive outcomes of an opportunity. The research paper will be a difficult challenge, but if we view it as an opportunity, we are more likely to do our very best and to achieve great things. The research paper is also an opportunity to develop our information literacy skills. Being literate in its most basic sense means being able to read. However, in the information age, it is not enough simply to be able to read. We also must be able to identify questions and learning objectives, to develop strategies for answering our questions through research, to find and evaluate appropriate sources, to think critically about the sources, and to use them to develop our own understanding of a topic and our position on issues. This is what it means to be information literate. As you learn more about research papers and as you write them in your various classes, be aware that you are learning how to learn, and you are developing your information literacy skills so that you will be a more effective evaluator and user of information.

DISCUSSION QUESTIONS

1. What was your view of research writing before reading this chapter? In what ways has your view of research writing changed (or not) after reading this chapter?

2. What is information literacy and how is it related to the research paper?

3. What is the function of the research paper in higher education? What critical thinking skills can you develop by writing research papers?

4. What is plagiarism and how can you avoid it?

5. What are the two main reasons for including proper citation in your research papers?

GROUP ACTIVITIES

1. As a group, pick a topic in which all group members have some interest. Individually, conduct some research, make a list of ten sources on that topic, then share with each other what sources you found. Discuss what strategies you used to find them.

2. Pick some topic or issue for a group presentation. Assign research roles for each team member. Compile your information and organize your findings into a cohesive presentation. Present your findings to the class and prepare for a question-and-answer period. Submit to your professor a properly formatted bibliography of your sources (using the MLA or APA format).

3. Pick some topic or issue for a team research paper. Assign research roles for each team member. Compile your information and organize your findings into a cohesive research paper. Consider using the division of labor method in which different team members write different sections of the paper. Be sure to read it through carefully and to smooth out the language such that all the sections fit together nicely to advance your main focus or purpose. Be sure to format the paper properly, using either the MLA or APA format.

WRITING ACTIVITIES

1. Pick a topic or issue that you care deeply about and then conduct some preliminary research. From your findings, develop five research questions that could be pursued on that one topic.

2. Pick a topic or issue that you care deeply about and identify a narrow research question. Conduct library and online research and compile a list of ten sources. Write a short essay (500–1,000 words) in which you analyze your process and explain what you learned about finding sources. Be sure to explain how and why you chose those ten sources; that is, explain what evaluative criteria you used when choosing your sources.

3. Choose a topic or issue you care deeply about. Identify a narrow research question and locate ten good sources. With your research question in mind, narrow those sources down to five of the best sources. Write an annotated bibliography of those sources: list each source in alphabetical order, using the MLA or APA format; after each entry, write a brief paragraph in which you summarize what the source says and explain how you would use that source in a research paper.

4. If you have done any one or all three of the above activities, next write a research paper based upon the work you have already completed (identifying a research question, compiling a list of sources, and narrowing your sources in order to analyze and to take notes on them). Write a well-focused, clearly organized, and fully developed research paper in which you answer your main research question using the sources you found. Format the paper using the MLA or APA format.

PART THREE

A Critical Thinking Reader

14

Readings

What's So Great about America?
Dinesh D'Souza

Dinesh D'Souza is widely considered to be among America's most prominent Asian Americans, one of the most important public-policy special-
ists, and one of America's most important conservative thinkers. D'Souza
graduated Phi Beta Kappa from Dartmouth College in 1983, where he wrote
for the nationally recognized student paper, *The Dartmouth Review*. From
1985 to 1987 he was managing editor of *Policy Review*, and from 1987 to
1988 he served as the senior policy analyst for President Ronald Reagan.
He was the John M. Olin Fellow at the American Enterprise Institute and
is now the Robert and Karen Rishwain Fellow at the Hoover Institution of
Stanford University. He is the author of several best-selling books, including *What's So Great about America* (2002), *Letters to a Young Conservative*
(2002), *Illiberal Education* (1991), *The End of Racism* (1995), and *Ronald
Reagan: How an Ordinary Man Became an Extraordinary Leader* (1997).
D'Souza's articles have appeared in nearly every major newspaper and
news magazine in America, and he speaks at top universities and business
groups across the nation. Learn more at dineshdsouza.com.

Essay Classification: Informative; argumentation/persuasion

IN RECENT YEARS, WE'VE heard a great deal about "why they hate us"
and about why America is so bad. What the critiques often miss is

what is good and even great about America. As an immigrant who grew up in Mumbai, India, I believe that the patriotism of Americans would be strengthened if people had a better understanding of why this country is unique.

In my book *What's So Great about America*, I ask: Why do millions of immigrants seek every year to come to America? Why is the idea of America so fascinating and attractive to people—especially young people—around the world?

Critics of America, both at home and abroad, have an easy explanation for why the American idea is so captivating and why immigrants want to come here. The reason, they say, is that America represents "the bitch goddess of success." In this view, immigrants flock to the United States for the sole purpose of getting rich. The critics hope to demean America by associating it with greed and selfishness. Their explanation, however, is so partial that it amounts to a distortion. It misses the deepest source of America's appeal.

There is enough truth in the critics' account to give it a surface plausibility. Certainly America offers a degree of mobility and opportunity unavailable elsewhere, not even in Europe. Even more significant, America gives a better life to the ordinary guy than does any other country. Let's be honest: rich people live well everywhere. America's greatness is that it has extended the benefits of affluence, traditionally available to the very few, to a large segment in society. We live in a nation where "poor" people have TV sets and microwave ovens, where construction workers cheerfully spend $4 on a nonfat latte, where maids drive very nice cars, where plumbers take their families on vacation to the Caribbean. Recently I asked an acquaintance in Bombay why he has been trying so hard to relocate to America. He replied, "I really want to move to a country where the poor people are fat."

The typical immigrant, who is used to the dilapidated infrastructure, mind-numbing inefficiency, and multilayered corruption of Third World countries, arrives in America to discover, to his wonder and delight, that everything works: the roads are clean and paper-smooth, the highway signs are clear and accurate, the public toilets function properly, when you pick up the telephone you get a dial tone, you can even buy things from the store and then take them back. The American supermarket is a thing to behold: endless aisles of every imaginable product, 50 different types of cereal, innumerable flavors of ice cream. The place is full of unappreciated inventions: quilted toilet paper, fabric softener, cordless phones, disposable diapers, and roll-on luggage.

So, yes, in material terms America offers the newcomer a better life. Still, the material allure of America does not capture the deepest source of its appeal. Consider how my own life would have been different had I never come to America. I was raised in a middle-class family in Mumbai. I didn't have luxuries, but I didn't lack necessities. Materially my life is better in the United States, but the real difference lies elsewhere.

Had I stayed in India, I would probably live my entire existence within a five-mile radius of where I was born. I would undoubtedly have married a woman of my identical caste and religious and socioeconomic background. I would have faced relentless pressure to become an engineer, like my father, or a doctor, like my grandfather. My socialization would have been entirely within my own ethnic community. I would have had a whole set of opinions that could be predicted in advance.

Because I came to America, though, I have seen my life break free of these traditional confines. In college I became interested in literature and politics, and resolved to make a career as a writer, which is something you can do in America, and cannot easily do in India. I married a woman of English, Scottish, French, and German ancestry.

Eventually I found myself working in the White House, even though I was not an American citizen. I cannot imagine another country allowing a noncitizen to work in the inner citadel of its government.

In most of the world, even today, your identity and your fate are largely handed to you. In America, by contrast, you get to write the script of your own life. What to be, where to live, who to love, who to marry, what to believe, what religion to practice—these are all decisions that, in America, we make for ourselves. Here we are the architects of our own fate.

The "self-directed life" is the incredibly powerful idea that is behind the worldwide appeal of the United States. Young people throughout the world find irresistible the prospect of being in the driver's seat of their own destiny. So, too, the immigrant discovers that America permits him to break free of the constraints that have held him captive, so that the future becomes a landscape of his own choosing.

CRITICAL THINKING QUESTIONS

1. What is D'Souza's main thesis? Comment on how he sets up his thesis in the introductory paragraphs.

2. To make his case, D'Souza presents information, facts, and personal testimony. What facts or information did you find surprising? Why?

3. The political left in America and abroad are quick to blame America for the world's problems and to focus on the sins of America's past and present. D'Souza notes that such critics miss the bigger picture and ignore the uniquely good aspects of America. Discuss some of these unique qualities. Do you agree or disagree that these are important good elements of America? Explain.

4. In your own opinion, what is so good or not so good about America? Explain.

≈

My Dad's Barbershop—and Personal Responsibility
Larry Elder

Larry Elder is a native of South Central Los Angeles, and he received his bachelor's degree in political science from Brown University and a law degree from the University of Michigan. He worked in a law firm in Cleveland, Ohio, before opening his own attorney recruiter business, Lawrence A. Elder and Associates. He hosted a television program on PBS and then on a local Fox News affiliate. His articles regularly appear in leading newspapers and newsmagazines across the nation, he writes a monthly newsletter called "The Elder Statement," and his newspaper column is syndicated through Creators Syndicate. He is also the best-selling author of such books as *The Ten Things You Can't Say in America* (2000) and *Showdown: Confronting Bias, Lies, and the Special Interests that Divide America* (2002). The following essay appeared in *Townhall.com* in 2005.

Essay Classification: Personal narrative; argumentation/persuasion

WHILE OFF FOR THE holidays, I took my 90-year-old, former Marine, Republican dad to his inner-city barbershop. Dad goes to the same barbershop that my brothers and I went to when we were growing up. Different people now own the shop, and I hadn't set foot in there in probably 35 years. Is it still, I asked Dad, the same "afro-centric," white-man-done-me-wrong, trash-talking joint? "Yes," sighed my father, who taught my brothers and me to overcome racism through hard work and personal responsibility.

When we get there, it's packed. Two barbers, cutting hair, with about six or seven people waiting. But the walls no longer sport posters of an angry, finger-pointing Malcolm X, or Elijah Muhammad, the founder of the anti-Semitic Nation of Islam, or Marcus Garvey, who urged blacks to leave racist America and return to Africa. I remember them staring down at me as my barber ranted about how "the white man" oppresses us. But on this day, as my dad and I walk in, one of the barbers recognizes me.

Barber: Mr. Larry Elder, how you doin'?

Larry: This is my dad. (My taciturn dad never told him that the notorious Sage from South Central was his son.) How many ahead of him?

Barber: Two.

The barber offered to take my dad right away, cutting in front of others, but dad and I quickly refused. As we waited, one of the barbers and I began talking about what the barber called the "problem of racism." I argued that racism no longer posed a significant obstacle to black progress. What other country could produce a Colin Powell, a Condi Rice, an Oprah Winfrey, a Tiger Woods, a Barack Obama and a Snoop Dogg?

Larry: What about my dad? How did he manage? How do you compare what it's like now to what it was like then? He grew up in the Jim Crow South during the Depression, when black adult unemployment was 50 percent. He dropped out of school at age 13, after his mother threw him out of the house in favor of her then-boyfriend. Hard jobs followed, and he served in World War II. When he came out, he worked two full-time jobs as a janitor, cooked for a family on the weekends and went to night school to get his high school G.E.D. He saved his money and somehow managed to start a restaurant when he was in his 40s, which he ran until he was in his 80s. If racism didn't stop him then, how can racism stop you today? And he votes Republican!

Most of the customers, and the barbers, start laughing. But another customer could take it no longer.

Customer: But you have to admit, Elder, that the playing field is not level. White people have more money and more property than we do.

Larry: (Turning to him.) Let's say I'm white and I got money. (Laughter.) Either I worked for it or my dad worked for it, or my grandfather worked for it and I inherited it. Still, it's my money. And guess what—I'm not giving it to you! I'm sorry about Rodney King. I'm sorry about Emmett Till. I'm sorry about Rosa Parks. I'm not giving you my money. I'm sorry they turned water hoses and dogs on Martin Luther King. I'm sorry about Rosewood. I'm sorry about the Tuskegee Experiment. I'm not giving you my money. I'm sorry about slavery. I'm sorry about Jim Crow. But I never owned a slave, and I don't use the 'N' word. I am not giving you my money.

The barbers laughed.

Larry: Now, what are you gonna do about it? Take it from me? Hah! I believe in the 2nd Amendment, and I own a gun. (More laughter.) Try and come and get it. (More laughter.) Try and take it from me through politics, and I'm gonna vote Republican to keep my taxes down. (More laughter.) Now I ask you again, what do you intend to do about it? Let me offer a suggestion—invest in yourself. Get an education, learn a trade or a skill, get a job, and get your own stuff. So you can BMW—bitch, moan and whine—all you want. But I am not giving you my money.

By now, most of the men in the barbershop, including the barbers, laughed.

Barber: The man makes sense.

Larry: When can we blacks get to the point where you and I can have a disagreement—about racism, affirmative action, the war in Iraq, whatever—without someone who thinks like me being a sellout or an Uncle Tom? Is that at all possible? Am I asking too much?

Barber: (Smiling.) No, man, that's not asking too much.

While driving home, my dad said, "That was something, Larry."

"No, Dad," I said, "*you* are something. Besides, I said nothing you hadn't heard before—or said."

CRITICAL THINKING QUESTIONS

1. Elder discusses a very sensitive issue: how the black community deals with racism and its effects on individuals and communities. How does his use of personal narrative defuse some of the tension?

2. Discuss Elder's main point or conclusion regarding how discrimination (regardless of its form) should be handled. To what extent do you agree or disagree with Elder? Explain.

3. In the midst of the barbershop debate, one of the barbers, between laughs, noted that Elder's points made sense. How so? Do you agree or disagree? Why?

4. Were you surprised to learn that Elder, an African American from a poor background, is a conservative and votes Republican, as does his conservative father? Why or why not?

5. Did you know that historically, African Americans since 1870 voted primarily Republican until the 1930s? Why was this the case? What changed?

6. Since the 1930s, some African Americans started to join the Democratic Party. After the 1960s African Americans have largely voted Democrat. Why? Do African Americans seem to still have the same grievances today as in the 1960s? What does this say about Democratic leadership for minorities?

7. Elder notes that conservative African Americans are often ridiculed and dismissed as "Uncle Toms" or "sellouts" or "wanna bes" (i.e., wanna be white). Is this fair? Given the nobility, hard work, and success of African American conservatives like Elder and his father, should the black community consider more carefully their allegiance to the Democratic Party and at least investigate conservatism and the Republican Party? What should both parties do to address social concerns of African Americans and other minorities? Explain.

Curing Poverty or Using Poverty?
Thomas Sowell

Thomas Sowell was born in North Carolina and grew up in Harlem. He dropped out of high school and entered the Marines, serving as a photographer in the Korean War. After the service, he studied economics at Harvard University and graduated magna cum laude. He later received his master's in economics from Columbia University and his doctorate in economics from the University of Chicago. He has held professorships at such universities as Cornell, Rutgers, Amherst, Brandeis, and UCLA. He has published a dozen books and numerous articles and essays on economics, social justice, and civil rights. He is the winner of the prestigious Francis Boyer Award from The American Enterprise Institute, and he is currently a senior fellow at the Hoover Institution in Stanford University. The following essay appeared in *Townhall.com* in 2006.

Essay Classification: Argumentation/persuasion; informative

"CHINA IS LIFTING A million people a month out of poverty." It is just one statement in an interesting new book titled *The Undercover Economist* by Tim Harford. But it has huge implications.

I haven't checked out the statistics but they sound reasonable. If so, this is something worth everyone's attention.

People on the political left make a lot of noise about poverty and advocate all sorts of programs and policies to reduce it but they show incredibly little interest in how poverty has actually been reduced, whether in China or anywhere else.

You can bet the rent money that the left will show little or no interest in how Chinese by the millions are rising out of poverty every year. The left showed far more interest in China back when it was run by Mao in far left fashion—and when millions of Chinese were starving.

Those of us who are not on the left ought to take a closer look at today's Chinese rising out of poverty.

First of all, what does it even mean to say that "China is lifting a million people a month out of poverty"? Where would the Chinese government get the money to do that?

The only people the Chinese government can tax are mainly the people in China. A country can't lift itself up by its own bootstraps that way. Nor has there ever been enough foreign aid to lift a million people a month out of poverty.

If the Chinese government hasn't done it, then who has? The Chinese people. They did not rise out of poverty by receiving largess from anybody.

The only thing that can cure poverty is wealth. The Chinese acquired wealth the old-fashioned way: They created it.

After the death of Mao, government controls over the market began to be relaxed—first tentatively, in selected places and for selected industries. Then, as those places and those industries began to prosper dramatically, similar relaxations of government control took place elsewhere, with similar results.

Even foreigners were allowed to come in and invest in China and sell their goods in China. But this was not just a transfer of wealth.

Foreigners did not come in to help the Chinese but to help themselves. The only way they could benefit, and the Chinese benefit at the same time, was if more total wealth was created. That is what happened but the political left has virtually no interest in the creation of wealth, in China or anywhere else, despite all of their proclaimed concern for "the poor."

Since wealth is the only thing that can cure poverty, you might think that the left would be as obsessed with the creation of wealth as they are with the redistribution of wealth. But you would be wrong.

When it comes to lifting people out of poverty, redistribution of income and wealth has a much poorer and more spotty track record than the creation of wealth. In some places, such as Zimbabwe today, attempts at a redistribution of wealth have turned out to be a redistribution of poverty.

While the creation of wealth may be more effective for enabling millions of people to rise out of poverty, it provides no special role for the political left, no puffed up importance, no moral superiority, no power for them to wield over others. Redistribution is clearly better for the left.

Leftist emphasis on "the poor" proceeds as if the poor were some separate group. But, in most Western countries, at least, millions of people who are "poor" at one period of their lives are "rich" at another period of their lives—as these terms are conventionally defined.

How can that be? People tend to become more productive—create more wealth—over time, with more experience and an accumulation of skills and training.

That is reflected in incomes that are two or three times higher in later years than at the beginning of a career. But that too is of little or no interest to the political left.

Things that work for millions of people offer little to the left, and ultimately the left is about the left, not about the people they claim to want to lift out of poverty.

CRITICAL THINKING QUESTIONS

1. Can you list any communist regime or far-left government that has successfully reduced poverty and increased wealth? Consider such nations as the former Soviet Union, China, Cuba, North Korea, Cambodia, Vietnam, and the numerous communist or leftist dictatorships of Africa and Central and South America. How successful have these governments been in alleviating poverty?

2. According to Sowell, what is the new China doing now which its citizens did not do before? What is this "new" model of economics used by China? Is it really new? Why is it successful?

3. Why do those on the political left ignore historical realities such as failed communist states and the material successes of capitalism and free enterprise? What happens to the political left if individuals are empowered to earn and create wealth themselves so that they are not dependent upon the government?

4. What is the difference between the creation of new wealth and redistribution of static or unchanging wealth? Which would you prefer and why?

5. Conservatives advocate individual economic freedom and the creation of wealth; liberals advocate dependence upon the state or government programs and redistribution of wealth. Given what you've learned from Sowell about creation of wealth versus redistribution of wealth, would you rather support economic conservatives or liberals? Why?

∾

Why I'm Optimistic about America
Daniel J. Boorstin

Daniel J. Boorstin was a leading American historian and writer. He received his undergraduate degree with honors from Harvard and later earned a Ph.D. from Yale University. President Gerald Ford appointed Boorstin to be Librarian of Congress and he served there from 1975 to 1987. He was also director of the Smithsonian's National Museum of History and Technology. He was a lawyer and university professor and the author of over 20 books on history, sociology, and intellectual history. In 1973 he won the Pulitzer Prize in history for his book *The Americans: The Democratic Experience*. Boorstin's theoretical concept of "pseudo-events," discussed in his book *The Image: A Guide to Pseudo-Events in America* (1962), informed decades of social theory and laid the foundations for theorizing postmodernity and hyperreality. In the following essay, Boorstin provides specific arguments for his optimism concerning America, even in the face of such negative views from many detractors within the country and its critics abroad. The following essay appeared in *Parade* in 1995.

Essay Classification: Informative; synthesis; argumentation/persuasion

You ASK WHAT IS the basis for my optimism. With a Europe in disarray in a century plagued by two murderous World Wars, by genocides without precedent—the German-Nazi massacre of six million and the Stalin-Soviet massacre of 30 million—how can I speak so hopefully about the American future?

One answer is very personal. I was raised and went to public school in the 1920s in Tulsa, Oklahoma, which then called itself "The Oil Capital of the World," but could perhaps have been called "The Optimism Capital of the World." Only ten years before my family came to Oklahoma, the Indian Territory had been admitted to the Union as the forty-sixth state.

The city thrived on "booster" pride, and before I graduated from Central High School, it boasted two daily newspapers, three skyscrapers, houses designed by Frank Lloyd Wright, and a public-school system superintended by the former U.S. Commissioner of Education. The Kiwanis, Rotary, and Chamber of Commerce competed furiously in projects of civic improvement. For our high school English classes, we memorized and declaimed patriotic orations—from Patrick Henry's "Give Me Liberty or Give Me Death" and Lincoln's "Gettysburg Address" to Henry Grady's "The New South" and Emile Zola's "Plea for Dreyfus." We wrote speeches on the virtues of the federal Constitution for a national contest, which held its finals before the Supreme Court in Washington.

Of course there were dark shadows—like the relentless racial segregation, the brutal race riots of the 1920s, and the Ku Klux Klan. But these were not visible or prominent in my life. The city burgeoned, proudly built a grand new railroad depot, a university, an elegant public library and a city hall—and soon it was embellished by art museums of national rank.

My father was one of the most enthusiastic "boosters," and the growing city seemed to justify his extravagant optimism. I came to sympathize with that American frontier newspaperman who was attacked for reporting as facts the mythic marvels of his upstart pioneer village—including its impressive hotel and prosperous Main Street. In America, he said, it was not fair to object to the rosy reports of community boosters simply because they had "not yet gone through the formality of taking place." I suppose I have never been cured of my distinctively American Oklahoma optimism, bred in the bone and confirmed by the real history of Tulsa.

Another reason for my optimism is in American history. The exhilarating features of our history and culture have in the past been captured in the idea of "American Exceptionalism." This is a long word for a simple idea: the traditional belief that the United States is a very special place, unique in crucial ways. American Exceptionalism is a name too for a cosmopolitan, optimistic, and humanistic view of history—that the modern world, while profiting from the European inheritance, need not be imprisoned in Old World molds. And, therefore, that the future of the United States and of its people need not be governed by the same expectations or plagued by the same problems that had afflicted people elsewhere.

How have we lost sight of this beacon?

We have been seduced by the rise of our country as a "superpower." For while power is quantitative, the uniqueness of the United States is not merely quantitative. We have suffered, too, from the consequences of our freedom. Totalitarian societies exaggerate their virtues. But free societies like ours somehow seize the temptation to exaggerate their vices. The negativism of our press and television reporting are, of course, the best evidence of our freedom to scrutinize ourselves. Far better this than the chauvinism of self-righteousness which has been the death of totalitarian empires in our time.

Yet we must never forget that, while to the Old World we were the Unexpected Land, we have ever since been the Land of the Unexpected. The main features of the culture of our United States are just what the wise men of Europe, looking at their own past, could not have conjured up. A short list of the American surprises includes what we have done here with four basic elements of culture—religion, language, law, and wealth.

Religion. By the time of the European settlement of North America, the history of the rising nations of Western Europe had been punctuated by torture and massacre in the name of religion. There was the notorious Spanish Inquisition of the 15th century (1478), the bloody Massacre of Bartholomew (1572) in France and, in Germany during the very years of the Puritan settlements in New England, the Thirty Years War (1618–1648), which spread into a general conflict between Protestant and Catholic Europe. In that war alone, some 10 percent of the German population was slaughtered in the name of religious orthodoxy.

This seemed not to augur well for a nation like ours, whose Pilgrims were obsessed with religion and had fled England to fulfill their passionate dream. Their religious faith gave them courage to brave the ocean-crossing, the hardships of an unknown land, and the risks of hostile natives, despite their lonely remoteness from ancestral homes.

Who could have predicted that the United States, unlike the nations from which our people came, would never suffer a religious war? That the Protestants and Catholics who had tortured and massacred each other in Europe would establish peaceful neighboring communities from New England to Maryland and Virginia? That Jews would here find asylum from ghettos and pogroms? That—though the United States would remain conspicuously a nation of churchgoers—the separation of church and state would become a cornerstone of civic life? Or that public-school principals in the twentieth century would be challenged by how to promote a holiday spirit without seeming to favor or neglect Christmas, Hanukkah, or Kwanzaa?

Language. In Europe, languages had made nations. Spanish, Portuguese, English, French, German, and Italian had produced their own literatures—even before there was a Spain, a Portugal, an England, a France, a Germany, or an Italy. But the United States was the first great modern nation without its own language. Our country has been uniquely created by people willing and able to borrow a language.

Oddly enough, the English language has helped make us a congenitally multicultural nation, since most Americans have not come from the land of Shakespeare. So we have learned here that people do not lose their civic dignity by speaking the language of a new community. The English language has been invigorated and Americanized by countless importations of words from German, Italian, French, Spanish, Yiddish, and American Indian tongues, among others.

The surprising result is that, without a unique national language, our community has developed a language wonderfully expressive of the vitality and variety of our people. Perhaps we should really call Broken English our distinctive American language, for it bears the mark of our immigrant history.

Law. Nowadays, we can be puzzled at the spectacle of peoples from Russia to South Africa contending over how, whether, and when to adopt a "constitution." They seem to have the odd notion that a "constitution" can be created instantly by vote of a legislature or by a popular election. All this offers a sharp contrast to our Anglo-American experience.

The tradition of a fundamental law—a "constitution"—that we inherited from England reached back to at least the 13th century. The byproduct of a nation's whole history, the unwritten English constitution was a pillar of government and of the people's rights. No one could have foreseen that such a tradition would find a transatlantic written reincarnation in the deliberations of 55 colonials meeting in Independence Hall in Philadelphia in 1787. So our United States was created by a constitution. With another surprising result—that our parvenu nation at the end of the 20th century now lives by the most venerable (and probably most venerated) written constitution in the world. And that the constitution would survive by its very power to be amended (with difficulty).

Yet who could have predicted that a nation whose birth certificate bore the declaration that "all men are created equal" should have been one of the last to abolish slavery? Slavery was abolished in the British Empire in 1833. Still, three decades passed before Lincoln's Emancipation Proclamation of 1863 freed slaves in the Southern secessionist states, followed by the Thirteenth Amendment to the Constitution outlawing slavery in all the United States (1865). The slave trade survived only in certain Muslim states and in parts of Africa.

On the other side, we must note that our only civil war was fought in a struggle to free a subject people. For this, too, it is hard to find a precedent. And a legacy of the history of slavery in the United States has been the equally unprecedented phenomenon of a conscience-wracked nation. This has led us to create a host of novel institutions—"equal opportunity" laws, "affirmative action," among others—in our strenuous effort to compensate for past injustices.

We should not be surprised that Russians are obsessively suspicious of foreigners coming to their country—after their long domination by the Mongols, their invasion by Napoleon and his forces of "liberation" who burned Moscow, and by the Germans in World War II who left 20 million casualties. No wonder the Russians see the foreigner as the invader or the agent of invaders.

In the United States, we have been luckily free of this stereotype. Instead our vision of the newcomer has been refracted in the experience of our own recent immigrant ancestors. "Strangers are welcome," Benjamin Franklin explained in his *Information to Those Who Would Remove to America* (1782), "because there is room enough for them all, and therefore the old inhabitants are not jealous of them." This has been the mainstream of our history: welcoming the newcomer as worker, customer, community-builder, fellow-citizen-in-the-making. The uniquely American notion of a Nation of Nations was never more vivid than today.

Wealth. We are told that the United States is a *rich* nation. But what really distinguishes us is less our wealth than our radically novel way of measuring a society's material well-being.

Wealth—which was at the center of English mercantilist thinking before the American Revolution—was a static notion. The wealth of the world, measured primarily in gold and silver treasure, was supposed to be a fixed quantity, a pie that could be sliced one way or another. But the size of the pie could not be substantially increased. A bigger slice for Great Britain meant a smaller slice for France or Spain or somebody else, and one nation's gain was another's loss.

Our New World changed that way of thinking. People have come here not for wealth but for a better "way of life." America blurred the boundary between the material and the spiritual. All this was reinforced by the spectacular progress of our technology, exploiting the resources of a rich, little-known and sparsely populated continent.

The American Revolution then was, among other things, a struggle between the time-honored idea of "wealth" and a New World idea of "standard of living." This characteristically American idea appears to have entered our language only at the beginning of this century. It could hardly have been conceived in an Old World burdened with the legacy of feudal "rights," landed aristocracies, royal courts, sacrosanct guild monopolies and ancestral cemeteries. Wealth is what someone possesses, but a standard of living is what people *share*. Wealth can be secretly hoarded, but a standard of living can only be publicly enjoyed. For it is the level of goods, housing, services, health, comfort, and education agreed to be appropriate.

All these remarkable transformations of the culture of the Older World add up to American Exceptionalism.

Recently, we have heard apologies for expressions of belief in American uniqueness—as if it were somehow provincial or chauvinist. But our ex-Colonial nation in this post-Colonial age would do well to see what the prescient French man of letters Andre Malraux observed on his visit to President Kennedy in the White House in 1962: "The United States is today the country that assumes the destiny of man. . . . For the first time, a country has become the world's leader without achieving this through conquest, and it is strange to think that for thousands of years one single country has found power while seeking only justice."

And, he might have added, while seeking community. We must see the unique power of the United States, then, not as the power of power, but as the power of example. Another name for history.

The depressing spectacle today of a Europe at war with itself has offered us a melodrama of those same ghosts of ethnic, racial, and religious hate that generations of immigrants have come to America to escape. Now, more than ever, we must inoculate ourselves against these latent perils. Luckily, the states of our federal union are not ethnic, racial, or religious enclaves. Luckily, we have remained a wonderfully mobile people. There is no better antidote to these perils abroad than a frank and vivid recognition of the uniqueness of our history—of the special opportunities offered us. Nor could there be greater folly than refusing to enjoy the happy accidents of our history.

The uniqueness that Jefferson and Lincoln claimed for us, we must remember, was for the sake of *all* mankind. Our Declaration of Independence takes its cue from "the course of human events." The Great

Seal of the United States on our dollar bill still proclaims "Novus Ordo Seclorum"—a new order of the centuries. When before had people put so much faith in the unexpected?

CRITICAL THINKING QUESTIONS

1. Are you personally optimistic, pessimistic, or somewhere in between regarding America, its current state of affairs, and its future? Explain.

2. Is Boorstin's optimism about America simply a subjective personal opinion, or are there some objective and verifiable reasons to be optimistic about America? Explain.

3. What are some key historical realities Boorstin highlights that distinguish America from Europe or the Old World? How do these differences contribute to his optimism?

4. Some people are very pessimistic about America and often focuses upon its vices. In what sense is this pessimism warranted? After having read this article, what are some reasons to have hope in the potential for America's future? Explain.

5. Comment on Andre Malraux's observation that "The United States is today the country that assumes the destiny of man. . . . For the first time, a country has become the world's leader without achieving this through conquest, and it is strange to think that for thousands of years one single country has found power while seeking only justice." What does this statement mean to you? Does it still apply to America today? Why or why not?

~

EDUCATION

The Hollow Curriculum
Robert N. Sollod

Robert N. Sollod, PhD, is a professor of psychology at Cleveland State University. He has published numerous articles analyzing the theoretical role of spirituality in psychotherapy and assessing its practical application in clinical psychology. Another of his academic specialties is theories of personality, and he has coauthored a book with Christopher F. Monte titled *Beneath the Mask: An Introduction to Theories of Personality* (2003). He also specializes in the relationship of religion and higher education, and the following essay was first published in *The Chronicle of Higher Education* in 1992.

Essay Classification: Argumentation/persuasion; informative

THE PAST DECADE IN academe has seen widespread controversy over curricular reform. We have explored many of the deeply rooted, core assumptions that have guided past decisions about which subjects should be emphasized in the curriculum and how they should be approached. Yet I have found myself repeatedly disappointed by the lack of significant discussion concerning the place of religion and spirituality in colleges' curricula and in the lives of educated persons.

I do not mean to suggest that universities should indoctrinate students with specific viewpoints or approaches to life; that is not their proper function. But American universities now largely ignore religion and spirituality, rather than considering what aspects of religious and spiritual teachings should enter the curriculum and how those subjects should be taught. The curricula that most undergraduates study do little to rectify the fact that many Americans are ignorant of religions and spiritual teachings, of their significance in the history of this and other civilizations, and of their significance in contemporary society. Omitting this major facet of human experience and thought contributes to a continuing shallowness and imbalance in much of university life today. Let us take the current discussions of multiculturalism as one example. It is hardly arguable that an educated person should approach life with knowledge of several cultures or patterns of experience. Appreciation and understanding of human diversity are worthy educational ideals. Should such an appreciation exclude the religious and spiritually based concepts of reality that are the backbone upon which entire cultures have been based?

Multiculturalism that does not include appreciation of the deepest visions of reality reminds me of the travelogues that I saw in the cinema as a child—full of details of quaint and somewhat mysterious behavior that evoked some superficial empathy but no real, in-depth understanding. Implicit in a multicultural approach that ignores spiritual factors is a kind of critical and patronizing attitude. It assumes that we can understand and evaluate the experiences of other cultures without comprehension of their deepest beliefs.

Incomprehensibly, traditionalists who oppose adding multicultural content to the curriculum also ignore the religious and theological bases of the Western civilization that they seek to defend. Today's advocates of Western traditionalism focus, for the most part, on conveying a type of rationalism that is only a single strain in Western thought. Their approach does not demonstrate sufficient awareness of the contributions of Western religions and spirituality to philosophy and literature, to moral and legal codes, to the development of governmental and political institutions, and to the mores of our society.

Nor is the lack of attention to religion and spirituality new. I recall taking undergraduate philosophy classes in the 1960s in which Plato and Socrates were taught without reference to the fact that they were contemplative mystics who believed in immortality and reincarnation. Everything that I learned in my formal undergraduate education about Christianity came through studying a little Thomas Aquinas in a philosophy course, and even there we focused more on the logical sequence of his arguments than on the fundamentals of the Christian doctrine that he espoused.

I recall that Dostoyevsky was presented as an existentialist, with hardly a nod given to the fervent Christian beliefs so clearly apparent in his writings. I even recall my professors referring to their Christian colleagues, somewhat disparagingly, as "Christers." I learned about mystical and spiritual interpretations of Shakespeare's sonnets and plays many years after taking college English courses.

We can see the significance of omitting teaching about religion and spirituality in the discipline of psychology and, in particular, in my own field of clinical psychology. I am a member of the Task Force on Religious Issues in Graduate Education and Training in Division 36 of the American Psychological Association, a panel chaired by Edward Shafranske of Pepperdine University. In this work, I have discovered that graduate programs generally do not require students to learn anything about the role of religion in people's lives.

Almost no courses are available to teach psychologists how to deal with the religious values or concerns expressed by their clients. Nor are such courses required or generally available at the undergraduate level for psychology majors. Allusions to religion and spirituality often are completely missing in textbooks on introductory psychology, personality theory, concepts of psychotherapy, and developmental psychology.

Recent attempts to add a multicultural perspective to clinical training almost completely ignore the role of religion and spirituality as core elements of many racial, ethnic, and national identities. Prayer is widely practiced, yet poorly understood and rarely studied by psychologists. When presented, religious ideas are usually found in case histories of patients manifesting severe psychopathology.

Yet spiritual and mystical experiences are not unusual in our culture. And research has shown that religion is an important factor in the lives of many Americans; some studies have suggested that a client's religious identification may affect the psychotherapeutic relationship, as well as the course and outcome of therapy. Some patterns of religious commitment have been found to be associated with high levels of mental health and ego strength. A small number of psychologists are beginning to actively challenge the field's inertia and indifference by researching and writing on topics related to religion and spirituality. Their efforts have not as yet, however, markedly affected the climate or curricula in most psychology departments.

Is it any wonder that religion for the typical psychotherapist is a mysterious and taboo topic'? It should not be surprising that therapists are not equipped even to ask the appropriate questions regarding a person's religious or spiritual life—much less deal with psychological aspects of spiritual crises.

Or consider the field of political science. Our scholars and policy makers have been unable to predict or understand the major social and political movements that produced upheavals around the world during the last decade. That is at least partly because many significant events—the remarkable rise of Islamic fundamentalism, the victory of Afghanistan over the Soviet Union, the unanticipated velvet revolutions in Eastern Europe and in the Soviet Union, and the continuing conflicts in Cyprus, Israel, Lebanon, Northern Ireland, Pakistan, Sri Lanka, Tibet, and Yugoslavia—can hardly be appreciated without a deep understanding of the religious views of those involved. The tender wisdom of our contemporary political scientists cannot seem to comprehend the deep spirituality inherent in many of today's important social movements.

Far from being all anachronism, religious conviction has proved to be a more potent contemporary force than most, if not all, secular ideologies. Too often, however, people with strong religions sentiments are simply dismissed as "zealots" or "fanatics"—whether they be Jewish settlers on the West Bank, Iranian demonstrators, Russian Baptists, Shiite leaders, anti-abortion activists, or evangelical Christians.

Most sadly, the continuing neglect of spirituality and religion by colleges and universities also results in a kind of segregation of the life of the spirit from the life of the mind in American culture. This situation is far from the ideals of Thoreau, Emerson, or William James. Spirituality in our society too often represents a retreat from the world of intellectual discourse, and spiritual pursuits are often cloaked in a reflexive anti-intellectualism, which mirrors the view in academe of spirituality as an irrational cultural residue. Students with spiritual interests and concerns learn that the university will not validate or feed their interests. They learn either to suppress their spiritual life or to split their spiritual life apart from their formal education.

Much has been written about the loss of ethics, a sense of decency, moderation, and fair play in American society. I would submit that much of this loss is a result of the increasing ignorance, in circles of presumably educated people, of religious and spiritual world views. It is difficult to imagine, for example, how ethical issues can be intelligently approached and discussed or how wise ethical decisions can be reached without either knowledge or reference to those religious and spiritual principles that underlie our legal system and moral codes.

Our colleges and universities should reclaim one of their earliest purposes—to educate and inform students concerning the spiritual and religious underpinnings of thought and society. To the extent that such education is lacking, our colleges and universities are presenting a narrow and fragmented view of human experience.

Both core curricula and more advanced courses in the humanities and social sciences should be evaluated for their coverage of religious topics. Active leadership at the university, college, and departmental levels is needed to encourage and carry out needed additions and changes in course content. Campus organizations should develop forums and committees to examine the issue, exchange information, and develop specific proposals.

National debate and discussion about the best way to educate students concerning religion and spirituality are long overdue.

1. According to Sollod, what has been missing from recent discussions of curriculum reform in higher education?

2. Do you agree with Sollod that issues of spirituality and religion should be part of higher education curriculum? Why or why not?

3. Discuss some of Sollod's main arguments for including religion and spirituality in higher education curriculum. Are his arguments reasonable? Why or why not?

4. What is the difference between informing students and indoctrinating them? Discuss what you think Sollod seeks in curriculum reform?

5. Sollod notes that religion and metaphysical traditions, particularly Christian thought in the West, informs so much of knowledge. According to Sollod, what happens when we ignore theological and metaphysical knowledge in higher education? Can we really claim to be "educated" if we ignore such knowledge? Explain.

∼

On Tour with the PC Thought Police
Author name omitted by request

Essay Classification: Informative (personal narrative); argumentation/persuasion; evaluative

NOT LONG AGO I was enjoying an elegant lunch at the Opera Cafe in former East Berlin, aside the very square where just over sixty years ago Brownshirt thugs and their young student collaborators burned books to demonstrate the Third Reich's determination to snuff out un-Nazi thought crimes. As my colleague Tom Grant reminded me of the dark history of our immediate environs, I couldn't help but think how far the world had come since those times.

We, too, were flanked by energetic young activists, but none of us had come to Berlin to goose-step or demonize racial enemies. We had come here, rather, to meet with the Chancellor of a humbled post-Holocaust, post-Communist Germany as representatives of its enlightened, tolerant, multiracial conqueror, the United States of America.

In our ranks were Jews, blacks, even homosexuals, all of whom would have been harassed, beaten, and possibly murdered in this neighborhood in the 1930s; and yet in the year 2000, we were being feted by the Germans as heroes.

Like most students studying abroad, the members of our group arrived in Germany a year ago full of questions about how things are done differently in European society than elsewhere. Unlike most, we actually had the chance to put these questions to leaders who could answer them.

The flip side to this red carpet treatment was that we were expected to "represent" America, demonstrating respect for our German patrons by asking intelligent, pointed questions worthy of "future leaders" of our great democracy.

Sadly, I can't say we lived up to our billing. No matter what we talked about, or with whom, our discussions descended into the same rut, with our German host trying to fend off unwelcome and usually inappropriate questions about race, gender, and homosexuality (for future convenience let's just call this "RGH").

Thus, we might be sitting with high-ranking members of the Interior Ministry, talking about the trillions of Deutschmarks sunk into the reconstruction of East Germany's economic infrastructure since reunification in 1990 to little apparent effect (unemployment there still stands at over 20%); but before we got to the bottom of this unbelievable bureaucratic boondoggle we would veer off onto the theme of gay rights for no apparent reason.

Or we'd be learning about Porsche's marketing strategy for its new SUV vehicle, only for our resident feminist to sideswipe our presenter with a loaded question about why women were underrepresented on the factory floor.

So long as our German hosts played along, our group's PC venom spewed straight out of the well-worn RGH playbook: a deputized member of their ranks would hijack intelligent discussion on some unacceptably normal and actually informative theme, force us at rhetorical gunpoint into a sharp U-turn in mid-air, and before we knew it we had touched down on planet RGH. A half-decade spent in the American university system had taught me to expect this.

What I had not yet seen was what transpired when intelligent, confident adults offered real resistance to the hijackers. The scene of the biggest thought crime scandal was the German Defense Ministry. Our poor host, Jürgen Quensell, had clearly not spent much time at NATO's political charm school in Brussels.

Unschooled in postmodern, press-friendly PC speak, Mr. Quensell spoke unapologetically with us as if we were adults who respected military institutions and took questions of international security seriously—and in doing so he stepped on all three land mines in the RGH arsenal one right after another.

The biggest blow-up was over race. Our interlocutor tripped up immediately here, speaking quite openly about what he (and just about every other military expert in Europe, mind you) considers the greatest security threats of the next several decades: Islamic terrorism and mass immigration from poverty-stricken Africa.

There was nothing remarkable about this, as far as I could tell—except that our speaker actually added a little color to his analysis, invoking a famous scene from the BBC film *The March*, in which four million unarmed blacks set off across the deserts of North Africa, intending to invade Europe without immigration visas. In such a situation, Mr. Quensell intoned, he would not hesitate to react just as the generals did in the film: firing on the invaders as soon as they threatened European shores. Worse, he implied in his remarks that some such mass emigration from Africa may be inevitable, as most Africans were in his view "unable to govern themselves."

Compared to such shockingly incorrect opinions about Africans, Mr. Quensell's PC slips on gender and sexuality were both mild and reassuringly predictable. He didn't like the ideas of gays serving openly in the military, and he thought that the contribution of women to national security was best served by the raising of boys, who are required by German law (unlike girls, it seems apropos to mention) to do military service.

How, then, did our group of PC activists respond to this free-thinking provocateur? Did they take him to the mat on the issues, arguing that national security might actually be improved if women, too, were forced to serve in the armed forces like men were; or if gays were allowed to serve openly, thus improving their own morale (if not that of heterosexual men put off by them)? Or question the dark scenarios of African demographic explosion and aggressive Islamic terrorism?

No, these armchair liberals merely pouted and grimaced, and then once we had left the building and the objectionable speaker no longer bothered them, our self-appointed group spokesman, a historian of pre-Holocaust German Jewry, wrote a letter to Chancellor Schroeder in which he asked that Mr. Quensell be fired for his violations of international RGH protocols.

What, after all, could a German Chancellor do, when an American Holocaust scholar (himself Jewish) accuses him of harboring racists in the German army? In the RGH playbook, this was roughly the equivalent of nuclear blackmail. Mr. Schroeder is an astute politician, and when we finally got to meet him in person, the Chancellor wasted little time dealing with the matter. "Der muss weg," he declared of the politically incorrect Mr. Quensell: he must go.

When it seemed prudent for reasons of civility, I kept my opinions to myself this past year, but there were several occasions when I simply could not be silent. Invariably, though, my interventions were deflected by subtle imputations of RGH guilt.

Our unelected leader (the historian of German Jewry) had the habit of conducting post-discussion group huddles in the manner of a football quarterback—at some six feet four inches tall, he cut a natural figure as our "PC QB"—and I was often the odd man out of the huddle. When, on leaving the Defense Ministry, I played devil's advocate, claiming it was possible to argue the efficacy of excluding gays and women from positions of military command for reasons of unit cohesion, I overheard him whispering to the huddlers, "I can't believe one of us defended that guy."

Gradually, I began taking pride in my propensity for asking "dumb" questions, as when I interrupted a strained argument between one of our gay militants and a conservative Christian politician about the "racism" that lay behind Bavaria's requirement of a blood test for residency certification to ask, "What is racist about blood tests?"

To this day, I am not sure of the answer to this question—I was shushed no less than four times by the homosexual members of our group, one of whom whispered to me at last in exasperation, "Well, *we* all know what's racist about it, Sean; can't you just drop it?" That settled that.

During a group lunch not long after this event, I got trapped in one of those only-on-planet-RGH conversations that simply boggles the imagination. We were talking about the issues facing boys growing up in

America, speculating about the psychological and social factors underlying the recent spate of schoolyard shootings.

Amazingly, the men at the table reflexively deferred to the one woman present, our group's most radical lesbian feminist, for the presumably expert analysis she could offer as . . . well, I wasn't really sure why we were deferring to her. Having once been a young man myself, I took offense at her predictable diatribe against the evils of "patriarchal" society, which socializes boys against their own selves to be aggressive and violent.

I offered instead an argument that viewed unmediated nature as the culprit—all young men, so far as I know, fantasize about avenging their enemies, pulverizing the mean kids who make fun of them, and so forth; but most of them have something, either sports or Boy Scouts or church groups or whatever, that channels their potent physical energies and frustrations away from destructive vengeance seeking.

Anyway, the substance of my argument was immaterial: our feminist lesbian expert on adolescent male psychology cut me off before I was finished. "That's not what I'm saying," she angrily intoned, both upset and confused by my remarks. "That's right, I'm disagreeing with you," I replied, producing a look of profound shock on her face such as I had never encountered. Not only was this homosexual woman, contrary to all available logic, apparently quite accustomed to being consulted as an expert on adolescent male psychology, *but she had not imagined that someone might disagree with her in such a conversation.*

How had this become possible? Had no one contradicted this woman during her entire graduate student career? Did no one dare offer her the slightest give-and-take during undergraduate dorm room jam sessions? Had the PC brownshirts staged a secret coup, switching the entire American university archipelago over to an RGH-only frequency back in 1997 without my noticing it?

Perhaps it is fear that keeps the silent majority of tuition-paying undergraduates from speaking out more often when thoughtful dissent is called for. Maybe students have simply acquiesced in the new orthodoxy, feeling that the risks ensuing from provocation of an RGH incident— a bad grade, unspoken ostracism from peers, or outright name-calling (racist! sexist! homophobe!)—outweigh the more intangible benefits that accrue from sticking up for honor, morality, or the truth.

But this is no time for surrender. Especially because Americans are now reaping the benefits of unprecedented wealth and global power, because in our every action we influence not only our fellow citizens, but virtually everyone on the planet, we must be careful about the example we set.

Silent dissenters, please speak out now, before these fanatical thought policemen ruin America's reputation for good. Millions of people around the world still look to our country as a beacon of freedom of expression. Let us remember our better selves, that we may no longer disappoint them.

CRITICAL THINKING QUESTIONS

1. Even though this is a personal narrative, there is still a clear thesis and focus. What is it? Where does the author provide the thesis?

2. How does the author use personal narrative to provide illustrations, explanations, and evidence in support of his thesis?

3. What does this essay reveal about the dangers of applying a narrow ideological worldview to reality? What happens if we approach learning situations from too specific and narrowly defined preconceptions and presuppositions?

4. What does this essay suggest about the intellectual, rational, and emotional limitations of strict political correctness that is the norm on most university campuses? To what extent is political correctness concerned with free thought, intellectual honesty, and openmindedness? Explain.

5. How tolerant of views different from their own were the political correctness advocates in this essay? To what extent are such individuals really committed to open dialog and debate and to what extent are they interested in forcing their own perspective on others through threats, vilification (ad hominem attacks), policy procedures, and the courts? Discuss examples from this essay and from your own experiences or cases in the news.

6. Discuss the extent to which you as a student feel empowered or free to disagree with prevailing political correctness orthodoxies on campus and to voice your opinion in open dialog and debate?

～

"The Moral Courage of the Human Mind": The Perils of Intellectual Freedom on Today's Campus

Mark Linville

Mark D. Linville holds the PhD in philosophy from the University of Wisconsin-Madison. He has published numerous journal articles on philosophy of religion and ethics and has written for *Christianity Today*, *Touchstone*, and *Salvo*. He is also a frequent contributor to the *Wittenburg Door*.

Essay Classification: Informative; critical evaluation; argumentation/ persuasion

> But the peculiar evil of silencing the expression of an opinion is, that it is robbing the human race; posterity as well as the existing generation; those who dissent from the opinion, still more than those who hold it. If the opinion is right, they are deprived of the opportunity of exchanging error for truth: if wrong, they lose what is almost as great a benefit, the clearer perception and livelier impression of truth, produced by its collision with error.
>
> —John Stuart Mill, On Liberty

B ROOKE ALDRICH, A FRESHMAN at the University of Delaware (UD), sounds like a nice person. "I personally have no problem with anyone of any background, race, sexual identity, or any religion," she told reporters in November. "I accept people for who they are as people." But the Animal-Science major learned that she was actually deluding herself on this score in a "Diversity Facilitation Training" session that university residence-life officials sponsored in her residence hall last fall.

The program utilized a manual written by a Dr. Shakti Butler, which, like some bad parody of the Geometric Method, begins with a set of axioms and definitions, and then proceeds inexorably to the conclusion that people such as Brooke, wittingly or not, share solidarity with those who would burn crosses and don bed sheets or jackboots. Students in the mandatory sessions learned that all and only "white people" are racists and that "racist" is synonymous with "white supremacist." Butler believes that racism involves racial prejudice *plus* the privilege and power bestowed by an inherently white-supremacist system. We thus have the makings of a compelling argument with a surprising conclusion: All and only white people are racists; all and only racists are white supremacists; Brooke is a white person; therefore, Brooke is a racist; therefore, Brooke is a white supremacist. *Quod est demonstratum.*

Dr. Butler is of course free to define "racist" however she sees fit. (I only hope that she will reciprocate and afford me equal latitude with "idiot.") But why should her definition be accepted by anyone else? Among other things, it implausibly characterizes a young lady with race-indifferent benevolence as a racist, while rescuing from any such charge Kamau Kambon, onetime visiting professor at North Carolina State University, who advocates racial genocide against "white people" ("The only solution in my estimation is to exterminate white people from the face of the earth," Kambon said to applause at Howard University).

Clearly, the views presented in such diversity-training sessions are controversial, some might even say morally repugnant. But the problem isn't with the assertions themselves. Dr. Butler is entitled to hold and express such beliefs, and to do so within an academic setting. Let her ideas be aired, assessed, and openly debated in the classroom or in other campus forums. This contributes to the sort of intellectual diversity—that clash of opposing ideas defended by John Stuart Mill—that inspires careful, critical, and autonomous thinking. Rather, what's dangerous here is that such views were foisted upon an essentially captive and impressionable audience, and with no room for argument or debate. Thus, the impression conveyed is that anyone who denies them must be stupid, ignorant, or wicked. This is *indoctrination*; not education.

The New Orthodoxy

The program at UD is indicative of a mindset shared by many college administrators and faculty around the nation who think it their mission as educators to imbue their students with a comprehensive and well-defined political outlook. The shared assumption is that, as a society, we have been systematically programmed to think within categories that are essentially racist, sexist, classist, and "homophobic." The only cure for such is to reprogram or reeducate ourselves. Thus, on many university and college campuses, there is a concerted effort on the part of faculty, administrators, and student groups to establish a new orthodoxy—the orthodoxy of the extreme Left—and to silence and shame any and all dissenters. This orthodoxy manifests itself in a variety of ways, including sensitivity-training sessions as the one just described, various campus speech codes that characterize as "hate speech" expressions of religious or conservative views (opposition to abortion or gay marriage, for instance), loyalty oaths and litmus tests for faculty, students, and staff, and dogmatic and one-sided presentations by leftist professors. In some cases, entire programs of study have been established with the clear intention of preparing social activists of a decidedly leftist mindset to become "catalysts of change." The sad truth is that on many college campuses, the far Left enjoys the power of the status quo, so conservative voices are either quite literally shouted down (as was the case with David Horowitz on a recent visit to Emory University) or shut out altogether.

The nearly inevitable result is that "intellectual pacification" is had at the sacrifice of "the moral courage of the human mind," as J. S. Mill put it. Indeed, Mill goes on to describe this situation as that

> state of things in which a large portion of the most active and inquiring intellects find it advisable to keep the general principles and grounds of their convictions within their own breasts, and attempt, in what they address to the public, to fit as much as they can of their own conclusions to premises which they have internally renounced.

A society in such a state, Mill argues, "cannot send forth the open, fearless characters, and logical, consistent intellects who once adorned the thinking world." Mill's concern was for society at large. How much more does his argument apply to the university, whose central mission should be to "send forth" precisely such individuals? Let's consider a few examples from recent years.

Academic Misconduct

As recently as 2005, freshmen at Ohio State University (OSU) at Mansfield underwent mandatory anti-homophobia sensitivity training during their orientation. Mansfield, of course, is the same OSU campus where a librarian was charged with sexual harassment for recommending the anti-gay book *The Marketing of Evil* as potential reading material for incoming freshmen. The book itself was subsequently banned as "hate speech."

A women's studies course at the University of South Carolina at Columbia established guidelines for class discussion that included an acknowledgement "that racism, classism, sexism, heterosexism, and other institutionalized forms of oppression exist," and that "one mechanism of institutionalized racism, classism, sexism, heterosexism, etc., is that we are all systematically taught misinformation about our own group and about members of other groups." But what of those students who are not convinced that any or all of these "institutionalized forms of oppression exist," or who believe that heterosexuality is in fact normative? Perhaps the instructor should have warned off the conservative students who were considering her class in the way that conservatives have been warned off elsewhere. For instance, the course description for "The Politics and Poetics of Palestinian Resistance" offered at UC-Berkeley included this warning: "Conservative thinkers are encouraged to seek other sections."

At a California community college, an instructor in a class on "Human Heredity" was terminated recently for discussing the "nature versus nurture" debate with regard to homosexuality, articulating and perhaps defending the "nurture" perspective. Apparently, no one had informed this professor that the debate on this subject was over, making expressions of the "losing" side intolerable.

Bucks County Community College (BCCC) found a way to avoid such a debacle; it required new faculty applicants to describe their "commitment to diversity." A BCCC professor who was upset by the requirement called it "a diversity loyalty oath." He added that "a college campus should be a marketplace of ideas—diversity of thinking, a robust discussion, civil argumentation, testing of ideas, for people with all kinds of wonderfully diverse political, cultural and social viewpoints." He suggested that the *cultural* diversity sought in the application process stifles the *intellectual* diversity that makes for a vibrant campus community. He may be right. But feel free to disagree with him. After all, that is what the marketplace of ideas is all about.

At Citrus College in California, Rosalyn Kahn, a professor in a speech class, offered extra credit to students who agreed to write to President Bush protesting the impending invasion of Iraq. She refused credit to students offering to send letters of *support* to the president. Such inappropriate politicizing of the classroom reminds me of C. S. Lewis's famous complaint in *The Abolition of Man* that the authors of a book on grammar spent their time fobbing off a half-baked philosophy of subjectivism rather than helping their readers gain a real facility with the language. One fears that there is an army of Rosalyn Kahns who are substituting "Why Bush is a Fascist 101" for "Late Victorian Novelists" and lectures on "How to Combat Homophobia" for calculus.

At Washington State University (WSU) in Pullman, Ed Swan, a student in the College of Education, made the mistake of expressing his Christian and conservative views in a class discussion. Although he managed superior grades, the result was that several professors in the department gave him failing marks on his "dispositions evaluation," which included an assessment of his character based in part upon his commitment to "diversity" and "social justice." Because of his failing marks, he was told that in order to stay in the program, he would have to sign a contract agreeing to attend a National Coalition Building Institute training session (read: sensitivity training) and to meet with Melynda Huskey, the Assistant Vice President for Equity and Diversity and the director of WSU's LGBT office, who, according to Swan, "was confrontational and made the matter a personal one."

The theory behind "dispositions evaluations" is that "pre-service teachers" should be assessed on their character before being trusted with the nation's youth. The trouble with the theory is that it permits this character assessment to be conducted from a strict ideological framework. Critics thus insist that it puts faculty and administrators—particularly those with leftist propensities—in the position of "ideological gatekeepers" who can create a pool of teachers sanitized of the likes of Ed Swan.

It is difficult not to agree with such critics. Consider the "conceptual framework" within which (until a 2007 revision and softening of the language, perhaps due to increased public scrutiny) the College of Education at the University of Alabama has worked. It is "committed to preparing individuals to promote social justice, to be change agents, and to recognize individual and institutional racism, sexism, homophobia, and classism." Clearly, this institution has formally adopted a one-sided political agenda with specific and hotly contested views on race, gender, and sexual orientation. This is not a unique or isolated case. Such are the goals of many NCATE (National Council for Accreditation of Teacher Education)-accredited schools nationwide. This is not teacher training; it is *missionary* training.

Believers Beware!

The new orthodox agenda is not limited to schools of education. Social-work programs around the country are almost universally premised upon its principles. Consider the department's stance on "homophobia" at St. Cloud State University:

> Because homophobia is so deeply embedded in our culture, it is likely that many social work students, as many other people in society, will have preconceived negative stereotypes about gay males and lesbians.... The Department's intent is to introduce knowledge and values that will challenge and help to combat these attitudes and stereotypes. Students' openness to learning is essential because those who hold negative attitudes and stereotypes about diverse populations can do serious harm to clients in their future social work practice. To prevent this, students must be open to examining their prejudices, including their homophobia.

The language here is interesting. Since the department thinks that the harboring of negative attitudes toward homosexuals "can do serious harm," and since it undoubtedly does not wish to foster mayhem and mischief, its insistence that students merely "examine" their prejudices is an understatement. "Examine" does not refer to the Socratic exercise that *may* possibly *vindicate* currently held beliefs. Rather, it is a euphemism for "root out and eliminate." Note also that the language is vague. Does the belief that homosexuality is immoral, a belief held by not a few people within our society, qualify as such an unacceptable "prejudice" or "stereotype" to be combated?

St. Cloud's undergraduate program in social work is accredited by the Council on Social Work Education (CSWE), and here is the rub. Accreditation through CSWE is contingent upon adherence to its requirement that graduates of all accredited programs demonstrate a commitment to "social and economic justice." We may suppose that all thinking persons of good will are concerned for "social justice." But in the hands of zealots, "social justice" may be defined in an exclusive and controversial way. The Foundation for Individual Rights in Education (FIRE), a nonpartisan organization dedicated to the preservation of constitutional and academic freedom, has argued that such language is vague and politically loaded—that it virtually mandates that potential graduates be evaluated for their political views.

What of those students of differing political and moral persuasion who have a heart for helping people through social work? Take the plight of Emily Brooker at Missouri State University, whose social-work professor gave the class an assignment that violated her conscience. Students were asked to write and sign letters to the Missouri Legislature advocating gay adoption. She refused, saying that to do so would violate her Christian convictions. The professor then accused her of violating the school's Standards of Essential Functioning in Social Work Education. The accusation resulted in her appearance before a college ethics committee where faculty members grilled her with such questions as, "Do you think gays and lesbians are sinners?" "Do you think I am a sinner?" Brooker claims that faculty told her that she would have to "lessen the gap" between her beliefs and the requirements of the national code of ethics embraced by the department. She sued the university, and the case was quickly settled out of court. David French, director of the advocacy group that defended Brooker, argued that "the university is supposed to be the marketplace of ideas, and professors should be tolerant of the opinions of Christian students as well as those of non-Christian students."

Brooker's case drew national attention, prompting a piece in *The Washington Post* by Alan Cooperman: "Is There Disdain for Evangelicals in the Classroom?" Cooperman cites a survey of some 1,200 college and university faculty that reveals that 53 percent of college professors professed "unfavorable" attitudes—where "unfavorable" was the most negative category in the survey—toward evangelical Christians. Interestingly, the majority "expressed positive feelings toward Jews, Buddhists, Roman Catholics and most other religious groups."

Cary Nelson, then president of the American Association of University Professors, insists that such attitudes reflect "political and cultural resistance" rather than a "religious bias." In particular, says Nelson, they stem from the association between Evangelicalism and Republican politics, as well as the perception that Evangelicals ostensibly eschew a scientific understanding of the world. This is minimally helpful in that religious beliefs typically *inform* social and political issues—such as gay rights and abortion, on the one hand, and a commitment to a theistic metaphysics incompatible with naturalistic assumptions, on the other. As Brooker's case illustrates, there is a clash between "personal belief" and the expectations of the new orthodoxy. David French makes an appearance in the Cooperman editorial as well. He is quoted as saying that "on many campuses, if you're an evangelical Christian, you're going to have to go through classes in which you're told that much of what you believe religiously is not just wrong, but worthy of mockery."

Religious groups around the country are increasingly finding that they are not particularly welcomed by college and university administrators. Administrators at the University of Wisconsin (UW)-Superior, for example, "derecognized" the campus chapter of InterVarsity Christian Fellowship (IVCF) on the grounds that the student group employed discriminatory policies. It seems that IVCF limited their leadership positions to Christians. Imagine that! One wonders what the policies of the UW-Superior's "Queer and Allied Student Union" would dictate in the event that a "homophobic," IVCF type were to seek a position of leadership.

Similar cases are cropping up everywhere around the country. The current chancellor at my own alma mater, the University of Wisconsin-Madison, recently attempted to refuse recognition or funding to the UW-Madison Roman Catholic Foundation (UWRCF), one of several faith-based student groups on campus, on the grounds that the group was "too religious." The Center for Academic Freedom subsequently filed suit against the university, and the UW-Madison's policies were eventually ruled unconstitutional.

Lady Liberty

Most of the cases that I mention here involved the intervention of organizations such as FIRE and the Alliance Defense Fund (ADF). And thus far, as these encroachments of constitutional liberties have been brought before the public eye and into the courts, they have in turn melted away like a late spring snow in the noon sun. For example, the harassment charge against the OSU librarian was dropped the very day that it was formally challenged. One now finds dead links on university Web pages where, presumably, references to sensitivity-training sessions once appeared. As I've noted, the language of "conceptual frameworks" and mission statements have also been revised of late, as the original, militant language has invited scrutiny and the potential for constitutional challenges. (One advocate of freshmen diversity training noted that the prudent advice among the politically orthodox is "Don't F-up and get us sued.")

Notably, under pressure from organizations such as FIRE, the diversity training at UD, the story with which I opened, was discontinued in November 2007 as well. This had to be terribly discouraging to the residence-life officials at UD, especially considering that in early 2006, they had basked in the glow of several "social justice awards" from the American College Personnel Association (ACPA) and the Commission for Social Justice Educators (CSJE). "The number and quality of the department's initiatives in the areas of diversity, multiculturalism, and the eradication of oppression are remarkable. I am proud of the staff's work and pleased that it is receiving national recognition," beamed one administrator. Another staff member noted that "getting recognized with such prestigious honors also spurs the mission of social justice on to greater heights." Presumably, the mandatory residence-hall sessions were part of this ascent to the summit.

It turns out that UD residence-life officials had already planned the "Second Annual Residential Curriculum Institute" for January 2008, this time with the program being held up as a model for attendees from res-life departments around the country. The November dismantling of the diversity program resulted in a dramatic and somber introduction to that conference. The opening female speaker held a large, lit candle and stood before a plate of smaller, unlit candles of diverse colors. The large candle represented "the knowledge and responsibility that we have as student affairs and residence life professionals." The smaller candles were the students "to whom we pass on that light"—students, this person indicated, who need to learn about social justice, multiculturalism, diversity, and sustainability. She then blew out the large candle. "Our light went out," she said. And in an obvious reference to the discontinuation of the residence-life program, she added that it was "hate, fear, ignorance and stupidity" that was responsible for putting it out. She then relit the candle to indicate that the present conference would serve to renew the noble mission that would never again succumb to the forces of darkness.

I do not question the good intentions of this candle-bearing speaker. I agree with her that a light is in danger of being extinguished, though not the one she herself was holding. This one is borne high by a solitary figure standing in a harbor where people of diverse beliefs and national origins have caught their first glimpse of a country that was conceived in liberty—a nation once determined to avoid imposing an official orthodoxy upon its citizens.

Ascend and Challenge

Despite the laudable efforts and noteworthy successes of groups such as FIRE and ADF, proponents of the diversity gospel do not intend to go away. And for every case that is brought to the attention of these advocacy groups, countless more go unreported. Students are typically unaware of their constitutional and moral rights, so they don't always realize that they're being violated by coercive campus policies and programs. Even where campus officials have refrained from the Orwellian tactics previously described, the far Left has succeeded in creating a "plausibility structure" that strongly discourages expressions of Christian conviction or conservative outlook. John Stuart Mill was as much concerned about mere "social intolerance," resulting in one being "ill-thought of and ill-spoken of," as he was about more obvious forms of oppression. After all, such snubs are nearly as effective in silencing dissenters, yet they do not invite legal challenges from advocacy groups.

As goes today's university, so goes tomorrow's society. Those campus administrators and faculty who promote the new orthodoxy understand this principle. They are utopians who envision a society purged of habits of mind that they view as oppressive and thus engaged in what Dinesh D'Souza describes as a "revolution from the top down." Charles Malik also understood the profound influence that the academy has upon a culture. In a speech titled "The Two Tasks of Evangelism," delivered in 1980 at the inauguration of Wheaton College's Billy Graham Center, Malik urged evangelicals to eschew the anti-intellectualism that characterized them. The consequences of continuing down their current path, he said, was that "the arena of creative thinking [would be completely] vacated and abdicated to the enemy."

The same might be said of social conservatives in general. FIRE maintains that "it is essential that our nation's future leaders be educated members of a free society, learning to debate and to resolve differences peacefully, without resorting to administrative coercion." I agree. Much of the blame for the current condition of universities rests upon the shoulders of the ideological gatekeepers described here. But the situation is exacerbated by those with solid moral and intellectual viewpoints who choose not to ascend the Ivory Tower of Academia. It is not enough that real debate and dialogue be permitted at our nation's colleges and universities. We must likewise encourage those with both the academic wherewithal *and* a commitment to true intellectual diversity to rise to the challenge and join this battle for the heart and mind of the culture.

CRITICAL THINKING QUESTIONS

1. Does your university have diversity training seminars as part of the residence life programs? What are their stated goals and objectives? Do you find that some views, cultures, and lifestyles are privileged over others? Explain.

2. What is intellectual diversity? To what extent do you feel your university encourages true intellectual diversity? Why or why not?

3. Is it logically consistent to exclude or to silence some theories, political views, religious values, or philosophical principles in the name of tolerance? Why or why not?

4. It is quite common for proponents of liberal ideologies to criticize religious institutions for holding too rigidly to orthodoxies. Do you see any irony in the extent to which these ideologues hold fast to their own set of orthodoxies? Explain.

5. Linville cites numerous examples in which conservative and religious students were discouraged from taking certain classes because their views did not match those of the professor. What kind of message does that send about the open-mindedness of such professors? What message does it send to students when university administrations allow for this type of discrimination? Do you think a religious or conservative professor would be allowed to discriminate against liberal or nonreligious students in the same way? Why or why not?

6. What are "disposition evaluations"? Do you think a student should be graded based upon the degree to which they agree or disagree with certain political views and moral values? Why or why not?

$\sim$

Patrolling Professors' Politics: Conservative Activists and Students Press Campaigns against Perceived Bias on Campuses
Sarah Hebel

Sarah Hebel is a government-and-politics reporter for *The Chronicle of Higher Education*. The following article appeared in volume 50, issue 23 (2004) of *The Chronicle*.

Essay Classification: Informative

GERALD WILSON, A HISTORY professor at Duke University, says a student's question on the first day of class last semester caught him off guard: "Do you have any prejudices?"

Unsure what the young man meant, Mr. Wilson decided to reply with a joke. "Yeah, Republicans," he recalls saying. (He found out later that the student was asking about writing styles.)

"Everybody laughed," the professor says.

Well, not quite everybody.

Matt Bettis, a senior in the class, thought the comment among others was inappropriate and sent an e-mail message to Mr. Wilson telling him so. The professor apologized to Mr. Bettis, who had dropped the course, "American Dreams/American Realities."

"I was absolutely dumbfounded," Mr. Bettis later wrote about Mr. Wilson's comments in a letter to Students for Academic Freedom, a national group that is collecting stories about political bias on campuses. "What worried me was the excited and proud manner in which he stated it, thus implying that his politics would be a large part of the classroom experience."

While Mr. Wilson calls the incident "regrettable," he says his remark reflected his tendency to use humor to engage students. "Everybody knows I'm very political," he says. "But, dear God, I make jokes about Democrats as well as Republicans. This is a course where we're going to talk about different viewpoints."

To some college students—and legislators—who hold conservative views, however, comments like Mr. Wilson's raise a red flag. Professors who unnecessarily interject their political views into the classroom contribute to conservative students' feelings of isolation on campuses that often seem to be dominated by faculty members with liberal views, these critics say. Several students who say they have Republican leanings argue that their grades have suffered or that their participation in classroom discussions has been stifled by liberal professors.

"Our institutions of higher education have become institutions of indoctrination," declares Stephen Miller, a freshman at Duke. "That's a frightening trend."

Now conservative activists are fighting back. David Horowitz, president of the California-based Center for the Study of Popular Culture, is leading a national campaign to change campus climates. The centerpiece of his efforts is an "Academic Bill of Rights," which he is urging Congress and state legislatures to adopt. It enumerates several principles that colleges should follow, among which is that they should foster a variety of political and religious beliefs in such areas as making tenure decisions, developing reading lists for courses, and selecting campus speakers.

Republican members of the U.S. House of Representatives have introduced as legislation a version of the proposal. In Colorado, a visit paid by Mr. Horowitz to state officials led the president of the State Senate, a Republican, to ask the heads of the state's 29 public institutions to specify their processes for handling complaints about bias and the steps they are taking to promote "intellectual diversity" in classes and faculty recruiting. Now Colorado's Republican lawmakers are pushing for legislation that would force college governing boards to develop and publicize processes for resolving students' complaints about bias.

Mr. Horowitz says he believes that his proposal, or similar ones, could be introduced in as many as a half-dozen more state legislatures, which he declines to identify, as well as in the U.S. Senate, by this spring. He is also urging campus administrators and student-government leaders to adopt policies that would spell out students' rights to academic freedom.

"The university should not be a political place," says Mr. Horowitz. "It's a place where there ought to be reasoned discourse." He has conducted studies finding that at 32 universities he deemed "elite," Democratic professors and administrators outnumbered Republican colleagues by a ratio of more than 10 to 1.

He says he took a lot of time crafting his bill of rights so that it would protect faculty members and students who hold views across the political spectrum. Practically, though, most of the students and politicians who are backing such legislation are Republicans who complain of liberal bias on campuses. As viewpoint-neutral as Mr. Horowitz's proposal may be, some argue that the principles it lays out are likely to give other conservative activists and lawmakers ammunition to push more controversial plans in the name of intellectual diversity. For instance, Stanley Fish, dean of the College of Liberal Arts and Sciences at the University of Illinois at Chicago, argues in this week's *Chronicle Review* that lawmakers may try to use the goal of ideological balance as a rationale for requiring institutions to hire additional conservative scholars or to monitor students' assigned reading to make sure it is sufficiently "pro-American."

"It is obvious that for Horowitz these are debating points designed to hoist the left by its own petard," writes Mr. Fish, "but the trouble with debating points is that they can't be kept in bounds."

A Matter of Balance

Many university administrators, faculty members, and state lawmakers believe that Mr. Horowitz's plan, or similar proposals, would invite too much meddling by lawmakers in academic matters. Some insist that such legislative efforts might actually hinder debate on campuses and restrict professors' ability to appropriately balance classroom discussions of significant scholarly ideas.

The American Association of University Professors issued a statement saying that Mr. Horowitz's proposal would encourage state and campus officials to exert oversight on faculty members on academic matters rather than trust their professional judgment. The group took specific exception to language in the proposal that would encourage institutions to make faculty employment decisions "with a view toward fostering a plurality of methodologies and perspectives."

"The danger of such guidelines is that they invite diversity to be measured by political standards that diverge from the academic criteria of the scholarly profession," the statement reads. For example, it said, a political-theory department might be required to hire a professor espousing Nazi philosophy if a college were forced to provide a real "plurality of methodologies and perspectives" in its academic courses.

Mr. Horowitz argues that the group has misread his proposal, and that it clearly states that professors' independence should be protected. He says he wants to promote "intellectual diversity," not "political pluralism."

"Political balance implies political interference (to correct any imbalance)," he wrote to the AAUP. "By contrast, intellectual diversity calls for intellectual standards to replace the existing political ones." Political bias, rather than academic standards, has driven too many decisions by professors and other people on campuses, he says, citing a course in "Modern Industrial Societies" that he sat in on at Bates College a few years ago. The sole text, he says, was a 500-page document, put together by editors of the *New Left Review* that included only Marxist views.

In a letter to the editor of the Web site *Salon,* which ran an article about Mr. Horowitz's visit to Bates, the professor, Kiran Asher, replied that the text that Mr. Horowitz complained about included "serious engagement of such conservative icons" as Francis Fukuyama. Ms. Asher, who is no longer at Bates, added that she also required her students to read *The Economist,* which she called "not exactly a bastion of leftist doctrine."

Colorado at Center Stage

Across the country, college students who hold conservative views are coming forward with dozens of reports of incidents in which they assert that professors treated them differently than their more-liberal peers. On Web sites that collect such anecdotes and in other forums, the students tell stories of faculty members who made demeaning jokes about Republicans and spent class time urging students to protest the war in Iraq. Some of the students expressed the belief that their conservative opinions, no matter how well argued, have resulted in low grades. Others describe reading lists that include controversial material that is unrelated to the subject matter.

Much of the debate in the past several months has centered in Colorado. State Senator John Andrews, president of the chamber, who surveyed the state's public colleges about their policies, says he has long been concerned about bias against conservative students and faculty members. After reviewing the colleges' policies on academic freedom, he concluded that they are well established but that the procedures for filing complaints are "more ragged" and not well known to students.

Following up, State Rep. Shawn Mitchell, a Republican, introduced legislation last month that would require the governing boards of public colleges in Colorado to create and make known a process for students to challenge any discrimination they experience because of their political beliefs.

The proposal also would amend Colorado's existing "bill of rights" for students by spelling out the protections against political discrimination that students should be guaranteed. The legislation requires, among other things, that students' grades be unaffected by their political or religious views, that professors refrain from introducing controversial topics unrelated to their courses, and that student fees be distributed among campus groups only on a viewpoint-neutral basis.

"This isn't about stifling political debate," Mr. Mitchell says. "It's about allowing political debate and trying to create a fair environment for everyone."

Some members of Colorado's legislature, however, say legislation to reaffirm the political rights of students isn't high on their agendas.

"There are some huge challenges facing Colorado's higher-education system; this isn't one of them," says State Representative Andrew Romanoff, a Democrat who is minority leader in the House of Representatives. "I haven't heard from any of my constituents who have identified the liberal-college conspiracy as a problem worth our time."

Instead, he says, his colleagues should focus on improving high-school graduation rates and college participation among Colorado residents, and providing more money for financial aid.

Robert Nero, spokesman for the University of Colorado System, argues that the legislation is unnecessary because the institution has adequate policies to protect students, and that it would be "demoralizing to the faculty."

Administrators also believe it would be harder to draw top scholars to Colorado if the legislation passed, he says, because it would appear that lawmakers were "micromanaging" university affairs.

Mr. Horowitz acknowledges that involving lawmakers was not his first choice as a tactic for raising the issue of bias on campuses. But he decided to take that approach, he says, after public-university officials in various states failed to adopt stronger policy statements about the issue.

"I at least wanted to open the discussion," he says, arguing that his proposed legislation would make a difference in protecting students. "You can tell," he says, "by the resistance."

Campaigns on Campuses

As Mr. Horowitz works to drum up support, students on some campuses are taking their own actions. Student-government leaders at Occidental College, Utah State University, and Wichita State University have adopted a "Student Bill of Rights" modeled after Mr. Horowitz's.

At the University of Colorado at Boulder, the College Republicans last month placed a form on their Web site for students to report experiences of bias based on political beliefs. The group says it wants to use the stories to help demonstrate the extent of the discrimination they see on the campus as they talk with state lawmakers and university administrators.

One Boulder student who has filed a complaint through the Web site is Meaghan McCarty, a junior. In her "Social Problems" class, she says, the professor would often speak over her and try to discredit her arguments during class discussions of issues like poverty. When she raised her concerns with the professor after class, Ms. McCarty says, he told her that no one agreed with her, and that she should consider taking a course with a more conservative professor. Ms. McCarty's professor could not be reached for comment.

"I'm not here for my views to be popular," Ms. McCarty says. But "it goes too far when a professor starts to stifle students' own thoughts. There should be less of their own opinion and more facts from both perspectives."

While many professors agree that courses should include healthy debates, some worry that legislation aimed at protecting students from political bias would place too much emphasis on simply balancing facts in course material.

"Learning is simply more than facts," says Mr. Wilson, the Duke professor. "What we need is intelligent discourse on these kinds of things. To do that, we should have flexibility and freedom."

But students who support Mr. Horowitz's campaign argue that his bill of rights seeks to foster just the kind of wide-ranging discourse that Mr. Wilson seeks, by protecting the expression of more viewpoints. "When students like myself feel alienated, that drastically compromises the educational environment," says Mr. Miller, the Duke freshman. "We need a completely, utterly, entirely unbiased pursuit of knowledge."

As part of a national effort to protect students with unpopular political views from discrimination on campuses, the group Students for Academic Freedom is collecting anecdotes from students who believe they have been treated unfairly. The group's Web site (http://www.studentsfora-cademicfreedom.org) contains an "Academic Freedom Complaint Form." It lists several ways in which, the group believes, students' academic freedom can be violated, including:

- Requiring readings or texts that cover only one side of an issue.

- Gratuitously singling out political or religious beliefs for ridicule.

- Introducing controversial material that is unrelated to the subject.

- Forcing students to express a certain point of view in assignments.

- Mocking national political or religious figures.

- Conducting political activities in class (e.g., recruiting for demonstrations).

- Allowing students' political or religious beliefs to influence grading.
- Using university funds to hold one-sided, partisan teach-ins or conferences.

EXCERPTS FROM THE ACADEMIC BILL OF RIGHTS

Following are excerpts from the "principles and procedures" that the Academic Bill of Rights says universities should follow. The full text of the proposed code is available online at http://www.studentsforacademic-freedom.org:

- All faculty shall be hired, fired, promoted, and granted tenure on the basis of their competence and appropriate knowledge in the field of their expertise and, in the humanities, the social sciences, and the arts, with a view toward fostering a plurality of methodologies and perspectives. No faculty shall be hired or fired or denied promotion or tenure on the basis of his or her political or religious beliefs.

- No faculty member will be excluded from tenure, search, and hiring committees on the basis of their political or religious beliefs.

- Students will be graded solely on the basis of their reasoned answers and appropriate knowledge of the subjects and disciplines they study, not on the basis of their political or religious beliefs.

- Curricula and reading lists in the humanities and social sciences should reflect the uncertainty and unsettled character of all human knowledge in these areas by providing students with dissenting sources and viewpoints where appropriate. While teachers are and should be free to pursue their own findings and perspectives in presenting their views, they should consider and make their students aware of other viewpoints. Academic disciplines should welcome a diversity of approaches to unsettled questions.

- Exposing students to the spectrum of significant scholarly viewpoints on the subjects examined in their courses is a major responsibility of faculty. Faculty will not use their courses for the purpose of political, ideological, religious or antireligious indoctrination.

- Selection of speakers, allocation of funds for speakers programs and other student activities will observe the principles of academic freedom and promote intellectual pluralism.

- An environment conducive to the civil exchange of ideas being an essential component of a free university, the obstruction of invited campus speakers, destruction of campus literature or other effort to obstruct this exchange will not be tolerated.

- Academic institutions and professional societies formed to advance knowledge within an area of research, maintain the integrity of the research process, and organize the professional lives of related researchers serve as indispensable venues within which scholars circulate research findings and debate their interpretation. To perform these functions adequately, academic institutions and professional societies should maintain a posture of organizational neutrality with respect to the substantive disagreements that divide researchers on questions within, or outside, their fields of inquiry.

CRITICAL THINKING QUESTIONS

1. Have you experienced a teacher or professor making what was in their view merely a humorous negative comment about a particular political party or point of view? Is such humor harmless? Why or why not?

2. What constitutes ideological indoctrination in the classroom? Discuss any examples from your own experience.

3. Most colleges and universities have very specific codes of speech and conduct pertaining to race, sex, class, religion, and sexual orientation. Should there be similar codes pertaining to political perspectives and ideologies? Why or why not?

4. The article cites a statistic that says Democrat professors and administrators outnumber Republican colleagues by more than 10 to 1. How do you feel about such a statistic? Can universities claim to be fair and balanced in the classroom when faculty from one party are so outnumbered by faculty from another party? Explain.

5. Most universities support affirmative action for hiring faculty and student enrollment to ensure racial and sex diversity. Why do they

oppose similar affirmative action criteria for political and intellectual diversity? Is this a contradiction? Why or why not?

6. If the university is about academic freedom and the free inquiry into ideas, is it logically consistent for some professors to silence students who have different points of view? Why or why not?

~

Science and Faith

Religion and Science
C. S. Lewis

C. S. Lewis was a professor of English language and literature at Oxford University and later became the Chair of Medieval and Renaissance English Literature at Cambridge University. Lewis was born into a Christian family, but he was a practical atheist for much of his early life. Through philosophical examinations of morality, the existence of evil, and the problem of pain, he rejected atheism and became a theist. After reading the works of G. K. Chesterton and having literary, philosophical, and theological discussions with J. R. R. Tolkien, Lewis became a Christian at age 33. He applied a keen philosophical mind to his religious faith and became the leading twentieth-century Christian apologist (one who explains and defends the Christian faith). In addition to his impressive literary scholarship, he wrote dozens of books dealing with various philosophical questions of Christianity. Some of his books include *The Pilgrim's Regress* (1933), *The Problem of Pain* (1940), *The Screwtape Letters* (1942), *The Abolition of Man* (1943), *Mere Christianity* (1952), and *Surprised by Joy* (1955). Along with J. R. R. Tolkien, Charles Williams, and others, Lewis founded the Inklings, a literary and philosophical society that produced some of the greatest works of literary fantasy of the twentieth century, including Tolkien's *The Hobbit* and *The Lord of the Rings* and Lewis's *The Chronicles of Narnia, Out of the Silent Planet, Perelandra, That Hideous Strength*, and *Till We Have Faces*. The following short essay comes from a collection of Lewis's essays titled

God in the Dock edited by Walter Hooper in 1970. Lewis died in 1963 on the same day John F. Kennedy was assassinated.

Essay Classification: Informative; synthesis; argumentation/persuasion; evaluative

"MIRACLES," SAID MY FRIEND. "Oh, come. Science has knocked the bottom out of all that. We know that Nature is governed by fixed laws."

"Didn't people always know that?" said I.

"Good Lord, no," said he. "For instance, take a story like the Virgin Birth. We know now that such a thing couldn't happen. We know there *must* be a male spermatozoon."

"But look here," said I, "St. Joseph—"

"Who's he?" asked my friend.

"He was the husband of the Virgin Mary. If you'll read the story in the Bible you'll find that when he saw his fiancée was going to have a baby he decided to cry off the marriage. Why did he do that?"

"Wouldn't most men?"

"Any man would," said I, "provided he knew the laws of Nature—in other words, provided he knew that a girl doesn't ordinarily have a baby unless she's been sleeping with a man. But according to your theory people in the old days didn't know that Nature was governed by fixed laws. I'm pointing out that the story shows that St. Joseph knew *that* law just as well as you do."

"But he came to believe in the Virgin Birth afterwards, didn't he?"

"Quite. But he didn't do so because he was under any illusion as to where babies came from in the ordinary course of Nature. He believed in the Virgin Birth as something *supernatural*. He knew Nature works in fixed, regular ways: but he also believed that there existed something *beyond* Nature which could interfere with her workings—from outside, so to speak."

"But modern science has shown there's no such thing."

"Really," said I. "Which of the sciences?"

"Oh, well, that's a matter of detail," said my friend. "I can't give you chapter and verse from memory."

"But, don't you see," said I, "that science never could show anything of the sort?"

"Why on earth not?"

"Because science studies Nature. And the question is whether any-thing *besides* Nature exists—anything 'outside.' How could you find that out by studying simply Nature?"

"But don't we find out that Nature *must* work in an absolutely fixed way? I mean, the laws of Nature tell us not merely how things *do* happen, but how they *must* happen. No power could possibly alter them."

"How do you mean?" said I.

"Look here," said he. "Could this 'something outside' that you talk about make two and two five?"

"Well, no," said I.

"All right," said he. "Well, I think the laws of Nature are really like two and two making four. The idea of their being altered is as absurd as the idea of altering the laws of arithmetic."

"Half a moment." said I. "Suppose you put sixpence into a drawer today, and sixpence into the same drawer tomorrow. Do the laws of arith-metic make it certain you'll find a shilling's worth there the day after?"

"Of course," said he, "provided no one's been tampering with your drawer."

"Ah, but that's the whole point," said I. "The laws of arithmetic can tell you what you'll find, with absolute certainty, *provided that* there's no inter-ference. If a thief has been at the drawer of course you'll get a different re-sult. But the thief won't have broken the laws of arithmetic—only the laws of England. Now, aren't the laws of Nature much in the same boat? Don't they all tell you what will happen *provided* there's no interference?"

"How do you mean?"

"Well, the laws will tell you how a billiard ball will travel on a smooth surface if you hit it in a particular way—but only provided no one inter-feres. If, after it's already in motion, someone snatches up a cue and gives it a biff on one side—why, then, you won't get what the scientist predicted."

"No, of course not. He can't allow for monkey-tricks like that."

"Quite, and in the same way, if there was anything outside Nature, and if it interfered—then the events which the scientist expected wouldn't follow. That would be what we call a miracle. In one sense it wouldn't break the laws of Nature. The laws tell you what will happen if nothing interferes. They can't tell you whether something *is* going to interfere. I mean, it's not the expert at arithmetic who can tell you how likely some-one is to interfere with the pennies in my drawer; a detective would be more use. It isn't the physicist who can tell you how likely I am to catch up a cue and spoil his experiment with the billiard ball; you'd better ask a psychologist. And it isn't the scientist who can tell you how likely Nature is to be interfered with from outside. You must go to the metaphysician."

"These are rather niggling points," said my friend. "You see, the real objection goes far deeper. The whole picture of the universe which science has given us makes it such rot to believe that the Power at the back of it all could be interested in us tiny little creatures crawling about on an unimportant planet! It was all so obviously invented by people who believed in a flat earth with the stars only a mile or two away."

"When did people believe that?"

"Why, all those old Christian chaps you're always telling about did. I mean Boethius and Augustine and Thomas Aquinas and Dante."

"Sorry," said I, "but this is one of the few subjects I do know something about."

I reached out my hand to a bookshelf. "You see this book," I said, "Ptolemy's *Almagest*. You know what it is?"

"Yes," said he. "It's the standard astronomical handbook used all through the Middle Ages."

"Well, just read that," I said, pointing to Book I, chapter 5.

"The earth," read out my friend, hesitating a bit as he translated the Latin, "the earth, in relation to the distance of the fixed stars, has no appreciable size and must be treated as a mathematical point!"

There was a moment's silence.

"Did they really know that *then?*" said my friend. "But—but none of the histories of science—none of the modern encyclopedias—ever mention the fact."

"Exactly," said I. "I'll leave you to think out the reason. It almost looks as if someone was anxious to hush it up, doesn't it? I wonder why."

There was another short silence.

"At any rate," said I, "we can now state the problem accurately. People usually think the problem is how to reconcile what we now know about the size of the universe with our traditional ideas of religion. That turns out not to be the problem at all. The real problem is this. The enormous size of the universe and the insignificance of the earth were known for centuries, and no one ever dreamed that they had any bearing on the religious question. Then, less than a hundred years ago, they are suddenly trotted out as an argument against Christianity. And the people who trot them out carefully hush up the fact that they were known long ago. Don't you think that all you atheists are strangely unsuspicious people?"

CRITICAL THINKING QUESTIONS

1. Many religious skeptics assume that religion is based upon primitive knowledge and that religious believers must be primitive in their thinking as well. How does Lewis refute that claim with his illustration of Joseph's reaction to finding out his fiancée, Mary, was pregnant with Jesus before they were married and before they had sexual intercourse? What does this say about their knowledge of biology? Were they stupid primitives?

2. Science deals primarily with nature and natural causes. As such, does it in any way prove that there is no supernatural causality? Or, does it merely assume there is no supernaturalism? Can scientific naturalism ever prove the existence or nonexistence of the supernatural? Explain what Lewis says on this matter.

3. The skeptic in the article notes that natural laws are like the laws of arithmetic and cannot be altered, thus only the natural can occur. How does Lewis refute this claim?

4. According to Lewis's explanation of nature, natural law, and the possibility of supernatural interference, what, then, is a miracle? Given this explanation, is the possibility of a miracle so outlandish as not to be believed rationally? Explain.

5. If physics (natural science) tells us about the natural world, what does metaphysics (theology) tell us about?

6. Many skeptics assert that Christians—past and present—do not know or understand science and just make things up. Is this true? What does Lewis teach us about this issue?

∾

By Design or by Chance?
Denyse O'Leary

Denyse O'Leary is a journalist based in Toronto who has covered the origins debate and intelligent design for years. She focuses on issues related to science, religion, and faith, and she has a special interest in neuroscience. She hosts her own blog called Post-Darwinist and assists William Dembski, a leading intelligent design scientist, in moderating his blog called Uncommon Descent. She is the faith and science columnist for *Christian Week* and her articles have appeared in *Christianity Today, Faith Today,* and *Christian Times.* Her books include *Crisis of Understanding: Homosexuality and the Canadian Church* (1988), *No Easy Answers: The Silent Agony of Crisis Pregnancies and Abortion* (1988), *Faith and Science: Why Science Needs Faith in the Twenty-First Century* (2001), and *By Design or By Chance?: The Growing Controversy on the Origins of Life in the Universe* (2004). The following is an excerpt from *By Design or by Chance.*

Essay Classification: Informative; synthesis; argumentation/persuasion

BEFORE THE EIGHTEENTH CENTURY, most people believed that the universe and time began when God created it. But from the eighteenth century until the mid-twentieth century, many scientists doubted that the universe even had a beginning. The idea of a beginning to the universe was considered a religious belief. Typically, scientists accepted an eternal universe, of never-ending binding and unbinding atoms over an infinity of space and time. Listen carefully to the scripts of some old science fiction movies, and you will still hear the echoes from the eternal void.

Then, in 1927, an obscure Belgian priest and cosmologist, Georges Lemaître (1894–1966), an early follower of Einstein, proposed that the universe popped into existence between 10 and 20 billion years ago, beginning with a single point.

Lemaître's theory was revolutionary. It overturned a century and a half of science. Initially, many scientists did not like the theory much, and some, like Arthur Eddington (1882–1944), said so. His comment was: "Philosophically, the notion of a beginning to the present order is repugnant to me. I should like to find a genuine loophole." To most scientists of the day, it sounded too much like religion. Thus, Lemaître, a priest, was in the unusual position of trying to focus attention on the science that supported his idea, while many atheists were more concerned with the religious implications. This odd turnabout continues to the present day, as we will see.

The Difference a Beginning Makes

If the universe has existed forever—or waxes and wanes in cycles—absolutely anything can happen, given the infinite amount of time available.

Now, just for a moment, let's picture the universe as a Universal Lottery. Perhaps neither you nor I are in the habit of buying lottery tickets, but for our illustration we must use the assumptions of scientists who view the universe that way. Well then, suppose we have pooled our money and bought a book of ten consecutive lottery tickets.

There is nothing unusual about our winning a lottery in which we have bought tickets. Indeed, suppose the universe is eternal. Over time, if tickets continue to be drawn indefinitely, our numbers will eventually come up. In fact, they will come up an infinite number of times, long after we are no longer around to claim our reward.

An eternal universe would work that way. All physically possible events would happen at some point. Its Universal Lottery is not guided by anyone because no guidance is needed. It just goes on drawing tickets forever. So the universe goes on and on, eternally evolving new and surprising situations—eventually it evolves into the very situation we are now experiencing.

However ... if the universe has a beginning—even if that beginning was a very long time ago—what happens to our Universal Lottery? Think about it. Here are some ways in which the Universal Lottery must change:

1. The number of tickets that can win shrinks dramatically. That is because only a certain number of draws can be made in the allowable time. Perhaps none of our tickets will be drawn.

2. Lots of unlikely things can still happen. For example, one of our tickets might win the lottery anyway.

3. However, every unlikely thing cannot happen because there is not enough time.

Suppose that in our Universal Lottery, there are fifty billion tickets. The odds that a ticket in our book will be a winner are very small but possible. Yet, what if, suddenly, every one of our ten tickets is called in perfect order, in a row, as a prizewinner. We know that is highly unlikely, even impossible. The lottery, which is now time limited, could not possibly randomly draw every ticket in our book, and no others, in the exact order in which the tickets are numbered. The lottery must have been "fixed"—designed so that we would win. That is indeed the universe we are living in. It appears fixed so that we would win.

Now, science is turning away from the concept of an eternal universe. The universe is thought by most cosmologists to have begun no more than 14 billion years ago. Its future life is estimated at about 100 trillion years. That sounds like a lot of time, and it is. The important thing to see, however, is that any finite amount of time, even if it is very large, enables us to calculate the odds of a given event.

As we will see, from the science evidence available today, our tickets have come up an amazing number of times. The coincidences that enable us humans to exist—which is what the Universal Lottery represents—now seem statistically impossible. Unless, that is, there is some sort of design at work.

The next question is: Does this mean that there would be an impact on "modern" culture? The answer is yes. Let's look at the ways.

Why "Modern" Culture Is On the Way Out

It may not be apparent at first glance, but the concept of the universe as an endless lottery of meaningless events actually shaped the "modern" culture of our society, from about the 1850s on. Modern culture, better known as "modernism," was the culture created by the theories of Darwin, Marx, and Freud. We humans were believed to be just an accident, living on a mediocre planet, circling a suburban star, in an irrelevantly repetitious universe. For culture, that means, among other things, "no God," "no meaning," "no purpose," and "no rules!" Not surprisingly, we have all heard these themes sounded every day from every source. They have driven the key questions that dominate modern society, such as:

- "Can we find meaning in a world without God?" (God's absence is taken for granted because there is no need for a creator in an eternal universe.)

- "How can a human life be important?" (If we just happen to exist, then we aren't important.)

- "What kind of morality should we have, if any, if God does not exist?" (A random universe can offer no moral guidance, and it is presumptuous to assume that we can really decide between right and wrong, or determine truth.)

Henri Frederic Amiel expressed this modern view clearly when he wrote, in 1868:

> The universe is but a kaleidoscope which turns within the mind of the so-called thinking being, who is himself a curiosity without a cause, an accident conscious of the great accident around him, and who amuses himself with it so long as the phenomenon of his vision lasts.

And, continuing the theme well over a century later, in 1986, zoologist Richard Dawkins wrote:

> Natural selection, the blind, unconscious, automatic process which Darwin discovered, and which we now know is the explanation for the existence and apparently purposeful form of all life, has no purpose in mind. It has no mind and no mind's eye. It does not plan for the future. It has no vision, no foresight, no sight at all. If it can be said to play the role of the watchmaker in nature, it is the blind watchmaker.

Yet, even as art, literature, and science were churning out endless riffs based on these propositions, a critical change was taking hold in science. A key moment was Lemaître's idea. Once science accepted the idea that the universe might have a beginning—and perhaps an end—it confronted a radically different picture of the universe from the "meaningless universe" of modernism. In some ways, it is a scarier one. But because it comes from the findings of contemporary science, it will have as much of an impact on our culture as the meaningless universe of modernism did. Key new findings in science usually do change culture and society.

What Does This Mean for Religion?

Many people, sensing a change in the wind, assume that the basic assumptions of modernism are false. Increasing numbers are looking elsewhere for answers. Ironically, one outcome is a worldwide resurgence of traditional religion. In North America, for example, liberal religious denominations that have aligned themselves with modernist philosophy are stagnant and graying, while nonmodernist ones are growing rapidly.

Some commentators argue that this situation simply reflects the "political muscle" of orthodox religious believers. In other words, it is merely a political event. They are mistaken. The change is a fundamental shift in how people look at questions about God, life, and the universe. It is a result of a change in the picture of the universe provided by science.

Shortly before he died, in 1966, Lemaître, who in his life had never sought or received much publicity, learned a critical piece of news. Two American physicists had discovered what is called the "signature" of the Big Bang: the microwaves that have been spreading throughout the universe ever since it took place. The idea that the universe has a beginning is now overwhelmingly accepted by cosmologists. But that did not happen without conflict. And what is even more interesting, the conflict had far more to do with defending the modernist religion of a meaningless, God-free universe than with science evidence.

So Evolution Means What?

Evolution is the theory that all life forms are descended from one or several common ancestors that were present on the early earth, three to four billion years ago. It includes the process by which one species is transformed into another, for example a dinosaur species into a bird species. There have been a number of models of how evolution works, including models that assume divine guidance or perhaps divine intervention at various points along the way.

So Darwinism Means Exactly What?

The fundamental principle of Darwinian evolution is common descent by fully naturalistic means. Common descent is the belief that all life forms, including ourselves, are descendants of a common ancestor (or possibly several common ancestors) billions of years ago. Scientists differ, often sharply, about the details. "Naturalistic means" is a way of saying that natural law acting on chance events explains everything that happens. Life came into existence by chance and developed by chance, without design, guidance, or intervention by God or an intelligent designer. Or, if there were any divine design, guidance, or intervention, it could never be scientifically detectable.

In his epoch-making *On the Origins of the Species,* published in 1859, Englishman Charles Darwin argued that there was no actual design to nature; the laws of nature acted by chance and created all the life forms that we see from a common ancestor. The fittest ones survived by developing endless adaptations (changes). In other words, Darwin provided a theory for how life forms develop from a common ancestor without design or outside intelligent influence.

He called the process natural selection. Scientists liked Darwin's simplification. It especially suited the materialistic world of nineteenth-century England. It provided a powerful support for a belief that was already rapidly growing among intellectuals that the universe was Godless and meaningless, and that human beings were a random outcome of its processes. Thus, Darwin became the popular central figure in biology in the same way that Freud had in psychology, and Marx in politics. The fact that these men were elevated as dominant figures did not, of course, mean that everyone agreed with them. It did mean that everyone had to take their claims seriously, and if they disagreed, they had to construct a viable alternative view.

From the beginning, scientists identified problems with Darwin's assumptions. These problems did not attract much attention, because scientists assumed that they would just be sorted out one day. For example, Darwin thought that the world under the microscope consisted of simple jellies and crystals that could easily form randomly. He could not have been more wrong. It was only with the dawn of biochemistry in the 1950s—when scientists were able to look into cells deeply and in detail—that they realized how wrong he was. The world at a microscopic level is almost as complex as the world above it.

It was difficult to understand how complex cells can be created simply by law acting on chance. We do not know of an "early, simple version" of cells or organs. Even the "simple" version had to be complex in order to exist. Respected scientists, such as Fred Hoyle, checked out of believing in a simple Darwinist explanation for the origin of life in the early 1970s, for precisely this reason. So why is Darwinism still entrenched?

Darwinism continues partly because it is the historical model of biology and partly because it underwrites the modernist religion. But more and more of the evidence supporting Darwinism just does not withstand close scrutiny.

The growing political uproar around the teaching of evolution is fueled by the fact that Darwinism is the only model of evolution that is permitted in most school systems. Indeed, some teachers have been forbidden even to bring up known problems with the theory. This is because modernism is the unacknowledged religion of tax-supported public school systems, and Darwinism is one of modernism's most important teachings. Just as you would not be permitted to argue against Christianity in the pulpit of a traditional church, so teachers are not permitted to argue against Darwinism in the lectern of a modernist school or university.

What's Intelligent Design (ID) Theory?

ID theory started to take shape in the late 1970s, as an outcome of information theory. Faced with the enormous complexity of living things—for example, the fact that complete instructions for creating DNA would be as long as the DNA code itself—ID theorists argue that it makes more sense to assume that the information is a language. In other words, it is a product of design. This is the complete opposite of Darwinism.

Reintroducing design would, of course, change the way many problems in science are perceived. The ID scientist does not try to figure out how things happened by chance, but rather looks for intentional patterns that suggest general laws of development. The laws that prevail in one situation may shed light on another. Darwinists view ID as heresy because they are committed to a "no-design model" and would prefer to continue looking for solutions to the mystery of life via law and chance.

Isn't This Just "Religion" Versus "No Religion" All Over Again?

No. All parties to the debates have a religious stance of some type. Many atheists who are Darwinists actively promote a "no-God religion," which they think is better suited to the times we live in than traditional religions. Many other Darwinists are religious people, sometimes devout Christians. One example is the American biochemist Ken Miller, a practicing Roman Catholic who is the author of *Finding Darwin's God*. During my research, I also ran across a number of atheists or agnostics who are non-Darwinists or post-Darwinists.

In the end, the conflict is between those who think that Darwinism can survive the collapse of modernism—a collapse that has already taken out Marx and Freud—and those who think that, on the contrary, design belongs as much in biology as in cosmology.

The Best Arguments for Design

Design advocates point to the sheer complexity of life forms as their strongest argument. Within the 14 billion or so years that are the age of the present universe, does either chance or necessity produce the complex molecular machines that form cells, the building blocks of animals and plants? Or is there an element of design?

Fred Hoyle was one scientist who was aware of the problems that the origin of life presented to scientists' materialist worldview. He had to admit, against his preferences, that life forms look as though they are designed. He compared Darwin's belief that life just happened somehow to the hope that a tornado in a junkyard would somehow manufacture for us a Boeing 747.

Hoyle did not like design, and he continued to propose alternatives to the end of his life, as he did with the Big Bang. But he never found one that really worked.

Some scientists, especially biochemist Michael Behe of Pennsylvania's Lehigh University, author of the controversial *Darwin's Black Box* (1996), have begun to argue that Darwinism—which explains everything in terms of law and chance—does not account for either the existence or the evolution of the complex machinery of cells. And we cannot talk about life without talking about cells. Every life form is either a cell or a highly organized, interconnected, indivisible nation of cells. Or, as Davies puts it: "Even a simple bacterium is a vast assemblage of intricately crafted molecules, many of them elaborately customized."

Behe calls some of the machinery in cells "irreducibly complex." He means that there are no "simple" cell systems that could just arise by chance from the six organic elements (calcium, carbon, hydrogen, nitrogen, oxygen, and phosphorous) and then evolve into complex cell systems. That is because there is no simple way of doing the jobs that these systems do. A creature with a simpler arrangement could not live at all. A little malfunction here or there, and the cell does not evolve to a higher form of life; it dies. One reason that cells are complex is that they must use molecular machinery to force elements and chemicals to do things that they do not normally do.

Behe is a key proponent of intelligent design theory. According to him, the cell works the way it does because at least some of its complex machinery was intelligently designed. Science cannot understand life as long as it excludes design.

Needless to say, Behe was soon roundly denounced by the Darwinist establishment. As Thomas Woodward puts it in *Doubts About Darwin: A History of Intelligent Design*, Behe's dissent was "the first time sophisticated skepticism of naturalistic evolution was brought to center stage in American society." The reaction was predictable. One of the world's foremost philosophers of evolution, Michael Ruse, has said of Behe, "I think he is wrong, wrong, wrong." Ruse directs his readers to Darwinist author Ken Miller to be rightly instructed.

To understand Ruse's and other Darwinists' responses, we need to keep in mind that Darwinian evolution is not just a theory. Darwinism eliminates design, and to the Darwinist, eliminating design is science. The fact that Behe is not a creationist and accepts a role for evolution does nothing to turn aside shock and anger at his views.

CRITICAL THINKING QUESTIONS

1. What is the central irony in the current debates about the origin of the universe that O'Leary notes early in her essay?

2. Why does the eternal universe theory appeal to atheists? What do atheists fear about the Big Bang theory or any theory that clearly implies or demonstrates that the universe had a beginning?

3. What does the current scientific evidence seem to suggest about the nature of the universe—is it eternal or did it have a beginning? Discuss the evidences presented by O'Leary.

4. Who seems to be operating more by faith than by reason and evidence, the theist who argues the universe had a beginning or the atheist who argues the universe is eternal? Explain.

5. Discuss O'Leary's use of the lottery metaphor. How does she use it to explain the notion that the universe must be designed and thus there must be a Designer? Is this a convincing metaphor? Why or why not?

6. In what way is modernism a type of religion and Darwinism one of its central doctrines? Is it fair and reasonable to forbid discussing the many scientific and logical problems with Darwinism in schools? Explain.

The Gods Must Be Tidy: Is the Cosmos a Work of Poor Engineering or the Gift of an Artistic Designer?

Jonathan Witt

Jonathan Witt received his PhD in English from the University of Kansas and was a professor at Lubbock Christian University. Currently he is a senior fellow and writer in residence at the Discovery Institute. The following essay appeared in *Touchstone Magazine* in 2004.

Essay Classification: Synthesis; informative; evaluative

WHEN AS A BOY I read "The Scouring of the Shire" near the end of J. R. R. Tolkien's *The Lord of the Rings*, I could not understand why Tolkien felt the need to tack on such an anticlimactic and shabby bit of evil. Only later, as I began to notice modernity's penchant for ugliness in the world beyond Middle Earth, did I understand that the scouring of the Shire bespoke a present evil, a malevolence insidious precisely because it lacked the stark drama of the trenches or the gas chambers.

I came to understand that the demolition of the hobbits' lovely village possessed the striking lines of caricature not because it was unrealistic but rather because the depiction is so sharp and trenchant. Familiarity may breed contempt, but it can also breed cataracts, an incapacity to see a thing vividly, truly.

God of the Nazis

The twentieth century was, in its darkest moments, an arresting illustration of the will to power, but it also exhibited a less imposing if somewhat more curious urge: what could be aptly termed the will to ugliness. The perversely drab "pre-fabs" of postwar England, the American slum projects constructed by a later generation, the willfully dissonant monstrosities of much modern high architecture, the willfully tortured, obscure, and graceless prose of the deconstructionists, even the black-eyed and anorexic grotesques of the Paris catwalks—all bespeak an age driven to throw up trappings repulsive in their embrace of detachment and death.

The cultural pedigree of this modern predilection for ugliness is old, various, and to some degree mysterious. But here I want to suggest that Darwinism—in which I include its DNA-inspired mutation, neo-Darwinism—has contributed to this will to ugliness not merely by underwriting a vision of the world as a godless accident, but also in the very way it critiques and thereby dismisses the idea of an Author and Designer of life.

What I call the a-teleological macroevolutionists—those who argue that the cosmos is the product of chance and has no intrinsic end or purpose—argue that life emerged by natural selection without design from single-celled organisms, and they claim to use strictly scientific methods to support their position. In truth, however, they often slip into what is essentially an aesthetic and theological argument against a designer.[1] Others have noted this, but what has not been fully explored is the dubious nature of the evolutionists' aesthetic argument.

Consider one especially prominent example, evolutionist Richard Dawkins's critique of the mammalian eye in his *The Blind Watchmaker: Why the Evidence of Evolution Reveals a Universe Without Design*:

> Each photocell is, in effect, wired in backwards, with its wire sticking out on the side nearest the light.... This means that the light, instead of being granted an unrestricted passage to the photocells, has to pass through a forest of connecting wires, presumably suffering at least some attenuation and distortion (actually probably not much but, still, it is the *principle* of the thing that would offend any tidy-minded engineer!)[2]

Never mind for the moment that it has been clearly demonstrated that the backward wiring of the mammalian eye actually confers a distinct advantage by dramatically increasing the flow of oxygen to the eye.[3] Let us ignore that brilliant bit of engineering and look at Dawkins's intriguing obsession with neatness. O brave new world whose supreme designer distinguishes himself first and foremost by his tidy-mindedness! Aldous Huxley has ably dramatized the horror of a society so engineered.

Do we really wish to substitute the exuberantly imaginative, even whimsical designer of our actual universe for a cosmic neat freak? Such a deity might serve nicely as the national God of the Nazis, matching Hitler stroke for stroke: Hitler in his disdain for humanity's sprawling diversity; the tidy cosmic engineer in his distaste for an ecosystem choked and sullied by a grotesque menagerie of strange and apparently substandard species. Out with that great big prodigal Gothic cathedral we call the world; in with a modern and minimalist blueprint for a new and neater cosmos.

Bye, Panda

One of the first things that would have to go is the panda—if not the whole bear, then certainly his two thumbs. In Stephen Jay Gould's book *The Panda's Thumb,* the late Harvard paleontologist has this criticism for his title character:

> An engineer's best solution is debarred by history. The panda's true thumb is committed to another role, too specialized for a different function to become an opposable, manipulating digit. So the panda must use parts on hand and settle for an enlarged wrist bone and a somewhat clumsy, but quite workable, solution. The sesamoid thumb wins no prize in an engineer's derby. It is, to use Michael Ghiselin's phrase, a contraption, not a lovely contrivance.

Now one might take the usual defend-the-engineer tack here, and any design advocate trained in such matters certainly should scrutinize Gould's assumptions as to the inferiority of the panda's thumb. Gould even provides a small opening when he concedes that the sesamoid thumb is "quite workable" and "does its job." Indeed, when he finally witnessed a panda firsthand, he "was amazed by their dexterity and wondered how the scion of a stock adapted for running could use its hands so adroitly."

By Gould's account, the panda's thumb makes a fine peeler for bamboo, the panda's principal food, and investigation may demonstrate that it is actually superior to an opposable thumb for such work.[4]

However, do not hold your breath waiting for pandas to take up flyfishing or needlepoint. For versatility, the opposable thumb is the clear blue ribbon winner. Which raises the obvious question: If an intelligent designer designed the world, did he not think of the opposable thumb until after he designed the panda? And was he too tired to go back and upgrade that poor panda?

To such a question the Darwinian community collectively responds thus: "Obviously not. If there's a designer out there running the show, he's a real bumbler, a second-rate engineer who could not get a job in a third-rate Swiss watch factory. Since the idea of a second-rate designer is patently ridiculous, there is no designer."

This argument is rife with problems already underscored by design thinkers like William Dembski in his book *The Design Revolution.* The most basic failing of this line of reasoning is that even if the panda's thumb is proven to be less useful than it could be, that doesn't negate the evidence that the whole panda has the mark of design. It's a creature dependent upon an architecturally marvelous cathedral of complex, specified information, the sort we know from experience is fashioned only by intelligent agents.

Indeed, the panda would remain so even if it had no thumbs at all. The Yugo, I'm told, was a badly designed automobile, but no sane person would argue that with all its problems, it wasn't designed. The same logic applies to a panda or a duck-billed platypus or an ostrich.

But the point here is that these anti-design arguments by Dawkins, Gould, and other Darwinists are not scientific ones. They are aesthetic arguments, expressing an idea of what the universe should look like—that is, that it should satisfy the tidy-minded engineer. But who is to say that the Darwinists' taste is that of the cosmic designer, if there is one? Who is to say that the designer should value tidiness over, say, whimsy?

Bad Art

Recently, something else struck me about this effort to call attention to the apparently jury-rigged quality of certain elements of the cosmic "watch" and then declare that such things could not have been designed: Critics of intelligent design tuck some idiosyncratic and highly dubious aesthetic presuppositions into the metaphor of the cosmos as watch. These include an overemphasis on tidiness, a de-emphasis on beauty, and a dismissal of any possibility that the creator might wish to commune with his creation. Surely a perfect watchmaker would wind up his perfect (tidy, efficient, functional) watch and step away, freed by the perfection of his instrument from the need to tinker any further with it.

We can see how Enlightenment thinkers arrived at this metaphor of the watch, confronted as they were with fresh insights into the orderly, mathematically precise nature of the cosmos. And contemporary astrophysicists, even those who resist the idea of a cosmic design, now tell us that the laws and constants of the cosmos are, in fact, finely tuned to an almost unimaginable degree, such that even very small changes in a few of them would render complex life utterly impossible. So at least in one sense, the universe is watch-like.

But all metaphors break down if pressed far enough, and this one breaks down pretty quickly. Where a single metaphor crowds out all others in a matter as complex as our living world, it produces an intellectually impoverished and very misleading stick-figure rendering of the subject.

Thus, the thinking person is wise to ask, to what *extent* is the universe watch-like? To what extent should it be watch-like?

To cling to the watch analogy in a critique of the notion of a wise cosmic designer fails to face an obvious (and theological) question: Is this an adequate way to speak of the hypothetical designer? Is his satisfying the aesthetic demands of the Darwinists a sufficient test of his existence? To put it another way, if there is a cosmic designer, what does he need a watch for? He doesn't. One would be hard-pressed to name a major religion that posits a transcendent god who uses the universe primarily as a tool.

Not even the god articulated by the orderly minds of Plato and Aristotle fits the bill. Whether we think of the morally compromised gods of Mount Olympus meddling in the affairs of their various mortal off-spring; or of Plato's "the One" (what he also called "the Good" or "Father of that Captain and Cause"); or the holy God of the Bible, father and shepherd and husband of his people, the deity is not construed as one in-terested in the world primarily as a tool for himself. Indeed, whenever he is construed as a personality, and not merely as some sort of nonsentient organizing First Principle, he is depicted as one interested in the world itself, as a creator who delights in the work of his hands.

The Lover's Watch

Dare we use the word "love" in this context? Dare one suggest that the designer loves his creation in a way the watchmaker does not love the watch he makes, that the Creator would no more think of his creation as a tool than would a bridegroom his bride or a father his children? The fact that such terms as *love* and *bridegroom* strike many as inappropri-ate to the evolution/design debate merely testifies to how thoroughly the utilitarian assumption behind the metaphor of the watch has permeated Western thinking.

Certainly, we could try to discuss the matter without consider-ing the designer's attitude toward his creation (that is, whether he is a watchmaker or a bridegroom or father). But the evolutionists have already smuggled this issue into the debate by assuming that, if there were a designer, he would be some sort of disinterested and hyper-tidy watchmaker. Having smuggled in this highly questionable point, they then regard as beneath consideration any idea of a designer who (as they put it) "meddles in his creation."

Or they dismiss the notion that an omnipotent and omniscient designer might fashion a creature short of an optimal design. Here they not only make a theological claim but ignore a key question at once practical and aesthetic: How do concerns about ecological balance impinge upon a critique of animal structures?

Must the cosmic designer's primary concern for pandas be that they are the most dexterous bears divinely imaginable? From a purely practical standpoint, might opposable-thumbed über-pandas wreak havoc on their ecosystem? From a purely aesthetic standpoint, might not those charming pandas up in their bamboo trees with their unopposing but quite workable thumbs be just the sort of humorous supporting character this great cosmic drama needs to lighten things up a bit? If Shakespeare could do it in his tragedies, why not God?

Pandas as comic relief? To spurn the notion as if it were patently ridiculous and beneath consideration is merely to expose one's utilitarian presuppositions. Why, after all, should the designer's world read like a dreary high-school science textbook, its style humorless, homogenous, and suffocating under the dead weight of a supposedly detached passive voice? Why should not the designer's world entertain, amuse, and fascinate, as well as "work"?

In summary, virtually the entire bad-design versus good-design discussion is framed by an engineer's perspective, not an artist's or mystic's. When I mentioned this to the philosopher Jay W. Richards a few years ago, he responded in a letter: "After all, why do we assume that God created the universe to be a watch, in which a self-winding mechanism makes it 'better'? Maybe the universe is like a piano, or a novel with the author as a character, or a garden for other beings with whom God wants to interact. It's amazing how a simple image can highjack a discussion for a century and a half."

What is worse, Darwinists like Gould and Dawkins commit the error called atomism: the idea that, in Gould's own words, "wholes should be understood by decomposition into 'basic' units." In other words, they assume not only that nature is a kind of watch but that each individual design is its own watch—its own machine—meant to be judged in relative isolation. They evaluate the panda's thumb by how well it works as a thumb, not by how well it fits into the whole life of the panda, including its place in its own environment.

This is, at the most practical level, to misunderstand pandas. At the aesthetic level, it is to declare that an artist who might have created pandas could not have been thinking (as artists do) of the whole work.

Unaesthetic Shakespeare

Interestingly, the god of the English canon, William Shakespeare, came in for much the same criticism by the tidier-minded among his neoclassical critics as the God of the cosmos has come in for from the tidier-minded scientists. This actor turned playwright lacked classical restraint, the argument went.

In 1726 Lewis Theobald perhaps initiated the century's long criticism of Hamlet's coarse speech when he commented on a particularly bawdy line spoken by Hamlet to Ophelia: "If ever the Poet deserved Whipping for low and indecent Ribaldry, it was for this Passage."[5]

Another regarded Shakespeare's general habit of mingling the low with the high, the comic with the tragic as a "wholly monstrous, unnatural mixture."[6] With only a little more restraint, a third lamented the bard's tragedies: "How inattentive to propriety and order, how deficient in grouping, how fond of exposing disgusting as well as beautiful figures!", how often he compels the audience "to grovel in dirt and ordure."[7]

Happily, most neoclassical Shakespearean critics were enthusiastic, and yet, as one modern critic noted, even the admiration of the more sympathetic critics was always "modified and tempered . . . by regrets that Shakespeare had elected, either through ignorance or by design, to embrace a method that discarded all classical rules."[8]

What do we make of such criticism today? To use Freud's language, itself rude and vulgar, such criticism strikes us as anal-retentive. What emotionally whole and thoroughly sane admirer of Renaissance drama would want to substitute for the works of the "myriad minded" Shakespeare, the relatively impoverished fare left over after unsympathetic neoclassical critics tidied him up?

Perhaps the relevance of the analogy is becoming clear. The criticism of Shakespeare is akin to the evolutionists' criticisms of the cosmic designer. In each case the critic believes the respective artist in question should build all of his characters according to some rigid set of criteria that ignores broader concerns, be they ecological, aesthetic, or otherwise. Proponents of this line of argument value tidiness over other and often more vital aesthetic criteria like intricacy, harmony, variety, imaginative exuberance, freedom, even moral complexity.

A Queer Assumption

The Darwinists' aesthetic criticism moves from the unconvincing to the positively odd in a further and even queerer assumption: the conviction that no all-knowing and all-powerful designer would restrict himself to the materials at hand, even when such designs are clearly superb. Darwinists are quite fond of this argument, apparently considering it irresistibly persuasive to all but the most irrational mind.

I saw an especially brazen instance of this strange aesthetic dogma at a debate at Texas Tech University between Darwinist James Carr and intelligent design microbiologist Michael Behe. Arguing against Behe, Carr used the similarities in the genetic code of chimps and humans as a bad-design argument. What all-powerful creator would need to recycle his materials like this, he argued. It was almost as if he considered it unmanly of the Fellow Upstairs.

Gould leveled essentially the same criticism against a would-be cosmic designer in his description of Charles Darwin's study of orchids:

> Orchids manufacture their intricate devices from the common components of ordinary flowers, parts usually fitted for very different functions. If God had designed a beautiful machine to reflect his wisdom and power, surely he would not have used a collection of parts generally fashioned for other purposes. Orchids were not made by an ideal engineer; they are jury-rigged from a limited set of available components.[9]

Or as one writer Gould quoted put it, nature is a superb tinkerer, not a divine artificer.[10]

The argument that no cosmic designer would so often recycle his creative material is a common tactic, one Darwin himself employed. In a letter to Asa Gray around 1861 Darwin wrote, "Your question what would convince me of Design is a poser. . . . If man was made of brass or iron and no way connected with any other organism which had ever lived, I should perhaps be convinced."[11]

Certainly humans made of iron or brass would create enormous difficulties for a Darwinian explanation of humankind's existence. But the tenor of this comment fits Darwin's attitude to the similarities among the species. His unstated assumption seems to be that the similarities are not merely one missed opportunity for the natural world to reveal its design and thus falsify his theory, but a positive argument against a cosmic designer.

Darwin's Design

Most of us would respond, "But why?" The only logical way to use the similarities as an argument against a designer is to take as an aesthetic premise the assumption that no omniscient and omnipotent designer would design in such a way. In other words, one would have to assume that using the ho-hum materials at hand instead of consistently elevating higher works of art with newer and "better" materials violates some pre-established and widely accepted aesthetic principle. "Why," Darwin asked in *The Origin of Species,* "should the sepals, petals, stamens, and pistils in any individual flower, though fitted for such widely different purposes, be all constructed on the same pattern?"[12]

Ironically, Darwin unwittingly suggested a very un-Darwinian answer in a letter to his sister. Expressing his admiration for the Duke of Northumberland's home, Darwin wrote, "His house was very grand; much more so than the other great nobility, and in much better taste." The young biologist did not attribute the house's nobility and beauty to a prodigal use of variously distinct materials or motifs—quite the contrary. "Every window in his house was full of straight lines of brilliant lights, and from their extreme regularity and number had a beautiful effect. *The paucity of invention* [emphasis mine] was very striking, crowns, anchors, and 'W.R.'s' were repeated in endless succession."[13]

So why should Darwin be surprised that an intelligent designer of the world would proceed in the same way? Conventional wisdom in the field of aesthetics all but demands such an artistic method. Pattern and variation are interdependent concepts fundamental to art. Where would Schubert's "Theme and Variations" be without the theme? The point is so basic one feels silly making it.

Should the later movements of Beethoven's Fifth Symphony be censured for continuing to build off an original motif? Do we exclaim with the woman at the first performance of *Bolero* that Ravel must be mad for building on his central motif? Do we not instead admire the way he built so exquisitely and powerfully on the central motif till the climactic grandeur of the finale? Ought we to demote Monet from the first rank of the impressionists because he had the bad taste to paint poplars and haystacks over and over again? Do we not instead marvel at the fecundity of his imagination, at the subtly of his observation and insight?

No one, not even his harshest eighteenth-century critics, accuses Shakespeare of bad art on the grounds that *Much Ado About Nothing* and *Othello* share virtually the same plot, creatively altered to produce radically different plays. Few if any object to Shakespeare's repetition of motherless girls as heroines, or to his girls-disguised-as-boys theme, or to his repetitive use of the sonnet form for his poetry.

Unimaginable Genius

Where the atomist or reductionist regards elements in isolation (and properly so within certain intellectual disciplines), the artist seeks variety within unity, rhythm, and harmony, qualities fundamental to the creation of beauty. Notice I am not claiming a seat of honor for some culturally narrow artistic practice—say, the English sonnet—but rather appealing to principles broad and fundamental in the history of the world's art.

If there is an intelligent designer behind this astonishingly complex work of art we call the world, it's quite sensible to suppose he would be at least as artistically savvy as the artistically gifted among his creatures, that he would cultivate harmony and unity through the creative reuse of common materials. Now, the Darwinist might complain, "What is all this artistic, aesthetic balderdash? We are scientists, not poets or starry-eyed mystics. Leave the artists to their pattern-making and let us get back to our hard-nosed, empirical science." Fine, but if they wish to avoid an argument about aesthetic principles, they should not assume within their arguments aesthetic principles that are at best highly debatable, and at worst contrary to the canons of art.

In the meantime, those who reject such dubious reasoning, who understand that the world is the handiwork of unimaginable genius, could do worse than to follow the aesthetic lead of those humble and beautiful hobbits who returned to their desecrated Shire carrying elven soil: We can take a soil richer than the dead ground of materialism and sprinkle it wherever we can, honoring the miracle of creation's growth even as we tend to our proper role as stewards and gardeners of a world between Heaven and Hell, a place we might aptly call Middle Earth.

Notes

1. See, for instance, Paul Nelson's "The Role of Theology in Current Evolutionary Reasoning," *Biology and Philosophy* 11 (1996), pp. 493–517; William Dembski's *Intelligent Design* (InterVarsity Press, 1999) and *The Design Revolution* (InterVarsity Press, 2004); and Cornelius G. Hunter's *Darwin's God* (Brazos Press, 2001).

2. W. W. Norton, 1996, p. 93.

3. Excerpts from "The Inverted Retina: Maladaptation or Pre-adaptation?" *Origins and Design* 19:2 (2000): 14 June 2000, www.arn.org/docs/odesign/od192/invertedretina192.htm.

4. W. W. Norton, 1980, pp. 21, 22, 24.

5. Quoted in Paul S. Conklin, *A History of Hamlet Criticism: 1601–1821* (Humanities Press, 1968), p. 53.

6. Charles Gildon, quoted in Herbert Spencer Robinson, *English Shakespearian Criticism in the Eighteenth Century* (Gordian Press, 1968), pp. 26–27.

7. Edward Taylor, "From *Cursory Remarks . . .*", in *Shakespeare: The Critical Heritage, 1774–1801,* edited by Brian Vickers (Routledge & Kegan Paul, 1981), pp. 130–32. This Taylor is not to be confused with the wonderful American poet Edward Taylor, the last of the metaphysical poets, who spent a great deal of time in the "dirt and ordure" exploring the mysteries of the divine and the human.

8. Robinson, *English Shakespearian Criticism,* p. xii.

9. *The Panda's Thumb,* p. 20.

10. François Jacob, quoted ibid., p. 26.

11. "To Asa Gray," 17 September 1861(?), volume 2 of *Life and Letters of Charles Darwin,* edited by Francis Darwin, ftp://sailor.gutenberg.org/pub/gutenberg/etext00/2llcd10.txt.

12. Sixth London Edition (1872), ftp://sailor.gutenberg.org/pub/gutenberg/etext99/otoos610.txt.

13. 9 September 1831, volume 1 of *Life and Letters of Charles Darwin,* ftp://sailor.gutenberg.org/pub/gutenberg/etext00/1llcd10.txt.

CRITICAL THINKING QUESTIONS

1. Why does Witt begin his essay by raising issues and questions of aesthetics and notions of beauty?

2. Some evolutionists and those who claim the universe cannot have a Designer argue from the view that some things just don't seem tidy enough to be designed by a supremely intelligent Designer. How does Witt answer such claims? Do you find his arguments compelling? Why or why not?

3. Anti-design scientists claim that there can't be a Designer because there seem to be imperfections in the supposed design or that some elements are not designed as they think they should be. Are these scientists making scientific judgments here or aesthetic ones? Why is it important to distinguish the two? Explain.

4. Many Darwinists and anti-design scientists conclude that there cannot be a Designer because the way the universe appears to them is not the kind of universe they think a supreme Designer would create. What is the main logical error in this argument?

5. What assumptions have the Darwinists made about the way they think a Designer, if there is one, would be like and how this Designer would view his creation? How does Witt address this assumption?

6. Why does Witt posit the possibility that maybe the Designer is more like an artistic Shakespeare than a utilitarian tidy engineer?

7. Darwinists claim that an omniscient and omnipotent Designer would not use variations of a single design in different creations, and they conclude that since we see similarities between species there can be no Designer. How does Witt answer this argument? Which position makes more sense to you? Why?

∾

What Is Scientific Naturalism?
J. P. Moreland

J. P. Moreland is Distinguished Professor of Philosophy at Talbot School of Theology, and he is the director of the Eidos Christian Center. He has written, edited, coauthored, and contributed to over forty books, including *Love Your God with All Your Mind: The Role of Reason in the Life of the Soul* (1997), *Scaling the Secular City: A Defense of Christianity* (1987), *The Creation Hypothesis: Scientific Evidence for an Intelligent Designer* (1994), and *Philosophical Foundations for a Christian Worldview* (2003). He has also written over sixty articles in numerous philosophical and theological academic journals. The following essay was written specifically for undergraduate students and posted on TrueU.org in 2005.

Essay Classification: Informative

IN 1941, HARVARD SOCIOLOGIST Pitirim A. Sorokin wrote a book entitled *The Crisis of Our Age.* In it Sorokin claimed that cultures come in two major types: sensate and ideational.

A sensate culture is one in which people only believe in the reality of the physical world we experience with our five senses. A sensate culture is secular, this-worldly, and empirical. By contrast, an ideational culture embraces the physical world, but goes on to accept the notion that a non-physical, immaterial reality can be known as well, a reality consisting of God, the soul, immaterial beings, values, purposes, and various abstract objects like numbers and propositions.

Sorokin claimed that a sensate culture will eventually disintegrate because it does not have the intellectual resources necessary to sustain a public and private life conducive to human flourishing. After all, if we can't know anything about values, life after death, God, and so forth, where can we find solid guidance toward a life of wisdom and character?

Sorokin's claim should come as no surprise to students of the Bible. Proverbs tells us that we become the ideas we cherish in our inner being and Paul reminds us that we transform our lives through a renewed intellectual life. Scripture is quite clear that our worldview will determine the shape of our cultural and individual lives. Because this is so, the worldview struggle raging in our modern context has absolutely far-reaching and crucial implications.

The dominant worldview in Western culture is scientific naturalism. In this article and the one to come, I intend to examine scientific naturalism and its central creation myth—evolution—in order to accomplish two ends. First, I want to explain why it is that so many people accept evolution when the evidence for it is far from conclusive, even quite meager. Second, I want to issue a warning for Christians who think that theistic evolution is a benign option for believers attempting to integrate science and theology. To accomplish these ends, I will answer the question, "What is scientific naturalism?" Then, in my next article, I will argue that evolution is embraced with a type of certainty that goes well beyond the evidence for it and close with a plea to Christians who advocate theistic evolution.

Just what is scientific naturalism (hereafter, naturalism)? Succinctly put, it is the view that the spatio-temporal universe established by scientific forms of investigation is all there is, was, or ever will be. Brains and buffaloes exist (for instance), but minds and moral values must not, because they are invisible to the five senses and therefore invisible to scientific enquiry.

There are three major components of naturalism.

First, naturalism begins with an epistemology—a view about the nature and limits of knowledge—known as scientism. Scientism comes in two forms: strong and weak.

Strong scientism is the view that we can only know things that can be tested scientifically. According to strong scientism, scientific knowledge exhausts what can be known; if some belief (for instance, a theological belief) is not part of a well established scientific theory, it is not an item of knowledge.

Weak scientism admits that some claims in fields outside of science (like ethics) are rational and justified. But scientific knowledge is taken to be so vastly superior that its claims always trump the claims made by other disciplines.

The first component of naturalism, then, is the belief that scientific knowledge is either the only kind of knowledge there is or an immeasurably superior kind of knowledge.

The second major component of naturalism is a theory about the ultimate cause of things, a story that tells us how everything in the universe has come to be. The central components of this story are the atomic theory of matter and the theory of evolution.

According to the atomic theory of matter, the smallest parts of the ordinary physical universe (that is, the chemical elements listed in the Periodic Table) originate in the combining of protons, electrons, and neutrons, and larger chunks of the physical universe (everything from rocks to planets) originate in the combining of chemical elements.

According to the theory of evolution, lions, tigers and bears (oh, my!) originate in the combining of organic chemicals, and this is also true of you and of me. The details of this story are not of concern here. But two broad features are of critical importance.

First, explanations of macro-changes in things are always in terms of micro-changes—causation starts at the bottom and works its way up, small to large, micro to macro. Second, everything happens because of earlier events plus the laws of nature.

The second component of naturalism, then, is a story telling us that everything that's ever happened can be exhaustively explained in terms of earlier events and the laws of nature, and each particular event can be exhaustively explained by the combining of chemical elements, which in turn can be exhaustively explained by the combining of electrons, neutrons, and protons.

The third major component of naturalism is a theory about reality in which physical entities are all there is. God and angels are just imaginary fictions. The mind is really just the physical brain, free decisions are merely the results of prior events plus the laws of nature, and there is no teleology or purpose in the world—*that is,* life is ultimately meaningless. History is just one ultimately accidental event following another. The world is simply one big cluster of physical mechanisms affecting other physical mechanisms.

To briefly review: The three major components to naturalism are:

1. Scientism: The belief that scientific knowledge is either the only form of knowledge or a vastly superior form of knowledge.

2. The belief that the atomic theory of matter and the theory of evolution explain all events.

3. The belief that nonphysical things don't exist and that the world isn't here for any purpose.

So far, I have been using the term "evolution" without defining it, but in reality, it can be used to mean three different things: the fact that organisms go through minor changes over time, the idea that all life has a common descent, and the blind watchmaker thesis. It is the third notion of evolution that is crucial to the naturalist. And it is precisely this sense of evolution that has far less evidence in support of it than is often realized.

The blind watchmaker thesis declares that the processes and mechanisms of evolution are solely naturalistic, meaning that they occur without the specific involvement of any deity. According to the blind watchmaker thesis, our "creator" is not a conscious designer like a watchmaker designing a watch. Rather, we have been created by a set of accidental physical processes that are not the result of intelligence and do not have any purpose behind them.

So understood, a theistic evolutionist could accept the blind watchmaker thesis, but only if he limits God's activity to that of a first cause, the being that tipped over the first domino, not knowing what would happen. For the theistic evolutionist to be both a theist and an evolutionist, he must believe in God, but think of God as no more than a being who sustains the world's existence as history unfolds accidentally, according to natural law and "chance."

Whether or not you agree with these statements, one thing seems clear: The certainty claimed for evolution and the ferocity with which belief in it is held go far beyond what is justified by scientific evidence and empirical testing.

No one could digest Phillip Johnson's *Darwin on Trial* (InterVarsity, 1991), Michael Denton's *Evolution: A Theory in Crisis* (Adler & Adler, 1986), or *The Creation Hypothesis* (which I edited, InterVarsity, 1994) without realizing that a serious, sophisticated case can be made against the blind watchmaker thesis even if one judged that, in the end, the case against the blind watchmaker thesis is not as persuasive as the blind watchmaker thesis itself.

The problem is, most intellectuals today act as if there is simply no issue here and presume that if you do not believe in evolution, then you must believe in a flat earth or something equally absurd. Why is this?

Why do so many people, including some well-intentioned Christians, heap so much scorn on creationists (young-earth and progressive) who reject the evolutionary story, and why do so many people act as though no informed, modern person could believe otherwise? I believe the answer lies in two directions, neither of which is purely scientific or subject to verification by our five senses.

Can this really be true? Can it really be the case that intelligent, well-informed scientists often don't know what they are rejecting when they reject creationism or intelligent design? And is it really true that the fervency and dogmatic acceptance of evolution is the result of factors that have nothing to do with scientific evidence? If so, what are those factors? I'll answer these questions next time!

Notes

1. In general, a theory, idea, or sentence is *epistemological* if it has to do with *knowledge*—if it has to do with good versus bad manners of believing. Put another way, a theory, idea or sentence is epistemological if it tells us what sorts of things we *should* believe and what sorts of things we should *not* believe.

CRITICAL THINKING QUESTIONS

1. What is the difference between a sensate and an ideational culture? Which one seems more freethinking and open minded? Explain.

2. What is scientific naturalism? Explain Moreland's definition. Had you heard of this school of thought or perspective before reading this essay? Do you believe the core tenets of this belief? Why or why not?

3. What is weak and strong scientism? What are the positive and negative aspects of these beliefs or worldviews?

4. To what extent are naturalism and evolution based upon philosophical assumptions that cannot be tested in a lab or observed empirically? Is this science as scientific as scientists lead us to believe? Explain.

~

What Is the Relation between Science and Religion?
William Lane Craig

William Lane Craig received his BA at Wheaton College, two MA degrees at Trinity Evangelical Divinity School, a PhD at University of Birmingham (England), and a DTheol at University of Munich (Germany). He has taught Philosophy of Religion at Trinity, pursued research at the University of Louvain (Belgium), and is currently Research Professor of Philosophy at Talbot School of Theology. He has written or edited over thirty books, including *Reasonable Faith, The Kalam Cosmological Argument, Creation Out of Nothing, Philosophical Foundations for a Christian Worldview,* and *Assessing the New Testament Evidence for the Historicity of the Resurrection of Jesus.* Also, he has published over one hundred articles in professional journals of philosophy and theology. The following article was published in 2007 on his Web site, ReasonableFaith.org.

Essay Classification: Informative; evaluative; argumentation/per-suasion

BACK IN 1896 THE president of Cornell University Andrew Dickson White published a book entitled *A History of the Warfare of Science with Theology in Christendom.* Under White's influence, the metaphor of "warfare" to describe the relations between science and the Christian faith became very widespread during the first half of the twentieth century. The culturally dominant view in the West—even among Christians—came to be that science and Christianity are not *allies* in the search for truth, but *adversaries.*

To illustrate, several years ago I had a debate with a philosopher of science at Simon Fraser University in Vancouver. Canada, on the question "Are Science and Religion Mutually Irrelevant?" When I walked onto the campus, I saw that the Christian students sponsoring the debate had advertised it with large banners and posters proclaiming "Science *vs.* Christianity." The students were perpetuating the same sort of warfare mentality that Andrew Dickson White proclaimed over a hundred years ago.

What has happened, however, in the second half of this century is that historians and philosophers of science have come to realize that this supposed history of warfare is a myth. As Thaxton and Pearcey point out in their recent book *The Soul of Science,* for over 300 years between the rise of modern science in the 1500s and the late 1800s the relationship between science and religion can best be described as an *alliance.* Up until the late 19th century, scientists were typically Christian believers who saw no conflict between their science and their faith—people like Kepler, Boyle, Maxwell, Faraday, Kelvin, and others. The idea of a warfare between science and religion is a relatively recent invention of the late nineteenth century, carefully nurtured by secular thinkers who had as their aim the undermining of the cultural dominance of Christianity in the West and its replacement by naturalism—the view that nothing outside nature is real and the only way to discover truth is through science. They were remarkably successful in pushing through their agenda. But philosophers of science during the second half of the twentieth century have come to realize that the idea of a warfare between science and theology is a gross oversimplification. White's book is now regarded as something of a bad joke, a one-sided and distorted piece of propaganda.

Now some people acknowledge that science and religion should not be regarded as foes, but nonetheless they do not think that they should be considered friends either. They say that science and religion are mutually irrelevant, that they represent two non-overlapping domains. Sometimes you hear slogans like, "Science deals with facts and religion deals with faith." But this is a gross caricature of both science and religion. As science probes the universe, she encounters problems and questions which are philosophical in character and therefore cannot be resolved scientifically, but which can be illuminated by a theological perspective. By the same token, it is simply false that religion makes no factual claims about the world. The world religions make various and conflicting claims about the origin and nature of the universe and humanity, and they cannot *all* be true. Science and religion are thus like two circles which intersect or partially overlap. It is in the area of intersection that the dialogue takes place.

And during the last quarter century, a flourishing dialogue between science and theology has been going on in North America and Europe. In an address before a conference on the history and philosophy of thermodynamics, the prominent British physicist P. T. Landsberg suddenly began to explore the *theological* implications of the scientific theory he was discussing. He observed,

> To talk about the implications of science for theology at a scientific meeting seems to break a taboo. But those who think so are out of date. During the last 15 years, this taboo has been removed, and in talking about the interaction of science and theology, I am actually moving with a tide.

Numerous societies for promoting this dialogue, like the European Society for the Study of Science and Theology, the Science and Religion Forum, the Berkeley Center for Theology and Natural Science, and so forth have sprung up. Especially significant have been the ongoing conferences sponsored by the Berkeley Center and the Vatican Observatory, in which prominent scientists like Stephen Hawking and Paul Davies have explored the implications of science for theology with prominent theologians like John Polkinghorne and Wolfhart Pannenberg. Not only are there professional journals devoted to the dialogue between science and religion, such as *Zygon* and *Perspectives on Science and Christian Faith,* but, more significantly, secular journals like *Nature* and the *British Journal for the Philosophy of Science* also carry articles on the mutual implications of science and theology. The Templeton Foundation has awarded its million-dollar Templeton Award in Science and Religion to outstanding integrative thinkers such as Paul Davies, John Polkinghorne, and George Ellis for their work in science and religion. The dialogue between science and theology has become so significant in our day that both Cambridge University and Oxford University have established chairs in science and theology.

I share all this to illustrate a point. Folks who think that science and religion are mutually irrelevant need to realize that the cat is already out of the bag; and I daresay there's little prospect of stuffing it back in. Science and religion have discovered that they have important mutual interests and important contributions to make to each other, and those who don't like this can choose not to participate in the dialogue, but that's not going to shut down the dialogue or show it to be meaningless.

So let's explore together ways in which science and religion serve as allies in the quest for truth. Let me suggest six ways in which science and religion are relevant to each other, starting with the most general and then becoming more particular.

1. *Religion furnishes the conceptual framework in which science can flourish.* Science is not something that is natural to mankind. As science writer Loren Eiseley has emphasized, science is "an *invented* cultural institution" which requires a "unique soil" in order to flourish.[1] Although glimmerings of science appeared among the ancient Greeks and Chinese, modern science is the child of European civilization. Why is this so? It is due to the unique contribution of the Christian faith to Western culture. As Eiseley states, "it is the Christian world which finally gave birth in a

clear, articulate fashion to the experimental method of science itself."[2] In contrast to pantheistic or animistic religions, Christianity does not view the world as divine or as indwelt by spirits, but rather as the natural product of a transcendent Creator who designed and brought it into being. Thus, the world is a rational place which is open to exploration and discovery.

Furthermore, the whole scientific enterprise is based on certain assumptions which cannot be proved scientifically, but which *are* guaranteed by the Christian worldview; for example: the laws of logic, the orderly nature of the external world, the reliability of our cognitive faculties in knowing the world, and the objectivity of the moral values used in science. I want to emphasize that science could not even exist without these assumptions, and yet these assumptions cannot be proved scientifically. They are philosophical assumptions which, interestingly, are part and parcel of a Christian worldview. Thus, religion is relevant to science in that it can furnish a conceptual framework in which science can exist. More than that, the Christian religion historically *did* furnish the conceptual framework in which modern science was born and nurtured.

2. *Science can both falsify and verify claims of religion.* When religions make claims about the natural world, they intersect the domain of science and are, in effect, making predictions which scientific investigation can either verify or falsify. Let me give some examples of each.

First, examples of falsification. Some examples are obvious. The views of ancient Greek and Indian religions that the sky rested on the shoulders of Atlas or the world on the back of a great turtle were easily falsified. But more subtle examples are available, too.

One of the most notorious examples was the medieval church's condemnation of Galileo for his holding that the earth moves around the sun rather than *vice versa*. On the basis of their misinterpretation of certain Bible passages like Psalm 93.1: "The Lord has established the world; it shall never be moved," medieval theologians denied that the earth moved. Scientific evidence eventually falsified this hypothesis, and the church belatedly came to admit its mistake.

Another interesting example of science's falsifying a religious view is the claim of several Eastern religions like Taoism and certain forms of Hinduism that the world is divine and therefore eternal. The discovery during this century of the expansion of the universe reveals that far from being eternal, all matter and energy, even physical space and time themselves, came into existence at a point in the finite past before which nothing existed. As Stephen Hawking says in his 1996 book *The Nature of Space and Time*, "almost everyone now believes that the universe, and time itself, had a beginning at the big bang."[3] But if the universe came into being at the Big Bang, then it is temporally finite and contingent in its existence and therefore neither eternal nor divine, as pantheistic religions had claimed.

On the other hand, science can also verify religious claims. For example, one of the principal doctrines of the Judaeo-Christian faith is that God created the universe out of nothing a finite time ago. The Bible begins with the words, "In the beginning God created the heavens and the Earth" (Genesis 1:1). The Bible thus teaches that the universe had a beginning. This teaching was repudiated by both ancient Greek philosophy and modern atheism, including dialectical materialism. Then in 1929 with the discovery of the expansion of the universe, this doctrine was dramatically verified. Physicists John Barrow and Frank Tipler, speaking of the beginning of the universe, explain, "At this singularity, space and time came into existence; literally nothing existed before the singularity, so, if the Universe originated at such a singularity, we would truly have a creation *ex nihilo* (out of nothing)."[4] Against all expectation, science thus verified this religious prediction. Robert Jastrow, head of NASA's Goddard Institute for Space Studies, envisions it this way:

> [The scientist] has scaled the mountains of ignorance; he is about to conquer the highest peak; as he pulls himself over the final rock, he is greeted by a band of theologians who have been sitting there for centuries.[5]

A second scientific verification of a religious belief is the claim of the great monotheistic faiths that the world is the product of intelligent design. Scientists originally thought that whatever the initial conditions of the universe were, eventually the universe would evolve the complex life forms we see today. But during the last forty years or so, scientists have been stunned by the discovery of how complex and sensitive a balance of initial conditions must be given in the Big Bang in order for the universe to permit the origin and evolution of intelligent life in the cosmos. In the various fields of physics and astrophysics, classical cosmology, quantum mechanics, and biochemistry, discoveries have repeatedly disclosed that the existence of intelligent life depends upon a delicate balance of physical constants and quantities. If any one of these were to be slightly altered, the balance would be destroyed and life would not exist. In fact, the universe appears to have been incomprehensibly fine-tuned from the moment of its inception for the production of intelligent life. We now know that life-*prohibiting* universes are vastly more probable than any life-*permitting* universe like ours. How much more probable?

The answer is that the chances that the universe should be life-permitting are so infinitesimal as to be incomprehensible and incalculable. For example, Stephen Hawking has estimated that if the rate of the universe's expansion one second after the Big Bang had been smaller by even one part in a hundred thousand million million, the universe would have re-collapsed into a hot fireball.[6] P. C. W. Davies has calculated that the odds against the initial conditions being suitable for later star formation (without which planets could not exist) is one followed by a thousand billion billion zeroes, at least.[7] He also estimates that a change in the strength of gravity or of the weak force by only one part in 10,100 would have prevented a life-permitting universe.[8] There are a number of such quantities and constants present in the big bang which must be fine-tuned in this way if the universe is to permit life. So improbability is multiplied by improbability until our minds are reeling in incomprehensible numbers.

There is no physical reason why these constants and quantities should possess the values they do. The former agnostic physicist Paul Davies comments, "Through my scientific work I have come to believe more and more strongly that the physical universe is put together with an ingenuity so astonishing that I cannot accept it merely as a brute fact."[9] Similarly, Fred Hoyle remarks, "A common sense interpretation of the facts suggests that a superintellect has monkeyed with physics."[10]

Our discovery of the fine-tuning of the big bang for intelligent life is like someone's trudging through the Gobi Desert and, rounding a sand dune, suddenly being confronted with a skyscraper the size of the Empire State Building. We would rightly dismiss as mad the suggestion that it just happened to come together there by chance. And we would find equally insane the idea that any arrangement of sand particles at that place is improbable and so there is nothing to be explained.

Why is this? Because the skyscraper exhibits a complexity which is absent from random arrangements of sand. But why should the complexity of the skyscraper strike us as special? John Leslie says it is because there is an apparent explanation of the complex skyscraper that is not suggested by just a random arrangement of sand grains, namely, intelligent design.[11] In the same way, Leslie concludes, the fine-tuning of the initial conditions of the universe for life points to the apparent explanation of intelligent design.

Thus, science can both falsify and verify the claims of religion.

3. *Science encounters metaphysical problems which religion can help to solve.* Science has an insatiable thirst for explanation. But eventually, science reaches the limits of its explanatory ability. For example, in explaining why various things in the universe exist, science ultimately confronts the question of why the universe itself exists. Notice that this need not be a question about the temporal origin of the universe. Even if spacetime is beginningless and endless, we may still ask why spacetime exists. Physicist David Park reflects, "As to why there is spacetime, that appears to be a perfectly good scientific question, but nobody knows how to answer it."[12]

Here theology can help. Traditional theists conceive of God as a necessary being whose nonexistence is impossible, who is the Creator of the contingent world of space and time. Thus, the person who believes in God has the resources to slake science's thirst for ultimate explanation. We can present this reasoning in the form of a simple argument:

1. Everything that exists has an explanation of its existence (either in the necessity of its own nature or in an external cause).

2. If the universe has an explanation of its existence, that explanation is God.

3. The universe exists.

4. Therefore the explanation of the existence of the universe is God.

4. *Religion can help to adjudicate between scientific theories.* Lawrence Sklar, a prominent philosopher of science, has remarked, "The adoption of one scientific theory rather than another, sometimes in very crucial cases indeed, rests as much upon ... philosophical presuppositions as it does upon the hard data...."[13] Particularly in cases in which two conflicting theories are empirically equivalent, so that one cannot decide between them on the basis of the evidence, metaphysical concerns, including religious concerns, come into play.

An excellent example is the Special Theory of Relativity. There are two ways to interpret the mathematical core of Special Relativity. On

Einstein's interpretation, there is no absolute "now" in the world; rather what is now is relative to different observers in motion. If you and I are moving with respect to each other, then what is now for me is not now for you. But on H. A. Lorentz's interpretation, there *is* an absolute now in the world, but we just cannot be sure *which* events in the world are happening now because motion affects our measuring instruments. Moving clocks run slow and moving measuring rods contract. The Einsteinian and the Lorentzian interpretations are empirically equivalent; there is no experiment you could perform to decide between them.[14] But I want to argue that if God exists, then Lorentz was right. Here is my argument:

1. If God exists, then God is in time.

    This is true because God is really related to the world as cause to effect. But a cause of a temporal effect must exist either before or at the same time as its effect. So God must be in time.

2. If God is in time, then a privileged observer exists.

    Since God transcends the world and is the cause of the existence of everything in the world, His perspective on the world is the true perspective.

3. If a privileged observer exists, then an absolute now exists.

    Since God is a privileged observer, His "now" is privileged. Thus, there is an absolute now, just as Lorentz claimed.

This is a very startling conclusion, indeed. But I am firmly convinced that if God exists, then a Lorentzian, rather than Einsteinian, theory of relativity is correct. It is hard to imagine how religion could have any greater relevance to science than this, to show that one theory is wrong and another is right.

5. *Religion can augment the explanatory power of science.* One of the pillars of the contemporary scientific view of the world is the evolution of biological complexity from more primitive life-forms. Unfortunately the current neo-Darwinian synthesis seems to be explanatorily deficient in its explanation of the gradual rise of biological complexity. In the first place, the neo-Darwinian mechanisms of random mutation and natural selection work far too slowly to produce, unaided, sentient life. In their *Anthropic Cosmological Principle*, Barrow and Tipler list ten steps in the evolution of *homo sapiens*, including such steps as the development of

the DNA-based genetic code, the origin of mitochondria, the origin of photosynthesis, the development of aerobic respiration, and so forth, each of which is so improbable that before it would have occurred, the sun would have ceased to be a main sequence star and incinerated the earth.[15] They report that "there has developed a general consensus among evolutionists that the evolution of intelligent life, comparable in information processing ability to that of *homo sapiens* is so improbable that it is unlikely to have occurred on any other planet in the entire visible universe."[16] But if this is the case, then one cannot help but wonder, why, apart from a commitment to naturalism, should we think that it evolved by unaided chance on this planet? Second, random mutation and natural selection have trouble accounting for the origin of irreducibly complex systems. In his recent book *Darwin's Black Box*, microbiologist Michael Behe explains that certain cellular systems like the cilia or protein transport system are like incredibly complicated, microscopic machines which cannot function at all unless all the parts are present and functioning.[17] There is no understanding within the neo-Darwinian synthesis of how such irreducibly complex systems can evolve by random mutation and natural selection. With respect to them current evolutionary theory has zero explanatory power. According to Behe, however, there is one familiar explanation adequate to account for irreducible complexity, one which in other contexts we employ unhesitatingly: intelligent design. "Life on Earth at its most fundamental level, in its most fundamental components," he concludes, "is the product of intelligent activity."[18] The gradual evolution of biological complexity is better explained if there exists an intelligent cause behind the process rather than just the blind mechanisms alone. Thus, the theist has explanatory resources available which the naturalist lacks.

6. *Science can establish a premise in an argument for a conclusion having religious significance.* The medieval theologian Thomas Aquinas always assumed the eternity of the universe in all his arguments for the existence of God, since to assume that the universe began to exist made things too easy for the theist. "If the world and motion have a first beginning," he said, "some cause must clearly be posited for this origin of the world and of motion" (*Summa contra gentiles* 1. 13. 30). Moreover, there was simply no empirical way to prove the past finitude of the universe during the Middle Ages. But the application of the General Theory of Relativity to cosmology and the discovery of the expansion of the universe during

this century appears to have dropped into the lap of the philosophical theologian precisely that premiss which had been missing in a successful argument for God's existence. For now he may argue as follows:

1. Whatever begins to exist has a cause.

2. The universe began to exist.

3. Therefore, the universe has a cause.

Premiss (2) is a religiously neutral statement which can be found in almost any text on astronomy and astrophysics. Yet it puts the atheist in a very awkward situation. For as Anthony Kenny of Oxford University urges, "A proponent of the big bang theory, at least if he is an atheist, must believe that ... the universe came from nothing and by nothing."[19]

But surely that is metaphysically impossible. Out of nothing, nothing comes. So why does the universe exist instead of just nothing? It is plausible that there must have been a cause which brought the universe into being. Now from the very nature of the case, as the cause of space and time, this cause must be an uncaused, changeless, timeless, and immaterial being of unimaginable power which created the universe. Moreover, I would argue, it must also be personal. For how else could a timeless cause give rise to a temporal effect like the universe? If the cause were an impersonal set of necessary and sufficient conditions, then the cause could never exist without the effect. If the cause were eternally present, then the effect would be eternally present as well. The only way for the cause to be timeless and the effect to begin in time is for the cause to be a personal agent who freely chooses to create an effect in time without any prior determining conditions. Thus, we are brought, not merely to a transcendent cause of the universe, but to its personal creator.

All this is not to make some simplistic and naive judgment like "Science proves that God exists." But it is to say that science can establish the truth of a premiss in an argument for a conclusion having religious significance.

In summary, we've seen six different ways in which science and religion are relevant to each other:

1. Religion furnishes the conceptual framework in which science can flourish.

2. Science can both falsify and verify claims of religion.

3. Science encounters metaphysical problems which religion can help to solve.

4. Religion can help to adjudicate between scientific theories.

5. Religion can augment the explanatory power of science.

6. Science can establish a premiss in an argument for a conclusion having religious significance.

Thus, in conclusion, we have seen that science and religion should not be thought of as foes or as mutually irrelevant. Rather we have seen several ways in which they can fruitfully interact. And that is why, after all, there is such a flourishing dialogue between these two disciplines going on today.

Notes

1. Loren Eiseley, "Francis Bacon," in *The Horizon Book of Makers of Modern Thought* (New York: American Heritage Publishing, 1972), pp. 95–96.

2. Loren Eiseley, *Darwin's Century* (Garden City, NY: Doubleday, 1958), p. 62. I am indebted for the Eiseley references to Nancy Pearcy and Charles Thaxton, *The Soul of Science* (Wheaton, IL: Crossway Books, 1994).

3. Stephen Hawking and Roger Penrose, *The Nature of Space and Time,* The Isaac Newton Institute Series of Lectures (Princeton, NJ: Princeton University Press, 1996), p. 20.

4. John Barrow and Frank Tipler, *The Anthropic Cosmological Principle* (Oxford: Clarendon Press, 1986), p. 442.

5. Robert Jastrow, *God and the Astronomers* (New York: W. W. Norton, 1978), p. 116.

6. Stephen W. Hawking, *A Brief History of Time* (New York: Bantam Books, 1988), p. 123.

7. P. C. W. Davies, *Other Worlds* (London: Dent, 1980), pp. 160–61, 168–69.

8. P. C. W. Davies, "The Anthropic Principle," in *Particle and Nuclear Physics* 10 (1983): 28.

9. Paul Davies, *The Mind of God* (New York: Simon & Schuster: 1992), p. 16.

10. Fred Hoyle, "The Universe: Past and Present Reflections," *Engineering and Science* (November, 1981), p.12.

11. John Leslie, *Universes* (London: Routledge, 1989), pp. 10, 121.

12. David Park, *The Image of Eternity* (Amherst: University of Massachusetts Press, 1980), p. 84.

13. Lawrence Sklar, *Space, Time, and Spacetime* (Berkeley: University of California Press, 1976), p. 417.

14. Actually, this statement bears qualification; for as a result of the Aspect experiments verifying the predictions of quantum mechanics with respect to Bell's Theorem, we now have substantial empirical grounds for affirming relations of absolute simultaneity between distant events, thus vindicating the Lorentzian interpretation.

15. Barrow and Tipler, *Anthropic Cosmological Principle*, pp. 561–65.

16. Ibid., p. 133.

17. Michael J. Behe, *Darwin's Black Box* (New York: Free Press, 1996).

18. Ibid., p. 193.

19. Anthony Kenny, *The Five Ways: St. Thomas Aquinas Proofs of God's Existence* (New York: Schocken Books, 1969), p. 66.

CRITICAL THINKING QUESTIONS

1. Before reading this essay, did you think that science and religion were incompatible and diametrically opposed to each other? Why or why not?

2. Have you ever had a science teacher or some other scientifically minded person suggest that religion should stay out of science? Have you had a pastor or religious friend say that science should stay out of religion? How does this article address these two perspectives?

3. Summarize the six ways that Craig suggests that science and religion are relevant to each other. Comment on these ideas.

4. Many scientists often say that science deals with empirical facts only. According to Craig, in what ways does science come up against metaphysical questions? How can theology or a theistic understanding of reality help science deal with these metaphysical questions?

5. Science also faces various ethical questions in how experiments are carried out and how conclusions are applied in lived experience (through technology and its uses). How can religion support science in its ethical operation?

~

SCIENTIFIC ETHICS AND THE HUMAN BEING

The Moral Imperative for Human Cloning
Ian Wilmut

Ian Wilmut received his doctorate from Cambridge University, and his research focuses on animal genetic engineering. He is considered the father of animal cloning for his groundbreaking genetic work on Dolly, the first lamb to be cloned. Wilmut has been very outspoken in his opposition to human cloning; however, as he reconsiders the potential medical benefits, he may be softening his opposition. This essay was published in 2004 in *New Scientist*.

Essay Classification: Argumentation/persuasion

HUMAN CLONING IS FINALLY here. But while the Korean team has overcome some technical obstacles, the political barriers to realizing cloning's medical potential remain. Many people object to the idea of any human cloning research, even for medical reasons, claiming it will inevitably open the door to reproductive cloning or, more generally, that experimenting with embryos is immoral. I believe the opposite: cloning promises such great benefits that it would be immoral not to do it.

That is why a number of United Kingdom labs, including my own, plan to apply to the relevant authorities for permission to study human cloning here in the UK. And while I remain implacably opposed to reproductive cloning per se, I do envisage that producing cloned babies would be desirable under certain circumstances, such as preventing genetic disease.

The therapeutic promise of human cloning lies in embryonic stem cells, or ES cells. Derived from 6-day-old embryos, ES cells can form any cell type in the body, such as nerve or blood cells. It is possible to extract such cells from spare IVF embryos. But this has a drawback. Researchers have no control over the genetic make-up of the cells in these embryos. This presents a problem if such stem cells are used to regenerate tissue destroyed by accident or disease: if they don't genetically match the patient, they could trigger an immune response.

Cloning, however, could overcome this problem and provide patients with tissue-matched stem cells. Although critics often claim therapeutic cloning would be too expensive and impractical, I think many of the problems can be tackled. But even if therapeutic cloning doesn't make it to the clinic, there are other compelling reasons why we need to develop human cloning technology.

The most imminent development is likely to be using cloning to study disease, particularly inherited conditions. At present, it is often impossible to safely take samples of affected cells from living patients, especially those suffering from genetic diseases that affect the brain and heart such as Parkinson's disease or inherited heart arrhythmias. What's more, by the time a patient develops symptoms, their disease has been progressing for some time. This makes it hard to find out whether the changes we see in their cells are directly related to the cause of that disease, or whether they are merely secondary effects. Ideally, we would like to be able to monitor the progress of the disease as it develops inside the cells, so that we can home in on its cause.

Cloning would allow us to recreate these diseased cells, with the same genetic make-up, outside the patient's body, and watch them develop from scratch. In principle, we could take, say, a skin cell, make a cloned embryo and then use its stem cells to create cultures of any cell type we wanted. These cell cultures would give us the power to do the kind of sophisticated genetics that we can often only do in animals.

Our team plans to start cloning ES cells from people with the neurodegenerative condition ALS, or Lou Gehrig's disease. This progressive and fatal paralysis strikes people in middle age, robbing them of their ability to move, speak, or breathe unaided. It is incurable and most victims die within five years of being diagnosed.

The disease affects nerve cells called motor neurons, which are found in the brain and spine. Owing to their location, it is impossible to remove living motor neurons for study. Partly because of this, we have little idea of what causes ALS. We do know that about 10 per cent of cases are inherited and that a fifth of these are caused by mutations in a gene called SOD1. But the cause of the majority of cases is a mystery.

Using cloning to create cultures of motor neurons from such patients would help us to track down the causes of the disease. What damages these cells? Does the damage come from within, or from faulty interactions with other cells? What's more, being able to study which genes are switched on or off in such cells could tell us what might be going wrong in the 60 per cent of ALS patients who did not inherit their condition. Cloning might even give us the chance to test new therapies.

For all these reasons, my colleagues and I are preparing to apply for a license to clone cells from ALS patients in the UK. As well as benefiting ALS research, we hope our techniques could be adapted for research into other neurodegenerative diseases, such as Parkinson's and Alzheimer's.

Human cloning also has the potential to revolutionize other areas of biomedical research. One key area is developing and testing new drugs. It is a surprising fact that bad reactions to prescription drugs, even when those drugs are used correctly, kill thousands of people every year. At the moment, drug companies have no reliable way of predicting who will react badly.

In most cases, the variation from person to person is due to differences in the genes that code for the liver enzymes that break down drugs. Human cloning could help in a number of ways. Researchers could clone and create cultures of liver cells from families who had suffered bad reactions to drugs. Such reactions often involve many different enzymes, and being able to study gene activity in the liver cells of susceptible people would let researchers identify variations in the key enzymes.

Findings from such research could allow drug companies to test their new drugs more safely and effectively by letting them screen out susceptible individuals from their trials. Such patients could also be warned that certain drugs are not suitable for them. Drug companies currently use postmortem liver samples as part of their extensive preclinical drug safety tests. However, these samples are often pooled, and the drug sensitivities of the donors are unknown.

Although research is likely to be the first beneficiary of human cloning, the most exciting developments will come as "therapeutic" cloning: ways to repair or cure diseased organs or repair genetic defects. Transplants of stem cells that are genetically identical to their recipients promise new treatments, such as repairing damaged heart muscle following a heart attack.

Of course, this is still some way off. We have technical problems to solve, such as how to get human ES cells to reliably form different cell types. There are safety aspects, too: we need to know these cells won't cause problems such as cancer. Lastly, human eggs are in short supply and this threatens to limit the use of therapeutic cloning. However, these problems can be addressed.

It is true that therapeutic cloning is unlikely to be practical for routine use. But not all diseases are equal in terms of expense, and treatments could be targeted to maximize benefit. An older person with heart disease, for example, could be treated with stem cells that are not a genetic match, take drugs to suppress their immune system for the rest of their life, and live with the side-effects. A younger person might benefit more from stem cells that match exactly.

What's more, therapies are likely to become cheaper and easier to use as the technology progresses. One way of overcoming the human egg shortage could be to use cow eggs, strictly for making stem cells. I personally wouldn't have an issue with it from a moral point of view because essentially, you can just see eggs as bags of proteins. But you would have to be even more careful about the safety aspect.

The most radical use of human cloning technology is to treat inherited disease—particularly those affecting whole organs that can't be replaced by stem cells, such as the lungs. It would also solve many of the problems that have recently plagued gene therapy, such as the risk of causing cancer.

At the moment, people carrying certain genetic diseases can try to avoid passing them on by undergoing IVF and having the embryos tested so that only healthy ones are implanted. But if none of the embryos created is suitable, the couple face another round of invasive treatment to create more.

There is another way. In March 2003, Thomas Zwaka and James Thomson at the University of Wisconsin in Madison reported that they had found a way of precisely replacing faulty genes in ES cells with healthy copies. This precision means there is little chance of a gene landing in the wrong place and causing problems. But how can the therapeutic gene be sent to every cell in the body?

This is where cloning could help. First, you would create an ordinary embryo using IVF. Then you would take the ES cells from it and correct the diseased gene with genetic engineering. However, ES cells by themselves cannot be used to reconstitute the embryo they came from. To do this, you would take the nucleus from one of these corrected ES cells and transfer it into an egg. The resulting embryo would be the identical twin of the original embryo, but with the diseased gene corrected in every one of its cells. This embryo could then be implanted in its mother's womb to develop into a baby. Although such a child would be a human clone, it would be a clone of a new individual, not a clone of one of its parents. This form of cloning would not create the same ethical and social problems as reproductive cloning.

Of course the question of safety still applies. For now, we still know far too little about what happens to the genes in a nucleus during cloning to consider creating a child in this way. But that should not hold us back from developing a technology that has such great potential to help so many people. Human cloning must not be banned. It could save many thousands of lives.

CRITICAL THINKING QUESTIONS

1. In an earlier article, Wilmut argued against human cloning; how has Wilmut modified his position on human cloning? What is his main reason for this change of view?

2. In his earlier article, he argued that it would be unconscionable to subject humans to experimental cloning, because the death rate for cloned fetuses would be too high to justify ethically. Yet, now he claims a moral obligation to clone humans for therapeutic reasons to cure disease. However, cloning a person to harvest stem cells for therapeutic use requires the destruction of the fetus. In such instances, the death rate is 100 percent. Is this a moral contradiction? Why or why not?.

3. Wilmut makes the point that genetic diseases could be detected in the embryonic stage, and that the embryo could be cloned with the clone having the defect removed. Why is this an appealing argument? What happens to the host embryo with the defect? Are we morally justified in destroying embryos with genetic defects? How are we to determine which defects warrant death and which ones do not?

4. Wilmut admits that the science of human cloning still requires much development for any of the possible cures he mentions to be achieved. In his earlier article he discusses the immorality of subjecting humans to failed trials, which would be much higher than the number of failed attempts to clone Dolly. He doesn't mention this point in the second essay. Why?

~

Is Therapeutic Cloning on the Skids?
Michael Cook

Michael Cook is the editor of *MercatorNet*, an online journal that investigates contemporary issues in terms of universally accepted moral values, common sense, and evidence, and the editor of *BioEdge*, a bioethics newsletter. The following essay comes from *MercatorNet* and first appeared November 17, 2007.

Essay Classification: Informative; evaluative; argumentation/persuasion

THREE KINDS OF FAILURES are guaranteed a berth on the front page of even the most sober newspapers at the moment: Britney Spears and relationships, Barry Bonds and drugs, and scientists and cloning. There's something irresistible about talented people on the skids. And of the three, cloning is by far the saddest story.

First, the good news. A few days ago it was announced that researchers at Oregon Health and Science University in Portland have successfully cloned primate embryos and used them to make embryonic stem-cell lines. Until a Korean cloned human embryos back in 2004, the difficulties seemed almost insurmountable. But that turned out to be a calculated fraud. Disheartened stem cell researchers once again fretted that human cloning to cure dread diseases might actually be impossible.

Shoukhrat Mitalipov and his colleagues merged skin cells from a nine-year-old rhesus macaque male with unfertilized monkey eggs whose DNA had been removed. It was far from an efficient process. After tweaking conventional cloning techniques, they produced only two embryonic stem-cell lines from 304 eggs. But at least it wasn't a fraud.

Stem cell scientists greeted the news ecstatically. "Like breaking the sound barrier," says Robert Lanza, with Advanced Cell Technology in Los Angeles. Even serious newspapers like the *London Times* sprinkled stardust on the results: "First cloning of monkey embryo raises hope of a great leap in medical science."

Now, the bad news. The scientist who cloned Dolly, Ian Wilmut, the world's most prominent expert in cloning, has abandoned his plans to clone human embryos. He believes that an "extremely exciting and astonishing" Japanese method of creating stem cells is more effective and carried no ethical baggage. "His announcement could mark the beginning of the end for therapeutic cloning," says the London *Daily Telegraph*.

This confirms what critics have been saying for years. What's baffling about the pubic infatuation with embryonic stem cells, which are obtained by dissecting and killing early stage embryos, is that they have not cured anyone or been useful for anything.

A very thorough summary of current research into therapeutic cloning was presented to the German Parliament (the Bundestag) earlier this year. In it Dr. Lukas Kenner, of the Ludwig Boltzmann Institute for Cancer Research in Vienna, reminded the German government that only a single experimental study has demonstrated that therapeutic cloning is possible, at least in mice. However, to the surprise of the researchers, the cloned cells were incompatible with the patient's immune system. That was in 2002, and in the five ensuing years, no one, not even the original authors, have "produced animal experimental evidence of the core hypothesis of the feasibility of immunocompatible 'therapeutic cloning' that overcomes the hurdle of immune rejection."

Of course, maybe someday embryonic stem cells will eventually work as a scientific tool. But only dazzled journalists, a few starry-eyed scientists and a lot of vote-hungry politicians are prepared to invest money in a maybe—other people's money, that is. Earlier this month Governor Jon Corzine and other leading politicians lobbied hard to persuade New

Jersey voters to authorize spending $450 million on stem cell research. The voters snubbed them. A baffled Mr. Corzine now wants pharmaceutical companies to step up to the plate. Fat chance.

The hoopla over monkey cloning shows the enormous pressure on scientists to wring good news out of the tiniest advances. In this hyper-competitive atmosphere, some are bound to exaggerate or even fake their results. This has already happened—and not just in Korea. Last year it was discovered that a scientist at the University of Missouri-Columbia had digitally altered images of mouse embryos in an article in the leading journal *Science*.

The California Institute for Regenerative Medicine, which has the world's biggest stem cell budget—$3 billion over 10 years, mostly for embryonic stem cells—has already had problems with two of its grants.

And this week a long investigation at the Monash University in Melbourne, Australia, concluded that a senior stem cell scientist had been negligent and had presented inaccurate research results. His project was adult stem cells and lung regeneration.

The significance of this event is that the hapless fellow's supervisor was the newly appointed head of the California Institute, Professor Alan Trounson. The Monash vice-chancellor found that Trounson himself had been negligent in approving the results without examining them—although, it must be stressed, he was not personally involved.

If Professor Trounson cannot supervise a $1 million grant properly, how will he manage with $3 billion sloshing around in the trough? The California funds are so immense that some scientists worry that too much money might be chasing too few high-quality research projects. "We have to have very discerning review boards so it doesn't become a boondoggle for companies that haven't succeeded," Dr Irving Weissman, a prominent stem cell researcher at Stanford University, has said. Furthermore, only Californian scientists will be allowed to paddle in this sea of money, so the number of qualified researchers is relatively small.

Too much hype. Too many daydreams. Too much taxpayers' money. Too few researchers. Too little supervision. It's the kind of brew that rogues and rascals thrive on. We can expect more stem cell scandals in the years to come unless scientists follow Ian Wilmut's lead and abandon therapeutic cloning.

CRITICAL THINKING QUESTIONS

1. What is your view of therapeutic human cloning? Discuss how your view has been augmented, enhanced, or changed by reading this essay.

2. Ian Wilmut, the scientist famous for cloning Dolly, first opposed human cloning, then embraced it for therapeutic reasons, and now seems to be favoring a new method for generating human stem cells that does not involve human cloning. Why do you suppose he has changed his mind yet again?

3. What is the main reason that many scientists want to pursue embryonic stem cell research that necessitates human cloning? Is there any evidence of success to support their enthusiasm? Why do you think they continue to insist on pursuing ethically controversial research when more promising answers lie in strategies that do not present ethical problems?

4. Should taxpayer money be used to fund ethically controversial research like human cloning and adult stem cell research? Why or why not?

~

Screwtape Revisited
Meghan Cox Gurdon

Meghan Cox Gurdon is a book reviewer and a columnist, and her work appears in *The Wall Street Journal*, *The National Review*, and *The Weekly Standard*. The following essay was published in 2005 by *The National Review*.

Essay Classification: Informative; argumentation/persuasion

With gratitude (and apologies) to C. S. Lewis.

"DON'T SLINK ALONG THE walls, boy, come in!" The voice is richer than the nephew remembers, vinous and lordlier, but with a reassuring tinge of malice just beneath the surface.

"By his tail, Uncle, this *is* fine," gasps Mildew, stepping cautiously into the center of the vast chamber that is his uncle's new office. The walls are hung with scarlet velvet; the temperature an agreeable Fahrenheit 911.

Screwtape stands in one corner behind a magnificent expanse of polished wood. "These desks are only given to the highest ranks," he says proudly. "Solid wormwood!" At the familiar name, the visitor flinches and slows his approach. Screwtape chuckles. "Shame about your brother, really," he murmurs, and just the tip of a red tongue flickers from his lips. "But let us hope you are made of more ambitious stuff?"

Mildew exhales loudly, as one bursting some inner restraint, and smiles. "Oh, I think so, Uncle. It is why I have been so eager to see you. Why I am so honored to see you—*here*."

"Wormwood," Screwtape repeats, pouring out two glasses of old *Pharisee* and handing one to his nephew. "It came with the promotion. So did the chairs. Sit down. They're Corinthian leather."

Mildew laughs politely and raises his glass. "To the Father of Lies."

"To the Father of Lies."

They drink, and put down their glasses. Screwtape looks hard at his nephew, his fingers moving the stem of his glass back and forth along the polished surface of the desk.

"I wonder, young Mildew, if you understand *why* I have been promoted—one might say exalted, even—to such heights?"

"I have heard," Mildew begins, and blushes. "The fact is, Uncle, I have heard things that seem impossible. Is it really true that you have found a way to get them to *eat*—"

"—their young?" Screwtape interrupts with a hungry smile. "Yes. Yes! I have found the key, the *key*, my boy, to unlocking the worst in the human heart. Oh, massacres are entertaining enough, and reasonably productive. Rapine and thieving and savagery and the usual nonsense go a good distance to wrecking men's souls, but not in sufficient numbers. Not for us to win for good—that is, ha-ha, for ill. We must forever be stoking grievances, feeding pride, and constantly thrusting and parrying with the Enemy and his agents. No, the beautifully corrupting key that *I* have found is vanity."

"I've read about that," Mildew says, remembering. "In first year college, Know Thine Enemy 101, I think it was. *All is vanity, saith the preacher*," the nephew quotes, his mouth twisting as if he has bitten a bad snail.

Screwtape grimaces companionably. "Indeed. Fortunately most of them don't bother with *that* any more."

"But how do—"

Screwtape presses on. "What does Man want? He wants sex, he wants comfort, he wants to be *young*. He does not want to be told he can't have what he wants, or to be inconvenienced, or, worse, to be told his desires are *wrong*. This is where the Enemy's agents end up doing our work for us, Mildew, countless times!" Screwtape chortles. "Man is a creature of appetites, Mildew. Remember that."

"Appetites, yes, but eating their young, Uncle? I feel sure that I read somewhere that humans are naturally revolted by cannibalism. The Enemy's doing, no doubt, but still, there it is."

Screwtape fixes his nephew with a shriveling glare. "We are not inducing them to *broil* the little tykes, dear boy, this is no *fricassee* of first-graders." He sighs heavily, a sufferer of fools, but then brightens, clearly distracted by a pleasing thought. "That's an idea, though. Must get Singer to write something up for me on that . . . excellent. Now, where—"

"Not broiling them."

"Yes. My achievement, the reason for *this*—" Screwtape gestures largely about the handsome apartment—" is that I have managed, by appealing to man's love of self, his vanity, to convince millions that it is not cannibalism, but *progress*, to turn tiny human infants into medicine. The strong picking the weak apart, cell by cell, to be *consumed* by the strong? Brilliant!"

The uncle pours another red gout of *Pharisee* into each glass, and leans forward. "There are some envious *others*—" he continues softly, glancing around as if to suggest malevolent eavesdroppers,"—who begrudge my rise. To them I say," and here Screwtape raises his voice, "Vanity is a rusty key that was left lying about, and it was I alone who saw what it could unlock at *this* point in human history.

"It is true," Screwtape continues with a shrug, "that much of the groundwork was already laid. We had already convinced people of the rightness of destroying inconvenient life. Now they talk quite coolly of 'blastocysts,' and 'clumps of cells' and 'surplus embryos.' *My* genius was to recognize that they needed just a little push to be convinced, with their mania for recycling, that by harvesting something that would otherwise be chucked out, they are doing a positive good! Think of it: They believe they occupy 'the moral high ground.' Oh, the profits for *us*—"

"But Uncle," Mildew interjects, very respectfully, "there is one point I do not understand. Humans have shown great resistance to the genetic modification of fruits and vegetables—"

Screwtape sees where this is going, and gives what might almost be called a tender smile, were not so many sharply-pointed teeth involved.

"All of Europe was up in arms over plans to make a more tender ear of corn, Uncle, do you remember? Frankenfood, they called it. Gigantic monster *tomatoes* were inflated and displayed for country folk. I do not mean to contradict you, Uncle, but if people fear an altered cob, surely they will not accept a genetically modified human being? After all, that's what this cell-picking is about, isn't it?"

"Do you think," says the uncle witheringly, "that people who believe that life on earth is the only one they have, that once they die there is nothing, that there are no consequences to their choices—one of Our Father Below's most successful slogans, by the way, *choice*—do you think, my boy, that they will hesitate if we give them the chance to cut and sew their medical destinies for the mere price of another's life? As Our Father pointed out to the Enemy during that unfortunate incident involving the man Job, 'A person will give up everything in order to stay alive.'"

Mildew tries to hold his uncle's eye, but cannot. He looks down and fiddles awkwardly with his tie.

"No, my boy," Screwtape continues in kinder tones. "We are on the brink of wondrous things. This is better than the eighteenth century, when we convinced whole societies that black-skinned persons were *things* rather than people—"

"Bought and sold and damnation aplenty," Mildew nods, impressed, "but it didn't last."

"No thanks to Him," Screwtape snaps. "But we are winning now, I can feel it, Mildew. Think of this: In some rich societies, people are not just destroying blastocysts, not merely dismantling children in the womb, they are euthanizing newborn babies!" Screwtape pats the place where his heart would be, were he to have one. "That's one of my father's, you know. *Euthanize.* So clean, so *modern*-sounding. He got a bonus for that one. But not wormwood."

"The one I love," Mildew interjects enthusiastically, "is *The Right to Die*. It's so *devilishly* clever."

Screwtape looks thoughtfully into his empty glass. "It has potential, once we get the strong to use it regularly against the weak in the guise of being humane." The uncle frowns. "Unfortunately we're running into some difficulties with that slogan. This Florida case is not going as hoped. *Right to Die* tests well in some markets but the Enemy, blast Him, *will* keep enlisting these poisonous little brutes with their claptrap about the Culture of Life and whatnot. Things may improve when we are rid of that turbulent chief priest of His. It can't be long now."

Screwtape shakes his head as if to clear it.

"More wine? Let's finish the bottle, with a toast to a glorious future. These are heady times, Mildew, and we can use the Enemy's words against Him. He wants these creatures to believe that each one of them has value. The Enemy actually *does* value them, however tiny or aged, however mewling or puking or cleft of palate, if you can imagine it.

"The wonderful thing for us? It is increasingly easy to take that Enemy-given sense of intrinsic worth and twist it into cruel self-interest. With man's vanity, and a little medical breakthrough here and there, we can tempt them with the prospect of a life without illness, inconvenience, or parasitical relatives. It will, for humans, be heaven on earth."

Screwtape chuckles darkly. "And afterwards? Why, we'll get to meet them down here. *In person.* And the loveliest bit of all is that their good intentions will have brought them here."

Uncle and nephew, grinning, raise their glasses once more.

"To the Father of Lies!"

CRITICAL THINKING QUESTIONS

1. Who was C. S. Lewis? What do you know about his famous book, *The Screwtape Letters*?

2. What is satire? How does Gurdon use satire to provide information and to express a point of view?

3. In this satire, who is "the father of all lies" and who is "the Enemy"? Who is Screwtape and why is he having this conversation with his nephew Mildew?

4. What is the basic nature of humanity, as explained by Screwtape?

5. What larger social, political, and ethical point regarding fetal stem cell research and euthanasia is Gurdon making through this satire? To what extent do you find this satirical approach effective or not? Explain.

6. What are the consequences of the idea that there are no absolute standards of right and wrong and that we are free to define human beings as we see fit? How are slavery, abortion, euthanasia, and fetal stem cell research related in this context?

∼

Breeding between the Lines: Rewriting the "Book of Life"
Les Sillars

Les Sillars is associate professor of journalism and acting chairperson of the Department of Government at Patrick Henry College in Purcellville, Virginia. He has contributed to the third edition of *The Responsible Reporter* and to *The Modest Republic*. He is the mailbag editor at *World Magazine* and a contributing editor at *Salvo Magazine*. His byline has also appeared in the *National Post* (Toronto), the *Washington Times*, and the *Reader's Digest* (Canada). He grew up near Calgary, Alberta, and holds a doctorate in journalism from the University of Texas at Austin.

Essay Classification: Informative, evaluative

ONE JUNE 26, 2000, President Bill Clinton announced the completion of the first draft of the "most important, most wondrous map ever produced by humankind." Researchers had "mapped" the human genome; that is, they had determined the sequence of the roughly 3 billion base pairs of nucleotides that make up human DNA. "Today," he added at the White House press conference, "we are learning the language in which God created life. With this profound new knowledge, humankind is on the verge of gaining immense new power to heal."

On the platform with him was Francis Collins, head of the National Institutes of Health's Human Genome Project. The ten-year-old government program, involving an international consortium of research facilities, most in the United States, was supposed to take fifteen years, from 1990 until 2005. Project researchers had been making their results available for anyone to use freely.

Also on the platform was J. Craig Venter, then president of Celera Genomics, Inc. In 1998 Venter had announced that Celera was working on a competing map of the human genome. The private company had promised to finish the job faster, using a new and controversial "shotgun" sequencing method, and sell the information to researchers. Venter (according to his critics) intended to plunder the human genome by turning humanity's "book of life" into a for-profit library. The result was a hotly contested race: public versus private, establishment heavies versus scientific maverick, genial scientist/bureaucrat versus biological buccaneer. Neither group had actually finished sequencing the genome (the versions had major gaps and differed significantly) by the time of the press conference, but that minor point was largely lost in the hoopla. The White House manufactured a tie, with Collins and Venter crossing the finish line holding hands, so to speak, one hiding a grimace and the other a smirk.

Six years later, the revolutionary "immense new power to heal" is still on the distant horizon. Even so, the project has touched off a massive science education effort that is transforming how society views what it means to be human. Public and private institutions alike are producing what has become a flood of educational materials designed to attract students into careers in genetics and prepare society for the coming medical revolution. Many of these programs go beyond basic genetics. They presume that the interaction between genes and environment explains all biological development and thus all human activity; that free will is an illusion; and that people are just slightly more sophisticated than other organisms (just slightly, mind you, given that we have about the same number of genes as a roundworm). The idea is to help prepare society for what Venter described in a recent online essay as "a realistic biology of humankind."

Reality never had a chance to live up to the hype. The *New York Times* called sequencing the genome "a pinnacle of self-knowledge," and other publications gushed that we now know "what it means to be human." "Revolutionize" became a favorite word among science journalists who quoted Collins (and others) predicting treatments for everything from cancer to schizophrenia, along with genetically designed drugs and amazing abilities to diagnose, anticipate, and even prevent disease.

There has been progress; since 2000 researchers have used the map to make significant discoveries, especially about the relationship between genes, environment, and disease, and developed some diagnostic tools and a handful of treatments for some of the less genetically complicated illnesses. But it seems that the more scientists discover about the intricate inner workings of cells, the more complications they encounter.

That hasn't discouraged many in the scientific community from taking advantage of the publicity generated by the sequencing of the map. In Cold Spring Harbor on Long Island's North Shore, in a stately converted red brick school just a quarter mile up the road from a waterfront park named after Billy Joel, is the Dolan DNA Learning Center. (Billy wrote no songs about genetics, unfortunately, but somebody did post online an ode to genetics and evolution called "We Didn't Start the Theory" to be sung to the tune of Billy's "We Didn't Start the Fire," presumably while wearing white lab coats and dancing 'round a Bunsen burner.)

The center is an offshoot of Cold Spring Harbor Laboratory, a prestigious, private, and nonprofit research facility. The center provides genetics instruction for more middle and high school students than any other institution in the world—over 27,000 in 2004, according to its latest annual report. The day I was there, a class of middle schoolers wandered through a series of exhibits that included a ceiling-high replica of Watson and Crick's 1953 model of the chemical structure of DNA, a sequencing machine, and a video on DNA replication. Students charted their own phenotypes (physical characteristics) and flipped up covers to read that, according to twin studies, genes account for 60–80 percent of intelligence, 30–40 percent of personality, and 40–50 percent of interest in religion.

There are also a handful of classrooms, including one laptop-equipped octagonal space where students do exercises in "bioinformatics," which is computer-enabled data crunching. Because of the genome map and high-powered computers, high school students can do research here, such as genetic database searches and population modeling, that fifteen years ago was limited to PhDs in high-end research facilities. The center also offers summer camps and internship programs and sends out teachers to conduct seminars across the country.

One display confidently assures visitors that in the field of "pharmacogenomics" scientists are "designing medicines for the individual, based on their genome." It doesn't mention that, as *Genetics for Dummies* (2005) explains, "nobody knows how many genes are involved in drug reactions, and most of the genes that are involved haven't even been discovered yet." Similarly, the center states that researchers are working on gene therapies (using viruses or other agents to insert correct genes into cells with disease-causing genes) and so "attempting to treat the cause of the disease, rather than its symptoms." Absent is any discussion of the conspicuous lack of promising results for gene therapy since Jesse Gelsinger, a col-

lege student, died in a 1999 clinical trial. Even the journal *Genomics &*
Proteomics conceded in the headline to an article last fall that "few areas
of genomic research have been filled with as much unfulfilled promise as
gene delivery."

There is also a theater where a very helpful center worker loaded up
for me a video called *DNA: The Secret of Life*. The computer animations
show the astonishingly complex process of DNA replication and compare
DNA to software, blithely affirming that genetic science "confirm[s] the
evolutionary truth first recognized by Charles Darwin"—that all life descended from one organism. With the completion of the Human Genome
Project, "Now, finally, we have the total picture." At best, this is misleading; scientists do indeed have the "book of life," but cell development is
expressed in a language involving DNA, proteins, and cell structure that
researchers are only beginning to interpret.

Online, the DNA Learning Center's family of Web sites (Gene
Almanac; Your Genes, Your Heath; DNA from the Beginning, and others)
attracted over 5.4 million visitors in 2004, and traffic was probably much
higher in 2005 after the center made their sites more accessible to search
engines. In fact, search "genetics" and "education" on Google and information will practically pour out of your screen; I got over 38 million hits.
Hundreds of private Web sites offer a vast array of information and resources. Many are openly commercial "e-health portals," like mydna.com,
offering everything from "Ask Dr. DNA" to medical news to lab referrals.
Others, run by nonprofit organizations like universities and laboratories,
offer curricula, classroom exercises, illustrations, videos, and so on.

Many of the top-ranked Web sites on the search engine are from
government agencies, like Collins's National Human Genome Research
Institute (NHGRI), the Department of Energy, and The Centers for
Disease Control. Many other federal and state agencies offer online genetics information. One hot topic this time of year is the NHGRI-sponsored
National DNA Day (April 25) commemorating the actual completion
of the Human Genome Project in 2003. Last year thousands of students
downloaded videos of science speakers, participated in online chats with
geneticists, and worked through specially designed materials. (They also
could have sent DNA Day-themed e-cards to suspected relations after
purchasing paternity tests online; but that's another story.)

Francis Collins, in a video message posted on the official Web site,
says that "on DNA Day we all ought to reflect on the remarkable moment

we have in history. . . . We've crossed the threshold. For all of human history we didn't know our own instruction book. Now we know it."

After opening with a few scenes of a cheerful but wizened little boy with a genetic disease that causes premature aging, Collins encourages his young listeners to consider careers in genetics. They could help people like Sam, and genetically based medical practices are soon going to be a major part of the mainstream, he says.

Toward the end, Collins concedes, gravely, that genetic science raises some serious ethical issues. For example, an individual's genetic information could be used against him—health insurance companies might deny coverage to those whose genomes suggest that they are at increased risk of disease or employers might deny jobs based on genetic information. But, he assures the students, the "best solution is a legislative one," and Congress is working on laws against such things. And we all know how coldly logical and efficient Congress is, unsullied by politics and lobby groups and campaign contributions. So no problem there.

As for the possibility of designer babies, Collins says that the usual image of parents choosing their babies' physical and psychological traits is "not scientifically accurate" because environment plays such a large role in development; you can't guarantee results. But if genome-based medicine can decrease or even eliminate a child's chances of acquiring particular diseases through genetic engineering, why won't it be possible to increase the chances of a child having better brain functions? Or more height? Or smoother skin?

Collins also allows that some worry that genetically inferior folks will suffer discrimination analogous to racism. But he argues that, because humans are all over 99 percent genetically alike, genetics "ought to be a great way to reduce prejudice." He doesn't seem to think that the genetic differences that do exist, no matter how minor, might simply provide a justification for discrimination, backed by all the authority of science.

Keep in mind now that this promotional approach, which offers a utopian view of the possibilities while glossing over the dangers, has come before genetic science is even close to settling what's possible and what isn't. Collins is coauthor of a 2003 NHGRI paper, "A Vision for the Future of Genomics Research," that sets this out: "We have entered a unique 'educable era' regarding genomics; health professionals and the public are increasingly interested in learning about genomics, but its widespread application to health is still several years away. For genomics-based health care to be maximally effective once it is widely feasible . . . we must take advantage now of this unique opportunity to increase understanding."

Perhaps even more troubling is the tendency, if you buy the hype presented in much of the genomics educational materials, toward a sort of determinism—genes plus environment defines "what it means to be human." Some scientists are skeptical about this, but many of the leading lights and loudest voices take it for granted. In January, in a Web-zine called *The Edge*, Venter proposed that we are on the threshold of a "realistic biology of humankind," the result of genomic science that can "sort out the reality about nature or nurture": "It will inevitably be revealed that there are strong genetic components associated with most aspects of what we attribute to human existence, including personality subtypes, language capabilities, mechanical abilities, intelligence, sexual activities and preferences, intuitive thinking, quality of memory, will power, temperament, athletic abilities, etc."

The implications of genetic/environmental determinism are startling. "What some individuals consider a sacrosanct ability to perceive moral truths may instead be a hodgepodge of simpler psychological mechanisms," speculates Cornell University psychologist David Pizarro in the same issue of *The Edge*, "some of which have evolved for other purposes."

Free will and moral accountability will also be history. From Oxford biologist Richard Dawkins: "Retribution as a moral principle is incompatible with a scientific view of human behavior. As scientists, we believe that human brains, though they may not work in the same way as man-made computers, are as surely governed by the laws of physics. When a computer malfunctions, we do not punish it. We track down the problem and fix it, usually by replacing a damaged component, either in hardware or software." Dawkins pointedly adds that an "especially warped and disgusting application of the flawed concept of retribution is Christian crucifixion as 'atonement' for 'sin.'"

Venter warns that "when these new powerful computers and databases are used to help us analyze who we are as humans, will society at large, largely ignorant and afraid of science, be ready for the answers we are likely to get?" The danger, he adds, "rests with what we already know: that we are not all created equal." And what if ignorant, superstitious "society at large" balks at the notion that a human is nothing more than a pack of neurons and that some packs are more equal than others? Will scientists like Venter and Dawkins have to take charge for everybody's good?

Venter would probably say that such a suggestion is outrageous and unfounded, and perhaps it is unfair to Venter and Dawkins personally. But scientists have a long history of attempting to exercise control over the direction society is headed. Consider again the Cold Springs Harbor Laboratory. From 1910 through 1940, it housed the Eugenics Record Office and was a central player in the American eugenics movement, a major social force early in the twentieth century whose supporters included such luminaries as the Rockefellers and Woodrow Wilson. Today, the laboratory houses the ERO archives, and the center's Web site has a very informative and blunt feature on the history of American eugenics and the laboratory's role in it. Oddly, though, while offering specific critiques of the weak science supporters used to justify the sterilization and suppression of the "feebleminded" and "social degenerates" (i.e., the poor, immigrants, and racial minorities), the feature implies eugenics is evil but never explains why.

That's understandable . . . in a sense. If naturalism—a philosophy that the Dolan Center takes for granted throughout its exhibits—is true, if we are only collections of DNA arranged by natural forces and there really is no ultimate meaning to it all, then it becomes hard to explain why eugenics is so awful. What's wrong with taking charge of our evolutionary destiny?

Indeed, eugenics is still widespread in an informal manner anyway, only now it's called "prenatal testing" and applied through abortion to unborn babies with Downs Syndrome and spina bifida. It seems likely that this practice will explode in popularity as genetic tests become available for more diseases. And it's a pretty small step, as well-known utilitarian philosophers like Princeton's Peter Singer have argued, from terminating lives inside the womb to terminating those who've recently left it. At the other end, given that growing cohort of graying Baby Boomers, the Medicare budget crunch will likely get here long before pharmacogenomically designed drugs, handing the pro-euthanasia forces that much more ammunition.

The similarities between yesterday's eugenics movement and today's promoters of genomics are startling: a desire that society, for its own good, adopt the best scientific principles available; a focus on public education; and a deep faith in government. When society finally agrees that the Venters and Dawkins of the world are right, then the criteria for judging human life will, of course, be much more *scientifically sound* than race and class, skin color, and country of origin. No, you will be judged on your genome (which at 3 billion base pairs is 255 times *smaller* than that of a salamander), and therefore the judgment will be sophisticated, precise, and irrefutable.

It would be uncharitable to say that those trying to educate the public about genetics are being deliberately deceitful about either the potential or pitfalls of genomic science. The scientific achievements are truly impressive, and the new "golden age of medicine" might eventually arrive. And some scientists, like Collins through the NIH, are attempting to educate the public about the ethical issues through in-depth materials, advisory panels, and so on. We need citizens informed about genetics, he says in the video, and "we're going to need all of you" to help make the decisions that ensure science moves forward "in a way we all believe is benefiting people in the maximum possible way."

And there are also a handful of think-tanks, like the Center for Bioethics and Human Dignity (cbhd.org), battling in the public arena this tendency toward determinism. But there is little incentive among those who produce these materials to dwell on the hazards. Government institutions need public support to make certain that legislators continue funding their work; private institutions want to develop markets for their research and the products that result by encouraging public acceptance of genomic-based medicine. The Human Genome Project sparked a cultural shift, and those pushing genetic science are taking advantage of it. As CBHD bioethicist C. Ben Mitchell explains, "The genie can't be put back in the bottle." The technology is coming; and though it may not bring a new golden age of medicine, it's certainly going to change how we view ourselves. The question is whether society buys the determinism that at present comes packaged with it. One way or another, we're going to get a "realistic biology."

CRITICAL THINKING QUESTIONS

1. What is the Human Genome Project and why is it so important? What are some of its potential medical applications?

2. What are some key ethical issues raised by the Human Genome Project?

3. What is "determinism" and how can research into human DNA further the potentially harmful logical outworking of genetic determinism?

4. What is your understanding of free will and moral accountability? How does genetic determinism threaten moral accountability and justice?

5. What is eugenics? Where in history have we seen eugenics in (horrific) practice? To what extent could information from the Human Genome Project be used to usher in a new era of eugenics? What can be done to benefit from the science of the Human Genome Project without necessarily slipping down the slippery slope to eugenics?

~

The Demolition of Man
Terry Graves

Terry Graves is a novelist and essayist who lives near Pittsburgh, Pennsylvania. A Roman Catholic, professed Secular Franciscan, veteran of both the Vietnam war and Harvard College, and former bureaucrat, he concentrates his research and writing where science, philosophy, religion, and the behavior of organizations overlap and impinge. He has published in e-zines and in print magazines such as *IntellectualConservative.com*, *Touchstone*, and *Saint Austin Review* on a very wide range of topics—school textbooks, disability activists and Christopher Reeve, Islamic influence in public schools, homosexual marriage, advertising, politics and language, and tort reform. A slightly different version of this essay first appeared in the *Fellowship of Catholic Scholars Quarterly*.

Essay Classification: Informative; evaluative; argumentation/persuasion

IN C. S. LEWIS AND *the Catholic Church*, Joseph Pearce devotes eighteen pages to Lewis's space trilogy, yet nowhere does he mention the lectures, later published as *The Abolition of Man*, that gave voice to what Lewis elsewhere called "the serious point" behind these books. In Lewis's own words, in a letter to an Anglican nun, the "serious point" is this: "that thousands of people in one way or another depend on some hope of perpetuating and improving the human race for the whole meaning of the universe—that a 'scientific' hope for defeating death is a real threat to Christianity."

Sixty years later, it is now tens or hundreds of millions who depend on that hope. Some go further, believing, as Jacques Barzun put it, "the fallacy ... that the method of science must be used on all forms of experience and, given time, will settle every issue." (Some call this fallacy *sciencism*; most, *scientism*.) For example, when asked why she supported embryonic stem cell research, Democratic congresswoman Marcy Kaptur took a brave stand: "The question should be left to scientists." Scientism is bipartisan: once when Republican Senator Arlen Specter was asked when life began, he replied, "I haven't found it helpful to get into the details." This blind trust in the people whose day job happens to be scientist is frightening: James Watson, a Nobel laureate for his pioneering work on DNA, reminded us, "in contrast to the popular conception supported by newspapers and by scientists' mothers, a goodly number of scientists are not only narrow-minded and dull, but also just stupid."

Of course, science cannot explain even its own bases: why matter and energy exist and why they are not chaotic. Those of us who reply, "God," might be told our answer begs those questions. Yet, even if He does, those questions persist. Still, this dependence on science—actually, on scientism and on, some, but not all, scientists—is to be expected, if only because so few are aware of an alternative: George Sayer wrote in *Jack*, his biography of Lewis, that few members of the audience at the *Abolition* lectures understood them—and this was at a university in 1943. And in that same letter Lewis noted that of about sixty reviews of the space trilogy's first novel, "only 2 showed any knowledge that my idea of the fall of the Bent One was anything but an invention of my own."

In this far less literate era, even fewer would trouble to pry Lewis's "serious point" out of a long essay like *The Abolition of Man*. Still fewer would find it hidden in the fantastic elements of the space trilogy's entertaining novels, set on, successively, Mars and Venus and in a literally demonic institution in Britain, the National Institute for Co-ordinated Experiments, or N.I.C.E.

This reluctance, or inability, to grapple with "the serious point" will be disastrous. What Lewis feared and foresaw is no longer science fiction:

under way are numerous scientific and pseudo-scientific efforts whose goals are to improve the human race and achieve personal immortality.

Unnatural Family Planning

In one of Bob Thaves's "Frank and Ernest" cartoons, the two stand in front of a "Biogenetic Research Lab." Frank complains to Ernest, "When I ask about cloning all I get is doubletalk." Of the efforts to remodel mankind, those using some form of genetic manipulation are the best known to us in the comic-strip-reading public, thanks to the controversy over cloning and stem cell research. But our lack of familiarity with these terms and their careless, even deceptive, use are among the reasons large-scale embryonic cloning has come upon us so quickly.

To clarify the doubletalk: the word *embryo* means, in humans, the first eight weeks after conception. As the National Institutes of Health (NIH) summarized: stem cells are unspecialized cells, found in both human embryos and adults, that can develop into specialized cells and also reproduce themselves for an extended period. Because of their potential for curing diseases, the federal government supports research on stem cells from both adults and embryos. *Harvard* magazine, in its July–August 2004 issue, explained that embryonic stem cells come from "a ball of four to 50 undifferentiated cells that forms in the first few days after a sperm fertilizes an egg." Columnist Susan Estrich and Mortimer Zuckerman, editor of *U.S. News and World Report,* are among the many who claim that fertility clinics in the U.S. have 400,000 frozen embryos that are likely to be "discarded"—that is, uh, well, *killed.* Other writers have carelessly claimed 400,000 such embryos are created every year. Instead, a Rand Corporation study found that number to have *accumulated* since the late 1970s, and that only 11,000 (2.2%) were slated to be "discarded"; of these, only about 275 (0.06875%) could create embryonic cell lines. Furthermore, as we shall see, even if 400,000 embryos were available, they could not begin to fulfill the demand.

There are two kinds of human cloning—research, or therapeutic, limited to a few cells for use in research or a medical therapy, and reproductive, where cells would be allowed to mature and be born. However, as David A. Prentice, a professor of biology at Indiana State University, told a committee of the Colorado legislature, the methods and the clones produced are precisely the same, differing only in how far the process is allowed to proceed. The intent of the cloning of embryonic stem cells is *not* to treat the embryo, whose cells are instead used to treat *others*—after the embryo is *killed*. In stark contrast, adult stem cells are harmlessly extracted from various parts of the body, such as blood, marrow, testicles, and even fat.

In the United States, there is no federal prohibition of research with embryos, only 1998 and 2001 presidential orders that limit the situations in which the federal government can pay for it. Even though research with embryos has continued in the United States and around the world, *all* the existing medical treatments instead use adult stem cells. As of this writing, no therapy using embryonic cells has even made it to phase 1 clinical (that is, human) *trials* (http://www.clinicaltrials.gov/ct2/results ?term=embryonic+stem+cells). The demonstrated power of adult stem cells is the reason that no one suggests diverting money from research with them—the request is always for more money, to be aimed at work with embryos. In general, adult stem cells have a thirty-year head start on the embryonic in the treatment of spinal cord injuries, Parkinson's, stroke, sickle cell anemia, cardiac damage, multiple sclerosis, and others, with, so far, no medical side effects. And in the stilted words of the sixteen authors of a *Nature* article, these adult cells are not "encumbered by ethical considerations."

There is good reason to expect that adult stem cell therapies will always be safer: in October 2004, fifty-seven biomedical researchers from major laboratories all over the United States wrote a letter (a copy of which was supplied to me indirectly by one of the signers) to then presidential candidate John Kerry. The letter warned that cloned embryonic stem cells are unstable, spontaneously accumulate genetic abnormalities, are prone to uncontrollable growth and tumor formation, as well as "serious and potentially lethal side-effects," and may be rejected by even the host that produced them. As these researchers were not, so to speak, Heinz 57, their letter received no media attention.

"Media attention" brings us to caveats necessary when interpreting its coverage of stem cell research—many who write of it appear not to know there is such a thing as adult stem cells; those who advocate embryonic stem cell research will not mention that successful therapies have used only adult stem cells; and any announced success in stem cell therapy will ignore or glide over the fact that it resulted from *adult* stem cells.

Judy Norigian, the pro-choice author of *Our Bodies/Our Selves*, opposed research with embryos at www.sfbg.com/38/53/cover_stem_cell

.html, citing the health risks for women who provide the eggs to create the embryos. In his "The Science of Human Cloning" (www.stemcellresearch .org/testimony/prentice_03-02-05.pdf), David Prentice spelled it out, estimating that treating just the seventeen million diabetics in the United States would need, at the very least, eighty-five million women (not the phantom famous 400,000, let alone 275!) to provide eggs. (Not that many American women *vote*.) Providing the eggs, Prentice continued, would carry with it significant health risks for the women and likely lead to their commercial exploitation, both here and abroad. Indeed, in the United States and the United Kingdom, private companies and institutions, Harvard, for one, have already begun to recruit women to act as donors.

The only certainty, then, about embryonic cell research is that millions of women must risk their health to donate eggs and a like number of fetuses will be killed. These are among the moral issues to which all thinking Americans should react, openly and loudly, much as we have the data from other research: that gathered by the Nazis in their horrific experiments on prisoners. (See http://www.jlaw.com/Articles/NaziMedEx .html.) This is not a perfect parallel: the Nazi data is tainted because of past events, whereas that from embryos is used to justify a *possible* future event. Too, a good experiment is, among other things, one whose results can be replicated by other experiments. The Nazis' experiments will, one hopes and prays, never be replicated. But for embryonic stem cell research, there are millions of abortions, and tens of millions of poor women in the world, with hundreds of millions of eggs, mere data vulnerable to endless replication.

But "cloning" and "stem cell" research are but two of many biomedical research efforts with moral implications. The Center for Genetics and Society (CGS) surveys them at www.genetics-and-society.org/analysis/ index.html. The center lists dozens of "troubling" technologies and dystopian urges, such as transhumanism and posthumanism; gender selection; gene transfer experiments; and inheritable genetic modification (IGM). About the last, four American bioethicists asserted that people should not be prohibited from creating genetically enhanced children (with, for example, higher IQs) and went on to argue that since this practice will likely create dramatic inequities, public policies should be adopted that make IGM freely available to all. University of Texas law school professor John Robertson introduced "procreative liberty" as a legal and ethical principle that argues against prohibitions on reproductive cloning and

IGM. Princeton biologist Lee Silver champions both and couples these with a libertarian social and political philosophy, arguing that a future in which humanity segregates into genetically engineered subspecies, the "GenRich" and the "Naturals," is "inevitable . . . whether we like it or not."

The huge CGS site is invaluable, because despite the center's preferences—it *favors* research cloning of embryonic stem cells—its presentations are thorough, skeptical, and evenhanded. Its analysis begins with this warning: "The motivations and visions driving the development of genetic technologies are varied. Some are quite troubling. Utopian beliefs, economic potentials, and exaggerated medical promise are playing as much of a role as the desire to alleviate human suffering."

The center's warning is, moreover, too brief: the economic potentials are not just private and corporate. Unlike scientific researchers in some foreign countries and academics here in the humanities or social sciences, biomedical scientists in universities and research institutes are, in a sense, self-employed. It is usually the individual researcher, not the institution(s) with which he is affiliated, who must seek out the money, especially from the NIH, or a tax-exempt nonprofit, or from a for-profit corporation. The NIH alone dispenses over $27 billion-with-*b* a year. With this money the researcher must pay for very expensive lab equipment and supplies and support graduate students and other researchers working for him. Costs, and grants, for each researcher are measured in the multimillions. Of course, when I wrote "costs" I meant "charges." As with the chicken and the oocyte, we do not know which came first, the multimillion dollar charges or the multimillion dollar NIH grants. Charges rise to meet the available funds, and the vendors of biological products that recently charged ten times the usual price for flu vaccine just might similarly overcharge researchers supported by the government, that shrewd buyer of $600 hammers.

So pressing is this need for money that it trumps both past accomplishments and the value of current work. For a researcher with no grants, even tenure is tenuous. Not for nothing has the American Association of Cancer Research urged its members to lobby for embryonic stem cell research: it is for the AACR just another source of money, and research follows the money. Johannes Kepler, who would know, wrote, "God has given every creature a way to make a living; for an astronomer, there is astrology"; were he alive today, Kepler might add, "and for other scientists, there is grantsmanship." The biomedical scientist may be self-employed in another way: a molecular biologist recently told me he estimated that 80 percent of established biomedical researchers have patent or other financial interests in their research, and a piece in *The Scientist* magazine about Madison, Wisconsin, stated "fully half" of the 250 biotech companies surrounding it derived from research done at the city's University of Wisconsin. Universities and other research institutions also have a major financial stake: one I know of takes almost *half*, off the top, of every grant its researchers bring in.

Biomedical research in this country is a very big, complex business, with scientists, students, government bureaucrats, suppliers, and institutions employed by or dependent on it. There is nothing necessarily wrong with this. Or necessarily right. It just is. *The Scientist* bills itself as "the number one cover-to-cover read in the industry" and brags, "Advertise with us and your business is guaranteed to be seen." One of its main categories of articles is "Biobusiness," so it is no surprise that it strongly supports research with embryos and shrugs off opposition to it. The scientific term for this outlay of billions of dollars is *hemanecrodentosis*, which is either from the Greek for "bled to death by lab rats" or something I just made up.

Another troubling motivation is crude partisan politics: that Bush has taken a strong stand against such research with embryos is apparently sufficient reason for others to plump for it, overlooking that the first presidential order restricting its funding came in 1998—from Clinton. Last but perhaps most is ideological opportunism: the strongly pro-abortion Anna Quindlen wrote in 2001 that "the use of the earliest embryo for life-saving [*sic!*] research might bring a certain long-overdue relativism to discussions of abortion across the board." But none of the definitions of moral relativism make sense in Quindlen's context. So, not being in the choir she preaches to, I can only conjecture that Quindlen meant instead a comparison of means and end: that the end justifies the means. This notion is in disrepute these days, perhaps why she did not so express it. (In Quindlen's defense, though, if the end does not justify the means, what does? Just wondering.) Now, here is an interesting means-end comparison: biomedical labs experiment on animals, especially on mice bred for that use. To obtain and use these experimental animals a researcher must receive special training, complete a novella-length protocol, and then seek approval from a dozen or more internal committees and outside agencies. These protocols are fussy even as to how mice will be, uh, well, *killed*, and which euphemism the protocol uses for this act—*euthanize* has replaced *sacrifice*. There is no protocol at all for embryos or, for that matter, aborted fetuses.

No matter; the mantra that abortion should be safe, legal, and rare never made any sense: if safe and legal, why should it be rare? The "exaggerated medical promise" of embryonic stem cells will bring "a certain long-overdue" update to the mantra, and abortion will be touted as safe, legal, and *useful*.

Mini-Me

A related technology (and issue) is human reproductive cloning—allowing the clone to mature and be born. The CGS names several groups that support it, such as the Raelian cult, which advertises, none too convincingly, that it has successfully cloned thirteen human babies. But far more oppose reproductive cloning, including the CGS itself and others who strongly support research cloning: Pitt's Gerald Schatten, who led the team that in December 2004 first cloned (through the blastocyst stage) a nonhuman primate, told *Science News* that he and most other researchers are "unhesitatingly" against human reproductive cloning. Schatten and "most other researchers" may believe that a cloned human baby will go from Raelian myth to real monster.

Despite what these trained professionals say, those readers who still wish to try this at home can go to eBay or, say, Stratagene of La Jolla, California (www.stratagene.com). There they will find a helpful instruction manual, "Human Clone Collection," along with warranty information and instructions on how to order its "Products." (The word *embryo* never appears in the manual.) Though the site warns its "Products" are for research only, they are, as Prentice said, precisely the same as clones intended for reproduction. If businesses and the GenRich are to treat children as "Products," will we then have IQ wars as we do automobile horsepower wars? Will *Consumer Reports*, which recently referred to unborn children as "uterine content," rate each year's new models? And what will happen to the inevitable "Product" recalls?

About the qualms of people like Schatten, David L. Bump wrote in *Science News* that "The researchers charging into this field think that we should pass laws to keep others from abusing their research. Ha! Do they really think they can keep this genie in a bottle?" A genie can grant favors; a better metaphor is that of Pandora's box. For this reason, the attempt by

Stanford's William Hurlbut, as reported by *Culture and Cosmos*, to devise a morally acceptable method of cloning will not stop others from doing it. Nor will the United Nations' resolution against human cloning, another hollow gesture not binding on even the nations that voted for it.

It is not that what can be done will be done. It is that anything funded will be attempted by, at least, any one of what University of Pennsylvania bioethicist Glenn McGee said were "a pretty good-sized group of not-so-credible scientists trying to make Mini-Me." Money for those dozens or hundreds of attempts to clone a human to a live birth will materialize from somewhere, probably somewhere tax-supported or, like the Raelians, tax-exempt.

And while groups like the Raelians may be crackpots, they are crackpots with money and influence. And lawyers: nowadays, a "right" claimed is very nearly a right earned. The Raelians shrewdly sponsor a Web site, www.HumanCloneRights.org, to promote what its name suggests, and attorney Mark Eibert (http://reason.com/opeds/eibert.shtml) said in 2001 he was preparing court challenges to establish human reproductive cloning as a legal right. Once established legally and politically as a "right," cloning, for example, will become a moot issue, a mere matter of personal preference. Too, the financial interests naturally attracted to such an activity will make it difficult to reverse politically.

This process is hardly new: Pearce considers that Lewis was, sixty years ago, representative of those who opposed "a drab egalitarian culture run by bureaucrats in which the sense of duty and responsibility would have no place amid the selfish demands for 'rights.'"

Let us pause for a moment to consider this: according to Schatten, most of the researchers who are willing to kill an embryo for the medical treatment of others are "unhesitatingly" against letting its clone develop into a living child. I oppose both, but the latter certainly seems the lesser of two evils—not that we should have to choose either. For a generation, many have cloaked opposition to abortion under the generic "pro-life," so much so that this "seamless garment" now has no hems either, stretched out of shape as it is to cover things such as racism. How open and loud, then, are we ready to be when—not if—an advocate of human reproductive cloning asks, "How can you call yourself pro-life yet oppose creating life, just because we did it without fornication?"

Furthermore, I doubt that the Center for Genetics and Society, the UN, and researchers like Schatten believe, given enough time, eggs, embryos, and money, that cloning could never produce a healthy child. Instead, perhaps they fear, as I do, what might follow: a return of eugenics.

Human Husbandry

The second approach to improving the species is eugenics, the control over who gets to mate with whom and how many children, if any, they may have, as in another Bob Thaves cartoon when a lab technician tells the hapless Ernest, "Sorry. We've examined your DNA and it's labeled 'Do not refill.'" A pro-eugenics group, Future Generations (www.eugenics.net), noted that Theognis of Megara wrote a poem in praise of eugenics about 520 b.c., and the concept of inherited nobility has always relied on the approach's supposed effectiveness. And not just nobility: in his *Millennium*, Felipe Fernandez-Armesto noted that in the Communist China of the mid-1960s, "class enmity was held to be genetically transmitted." Eugenics was popular and respectable from the mid-1800s through the 1930s, thanks to people themselves as respectable as Charles Darwin's cousin, Francis Galton, later knighted for his studies.

Among the places eugenics was popular was in Germany, long before Hitler, during the democratic Weimar Republic. Most might believe eugenics then died in the bunker with Hitler, but it did not. In 2004 Rolf Winau, a professor at a medical school in Berlin, wanted his colleagues to "exorcize their demons" about eugenics. Winau then let his *own* demons out for some exercise, as he urged researchers to overcome their moral revulsion against eugenics (http://www.lifesite.net/ldn/2004/jun/04062806 .html). But Germany has some of the strongest laws against eugenics and genetic manipulation, far stronger than those in the United States. The Center for Genetics and Society listed (as a cautionary) the many organizations and academics supporting eugenics in one form or another; most are here, in Britain especially, or in Europe. Some of its proponents, such as psychologist Richard Lynn, focus on the desire of parents to have children who are intelligent and free of genetic disease. Another quoted, with seeming approval, a 1939 reference to some unspecified humans as "noxious animals" (this from Harvard professor E. A. Hooten, by the way, not Hitler). Other sources the center surveyed seem at least tinged with racism and anti-Semitism, and all display a dull arrogance.

It is the disabled, the canaries in any eugenics coal mine, who most fear its current resurgence. At http://www.h-net.org/~disabil/, a posting noted that, for example, Britain's People Against Eugenics, or PAE, fear that cloning or other genetic manipulation will lead to Nazi-like eugenics and the abortion of disabled children. For good reason: in the fall of 2004, the Royal Society, no less, sponsored a conference whose topics included "Why We Are Morally Obliged to Genetically Enhance Our Children," "Gay science: Choosing Our Children's Sexual Orientation," and "Preventing the Existence of People with Disabilities."

Nevertheless, the PAE hastened to add that it "supports women's right to choose abortion." In effect, therefore, PAE supports the abortion of only healthy babies. So we have been practicing eugenics on a large scale for decades: abortion is a kind of postcoital eugenics. In his *Birth Control in America: The Career of Margaret Sanger*, David M. Kennedy quotes Sanger as saying, "Birth control is nothing more or less than the facilitation of the process of weeding out of the unfit, or preventing the birth of defectives or of those who will become defectives."

Necessarily, eugenicists will label some genetic traits as defects, others as benefits, and what was once the one may become the other. Just a few years ago, some behavior was to be excused because there supposedly was a "fat" gene or a "gay" gene. Will these be subject to manipulation? Deletion? Enhancement? These judgments about "defectives" are not just scientific, political, or even, as we shall see, ethical; they will, or at least should, begin as moral questions.

Lapsing Into Consciousness

Free will has no meaning without consciousness, something many insist is a meaningless illusion. As Nobel Prize winner David Hubel put it, "The word Mind is obsolete ... like the word *sky* for astronomers." Another Nobel laureate, Francis Crick, wrote, "You, your joys and your sorrows, your memories and ambitions, your sense of personal identity and free will, are, in fact, no more than the behavior of a vast assembly of nerve cells and their associated molecules." (Note that Crick wrote *You*, not *We*.) A Frank and Ernest cartoon put it better in a salute to Descartes: "I respond to external stimuli, therefore I am." (I cite cartoons to stress that the practical and moral aspects of these efforts to make us over are not rocket, or any other kind of, science, but rather scientism, just another rationale for what some people want other people to do.) Now, if all that people like Hubel and Crick meant is that nerve cells are how the Mind, or consciousness, instructs, say, the hand to grasp a pencil, then this would be neither novel or controversial. But it is far more ambitious than that; it is that the Mind is no more than the molecules. An extreme example: in his *Consilience* Edward O. Wilson argued that ethics is merely an extension of the cooperative behavior displayed by the organisms Wilson has studied— ants, by the way, not humans. Humans are for Wilson just another creature that, in our naiveté, we should not attempt to anthropomorphize.

But if Mind, consciousness, is an illusion, how did it evolve among humans? Assuming for the moment consciousness is not something magical or miraculous (a soul, for example), then it must be a product or byproduct of chemical reactions within the body, presumably within the brain, and must have arisen *via* evolution. But evolution is just another complex physical process like photosynthesis or the collapse of a black hole, no less and certainly no more. After all, like the other processes, evolution is not self-explanatory, an unmoved mover, so it should not be a cause in the other sense of being all-explanatory, the at once arrogant but defensive ideology it has become for some, a stunt double for the older notions of determinism and materialism. Nor is evolution purposeful: that would smack of (horrors!) Intelligent Design. Evolution lacks even a direction, such as toward more complexity. Cave fish have lost their eyes, and the tapeworm is a descendant of the more complex flatworm and has discarded its nervous system as superfluous in its environment. Species that are less successful than the tapeworm, at least as to number, are subject to the same pressures: our own senses are less acute than they once were. Looking at evolution for what it is, just another physical process, may be why creationists have been little perturbed by Spore, a videogame about evolution, which was "designed" by someone with the entirely suitable name of Will Wright. Wright purposely designed Spore, whose point is for its single player to control the evolution of a species. No wonder creationists disbelieve in evolution but can tolerate Spore: the game validates what they say about evolution, in that it has a Designer, a Single Player who is also the Designer, and a Purpose.

Instead, the physical process of evolution is merely adaptive and opportunistic: long before Darwin, Goethe wrote, "Life is a disease of matter." (This doubtless sounds even bleaker in the original German.) As the process of cancer changes healthy cells into cancer cells, the process of life converts inorganic into the organic, into biomass. If evolution were as self-this and all-that as some of its ideologues would have us believe, then we humans would not deserve condemnation as despoilers of the planet: the human species is evolutionarily quite successful, as there is now far more human biomass than there was even a hundred years ago, and most of our competition, other large mammals, now exists by our sufferance, if not for our sustenance. If this seems somehow to have upset the balance of nature we hear so much about (usually in tandem with ecosystems that invariably are fragile, as brides are always beautiful), consider that if nature had ever been balanced—that is, static—then inorganic compounds would never become organic, and there would have been no unicellular organisms, no dinosaurs, no australopithecines, no you, and no me. And if this seems somehow unfair, recall that quaint notions such as fairness are but the behavior of a vast assembly of nerve cells. Oddly, many of the people who believe in evolution as all-explanatory also disapprove of its outcomes, while many who think of it as godless rubbish nevertheless are content with the results.

Again, how did we evolutionary winners develop our minds, illusory as they may be? Mutation could cause isolated occurrences of the necessary processes, but Mind, *or even its illusion*, expends energy. Again assuming for the moment, this time that evolution explains all about how we became what we are: for the mutation of consciousness to become universal or even common, then evolutionarily speaking it must somehow confer some advantage on the creatures with it. Mind must pay its own way, must justify that expenditure of energy. But if the Mind is obsolete and personal identity and free will just nerve cells and molecules, then it would be just a captive passenger within the body, impotently observing what goes on around it. Furthermore—and this is crucial—the Mind therefore could not affect any form or behavior for natural selection to favor and spread throughout the species. If Mind is obsolete and illusory, then it must also be at best a needless distraction, at worst an impotent waste of energy. (Poet J. D. Smith so amended Goethe: "And thought a disease of life . . .") Instead, the edge would lie with those individuals who are not wasting energy on something useless like the Mind, like consciousness. And in the long run, it may, anyway. We may go the way of the flatworm.

So, still assuming that Mind is an illusory byproduct, then those of us who fancy we are conscious must be rare mutants whose peculiarity is as useless as a vermiform appendix, evolutionary dead-ends like the Neanderthals. And if we were to believe Hubel and Crick or any other flavor of materialist or determinist, science alone cannot prove to me that you possess consciousness—or to you that I do. But it is remarkable that the belief in one's own consciousness is so strong (so wasteful of energy!)

that most believe that, at least, everyone he knows also possesses it. For good reason: instead of a scattering of ineffectual mutations, the simpler explanation—and therefore the better scientific presumption—is that the Mind exists and with it consciousness and free will consciously affect behavior, a presumption that we are about to see has much to support it.

Ipsilon

Here I shall use the Greek letter *ipsilon*—also the ancient Y-shaped Christian symbol for free will—to represent the third and last approach to the reshaping of us and of human society. Call it will power or, paradoxically, its evil twin, brainwashing, or intense conditioning. Now that brainwashing is no longer the buzzword it was in the 1950s, this approach is overlooked by even, thankfully, those who might wish to misuse it or, worse yet, use it for our "own good." But brainwashing is more than just the plot device in *The Manchurian Candidate* and *A Clockwork Orange*. *Dorland's Medical Dictionary for Healthcare Consumers* defines it as "[A] ny systematic effort aimed at instilling certain attitudes and beliefs against a person's will, usually beliefs in conflict with prior beliefs and knowledge." That is, it differs only in degree from advertising and propaganda, which differ from each other only in what they are selling.

A fine source of background information about will power and its evil twin is *The Mind and the Brain* by Jeffrey Schwartz, MD, and science writer Sharon Begley. In it Schwartz, a neuropsychiatrist, relates his far-ranging search for an effective therapy for his patients with obsessive-compulsive disorder, or OCD. He reviews the various theories of dualism, materialism, and determinism and shows that those laymen—and scientists like Hubel—who profess to hold to them are seventy years or more behind in the pertinent science. Schwartz and Begley cite numerous peer-reviewed studies by Michael Merzenich and Edward Taub, among many others, that show a person can, within limits, rewire his brain, alter both its physical form and functions—and therefore his outward behavior—by an effort of conscious will. The limits of change are broad: the authors said what happens is a "wholesale remapping of neural real estate." Therefore, the crude diagrams that supposedly show which part of which side of the human brain does what are naïve and quite misleading. Instead, the brain's map varies from one person to the next and, for the same person, from one moment to the next.

This ability to "will" changes does not end in childhood and continues through old age. Examples: a Japanese learning English must first rewire his brain so as to *hear* the L sound before he can learn to *say* it, and Schwartz learned that his "OCD patients can, by changing the way they think about their thoughts, also change their brain." That is, they can willfully reduce their repetitive behaviors.

The brain adapts to outside influences; it also adapts to the mind's thoughts. Here are two of the experiments that dramatically illustrated this. In the late 1980s, Greg Recanzone and William Jenkins learned that if their lab "monkeys' *attention* was focused elsewhere while they received the same tactile stimulation that had otherwise produced massive cortical remapping, no such reorganization occurred [emphasis added]." In 1995, Alvaro Pascual-Leone had one group of human volunteers practice a five-finger piano exercise, while a control group merely thought about it. As expected, the physical exercise caused changes in the motor cortex of each member of the first group; but the same changes in the brains showed up, and to the same degree, in the control group that merely imagined they were practicing.

Both these experiments showed that the mind's attentiveness is both necessary and sufficient to bring about a physical change in the brain. Schwartz and Begley rely on quantum theory to show how our mind causes the brain to carry out the mind's will, to produce this rewiring, but the reader interested in their shade-tree quantum mechanics must read their book. Suffice for now to say that they begin their discussion by quoting the great physicist, Niels Bohr: "Anyone who is not shocked by quantum theory has not understood it."

No matter: how we exercise free will is far less important than that we do. Schwartz, who seems to lean spiritually toward Buddhism, believes strongly in free will and, indeed, blames "the cultural morass of the late twentieth century" on the philosophy of materialism. Most Christians, too, will readily affirm a belief in a conscious free will and may be impatient with, say, the deterministic defenses of attorneys whose clients are, in the lyrics from *West Side Story*, depraved on account of being deprived. Oddly, such pop materialism is never used to explain away good or beneficial behavior. Since Hubel believes he has no Mind and Crick no free will that guided their researches, did they refuse their Nobel Prizes? (Answer: No.) Like anyone else, materialists and other determinists do not just sit around waiting for their molecules to motivate them. Like Crick, they reserve their notions of inevitability, of helplessness, for *other* people.

Despite such inconsistencies, for generations we have absorbed some form of determinism with the very air we breathe. It must afford us comfort: even so staunch an advocate of free will as the Roman Catholic Church has inhaled, deeply: while section 1734 of its *Catechism* says: "Freedom makes man *responsible* for his acts to the extent that they are voluntary," its 1735 qualifies this into, literally, a nullity: "responsibility for an action can be diminished or even nullified by ignorance, inadvertence, duress, fear, habit, inordinate attachments, and other psychological or social factors." The Roman Church, and we, must learn to exhale.

An *ipsilon* has two branches, as a sword has two edges: if one is empowered by his own will, so are the wills of others. An outside will can bend one's own will to bring about major, long-lasting changes in the brain's wiring and, hence, in behavior. This happens, of course, to all of us, every day—it is how a child learns language and the violin and why "practice makes perfect." But if one's will power can effect these changes so haphazardly, it can also happen, indirectly, as a result of someone else's will. The process can be as innocent and beneficial as a tennis coach's helping with your forehand—or as insidious as advertising and propaganda or as sinister as brainwashing. Schwartz and Begley put it this way: "Several hundred 'trials' consisting of hearing spoken language spoken imperfectly ... [might] result in a new brain—and possibly a new impairment—in people. The brain changes causing these impairments could become so severe that Merzenich coined a term to capture their magnitude: *learning-based representational catastrophe.*"

Because it has three arms, the *ipsilon* has also been used as a symbol of the Trinity. But its three arms can also represent three kinds of behavior—moral; immoral; and conditioned, which is to say, amoral: a representational catastrophe. We must choose among them while we still can. As the prison chaplain put it in Anthony Burgess's *A Clockwork Orange*, "When a man cannot choose he ceases to be a man."

After this survey of these dangerous technologies, many readers will still believe there is no danger, that scientists' professional ethics and, especially, the democratic process will save us from these horrors. We can rely on neither one.

Ethic Cleansing

Archimedes is supposed to have said about the lever, "Give me a firm spot to stand, and I will move the Earth." The Center for Genetics and Society disapproves of many of the technologies its Web site discusses, such as inheritable genetic modification and reproductive cloning. But it gives no ultimate, bedrock reason why it does and presumably relies on some flavor of ethics, bio- or otherwise.

But some cautions are here in order, because nowadays anybody can hang out his shingle as an ethicist, bio- or otherwise. When Nobel laureate James Watson was trying to reassure Fr. Richard John Neuhaus about the Human Genome Project, he told Neuhaus that the project had set aside several million dollars "to get the best ethicists money can buy." But there is no reason to assume an ethicist's observations and experience are more nearly universal, or his assumptions about good and evil somehow better, than those of Joe Sixpack. For example, a baroness whose shingle reads "Britain's leading moral philosopher"—no mere ethicist she—recently urged, in her tweedy way, that the demented be "put ... down." Why? Because of the financial strain on the UK's National Health Service. "Put ... down": this phrase, redolent of stables and kennels, completes the link between animal husbandry and human husbandry.

At best, a body of ethics can be a more stringent application of ordinary morality. But it can also be a gentrified, upscale body of exceptions to morality, or even a low-cal, less filling substitute for it. For example, when Harvard's provost created a committee to review embryonic stem cell research because of the ethical issues it raised, its chair said, "Our starting point is academic freedom"—thereby effectively ending any reason for his committee's existence. A professional group's ethics and ethicists are not binding on even its own members. For example, for his book *What Scientists Think,* Jeremy Stangroom, coeditor of *The Philosopher's Magazine,* asked UK geneticist Steve Jones about, among other things, health insurance, IQ, and "the future of the human race." Jones averred, "I don't think biochemists are going to be the least bit interested in what philosophers think about genes. As I've said in the past, philosophy is to science as pornography is to sex: It's cheaper, easier, and some people prefer it." Imagine, then, how much Jones despises the opinions of mere ethicists and still more those of Joe Sixpack and the other taxpayers who pay for his research. Too, one has to wonder why Jones imagined anyone would be the least bit interested in what geneticists think about health insurance or, heaven help us, "the future of the human race." Jones' flippant attitude about the moral issue is not unusual: a company that was the first to sell a cloned cat has the cutesy name of Genetic Savings & Clone.

We forever hear, "You can't legislate morality"—but never the unspoken rest of the chant, "but I can, if I call it ethics." Professional ethics is no substitute for morality for even its profession and over the culture at large should have no authority whatsoever. The CGS is like Archimedes, without a firm spot on which to stand. It hopes to be a Pandora who can selectively swat down the evils she has released, while letting others fly away.

The Camel's Other End

Furthermore, the CGS disagrees that these ominous technological changes are inevitable, "whether we like it or not," arguing, "In a democratic society, people have the power to agree on the rules under which they wish to live." Ironically, this naïve statement remains on the CGS Web site even after the 2004 election, when the voters in California chose overwhelmingly to amend its constitution to establish and extravagantly fund the California Institute for Regenerative Medicine, or CIRM. Its purpose is to promote and perform research cloning of human embryos, though, just as coy as Stratagene's cloning manual, CIRM's official statement of over ten thousand words includes no form of the term *embryo* and instead uses *pluripotent* or, like Stratagene, *products*.

The center strongly opposed the CIRM, as did pro-life churches and some pro-abortion groups. (California's Council of Churches, representing 1.5 million Protestants and Orthodox, supported it, however.) Yet CIRM became law, thanks to its misleading official statement and mostly to a campaign of, fittingly, advertising and propaganda led and financed by the very people, biotech companies, and universities that stand to directly benefit from the $3 billion it will hand out—and by law must also have a solid majority on its board of directors. (Crime may not pay, but CIRM does.) Its opponents warned of not only the evils of embryonic stem cell research but also of the waste, cronyism, corruption, and other "economic potentials" built into CIRM.

The demonic N.I.C.E. of Lewis' space trilogy wants, as Pearce puts it, to implement "all the 'progressive' wonders of the eugenically correct state." So, while demons are neither necessary nor sufficient for evil, it would be, well, nice if N.I.C.E. could be seen as an ancestor of CIRM. But so far CIRM has not shown any sign of intelligent control, demonic or otherwise. It is not the camel's nose inside the tent flap; it is behaving more like the camel's other end. Since its creation, CIRM has managed to confirm the warnings of its detractors and to disappoint its supporters, some of whom now seek, too late, ways to rein it in—even while praising it with faint damnation. CIRM is not N.I.C.E.; it is a slippery slope into a money pit, or worse, and will become just another strand in the web of amoral and incompetent organizations that enmesh us.

If something as blatant and clumsy as CIRM elbowed its way into California's constitution, then the Center for Genetics and Society (and we) would be unrealistic to believe that mere rhetoric can derail other such efforts that will themselves, in the long run, grossly warp the electoral process. In the short run, Connecticut, New Jersey, and New York already seek to follow California into embryonic research; their announcements indicate they regard it as just good business, a way of keeping up with the Gomezes.

Unmoved Movers and Shakers

It may seem like comparing apples to clockwork oranges, but these three efforts—genetic manipulation, eugenics, and conditioning—to nudge evolution along and defeat death share three characteristics: they complement, not compete with, each other and, while they claim to have only the best intentions, are threats to any form of free society.

Lewis realized that the "culture run by bureaucrats" might not be egalitarian, only drab; he put these words into the mouth of one of the leaders of N.I.C.E: "Man has got to take charge of Man. That means, remember, that some men have got to take charge of the rest." And in *The Abolition of Man* he had already linked this taking charge directly with science: "What we call Man's power over Nature turns out to be a power exercised by some men over other men with Nature as its instrument."

There need be no grand conspiracy to dumb us down and take over our lives. Our Abolition, or Demolition, may just be our path of least resistance; we already seem content not to be self-governing, or even governed, but merely administered. And badly at that. Or our Demolition may be the lofty stuff of dreams, but we have dreamt them before—Hitler Youth and the *Lebensborn*, the New Soviet Man (who turned out to be an old Georgian thug), Mao's Great Proletarian Cultural Revolution, and the good doctors Frankenstein, Jekyll, and Mengele. Unlike Dr. Jekyll, who drank his own concoction, the controllers, the conditioners, the manipulators will try to exclude themselves from their own techniques, to be unmoved movers. Perhaps they truly believe that only they possess consciousness, have a mind. And if we allow such people such power over us and "the future of the human race," then they would be right. What we allow, we get, and what we get, we deserve.

It is possible that all these efforts will messily fail; the greater danger is that they will gloriously succeed. And the would-be unmoved movers likely will be caught up in their own systems, leaving no one free: all of us, the movers and the moved, are already bombarded with external stimuli of all kinds, every day. The technologies have already begun to enmesh their makers: in an introduction to Jacques Ellul's brilliant *Propaganda*, Konrad Kellen wrote, "Ellul regards propaganda as a sociological phenomenon rather than as something *made* by certain people for certain purposes. Propaganda exists and thrives; it is the Siamese twin of our technological society." That is, there need be no grand conspiracy to flood us with propaganda; we are inflicting it on ourselves. David Harris, a 1960s draft resister, once remarked, "I mean, the beautiful thing about American totalitarianism is that it's participatory." This remark is less remarkable than it seems; given the low level of technology, to enslave us all, we all must help out, must do our bit.

You reading this may not be at risk, but our children, and certainly their children, will be. It is already too late to stop at least some of these procedures from being attempted. For example, a culture that supports partial-birth abortion will do as it pleases with a clump of embryonic cells smaller than the period at the end of this sentence. Invisibility eases moral qualms: just as a stem cell is too small to see, abortion, probably the most common surgery performed in the United States, is never shown on television, not yet even on PBS's *Nova*, in an episode entitled, say, *The Miracle of Death*. PBS would sooner broadcast the equally hypothetical *Rick Steves Tours the Bordellos of Amsterdam* than it would *The Miracle of Death*.

Armed with the latest genetic and neuropsychiatric research, better techniques and chemicals, and decades of experience, successive generations of manipulators will grow more effective. Next time around, Raymond Shaw, the sniper in Richard Condon's *The Manchurian Candidate*, will carry out his mission, and the Ludovico conditioning technique Burgess invented for *A Clockwork Orange* will not need to be reversed so as to "cure" Alex, its protagonist, of his passivity. The time after *that*, Raymond and Alex may each be designed for his role from the moment of conception in some Petri dish. Of course, just so many ducks in somebody else's row, novelists in this bleak future will never think to write of such matters, and you would never read this essay because I would never think to write it.

Nor will these efforts be the last. For example, surgical and chemical interventions to control behavior are outside the scope of this essay because their use is limited to criminals and the mentally ill. For now. All depends on definition: for example, Freud was not the last to consider religion a form of mental illness, and the Soviet Union will not be the last to act on Freud's belief.

Milton wrote in Paradise Lost, "The mind is its own place, and in itself/Can make a heaven of hell." In the centuries since we have gone from striving for heaven to striving for heaven on earth. Now, to the extent we remain inward and quiet, we are ready to settle for a drab culture run by bureaucrats, an earth on earth, so long as it promises to be eternal. Instead, once we cannot choose, we shall remove man and woman, as well as God, from the equation, and our minds will make a hell on earth.

CRITICAL THINKING QUESTIONS

1. What is the difference between embryonic stem cell research and adult stem cell research? Which one has produced no medical treatments or cures? Which one has produced numerous practical medical cures? Why, then, do policy makers and the press push for federal funding for the one type that has produced no cures, that destroys human life, and that puts donor women at risk?

2. In what ways could human cloning create a world of biological inequality and discrimination?

3. According to Graves what is the connection between reproductive cloning and eugenics?

4. Many scientific materialists have argued that the mind is merely an illusion and that it is nothing but an emergent quality of the physical brain. However, how has recent research refuted this claim and thus reaffirmed the ancient understanding that there is the mind that is separate from yet related to the material brain?

∽

Better Than Human: The Transhumanist Transition to a Technological Future

John Coleman

John Coleman is a management consultant living in Atlanta. His articles have appeared in such periodicals as the *Birmingham News*, the *Tallahassee Democrat, Touchstone, Liberty* magazine, the *New Pantagruel*, and the *National Review Online*. The following article appeared in *Salvo* (Autumn 2006).

Essay Classification: Informative; evaluative; argumentation/persuasion

IT STARTED WITH WHAT Richard Dawkins refers to as "stable things." Before organic life arose on earth, this marvelous universe was nothing more than an interstellar light show. Stars, planets, and moons spun through the galaxy totally devoid of conscious intent, intelligence, or motive. You know the drill: no U2 concerts, no moody ex-girlfriends, no surprises.

Then a fascinating twist of fate altered the course of prehistory. Somewhere on earth, the right stable things swirled together to ignite something totally new. Boom! Splash! *Emergence*. Life arose and introduced the faintest twinkle of action to an elegant and predictable abyss. Time, for the first time, mattered. Our story gained some steam.

From emergence it wasn't far to replication and, subsequently, *evolution*. Over billions of years, DNA transformed into single-celled organisms that strove on in the muck until the survivors were selected for their biological eccentricities to move up the food chain. Trillions of deaths and thousands of centuries led to the gradual selection of ever more complex critters: puffer fish, newts, ostriches, and iguanas; and, suddenly, only a few thousand years ago, our hero took the stage.

The first man (or woman) skipped away from the world of the apes, and chance held its breath. Up to that point, everything had been trial and error, a painstaking game of genetic roulette.

But with man, conscious innovation outpaced unconscious accident. With tools and intelligence, man built spears and then towers and then automobiles. He corralled fire and co-opted the power of the atom. He created fascinating canvas art and laughably bad cinema, and in the time it took amoebas to jump from amoebas to, well, somewhat more advanced amoebas, the planet was transformed. Mankind won the battle for supremacy over stable (and unstable) things, and only one conundrum remained. For all his power, man had failed to change the universe's most complex creation—himself.

But fear not! Now we sit at the cusp of something more monumental than either emergence or evolution: *intelligent design*. Just as man unwrapped the complexities of space travel and microwave ovens, he has finally unraveled the secrets of silicon and DNA. And with these and other innovations, to quote acclaimed naturalist Edward O. Wilson, "Homo sapiens, the first truly free species, is about to decommission natural selection, the force that made us."

So, that is the process, ladies and gentlemen. Emergence. Evolution. Intelligent design. According to the Singularity Institute's Eliezer Yudkowsky in a speech delivered at the Immortality Institute's Life Extension Conference on November 5, 2005, far from competing theories, these are succeeding pieces in the puzzle of history. And within a century, we will radically redefine what it means to be human.

Shocked? Astounded? Don't be. If you believe the "transhumanists," this is a ride you have to take.

Our Posthuman Future?

Unless you are a prominent gerontologist, cryonicist, or president of the Francis Fukuyama fan club, it is quite possible that you have never heard of "transhumanism." Sporting a prefix generally reserved for transvestitism, transcendentalism, and the trans-Siberian railroad, transhumanism is a movement that hopes for the radical evolution of our species, and it is quickly attracting the attention of followers and critics alike.

Tracing its etymological roots to 1972 and New School University professor FM 2030 (who proved, once and for all, that alpha-numeric names are not solely the domain of rappers), "transhuman," short for transitory human, was first used to refer to a human evolutionary stage transitional to "posthumanity" and has grown to include a broad basket of varied philosophic and scientific beliefs.

Throughout the 1970s and 1980s, radical philosophers, futurists, scientists, body builders, and assorted science-fiction fanatics from all walks of life began to meet in hopelessly hip places like L.A. and New York to discuss the possibilities of rapid technological progress. In 1988, an Oxford-educated California man named Max More launched one of transhumanism's pioneering organizations, the Extropy Institute; and in 1998 transhumanism found a second home in Nick Bostrom and David Pearce's World Transhumanist Association.

Now, motivated and ambitious, this eclectic band stands for nothing less than the rapid metamorphosis of the human species into something "posthuman"—that is, better than human. According to Bostrom, "Transhumanists view human nature as a work-in-progress, a half-baked beginning that we can learn to remold in desirable ways." They "yearn to reach intellectual heights as far above any current human genius as humans are above other primates; to be resistant to disease and impervious to aging; to have unlimited youth and vigor; to exercise control over their own desires, moods, and mental states." And no method of advancement—chemical, digital, molecular, or robotic—is outside the realm of reasonable discussion.

Their first target is immortality, and leading the charge is a passionate blue-eyed Brit with a Rip-Van-Winkle beard named Aubrey de Grey. Of late, de Grey has become the crown prince of the "immortalist" movement with his razor-sharp wit, his confrontational (yet charming) personality, and his SENS (Strategies for Engineered Negligible Senescence) approach to fighting aging; and when I met de Grey at the 2005 Immortality Institute conference, I wasn't disappointed. Half scientist and half civil rights pulpit pounder, de Grey has a way of framing the issue of aging that tends to undermine his critics. He views it more as a disease, a silent killer, than the acceptable progression of nature, and he is fond of asking would-be opponents, "If you could stop 100,000 people from dying needlessly every day, why not do it?" That's a hard question to parry, and when you see him in a room surrounded by hundreds of people who have already signed up to have their heads cryogenically frozen in hopes of a future revival (including at least one gentleman in a "Bury funerals, not people!" t-shirt), you understand the kind of zeal the promise of immortality can inspire—whether the messenger is a Cambridge researcher like de Grey or an evangelist like Billy Graham.

Moving beyond de Grey's modest ambitions, however, the essence of the movement is not just a push for the mortal persistence of the individual human being but for his evolution—even postbiological evolution.

This is the message of inventor, author, and technological optimist Ray Kurzweil. The primary proponent of what Joel Garreau has referred to as transhumanism's "Heaven Scenario," Kurzweil doesn't stop at immortality but instead drives forward to the radical evolution of the human machine. In his book *Radical Evolution*, Garreau quotes Kurzweil as predicting that by 2029, "a $1,000 unit of computation . . . [will have] the hardware capacity of 1,000 human brains," and it will be "as hard to tell if a person is handicapped as it is to guess his original hair color." He is joined by academics like Trinity College's James J. Hughes, who envisions a futuristic family in which "one member is a cyborg, another is outfitted with gills for living underwater. Yet another has been modified to live in a vacuum." And if you think gills, cyborgs, and supercomputers are out there, wait until you see where they're leading: a phenomenon called "the singularity."

According to a Web site devoted to the topic (*singularity.org*), the singularity is "the rise of super-intelligent life, created through the improvement of human tools by the acceleration of technological progress reaching the point of infinity." In the abstract, it sounds like a mathematic equation; in practice, it looks eerily like the extinction of the human species.

The theory is that once we make smarter-than-human intelligence capable of replicating and improving itself, it will do so at such a rapid pace that within a short period of time the human species will become antiquated and unnecessary. However, "just because humans become obsolete doesn't mean *you* become obsolete," notes the Singularity Institute's Yudkowsky. "You are not a human. You are an intelligence which, at present, happens to have a mind unfortunately limited to human hardware." And in the future we will trade in these biological bodies, frail and prone to death, for new technological bodies into which we will "upload" our minds—a process kind of like burning a CD with *you* on it.

It's a lot for the uninitiated to take in, isn't it? So—let's review the future. Within decades we will start to enhance ourselves by means of chemical, genetic, and technological change. Drugs will alter our minds, leaving us happy and motivated around the clock. Gene therapy and biotechnology will allow us to defeat infirmity and then blur the line between diseases (like cancer) and less-than-optimal mental and physical states (like shortness). People will begin to live for hundreds and then thousands of years, adding mental features like telepathy and physical features like super-strong bone structure; and, finally, we will begin to merge with our technological creations: the machines. Like the Borg of *Star Trek* fame, we will share mental networks and create outer shells that never age. With the help of our mechanical progeny—the AI—we will become pure mental energy, until all that is currently human has faded away and we are Aristotelian gods—all-knowing, all-seeing, and left with nothing but the consideration of ourselves (or self).

"The twenty-first century could end in world peace, universal prosperity, and evolution to a higher level of compassion and accomplishment," write the National Science Foundation's Mihail C. Roco and William Sims Bainbridge in the 415-page policy document *Converging Technologies for Improving Human Performance*. "It is hard to find the right metaphor to see a century into the future, but it may be that humanity would become like a single, distributed and interconnected 'brain.'"

World peace. Immortality. Unlimited intelligence. Perfection.

Convinced? If you say "no," you're not alone.

The Skeptics of Utopia

In April of 2000, Sun Microsystems cofounder and chief scientist Bill Joy rocked the pages of *Wired* magazine with a stunning 11,000-word article titled "Why the Future Doesn't Need Us." In short (to borrow a metaphor from Garreau), where Kurzweil envisions heaven, Bill Joy senses hell.

"Biological species almost never survive encounters with superior competitors," writes Joy. "In a completely free marketplace, [with] superior robots ... biological humans would be squeezed out of existence." And Joy doesn't mean this in the happy-go-lucky transformative way that Yudkowsky does. Throughout his *Wired* piece, Joy notes the dangers of advanced robotics, AI, and nanotechnology—greater than those of conventional Weapons of Mass Destruction (WMDs) because they may soon be cheaply and readily available, virtually undetectable, and "self-replicating" (meaning that nasty little machines might make more of their nasty little selves without us wanting them to).

The ever-present danger of self-replicating nanotechnology even led author Eric Drexler to give it a name—the "grey goo problem"—which prophecies that incredibly simple self-replicating nanotechnological robots could go out of control searching for and assimilating resources to self-replicate (their only purpose) and end up consuming all life (and nonlife) on earth. Drexler notes that these machines "might be superior in an evolutionary sense, but this need not make them valuable." Read a little Drexler and Joy, and you start to think a little harder about the nightmare scenarios pictured in *The Matrix* and *The Terminator*. While I was once naïve enough to wonder what terrorists, rogue dictators, and disgruntled soccer moms might do with such technology, the real experts have a greater concern: what the technology might do with itself; and the consequences of the dangers they predict often take on blockbuster sci-fi proportions.

Pushing aside "grey goo," however, Johns Hopkins professor Francis Fukuyama has taken another line of attack—questioning the cultural and philosophical implications of transhumanism. In the September/October 2004 edition of *Foreign Policy*, Fukuyama brought infamy to the transhumanist movement when he labeled it "the world's most dangerous idea"; and, while his full considerations of the topic are detailed in the acclaimed *Our Posthuman Future*, Fukuyama's primary objections to transhumanism in *Foreign Policy* are twofold: It is a threat to the equality of rights, and it is an affront to the outstanding complexity of the human being.

First, Fukuyama sees the consciously directed evolution of individual human beings into "posthumans" as more than slightly problematic for that whole liberal conception of *equal rights*. As Fukuyama notes, "Underlying the idea of the equality of rights is the belief that we all possess a human essence that dwarfs manifest differences in skin color, beauty, and even intelligence"; however, if the transhumanists have their way, there will be a whole new strata of considerations to deal with—massive differences in physical and mental coordination, the possibility of conscious machines, radically altered animal species—and these new differences could rock to the core our current understanding of rights and dignity.

Second, Fukuyama sees human nature as irreducibly complex and the transhumanist desire to change it as rudderless and hasty—lacking an appropriate value system to replace the one it intends to undermine. "Transhumanism's advocates think they understand what constitutes a good human being," writes Fukuyama. "But do they really comprehend the ultimate human goods?" For Fukuyama, there are certain necessities to human life—limitation, jealousy, love—that make life livable and that bind us as a species, but the complexity of our current culture would collapse should this foundation be shaken. In short, the transhumanists might be willing to strip bare the current moral and cultural structures of the human race, but do they have anything solid with which to fill the vacuum once these things are gone?

Finally, many people have a more commonsensical objection, a practical combination of the other warnings brilliantly communicated by the Center for Bioethics & Human Dignity's Matthew Eppinette: all this utopianism and idealism are just a little scary, and the movement seems to ignore some of the basic historical lessons of past attempts at human perfection. "Transhumanism is both appealing and frightening because of the way they cast things," remarked Eppinette in a telephone interview last fall. He thinks the transhumanists underemphasize evil as a cause of suffering in the world and gloss over objections like Joy's and Fukuyama's in order to barrel ahead with new technologies and an unbounded faith in their ability to perfect the human condition. Meanwhile, they accept a total separation of the mind and body (Cartesian in its belief that humans are defined solely by their capacity for intelligence), and never question whether a life of enhancement would really be a "life" or whether we, in the end, would simply become the machines—the materialistic means by which we achieved those enhancements.

The movement, in total, is a process where the process (improvement, immortality, ascension) is the purpose. There is rarely a "why?"; there is only "why not?"

Sorry, But Your Soul Just Died

When all is said and done, the whole transhumanism debate may come to nothing more than a few wacky National Science Foundation reports and a few thousand cryogenically frozen futurists. While the ideas of transhumanism are discussed as if they are verging on reality, most of modern science is still light years behind even the modest predictions of radically prolonged lifespans and nanotechnological medicine. I was constantly reminded of this as I fought a cold—one of humanity's most persistently untreatable illnesses—throughout the Immortality Institute's conference. But moving beyond the feasibility of their proposals, it may not be the science that is most disconcerting about the transhumanist view of the future; these problems are obvious enough. It may be—as Eppinette, Fukuyama, and others hint—the psychology.

During his Immortality Institute conference speech on artificial intelligence, AI expert Ben Goertzel addressed two startling areas of inquiry: "human essence" and free will. Goertzel was quick to write off the idea of free will, noting that no person or thing can ever escape the determinism of physics or the determinism of the unconscious mind; and he was skeptical of any "human essence" that would make us a truly unique species. In his mind, the migration to human software won't be a difficult concept because our only defining characteristic is our intelligence. We represent the latest tool in the progression of nature to gradually uncover the mystery of itself; and our posthuman progeny, finally escaping the myths of essence and free will, could be just the ones to vanquish all illusion (we call it the "heart" or "self-consciousness" or the "soul") and know the universe perfectly. To quote Goertzel, getting rid of these illusions will allow us "to transmit what is truly valuable."

And in the back of my mind I wondered: What are these "truly valuable" things? What is the purpose of living forever if there is no purpose? What should I care about if I have no control? Why should I bother to love or be loved if it is all an illusion? How can I find beauty in a moment if I know that moment will never require sacrifice, never wither away? I know that all religions must have their "heaven scenarios," but doesn't this one seem a little bleak? To view all of human history—all poetry, courage, discovery, risk, faith, and love—as a mechanical misstep on the way to posthuman perfection is more than wickedly unromantic; it is devastating to even the simplest moral precept, the simplest sense of purpose, the simplest reason for life—particularly immortal life.

You see, the entire enterprise of transhumanism does, to some extent, rest on the "determinism of physics" and on the fundamental belief that we humans are mere cogs in a blind naturalistic process that will culminate in nothing but extinction and pure knowledge. Rather than giving us something valuable, it sounds eerily like the road to what Nietzsche predicted for the twentieth century: "the total eclipse of all values."

In his incomparable essay "Sorry, But Your Soul Just Died," Tom Wolfe writes of this century's Nietzsche (a neuroscientist, he predicts), who, having vanquished the idols "self" and "soul," finally rises to the podium to bring humanity word of an event. "He will say that he is merely bringing the news," writes Wolfe, "the news of the greatest event of the millennium: 'The soul, the last refuge of values, is dead, because educated people no longer believe it exists.'" And, suddenly, everything that most people have ever lived for will simply fall and wither away.

I guess my biggest question is this: Is all that is human—history, will, limitation, enigma, hope, individuality, vulnerability, that culminating cosmological weirdness of stability shacked up with instability—such an easy (or desirable) thing to dismiss?

CRITICAL THINKING QUESTIONS

1. What are the basic differences in principle and assumption between Neo-Darwinian evolution and Intelligent Design? Discuss
   the ultimate irony of humans using their intelligence, which supposedly emerged from nonthinking processes of evolution, to intelligently direct future human evolution.

2. Define and explain "transhumanism" and "posthuman." Discuss
   how you emotionally and intellectually respond to these concepts.

3. Summarize the main arguments of those in favor of transhumanism and those opposed to it. Which camp makes the stronger case?
   Why?

4. To what extent do many of these transhumanist theories rely upon
   physical and natural determinism? What, then, happens to the soul
   or our metaphysical selves in such a view?

~

SEX AND SEXUALITY

Bodies of Evidence: The Real Meaning of Sex Is Right Before Our Eyes

Frederica Mathewes-Green

Frederica Mathewes-Green is a columnist for *Beliefnet.com*, and she contributes to the Christian Millennial History Project. She has written such
books as *Facing East: A Pilgrim's Journey into the Mysteries of Orthodoxy*
(2006), *Gender: Men, Women, Sex and Feminism* (2002), *At the Corner
of East and Now: A Modern Life in Ancient Christian Orthodoxy* (2000),
and *Real Choices: Listening to Women, Looking for Alternatives to Abortion*
(1997). The following article appeared in *Touchstone* in 2005 and is drawn
from a speech to students given at a Veritas Forum at the University of
Virginia in 2005.

Essay Classification: Informative; argumentation/persuasion

ON JANUARY 24, 2005, I stood on the sidewalk of Constitution Avenue in Washington, D.C., as the March for Life surged by. There was a small band of pro-choice counter-protestors, and I positioned myself just past them because I was curious about how pro-lifers would react to their presence.

Now, I'm a convert from pro-choice to pro-life myself, and I have a strong interest in getting the two sides to understand each other's positions more clearly. I was one of the founders of a group called The Common Ground Network for Life and Choice, which sponsored ongoing dialogue groups in twelve cities and held two national conferences. So I have known and talked with many pro-choicers.

Just Say No to Sex

That's how I knew that this small band of counter-demonstrators was not typical. They were holding up sheets of black fabric painted in white. The first read, "Post-birth abortion for George W." The second read, "Pro-Choicers against Fascism." The third read, "Just say no to sex with pro-lifers."

There were about four or five men and two women, and they all looked to be in their twenties. As pro-lifers marched by, they chanted various things, like "Women's liberation, we won't go back." Then they sang the following song, to the tune of "Jesus Loves the Little Children":

> Jesus should have been aborted
> Mary wanted a career
> Abortion is a woman's right
> So we won't give up the fight
> Until you Christian ** go away.

An older man in a pro-life sweatshirt stood near them. When a passing woman flipped the bird at the pro-choicers, he yelled at her, "Have a little class!" When a young man walked up and spat on the ground in front of the group, he stepped after him, shouting a warning "Hey!" Otherwise, he didn't say anything; he just kept his eyes out for trouble. I sure admired that guy.

Then a young man who had already passed by came back to say something. Maybe he'd just thought of it, or maybe he said it to his friends and they told him to go back. He walked up to the group, looking nervous, and said: "You guys don't even know the real meaning of sex."

He turned quickly and walked away.

It took the group a moment to register what he'd said, and then they began to laugh. A young man said, "Yeah, well, at least we're having more of it than you are." One of the women said, "What does that even mean?!?"

I wondered the same thing. What did he mean? What is the meaning of sex?

I'm an old ex-hippie flower-child mother-earth type, so my first impulse in any question like that is to look at what nature appears to tell us. If you think of humans as part of nature, as animals like any other animal, what does it look like our body is designed to do? How is it designed to work?

For example, think about what the design of our bodies tells us about the foods we're made to eat. The human body is a complex organism, and we can see that it's designed to run on a complex kind of fuel. We know pretty instinctively which foods are good for our health, and which things we can tolerate but aren't good for us, and which things humans simply can't digest, even if other animals can. We have a sense of what our bodies are designed to consume.

Nature's Meaning

So let's set aside the idea that humans are different from or better than other animals and think of humans in their natural state. Whether we attribute extra meaning to humans or not, we are *at least* animals, sharing this planet with many other kinds of creatures.

From that perspective, the "meaning" of sex is pretty obvious. It's reproduction. Every living creature has two primary drives: first, to sustain its own life (which includes seeking food, shelter, and safety), and second, to pass on that life to a new generation. Creatures reproduce in many different ways, but humans and other mammals do so by sexual reproduction.

It seems that the reason sex feels good is so we'll want to do it, and be motivated to give birth to that new generation. It's the same way with food: the reason our taste buds register some flavors as delicious and others as bitter is so we'll eat things that are good for us and avoid others that might be poisonous.

These flavor preferences are something we're born with; they're not learned. Researchers have found that if they add a bit of sweetener to amniotic fluid, the unborn child will gulp it down more quickly. We're designed to like sweets, I suppose so that our earliest ancestors would keep going back to those brightly colored, vitamin-filled fruits hanging so conveniently within reach.

It's the same way with sex: It feels good so we'll want to reproduce. But there are some interesting ways that humans are different from other mammals, even from other primates. For us, sex feels good at any time in the fertility cycle. Other mammals mate only during fertile periods.

What's more, researchers suspect that only among humans is the female capable of orgasm. Of course, orgasm has nothing to do with conception; it's not related to the reproduction process at all. So both men and women are motivated to have sex for reasons that other animals, and even other mammals and primates, don't have. It looks like the "meaning of sex" for humans is something broader than simply reproduction.

You can see the same analogy with food. As far as I know, animals only eat what they need to, for the sake of nutrition. But humans eat for all kinds of reasons. We eat birthday cake, have a cup of coffee with a friend, munch popcorn during a movie. We eat for social reasons, or for comfort, or just out of habit. We don't eat solely for nutrition. Likewise, we don't have sex solely for reproduction.

Face to Face

This is shown by another way humans are unique. We're one of the very, very few mammals able to have sex face-to-face. Seeing each other's faces means something—not just during sex, but all the time. We are dependent on reading each other's faces; in fact, we can't resist looking at faces. We seem to be programmed that way.

Researchers have found that if a newborn baby is shown a set of different geometric shapes, his eyes will always go back to one that shows an oval with two dots toward the top—that is, a very rudimentary face with eyes. The baby will stare at those dots, those "eyes," and ignore squares, triangles, and rectangles placed alongside it. Consider this: The baby has been in a womb all his life, and has never before seen a face. But the minute he comes out, he knows what to look at. We're made that way.

There's something about a human face that attracts the eyes of other humans irresistibly. In an audience, if one person turns around backwards and starts scanning the crowd, the other audience members find it hard not to look at his face. Advertisers know this, and in print ads will often cut off the faces of people, or cover or obscure their eyes, so that you'll look at the product instead of staring at the faces.

Looking at faces meets a very deep human hunger. I think it's significant that humans are one of the few animals capable of looking into each other's faces during sex.

Sex is, if nothing else, about making a connection with another person, and that seems to be something that humans have trouble with. This seems to be the main way we're different from other animals. All our lives we look at each other from the outside and have trouble figuring out what's going on.

When a baby keeps his parents up all night crying, they'll be frantic trying to figure out what he's crying for. But animal parents don't have any such difficulty; they understand their babies' cries very well. When his girlfriend is crying, a young man may be totally baffled as to what's going on inside her, or what he should do to help. This can be true even among people who love each other very much. We spend much of our time going through life looking at each other from the outside, making guesses, feeling confused, and feeling, basically, lonely.

Since sex is the most obvious, the most *literal* way we connect with each other, we have to think about what role it's designed to play in this essential problem of loneliness. It's not an external activity added on to the other things we do in life. It's one of our most basic biological functions, and no matter how civilized humans get, it remains an activity that goes back to our most basic, animal selves.

From these clues, it looks like sex means something more to us than to most mammals, something that has to do with humans forging a deep connection with each other. The connection is not just physical or reproductive but involves the whole person. It seems that the "meaning of sex" is related to the profound human need to bond with another person in love, in trust, and to forge a relationship that will last for a lifetime.

Sex for a Lifetime

Let me say something about "for a lifetime." That's a leap. Why not just have a relationship for a little while? After all, it only takes a few minutes to conceive a child. Why should the father stick around at all? Most mammals don't form families that include monogamous dad. Bambi never saw his father until he was nearly grown. Most mammals mate and then part, and the mother raises the child alone, or as part of a herd.

There's evidence for why this isn't best for human babies, however. It has to do with how very, very premature human newborns are, in comparison with the children of other species. A newborn deer struggles to its feet and goes over to its mother to nurse. But a newborn baby won't walk for a year. He won't talk for much longer, and can't provide for his own food and safety for many years after that.

The scientist Stephen J. Gould referred to the newborn human as an "extrauterine embryo." He meant that we're born at a level of development that, in other mammals, would still be considered embryonic. It's estimated that for a human to be born at the developmental level of other mammals, pregnancy would need to last, not nine months, but twenty-one. And even after birth, our development proceeds much more slowly than that of other mammals.

This heightened vulnerability means that a human newborn requires more intensive parental care than other mammals do, and for a much longer time. A single parent will find it very hard, as we well know, to provide both the constant care a newborn needs, and also the food and shelter that both parent and child require. This is a job that really requires two people, at least for the first few years.

You have to keep in mind that the task of reproduction isn't finished at the moment of birth. If the single parent is overwhelmed and unable to provide care, and the baby dies, it's as if reproduction never took place. The child must grow, in fact grow up to the point where it can reproduce itself in turn, or the species will become extinct. Two parents make it much more likely that a baby will survive, and it seems that's the reason humans are among the few mammals—three percent—who mate for life.

Yet that still doesn't answer the question. Why "for life"—why not just for those first few vulnerable years? Even if the child needs two parents for survival in the early years, he'd be self-sufficient enough to get along with just one well before adulthood. By the age of ten, let's say, he'd be able to communicate, locate food, recognize danger, and so forth. Why should his dad stick around?

Sitting Together

Years ago, I was up in a theater balcony looking at the crowd below, and it suddenly struck me that there was a pattern all through the audience. This is one of those things that's so obvious you don't notice it.

What I saw was that everywhere a man and a woman were sitting next to each other. These couples were of all different ages; many had gray hair. Now, I can argue from nature that a newborn and a young child need father and mother to stick together. But why would this pattern continue decades after that, even till the end of life, when the children were long since grown? What makes people stick together when reproduction is over and done with?

I think that brings us back to the mystery of faces: the need to connect, the real "meaning of sex." The initial impulse of sexual attraction is physical pleasure. It's an inborn impulse, like grabbing a candy bar because it's sweet. But deeper levels of resonance are also involved.

Humans are different from other mammals. We don't just want someone for a night. We're looking for someone we can spend a lifetime with. Humans are made to mate for a lifetime, because we find ourselves in a world that seems enormous, dangerous, and confusing. In the midst of it we feel so small, so insignificant. Sure we want to have sex, but even more, we want to be loved.

Here's where I think my generation did the next generations a disservice. I was part of that hippie generation that very deliberately rejected the values of the older generation that came before us. Part of this was the "sexual revolution," an insistence on sexual freedom.

I think that, for us, "freedom" had a defiant quality; we were rebelling against something. I think that for young people thirty years later, it's a milder kind of freedom. It's like the freedom to choose between cheese-flavored and barbecue-flavored tortilla chips. It's a consumer freedom. It looks like sex is something you can select, take home, consume, and forget about.

But I think this seriously underestimates the deeper levels of meaning that sex has. Given the primal and complex role that sex has in the life of the human animal, it involves much more than just consuming pleasure. It's tangled up with all the deeper issues of trust, security, and loneliness. My generation just dismissed all that, as if it weren't there. As a result, we have not prepared our children to deal with it. The result is that they can get blindsided: you think you're just having fun and discover that something bad is happening to your heart.

I heard in a news story once that archaeologists had discovered what they thought was the oldest song ever written. Know what it was about? It was about a young man grieving because his girlfriend didn't love him any more. That's the human condition. It wasn't about sex; it was about love. We can't just drive our bodies around as if they were sports cars. We have hearts in here too, and they keep getting bruised, whether we think that should be happening or not.

Abandoned Children

It was this breezy attitude toward the sexual revolution that lay behind so much of the divorce in my generation. That's why so many of our children grew up without dads, or lived through their parents' divorce (and why so many of their children will as well): because my generation decided that you can change partners when the mood strikes, that you can make a commitment, break it, and make a new one, and that the whole meaning of sex is consumer pleasure.

We abandoned our children. Now they're growing up, and we haven't given them much guidance about how to do a better job. Many young people are afraid of marriage because they're afraid of divorce, and at the same time they really long for a safe, secure, happy home, even though they have no idea how to make one.

My generation has spread the idea that sex is about power rather than vulnerability. While there has always been a pattern of men treating women as conquests, the sexual revolution led women to think in the same way, that making men desire them was evidence of their power.

But that doesn't have anything to do with love; it can even be the opposite of love. I recently read a review of a book titled *Strip City,* written by a woman, Lily Burana, who traveled across the nation working at strip clubs. She says that we're living in an era of "sex-positive feminism." She calls herself a "gender warrior," and says that when she dances, she can feel "all the hearts in the room gathered into the palm of my hand."

Well, that's a lot of power. Yet she doesn't feel tenderness toward those gathered hearts. The reviewer says that Burana "relished taunting men because she is revolted by their erotic neediness." It's a battle, for this "gender warrior." Make war, not love.

Here's something else. Burana says that her work represents new liberation for women's sexuality. She says we live in a period when "the notion of female desire is being re-evaluated." But does stripping have anything to do with the woman's sexual desires? It looks like it's all about *male desire,* provoking and despising and ridiculing that. Once again, sex means male desire. For women, stripping isn't about a deeper understanding of their own sexuality, but about a substitute thrill: the experience of power. A power that doesn't have much to do with love.

And it's a funny kind of power. Dancers work in depressing places that stink of mildew and ammonia, exposing themselves to seedy old men. It's no great achievement if you get a guy to look at your body. Any girl could do that. The dancers are all interchangeable, and nobody cares about their name or history or personality. Nobody looks at their faces. An ex-stripper once told me, "I had to ask myself, if I had all the power, why was I the only person in the room with no clothes on?"

Power's Thrill

This world of strippers represents an extreme, but in many ways reflects the general assumptions in our culture about the meaning of sex. Instead of sex being about vulnerability, love, and sharing, it's about the thrill of power. Sexual liberation doesn't mean understanding women's desires, but women laboring to provoke male desire, competing with other women in an endless cycle of "how low can you go."

But men also have to be anxious about their physical appeal. We live in such a relentlessly consumer culture that we have come to see ourselves as competing products. The test is how much of a market share you can command, how many people you can stimulate to desire you. Both men and women have to present themselves as sexually desirable consumer items. In a culture that's already visually saturated, we have become much, much more anxious about maintaining unrealistic standards of appearance. It's all about market share.

But in real life, very few people have the kind of body they can be utterly, aggressively confident about. Most of us feel a little inadequate. We don't go into a sexual relationship feeling like a conqueror, but feeling vulnerable. We don't unveil a body that blasts the competition, but one marked by imperfections and sags and scars, parts that are too little and parts that are too big, things we feel worried about other people seeing.

We have to trust that the other person will love us enough that they won't make fun of us, that they won't make fun of us behind our backs to other people later on. It's funny that we try so hard to dress in ways that will make people stare at our bodies, when what we really want is for them to look at our eyes.

It turns out that sex is not about power, but vulnerability. My generation failed to tell you this. We failed to learn it ourselves, and you see the result in our trail of shattered marriages.

Sexual Connection

I don't know that I can give a short answer to the question of what the "real meaning of sex" is. I speak from a generation that made a lot of mistakes, and when I see how badly we've equipped our children to make sense of their own lives and relationships, it looks pretty sad. I guess the clue I would draw is that nature shows us that sex is not just for reproduction but also for that deep human connection we hunger for. It's designed to be part of healing the essential human condition of loneliness.

This is why Christians have always had an interest in how to handle sexuality. This deep human experience of alienation and loneliness, our difficulty in connecting with each other in love, is an aspect of the shattering of our relationship with God. It's probably not an exaggeration to say that all religions recognize that there is something wrong in the universe, either with our relationship to God and each other, or in our perception of that relationship. We feel out of sync. Every religion tries to address that experienced disconnect by helping humans recover unity through prayer, meditation, serving the poor, or other means.

Christians believe that God took the initiative to repair the damage by coming to earth in human form. This means that he blessed and affirmed the human body, the body he made at the beginning of creation. He showed that it is possible for a human body to contain the presence of God.

In Christ we, too, can become "partakers of the divine nature," as St. Peter says; we take on the presence of God like a coal takes on the illumination and warmth of fire. We live "in Christ" as St. Paul says, filled with the healing presence of God. Being bearers of God's light means that we're able to love each other and repair the tragic brokenness among the human race.

It is a sign, in fact a sacrament, of that union when two people unite with each other for a lifetime. We can't love each other very well. We do so in spite of flaws and failures, continuing to offer active love no matter what. Offering this love changes the person who gives it, molding him or her into the image of God.

Receiving this love, even this imperfect love, changes the person who receives it, day by day restoring him to the likeness of God. From all we can see in nature, humans are designed to mate for a lifetime, so that even when you're old and gray and nobody else in the world would find you sexy, you can still look over at a person who loves you just as much as he did when you were young.

The Mornings After

Everything you hear in ads and entertainment is telling you that your goal is to wake up next to someone gorgeous tomorrow morning. That's the rationale of consumer sex. But I think what humans really want is to wake up next to someone kind, fifty years from tomorrow morning.

The decisions you make today, and tomorrow—and tomorrow night—will have everything to do with whether that happens for you or not. It happened for me. I have been married thirty-one years, and until the end of my life I'll have beside me the man who fell in love with me when I was nineteen. If I get old and cranky, if I get breast cancer, if I get Alzheimer's, he'll stick with me, and I won't be alone, and I'll do the same for him. In this way we show the presence of God to each other, and grow into his likeness.

CRITICAL THINKING QUESTIONS

1. Frederica Mathewes-Green uses the natural law or design principle in her article. How is it similar to that of J. Budziszewski? What other points does she bring out that he did not?

2. The author ponders the question, why should humans mate for life? What is her answer? Do you agree or disagree? Explain.

3. The author also comes to the principle that humans are different than other animals and even other mammals. Why is this distinction important to make? What happens when we deny that humans are uniquely different than other animals?

4. In what ways did the previous generation that ushered in the "sexual revolution" do a grave disservice to the following genera- tions, according to this author? What elements of human sexuality did this "revolution" ignore and dismiss?

5. Many feminists and sexual liberators claim that sex is about power and the thrill of control. What does this author say in response to that assumption? What is sex really about? Do you agree with the author's conclusions? Why or why not?

6. Is all that occurs in nature to be considered "natural" and thus ac- ceptable for human behavior? What important distinction does the author make? Relate this to Budziszewski's definition of natural law or design.

~

Designed for Sex: What We Lose when We Forget What Sex Is For

J. Budziszewski

J. Budziszewski is professor of government and philosophy at the University of Texas, Austin. He has written several books on political science, natural law theory, and Christian apologetics, including *Natural Law for Lawyers* (2006), *What We Can't Not Know* (2004), *Ask Me Anything: Provocative Answers for College Students* (2004), *The Revenge of Conscience: Politics and the Fall of Man* (2004), *True Tolerance: Liberalism and the Necessity of Judgment* (1999), *Written on the Heart: How to Stay Christian in College* (1999), and *Case for Natural Law* (1997). He also writes regular columns for college students appearing on Boundless.org and TrueU.org, and he also writes for *Touchstone* and *Salvo*. The following article appeared in *Touchstone* in 2005.

Essay Classification: Informative; argumentation/persuasion

MIDNIGHT. SHELLY IS GETTING herself drunk so that she can bring herself to go home with the strange man seated next to her at the bar. *One o'clock.* Steven is busy downloading pornographic images of chil- dren from Internet bulletin boards. *Two o'clock.* Marjorie, who used to spend every Friday night in bed with a different man, has been binging and purging since eleven. *Three o'clock.* Pablo stares through the darkness at the ceiling, wondering how to convince his girlfriend to have an abortion. *Four o'clock.* After partying all night, Jesse takes another man home, not mentioning that he tests positive for an incurable STD. *Five o'clock.* Lisa is in the bathroom, cutting herself delicately with a razor. This isn't what my generation expected when it invented the sexual revolution. The game isn't fun anymore. Even some of the diehard proponents of that enslaving liberation have begun to show signs of fatigue and confusion.

Liberation Fatigue

Naomi Wolf, in her book *Promiscuities,* reports that when she lost her own virginity at age 15, there was "something important missing." Apparently, the thing missing was the very sense that anything could be important. In her book *Last Night in Paradise,* Katie Roiphe poignantly wonders what could be wrong with freedom: "It's not the absence of rules exactly, the dizzying sense that we can do whatever we want, but the sudden realization that nothing we do matters."

Desperate to find a way to make it matter, some young male homosexuals court death, deliberately seeking out men with deadly infections as partners; this is called "bug chasing." At the opposite extreme, some of those who languish in the shadow of the revolution toy with the idea of abstinence—but an abstinence that arises less from purity or principle than from boredom, fear, and disgust. In Hollywood, of all places, it has become fashionable to talk up Buddhism, a doctrine that finds the cure of suffering in the ending of desire, and the cure of desire in annihilation.

Speaking of exhaustion, let me tell you about my students. In the 1980s, if I suggested in class that there might be any problem with sexual liberation, they said that everything was fine—what was I talking about? Now if I raise questions, many of them speak differently. Although they still live like libertines, it's getting old. They are beginning to sound like the children of third-generation Maoists.

My generation may have ordered the sexual revolution; theirs is paying the price. I am not speaking only of the medical price of sexual promiscuity. To be sure, those consequences are ruinous: at the beginning of the revolution, most physicians had to worry about only two or three sexually transmitted diseases, and now it is more like two or three dozen. But I am not speaking only of broken bodies. I am speaking, for example, of broken childhoods. What is it like for your family to break up? What is it like to be passed from stepparent to stepparent to stepparent? What is it like to grow up knowing that you would have had a sister, but she was aborted?

A young man remarked in one of my classes that he longed to get married and stay married to the same woman forever, but because his own parents hadn't been able to manage it, he was afraid to get married at all. Women show signs of avoidance too, but in a more conflicted way. According to a survey commissioned by the Independent Women's Forum, Norval Glenn and Elizabeth Marquardt of the Institute for American Values found that 83 percent of college women say marriage is a very important goal for them. Yet 40 percent of them engage in "hooking up"—physical encounters (commonly oral sex) without any expectation of relationship whatsoever.

Do you hear a little cognitive dissonance there? Can you think of a sexual behavior *less likely* to get you into marriage? The ideology of hooking up says that sex is merely release or recreation. You have some friends for friendship and you have other friends just for hooking up— they're called "friends with benefits." What your body does is unrelated to your heart.

Don't believe it. The same survey reports that hooking up commonly takes place when both participants are drinking or drunk, and it's not hard to guess the reason why: after a certain amount of this, you may need to get drunk to go through with it.

Not Designed for It

The fact is that we aren't designed for hooking up. Our hearts and bodies are designed to work together. Don't we already know that?

In "Friends, Friends with Benefits, and the Benefits of the Local Mall," a *New York Times Magazine* writer who interviewed teenagers who hook up supplies a telling anecdote. The girl Melissa tells him, "I have my friends for my emotional needs, so I don't need that from the guy I'm having sex with." Yet on the day of the interview, "Melissa was in a foul mood. Her 'friend with benefits' had just broken up with her. 'How is that even possible?' she said, sitting, shoulders slumped, in a booth at a diner. 'The point of having a friend with benefits is that you won't get broken up with, you won't get hurt.'"

But let there be no mistake: when I say we aren't designed for this, I'm also speaking of males. A woman may be more likely to cry the next morning; it's not so easy to sleep with a man who won't even call you back.

But a man pays a price too. He probably thinks he can instrumentalize his relationships with women in general, yet remain capable of romantic intimacy when the right woman comes along. Sorry, fellow. That's not how it works.

Sex is like applying adhesive tape; promiscuity is like ripping the tape off again. If you rip it off, rip it off, rip it off, eventually the tape can't stick anymore. This probably contributes to an even wider social problem that might be called the Peter Pan syndrome. Men in their forties with children in their twenties talk like boys in their teens. "I still don't feel like a grown-up," they say. They don't even call themselves men—just "guys."

Now, in a roundabout sort of way, I've just introduced you to the concept of natural law. Although the natural-law tradition is unfamiliar to most people today, it has been the main axis of Western ethical thought for twenty-three centuries, and in fact it is experiencing a renaissance.

The hinge concept is *design*. I said that we're not *designed* for hooking up, that we're *designed* for our bodies and hearts to work together. We human beings really do have a design, and I mean that literally—not just a biological design, but an emotional, intellectual, and spiritual design. The human design is the *meaning* of the ancient expression "human nature." Some ways of living comport with our design. Others don't.

Flouting the Design

From a natural-law perspective, the problem with twenty-first-century Western sexuality is that it flouts the basic principles of the human *sexual* design. By talking with you about unexpected pregnancies and sexually transmitted diseases, a medical scientist or public-health professional might highlight the consequences of flouting the biological side of the human sexual design. By talking with you about women who wake up crying and men who are afraid to grow up or get married, a natural-law philosopher like me highlights the consequences of flouting the other side of the human sexual design. These two sides of human sexuality must be viewed together.

Now if we are going to be serious about the human sexual design, then we have to attend to its purpose. If it has more than one purpose, then these purposes have to harmonize. The first question to ask about our sexual design, then, is, "What is its purpose, or purposes? What is it *for*?" I'll answer that question in a moment. Before I can do so, I have to take time out to deal with two inevitable objections to natural law.

The first objection is that it is rubbish to talk about natural purposes, because we merely imagine them; the purposes of things aren't natural; they are merely in the eye of the beholder. But is this true? Take the lungs, for example. When we say that their purpose is to oxygenate the blood, are we just making that up? Of course not. The purpose of oxygenation isn't in the eye of the beholder; it's in the design of the lungs themselves. There is no reason for us to have lungs apart from it.

Suppose a young man is more interested in using his lungs to get high by sniffing glue. What would you think of me if I said, "That's interesting—I guess the purpose of *my* lungs is to oxygenate my blood, but the purpose of *his* lungs is to get high"? You'd think me a fool, and rightly so. The purpose of the lungs is built into the design of the lungs. He doesn't *change* that purpose by sniffing glue; he only violates it.

We can ascertain the purposes of the other features of our design in the same way. The purpose of the eyes is to see, the purpose of the heart is to pump blood, the purpose of the thumb is to oppose the fingers so as to grasp, the purpose of the capacity for anger is to protect endangered goods, and so on. If we can ascertain the purpose of all those other powers, there is no reason to think that we cannot ascertain the purpose or purposes of the sexual powers too.

The second objection is that it doesn't make any difference even if we *can* ascertain the purpose or purposes of the sexual powers, because an *is* does not imply an *ought*. This currently unquestioned dogma, too, is false. If the purpose of eyes is to see, then eyes that see well are good eyes, and eyes that see poorly are poor ones. Given their purpose, this is what it means for eyes to be good.

Moreover, good is to be pursued; the appropriateness of pursuing it is what it means for anything to be good. Therefore, the appropriate thing to do with poor eyes is to try to turn them into good ones. If it really were impossible to derive an *ought* from the *is* of the human design, then the practice of medicine would make no sense. Neither would the practice of health education.

Consider the young glue-sniffer again. How should we advise him? Is the purpose of his lungs irrelevant? Should we say to him, "Sniff all you want, because an *is* does not imply an *ought*"? Of course not; we should advise him to kick the habit. We *ought* to respect our design. Nothing in us should be used in a way that flouts its inbuilt purposes.

What Is Sex For?

Now that I have warded off the two inevitable objections, let us return to the question of the purpose or purposes of the sexual powers. Common sense tells us that their main purpose is procreation. Since common sense is no longer trusted these days, I'll give an explanation too. Forgive me for sounding like a philosopher, but the explanation is clearer if I use letters as placeholders.

Two conditions must be satisfied before you can say that the purpose of P is to bring about Q, and our answer satisfies both of them. First, it must be the case that P actually does bring about Q. This condition is satisfied because the sexual powers actually do bring about procreation; that's just birds and bees stuff. Second, it must be the case that the fact that P does bring about Q is necessary to explaining why P has come to be—why P exists in the first place. This condition is also satisfied, because the fact that the sexual powers bring about procreation is a necessary part of explaining why we have such powers.

To put this another way, if it weren't for the birds and bees stuff, then it would be mighty hard to understand why we have sexual powers at all. Even a Darwinist must concede the point. (By the way, if you have been worrying about a population explosion, you can stop. In the developed countries, the net reproduction rate is 0.7 and dropping, which means that the next generation will be only 70 percent as large as this one. Demographers are beginning to realize that the looming threat throughout most of the world is not explosion, but implosion.)

Besides procreation, two other purposes are also commonly proposed as the inbuilt purpose of the sexual powers, so let's consider each one. The first suggestion is that the purpose of the sexual powers is pleasure. That their exercise is pleasurable can hardly be doubted, but to call pleasure their purpose does not follow and is deeply misleading.

To see why, consider an analogy between sex and eating. The purpose of eating is to take in nutrition. But eating is pleasurable too. Suppose we were to say, then, that the purpose of eating, too, is pleasure. Then it would seem that any way of eating that gives pleasure is good, whether it is suitable for nutrition or not. Certain ancient Romans are said to have thought this way. To prolong the pleasure of their feasts, they purged between courses. I hope it is not difficult to recognize that such behavior is disordered.

The more general point I am trying to make is that although pleasure accompanies the exercise of every voluntary power, not just sex, it is never the purpose of the power. It only provides a motive for using it—and a dangerous motive, too, which may often be in conflict with the purpose and steer us wrong.

Unitive Intimacy

The other common suggestion is that the purpose of the sexual powers is union: the production of an intimate bond between the partners. This is a much more interesting suggestion, but only half-true. What I mean is that it makes an intriguing point, but that it is not correctly put.

Here's what's intriguing about it. We aren't designed like guppies, who cooperate only for a moment. For us, procreation requires an enduring partnership between two beings, the man and the woman, who are different but in complementary ways. But this implies that union isn't a *different* purpose, *independent* of procreation; rather, it arises in the *context* of procreation and characterizes the *way* we procreate.

A parent of each sex is necessary to make the child, to raise the child, and to teach the child. To make him, both are needed because the female provides the egg, the male fertilizes it, and the female incubates the resulting zygote. To raise him, both are needed because the male is better designed for protection, the female for nurture. To teach him, both are needed because he needs a model of his own sex, a model of the other, and a model of the relationship between them. Mom and Dad are jointly irreplaceable. Their partnership in procreation continues even after the kids are grown, because then they are needed to help them establish their own new families.

Sociologists Sara S. McLanahan and Gary Sandefur remark in their book *Growing Up with a Single Parent* that "if we were asked to design a system for making sure that children's basic needs were met, we would probably come up with something quite similar to the two-parent ideal." Of course—for it *is* designed, though not by us.

Another sociologist, René König, explains in the *International Encyclopedia of Comparative Law* that children, young ones especially, thrive less in orphanages than in the average family—even when care is taken to make the institutions homelike, and even when, to sociological eyes, they are better organized than an average family *in every respect,* hygienically, medically, psychologically, and pedagogically.

All this explains why the longing for unitive intimacy is at the center of our design. Without it, procreative partnerships could hardly be expected to endure in the way that they must endure to generate sound and stable families. So, to repeat, achieving union is a real purpose of the sexual powers, but it isn't a purpose separate from procreation; for humans, it comes as part of the procreative package.

Blessed Incompletion

Let me explain a little more about the nature of spousal union. Unitive intimacy is more than intense sexual desire leading to pleasurable intercourse. The sexes are designed to complement each other. Short of a divine provision for people called to celibacy, there is something missing in the man, which must be provided by the woman, and something missing in the woman, which must be provided by the man. By themselves, each one is incomplete; to be whole, they must be united.

This incompleteness is an incredible blessing because it both makes it possible for them to give themselves to each other, and gives them a motive to do so. The gift of self makes each self to the other self what no other self can be. The fact that they "forsake all others" is not just a sentimental feature of traditional Western marriage vows; it arises from the very nature of the gift. You cannot partly give yourself, because your Self is indivisible; the only way to give yourself is to give yourself entirely. Because the gift is total, it has to exclude all others, and if it doesn't do that, then it hasn't taken place.

We can say even more about this gift, because the union of the spouses' bodies has a more-than-bodily significance; the body emblematizes the person, and the joining of bodies emblematizes the joining of the persons. It is a symbol that participates in, and duplicates the pattern of, the very thing that it symbolizes; one-flesh unity is the body's language for one-life unity. (The next two paragraphs are closely indebted to the Oxford philosopher John Finnis.)

In the case of every other biological function, only one body is required to do the job. A person can digest food by himself, using no other stomach but his own; he can see by himself, using no other eyes but his own; he can walk by himself, using no other legs but his own; and so on with each of the other powers and their corresponding organs. Each of us can perform every vital function by himself, except one. The single exception is procreation.

If we were speaking of respiration, it would be as though the man had the diaphragm, the woman the lungs, and they had to come together to take a single breath. If we were speaking of circulation, it would be as though the man had the right atrium and ventricle, the woman the left atrium and ventricle, and they had to come together to make a single beat.

Now, it isn't like that with the respiratory or circulatory powers, but that is precisely how it is with the procreative powers. The union of complementary opposites is the only possible realization of their procreative potential; unless they come together as "one flesh"—as a single organism, though with two personalities—procreation doesn't occur.

Sexual Landscape

Why do I spend time on these matters? I do so in order to emphasize the tightness with which different strands are woven together by our sexual design.

Mutual and total self-giving, strong feelings of attachment, intense pleasure, and the procreation of new life are linked by human nature in a single complex of purpose. If it is true that they are linked by human nature, then if we try to split them apart, we split ourselves. Failure to grasp this fact is more ruinous to our lives, and more difficult to correct, than any amount of ignorance about genital warts. It ought to be taught, but it isn't.

The problem is that we don't want to believe that these things are really joined; we don't want the package deal that they represent. We want to transcend our own nature, like gods. We want to pick and choose among the elements of our sexual design, enjoying just the pieces that we want and not the others. Some people pick and choose one element, others pick and choose another, but they share the illusion that they can pick and choose.

Sometimes such picking and choosing is called "having it all." Having it all is precisely what it isn't. A more apt description would be *refusing* it all, insisting on having only a part, and in the end, not even having that.

Think of our sexual landscape as a square or quadrant with four corners, *A*, *B*, *C*, and *D*. Over in corner *A* are people—mostly men—who buy into the fantasy that they can enjoy greater sexual pleasure by instrumentalizing their partners and refusing the gift of self. By doing so, they fall pell-mell into what has been called the "hedonistic paradox": the best way to ruin pleasure is to make it your goal.

Pleasure comes naturally as a byproduct of pursuing something else, like the good of another person. When I talk with students, I illustrate the point with a Mick Jagger song they've all heard, although they think the Rolling Stones are a bunch of geezers. The song is "I Can't Get No Satisfaction." Nobody who has ever listened to the song imagined that Jagger suffered from a shortage of sex. The problem was that all that satisfaction wasn't satisfying anymore.

In corner *B* of the quadrant are other people—mostly women—who try to substitute *feelings* of union for union itself. We catch a hint of how common this is in the debasement of the language of intimacy. In today's talk, "I was intimate with him" means "I had sex with him," no more and no less. This euphemism is used more or less interchangeably with another one, "I was physical with him," and that tells you all you need to know.

The parties have engaged in a certain transaction with their bodily parts. There may have been one-flesh unity—in other words, their bodies may have been acting as a single organism for purposes of procreation—but there has not been one-life unity, because that would require mutual and total self-giving. Even so, the bodily transaction *produces feelings* of union, because that is what it is designed to produce.

One confuses these feelings with the things that they represent and are meant to encourage, wondering afterward why everything fell apart. After all, you "felt so close." You "seemed so committed." You "had such a good thing going." Yes, you had everything except the substance of which these feelings are designed to be a sign.

In corner *C* of the quadrant are couples, who imagine that by denying the procreative meaning of sexuality, they can enhance its unitive meaning—that by deliberately avoiding the so-called burden of children, they can enjoy a deeper intimacy. It doesn't work that way. Why should it? The unitive capacities of the spouses don't exist for nothing; they exist for their procreative partnership.

That is their purpose, and that is the matrix in which they develop. Children change us in a way we desperately need to be changed. They wake us up, they wet their diapers, they depend on us utterly. Willy-nilly, they knock us out of our selfish habits and force us to live sacrificially for others; they are the necessary and natural continuation of the shock to our selfishness that is initiated by matrimony itself.

To be sure, the spouses may try to live sacrificially for each other, but by itself, this love turns too easily inward. Let no one think that I am referring to couples who are childless through no fault of their own. For them, too, childlessness is a loss, but the decisive factor is not sterility, but deliberate sterility. In the natural course of things, if we *willfully* refuse the procreative meaning of union, then union is stunted. We are changed merely from a pair of selfish *me*'s to a single selfish *us*.

In corner *D* of the quadrant are people who think in exactly the opposite way. Instead of supposing that they can affirm the unitive meaning of sexuality without the procreative, they imagine that they can affirm the procreative meaning of sexuality without the unitive. The full shock of this way of life is not with us yet, but our technology allows it, and in most jurisdictions, so does our law.

Meet Amber, who lives alone, shares social occasions with Dave, in whom she has no sexual interest, and sleeps occasionally with Robert, in whom she has no social interest. Amber wants a child, but she doesn't want the complications of a relationship, and besides, she doesn't want to be pregnant. Where there's a will, there's a way. She contracts with Paul as sperm donor, Danielle as egg donor, Brooke as incubator, and Brian as visiting father figure to provide the child with "quality time."

Let us set aside our feelings and attend to what has happened here. Among humans, procreation takes place within the context of a unitive relationship. To destroy the unitive meaning of the procreative act is to turn it into a different kind of act. It's no longer procreation, but production; the child is no longer an expression of his parents' love, but a product. In fact, he has no parents. He was orphaned before his conception. His relation to his caretaker is that of a thing bought and paid for to the one who bought and paid for it.

The Counterrevolution

I've developed just four themes in this article; allow me to review them. The first is that we ought to respect the principles of our sexual design. Just as those ways of living that flout the bodily aspects of our design sicken and kill us, so those ways of living that flout the emotional, intellectual, and spiritual aspects of our design ruin us and empty life of meaning.

The second theme is that the human sexual powers have a purpose. As the purpose of the visual powers is to see and the purpose of the ingestive powers is to take in nourishment, so the purpose of the sexual powers is to procreate. This purpose is not in the eye of the beholder; apart from this purpose, we would have no way to explain why we have them.

Moreover, if we try to make use of the sexual powers in ways that thwart and violate this purpose, we thwart and violate ourselves.

The third theme is that the human design for procreation requires marital and family life. For guppies, it doesn't; they manage to procreate without them. For us, however, it does. To put this another way, we are made with a view to marriage and family, and fitness for them is one of our design criteria. No one invented them, no one is indifferent to them, and there was never a time in human history when they did not exist.

Even when disordered, they persist. Spouses and family members who are divided by disaster commonly undertake Herculean efforts to reunite with each other. Marriage and family are not merely apparent goods but real ones, and the rules and habits necessary to their flourishing belong to the natural law.

The final theme is that the spousal bond has its own structure, which both nourishes and is nourished by these institutions—because it has its own structure, it has its own principles. Among these principles are the following: happiness cannot be heightened by sexually using the Other; conjugal joy requires a mutual and total gift of Self. Feelings of union are no substitute for union; their purpose is to encourage the reality of which they are merely a foretaste. The procreative and unitive meanings of sexuality are joined by nature; they cannot be severed without distorting or diminishing them both.

These principles are the real reason for the commands and prohibitions contained in traditional sexual morality. Honor your parents. Care for your children. Save sex for marriage. Make marriage fruitful. Be faithful to your spouse.

Let the sexual revolution bury the sexual revolution. Having finished revolving, we arrive back where we started. What your mother—no, what your grandmother—no, what your great-grandmother told you was right all along. These are the natural laws of sex.

CRITICAL THINKING QUESTIONS

1. Comment on the essay's introduction. Does it effectively draw the reader in and establish the focus? Why or why not?

2. What have been some of the heavy physical, medical, and emotional/spiritual costs of the "sexual revolution"? Was this "revolution" really so liberating after all? Explain by discussing some of the examples and evidences raised by the author.

3. What are natural law and the design principle?

4. How does the author use the principles of natural law and design to explain the proper understanding of human sexuality? How does natural design help us understand the costs of violating the intended purpose and design of human sexuality?

5. As part of good persuasion, one must address oppositional perspectives. How does this writer refute objections to natural law and design principles? Are his refutations effective and convincing? Why or why not?

6. Discuss the three key natural functions or purposes of human sexuality. How are they related and dependent upon each other?

7. How has your understanding of human sexuality been enhanced or developed by considering it in terms of natural law or design?

∼

Birds Do It, Bees Do It
Sam Torode

Sam Torode is a writer whose work appears in *Christianity Today*, Boundless.org, and TrueU.org. He has coauthored such books as *Aflame: Ancient Wisdom on Marriage* (2005), *Body and Gift: Reflections on Creation* (2005), *Purity of Heart: Reflections on Lust and Love* (2004), and *Open Embrace: A Protestant Couple Rethinks Contraception* (2002). The following article appeared on TrueU.org in 2000.

Essay Classification: Evalutative; critical analysis; informative

FEMALES ARE NATURALLY PROMISCUOUS. That is the thesis of biologist Tim Burkhead's new book, *Promiscuity*. "Generations of reproductive biologists assumed females to be sexually monogamous," he writes. "But now it is clear that this is wrong. Females of most species routinely copulate with several different males."

Shocking, isn't it? At least the editors of *Newsweek* think so. The August 14, 2000, edition of *Newsweek* devotes a two-page spread to Burkhead's book and the evidence for "female promiscuity." The article, "Sex and the Single Fly" by Sharon Begley (pp. 44–45), summarizes the evidence for female promiscuity in a variety of species, then suggests two reasons as to why females are promiscuous.

First, multiple partners provide females with "increased resources," such as gifts of food or protection. Second, by shopping around, females seek out males that will provide superior DNA for their offspring. Female promiscuity is a tool of natural selection for enhancing the gene pool.

Begley's article is accompanied by photographs of promiscuous females spanning the animal kingdom: chimpanzees, damselflies, hyenas, penguins, and women (represented by the stars of television's *Sex and the City*). The implication is clear: women really aren't that different from their sisters of other species—they all want the same thing, and for similar reasons. As the caption next to the women of *Sex and the City* states, "For women, playing around can bring them more resources, as well as healthier kids."

The editors of *Newsweek*, I suspect, know full well that this notion of "female promiscuity" has little to do with "the single fly," and everything to do with the modern woman. It is telling that the article appears in the Society section, rather than under the heading of Science or Nature. The underlying assertion is that the sexual liberation of women is ordained by nature, while monogamy is the exception to the rule and can be harmful for the species in the long run.

Begley appears to believe that revelations of animal infidelity explode the superstition that women desire and benefit from monogamy. As if, all along, we thought that female chimpanzees were moral, upstanding mammals, but—alas!—"a 1997 study using DNA to run paternity tests found that 54 percent of baby chimps were fathered by males other than Mom's supposed partner."

Moreover, behold the birds of the air: "Thirty-five percent of baby indigo buntings, a pretty little songbird, are sired by a male other than the guy Mom came with." Why, the pretty little Lolitas!

And human beings? "In Bhutan, many women practice polyandry because in the poor valleys of the Himalayas a lone husband cannot support a family." We're no different from any other species, it turns out. Chimp, songbird, or human, all females are subject to the same laws of natural selection. In light of the astounding discovery of female promiscuity, *Newsweek* informs us, sexual behavior among all species is "becoming less mysterious."

I hate to break it to the folks at *Newsweek,* but any backyard biologist could tell you that damselflies are not sexually monogamous, any more than squirrels are sexually modest. And the news that "a clutch of grasshopper eggs can have several fathers" is not likely to shake up the average moral conservative's view of sexuality among grasshoppers, much less human beings.

This hubbub about "female promiscuity" is but another attempt to debunk traditional morality by treating human beings as mere hairless apes, comparing their behavior with that of other animals, and declaring that there is no moral law. This is an old game. In 1926, a London newspaper ran an article touting a similar scientific study, with the headline: "Do Whales Have Two Wives?" This riled the satiric pen of the great Christian apologist G. K. Chesterton, who discerned that the report was really about human, not cetacean, sexuality:

> We know how some people perpetually preach to us that there is no morality in nature and therefore nothing natural in morality. We know we have been told to learn everything from the herd instinct or law of the jungle; to learn our manners from a monkey house and our morals from a dog-fight. May we not find a model in a far more impressive and serene animal? Shall we not be told that Leviathan refuses to put forth his nose to the hook of monogamy, and laughs at the shaking of the chivalric spear?

Little has changed since Chesterton's time. (Except that today's scientists, no longer sexist, inquire whether whales have two *husbands.)* Now we are asked to believe that hyenas and penguins are sexually liberated, just like the women of prime-time television.

Female hyenas, Begley writes, "make males—many males—grovel for a chance to mate." Yes, the bold, independent hyena: poster-mammal of the sexual revolution. She's nobody's homemaker! Meanwhile, the lady penguin, it turns out, is a prostitute. "Adelie penguins proposition males, collecting a stone for their nest with each 'yes.'"

At the risk of stating the obvious, the female grasshopper who employs the services of several mates is not a loose woman. To talk of "promiscuity" among chimpanzees is to apply a standard of human judgment to a nonhuman. Is the female chimpanzee promiscuous by chimpanzees' standards? Of course not—there are no such standards, for beasts do not live by principles.

Morality, like language (the mind's grasping of universal, abstract concepts), is not a matter of evolution or development; it represents a radical break between man and the animals. It is not as though fish know only primitive precepts, while apes live by a more highly evolved moral code, and man by the most cleverly devised morality of all. Animals do not choose between right and wrong. Only men do.

The question "Do Whales Have Two Wives?" is laughable because whales have no wives at all. Similarly, when Begley writes of baby chimpanzees being "fathered by males other than Mom's supposed partner," she is smuggling in human categories through the back door, enabling her to speak of promiscuous women as akin to animal "Moms."

Can we expect to see a sequel in *Newsweek* on animal "parents" who eat their children, along with a sympathetic portrayal of human beings who do the same, explaining why this is beneficial for the species? Of course not. Nor can we expect *Newsweek* to report on a scientific study explaining the Nazi holocaust as the product of natural selection, citing examples of ape tribes that exterminate their "genetic inferiors." Not all animal behaviors are equally in vogue, it seems.

To say that human beings are mere clever animals, driven along by the blind forces of instinct and natural selection, is to deny both conscience and common sense. Intuitively, we know that our choices are freely made and that their consequences are eternal.

Chimpanzees do not exchange nuptial vows. Grasshoppers do not suffer heartbreak and betrayal. Damselflies and dragonflies know nothing of love, intimacy, and fidelity. Hyenas do not commit sin, repent, or seek forgiveness. And yet we should look to them to explain and justify the moral decisions we humans make?

Human sexuality forms a mysterious, spiritual bond that cannot be examined under a microscope or explained by natural selection. Among persons, sexuality is a means of sharing in grace and love; this can be fully realized only within the context of a monogamous marriage. Producing "genetically-superior offspring" may not require monogamy, but raising healthy children in a loving home does. This is so obvious, it takes an intellectual to deny it.

Those like Sharon Begley, who believe that studies of animal behavior make human sexuality "less mysterious," inhabit a flat, dreary world indeed. If you see no essential difference between human and animal sexuality, your mind is locked in a cage smaller than any found at the local zoo.

In the words of Hamlet, "There are more things in heaven and earth than are dreamt of in your philosophy."

CRITICAL THINKING QUESTIONS

1. Do you think human females are naturally promiscuous? Why or why not?

2. What main evidence is presented by the researchers to conclude that human females are naturally promiscuous?

3. Discuss Torode's critical analysis of these arguments and evidences. According to Torode, what are some of the main problems or logical failings of these recent arguments?

4. Why is it a logical fallacy to talk about "promiscuity" in chimps, grasshoppers, birds, or any other beast?

5. Is it a logical fallacy to gauge human behavior and to determine human morality according to animal behavior? Why or why not? Can we justify human behavior by comparing it to animal behavior? Why or why not?

6. Many feminists and social liberals often object to claims to "nature" or "natural design," saying that identities are social constructs. Is there any irony or contradiction, then, in looking to "nature" (the nonhuman animal kingdom) to argue that women are "naturally" promiscuous in an attempt to justify or to excuse promiscuous behavior? Explain.

7. If we are to resort to the natural law or design argument when addressing human sexuality and behavior, as does J. Budziszewski, then what (or whose) nature should we observe and study, human nature and design (including the physical, emotional, and spiritual designs) or brute animal nature? Explain.

∾

The Gay Invention: Homosexuality Is a Linguistic as Well as a Moral Error

R. V. Young

R. V. Young is professor of English at North Carolina State University and is the author of *A Student's Guide to Literature* (2000), *Doctrine and Devotion in Seventeenth-Century Poetry* (2000), and *At War with the Word: Literary Theory and Liberal Education* (1999). He has also written numerous articles for various journals and periodicals, including *John Donne Journal*, *Ben Johnson Journal*, *First Things*, *The Weekly Standard*, *The National Review*, *Culture Wars*, and *Touchstone Magazine*. The following essay appeared in *Touchstone Magazine* in 2005.

Essay Classification: Informative; argumentation/persuasion

FOR THOUSANDS OF YEARS, until the late 1800s, our ancestors were completely oblivious to the existence of a fundamentally distinct class of human beings. Indeed, during the long period of Greco-Roman antiquity and more than a millennium and a half of Christian civilization, man did not even have a name for this class.

Or so asserts an almost universal assumption fixed in the language almost everyone uses: that "heterosexuals" and "homosexuals" are two permanently and innately different kinds of human being, and that "sexual orientation" constitutes a difference comparable to the difference between male and female. Widespread acceptance of "homosexuality" and associated terms thus biases discussion of the subject before an argument is even formulated.

Terms Lacking

What might be called the philological evidence calls this notion into question. If it were true, someone would long ago have given this class a name. That no one did until very recently suggests that the notion is not true.

In the first footnote of the first chapter of *Greek Homosexuality*, which is generally regarded as the definitive treatment of its subject, Oxford classical scholar K. J. Dover points out that the ancient Greek language "has no nouns corresponding to the English nouns 'a homosexual' and 'a heterosexual.'" Such an observation would seem to call for more notice than is accorded by a single short footnote, but even the apparent concession is misleading, insofar as it suggests that the absence of these terms is a peculiarity of Greek.

In fact, Latin also lacks these terms and the same is true of Old and Middle English. Among modern European languages the word that corresponds to the English "homosexual" is generally a variant on the same word: in Spanish *homosexual* and in Dutch *homoseksueel*, for example. German also offers *gleichgeschlechtlich*, which is simply a combination of two Germanic roots, *gleich* and *Geschlecht*, that correspond to the Greek (*homo = same*) and Latin (*sexus = sex*) of the English word.

This English word is itself a very recent coinage. According to the *Oxford English Dictionary*, both "homosexual" and "homosexuality" first appeared in English in 1892, along with "heterosexual" and "heterosexuality," in an English translation of Richard von Kraft-Ebing's *Psychopathologia Sexualis* (1886) and turn up again five years later in Havelock Ellis's *Studies in the Psychology of Sex*.

In other words, only in the late nineteenth century, when physicians began discussing sexual perversion as a medical rather than a moral problem in Latin treatises intended only for the learned and required a neutral, clinical term, was there a perceived need to refer to "homosexuality." Moreover, it is not at all clear that the originators of the term had precisely in mind what is usually meant by "homosexuality" in contemporary parlance.

Kraft-Ebing, for example, does not write a separate chapter on this subject (Ellis, however, does); same-sex attraction is rather an attribute or additional characteristic of other specific activities—regarded by Kraft-Ebing as abuses of the sexual organs and the pleasure associated with erotic stimulation. Ellis says that the term actually originated in 1869 with an obscure Hungarian doctor, Benkert (or Kertbeny), and endorses its use because "its significance—sexual attraction to the same sex—is fairly clear and definite, while it is free of any question-begging association of either favorable or unfavorable character."

The Greek Example

Contemporary advocates of "homosexuality" often invoke the Greek example to make acts of sodomy seem acceptable or even normal. They assume that the Greeks believed in "homosexuality" in the modern sense because some Greeks praised the erotic relations of men and boys; they read the Greeks as if they were modern Americans or Europeans.

Of course our ancestors were quite aware of what are now called "homosexual" acts or behavior. Latin and Greek are both rich in words that designate the penetrating member and the penetrated orifices, as well as the active and passive participants. Interested readers may find in J. N. Adams's *The Latin Sexual Vocabulary* an abundance of such terms (usually with Greek counterparts). Almost all of them are obscene as well as pejorative, and their usage is almost always in a context of coarse humor or insult.

Clear verbal distinctions are drawn between those who take the active, male role and those who assume the passive female role; men who submit in the latter fashion are almost universally regarded with contempt, since they are ordinarily slaves or male prostitutes. The only real exception seems to come in the ancient Greek city-states with the pubescent boy (*eromenos*) who is the beloved of an older man (*erastes*), who is ideally a kind of intellectual mentor as well as lover to the youth.

This situation is discussed at length in Plato's *Symposium* (discussed in more detail shortly), and this is the principal cultural phenomenon that provides Dover the opportunity to give a generally favorable account of "Greek homosexuality." But his account undermines the claim implied in the title of his book. He begins his study by defining *homosexuality* as "the disposition to seek sensory pleasure through bodily contact with persons of one's own sex in preference to contact with the other sex." *Disposition* suggests a condition considerably less permanent or innate than the term *sexual orientation,* which has become a fixture in current discourse.

Still more revealing is Dover's rationalization of the absence of a Greek word for "homosexual" in that first, uncomfortable footnote. The Greeks, he wrote, "assumed . . . that (a) virtually everyone responds at different times both to homosexual and to heterosexual stimuli, and (b) virtually no male both penetrates other males and submits to penetration by other males at the same stage in his life."

This explanation amounts to an admission that the ancient Greeks did not recognize the existence of the permanent "homosexual orientation" that is nowadays taken as a given: "Since the reciprocal desire of partners belonging to the same age-category is virtually unknown in Greek homosexuality," Dover remarks, "the distinction between the bodily activity of the one who has fallen in love and the bodily passivity of the one with whom he has fallen in love is of the highest importance."

In a very defensive "Postscript" to the 1989 edition, Dover feels constrained to defend "my inclination to treat homosexuality as 'quasi-sexuality' or 'pseudo-sexuality'. My reasoning was simple: we have the word 'sex' because there is more than one sex, definable in terms of reproductive function, and I accordingly use 'sexual' to mean 'having to do with (difference of) sex.'" This acknowledgment that *heterosexual* and *homosexual* are incommensurable with *male* and *female* and *man* and *woman* practically dismantles the significance of Dover's title.

Not Socrates

Plato's *Symposium* is the most prominent work that seems to provide evidence for the notion that "homosexuality" was a normal and accepted aspect of ancient Greek society, since all but one of the characters in the dialogue gives a speech in praise of the god of love (*Eros*) and specifically designates pederasty, the desire of a man for a youth, as the ultimate expression of love.

The speech attributed to the comic playwright Aristophanes even suggests that "sexual orientation" is a permanent feature of human beings, since desire is, literally, a longing to be reunited with our "other half." Human beings were once, he says, creatures with four legs and four arms, two faces and two sets of genitals, and so on. Anxious about the threat of such formidable creatures, Zeus used his thunderbolts to split them in half, creating men and women as we know them now.

If one's other half were of the opposite sex in this mythical past, then he desires physical intimacy with a member of the opposite sex; but if one's other half were of the same sex, then union with the opposite sex fails to satisfy. It is difficult to judge the tone and import of this myth, especially as Aristophanes disparaged Plato's mentor Socrates in his comedy, the *Clouds*; but in any case it hardly constitutes a philosophical endorsement of same-sex erotic relationships.

There are, however, substantial reasons for finding the status of "homosexuality" in the *Symposium* problematic. The dialogue is set at a dinner party celebrating Agathon's victory in the Athenian tragedy competition. The guests are all artists and intellectuals—hardly a representative sample of moral opinion in fifth-century b.c. Athens.

Moreover, the one speaker who does not praise *Eros* as the inspiration of "boy-love" (*paiderastia*) is Socrates. Having declared himself incapable of matching the splendidly rhetorical speeches of the others, he instead expounds the wisdom of the "prophetess" Diotima (a nicely ironic touch, since so many of the other speakers admit to preferring boys because they find women so contemptible). According to her, Socrates says, the desire aroused by the sight of a beautiful body should lead us to seek not physical gratification, but rather the beauty of the soul, of which the body is merely an ephemeral expression, and this in turn should lead us up the steps of the "ladder of love" until we contemplate the Idea of the Beautiful itself.

A "Platonic relationship" is thus a spiritual affection, not a carnal satisfaction. The drunken tirade of the latecomer Alcibiades, which brings the dialogue to a close, ruefully upbraids Socrates for having refused his effort at seduction, thus making the point about Socrates' chastity clear for anyone who has missed it.

Yet the most revealing qualification of the praise of boy-love in the *Symposium* is not Socrates' exaltation of the idea of purely spiritual love, but a digressive comment in the discourse of the sophist Pausanias who, having denigrated the love of women and even of immature boys, concedes that even in Athens not everyone is happy about erotic relationships between men and youths. If a man finds out that another man seeks to become the lover of his son, Pausanias complains, the father puts the boy in the charge of a tutor who is instructed to keep the lover away. If the other boys find out about it, they ridicule the one who has drawn the attraction of the older man.

Thus even in Athens many men are uneasy about pederasty, failing to distinguish between the mere sensual indulgence of the followers of the "earthly Aphrodite" and the gratification of a virtuous lover, a follower of the "heavenly Aphrodite," who really has the boy's interest at heart. Given the genuinely transcendent vision of love offered by Socrates later in the dialogue, it is hard to see Pausanias's complaint as anything but a sample of ironically undercut special pleading.

A Kind of Fornication

Severe condemnation of any deviation from procreative sexuality seems, however, to have been in force in the ancient world only among the Hebrews, but it was incorporated into both the morality and the law of the Christian society emerging at the end of classical antiquity and became the standard view of the Western world.

On the basis of Genesis 19, Christians applied the term "sodomy" specifically to erotic acts between persons of the same sex. In his typically brisk, dispassionate style, St. Thomas Aquinas classifies "sodomitical vice" among "the species of lust contrary to nature," and says that it is not quite so grave a sin as bestiality, but worse than the failure of a man and woman to observe "the proper manner of lying together."

The worst form of this last is neglecting to observe the use of "the appropriate organ," meaning the deposit of semen somewhere other than in the vagina rather than "some other disorder pertaining to the mode of copulation." Obviously, sodomy between persons of the same sex is further down the scale of vice and a graver sin because it necessarily excludes the use of the proper organ.

St. Thomas thus points out that while even simple fornication is "against properly human nature, of which the act of generation is ordered to the appropriate education of children," sodomy is "against the nature of every animal" because it is not aimed at generation at all. Nevertheless, actions today designated "homosexual" are for Thomas just one manifestation of lust among others; the commission of such sins, even the persistent desire to commit such sins, does not constitute a particular class of persons.

Writing for university theology students, St. Thomas is considerably more explicit on the subject than most Christian writers. The author of a fourteenth-century preacher's manual, *Fasciculus Morum,* calls sodomy a "diabolical sin against nature" and passes over it "with horror, leaving it for others to expound" and Chaucer's Parson likewise calls it "thilke abhomynable synne, of which that no man unnethe oghte speke ne write."

Scriptural writers likewise tend to be reticent on the subject: The epistle of Jude, for example, refers to the sin of Sodom and Gomorrah as fornication and, in a curious circumlocution, the pursuit of "other flesh," and in writing to the Ephesians St. Paul shrinks from mentioning "things . . . done by them in secret" that "it is a shame even to speak of." This reluctance even to name or describe sodomy and other forms of lechery seems to undermine the argument that sodomy is of little consequence in the Bible because it is mentioned infrequently.

Although the lecherous act defined as sodomy is simply a sin like any other, its implications are grave, since in Romans St. Paul describes this particular sin as a punishment for the prior sin of unbelief, of a refusal to acknowledge God. From his perspective sodomy results not from an innate condition, "homosexuality," but from faithlessness. Similarly, the popular argument that Paul meant that sodomy is only a sin when it is committed by those who are "not really homosexuals," is (at best) problematic, since the authors of sacred Scripture, like the ancient Greeks and Romans, did not recognize the category, "homosexual," for which they had no term.

A Gay Argument

To be sure, some men and women who identify themselves as "gay" also reject the label "homosexual," or are at least indifferent to it. This viewpoint is very much in evidence, for example, in the essays and excerpts collected under the title *Reclaiming Sodom,* where we learn from Jonathan Ned Katz about the very different view of the matter in colonial New England:

> As sin, sodomy was an act "committed" or not "committed," an act (and inclination) for which one was "guilty" or "not guilty," ashamed or unashamed. As sin, the act of sodomy might be taught by "bad" example, but no one thought (as did late-Victorian doctors) of distinguishing between "acquired" sodomy and "congenital." A sodomitical impulse was an inherent potential of all fallen male descendants of Eve and Adam. Only in the twentieth century would the doctors' allegedly objective and scientific concept of "homosexuality" hide the negative value judgment explicit in the colonial concept of sodomy as a sin.

The candor of this passage is admirable even if one does not accept Katz's belief that the attitudes of the New England Puritans toward sex are irrelevant to us. We study them, he asserts, because "perceiving our own sex and affection as a historical, socially constructed form we better understand the possibility of reconstructing it."

Similarly, on the book's first page, the editor, Jonathan Goldberg, extols "the *productive* role that sodomy has played and can play as a site of pleasures that are also refusals of normative categories" (emphasis in original). In other words, to engage in sodomy is a deliberate means of rejecting traditional moral standards, what Goldberg elsewhere calls "heteronormativity." This attitude vindicates St. Paul's assertion that "use which is against nature" is punishment for those "who changed the truth of God into a lie and worshiped and served the creature rather than the Creator."

The "gay" liberation movement, like feminism, is a branch of the wider sexual revolution that depends upon the postulate that traditional morality is false and untenable because it assumes a stable human nature with corresponding norms of conduct—moral absolutes, in other words. Modern relativism has always maintained to the contrary that our "sexuality" is like every other human capacity and attitude, "constructed" by our social milieu; in Marxist terms it is an ideological "superstructure" arising from the inexorable evolution of the material "base."

Hence what we call our "nature" is really no more than a temporary accommodation to social pressures generated by the forces of the human environment; hence men commit sodomy not because they are innately "homosexual," but because the peculiar configuration of their desires in relation to the dynamics of a particular historical moment drives them to it. Since "human nature" is limitlessly malleable, human institutions like "marriage" and "family" lack a specific essence, and we may attach these terms to any arrangements that currently suit our fancy.

Katz and Goldberg, in other words, lay bare the hypocrisy of the claim that individuals are born with an innate and unchangeable "heterosexual" or "homosexual" orientation.

Sex Has New Meaning

So our public language asserts the reality of "homosexuality" as a permanent condition, though there is little if anything in our history (Greek, Roman, and Christian) to justify the idea and even some "gay" theorists do not accept it. The imposition upon an ingenuous public of the terms "homosexual" and "heterosexual" required a prior bit of linguistic legerdemain, namely, the redefinition of "sex" and the displacement of its principal original function by the term "gender."

Latin provides the root (*sexus* or *secus*, probably from "cut" or "sever," but more pertinently to "divide" or "halve") for the English word "sex" and for its Romance language equivalents. Since the twentieth century, the word "sex" first evokes the specific notion of sexual intercourse and everything associated with it rather than the simple division of a species into male and female, or the division of humanity into men and women. "Sex" now means primarily an activity rather than a state of being, as in the awkward and ugly, but ubiquitous, phrase, "having sex" (of which the *OED* attributes the first usage to D. H. Lawrence in 1929).

Once "sex" had acquired this new semantic profile, it became easier to substitute "gender" for "sex" as the denomination of the difference between male and female, man and woman. If the first change, however, was the gradual result of recreation replacing reproduction as the principal association of "sex" in Western culture, the introduction of "gender" as the differentiating term was deliberate and fraught with ideological baggage.

The first edition of the *OED* (1933) lists sporadic usages of "gender" for "sex" from the fourteenth through the nineteenth centuries, but notes that such usage is "now only *jocular.*" The second edition (1989) adds this to the entry: "In mod. (esp. feminist) use a euphemism for the sex of a human being, often intended to emphasize the social and cultural, as opposed to the biological, distinctions between the sexes." It gives 1963 as the date of the first such usage of "gender."

Before the sixties, "gender" was largely confined to marking the distinctions between masculine, feminine, and neuter nouns and pronouns in various languages. The gender of a noun is quite often purely arbitrary or, if you will, socially constructed; that is, there is no particular reason why the Spanish word for pen (*la pluma*) is feminine while a pencil (*el lápiz*) is masculine. Or why in Latin, French, and Spanish the hand (*manus, la main, la mano*) is feminine, while the foot (*pes, le pied, el pie*) is masculine.

The application of the term *gender* to the difference between men and women thus implies, without the argument ever being made, that the differential roles of men and women in family and society are as arbitrary as the gender of nouns. The routine use of *gender* to identify as men or women, test-takers, applicants for driver's licenses and insurance policies, and virtually all those who fill out almost any kind of document marks the bureaucratic imposition of the feminist view of the sexes on society as a whole.

Manipulated Words

Two linguistic developments over the past several decades have thus been effected by academic and media elites: *gender* has been substituted for *sex* as the designation of the distinction between men and women, and *homosexual* and *heterosexual* have been accepted as legitimate terms for distinguishable classes of persons.

The first development provides an official linguistic approval for the feminist notion that distinctions between men and women are based, not on the intrinsic nature of humankind, but on arbitrary social constructs. The second, conversely, asserts that the compulsion to commit sodomy results not from any disorder, moral, spiritual, or psychological, but from an inherent "homosexual" nature. Apart from the obvious contradiction, further ironies are involved in these verbal manipulations.

If sex is understood in its proper sense, then *homosexual* and *heterosexual* are senseless words. Etymologically, *sex* means the difference or division that makes men and women separate and complementary. To link the unique Latin word *sexus* with the Greek word for *same* is a contradiction in terms—an unnatural verbal conjunction. *Heterosexual,* on the other hand, is tautological: sex, by definition, requires someone "other" or "different."

Former President Clinton was technically correct in denying that he "had sex with that woman." What he was doing with Monica Lewinski did not require a woman, or even another human being. Orgasm can be reached by a variety of means, but only a man and a woman can engage in actual *sexual* intercourse and transform the physical difference into conjugal love: face-to-face in the much-maligned "missionary position," mutually acknowledging the personal identity of each spouse.

Homosexual and *heterosexual* can only make even a modicum of sense if sex means nothing more than carnal coupling in its myriad ways and is no longer associated with the natural complementary relation of men and women. To have recourse to this definition is, however, to rely on the social-constructivist relativism that drives the sexual revolution, which is an absurd basis for the assertion that homosexuality is an innate condition.

To deny that marriage is natural does not make the contrary alternatives "natural" in its stead (to assert thus is to commit the logical fallacy of affirming the consequent). If marriage is not natural, then nothing is, and the claim that a man is homosexual *by nature* undermines the very basis on which the term has been erected, because if sex is no more than erotic acts and urges, nothing permanent or intrinsic can be built on the shifting sands of gender.

Given the sinfulness of our nature and the mysterious blend of genetic features and external influences that shapes the specific character of particular human beings, it is probable that some individuals are, in fact, born with erotic proclivities toward persons of the same sex (or, for that matter, towards children or beasts or random promiscuity). Nevertheless, compulsive behavior arising from peculiar inclinations is not an adequate basis for establishing social institutions, much less for threatening those upon which society has long depended.

While men and women who are possessed by an urge to commit sodomy with others of the same sex should always be treated with justice and charity, they should not be allowed to determine the norms of moral discourse.

Reasonable Words

The words in which we express our ideas have consequences. To insist that words be used rationally and consistently is a first small step toward recovering moral reason. We should, therefore, refuse to accept *gender* as a relativistic substitute for the fundamental difference indicated by *sex,* while the latter term is expropriated to mean any kind of physical coupling. Above all, we should not acquiesce in the labels *heterosexual* and *homosexual,* when we are referring to men and women.

To concede the validity of such linguistic novelties is to allow the ideologues of the sexual revolution to control the terms of the debate. Male and female, masculine and feminine, designate normative components of actual human nature: anatomical, physiological, affective, and rational.

Homosexuality is now used to suggest that numerous urges and actions that deviate from these norms hold equivalent status as an element of human nature, but the peculiar use of a natural organ or faculty does not change its nature. A man can walk around on his hands, but that does not turn hands into feet; and society ought not to be obliged to redesign sidewalks and staircases to accommodate compulsive "handwalkers" (*manambulants?*), even if they are born with the inclination.

No really existing class of persons of a specific, distinct nature corresponds to the word *homosexual* in the way that men and women are distinct, complementary kinds of human being. A claim for specific "homosexual rights" is, therefore, frivolous, and the word is merely an ideological construct aimed at undermining the sexual norms inscribed in human nature.

The references are, in order, to: K J. Dover's Greek Homosexuality *(Harvard University Press, 1978 & 1989); Plato's* Symposium *189c–193d (Aristophanes), 198b–212b (Diotima), 180d–183e (Pausanias); St. Thomas*

Aquinas's Summa Theologicae *II 154 11 & 12 ad 4 and* De Malo *XV ad 7;* Fasciculus Morum *VII.Xi; Chaucer X.909;* Reclaiming Sodom, *edited by Jonathan Goldberg (Routledge, 1994), pp. 49, 58, and 1;* Symposium *190b.*

CRITICAL THINKING QUESTIONS

1. Many same-sex advocates argue that *homosexual* is a distinct class of humans, like *heterosexual.* Discuss Young's argument from language and history that suggests otherwise.

2. Advocates of same-sex attraction and behavior often point to ancient Greek civilization to argue that it was accepted and celebrated then and thus should be embraced and celebrated now. Does Young's historical research confirm or correct this argument? Explain.

3. Some argue that the Bible and the Judeo-Christian tradition are not clear in their position on homosexuality. What does the evidence outlined by Young from such Judeo-Christian writers as Paul, Jude, Aquinas, and Chaucer suggest?

4. Same-sex advocates argue that there is no moral absolute and that sexuality is simply a social construct. As such, they seek to redefine sexuality and to make same-sex attraction and behavior a new acceptable sexual construction. However, is sexuality merely a social construct? Review the articles by Budziszewski, Torode, and Frederica Mathewes-Green that discuss natural law and design. Can we know what sexuality ought to be by studying and understanding the natural design and function of human sexuality? Explain.

5. From the Latin root, what does the English word *sex* originally mean? Why have feminists and same-sex advocates encouraged the use of the word *gender* to replace the word *sex*? Is there any historical, biological, or linguistic justification for replacing the word *sex* with *gender*? Explain.

6. According to Young, why are the words *homosexual* and *heterosexual* nonsensical words?

7. Many same-sex advocates deny that man and woman are innate identities but instead are socially constructed genders. If this is

true, then is it logical to argue that homosexuality is an innate identity that constitutes a class of person? Explain.

~

Office Hours of Professor Theophilus: Homophobia—an Unfinished Story
J. Budziszewski

J. Budziszewski is professor of government and philosophy at the University of Texas, Austin. He has written several books on political science, natural law theory, and Christian apologetics, such as *Natural Law for Lawyers* (2006), *What We Can't Not Know* (2004), *Ask Me Anything: Provocative Answers for College Students* (2004), *The Revenge of Conscience: Politics and the Fall of Man* (2004), *True Tolerance: Liberalism and the Necessity of Judgment* (1999), *Written on the Heart: How to Stay Christian in College* (1999), and *Case for Natural Law* (1997). He writes regular columns for college students appearing on Boundless.org and TrueU.org, and he also writes for *Touchstone* and *Salvo*. The following is the first in a two-part series that appeared on Boundless.org and then on TrueU.org in 2000.

Essay Classification: Narrative; informative; argumentation/persuasion

"**A**RE YOU PROFESSOR THEOPHILUS?"
I turned. "That's me. Come in."
"My name's Lawrence. I'm gay. I came to complain about your talk about constitutional liberties yesterday. It was bigoted and homophobic. I'm filing a formal protest to the people who run the Student Union speakers series."
At least he's direct, I thought. I waved him to a seat.
"Help me out, Mr. Lawrence. How could—"
"Just Lawrence."
"Thank you. Now how could my talk have been 'bigoted and homophobic' when it didn't mention homosexuality?"
"I didn't actually hear the talk itself. I came in during Q&A."
"I see. And what did I say during Q&A?"
"You said gays have sex with animals."

I'm used to this sort of thing, so I merely observed, "I'm afraid you weren't listening carefully."

"I remember distinctly," he declared. "A girl asked your opinion of laws against discrimination on the basis of sexual orientation, and you said gays have sex with animals."

"No, what I said was 'sexual orientation' can mean many things. Some people are 'sexually oriented' toward the opposite sex; others toward the same sex; others toward children; others toward animals; others toward cadavers. I said that I wondered where this trend will end."

"Then you admit that gays don't have sex with animals?"

"You brought that up," I reminded him. "I have no information on the point. I'm only suggesting that not all 'orientations' are morally equivalent."

He said nothing, but showed no inclination to leave. "Do *you* think all 'orientations' are morally equivalent?" I queried.

"I won't even dignify that question with an answer," he said. "But I know what you think of my orientation. I'm sick of you phony Christians with your filthy hypocrisy about the love of God."

"So you've heard that I'm a Christian."

"Who hasn't? The holy, the sanctimonious, the Most Excellent Professor Theophilus of Post-Everything State University—what else would he be? The whole school reeks of you, of you and the other so-called Christian so-called professors. That's why I walked in on your Q&A. I wanted to see you spit venom."

"My goodness. Have I said anything venomous?"

"It's what you're thinking that's venomous."

"I see," I smiled. "Why don't you stop being bashful, and tell me what's bothering you?"

"You must think you're funny."

"I'm serious. Tell your complaints one by one, and I'll answer them."

"You couldn't answer them. I have too many."

"Try me. I'll give short answers."

He cocked his head and peered at me. "You mean it, don't you?"

"I wouldn't say it if I didn't."

"One at a time?"

"One at a time."

"All right, here's the first. Christians are hypocrites. You're always running down gays, but what about the other things your Bible condemns, like divorce and remarriage? It's other people's sins that bother you, not your own."

I laughed. "If you'd spent any time around me, you'd know that I'm just as hard on the sins of heterosexuals as on those of homosexuals. Easy divorce is a prime example of how one bad thing leads to another—in our case the loss of the ability to make any distinctions about sexual acts at all."

Ignoring the reply, he went on to his next complaint. "You're intolerant. You reject people like me just because we're different than you."

"Me reject you?" I said. "Aren't you the one who rejects what is different than yourself? Don't you reject the challenge of the other sex?"

"I don't need the other sex. I have a committed relationship with my partner."

"Research shows that homosexuals with partners don't stop cruising, they just cruise less. When they don't think straights are listening, gay writers say the same."

"So what if it's true? There's nothing wrong with gay love anyway."

I spoke quietly. "Tell me what's loving about sex acts that cause bleeding, choking, disease, and pain," I suggested. "You might start by explaining the meaning of the medical term 'Gay Bowel Syndrome,' or how people get herpes lesions on their tonsils."

"You're—how can you even say that?" he demanded. "How dare you tell me who to love?"

"I don't think I am telling you who to love."

"Oh, no? Then what are you telling me?"

"That there is nothing loving about mutual self-destruction."

"You must think my relationship with my partner is just dirt!"

"No, I respect friendship wherever I find it—your friendship with your partner included. It's just that sex doesn't make every kind of friendship better."

"Why not? Are you anti-sex or something?"

"Not at all," I said, "but would you say that sex improves the friendship of a father with his daughter?"

Seeing from his face that he didn't, I continued. "You get my point. Nor does sex improve the friendship of two men."

"That's where you're wrong. Gay sex is just as natural for some people as straight sex is for other people."

"What's 'natural,'" I said, "is what unlocks our inbuilt potential instead of thwarting it. One of the purposes of marital sex is to get you outside your Self and its concerns, to achieve intimacy with someone who is Really Other."

Was he listening to any of this? "I'm sorry, Lawrence—I really am—but having sex with another man can't do that. It's too much like loving your reflection. That's what I meant before about refusing the challenge of the other sex."

I was about to go on, but abruptly he changed the subject: "It's attitudes like yours that killed Matthew Shepard."

"Surely you don't imagine that the thugs who killed Matthew Shepard were Christians, do you?" I smiled at the absurdity of the thought, but seeing that he misunderstood my smile I made my face serious and tried again.

"Lawrence, I deplore the violence that killed Matthew Shepard, and I'm glad those men were caught. But shouldn't we also grieve the urge which caused Matthew Shepard to be sexually attracted to violent strangers?"

He said only, "You hate me."

I paused to study him. Did he really believe that, or was it a smokescreen?

"I don't hate you," I said. "I love you." I paused. "I'd like to be with you forever, in heaven."

Lawrence's face displayed shock, as though he had been hit in the stomach. Then he looked confused. The expression of confusion was instantaneously replaced by an expression of anger.

For one split-second, it had looked as if the shutters were open. *"God in heaven,"* I thought, *"I need help."* How could they be pried back up?

"My love isn't really the issue for you, is it?" I asked.

"What do you mean?"

"It's God's. God's love is the issue for you." For a few seconds there was no reaction.

Then it came. "You're bleeping right God's love is the issue for me," he said. *"Your* God's love. The lying God who says He loves man, but who hates me for loving men."

"Do you think God hates you?"

"Doesn't He?"

"What makes you say that?"

"Doesn't your Bible say that? It calls people like me an abomination."

"It calls what you *do* abomination. There's a difference."

"There's no difference. I do what I am."

I considered his point. "Could it be," I said, "that you want God to love you *less?*"

"Less!" he spat.

"Yes. Don't you know what love is?"

"Acceptance."

"Acceptance of what kills you? Consider another view: love is a commitment of the will to the true good of the other person."

"What?"

"I said love is a commitment of the will to the true good of the other person."

"I don't get what you're saying."

"Sure you do. The lover wants what's good for the beloved."

He hesitated. "I suppose."

"Good. Now think. If that's what love is, then a *perfect* Lover would want the *perfect* good of the Beloved. Do you see what that means? He would loath and detest whatever destroyed the beloved's good—no matter how much the beloved desired it."

I couldn't read the look on his face, so I plowed on. "That's what sin does—it destroys us. Yours destroys you, mine destroys me. And so the Lover doesn't 'accept' it; He hates it with an inexorable hatred. To cut the cancer out of us, He will do whatever it takes—like a surgeon. No, more than like a surgeon. If you let Him, He will even take the cancer upon Himself and die in your place."

Still inscrutable, he kept his eyes in front of him, just avoiding my own.

I asked, "What happens, then, if you refuse to let go of what destroys you? What happens if you say this to the divine and perfect Lover who wants your complete and perfect good—if you say, 'I bind myself to my destruction! Accept me, and my destruction with me! I refuse to enter heaven except in the company of Death!'"

Neither of us spoke.

Lawrence rose from his chair and walked out the door.

CRITICAL THINKING QUESTIONS

1. What does *homophobia* actually mean (its true, dictionary definition)? How is this term commonly used today? Is it fair and reasonable to automatically label someone who argues cogently against same-sex behavior as necessarily homophobic? Explain.

2. How does "Professor Theophilus" handle the student charging him with bigotry and homophobia? Discuss Theophilus's use of questions to respond to the student's charges.

3. In this exchange, who seems more rational, calm, fair, and reasonable? Who is intolerant of the other? Is it fair to characterize J. Budziszewski ("Professor Theophilus") as a bigot? Why or why not?

4. There are indeed many sexual orientations, but does that mean that all must be embraced and treated as morally equivalent? Explain.

5. This student claimed that Budziszewski is a hypocrite, a bigot, and a mean-spirited intolerant person who he assumed would "spit venom." Did Budziszewski ever "spit venom"? Was he ever intolerant? Who comes off as venomous and intolerant here?

6. The student claims that gay love and gay sex is natural. How does Budziszewski reply? How is he using the natural law/design argument here? Does it make sense? Why or why not?

7. Why is it important to distinguish the person from his/her actions? Does rejecting the behavior necessarily mean you reject the person engaging in the behavior? Explain.

8. What is the student's understanding of love? What is Budziszewski's understanding of love? How does this definition of love explain God's perfect love for humanity while objecting to (not accepting) the behavior that destroys a human's good?

~

Office Hours of Professor Theophilus: The Seeker—Homophobia, Part 2

J. Budziszewski

Essay Classification: Narrative; informative; argumentation/persuasion

"I T WASN'T EASY FINDING your office," said my visitor as he took a seat. "This building is like a rabbit warren."

"Yes," I said, "for the first couple of years I worked here, I had to leave a trail of crumbs each day to find my way back out. We haven't met, have we?"

"No, I'm over in Antediluvian Studies—I'm a grad student. My name's Adam, Adam Apollolas."

"M. E. Theophilus." We shook hands.

"You are the same Theophilus who wrote the 'Homophobia' dialogue for *Nounless Webzine,* aren't you? I was hoping to talk with you about it."

"Busted," I smiled. "What would you like to know about it?"

"Was it based on a real conversation?"

"Yes and no; it was a composite. A homosexual student really did visit to accuse me of saying that 'gays have sex with animals,' and the rest is from real life, too, but not necessarily from the same conversation."

"But it can't possibly be true that all of the homosexuals who speak with you are as angry and closed-minded as he was."

"No, of course not."

"Then why did you portray him that way in the dialogue?"

"Would you have me pretend that *nobody* in the homosexual life is angry and closed-minded? A good many are like that—you should see my letters—and I try to show my readers the dynamics of more than one kind of conversation. You see, when people have honest questions you try to answer them, but when they only churn out smokescreens, then you blow the smoke away."

"So you'd be open to different kinds of conversation."

"Of course," I said. I smiled. "Are we, perhaps, having one right now?"

His eyebrows lifted. "Am I that obvious?"

"It was just a shot in the dark, So, what did you really want to talk about?"

"I'm not very ideological, but I guess you could call me a Seeker. See, I've been in the gay life for five years, but lately I've been having second thoughts. I'm not asking you to convert me, understand? I thought I'd just hear what you have to say, then go away and think about it."

"What have you been having second thoughts about?"

He hesitated. "Are you going to use this conversation in one of your dialogues?"

"If I did, I'd make sure you couldn't be identified. You can speak freely."

"Well—" he hesitated again. "One thing is intimacy. I've never had problems finding sex, but it's more or less anonymous. That didn't bother me at first, but now it's getting me down."

"Is the sex always anonymous?"

"No, the first time I had gay sex was in a steady relationship. I've been in two or three others, too—for a month, two months, a year. But they were never what you'd call faithful, know what I mean? It's as though there had to be other sexual outlets for the relationship to work at all. I'm starting to want—I don't know. Something else."

"I follow you."

He paused. "Another thing. I want to be a Dad. That doesn't fit the stereotype, does it? Are you surprised to hear me say it?"

"Not at all."

"In that case, you're the only one. My friends don't get it. One said, 'Why don't you just get a turkey baster and make an arrangement with a lesbian?' But that's not what I want." Another pause. "I used to say to myself, 'Get used to it. You can't have everything you want.' But that doesn't work for me any more."

After a second he spoke again. "There's one more thing."

"What's that?"

"God."

"God? How so?"

"Oh, I go to church sometimes. Now *that* must surprise you."

"No. What kind of church?"

"Different kinds. I didn't go to any church at first. My family never went to church. Most of my gay friends don't have any use for God. Then I started going to a gay church, and that was OK for awhile. But I think I might want the real stuff, do you know what I mean? Or else nothing."

"I think so. You don't have any doubts about what the real stuff is?"

"No. I'm not saying I believe in Jesus, but—" He thought for a moment. "The gay church said you can be a Christian and still live a gay life. I don't think I ever really believed that. I read a book that the minister in the gay church recommended—"

"Yes?"

"The title was something like *Sex and Dirt*. I'm leaving something out. Hold on, it'll come to me."

"Never mind, I know the book."

"Oh, good. Then you probably remember how the author argues that when the Bible lays down rules about sex, they're just purity codes, not moral laws—so you don't have to keep them."

"Sure."

"He had me going for a while—right up to where he said 'that's why even having sex with animals is OK,' or words to that effect. Just what the guy in your dialogue accused *you* of saying gay people think. I could see that the author's conclusion followed from his premises—but after that, I didn't have any use for his premises, if you see what I mean."

"I see exactly what you mean. So where does all this leave you?"

"Like I said, I want to hear you out, and then I'll go away and think about it."

"That's fine, Adam, but just what is it that you want to hear me out about?"

"I think what I'm missing is the Big Picture about sex. If there *is* a Big Picture about sex."

"There is indeed a Big Picture about sex."

"Draw it, then. Paint it. Lecture me, even. That is," he added, "if you don't mind."

I had to laugh. "You asked me before if I was going to use this conversation in one of my dialogues. If I do, nobody will believe it. They'll call it contrived."

"Why?"

"Because you've set the stage too well. Your 'second thoughts' anticipate everything I'd like to say. And now you ask for a lecture!"

"After seven years of college, I'm used to lectures. You do your professor thing, and I'll listen. If I want to argue—believe me, I know how—I'll come back another day."

I collected my thoughts. "All right, Adam. The main point of Christian sexual morality is that human nature is *designed*. We need to live a certain way because we're designed to live that way."

He said, "I can see design in an organ like the heart. Human nature— that's a little too big for me."

"Then let's start with the heart. Do you see how every part works together toward its purpose, its function?"

"Sure. You've got nerves and valves and pumping chambers, all for moving blood."

"Right. If you think about the sexual powers instead of the heart, it's just the same. The key to understanding a design is to recognize its purposes. For the heart, the purpose is pumping blood; for the sexual powers—you tell me."

"Pleasure?"

"Think about it. Would you say pleasure is the purpose of eating?"

"No, I'd say nourishment is the purpose of eating, and pleasure is just the result."

"If you thought pleasure were the purpose of eating, what would you do if I offered you pleasant-tasting poison?"

"Eat it."

"And what would happen?"

"I'd get sick."

"But if you understood that nourishment were the purpose of eating and pleasure merely the result, *then* what would you do if I offered you pleasant-tasting poison?"

"Refuse it and ask for food instead."

"It's the same with the sexual powers. Pleasure is a result of their use, but not the purpose of their use. The purposes can tell you which kinds of sexual activity are good and which aren't; by itself, pleasure can't."

"So what are the purposes of the sexual powers?"

"You've told me already; you just didn't realize you were doing so."

"I have? When?"

"When you were telling me your second thoughts about the homo-sexual life. There were three of them. What was the first one about?"

"Intimacy. Bonding."

"And the second?"

"Having children."

"Then you won't be surprised to hear that one inbuilt purpose of the sexual powers is to bond a man with a woman, and another is to have and raise children."

"If bonding is good, why not use the sexual powers to bond a man with a man?"

"Has that worked in your case, Adam?"

"Well, no. That's what I was complaining about."

"You see, that's no accident. Bonding man with man is contrary to the design."

"You say that, but how do you *know?*"

"There are two reasons. First, man and woman are complementary. They're not just *different,* they *match.* There is something in male emotional design to which only the female can give completion, and something in female emotional design to which only the male can give completion. When same mates with same, that can't happen. Instead of balancing each other, they unbalance each other."

"What's the other reason?"

"The other reason is that the linkage of same with same is sterile. You've complained about that, too."

"But sometimes a man can't produce children with a woman, either."

"The mating of same with same isn't *accidentally* sterile, Adam, as the union of a particular man with a particular woman might be; it's *inherently* sterile. A husband and wife who are unable to have a baby haven't set themselves against their own inbuilt purposes. A man and man who have sex together have."

He grinned. "There's always the turkey baster."

"But when your friend made that suggestion, you refused, didn't you? What was your reason?"

"I'm not sure. I just think a kid needs a Mom and a Dad."

"That's exactly right. Male and female complement and complete each other not just in having children but in rearing them. Women are better designed for nurture, men are better designed for protection. Besides, two Dads can't model male-female relationships. Neither can two Moms. Neither can one."

Adam was silent as he digested this. "You know," he said finally, "this isn't at all what I expected you to talk about."

"What did you expect me to talk about?"

"Disease." He paused. "Now that I think about it, you didn't say much about disease in that dialogue I read either."

"I should think you already know the deadliness of your way of life."

"I suppose so. But it does seem unfair. Why should gay sex be less healthy than any other kind?"

"Don't we come right back to the design? Start with the fact that not all orifices are created equal."

"Hmmm."

"Hmmm?"

"I think I'll go do what I said I'd do: Go away and think about it all. In the meantime, Professor, I think you have a problem."

"Do I?"

"That is, if you do intend to use this chat of ours in one of your dialogues."

"And what might this problem be?"

"We've talked too long. Your dialogues are all 1,500 words. This one is way over."

I smiled. "I'll talk to my editor about it."

CRITICAL THINKING QUESTIONS

1. This student seems upset that Budziszewski represented the gay student in his first homophobia dialog as an angry, judgmental, and vitriolic individual. How does Budziszewski respond?

2. What is the difference between sex and intimacy? How does fidelity factor into this issue? Why wasn't this gay student emotionally and spiritually satisfied by gay sex (by his own admission)?

3. Why isn't Budziszewski surprised that this gay student desires true intimacy, wants to be a father, and desires a relationship with God? How does natural law/design explain this?

4. The student wants "the big picture" about sex. What does Budziszewski paint for him? Does this explanation make sense? Why or why not?

5. Budziszewski argues that just as an organ like the heart has a design and function based upon its purpose, so too does human sexual power. Summarize his main points regarding the design and

purpose of human sexuality. Do they make rational sense? Why or why not?

6. Explain the difference between understanding sex in terms of purpose versus pleasure. How can purpose tell you which kinds of sexual activity are good for you and which are not while the pleasure principle cannot (recall the food/poison analogy)?

7. According to natural law, design, and purpose, can sex bond a man to a man or a woman to a woman as sex bonds a man to a woman? Why or why not (consider carefully the issue of difference and complementarity between the sexes)?

8. What does natural design suggest about the proper natural makeup of the family? Can sameness properly raise a fully developed human being or is that best accomplished by parents of opposite yet complementary sexes? Explain.

~

Marriage Ain't What It Used to Be—Or Is It?
Mike D'Virgilio

Mike D'Virgilio is a prolific blogger and posts his views on politics, culture, and faith on MDVOutlook.com. He is also the founder of *The Culture Project* (thecultureproject.org). The following article was published by *Crux* in 2005 and is currently archived by *Salvo*.

Essay Classification: Evaluative; argumentation/persuasion

STEPHANIE COONTZ, A TEACHER of family history at a northwestern U.S. university, considered the changing state of marriage recently in the *Washington Post*. She wrote as a sociologist making observations about the state of marriage, but one gets the strong feeling she doesn't have much respect for traditional notions of marriage.

Coontz's basic contention is that once love became the driving force behind marriage, marriage changed for the worse. Individual choice, which had been held in check by a number of restraints over the centuries, effectively changed the social significance of marriage in the economy and culture. There is a bit of Marxist dialectic going on in Coontz's analysis.

These changes are somehow inevitable, she implies, and nothing can be done to alter their dynamics.

Because of this she derides any notion that these forces that work against marriage can be stopped or turned back, arguing that traditional notions of marriage are simply outmoded:

> What these campaigns have in common is the idea that people are willfully refusing to recognize the value of traditional families and that their behavior will change if we can just enlighten them.
>
> But recent changes in marriage are part of a worldwide upheaval in family life that has transformed the way people conduct their personal lives as thoroughly and permanently as the Industrial Revolution transformed their working lives 200 years ago. Marriage is no longer the main way in which societies regulate sexuality and parenting or organize the division of labor between men and women. And although some people hope to turn back the tide by promoting traditional values, making divorce harder or outlawing gay marriage, they are having to confront a startling irony: The very factors that have made marriage more satisfying in modern times have also made it more optional.

This is an interesting argument that is in many ways correct as far as it goes. Marriage, throughout history and in many cultures still, was a mandatory state in which the parties directly involved had little say. No one wants to go back to such times.

But is it true that marriage based on love is inherently less stable? Are we to throw in the towel and say that it is simply not possible to make marriage a more enduring social institution in our country? Coontz thinks so, but she is inferring an *ought* from an *is*. It is one thing to make observations about what marriage has become, and then base your conclusions on the behavior you observe. That is the way of the skeptic and cynic, who in effect believes in no higher ideal that can compel human behavior, whether that relates to marriage or anything else. It is another thing altogether to start with the ideal and then try to determine whether and how human behavior can fit into that ideal, even if we can only hope to approximate such ultimate fulfillment.

Here is how this cynical mentality is reflected in the article:

> Marriage is no longer the institution where people are initiated into sex. It no longer determines the work men and women do on the job or at home, regulates who has children and who doesn't,

or coordinates care-giving for the ill or the aged. For better or worse, marriage has been displaced from its pivotal position in personal and social life, and will not regain it short of a Taliban-like counterrevolution.

Notice that what "is" is what "should be." Coontz claims that only the repression of religious extremists can change marriage, and then only from the outside. Moral suasion has no place in this woman's world.

Thus Coontz makes two critical errors that underlie her conclusion of inexorable forces beyond human control. One is in the very foundation of her argument, the notion that marriage today is based on love. To most moderns, American or otherwise, love is fundamentally an emotion. Emotions of attraction, we believe, are very hard to control. Things change (it's a fact of life), and once they do, so will my emotions and so will my choices.

If, however, we look at love from a different, distinctly nonmodern perspective, we see a very different picture. This is the idea that love is a commitment to the well-being of another. As to where emotion fits into this idea of love, I would argue that emotion will always follow our obedience to the commitments we have made. There really is no such thing as being "in love," in my view, because real love is nothing like the lust and infatuation that tend to drive a new romantic relationship. The last thing on my mind during the first months of my courtship of my wife was self-sacrifice. Everyone who has fallen "in love" can attest to this.

When we see love as a commitment to another's well-being, traditional ideas of marriage makes great sense. The following words from the thirteenth chapter of the book of Corinthians in the Bible have great power regardless of one's religious beliefs or ability to apply them (but it is much easier with the grace of God and prayer):

> Love is patient, love is kind. It does not envy, it does not boast, it is not proud. It is not rude, it is not self-seeking, it is not easily angered, it keeps no record of wrongs. Love does not delight in evil, but rejoices in the truth. It always protects, always trusts, always hopes, always perseveres. Love never fails.

The irony of this biblical conception of love is that although it is the least self-centered idea of relating to others imaginable, it is also the most self-satisfying. Love truly given invites love in return. Note that phrase about keeping no record of wrongs; that is all but inconceivable for most people, yet is a key to enjoying a relationship with another person. Hence, regardless of what marriage looks like today or how cynical Ms. Coontz may be, traditional marriage would continue to be viable today if people were taught how to truly love instead of being encouraged to indulge in transitory emotions.

The second mistake Coontz makes is in accepting an obviously untrue assertion that has made marriage much weaker in the modern context:

> None of this means that marriage is dead. Indeed, most people have a higher regard for the marital relationship today than when marriage was practically mandatory. Marriage as a private relationship between two individuals is taken more seriously and comes with higher emotional expectations than ever before in history.

Coontz is dead wrong here. Marriage is most certainly *not* "a private relationship between two individuals." As soon as a couple decides to marry, their relationship changes from private to public. Now two families are involved and tied together. The dynamics of the relationship of each spouse to friends made prior to marriage change dramatically. The state now has a vested interest in the relationship unlike any considerations it may have had when the two individuals were not married. The couple becomes a legal unit in the eyes of the law. And need I mention children? Once two people marry, others become dependent on the success of that relationship.

(Of course, a couple who have children while living together without being married have people dependent on the success of their relationship, but that is what makes their relationship serious: the fact that it is like a marriage even though the couple has not seen fit to formalize it according to law and custom.)

Coontz states that marriage is taken "more seriously" now, which she indicates in the same sentence as meaning there are greater "emotional expectations" attached to the relationship between the couple. But that is exactly the problem with the modern vision of marriage. Marriage relationships are *less* fulfilling when they are viewed as merely private affairs. Self-centeredness is invariably less satisfying than openness to others.

When marriage is viewed from the broader perspective I have proposed, the paradigm changes entirely. Self-fulfillment is more a product of self-sacrifice than of selfishness. If you always get what you want and if things always go your way, if there are no struggles and no challenges in your life, you may well be the most miserable creature alive. So it is with personal relationships: it is when problems arise that we see who truly loves us.

The illusion that Coontz wishes to strengthen—the vision of marriage as an emotional attachment first and foremost—is the very thing that causes most people go into wedlock with an infatuated idea of an ideal marriage in which problems indicate that something is *wrong*. Nothing could be further from the truth. The fairy-tale idea of marriage—that people can live happily ever after—is actually true, but it doesn't mean the couple subsequently lives a frictionless life. It means they've learned to love one another in spite of themselves, and that they recognize that their marriage has profound repercussions for them, their children, their town, their city, their state, their country, their culture. They commit to the hard work involved in holding a family together, and they reap incalculable rewards for their effort.

Ms. Coontz may think that the "series" called traditional marriage has been "cancelled," but as program directors of the network called "my life," millions of Americans have a say in bringing this show back. If they did, I am convinced it would be a hit.

CRITICAL THINKING QUESTIONS

1. D'Virgilio begins his analysis by summarizing Stephanie Coontz's view of how marriage has changed in recent history. What is her position? How does D'Virgilio respond?

2. What is the logical fallacy of confusing an *is* for an *ought*? According to D'Virgilio, how has Coontz in her analysis of marriage committed this fallacy?

3. Do you agree with Coontz and other such skeptics and cynics that you are powerless against social, economic, and historical forces beyond your control and that you can do nothing to change your life or your society? Why or why not?

4. We are often confused about what love means and how it relates to marriage. What is D'Virgilio's definition and explanation of love? How can practicing this kind of love transform marriage into the stabilizing institution it was designed to be?

5. Should fulfillment in marriage be based on selfish desires or selfless self-sacrifice? Explain.

~

ABORTION

Unsafe, Deadly, and Legal
Janice Shaw Crouse

Dr. Janice Shaw Crouse is coauthor with Beverly LeHaye of *A Different Kind of Strength* (2001) and is the author of the Beverly LeHaye Institute report titled *Gaining Ground: A Profile of American Women in the Twentieth Century* (2000). Dr. Crouse was appointed by President Bush to the United States Delegation for the United Nations Children's Summit, held in May 2002, and she is a senior fellow at the Beverly LeHaye Institute. The following article appeared in *Touchstone* in 2003.

Essay Classification: Informative

ONE OF THE MOST important abortion mantras is "make abortion safe, legal, and rare." It is legal, but it is not necessarily safe, and it is certainly not rare. The United States has the highest legal abortion rate among Western nations. Over one million children are aborted in the United States every year.

It is not rare among American women. Since *Roe v. Wade* made abortion legal in the United States in 1973, over 40 million abortions have been performed. In 1973, out of 46.8 million women of childbearing age (ages 14–44), there were 745,000 abortions. By 1996, with 60.4 million women of childbearing age (ages 15–44), there were 1,366,000 abortions.

Abortion is not rare even among teenagers. The United States has the highest teen pregnancy rate in the world. Four in ten young women become pregnant at least once before they reach the age of 20—nearly one million a year. In 1997, 1.7 percent of younger teens (ages 15–17) and 4.3 percent of older teens (age 18 or 19) obtained an abortion.

Abortion is not rare among women who are not married. According to the Alan Guttmacher Institute, the abortion rate for unmarried women is four times greater than that of married women. Six million American women become pregnant every year—almost half of them are unmarried. Of those three million unmarried pregnant women, almost half have an abortion and almost half become single mothers. Very few of them marry the father of their child or give up the child for adoption.

Most of the unmarried women are living with the man who fathered their child, yet they do not even consider marriage and never consider giving the child up for adoption to a couple on the long list of infertile couples desperate to have a child. Ironically, young women today are told that marrying because you "have to" or giving up a child for adoption is "cruel." It is not considered cruel to abort the child they do not want.

Indeed, in some circles, abortion is considered a "brave" and "courageous" action because nothing could be worse for a child than being "unwanted." And, of course, it is argued in the same circles that nothing could be worse for a woman than to be saddled with a child that is "unwanted."

No Choice at All?

Actually, something is much worse—discovering that a man is willing to have sex with you but is unwilling to marry you, even when that sex results in a pregnancy. The truth behind the data is that abortion is overwhelmingly a choice of unmarried, rather than married, pregnant women. Over and over, crisis pregnancy center personnel hear unmarried women say that their "boyfriend" or "partner" is making them have an abortion. Choosing to have the baby is not an option the women believe is available to them when a boyfriend or lover is pressuring them to have an abortion. Often the man tells the woman he has gotten pregnant that if she does not "get rid of the baby," he is "out of here."

Increasingly, abortion is less a desperate teen's impulsive solution than a twenty-something's calculated choice between a man she wants and the baby he refuses to accept. In 1996, women ages 20 to 24 had over 400,000 abortions, about one-third of the total performed that year. These women are, of course, supposed to be responsible, mature, and informed. Yet their behavior has a high likelihood of producing pregnancy, and the men they are involved with are poor candidates for marriage and even worse candidates for fatherhood. Even so, a lifestyle of casual sex is commonplace, and the rate of cohabitation is continuing to rise dramatically.

Though the median age for a woman's first marriage is now the mid-twenties (it was 21 in 1973 and 24.8 in 1996), contrary to the feminist myth, women don't have as many choices as they have been led to expect.

Among cohabiting or sexually involved couples, the man determines if and when the couple gets married; a couple does not get married until the man is ready, regardless of how much the woman might desire marriage. Even when confronted with a pregnancy, too many men are unwilling to make a commitment or take responsibility. In this respect, too, trends have changed dramatically. In 1960, 60 percent of unmarried pregnant women married the father of their baby before the baby was born; in 1994, only 23 percent did.

And abortion is least rare among separated women. One author writes that they are at the highest risk for having an abortion, and in fact they are twice as likely as all women to have an abortion.

Unsafe Abortions

As the United States approaches the thirtieth anniversary of *Roe v. Wade,* this so-called women's rights issue is thoroughly entrenched in American culture, and special interest groups are now calling for abortion to be a "human" rights issue the United States should promote around the world. But nagging facts just will not go away. Abortion is not rare, and it has not been proven safe for women.

Abortion has made it easier for irresponsible men to turn their backs on women and the children they conceive. As we have seen, it has encouraged women into sexual relationships that deny them the security and commitment they need from the men with whom they have involved themselves. Women are left to deal with the consequences, and often they are not even aware of the worst complications of their choice to abort.

One of the major consequences of abortion, of course, is death—not just the baby's, but also the mother's. Pro-abortion rhetoric focuses on the danger of "back-alley" abortions, but legalized abortion is not safe. Abortion is four times deadlier than childbirth. Infertility can be another consequence. Evidence is mounting that there is a link between abortion and breast cancer—commonly called the ABC link. Eleven out of 12 studies of American women report an increased risk of breast cancer after an induced abortion, while 25 studies out of 31 conducted around the world indicate increased risk. A British study found that the risk of cancer was increased, on average, by 30 percent by one induced abortion.

Emotional and psychological consequences are less easy to quantify, but abortion-related emotional and psychological problems are not uncommon after an abortion. In fact, so many women have these problems that they have earned a medical name: postabortion syndrome.

There is good news: Between 1994 and 1998, the number of abortion clinics in the United States decreased by over 40 percent simply because not enough doctors were willing to provide the abortions and fewer women were asking for them. More and more doctors are refusing to perform abortions. Some medical schools are seeking legal provisions that require abortion training because too many medical students are declining to become licensed for the procedure.

Other good news is the increase in crisis pregnancy centers (CPCs). While abortion clinics are closing because of the decline in business, CPCs are springing up everywhere. In 1980 there were only 500 across the nation. By 1990 there were 2,000, and now there are at least 4,000.

Yet abortion is still not rare, not even safe, and prominent voices continue to support it not only as a right but also as *good* for society. "Abortion is good child policy," proclaimed a recent column in the *Chicago Tribune*. The author argued that New York City's crime rate is lower today because unwanted babies had been eliminated through abortion eighteen years ago. "The only children we ought to produce," he said, "are wanted children."

Nothing is heard more often these days than that certain policies and programs must be enacted "for the children." Yet America's culture is no longer child-friendly when the most Americans hope for is that abortion will be safe, legal, and rare, and when so many assert that children who are not wanted ought to be aborted. If you slaughter the innocents, you destroy the future.

CRITICAL THINKING QUESTIONS

1. Many pro-abortionists argue that having an abortion is courageous and brave, that it is cruel to have an unwanted baby, and that it is unfair for a mother to be burdened with an unwanted baby. Given the information in this article, do these arguments still seem convincing? What is crueler, killing the unborn baby or allowing him/her to live and giving him/her to a couple willing to love and raise him/her? Explain.

2. Pro-abortionists claim that legalized abortion is not about preserving a lifestyle, nor is it a form of birth control. What do the statistics

in this article seem to suggest about how abortion is used in the United States? Do you think this is morally acceptable? Why or why not?

3. Pro-abortionists argue that abortion must be kept legal to keep it safe. But, after more than thirty years of legalized abortion, how safe is it? What are some of the physical and emotional dangers of abortion?

4. Discuss the irony expressed in the last paragraph. Do you think this is an effective way to end this essay? Why or why not?

∼

Defending the Indefensible
David Mills

David Mills is the editor of *Touchstone* and the author of critical essays on C. S. Lewis. He edited the book *The Pilgrim's Guide: C. S. Lewis and the Art of Witness* (1999), and he wrote *The Saint's Guide to Knowing the Real Jesus* (2000). This essay appeared in *Touchstone* in 2000.

Essay Classification: Informative; argumentation/persuasion

IN A RECENT COLUMN, George Will described how *USA Today* and the *New York Times* both refused to run a pointed but visually inoffensive ad against partial-birth abortion. Placed by Focus on the Family, the cartoon's first four panels showed a baby being born, but the fifth showed him with his eyes closed and the caption, "Then he felt a sharp pain at the base of his skull! He jerked violently! And then . . . it was over!"

The *Times* thought the ad "too graphic," said Focus on the Family, and Will noted that *USA Today* "must have considered the ad in poor taste," since it was not fraudulent or libelous, the newspaper's other two reasons for turning down an ad. "If that moving but mild ad is objectionable to *USA Today* and the *Times*, then they probably consider any criticism of partial-birth abortion unfit for public consumption. Such censorship—in the name of compassion protecting the public's tender sensibilities—represents a novel understanding of the duties of journalistic institutions."

Transforming Reality

I do not believe, any more than George Will seems to, that these papers truly found the ad objectionable. It is not plausible, given the ads they do run and the stories they publish. They were acting, as a pro-choice media has acted for some time, to keep the reality of abortion out of public discourse.

But there is another way to hide a reality from others, and that is to lie about it. The most effective lies do not deny the reality, because to deny it implies that it might exist. The most effective lies transform the reality into something else entirely.

Something in us makes us give good names to the bad things we want to do, after which the good names keep us from feeling guilty when we do the bad things. In C. S. Lewis's "Screwtape Proposes a Toast," the senior devil Screwtape explains to the graduates of the Tempters' Training College how the competent devil uses language in his work of encouraging a human soul to damn himself.

The work begins, Screwtape says, when the subject's "consciousness hardly exists apart from the atmosphere that surrounds [him]," so that he does not quite realize what he is doing when he sins. To take advantage of this ignorance, he tells the graduate devils, "We have contrived that their very language should be all smudge and blur; what would be a *bribe* in someone else's profession is a *tip* or a *present* in theirs."

The tempter must then work to turn these not-quite-conscious choices to sin into habits and these habits into principles, and again he does so by encouraging the subject to change his language. The unconscious desire to be like everyone else "now becomes an unacknowledged creed or ideal of Togetherness or Being like Folks. Mere ignorance of the law they break now turns into a vague theory about it—remember they know no history—a theory expressed by calling it *conventional* or *puritan* or *bourgeois* 'morality.'"

We see people doing this sort of thing all the time, and most of us do it ourselves. In public life we see people doing it, not surprisingly, to the most vulnerable. People who would never hit a child or raise their voices even to a defiantly disobedient child, will speak of an unborn child as "tissue" or "the product of conception" or even more abstractly of "a woman's right to control her own body," in explaining why the "tissue" must be removed and the pregnancy (not the baby) "terminated."

"Improving" the Race

Children with Down syndrome, for example, are being aborted at an increasing rate, and many people who want them to be aborted do not want to say so, and so use the language to hide the fact that what they want to do is kill retarded children before they are born, and therefore advance the practice. This was the horrifying point of a story by Tucker Carlson in *The Weekly Standard* a year or two ago, titled "Eugenics, American Style."

Eugenics is the attempt to "improve" the human race by selective breeding and sometimes, as in the case of infants with Down syndrome, killing them before they are born. Seventy or eighty years ago many of the enlightened and progressive favored it. The feminist hero and founder of Planned Parenthood, Margaret Sanger, was a eugenicist, as were the great socialist wise man George Bernard Shaw and other leading humanitarians.

Many wanted to sterilize the poor and (as they thought them) unfit, so that there would, in time, be fewer poor unfit people and more people like them. (This strikes me, I must admit, and I am not being facetious, as a bad bargain.) Things were going nicely for the eugenicists until Hitler gave eugenics a bad name by being so good at it.

There is a problem of criteria, of course. As I wrote in these pages last year, the modern eugenicists really seem to think the value of a man's life defined by his intelligence. The less intelligent are "defective" because: they are less intelligent.

In this case, since many Christians are demonstrably smarter than many of the eugenicists, on their own grounds we could rule their quality of life defective and do something about them. They, after all, set the standards. People near the top of a slippery slope rarely seem to realize how easily someone higher up can give them a push.

In another of Screwtape's letters, by the way, he explains the demonic use of eugenics—and it is not the use you would expect, that it encourages men to kill other men for their own purposes. (Though Screwtape certainly approves of murder.) The vision of eugenics is one of those utopian promises that tie men, and especially the young, more firmly to this world, giving them time to become truly worldly.

"So inveterate is their [the young's] appetite for Heaven," wrote Screwtape, "that our best method, at this stage, of attaching them to Earth is to make them believe that Earth can be turned into Heaven at some future date by politics or eugenics or 'science' or psychology or what not. Real worldliness is a work of time—assisted, of course, by pride, for we teach them to describe the creeping death as Good Sense or Maturity or Experience."

A language that smudges and blurs is a great help in this movement into real worldliness. And I have often heard pro-abortionists speak of the choice to "terminate the pregnancy" as an example of good sense or maturity or experience.

The Language of Abortion

The most vulnerable, of course, are the first victims of other people's real worldliness. As Carlson explains, though "mildly to moderately retarded" (being not quite as bright as Forrest Gump), Down syndrome children can live at home, read, work, and live into late middle age.

Parents testify that such children are unusually loving and gentle and not as hard to raise as other people think. A charity that places these children for adoption never has fewer than 100 couples on its waiting list eager to adopt them.

Nevertheless, because they are expensive and troublesome and inconvenient, people do not want to have them, or for others to have them. Since the syndrome is usually discovered by amniocentesis, which is not performed till the sixteenth week of pregnancy, to abort the child requires tearing apart a fully formed human being, including some who are allowed almost to be born, and who could live were they born, whose skulls are crushed and their brains sucked out before the delivery is finished.

That is the reality. That is, for obvious reasons, the reality that must be hidden from sight.

Carlson began his article by reminding readers of the comments of soon-to-be Surgeon General Jocelyn Elders, who in 1990 claimed that abortion "has had an important and positive public-health effect" because it reduced "the number of children afflicted with severe defects." She noted that "the number of Down syndrome infants in Washington state in 1976 was 64 percent lower than it would have been without legal abortion."

Elders considers people who are not as smart as she is to be not just defective but *severely* defective, and killing them a benefit to the public health. One may think this morally deranged, but at least she said clearly and in public what she thinks.

Others—almost everyone else who shares her position—are not so honest. The Clinton administration argued that babies with "serious health problems" or a "serious fetal defect" should be exempted from the ban on partial-birth abortions. The abortionist it cited admitted that the most common "defect" he "treated"—"treated" by killing the child—was Down syndrome.

One doctor (one *doctor*) said that estimates of the high cost of raising a child with Down syndrome "provide a vivid picture of the value of research and prevention." By which he meant preventing not the syndrome but the births of the children suffering from it.

Another doctor, who is actually the director of the Down Syndrome Center of Western Pennsylvania, said that aborting a Down syndrome child (he used the usual euphemism "terminating the pregnancy") is not a "pro-life issue" but "a choice issue" and "an information issue."

Yet another doctor, an obstetrician with whose words Carlson ended the article, said that he approves of eugenics—he favors eliminating "babies [*sic*] who don't have much chance of a viable life"—though he dislikes the word. It has gotten "bad connotations over time. I think the better terms would be 'genetic counseling' and 'prenatal diagnosis' and 'having a country in which the option to exercise choice in whether to continue or terminate a pregnancy is a right of the people.'"

All Evasions

These are all evasions of the plain and obvious facts of the matter. As George Orwell noted fifty years ago in his essay "Politics and the English Language," "political speech and writing are largely the defense of the indefensible." He may have been exaggerating, but not much.

In his world, fifty years ago, "Millions of peasants are robbed of their farms and sent trudging along the roads with no more than they can carry: this is called transfer of population or rectification of frontiers." And perhaps more relevantly: "People are imprisoned for years without trial, or shot in the back of the neck or sent to die of scurvy in Arctic lumber camps: this is called elimination of unreliable elements."

And in our world, killing the unborn because they will someday do badly on their SATs is called "treatment" or "prevention" or "a choice issue" or "genetic counseling" or "prenatal diagnosis." What it is not called, except by indiscreet people like Ms. Elders (and remember that she was removed from office as quickly as her sex and color would allow), is killing a child before he is born because you think he will not live the sort of life he should and will cost too much to support.

These are lies, and our Lord said that Satan is the father of lies. As a friend, Louis Tarsitano, wrote me: "The worship of Satan requires human sacrifice because Satan, or any other creature, cannot make anything alive. To claim autonomous power, Satan and every other creature must kill. Satan and his children lie for a similar reason: they cannot make a truth."

During the Civil War, he continued, "Nathan Bedford Forrest shocked his more cultured fellow Americans (Confederates and Federals alike) with his dictum, 'War means fighting, and fighting means killing.' His candor was considered uncouth. Cultural elites live by the euphemism that hides the nasty means to their right-thinking ends.

"This applies as much to our modern abortion elite as to any other. Even the word 'eugenics' is too blunt, since any slob with a dictionary can discover what it means. General Forrest might well have said in today's America, 'Abortion means choice, and choice means killing.' How uncouth!"

It is not coincidental that the worship of Satan so often requires the sacrifice of small children. But even his worshippers cannot bring themselves to say this aloud, or in public, and so those who would kill children lie, by calling murder something else.

The author's essay on C. S. Lewis, George Orwell, and ideological language appeared in the book he edited, The Pilgrim's Guide: C. S. Lewis and the Art of Witness *(Eerdmans).*

"Screwtape Proposes a Toast" can be found in the 1996 Simon & Schuster edition of The Screwtape Letters *and in* The World's Last Night and Other Essays *(Harcourt Brace, 1984).*

CRITICAL THINKING QUESTIONS

1. Do you think it was fair and balanced for the *New York Times* and *USA Today* not to publish an ad that opposes partial-birth abortion? Should newspapers willingly support and advocate specific political views and social positions? Why or why not?.

2. According to Mills, how does changing our language about something alter our understanding and perception of reality? How have

the pro-abortion advocates used language to hide the facts of abortion (that an unborn human being is being destroyed)?

3. What is eugenics? Do you agree with the purpose of eugenics? Why or why not? In what way is abortion a method of eugenics? If you disagree with eugenics, can you also support abortion? Why or why not?

4. Do you agree that pro-abortionists have changed the language used to denote and to describe abortion facts and practices in order to defend the indefensible? Why or why not?

$\sim$

Who and What Are We? (What the Abortion Debate Is Really About)

Francis J. Beckwith

Francis J. Beckwith is a philosopher specializing in religion, politics, applied ethics, and jurisprudence. He is an associate professor of Church-State Studies and the associate director of the J. M. Dawson Institute of Church-State Studies at Baylor University. He has authored and edited numerous books, including *To Everyone an Answer: A Case for the Christian Worldview* (2004), *Law, Darwinism & Public Education: The Establishment Clause & the Challenge of Intelligent Design* (2003), *Do the Right Thing: Readings in Applied Ethics & Social Philosophy* (2002), *The Abortion Controversy 25 Years after Roe v. Wade: A Reader* (1998), and *Relativism: Feet Firmly Planted in Mid-Air* (1998). The following essay can be found on the TrueU.org Web site and first appeared there in 2005.

Essay Classification: Argumentation/persuasion

Where Children are Unwanted

> We live in a political world,
> Love don't have any place.
> We're living in times where men commit crimes
> And crime don't have a face

> We live in a political world
> Where courage is a thing of the past
> Houses are haunted, children are unwanted
> The next day could be your last.
>
> We live in a political world
> Turning and a'thrashing about,
> As soon as you're awake, you're trained to take
> What looks like the easy way out.
>
> —Bob Dylan, Political World (1989)

ABORTION IS AN ISSUE over which Americans are deeply divided, and there is little chance that this discord will be remedied anytime soon. Each side of this cultural divide consists of citizens sincere in their convictions. But the passions that fuel these convictions about abortion often distract us from understanding the issues that *really* divide us.

Now it may seem odd to say "the issues that really divide us," since it seems obvious to most people that what divides us is in fact only one issue, abortion. But that is misleading. After all, if abortion did not result in the death of an unborn human being, the controversy would either cease entirely or diminish significantly. So, what we disagree over is not really abortion. But rather, our disagreement is over the nature of the being whose life abortion terminates, the unborn.

But there is another issue that percolates beneath the abortion debate: What does it mean to say that something is wrong? Suppose, for example, you are arguing with a friend over the question of whether abortion should remain legal, and your friend says to you, "If you don't like abortion, then don't have one." Although this is a common response, it really is a strange one. After all, you probably oppose abortion because you think it is *wrong*, not because you dislike it.

This can be better understood if we change the issue. Imagine that your friend is a defender of spousal abuse and says to you, "If you don't like spousal abuse, then don't beat your spouse." Upon hearing those words, you would instantly conclude that your friend has no idea why you oppose spousal abuse. Your opposition is not based on what you like or dislike. It is based on what you have good reason to believe *is true*: one ought not to abuse a fellow human being, especially one's spouse. That moral truth has nothing to do with whether or not you like or dislike spousal abuse.

In the same way, pro-lifers oppose abortion because they have reasons to believe that the unborn are full-fledged members of the human community, no different in nature than you or me. And for that reason, the unborn has a right to life that ought to be enshrined in our laws. Thus, in order to defeat the pro-lifer's point of view, the abortion advocate must show that the unborn is not a full-fledged member of the human community. At the end of the day, the abortion debate is not about likes or dislikes. It is about who and what we are, and whether the unborn is *one of us*.

Is the Unborn One of Us?

There is no doubt that the unborn is a human being from conception, the result of the dynamic interaction, and organic merger, of the female ovum (which contains 23 chromosomes) and the male sperm (which contains 23 chromosomes). At conception, a *whole human being*, with its own genome, comes into existence, needing only food, water, shelter, oxygen, and a congenial environment in which to interact. These are necessary in order to grow and develop itself to maturity in accordance with its own nature.

Like the infant, the child, and the adolescent, the unborn is a being that is in the process of unfolding its potential—the potential to grow and develop itself but not to change what it is. This unborn being, because of its nature, is actively disposed to develop into a mature version of itself, though never ceasing to be the same being. Thus, the same human being that begins as a one-cell zygote continues to exist to its birth and through its adulthood unless disease or violence stops it from doing so. This is why it makes perfect sense for any one of us to say, "When *I* was conceived . . ."

Abortion advocates typically do not dispute that the unborn is a human being during all or most of its time in the womb. For example, philosopher David Boonin, in his book *A Defense of Abortion* (Cambridge University Press, 2002), writes:

> On the desk in my office where most of this book was written and revised, there are several pictures of my son, Eli. In one, he is gleefully dancing on the sand along the Gulf of Mexico, the cool ocean breeze wreaking havoc with his wispy hair. . . . In the top

drawer of my desk, I keep another picture of Eli. The picture was taken September 7, 1993, 24 weeks before he was born. The sonogram image is murky, but it reveals clearly enough a small head tilted back slightly, and an arm raised up and bent, with the hand pointing back toward the face and the thumb extended toward the mouth. There is no doubt in my mind that this picture, too, shows the same little boy at a very early stage in his physical development. And there is no question that the position I defend in this book entails that it would have been morally permissible to end his life at this point. (xiii, xiv)

Why does Professor Boonin hold this view? Like some other philosophers, Boonin maintains that the unborn, though a human being, lacks characteristics that are necessary for it to have a right to life. These characteristics typically include having a self-concept, a particular level of higher brain activity, and/or a desire for a right to life. But there are problems with this approach.

Consider first this example. Imagine that your father was involved in a car accident that put him in a temporarily comatose state. His physician tells you he will awake from the coma in nine months. His conscious experiences, memories, particular skills, and abilities will be lost forever and he will have no mental record of them. This means that he will have to relearn all of his abilities and knowledge as he did before he had any conscious experiences. But they would not be the same experiences and desires he had before. That is, he is in precisely the same position as the standard unborn child, with all the basic capacities he had at the beginning of his existence. Thus, if your father has a right to life while in the coma, then so does the standard unborn child.

Another problem with the Boonin-type view is that it provides no real moral reason to oppose seemingly immoral experiments on the unborn. Imagine that there is a scientist who is able to alter the unborn's brain development in such a way that the higher brain and its functions are prevented from arising. And thus, when the child is born, it never develops a self-concept or a desire for a right to life. In fact, its organs are harvested and donated to needy patients.

Suppose that this creation of "brainless" children becomes commonplace as a demand for donor organs increases. Yet, this seems deeply immoral, even if these children had not achieved the characteristics that Boonin and others believe are required in order to have a right to life. So,

Boonin's view cannot account for the wrong of purposely creating brainless children. Only the pro-life view can do that. For, according to *this* view, human beings are persons by nature and therefore should not be unjustly deprived of those goods—including their brains—that they are designed to acquire.

Conclusion: It's All About Who and What We Are

In the July 9, 2000, edition of the *Los Angeles Times* (Orange County edition), abortion advocate Eileen Padberg claimed that an implication of the pro-life position is that the unborn child "has more rights than" our "wives, sisters, and daughters."

But that is not what follows from the pro-life position. What follows is that *all* human beings, including wives, sisters (born and unborn), and daughters (born and unborn), retain their dignity and rights as long as they exist, from the moment they come into being.

Ironically, by excluding the unborn from the human community, Ms. Padberg diminishes, and puts in peril, the very rights she jealously, and correctly, guards. For she is saying that the government may exclude small, vulnerable, defenseless, and dependent unborn human beings from its protection for no other reason than because others consider the unborn's destruction vital to their well-being.

But Ms. Padberg would surely, and correctly, protest a government policy that allows for the exploitation and destruction of wives, sisters, and daughters by powerful people who believe they will live better lives by engaging in such atrocities against these women. So, if the unborn is one of us, then whatever is true of our worth and dignity is true of theirs as well.

CRITICAL THINKING QUESTIONS

1. Discuss how Beckwith introduces his essay. How does he achieve common ground? Is this an effective strategy? Why or why not?

2. What is really at issue, according to Beckwith, in the abortion debate? Is it abortion per se or the nature of what is being aborted? Explain why it is important to understand this distinction.

3. Beckwith claims the ultimate question in the abortion debate is simply, is the unborn "one of us"? Why is this the central question? How does Beckwith answer the question? What evidences and arguments does he give? Do you agree? Why or why not?

4. Beckwith is careful to articulate and refute the main points of his opposition (the abortion advocates). What key points does he explain and refute? Does he do a fair and honest job of explaining their points? How convincing are his refutations? Explain.

~

Oh the Humanity: Dred Scott and Roe v. Wade
Greg Koukl

Greg Koukl used to think that he was too smart to ever become a Christian. After careful consideration of various lines of argument and evidence, he is now a committed Christian and Christian apologist (one who provides logical defenses for the central teachings of Christianity). He has written numerous books, hosts a radio program, and is the founder and president of Stand to Reason. The following essay appeared in *Salvo* in 2007.

Essay Classification: Informative; argumentation/persuasion

ARE BLACK PEOPLE HUMAN beings? Believe it or not, there was a time when the Supreme Court's answer to this question was no, not if they were slaves.

It was 1856. Dred Scott, a black slave, had been taken north of the Mason-Dixon line into Illinois and Wisconsin, where slavery was prohibited by the Missouri Compromise. Scott sued for his freedom and lost. The Supreme Court ruled that the Compromise was unconstitutional. Congress, they said, had no authority to limit slavery in that way.

In the Court's mind, the choice to own slaves was an individual decision, a private matter with which each citizen must struggle apart from interference by the state. If a person, in an act of conscience, chose not to keep slaves, that was his own decision, but he could not force that choice on others. Every person had a private right to choose.

Dred Scott, as a slave, was declared chattel—human property. He was a possession of his owner, and the owner had a right to do whatever he wanted with his assets. Three of the justices held that even a "Negro" who had descended from slaves had no rights as an American citizen and thus no standing in the Court.

A civil war and 100 years of oppression stood between the slave as property and the slave as human being. Today, the dream of "Black America" has come true, by and large. Slavery is a thing of the past, and black individuals have been for the most part integrated into the mainstream of American life. In a climate of civil rights and civil liberties, the question "Are black people human beings?" sounds so bizarre it's almost comical. Who could ask such a thing today?

The question, however, is still being asked, this time with a twist: Is an unborn baby a human being? So far, our answer as a nation has been the same as that in *Dred Scott*. No, the Supreme Court has ruled; the child is the property of the woman who carries it. A woman has the right to do whatever she wants with her own property. Abortion is a private, individual decision that cannot be denied by others. Every person has a right to choose.

Much of the justification for this position focuses on the confusion about when life begins. However, the scientific community is of one mind on this. Biologically, the life of a new organism always begins at conception.

When a cat conceives, what kind of life is stirring in its womb? What kind of being is living there? It's not a dog being, is it? It's not a salamander being, or a mosquito being. A close look at its genetic structure shows that there's only one kind of being growing there, a feline being, a cat being.

If the biological life of any being begins at conception (as scientists agree), then any termination of pregnancy kills the life of an individual being, however rudimentary its development may be. If the cat's pregnancy is aborted, a kitten will die.

When a woman conceives, what kind of being has just started a new life? There's only one answer: a human being. From the very first day, a small human being is developing in his mother's womb. If the pregnancy is terminated, a life is lost, the life of a human being. There's no way around it.

In the case of humans, however, a new category has been added, distinct from biological life: personhood. When does this human being become a protected member of the human community?

Whether any baby is a "person" or not is a question for the lawmakers to decide. The legal concept of personhood is malleable. Lawmakers define who is protected by the law and who is excluded. The law says, for example, that even a company can be a "person" for purposes of tax and liability law and the like. On the other hand, black slave babies in 1856 were not persons according to the Taney Court.

In 1973, the Supreme Court, in the spirit of *Dred Scott,* relegated the unborn child to the status of chattel—mere human property. Their decision, however, will not change the fact that with every aborted pregnancy a living being loses its life. A human being.

CRITICAL THINKING QUESTIONS

1. Why does Koukl locate his discussion of abortion within the context of the *Dred Scott* Supreme Court decision? What is the argumentative point of this comparison? Is it effective? Why or why not?

2. What logical conclusions can we make if we decide that the unborn human being is the mere property of the pregnant woman? What actions could be legally and logically defended by these conclusions?

3. Why does Koukl discuss the nature or identity of the life conceived in a cat's womb? Is there any confusion as to what kind of life is there? Why, then, does there seem to be confusion as to what kind of life is present when a human conceives? Is there really any confusion, or is this just a smokescreen? Explain.

4. Why do some people discuss "personhood" of the unborn human instead of the biological identity? Does this linguistic move really change the reality of the identity of the unborn? Why or why not?

~

ANALYZING MEDIA

Public Sees Media Bias

Ted J. Smith

Ted J. Smith was an associate professor at Virginia Commonwealth University, teaching in the school of Mass Communications until his death in 2004. He was also a fellow at the Center for Media and Public Affairs, and he published articles in such journals as *The American Enterprise,*

Arkansas Historical Quarterly, Alabama Review, and *Journalism Quarterly.*
The following article was published in 2002 in *The American Enterprise.*

Essay Classification: Informative; synthesis

CBS CORRESPONDENT BERNIE GOLDBERG's book that showcases liberal bias in the media has had no discernible impact on establishment journalists. Nor should any have been expected. Bias is merely the latest addition to a huge body of literature, including at least 100 books and research monographs documenting a widespread left-wing bias in the news. Yet none of it has had much effect.

Journalists and their defenders discovered long ago that such materials could usually be ignored or dismissed as the fevered ravings of right-wing zealots. On those rare occasions when a book or article breaks through to a wider audience, all that's required is a bit of damage control. First, the author is rigorously excluded from the largest popular media (which is why Goldberg has appeared only once on any of the three major television networks, though his book spent weeks at the top of the *New York Times* bestseller list). Second, in the rest of the elite media the author is subjected to personal abuse (as by Tom Shales), and endless quibbling about details of his work (as in Michael Kinsley's review). Seldom does anyone bother to respond to the substance of his argument, and in the end the attention of the public moves elsewhere.

Because the media have the power to set the terms of debate, every critic can be marginalized, every study rendered "controversial." So journalists and their apologists can always claim that media bias has not been proved. That is why Tom Goldstein, dean of the prestigious Graduate School of Journalism at Columbia University, feels free to make the astounding assertion that, while most journalists may be liberal in their views, "no study ... has shown that the personal backgrounds and values of journalists are particularly relevant to how journalists report the news."

But there is a body of definitive evidence that proves a contrary view. Journalists like to claim that perceptions of media bias are purely a matter of perspective. They say the news is scrupulously fair and balanced, so when viewed by conservatives it appears skewed to the left, and from a liberal perspective it leans to the right. To test this contention, the Center for Media and Public Affairs (CMPA) commissioned a large-scale study of public attitudes about the press. Fielded by Louis Harris and Associates in November 1996, the telephone survey sought responses to 107 questions from a representative sample of 3,004 American adults. The unusually large sample made it possible to acquire accurate information about the views of various population subgroups.

Like earlier studies, the survey found that 74 percent of Americans see either "a great deal" (30 percent) or "a fair amount" (44 percent) of "political bias in news coverage." Fully 63 percent of the public believes the news media "tend to favor one side" in "presenting the news dealing with political and social issues." But unlike most studies, this one also asked respondents to "describe the views of the news media on most matters having to do with politics," giving them the choices of "very liberal, somewhat liberal, middle-of-the road, somewhat conservative, or very conservative." The responses are illuminating.

Among the whole public, a plurality of 43 percent described the news media as very (18 percent) or somewhat (25 percent) liberal. This compares to only 19 percent who described the media as very (6 percent) or somewhat (12 percent) conservative.

More important, the study examined 75 different subgroups of the U.S. population and found that in 73 of them more people see liberal bias than see conservative bias in the news. Even Democrats and self-described liberals came to this conclusion (see accompanying chart). This conclusively refutes the claim that perceptions of bias are solely a function of perspective.

The CMPA/Harris study also divided respondents into five levels of political participation and five levels of education. The results show a near-perfect linear progression: the higher the level of participation and education, the greater the perception of a leftist slant to the news. Among the most politically active citizens, who are presumably best able to make accurate assessments of bias, 55 percent see a liberal tilt, only 15 percent a conservative. The findings are even more striking for the educated elite (see chart).

The verdict is in; the people have spoken; the media are guilty as charged. The time has come to shift the debate from whether the news is biased to what can be done to correct it.

CRITICAL THINKING QUESTIONS

1. According to Smith, how does the media establishment usually respond to those journalists and writers who publish works that outline, detail, and prove liberal bias in the media? Is it fair to attack the person's character or to ignore the claims instead of discussing the issues and the substance of the analysis? Explain.

2. What are your own views of the mainstream media? Is there a bias? Explain and provide evidence and examples.

3. Many argue that any perceived bias is merely subjective perception and is thus not real at all. How does Smith address this issue? What do his research and statistics prove?

4. Smith concludes by suggesting that the real focus now should be on how to address this liberal bias, now that we empirically know it exists. What do you think can or should be done, if anything? Explain.

∼

Clouds of Conspiracy: Is Media Bias Real? Look No Further than Global Warming

Raymond J. Keating

Raymond J. Keating a columnist for *Newsday* in New York City and a contributing editor of *Salvo*. He is the author of books on media and politics. The following article appeared in *Salvo* in 2007.

Essay Classification: Informative; analytical/evaluative

RIGOROUS ANALYSIS OF MEDIA bias really began in 1981, when Robert Lichter and Stanley Rothman surveyed journalists at top media outlets on their political views and voting habits. The findings? Overwhelmingly liberal. Not exactly shocking, but it was nice to have the data. In the following years, survey after survey confirmed the media's leftist leanings.

For example, a 2005 survey of 300 journalists by the University of Connecticut's Department of Public Policy found that 52 percent of news reporters voted for John Kerry, the Democrat in the 2004 presidential election, versus 21 percent who voted for President George W.

Bush, the Republican. In addition, 33 percent said they were Democrats, while 10 percent said they were Republicans. And self-identified liberals came in at 28 percent, as opposed to the 10 percent who called themselves conservatives.

Similarly, a UCLA-led study released in late 2005 found that "almost all major media outlets tilt to the left." Tim Groseclose, a UCLA political scientist and lead researcher on the study, said that he "suspected that many media outlets would tilt to the left because surveys have shown that reporters tend to vote more Democrat than Republican." But he was "surprised at just how pronounced the distinctions are." Coauthor Jeffrey Milyo, a University of Missouri economist and public policy scholar, added that "overall, the major media outlets are quite moderate compared to members of Congress, but even so, there is a quantifiable and significant bias in that nearly all of them lean to the left."

Some journalists make their political preferences clear by how they spend their own money. After all, political donations are not exactly subtle. A 2007 investigation by MSNBC.com reporter Bill Dedman tracked journalists who made political contributions to federal candidates, political action committees, and political parties between January 2004 and the first quarter of 2007. The good news? Only a tiny percentage of journalists made political contributions. The predictable news? Out of the 143 journalists identified as making political contributions, 125—or 87 percent—gave to Democrats or liberal causes, while only 16 percent gave to Republicans.

Does this liberal bias manifest itself in news coverage? Let's consider just one of the hot-button issues that currently divides liberals and conservatives: global warming.

Media-Made Global Warming?

The story of man-made climate change, or global warming, has everything a left-leaning journalist could possibly desire: it's about the environment, always a fave topic, and it pits those who care about the earth against big bad business and the presumably insensitive, self-absorbed consumer—likewise topics about which liberals love to write. And because there are scientists out there who argue that the case on global warming is already closed—that it is definitely mankind's CO_2-spewing actions that are changing the climate—most major media outlets have shown themselves eager to run regular "news" stories that present man-made global warming as fact, insisting that no disagreement exists among scientists.

For example, a keyword search of the *New York Times* (April through June of 2007) resulted in 43 stories or analyses that focused on—or included—the topic "climate change," none of which featured any substantive quotes or explanations that departed from the environmentalist party line on global warming.

A few articles *did* note disagreements between environmental groups over how best to deal with the problem, but none quarreled with global warming itself. And while most economic studies have tied the reduction of emissions to substantial costs for consumers, businesses, and nations, only three of the pieces in question acknowledged—not through research, mind you, but just via statements from interested parties—some "possible" costs. In contrast, many of these articles quoted politicians who declared that fighting global warming would be just dandy for the economy.

Other articles focused on the people pushing our nation's spy agencies to focus on climate change; how poor nations will suffer most from global warming's fallout; the businesses that are aboard the climate-change fight; and even an artist going around New York City using blue chalk on streets and sidewalks to mark a flood line based on global warming projections.

Just in case you were wondering, it is not at all difficult to find climate scientists and experts who disagree with the absolutist position on man-made global warming. Over 17,000 scientists have signed the Global Warming Petition Project from the Oregon Institute of Science and Medicine. Here's what the petition states:

> There is no convincing scientific evidence that human release of carbon dioxide, methane, or other greenhouse gasses is causing or will, in the foreseeable future, cause catastrophic heating of the Earth's atmosphere and disruption of the Earth's climate. Moreover, there is substantial scientific evidence that increases in atmospheric carbon dioxide produce many beneficial effects upon the natural plant and animal environments of the Earth.

Despite such findings, however, media outlets such as the *New York Times* continue to proceed as if the global warming threat isn't a theory at all, but rather as demonstrable as gravity. Not only that, but when they are forced to admit that there are some who do disagree with such certainty, they often portray these individuals as idiots—or worse.

Take Brian Montopoli's recent interaction with CBS News correspondent Scott Pelley. On CBS's "Public Eye" blog, Montopoli describes their conversation:

> Pelley's most recent report, like his first, did not pause to acknowledge global warming skeptics, instead treating the existence of global warming as an established fact. I again asked him why. "If I do an interview with Elie Wiesel," he asks, "am I required as a journalist to find a Holocaust denier?" He says his team tried hard to find a respected scientist who contradicted the prevailing opinion in the scientific community, but there was no one out there who fit that description. "This isn't about politics or pseudo-science or conspiracy theory blogs," he says. "This is about sound science."

Global warming skeptics equivalent to Holocaust deniers? No respected scientist disputes the man-made global warming theory? Pelley is a classic example of a biased reporter who cannot fathom that he might possibly be biased. Somewhat ironically, this ostensibly "open-minded" liberal won't even consider that an alternative viewpoint is possible.

Similarly, the Weather Channel's Heidi Cullen suggested that if any meteorologists do not agree with the man-made global warming theory, then perhaps the American Meteorological Society should give those individuals the boot. On her Weather Channel blog last December, she wrote: "If a meteorologist can't speak to the fundamental science of climate change, then maybe the AMS shouldn't give them a Seal of Approval."

Are there exceptions to global warming bias in the media? Of course; but they seem to be a small minority. Lawrence Solomon, a columnist for Canada's *Financial Post,* started a series in late 2006 on global warming dissenters and deniers. In a 2007 news column, Solomon explained that when starting out, he accepted "the prevailing view that scientists overwhelmingly believe that climate change threatens the planet" and was only looking to do a few profiles on the dissenters to allow them "to have their views heard." He was not prepared for the information that he encountered. What did he learn?

> Somewhere along the way, I stopped believing that a scientific consensus exists on climate change. Certainly there is no consensus at the very top echelons of scientists—the ranks from which I have been drawing my subjects—and certainly there is no consensus among astrophysicists and other solar scientists, several of whom I have profiled.

Solomon admits that many scientists *do* agree with global warming theory, but he wanted the world to know that there were also some who do not; he came to that conclusion after interviewing top scientists. How unbiased. How unique.

The Right to Choose

According to a new Zogby poll on public attitudes in the United States toward global warming, 70 percent of Americans believe that man-made climate change is a fact. Clearly, media bias can, and does, influence our culture. The point here is not whether global warming is truly occurring, but whether the media covers the topic in a fair and complete fashion, which they do not. And if this is the case with global warming, on how many other issues is media bias influencing people's views?

Thankfully, we are becoming less and less reliant on legacy media outlets. As the Internet and broadband technology leap ahead, media competition and choices for the public expand, too. And in the end, more choice just might be the answer to media bias.

Even so, bias will never be wiped out completely. Many in the news media are so imbued with their ideology that they are not even aware of their biases. Many strive for fairness but come up short. Many others do not even try. With expanding options, however, there will be more from which news consumers can pick and choose, and hopefully, balance and a well-grounded perspective will be recognized, and the truth will not be lost.

Supplementary Article Sidebar Information:

Cramping Their Style

You know media bias has gotten out of hand when news outlets begin controlling the language choices of their reporters. Well, that's exactly what is happening within two very prominent new agencies. Both the *New York Daily News* (NYDN), the sixth largest paper in the United States, and the Associated Press (AP) use linguistic style guides that give preferential treatment to those who support abortion. For example, the AP demands that its writers avoid using the word *pro-life,* preferring instead *anti-abortion.* It likewise insists that abortion advocates be described as supporters of *abortion rights,* as opposed to *pro-abortion* or even *pro-choice.* The NYDN has a similar set of requirements, stipulating that writers should use *abortion foes* and *abortion opponents* instead of *pro-life* and *pro-lifers,* but then takes the matter a few steps further. Indeed, it also requires its writers to replace *unborn child* with *fetus,* and to replace *mother* with *woman* in the phrase, "when the life of the mother is at stake." So much for objective reporting.

Telling the Truth Slant: Other Examples of Media Bias

"Tell the truth," Emily Dickinson once wrote, "but tell it slant." It's a sentiment that could serve as the unacknowledged motto of the mainstream media. Under the guise of "straight" reporting, our major news sources manipulate how we perceive and respond to current events in a variety of ways, from story selection to carefully worded headlines to outright disinformation. Here are just six examples of the rampant media bias to which we have been subjected in recent months:

1. The Associated Press's June 5 story on the 16-count indictment of Louisiana Congressman William Jefferson for bribery, racketeering, wire fraud, money laundering, obstruction of justice, and other offenses never mentioned Jefferson's party affiliation—Democrat— although it did identify the party affiliation of other politicians mentioned in the story, including California Democrat Nancy Pelosi and Ohio Republican John Boehner.

2. The media ran more than 6,000 stories and innumerable photos on the abuse of prisoners at Abu Ghraib. But nine days after evidence showing how al-Qaeda tortures its victims—including tools, drawings, and photos—was released, ABC, CBS, NBC, the *New York Times,* and the *Washington Post* had yet to run a story with photos on the material, which was discovered by U.S. soldiers in Iraq in April and declassified in May.

3. After his release from prison on June 1, assisted-suicide activist Jack Kevorkian was interviewed by Mike Wallace on CBS's *60 Minutes.* Among the things not shown or mentioned in the interview were: the hug between Wallace and Kevorkian when the two met; the fact that Wallace is a euthanasia proponent himself; Kevorkian's advocacy of human vivisection, which in his book *Prescription Medicide* he calls "obitiatry"; the facts that most of Kevorkian's assisted-suicide victims were not terminally ill and that he has never advocated that euthanasia be limited to the terminally ill.

4. The June 12th dedication of a new memorial in Washington, D.C., that commemorates the more than 100 million victims of communism around the world, received scant media coverage, according to Michael Chapman of NewsBusters:

> From yesterday's dedication of the memorial, there has been some print coverage, yet most of the stories have been buried inside the papers. For instance, *Los Angeles Times,* p. 15; *Chicago Tribune,* p. 3; *Miami Herald,* p. 17; and the *Washington Post* (registration required) placed the story in its Style section but did run a page 1 story in its free "express" newspaper, distributed around D.C. But, so far, I have not seen any network news coverage and only one mention on MSNBC in a Financial Times article on the MSNBC Web site.

The AP's coverage of the dedication was headlined, "China Denounces Anti-Communism Memorial," and led with the paragraph, "China criticized the United States' 'Cold War' thinking Wednesday after President Bush attended the opening of a Washington memorial for those killed in communist regimes." The story by Scott McDonald devoted four of its first six paragraphs to China's complaints, one to China's current political situation, and one to the dedication ceremony.

5. ABCNews.com's coverage of the Massachusetts Legislature's vote defeating the state's marriage amendment ballot measure carried this headline:

Gay Marriage Safe in Massachusetts: A Vote to Redefine Marriage as a Union Between a Man and a Woman Was Defeated

6. Michael Medved noticed that the BBC described the terror suspects arrested for planning the car bombings in London and Glasgow in June as arising from "the disfranchised South Asian community," and commented:

> Well first, it's ridiculous to describe successful physicians as disfranchised in any way. Second, the reference to "South Asian community" is misleading—like the description of one of the plotters as "Indian." The refusal to use the words "Muslim" or "Islamist" to identify these terrorists—echoed by the official policy of the new Prime Minister, Gordon Brown—suggests

that the would-be bombers might be Hindu—since Hinduism is the primary religion of South Asia, and certainly of India.

Of course, they're all Muslim, and at least two are from the Middle East, not Pakistan. The press identifies the ringleader, Mohammed Asha, as Palestinian, even though he spent his life in Saudi Arabia, Jordan and Britain—another distortion from media outlets that often ignore or deny the truth about terrorism and about Islam.

CRITICAL THINKING QUESTIONS

1. For years, the mainstream news media (ABC, NBC, CBS) and such cable news networks as MSNBC and CNN have denied political bias in their reporting. Based upon the information in this article and from your own experience, is there political bias in the news media? Is it largely liberal or conservative? Explain and give examples from your own experience.

2. What is your general understanding of the debate surrounding man-caused global warming? What is the perspective of most news media outlets on this topic? Are they reporting the facts fairly and accurately? Why or why not? What potential policy effects can this bias have?

3. The media clearly influences public opinion, thus making media bias all the more troubling. What, then, is the responsibility of the informed citizen when it comes to investigating the facts of an issue? Discuss.

4. Discuss other examples of media bias in the news, film, TV, and advertising.

Bibliography

Budziszewski, J. "Designed for Sex: What We Lose When We Forget What Sex Is For." *Touchstone: A Journal of Mere Christianity* (July–August 2005): 22–27.

Chesterton, G. K. *The Everlasting Man.* 1925. San Francisco: Ignatius Press, 1993.

———. "The Fear of the Film." *Selected Essays of G. K. Chesterton.* Ed. Dorothy Collins. London: Methuen, 1949. 226–30.

———. *Orthodoxy.* 1908. San Francisco: Ignatius Press, 1995.

Copan, Paul. *"That's Just Your Interpretation": Responding to Skeptics Who Challenge Your Faith.* Grand Rapids: Baker Books, 2001.

Dembski, William A. *Intelligent Design: The Bridge Between Science and Theology.* Downers Grove, IL: InterVarsity Press, 1999.

———, ed. *Uncommon Dissent: Intellectuals Who Find Darwinism Unconvincing.* Wilmington, DE: ISI Books, 2004.

D'Souza, Dinesh. *Letters to a Young Conservative.* New York: Basic Books, 2002.

Frankl, Viktor. *The Doctor and the Soul: Introduction to Logotherapy.* New York: Knopf, 1982.

Geisler, Norman L., and Frank Turek. *I Don't Have Enough Faith to Be an Atheist.* Wheaton, IL.: Crossway Books, 2004.

Guinness, Os. *The Call: Finding and Fulfilling the Central Purpose of Your Life.* Nashville: W Publishing Group, 2003.

Jackson, Rosemary. *Fantasy: The Literature of Subversion.* New York: Routledge, 1981.

Johnson, Phillip E. *The Wedge of Truth: Splitting the Foundations of Naturalism.* Downers Grove, IL: InterVarsity Press, 2000.

Koons, Robert C. "The Check Is in the Mail: Why Darwinism Fails to Inspire Confidence." Dembski, *Uncommon Dissent* 3–22.

Lewis, C. S. *God in the Dock: Essays on Theology and Ethics.* Grand Rapids: Eerdmans, 1970.

———. *The Problem of Pain.* 1940. New York: HarperCollins, 1996.

———. *The Screwtape Letters.* 1942. New York: HarperCollins, 1996.

Moreland, J. P., ed. *The Creation Hypothesis: Scientific Evidence for an Intelligent Designer.* Downers Grove, IL: InterVarsity Press, 1994.

Morse, Jennifer Roback. "First Comes Marriage." *Touchstone Magazine: A Journal of Mere Christianity* Jan.–Feb. 2006. 13–14.

Muggeridge, Malcolm. *Christ and the Media.* Vancouver: Regent College Publishing, 1977.

Oller, John W., Jr., and John L. Omdahl, "Origin of the Human Language Capacity: In Whose Image?" Moreland 235–69.

Pearcey, Nancy R. "Darwin Meets the Berenstein Bears: Evolution as a Total Worldview." Dembski, *Uncommon Dissent,* 53–73.

Rosenthal, Peggy. "Why We Need the Arts in Time of War." *The Crux Project Archives. Salvo Magazine.* Accessed September 6, 2008. http://www.salvomag.com/new/ articles/ archives/art/rosenthal.php.

Ross, Hugh. "Astronomical Evidences for a Personal, Transcendent God." Moreland 141–72.

Scully, Matthew. *Dominion: The Power of Man, the Suffering of Animals, and the Call to Mercy.* New York: St. Martin's Press, 2002.

Spencer, Kathleen L. "Purity and Danger: *Dracula*, the Urban Gothic, and the Late Victorian Degeneracy Crisis." *ELH* 59 (1992): 197–225.

Sproul, R. C. *The Consequences of Ideas: Understanding the Concepts That Shaped Our World.* Wheaton, IL: Crossway Books, 2000.

Wells, David F. *No Place for Truth: Or, Whatever Happened to Evangelical Theology?* Grand Rapids: Eerdmans, 1993.

Willard, Dallas. *The Divine Conspiracy: Rediscovering Our Hidden Life in God.* New York: HarperCollins, 1997.

Wise, Kurt P. "The Origin of Life's Major Groups." Moreland 211–34.

Wordsworth, William. Preface to *Lyrical Ballads. Norton Anthology of English Literature* (6th ed.), vol. 2. Ed. M. H. Abrams. New York: Norton, 1993. 141–52.

Zacharias, Ravi. *Can Man Live without God?* Dallas: Word Publishing, 1994.

———. *Deliver Us from Evil: Restoring Soul in a Disintegrating Culture.* Dallas: Word, 1996.

———. *The Real Face of Atheism.* Grand Rapids: Baker Books, 2004.

———. *Recapture the Wonder.* Nashville: Integrity Publishers, 2003.

Credits